THE HOME SCHOOL SOURCE BOOK

Second Edition, Revised

DONN REED

BROOK FARM BOOKS

GLASSVILLE, NEW BRUNSWICK
BRIDGEWATER, MAINE

This book incorporates material previously published, in somewhat different form, in THE FIRST HOME-SCHOOL CATALOGUE (1982, 1986), THE HOME-SCHOOL CHALLENGE (1985), "efficient instruction elsewhere" (1984), and THE HOME SCHOOL SOURCE BOOK, First Edition (1991), and in Home Education Magazine, Harrowsmith, Nurturing, The New Nativity, and other periodicals.

Portraits of Jean and Donn on p. 1, of Jean on p. 287, and illustrations of Donn and Gus on pp. 80 and 84 are by Chuck Trapkus, Rock Island, Illinois.

Special thanks to The Learning Works, Inc., P.O. Box 6187, Santa Barbara, CA 93160 for generous permission to make extensive use of material from The Clip Art Carousel (copyright © 1986 and 1989 by The Learning Works, Inc.). (See Art, "Clip Art Carousel"; Science, "Reproducible Science Series"; Education, Learning, & Teaching Aids, "The Learning Works"; and Index, "The Learning Works.")

Published simultaneously in Canada and the United States by Brook Farm Books, Glassville, New Brunswick, and Bridgewater, Maine. Printed and bound in the United States of America.

PUBLISHER'S CATALOGUING IN PUBLICATION DATA
Reed, Donn.

The home school source book, second edition, revised.
Includes index.
ISBN 0-919761-26-7

1. Home schooling. 2. Domestic education - United States. 3. Domestic education - Canada. 4. Instructional materials - United States. 5. Instructional materials - Canada. 6. Children - Books and reading - Bibliography. 7. First home-school catalogue - see Home school source book. 8. Reed, Donn. I. Title.

DEDICATION

For Jean--

Whose constant inspiration, support, patience, hard work, and companionship have made this and all things possible; this book, like so many other parts of our lives, is hers as much as mine;

And for Cathy, Karen, Susan, and Derek--

Who have taught us far more than we have taught them; whose curiosity, interests, hopes and fears, increasing awareness, perceptions, and interpretations have all added to our knowledge of ourselves as parents and as people;

All five of whom have given me a life of warmth and meaning far beyond my reasonable expectations; I look back over our lives together, and am very glad we chose to do it all our way.

And our adventure continues...

ORDERING FROM BROOK FARM BOOKS

Part II, the Catalog & Directory of this Source Book, offers you a comprehensive guide to more than 3000 individual items, sources of material and/or information, support groups, and other materials especially useful to children and adults learning at home. More than 1,500 of these items can be ordered directly from Brook Farm Books, which gives you consolidated ordering of materials from scores of publishers, manuracturers, and other suppliers.

INSTRUCTIONS FOR ORDERING FROM BROOK FARM BOOKS ARE ON PAGE 288.

Our criteria for items we sell are the same as for items we use ourselves: they must be fun, challenging, constructive, informative, and relevant to steady mental, physical, and moral growth.

We don't have a large company. Jean and I "process" all orders, from opening the mail to sending out the orders; from keeping records to emptying the wastebasket. We welcome personal correspondence with all readers and customers.

TO ORDER MORE COPIES OF THIS BOOK

Additional copies of THE HOME SCHOOL SOURCE BOOK, Second Edition, Revised, may be ordered from BROOK FARM BOOKS, P.O. Box 246, Bridgewater, ME 04735, for $15.00 each plus $1 postage. ($20 plus $1.50 postage, in Canadian funds, from Brook Farm Books, Glassville, N.B. E0J 1L0.)

QUANTITY DISCOUNTS

Home school support groups and organizations ordering 10 or more copies of THE HOME SCHOOL SOURCE BOOK at one time will receive a discount of 20% -- $12.00 per copy, *postpaid* (you save $4 per copy). All copies must be sent to the same address, and orders must be prepaid.

ITEMS *NOT* SOLD BY BROOK FARM BOOKS

Ordering instructions are usually given with the listing. If any necessary information (such as price) is missing, write to the publisher or supplier. If it's a small company, send a #10 SASE with your request for information. Using a letterhead, order form, or, at least, a rubber stamp, will often get you better service, and sometimes a substantial discount.

"UNKNOWN" -- "FORWARDING ORDER EXPIRED" -- "RETURN TO SENDER"

For every inquiry which is returned to you with the above words, or an equivalent, I sincerely apologize. I've tried to ascertain the accuracy of all listings, but companies, like people, sometimes move and then seem to disappear. Usually, the best one can do in such a case is to look for similar services or materials from other companies.

"REGISTER" YOUR HOME SCHOOL SOURCE BOOK

If you didn't buy your SOURCE BOOK from Brook Farm Books, please send us your name and address, telling us when and where you bought it, so we can add your name to our files for future mailings (such as notice of the next edition). We do not sell, rent, or trade our mailing list; your name will stay with us.

DONN REED was born and raised in Vermont, and has travelled by bus, thumb, and pickup truck through much of the United States, Mexico, and Canada.

He has worked as a carpenter, laborer, radio announcer, truck driver, dishwasher, warehouseman, librarian, teacher, foundry worker, peace marcher, janitor, psychiatric aide, tax assessor, sawmill edgerman, migrant field worker, pandhandler (one day), clerk-typist, reporter, columnist, and newspaper editor.

He served three years (of a six-year sentence) in five federal prisions and about forty city and county jails for his refusal to carry a draft card. While in prison, he attended a summer workshop in Adult Literacy at the University of Denver, and later received a Meritorious Service Award from the U.S. Bureau of Prisons for his work with adult illiterates in the prison.

His articles have appeared in *Today*, *Nurturing*, *Harrowsmith*, *Home Education Magazine*, and other periodicals.

Jean and Donn Reed live on a fifty-acre homestead in New Brunswick, Canada, about thirty miles from Maine. Jean plays classical guitar and makes doughnuts. Donn splits firewood, milks the cow, and plays with his typewriter.

C O N T E N T S

INTRODUCTION 1

1

When Henry David Thoreau began his famous experiment in living at Walden Pond, his purpose, he wrote later, was to determine what things and conditions are essential to life. In most parts of the world, he said, only four things are essential for physical survival: food, clothing, shelter, and heat.

"At the present day," Thoreau went on to say (in the mid-1800's), "and in this country, as I find by my own experience, a few implements, a knife, an axe, a spade, a wheelbarrow, etc., and for the studious, lamplight, stationery, and access to a few good books, rank next to necessaries, and can all be obtained at a trifling cost."

When Jean and I began our "experiment" in homeschooling, part of our purpose was to determine what things and conditions are most useful, if not essential, in learning. What are the "necessaries" of teaching at home -- not just the physical materials, such as books and pencils, but the methods, the attitudes, and the objectives? What knowledge is really useful or essential in life, and what are the best ways of obtaining or imparting it?

There were no books or magazines about homeschooling then; no directories or catalogs of materials; and we didn't know any other homeschoolers. We found and chose learning materials by hit-or-miss: browsing in book stores, buying discarded library books, searching through garage sales and used book stores; buying activity books in toy stores; borrowing from public libraries and, when we could, from schools.

When a school principal loaned us a school supplies catalog, we discovered wonderful possibilities which we hadn't even suspected -- books, charts, posters, toys, games, science kits, film strips, models, and much more. The rustic, rural lifestyle which we prefer seldom generates much money (although we have no objection to money, in itself), but that period of discovery was one of the fortunate exceptions during which I was earning a good wage. We spent several hundred dollars on our first order.

When the packages arrived, it was like a childhood Christmas morning for all of us. In the weeks following, we remained very happy with most of the purchases. Some items, however, proved to be very disappointing, and we began to learn that an item isn't necessarily good, or even worth the postage, just because it's offered for sale to professional educators. (The same is true today of items offered to homeschoolers by some of the companies which have discovered the "new" and lucrative market. As always, caveat emptor.)

Once we discovered the scores of suppliers and hundreds of educational book publishers, our problem was no longer finding materials, but deciding what would be most useful. How we wished for a comprehensive guide to the materials available! It would have saved us hundreds of dollars, as well as hundreds of hours wasted in trying to use worthless materials.

We continued our search, gradually sifting the excellent from the moderately good and the worthless. Experience was certainly our best teacher.

As public schools continued to get worse, homeschooling became more common, and parents began coming to us for advice about teaching at home. In offering ideas and suggestions, we often discussed the need for a comprehensive directory of materials. One evening, after a couple had left with an armload of borrowed books and many pages of notes, Jean said to me, "No one else is doing it. Why don't you?"

I laughed -- but she was serious, and the idea grew on me.

Even after teaching at home for more than ten years, we had had no contact with other homeschoolers, and knew nothing about the growing number of home-school newsletters and support groups. Guessing that the finished book would be about a hundred pages, and would take a month or two to finish, I began making notes, I wrote to publishers, government agencies, and home-school organizations. My notes grew. After eight months of research, evaluating, and selecting, I had compiled nearly 240 pages of sources, resources, organizations, and publications. This was another period of very low income for us, so we decided to finance the publication by selling some of the listed items ourselves (which we still

do). After considering scores of titles, I finally called my book THE FIRST HOME-SCHOOL CATALOGUE
-- because that's what it was. I typed it on an
ancient Royal and put illustrations in with Glue-
Stick. I made fifty copies of the book on a photocopier and had covers printed. Jean and I col-
lated the pages on our kitchen table, bound them,
glued on the covers, and had the books trimmed at
a print shop. In the spring of 1982, I mailed a
few review copies, ran two small ads, and waited.

The response more than paid me for all my time
and work. THE FIRST HOME-SCHOOL CATALOGUE seemed
to be a welcome addition to the home-school movement. It was a very crude book, with no professional expertise whatsoever, but no one mentioned
that, nor the many faults and serious omissions
of which I was very aware. Orders for the Catalogue came from all the Canadian provinces, nearly all of the United States, and even from Spain,
Greece, Puerto Rico, Japan, Indonesia, and many
other countries, and were quickly followed by enthusiastic letters of appreciation -- "Thanks for
the information," "Great," "Loved it."

"I like it very much," wrote John Holt; "a wonderful venture." The Mother Earth News said its
"listings, honest reviews, and advice...should be
invaluable to any home-schooling parent."

I was very happy with the positive response,
but felt the high praise had been earned more by
my intention than by an actual accomplishment.
Almost immediately, I began planning extensive
additions, revisions, and improvements. I published the second edition in 1986.

[I had planned to call the next edition THE
SECOND HOME-SCHOOL CATALOGUE, but by then two
other resource guides had been published (one in
1985, the other in 1986), each claiming to be the
first; so, in weak self-defense, I kept my original title. It's true that imitation can be flat-
tering, but an omission of polite acknowledgement
reduces its sincerity.]

The changing needs of our four children, the
many new products available, and questions and
suggestions from readers have all kept me searching and evaluating. Most home-school services and
organizations freely exchange ideas and information; but, as in many growing movements, a few
have become very competitive. Many new organizations have begun, most of them providing real and
needed services, but a few apparently trying to
displace others. A few reviewers of books and
other materials for home-schoolers, relying for a
large part of their income on advertisers, praise
and recommend everything sent to them, even when
the products are contradictory in philosophy or
purpose, sometimes without fully examining the

material being reviewed. "He who praises everybody," wrote James Boswell, "praises nobody."

Jean and I believe learning materials should be
fun, challenging, constructive, informative, and
relevant to steady mental, physical, and moral
growth. We depend on orders from customers to
continue the publication of this Source Book, but
we absolutely will not sell or recommend any item
which doesn't meet our criteria. This book lists
a few items with which we don't agree, and you
can't buy them from us, but we don't mind telling
you where you can buy them if you want them. We
also recommend many items which we don't sell,
sometimes because they are available only from
other suppliers, sometimes because we can't give
you as low a price as other suppliers can.

As you'll see, I have strong opinions. Whether
you agree or disagree with me, you'll always know
where I stand, and will not be misled by indis-
criminate praise and false "objectivity." We want
to make money, but we want to make it honestly.

Most people who are not home-schooling, whether
or not they approve of it, assume that its goals
are similar to those of public schooling -- to
prepare young people for jobs or careers or further education, to make a living, and to be relatively good citizens of the society in which they
live. Many home-schoolers agree with those goals,
but believe that education at home will provide a
better foundation than the public schools can.

We are among the many others who want to reach
further, to aim higher. Money-earning skills are
certainly useful and perhaps even necessary; but
there are other skills of far greater importance.
This is, and will continue to be, a period of
rapid and radical change -- in society, in government, and in the ecology of our planet. We
have the duty, as parents and educators, to help
our children prepare to meet those changes creatively and responsibly; to help them develop
skills and attitudes with which they can make
positive contributions to the world. The ability
to evaluate, to make responsible judgements, to
resolve conflicts peacefully, and to give helpful
counsel to others will be of much more worth to
our children and to the world than business management, welding, or engineering.

Of equal importance, we want our children to be
happy now, as children. Childhood is important in
itself; it shouldn't be spent only in preparation
for adulthood.

In selecting learning tools and materials -- to recommend, to sell, or to use ourselves -- we always try to keep these objectives in mind -- to find kits, books, models, and other learning materials which help us define and develop more fully the values and skills which we believe are needed for happy, purposeful, creative lives, as children and as adults.

We hope you find this book useful. We welcome personal correspondence with all our readers. If you have any questions, comments, or suggestions, please write.

Jean & Donn Reed
Brook Farm

4 "WE WOULD BETTER WAIT AND SEE"

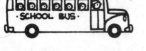

"We would better wait and see," our provincial Minister of Education was quoted as saying, referring to the possibility of closing the public schools if 3,000 janitors, secretaries, and bus drivers decided to strike.

A staff writer for The Telegraph-Journal of Saint John, New Brunswick, went on to tell his readers about the Treasury Board's efforts to ensure that many non-teaching employees would be forced to work in the event of a strike: "The Board has been only successful in having 132 non-teaching employees designated essential."

Did he think the Board should have been more than successful? Wasn't success enough? Perhaps the adverb was meant to be an adjective, to modify the number of employees, "only 132," rather than to diminish the Board's success.

The 132 employees whom the Treasury Board designated as "essential" should have been congratulated. Apparently, it wasn't their jobs which were essential, but the 132 employees themselves. Kings, queens, prime ministers, and presidents will all be replaced someday, so even they are not essential, but the writer brought to our attention 132 people with a sinecure greater than that of the Twelve Disciples -- at least in the opinion of the Treasury Board.

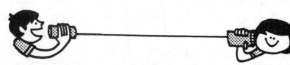

Part of the problem, according to the Chief Negotiator, was that for more than six months the Treasury Board "constantly refused to negotiate in a serious tone."

According to all of my several dictionaries, "constantly" means "happening or continuing all the time; happening repeatedly." Those Treasury Board members must have been as busy as naughty schoolboys writing their penances on the chalkboard: "We will not negotiate in a serious tone, we will not negotiate in a serious tone, we will not..." and so on, over and over, for six months.

The Chief Negotiator didn't say that the Treasury Board had refused to negotiate, but that it had refused to do so "in a serious tone." Did the Board make flippant remarks? Giggle during meetings? Make faces at non-essential employees?

"The only reason Charlie got to be Minister of Education," a neighboring farmer told me recently, "is that he sat behind me in grade school and copied all my answers."

Another question pops up constantly, in a serious tone: If the school employees, whether essential or non-essential, go out on strike, and the schools are all closed, and the students spend the day watching Sesame Street and cleaning their fingernails, will it make any appreciable difference in the education of tomorrow's writers, educators, and politicians?

We would better wait and see.

Dad, are you and Mom gonna go on strike, too?

WHY WE TEACH AT HOME

5

When Jean and I were expecting our first baby, in 1966, there was very little literature about natural birth. We had read enough to know that we wanted an undrugged birth, but we took for granted the "necessity" of birth in a hospital.

From the beginning, we felt that both the pregnancy and the birth were ours, together. All we asked was permission for me to be present during the delivery.

"Oh, no," the doctor said, "we have enough problems without having fainting husbands all over the floor."

So Jean and I decided, tentatively, to have the baby at home.

We began studying all the books we could find on childbirth, gynecology, and relaxation techniques (such as yoga breathing). We left the question of "where" open to the last minute. We bought and familiarized ourselves with the few supplies necessary for a homebirth, but we kept our suitcases packed, ready to throw into the car. If either of us felt even a little insecure or worried about having the baby at home, we'd go to the hospital.

The time came, and we felt fine. We tingled with anticipation and quiet excitement. The labor was long and tiring, but completely without pain. Throughout the labor, I stayed with Jean, rubbing her back, moistening her lips, and being a brace for her legs -- except a few times between contractions when I tried to find food for myself. Each time I put on a pot of coffee or a pan of canned beans, another contraction began and I ran back to help.

Cathy was born in a little log cabin in northern Vermont, forty miles from the nearest hospital. She began nursing right away, while I massaged Jean's uterus to reduce the possibility of excessive bleeding.

The only thing that went wrong with Cathy's birth was that I burned three pans of beans and boiled away six pots of coffee.

Karen was born in 1968, in our home in Vermont, with six feet of snow drifted outside the windows. This birth was not only painless, but very actively pleasurable. We had never read about this aspect of birth, and it took us both by surprise. What a long way from the pain and agony of conventional myth! (Years later, a sympathetic doctor said, "Yes, I've seen it a few times. It may even be that many women have orgasms during birth, but interpret them as pain -- because the sensations are more intense than anything they've experienced previously, and because they have been conditioned to expect pain."

Susan was born in 1970, and Derek in 1972, both in a log cabin in the mountainous Central Interior of British Columbia, also forty miles from the nearest hospital. Both births were a lot of work but relatively easy, completely painless, and physically pleasurable.

Active fatherhood -- that is, participating as a full partner in parenting -- has many rewards, but one of the greatest is hearing that first little cry of "Hello" and of cradling the new son or daughter even before he or she is fully born.

Jean nursed each of the babies for at least a year. For the first six weeks or more, we never put the babies down or left them alone; we always held them, carried them, and cuddled them. They never woke up crying, wondering where they -- or we -- were.

"It's good for them to cry," several neighbors and relatives told us. "It develops their lungs."

Others told us, "You give them too much attention. It isn't good for them. They'll become too dependent on you."

The babies slept with us, despite the many warnings (from people who had never tried it) that "You'll roll on the baby in your sleep!" It never happened, of course. When the baby became hungry during the night, Jean had only to turn over, still half-asleep, help the baby find the nipple, and doze off again. No fumbling for the light switch, no grumbling at being awakened, no crying, no frustration.

There was only one instance when it didn't quite work -- that is, not right away. I woke up enough to hear Cathy's murmur of hunger change to a cry of indignation, and I turned on the bedside light to see why Jean wasn't feeding her. Jean, still asleep, was trying with great determination to put her nipple into Cathy's ear. (A reader of Nurturing Magazine, in which part of this story appeared, wrote me, "Ah, the old nipple-in-the-ear trick -- I've done it myself many times!")

Cathy was visiting neighbors with her grandmother when Karen was born, so she missed the birth -- by just a few minutes. Both Cathy and Karen were with us during Susan's birth, and all three welcomed Derek into the world.

The objections and fears which many people have about home-birth are not greatly different from their feelings about home-school: "Something will go wrong," "You need the experts," "You're sheltering them too much," and so on.

Our main reason for having home-birth was that we loved our children (yes, even before they were born), and we wanted them to have the best start in life. We began teaching them at home for the same reason.

In education, as with birth, it was the narrow-mindedness and insensitivity of the "experts" and "trained professionals" which led us to realize that we could probably do much better without their help.

We are confirmed do-it-yourselfers in many areas of life -- child-birth, house-building, food production, etc. -- and so we thought about teaching our children at home, but didn't have any definite reason for doing so, and assumed that contact with other children would be enjoyable and beneficial.

We had read some of John Holt's books (HOW CHILDREN FAIL, HOW CHILDREN LEARN, etc.) and various other books about education, but we thought that small rural schools might somehow have escaped the negative attitudes and academic failings which most of the books described.

We were wrong. In nearly every instance, our children returned from school much poorer than they had been when they left home. Each of them had learned to read and to enjoy books at least a year or two before entering school. They soon learned, in the public schools, that reading is a very serious chore; they not only lost interest in reading, but actually lost a great deal of reading ability. They became ill-mannered and bigoted. Far from being "broadened" by social contacts, they were coerced into becoming very narrow and intolerant.

Cathy had always enjoyed books, from the time she was old enough to look at them. Before she was two, she spent hours with her favorites, studying minute details in the pictures and asking us about the letters. By the time she was six, she was entirely familiar with the alphabet, basic phonics, shapes, colors, and seemed to have an intuitive grasp of elementary psychology (but without knowing any of its jargon). She enjoyed working with us in the garden, the barn, and the kitchen. We talked about school, and decided to give it a try.

Each morning, we drove to the corner, where Cathy boarded the school bus and rode to the two-room schoolhouse twenty miles away. In the afternoon, we met her at the corner to bring her home.

Cathy liked school, she told us. She had many friends and she liked the teacher. Each day, she was eager to meet the bus, and came home with excited stories of new games and new friends.

She began sucking and chewing her lower lip, until it was always red and swollen. She stopped reading, and had no interest in books. She became bossy and whiney. The redness of her lower lip spread down toward her chin.

Cathy's teacher told us she hadn't noticed any problems. Cathy insisted there was nothing wrong; she got along with the other children, she still liked her teacher, and the work was very easy, even if a little boring. She continued to chew her lower lip, and often screamed at us and gave us belligerent orders.

During the two-week Christmas vacation, she stopped chewing her lip, and the redness almost disappeared from her lip and chin. Toward the end of her vacation, she looked into a few of her favorite books. She became more pleasant to live with, more friendly and agreeable and cooperative -- as she had always been before she started school.

When she returned from the first day at school after vacation, her lower lip was red and swollen. She refused to pick her coat up from the floor, and she was snappy and bossy.

We never returned her to the school. For the rest of that winter and through the following summer, she occasionally looked through her books, but had no interest in reading. We left her alone, and didn't try to give her any "school" work.

In the fall Cathy entered school again, in the second grade. Despite having "missed" half of the first grade, she had no difficulties with second-grade work. Her teacher was pleasant, competent, and understanding. Cathy finished the school year with high marks and still had a pleasant personality. We concluded that the first year must have been an unfortunate exception.

Karen, like Cathy, had learned basic reading and math skills long before she entered formal schooling. Her first grade teacher was one of the most loving and dedicated teachers our children ever encountered. Karen's first grade experience was nearly everything we thought public education should be -- a continuation of skills already learned and the introduction of new subjects and new concepts, both academically and socially. We could see Karen growing, rapidly and happily.

Cathy's third grade teacher was often hoarse from yelling at her students. One of her favorite punishments for any misbehaving boy was to have him sit on her lap, making him the unhappy object of his classmates' coarse jokes and teasing.

What happens in the mind of a child for whom a customary act of affection becomes a dreaded punishment and humiliation?

As it happened, Cathy was a model student, academically and socially, and became the teacher's pet. She disliked the teacher's screaming and bullying, but was relieved (as we were) that she was never the object of the teacher's tirades.

We felt it was a very unhealthy environment, whether or not Cathy was learning anything positive or useful. And she wasn't.

Given a writing assignment, Cathy wrote:

One day I was sweeping the floor. I swept the edge of the counter, and I swept a spray can out. It said Spray a broom. I sprayed the broom. The broom said Hi who are you? I'm Cathy I said will you come to the zoo with me? Of course I will I am your friend. So we went to the zoo. We saw a lion and it was loose. We told someone at the zoo. The end.

Not too bad, really. I know many adults who couldn't do as well. But it was much less than we thought should have been achieved in thirty hours a week, four weeks a month, nine months a year, for over two years.

Even worse, Cathy was bored.

"What did you do in school today, Cathy?"

"Oh, nothing. Just more second grade work. I did it all last year. When will I start learning something new?"

From asking that question to becoming an eight-year-old dropout, with full parental approval and encouragement, was a very short step.

A dropout. No education? How would she get anywhere in life?

Cathy began "going to school" at home. Not yet free of our own educational conditioning, we eased ourselves into the formal teaching business by subscribing to a correspondence course from Calvert School. Each weekday, from nine in the morning until noon, Jean was Cathy's teacher. In those three hours, they easily covered more than two daily lessons, including arithmetic, geography, Greek mythology, art, literature, spelling, history, science, and composition.

At the same time, Jean was raising and teaching Susan and Derek. Karen was doing well in first grade in the public school. (I was taking life easy as an edgerman in a sawmill.)

As a hobby, Cathy studied dinosaurs and fossils, and this was only one of many areas in which we found Cathy was often the teacher and we were the pupils.

Ten weeks after leaving the public school, Cathy wrote:

A JOURNEY TO THE PAST

I found a time machine. I am going back to 120 million years ago. Dinosaurs roamed the earth and volcanoes erupted a lot.

They liked it warm and wet and it never snowed. I saw a Stegosaurus, like a duck; it ate plants. It didn't frighten me but it was about 11 feet tall and four feet wide. I rode on a Triceratops, a three-horned dinosaur. I saw a Tyrannosaurus. I ran back to the time machine and I went to another part of the jungle. I saw a Teranodon, a bird without teeth. I had a ride on it. It took me to an Ankylosaurus and I took the Ankylosaurus home with me.

Did you notice she missed the "p" in "pteranodon"? You wouldn't miss it, of course; and I just looked in my dictionary for the spelling.

But how much can you expect of an eight-year-old kid, only halfway through third grade?

In spite of a few good experiences with the public schools, we were finally beginning to learn our own lesson. For the next three years, we taught all four of our children at home. Then Cathy wanted to try public school again, to be able to spend more time with others her age. After much discussion, we reluctantly agreed to let her try. Her teacher proved to be the second of the best teachers our children ever had in public school, and we never regretted Cathy's year with her.

The next year was quite different. Cathy's English and history teacher, with a Master's degree in education, couldn't spell, punctuate, or construct a proper sentence. He taught his students to use colons and semi-colons interchangeably. He taught them a punctuation device which he called "dot-dot-dot," and met my objection with the explanation that the word "ellipsis" would be too difficult for eighth graders to remember. He taught that capitalization of the first letter in a sentence is a matter of personal preference.

I haunted him, two or three times a week, after school hours and occasionally at class time, but wasn't surprised that it did no good. He wasn't overly anxious to discuss his methods, although he tried to assure me that his own training had been quite thorough, and that he certainly knew more about English and teaching than anyone without formal training in those subjects.

Cathy and her class were told to find Rio Blanco on a map of Brazil. She spent over an hour searching through her school atlas, our own atlas (which is better), and the Encyclopedia Britannica. Failing to find Rio Blanco anywhere, Cathy was finally convinced that the teacher had made another spelling mistake, and he later admitted it (with a shrug, and not seeming embarrassed). Cathy had learned a lesson, but not the one her teacher had intended. That wasn't the only hour of her life wasted by a teacher's careless spelling or sloppy handwriting.

I made a list of words which the teacher consistently misspelled on assignment sheets, and showed the list to the principal.

"What grade level," I asked, "should have complete mastery of the spelling of these words?"

He looked the list over and said, "Third grade. A fourth grader who didn't know these words would be considered slow."

I said it seemed to be a great waste of time for the teacher, for his students, and for me -- the latter because I often needed to correct the teacher's assignments before allowing Cathy to work on them.

The principal insisted I must be mistaken about the teacher's having misspelled the words, and suggested that Cathy had copied them incorrectly. I showed him the teacher's assignment sheets. He suggested I take my complaints directly to the teacher. I told him I had done so, several times, and was less than satisfied. He said he would have to side with his teachers, on the assumption that they would not be teachers if they didn't know what they were doing.

A few days later, the principal wrote me a letter (so he could put a carbon copy in his office files), saying that the teacher we had discussed (but whom he didn't name) was a Trained Professional (his capital letters), and therefore must know what he is doing. The Trained Professional's qualification to teach, he went on to say, was proven by the fact that he had been hired by the school board.

Mark Twain once remarked that God made a fool for practice, and then made school boards. That's a harsh judgement, and may be extreme. Was the mistake Twain's or God's? As far as I know, neither was a Trained Professional, except that Twain had a license to pilot a river boat.

Jesus told the sick man to pick up his bed and walk. Henry David Thoreau advised his contemporaries to throw down their beds and run. Anyone who is only a Trained Professional -- that is, who has nothing more to offer than his Trained

Professionalism -- has little chance of doing either.

Since that time, we have taught our children at home, and have seen no reason to try the public schools again.

The kids have all been active, according to their ages and interests, in ball games, 4-H, youth groups, dances, overnight slumber parties, national exchange trips, and jobs in town. They have been concerned about global problems, such as hunger, human rights, and the death penalty.

It has now been twenty-three years since our first home-birth, and seventeen years (not counting the years from birth to age six!) since we began teaching at home. Three of our kids have left home now; Derek, 17 as I write this, may stay with us another year or so, or may decide to strike out on his own soon.

School at home isn't always easy, but, whenever problems have arisen, we have tried to treat them not as interruptions of our education, but as parts of it. In facing problems and working with them, we have learned more about ourselves and each other and the world.

We're increasingly convinced that education at home has made our children happier, healthier, and stronger -- physically, mentally, and spiritually. Our children have remained bright, curious, and creative -- and, we hope, have helped us to remain so, too.

WHY THE MOVEMENT IS GROWING

"For the first time in the history of our country," says the United States National Commission on Excellence in Education, **"the educational skills of one generation will not surpass, will not equal, will not even approach, those of their parents."**

"To be culturally literate is to possess the basic information needed to thrive in the modern world," says E. D. Hirsch, Jr., in his best-selling CULTURAL LITERACY: WHAT EVERY AMERICAN NEEDS TO KNOW. As evidence that far too many school students are not learning this necessary knowledge, Hirsch offers the steadily-declining scores on Verbal Scholastic Aptitude Tests, and reports of the National Assessment of Educational Progress that student knowledge in key areas is shrinking.

A 1988 special edition of Instructor, a magazine for public school teachers, says, "Unfortunately, two recent surveys may back Hirsch up. The National Endowment for the Humanities assessed the study of history, literature, and languages in the nation's public schools and reported that 'America's elementary and secondary schools are failing to teach students about their shared past and culture.'

"In a related study [the article continues], Diane Ravitch, professor of history and education at Columbia University, and Chester E. Finn, Jr., the U.S. Assistant Secretary of Education for Research and Improvement, analyzed a 1986 assessment of 7,812 high school juniors and gave them failing marks on their knowledge of literature and history."

The public schools throughout North America are failing, even by their own standards, which most critics agree are misguided and poorly-conceived at best. Too many children are being labeled "learning-disabled" and put into special remedial classes with "high-interest, low-vocabulary" readers and text-books. Tenth-graders are reading on a third-grade level. How did they get to tenth grade without learning to read much more than their own names?

More and more people are teaching their own children in their homes. Some parents have no particular quarrel with the public schools, but simply feel that children shouldn't be taken from the family at an early age, if at all. A reason given more frequently is the steadily-declining level of academic instruction in the public schools.

Parents are no longer accepting the weak promises and weaker excuses of the schools. They want their children to receive a proper education, even if it means removing them from the schools.

"Dear Mr. Reed,

"I hope you receive this and are still in business! I saw your ad in a 1985 issue of Nurturing Magazine that I borrowed from a friend. Today is the last day of school for our three girls. Yesterday, they brought home the year's "work" -- what a pathetic example of wasted time! Six pages of a notebook for the entire year's effort for science; maybe twelve pages for social studies. The story my sixth-grade student wrote had no punctuation or proper grammar. I have told the girls of my dissatisfaction. They like the social aspect of school -- but I have to look out for their welfare. I don't feel they are getting an education that will help them in years to come. They need something better!"

In 1979 the Wall Street Journal reported that the U.S. Census Bureau estimated that one percent of the country's 32 million school-age children were not in school. I think it's safe to assume that the number is much greater now than it was ten years ago. If we eliminate those who may not be receiving any education at all, in the conventional sense, even including the thousands of runaways and other street kids whose "education" is probably not very desirable (whether we guess the number to be half, two-thirds, or even nine-tenths), we're still left with a number of children receiving their education "at home" -- i.e., out of the public school system -- far beyond the number which any Department of Education is willing to admit.

An article in The New York Times back in 1981 suggested the number might be fifty thousand. A more recent article in **Learning**, a magazine for professional teachers, suggested a million. Home-school groups throughout the United States and Canada report phenomenal growth in recent years, many of them from hundreds to thousands.

Not very many years ago, a grade level lower than 70 was failing. In most schools today, any grade over 60, and sometimes 55 or even 50, is accepted as a passing grade -- and often that "passing" grade is achieved by comparison with a class average, rather than with the overall requirements of a course. If the class average is 50, a passing grade need be no more than 25.

Most school suppliers' catalogs have a high

percentage of "high-interest, low-vocabulary" readers -- books written on a reading level several years below the grade for which they are intended. In such catalogs, notations such as "Interest level, grades 11-12; reading level, grades 3-4" are common. There has always been some need of such books, especially in teaching remedial reading to the few students who somehow got behind, and in teaching adult illiterates; but now the growing failures of the public schools are making it necessary for nearly half of all textbooks, in nearly all subjects, to be written with "high interest" and "low vocabulary."

Several publications have reported the results of a two-year survey of high school students in southern California, in which a junior at USC was shocked to learn that the United States had been fighting against Japan in World War II, and asked, "Who won?" A journalism student at USC didn't know if Germany had been an enemy or an ally of the U.S. during World War II. A junior at UCLA thought Toronto is a city in Italy; another guessed that Stalin was the U.S. president just before Roosevelt; and another thought Lenin was a drummer with the Beatles before Ringo Starr.

Design for Change, a children's rights organization, reported in 1985: "Of the 39,500 students who entered Chicago public high schools in the fall of 1980, only 18,500 were graduated in 1984. Of those who did graduate, only 6,000 had 12th grade reading ability, while 5,000 had only 8th grade reading skills or less."

A survey in 1987 by the National Assessment of Education Progress (NAEP) of high school seniors in seven major cities disclosed that in Dallas, 25 percent of students tested couldn't identify the country that borders the United States on the south; in Boston, 39 percent couldn't name the six New England states; in Minneapolis-St. Paul, 63 percent couldn't name all seven continents; in Baltimore, 45 percent couldn't find the United States on a world map; in Hartford, 48 percent couldn't name three African countries; in Kansas City, 40 percent couldn't name three countries in South America; and in Atlanta, 42 percent couldn't answer the question, "When it is noon in Atlanta, what time is it in San Francisco?"

"We have a situation," said the director of the U.S. National Council for Geographic Education, "where Johnny not only doesn't know how to read or add, he doesn't even know where he is."

A newspaper article written by a recent college graduate reported, "The body of a man found in the Saint John River last week is still trying to be identified."

Another paper told readers about a business-woman, who, "having been closed for two years, re-opened the store."

A newspaper editor showed me a letter he had received from a recent high school graduate asking for a job as a "sprots writter."

Learning problems frequently come from problem teachers who seek to excuse their inability to convey knowledge to their students by saying the students are hyperactive, retarded, disturbed, disabled, or -- more recently -- have an Attention Deficit.

One of the students in an Adult Literacy class I taught some years ago was a man with a measured IQ of 50. Previous teachers had tried briefly to teach him, but were quick to decide that he was incapable of learning, and therefore not worth the time it would take to work with him. He was living away from home, and the high point of each day for him was "writing" -- dictating -- a letter to his mother. One day, I typed the letter he had just dictated to me, then asked him to read it to me. None of the symbols meant anything to him, although I'd been working with him for several weeks. I pointed out the letters which spelled MOM, naming them and sounding them, then pronouncing the word again. "This is the word that means your mom," I told him. He repeated the sounds and the word after me, lovingly, wonderingly, studying the letters. I moved his finger, tracing the shapes of the letters as I said them. Then I guided his hand with a pencil in it to draw the letters. He printed **M O M** over and over for hours. With that word as his personal key, he progressed from total, "hopeless" illiteracy to a sixth-grade reading and writing level -- in less than six months. He could read comic books, magazines, newspapers, street signs, a driver's manual, and thousands of books. The psychologists and educators who had pronounced him incapable of learning decided their tests had been wrong, and were baffled when his IQ still tested at 50. Retarded? Disturbed? Attention Deficit? When I read those weak excuses for the schools' failures, I have a definite Belief Deficit.

Teachers today are rated more for their accuracy and punctuality in keeping attendance records than for their achievements in providing an environment in which students can learn. In most cases, the teachers themselves are not at fault, at least when they begin their careers. They have high ideals and higher hopes, but they are soon beaten down by the quasi-scientific theories of statisticians and pompous educational psychologists who can't get past the first four letters of analysis.

An article in the national homeschool magazine

Growing Without Schooling (December 1983) told of a Minnesota judge who ruled that a mother's actual ability to teach is unimportant if she isn't legally "qualified." The mother had offered her daughter's educational progress as evidence of the effectiveness of her teaching, but the judge ruled that if the mother doesn't have legal certification, then her being a good teacher in fact is irrelevant.

In the same state, according to an article in **Learning Magazine,** several teachers who had been out on strike were given up to 33 credits needed for the renewal of their teaching certificates, "on the theory that the teachers learned communication and political organization skills during the walkout."

Time reported in October 1983 that "when one-third of Houston's public-school teachers took a competency exam last spring, some 60 percent failed the reading section."

A study titled "What's Happening in Teacher Testing," released in 1987 by Chester Finn, Jr., of the U.S. Department of Education, says that 28 percent of the applicants to teacher education programs are being rejected, and that 17 percent of teacher graduates who apply for teaching licenses are being turned down. In spite of this, says the report, passing scores are still set so low that many "incompetents" are being licensed and subsequently hired. In some states, says the report, teachers can be certified even if they miss more than half of the questions on the National Teacher Examinations.

Joseph Weizenbaum, a professor of computer science at MIT, in an interview published in **Science Digest** (August 1983), said, "[F]ully half of all math and science teachers are operating on emergency certificates." That is, when there aren't enough qualified instructors to go around, unearned certificates are given to teachers whose training is in completely different and often unrelated fields.

The same school authorities who issue these "emergency certificates" would undoubtedly scoff at mail-order diploma mills which will sell a phony Ph.D. for a few hundred dollars. Is there really any difference?

It's probably still true, as we've been told for so long, that high school graduates earn more money than dropouts, but it's not always because they're better educated. It's often because employers also have been taught that there is magic in the graduates' parchment coupons with the Olde Englishe lettering. Indeed, a few decades ago, there may have been some magic there, but today most of it is no more than clumsy legerdemain.

Public schools teach students how to pass tests -- by memorizing facts and formulas, by guessing, or by cheating. If teachers did not announce tests days and weeks in advance, and then tell their students what to study in preparation, and

even what questions to expect, and on what pages they should look for the answers, and then just as often give a "pre-test" for practice, nearly all the students would fail. Even with all this rigorous coaching, most students would still fail if the test were unexpectedly postponed for two weeks, during which time everything would be forgotten again. It's only by such hocus-pocus that teachers are able to help most students "pass" their tests; the marks are duly recorded, and the year is considered a success. Next year, two or three months will be spent in "review" of last year's subjects before a new field or higher level can be introduced.

Sixty, forty, even twenty years ago, "average" students learned more and retained more than most of today's top students. "But we have more subjects to cover," protest the teachers. That's true, but so what? The larger range of subjects supposedly being presented is no excuse for dim mediocrity in all of them.

The academic failures of the public schools are unimportant beside their much greater failure to provide an environment in which children can grow in moral strength and integrity. Most parents, whether or not they consider teaching at home, are worried about drugs, violence, sexual promiscuity, and teenage pregnancy.

Several magazines and newspapers have repeated a comparison of two surveys of public school teachers:

In 1940, the most serious problems they had to deal with were talking without permission, chewing gum, making noise, running in the halls, getting out of turn in line, and wearing improper clothing.

In 1980, their major concerns were rape, burglary, robbery, assault, arson, bombings, murder, suicide, vandalism, extortion, drug and alcohol abuse, gang warfare, pregnancies, abortions, and venereal disease.

These "problems" are the fault of society in general, not of the schools and teachers, but the schools are doing little or nothing to change them.

On an administrative level, the schools try to produce obedient, unquestioning citizens, good consumers, productive (but not creative) workers.

On a social level -- admittedly not through deliberate design usually, but nonetheless a fact -- the schools promote religious intolerance, racial bigotry, drug abuse, sexual promiscuity, lying, cheating, emotional insincerity, philosophical skepticism, fake sophistication, and intellectual apathy.

A few years ago, my father-in-law, a firm opponent of homeschooling, wrote to us, "Your lessons on morality are fine for your homeschool, but they have no validity in the real world."

Obviously, we disagree; but his statement seems to reflect the opinions of a disproportionate segment of society. Corporate advertising, popular music, television, and the majority of public schools are bombarding our society with the dictum, "If it feels good, do it."

"You can't shelter your children forever," the self-appointed experts tell us. "They'll have to be exposed to these things sooner or later."

That's true, we answer; we can't shelter them forever -- nor do we want to. We just want to shelter them until they are strong enough to face these issues by themselves without being overwhelmed by them. Most adults would have great difficulty in resisting a constant daily barrage of sex and drugs and violence. How, then, can we expect our children -- who are still learning to examine, evaluate, and judge -- to put such "problems" into their proper perspective?

Such issues and problems are facts of life in today's world, and our children need to be aware of them and to be prepared to deal with them; but they don't need -- and should not have -- daily exposure to them, especially among their friends and acquaintances. Such problems are symptoms of an unhealthy society, a society with an illness which, we hope and believe, isn't fatal, but is certainly dangerous and highly contagious.

More and more people, fortunately, are resisting the trend toward laissez-faire ethics.

"As any parent knows, teaching character is a difficult task," William J. Bennett, then-Secretary of Education, told the National Press Club, in Washington, D.C., March 27, 1985. "But it is a crucial task because we want all our children to be not only healthy, happy, and successful, but decent, strong, and good. None of this happens automatically; there is no genetic transmission of virtue. It takes conscious, committed effort ...Not all teachers are parents, but all parents are teachers, the indispensable teachers. And, as teachers, parents always have had the first and largest responsibility for educating their children... And in some cases parents discover that their children are unlearning in school the lessons they have learned at home."

To protect our children from the harmful influences of a chaotic society until they are better able to handle them is not only our right, but our duty and responsibility -- even if it means (although of course it doesn't) that they receive no academic education at all.

Hardly a day goes by without an article about homeschooling in a major newspaper or magazine. Publications which promote and celebrate family closeness are becoming much more numerous. There are now hundreds of home school newsletters, organizations, and support groups.

Professional educators are beginning to realize that all their training and certification are not helping them teach, and that most parents could educate their own children far better, and in less time, than the schools can. The teachers may have to find other work -- or throw out the schedules and formulas and remedial classes, and get back to real teaching.

My grandmother wanted me to have an education, so she kept me out of school.
Margaret Mead

PERMISSION TO TEACH
AT HOME

> Alice began to feel very uneasy. To be
> sure, she had not as yet had any dispute
> with the Queen, but she knew that it
> might happen any minute. "And then,"
> thought she, "what would become of me?
> They're dreadfully fond of beheading
> people here."
>
> Lewis Carroll

Home-schooling is permitted in most of the United States and all of the Canadian provinces. Requirements and conditions vary from extremely lenient to very strict, with the majority in between but leaning toward the more permissive.

Information, suggestions, and advice about dealing with education laws were very difficult to find fifteen years ago, or even ten, but now such information is easily obtained.

Begin with a copy of the Education Act for your state or province, which your public library will have or be able to get. Ask your Department of Education for a copy of all laws regarding home education, but don't get into a lengthy dialogue yet; and don't take the word of teachers, principals, or education officials as infallible. Sometimes they don't know the laws but will gladly offer opinions or even guesses as if they were facts. Sometimes, they will even lie. (A couple in one state was told that home-schooling is allowed only in the first four grades, and another couple in the same state was told that home-schooling is allowed only after the first four grades. In fact, it's allowed there on all grade levels.)

The best single source for legal information and advice for most home-schoolers is HOLT ASSO-CIATES, INC., 2269 Massachusetts Ave., Cambridge, MA 02140. This organization, founded by John Holt in 1970 and continuing his work since his death in 1985, publishes the bimonthly magazine "Growing Without Schooling," operates a home-school book and music store, and offers many other publications, large and small, about home-schooling. Send a #10 self-addressed, stamped envelope for more information and a catalog.

John Holt's **TEACH YOUR OWN,** the only one of his books specifically about home-schooling, has many invaluable suggestions for dealing with officials and the law, as well as extensive information, with examples, about many other aspects of home-schooling. (This book, described more fully later on, is available from Holt Associates, Brook Farm Books, and most bookstores.)

Most states and provinces have at least one home-school support group or newsletter, and some have several. Most of these groups can give up-to-date information about requirements in their own areas, as well as suggestions for dealing with them, or can refer you to other groups which can help you. Some have detailed "legal packets," with both general and specific information and suggestions, including sample letters, curriculum plans, and strategies for dealing with hostile authorities. Many of these organizations are listed later in this book.

Another excellent source of general information is HOME EDUCATION PRESS, P.O. Box 1083, Tonasket, WA 98855, which publishes the national bimonthly "Home Education Magazine," and several books and booklets on home-schooling. (See Support Groups & Organizations.)

STORY OF A BILL: Legalizing Homeschooling in Pennsylvania, by Howard Richman ($6.95, postpaid, from PENNSYLVANIA HOMESCHOOLERS, RD 2 Box 117, Kittanning, PA 16201), is the exciting, informative story of how homeschoolers in that state fought and won a five-year battle for the legalization of home education, and how the legislators finally applauded them. Very interesting reading, and an excellent blueprint for others in the same predicament, with many suggestions for similar action in other states.

BETTER THAN SCHOOL, by Nancy Wallace (see Education), although not a "how-to" book, is in part the story of a long and finally victorious battle with public school authorities, and has many good ideas for others who face a similar situation.

CLONLARA SCHOOL, 1289 Jewett Street, Ann Arbor, MI 48104, offers many very useful services, including legal representation. Send a #10 SASE for full information about the HOME BASED EDUCATION PLAN and other services. (See Organizations.)

Useful information may also be gotten from the NATIONAL HOMESCHOOL ASSOCIATION, PO Box 157290, Cincinnati, OH 45215 (see Organizations).

An appendix in Ted Wade's THE HOME SCHOOL MANUAL (See Education) lists the requirements of each state and the Canadian provinces, and is updated fairly regularly, but not annually.

One of the most informative (and interesting) books about dealing with the legal aspects of home-schooling is **TAKING CHARGE THROUGH HOME SCHOOLING: Personal and Political Empowerment,** by M. Larry and Susan D. Kaseman (see Education).

The National Committee for Citizens Rights in Education, Ste. 410, Wilde Lake Village Green, Columbia, MD 1044, offers a variety of publications which may be useful.

The HOME SCHOOL LEGAL DEFENSE ASSOCIATION, P.O. Box 2091, Washington, DC 20013, offers complete legal representation at no charge beyond an annual fee of $100 -- if you qualify. Just as sick people have trouble obtaining health insurance, only applicants not yet facing legal action are eligible for representation by the HSLDA. The HSLDA is very conservative Christian and the membership application requires a description of the applicants' religious affiliations and beliefs, although particular affiliation doesn't seem to be a requirement. However, applicants must agree in a legal contract to "exercise diligence in teaching our children in a responsible way" -- as defined by the HSLDA -- and to "use an organized curriculum and a clearly recognizable program of education," which automatically eliminates many home-schoolers who prefer a freer approach to learning. A very valuable service if you need it, and if you can get it.

If you're in a hurry for a quick reference to the bare-bones legislative requirements of all the states, or if you want to compare laws of different states, order **HOME SCHOOLING LAWS: All Fifty States,** from the author, Steve Deckard, Ed.D., 228 Central Drive, Briarcliff Manor, NY 10510, for $18.00, postpaid. This small book has basic information from each state, without interpretation. For about the same cost in stamps and envelopes, you can get the same information directly from the various states' departments of education, and you can get interpretations and actual procedures from the respective home-school support groups and newsletters.

* * * * *

Two of the cardinal points in our homeschooling are that individuals are always more important than government, and that individuals can effect meaningful changes in society. Might does not make right, and we want our children to know it. We tell them that freedom is a very fragile and elusive condition. We agree with Thomas Jefferson that "eternal vigilance is the price of liberty," not only in a broad, political sense, but also in our immediate, personal lives; not only against foreign governments, but against soft-drink ads, religious fanatics, and repressive forces in our own government, including a few education authorities.

If the government has particular rules and regulations regarding subjects taught or hours observed, we'll try to meet them -- if such compliance doesn't interfere with the education of our children. If the government comes to us to discuss, negotiate, or offer a compromise, we're willing to listen and participate and consider. We don't want broadside confrontation with school officials. But if the government comes to us with orders and demands, as if it is right simply because it is stronger, then we resist. That which is demanded may be right -- but the demand, as such, is wrong.

We are convinced -- not by anyone's scripture, but by observation and reason -- that teaching our own children is not merely a privilege to be granted by the government, but is an intrinsic right. Whether that right is God-given or a sine qua non of natural, universal law (not forgetting they may be one and the same), the instruction to render unto Caesar only that which is Caesar's is completely pertinent, both literally and symbolically. As Emerson wrote in "Self Reliance," we cannot consent to pay for a privilege where we have intrinsic right.

We never ask for permission to teach at home. A request for permission would imply a willingness to abide by the response, whether positive or negative. The request might be denied, and then where would we be? We have no such willingness, so we usually just go about our business, and expect the government to do the same.

But people who build their home in the woods and don't put their children on the rural school bus don't blend into the woodwork, even if they dress conventionally and drive an ordinary eight-year-old car. Word gets around, although it's often like the old game of "Telephone," in which the players sit in a circle and a message is whispered from one to the next, and finally back to the one who began it, usually becoming considerably distorted as it passes through one head after another.

OFFICE OF THE SUPERINTENDENT OF SCHOOLS
Fredericton, New Brunswick
October 27, 1980

Dear Mr. Reed:

It is my understanding that you have recently moved to this area from British Columbia. It has been brought to my attention that you have four school age children for whom you are responsible. The Province of New Brunswick requires any person from seven to fifteen years of age inclusive to be in attendance at school. I have included the appropriate sections for your information.

59(1) In sections 59 to 66 inclusive "child" means any person from seven to fifteen years of age inclusive.

59(2) Except as provided in this section, every child shall attend school in the school selected by the school board in that school district provided for in section 5.

59(3) Where

(a) in the opinion of the Minister, a child is under efficient instruction elsewhere,

(b) a child is unable to attend school by reason of his own sickness or other unavoidable cause,

(c) the child is officially excluded from attendance under sections 45, 46, or 53,

(d) the child has completed the course prescribed for grade twelve, or

(e) the Minister certifies in writing to the school board that the child should be exempt from school attendance,

the child shall not be required to attend school.

59(4) A school attendance officer shall examine every case of non-compliance with subsection (2) within the district for which he is employed.

59(5) When the examination warrants it, the school attendance officer shall notify in writing the parent of a child of the fact and the consequence of non-compliance.

59(6) Upon receipt of the notice mentioned in subsection (5), unless the child is excused from attendance as provided by this Act, the parent shall cause the child to attend school forthwith.

59(7) A parent who violates subsection (6) is guilty of an offense and on summary conviction is liable to a fine of twenty dollars for the first offense and forty dollars for each subsequent offense and in default of payment is liable to imprisonment in accordance with subsection 31(3) of the Summary Convictions Act, or to both fine and imprisonment. 1966, c24, s.47.

Unless you receive special permission from the Minister of Education to exempt your children from the public school system, you must enroll them without further delay.

Yours truly,
Garth Hathaway

When the Superintendent wrote, "It has been brought to my attention," he didn't say by whom. Certainly not by us. In these days of neighborhood watchers and satellite surveillance, there seems little need of our volunteering to the government what our intentions are.

Not knowing what kind of nut he might have to deal with, the Superintendent let loose with both barrels, sections and sub-sections, including the penalties of fines and imprisonment for non-compliance with the rules. With the exception of 59(3)(a), **"in the opinion of the Minister, a child is under efficient instruction elsewhere,'** there was no mention of the child receiving an education, but only of his obligation to attend school; or, rather, my obligation to cause him to do so.

The Superintendent offered no arguments about

Dad, if they put you in jail for teaching us at home, will they let you teach us in jail?

the need of learning or the general advantages of dispelling ignorance; only the potential threat of losing my money or my freedom, or both, if I didn't comply without further delay.

"Thus the State never intentionally confronts a man's sense, intellectual or moral, but only his body, his senses," wrote Henry David Thoreau. "It is not armed with superior wit or honesty, but with superior physical strength."

My visceral inclination, held in check by reason, was to write back that I feel the government has no business interfering in the education of my children, and to refuse to answer questions or entertain an assessment of our books and program. However, we must refrain from the satisfaction of self-righteous paranoia. Government isn't always bad, nor are the public schools. Whether or not the school authorities are right, most of them sincerely believe they are. To challenge their beliefs or their authority is no better than waving the seat of one's pants at a mad bull.

We've known parents who have responded to such reminders of the government's strength with counter-threats, accusations, and ultimatums. Usually, it's fruitless. What would we have gained? Nasty letters, more threats, and probably loss of the one thing we wanted most -- the opportunity to teach our children at home.

We were certain that our children were "under efficient instruction elsewhere," so the next step was to convince the Minister of Education. Since he and I were not yet on speaking terms, I wrote back to the Superintendent, with extensive details of our kids' previous education, including specific courses and books, to indicate that we were taking the matter seriously; and listing many of our educational materials -- "more than 2000 volumes, including an encyclopedia, various reference books, dictionaries, atlases; non-fiction works on art, music, philosophy, psychology, medicine, astronomy, history, literature, religion, science, botany, biology; novels, short stories, essays; posters, charts, flash cards, records, cassette tapes, microscope, chemistry sets, electronic kits; models of the human body, vital organs, and the solar system; a world globe and a moon globe" -- to point out that we had spent a great deal of money as well as thought, and also implying that our school's inventory, per capita, was superior to that of most public schools.

In closing, I wrote, "I hope this information will be of use to you. If you have any further questions about Brook Farm School, please do not hesitate to write or to visit us at any time. Thank you again for your concern, and for any

help you are able to give us."

I didn't "request permission" to teach at home, but neither did I underline that omission.

I used the name "Brook Farm School" frequently in the letter (and earlier had had letterheads printed) to impress upon the Minister and his representatives that ours is a "real" school, not just a home with books. Subsequent letters from school authorities were addressed to Brook Farm School, and authorities usually used the name in referring to our educational program.

Many home-schooling parents are "invited," in a peremptory manner very like a court summons, to present their case in person before a school official or board. Failure to comply may mean automatic dismissal of the request for exemption. Those in this situation should prepare themselves with as much material as possible -- laws, precedents, examples, educational theory, etc. -- and proceed cautiously, a step at a time.

Some home-school writers feel it's best not to invite officials to one's own home, but in our experience it has always worked out well. We think it's almost always best, if possible, to invite the superintendent or examiner to our home -- and to get the jump on him, by inviting him before he invites us. "To look over our material" is a good pretext, and not untrue. It has saved us the bother of collecting material, leaving home, tapping our feet in a waiting room, and facing the lion in his own den. People, like most other animals, are usually more at ease on their own territory; we feel more comfortable in our own homes. The visiting official is aware that he's a guest, and even if his basic attitude is hostile, he'll be less antagonistic than if we were in his office.

Not all school officials are suspicious or opposed to home-schooling. Most of those who have come to examine our materials and our children have been curious, friendly, and cooperative, and our visits have been genuinely friendly, with no need for verbal fencing. Officials in person are often much more human than in their letters. They never know when their letters may be taken from the file, or by whom, so in their letters they'll be careful not to depart from the most conservative and official position. If they know they're speaking off the record, they may be freer and more helpful. (Two visiting officials admitted to us that if they were not working for the school system they would definitely teach their own children at home.)

In THE POWER OF NON-VIOLENCE, Richard B. Gregg refers to disarming an antagonist with love and sympathy as "moral jiu-jitsu." True peacefulness is not a tactic, but an attitude of being, so inviting an official to our home is not really equivalent; however, the changes in our relationship can be so marked that it might certainly be a kind of psychological jiu-jitsu.

On the few occasions we were visited by an officious Mrs. Grundy and a suspicious Mr. Crabapple, we invited them in graciously. We introduced our children to them, and included the children in our discussions. Sometimes the officials wanted to talk with the children, to see if they could speak with some semblance of knowledge and intelligence; other times, they suggested that we might talk more freely if the children were excused. We explained that the children found adult conversation, particularly about education, stimulating and informative, and that they might as well stay. Besides, we said, we had to get back to our studies soon, which let the officials know that they were interrupting a serious school. We invited them into the kitchen (less formal than the living room, and therefore more relaxing), offered chairs, and put examples of the kids' work on the table. Without asking, we served tea or coffee, and one of the kids passed a plate of cookies. The informality and homey warmth was somewhat contagious. We stood by the visitors' shoulders occasionally to point out something in the material in front of them, causing them to look up at us -- the eternal pose of a student with a hovering teacher, to reawaken a little of their own childhood conditioning toward authority. We tried to keep them slightly off balance -- "jiu-jitsu" -- but not uncomfortably

so. If they relaxed, then we did, too; but we stayed on guard, not wanting to lose any psychological advantage we had gained.

We seldom attacked the school system. It would only have made them more defensive, and then more offensive. We just told them of our own materials, methods, and objectives. We knew we'd never convince the officials that our standards are superior to theirs, so we didn't try; instead, we tried to help them see that our educational program was good, not only by our standards, but also by theirs.

We read books and magazines about public education so we can talk the officials' language, use their terminology, and relate to their frames of reference. We can win and let them think they have won, but not by lying or deceit. Being imprisoned or having our children kidnapped by the state would certainly defeat our purpose, but avoiding either of those circumstances by deceit and subterfuge might defeat our larger purpose.

As the officials talked, even if they were telling us that we were depriving our children of all the advantages of life, we remained friendly, pleasant, and politely informal. No matter how antagonistic or unreasoning they were, we stayed calm and friendly (outwardly, at least), which confused them. Anger, no matter how thoroughly provoked it might have been, would have been taken as a sign of weakness, and as cause for a stronger position on their part. If they began a long harangue, we excused ourselves to get more of the children's school work, and talked about it as if we hadn't interrupted a speech about

something else.

We felt an attitude of firm commitment was of prime importance. If we had any doubts or reservations about our methods or materials, or about our ability to teach, we didn't let them show. Our manner exuded self-confidence and calm determination. Usually, school officials were as desirous of avoiding a serious confrontation as we were. Once they realized we wouldn't change our position, even under heavy pressure, they always gave in.

This approach won't work all the time, for everyone, but it has worked well for us, and many readers have said it worked well for them.

"Dear Donn and Jean and family,
"Your book reached us on September 3, and I started reading it after lunch... About three hours later we were paid an unexpected and rather unpleasant visit from our local school representative in regard to our failure to register our daughter for first grade... I'm sure that if I had not just read your remarks, I would have reacted differently to his aggressive attitude, and perhaps pushed him into taking further steps. However, I checked my annoyance and tried to explain our position reasonably, calmly but firmly. He eventually left, unconvinced... but we have never heard another word... I don't expect this to go on forever, but it gives us a much-needed breathing space..."

DEPARTMENT OF EDUCATION
Office of the Minister
February 3, 1981

Dear Mr. Reed:

I have arranged for the Coordinator of Elementary School Programs in my Department and the School Supervisor in Districts 30 & 31 to conduct an assessment of the instructional programs that you are providing in your home for your four children. It is my understanding that the Supervisor has discussed these programs in some depth with you and that he has communicated this information to the Coordinator.

It is reported to me that the instructional programs that you are using with your four children are adequate and that you have a good supply of books and materials.

In light of the positive report that I have received, I am willing to approve the exemption of your four children from attendance at public school for the current school year.

Should you wish to continue this arrangement beyond the current school year, you should make an application to me during the coming summer and

before the opening of school in September.
Yours very truly,
Charles G. Gallagher
Minister of Education

B R O O K   F A R M   S C H O O L
Glassville, New Brunswick EOJ 1L0
August 15, 1981

Dear Mr. Gallagher:

As you requested, we are informing you of our intention to teach our children at home again this year.

Thank you for your attention and consideration.
Yours truly,
Donn Reed

Office of the Superintendent
September 30, 1981

Dear Mr. Reed:

You will recall that the School Supervisor came to visit the Brook Farm School to determine the suitability of your curriculum for your four children. You were subsequently given permission, by the Minister of Education, to teach in your home school instructional program for the school year 1980-1981.

Unless you plan to enroll these students in the school system, approval from the Minister of Education must be received for exemptions covering the 1981-1982 school year.

Please enlighten me with respect to your intentions relative to the education of your children for the 1981-1982 school year.
Yours truly,
Garth Hathaway
District Superintendent

B R O O K   F A R M   S C H O O L
Glassville, New Brunswick EOJ 1L0
October 10, 1981

Dear Mr. Hathaway:

Thank you for your concern.

We wrote to the Minister on August 15, informing him of our intention to teach our children at home again this year, but have not received a reply.

Yours truly,
Donn Reed

OFFICE OF THE MINISTER
November 17, 1981

Dear Mr. Reed:

I have been advised that a follow-up assessment of the instructional programs that you are providing in your home for your four children has been conducted by the District School Supervisor. He has been in touch with the Coordinator of Elementary Education in this Department, and there is general agreement that the instructional programs that you are using with your four children are adequate and that you have a good supply of books and materials.

In light of the positive report that I have received, I am willing to approve the exemption of your four children from attendance at public school for the current school year ending June 30, 1982.

Should you wish to continue this arrangement beyond the current school year, you should make an application to me before the opening of school in September, 1982.

> Yours very truly,
> Charles G. Gallagher
> Minister of Education

The following August, I wrote again, telling the Minister that we intended to continue teaching at home. We received no answer, nor any more letters from the Superintendent asking us to enlighten him with respect to our intentions relative to the education of our children. Although my letter had been one of declaration rather than of application, I felt it was close enough to the Minister's instruction to have fulfilled my obligation. No one had objected to my wording -- not to me, anyway -- so I assumed the absence of further inquiry was not because I had offended them.

The following year, feeling that the Department of Education was behind in its correspondence, and owed me a letter, I wrote neither application nor declaration. There the matter stood for half

a dozen years. We received letters from other home-schoolers in the province who were being harassed by the Department of Education or by their local school boards, but we received no more letters, no more assessments, and our children never had the privilege of being tested by school authorities.

We decided our file must have been misplaced, or the authorities had given up on us as a lost cause.

Then, after being ignored by the authorities for several years, we received a letter explaining that home-schoolers in the province were now in the charge of a new special branch, and asking us to fill out and return a long questionnaire which was also enclosed. The questions seemed reasonable and non-threatening, so we answered them. A few weeks later, the administrator of the new special branch came to visit. We had many similar ideas about education, and she had no objections to our homeschooling, and she liked our homemade cookies.

Probably the cookies had nothing to do with the letter we received a few weeks later from the Minister of Education, granting exemption of our children from public school for the current school year, saying that our supplies seemed adequate, and telling us to apply again next summer if we planned to continue this practice.

We no longer felt ignored, but the renewed official stamp of approval didn't have any noticeable effect on the efficiency of our instruction elsewhere. Probably the Department had been

changing from human files to computer files, and it took six years for modern technology to bring us out of limbo.

Most of our experience has been limited to places where the grounds for exemption are not clearly or rigidly defined (as with New Brunswick's ambiguous phrase, "efficient instruction elsewhere"), or where home education is more or less well-accepted (such as British Columbia, where many people live several miles beyond any school bus line). Even in such areas, officials may bluster and threaten, and sometimes impede education, but they're not immovable obstacles.

A few of the states make no statutory allowance at all for home-schooling. If we were in such a place, our approach might not work, but our attitudes would still be the same, so we'd probably try it anyway. I prefer not to wave flags (or the seat of my pants) at bulls, mad or not, but I also agree with Kahlil Gibran, who says in THE PROPHET that "if it is a despot you would dethrone, see first that his throne erected within you is destroyed."

"Unjust laws exist," wrote Thoreau in CIVIL DISOBEDIENCE: "shall we be content to obey them, or shall we endeavor to amend them, and obey them until we have succeeded, or shall we transgress them at once?"

Across the United States and Canada, homeschool support groups have lobbied and petitioned state and provincial governments with great success, causing restrictive education laws to be significantly modified, but many homeschoolers are still subject to laws which they feel are too intrusive and demanding. "Men generally think," Thoreau said, "that they ought to wait until they have persuaded the majority to alter them. They think that, if they should resist, the remedy would be worse than the evil. But it is the fault of the government itself that the remedy is worse than the evil... As for adopting the ways which the state has provided for remedying the evil, I know not of such ways. They take too much time, and a man's life will be gone. I have other affairs to attend to..."

So do we all.

We cannot change all the unjust laws, nor constantly risk our freedom even by resisting them all, but we must begin somewhere. Let us begin with those laws which affect us most personally and deeply.

Five of my ancestors were on the Mayflower, and twice that number dropped their hoes to join the fighting in Concord and Lexington. Maintaining the tradition of their spirit, I simply do not accept the authority of any person or government to force me into an action which I believe is wrong. We would be very polite and tactful, but our final position would still be that no government has more right than we to determine our children's upbringing and education. If possible, without extreme danger of completely losing that for which we would be fighting, we would join Washington, Thoreau, and Gandhi in resisting the state's unwarranted demands. If necessary, we would emulate my Mayflower ancestors and go to another place where the demands were fewer and the restrictions more democratic.

Exodus to escape persecution has several worthy precedents.

Home-schooling should never be just an avoidance of the problems in or created by the public schools. It should also be a positive contribution to the improvement of the society in which we live. By insisting upon our right to choose the place and method of our children's education, we are helping to prepare a slightly better world for them; and we are showing them, by our own example, how they can make similar contributions.

We must be clear, however, about the difference between moral right and legal right. Government, at its root and in its simplest form, is neither more nor less than a contract between individuals for their mutual benefit and protection. The need for some form of government, and the corollary need for some means of enforcing it, is obvious. However unjust or immoral an individual law may be, the basic principle of law per se is just. Disobedience of a law willfully or on whim, simply because it is disagreeable or inconvenient, or because of greed or cowardice, strikes not only at the law but at the foundations of society itself. "Action from principle," wrote Thoreau, "the perception and the performance of right, changes things and relations; it is essentially revolutionary...Cast your whole vote; not a strip of paper merely, but your whole influence."

Your whole influence, and ours, will bring us all a little closer to true democracy, and beyond; to that time and place when people are governed, not by the wishes of the majority or the dictates of a minority, but by what is right and true.

To live outside the law, you must be honest.
Bob Dylan

Some homeschool support groups meet periodically to socialize and exchange views on home-learning experiences, difficulties, and successes. Others have picnics, campouts, group tours, and regular meetings. Some have libraries, to be shared by members. Many have information packets which include resource guides and other information useful to members and newcomers. Most publish newsletters with information and sometimes articles about home-schooling in their respective areas. Some groups are very active politically, presenting a unified front to legislators and school officials in seeking changes favorable to homeschoolers.

We have always lived in an area where there were no other home-schoolers, to say nothing of a support group. In fact, we had been teaching at home for several years before we learned that any support groups existed. We would welcome such a group, and would undoubtedly join, but at the same time we'd be somewhat cautious about our identification with them. We might wear buttons proclaiming "I'm a home-schooler" when attending a support group meeting or campout, but never when visiting our neighbors or going to town. In relating to our neighbors, we have always been very casual about our home-schooling, wanting to be known as people who happen to be home-schooling rather than as home-schoolers. There's a big difference. Home-schooling, although interwoven throughout our lives, is still not the most dominant facet of our being. We also do many other

things, none of which would be an adequate definition of our entire lives. Although we're glad to answer questions and to share information, we're not attempting to recruit converts to a new religion, and we carefully avoid any evangelistic stance which could easily antagonize people who would otherwise be friendly and interested (or not interested). We don't want our home-schooling to be a barrier between us and our neighbors. If the subject comes up, we're very open about our home-schooling, but we don't feel it's proper or even advantageous to answer our neighbors' comments about their children's problems in school with a smug reminder that our children don't have those problems. Self-righteous, proselytizing home-schoolers can quickly become as boring as recently-reformed smokers and drinkers. Besides, the only home-schoolers who don't have problems of their own don't have children.

Most support groups invite all home-schoolers in their areas to join; a few insist upon agreement with certain religious doctrines or educational philosophies. If you don't agree with the requirements of the group nearest you, start another: put a note on the supermarket bulletin board and a small ad in the local paper with your phone number, and you're bound to discover many others who share your views.

In rejecting the professional experts, we try to remember that amateur experts may not have all the answers, either. We read and listen, weigh and consider, and then take the course which seems best to us.

NATIONAL HOME SCHOOL ORGANIZATIONS

HOLT ASSOCIATES, INC., 2269 Massachusetts Avenue, Cambridge, MA 02140. Founded by John Holt in 1970, and continuing his work since his death in 1985. First and still foremost national clearinghouse of home-school information, maintaining files of current laws, recent decisions, and successful proposals to school districts; updating and publishing lists of home-schoolers willing to correspond with others, a Resource List of correspondence schools, private schools, and home-school groups; lists of helpful certified teachers, lawyers, and professors; and lists of people available for correspondence on special topics such as adoption, twins, and Down Syndrome. Staff members are available to speak to support groups or other interested people. Most

other home-school businesses and organizations which offer a few similar services have based their material on information originally obtained from Holt Associates. [My list of Support Groups (below) was borrowed primarily from the list compiled by Holt Associates.]

JOHN HOLT'S BOOK AND MUSIC STORE sells more than 300 books and materials, including art supplies and musical instruments, the selections based on quality and comformity with John Holt's philosophies.

Holt Associates' "Home School Information Packet" and John Holt's Book and Music Store catalog are free. (See also Education: Growing Without Schooling, the bimonthly magazine begun by John Holt in 1977.)

◆◆◆

HOME EDUCATION PRESS, P.O. Box 1083, Tonasket, WA 98855. Publisher since 1983 of the national bimonthly "Home Education Magazine" (see Index), and publisher of several books and pamphlets, including THE HOMESCHOOL HANDBOOK, THE HOME SCHOOL READER, ALTERNATIVES IN EDUCATION, GOOD STUFF, I LEARN BETTER BY

TEACHING MYSELF, and many others. Their booklets and pamphlets cover many special interest subjects. Back issues of their magazine are available.

Selected books from other publishers are also offered by Home Education Press. Write for a free catalog and list of services.

CLONLARA SCHOOL, 1289 Jewett Street, Ann Arbor, MI 48104, offers many very useful services, including the Home Based Education Program, which helps families find and choose suitable learning materials, design a satisfactory curriculum, maintain records for school officials; updated legal information; legal representation in court, if needed; regular advice and counseling, if desired; transcripts to other institutions, if requested; and a diploma. Send a #10 SASE for full information.

THE MOORE FOUNDATION, Box 1, Camas, WA 98607. Educational books, correspondence courses, educational research reports, a bimonthly newsletter, and much more, including several excellent books by Raymond and Dorothy Moore. (See Index: Moore, Raymond.) Send a #10 SASE for information.

NATIONAL HOMESCHOOL ASSOCIATION, P.O. Box 157290, Cincinnati, OH 45215. Originally a non-political, service organization only, the NHA was organized by a small number of home-schoolers who felt there was a need to unify the diversified home-school movement and to promote home-schooling more actively. Despite the strong resistance of many other home-school leaders who objected to increased centralization and an expected duplication of services already offered by many organizations, the NHA soon claimed to be "a grassroots organization" serving as a bridge between all existing networks and as a national clearinghouse of information. Some members have initiated new and very valuable services, including a Single Parent Network and an Apprentice and Mentorship Program. The membership has begun to grow slowly, but the NHA remains somewhat controversial, as many home-schoolers disapprove of its increasingly aggressive political stance, its continued upstaging (intentional or not) of other well-established organizations, and its more-recent insistence on the "political responsibility" of home-schoolers to provide a united front (through the NHA). The NHA publishes an annual Homeschool Travel Directory, which was begun by Holt Associates, and was later published by Home Education Press. The NHA publishes a quarterly newsletter and sponsors an annual conference. Annual family membership dues are $15.00. Write for more information.

NATIONAL HOMESCHOOL SERVICE, P.O. Box 167, Rodeo, NM 88056. When a majority of the founders and members of the National Homeschool Association voted to revise their apolitical stance and to publicize home-schooling more agressively, a few of the founders withdrew their support from the NHA and formed the National Homeschool Service, determined to remain a service organization only, not claiming or hoping to speak for the entire movement. At present, the National Homeschool Service Organization is devoted to helping with fund-raising for selected homeschool projects, developing a homeschool research library, and providing special interest clubs for homeschool children. Send a #10 SASE for further information.

OAK MEADOW, P.O. Box 712, Blacksburg, VA 24063. Home study courses, kindergarten through grade 8. "All Oak Meadow curricula are designed to cooperate with children's natural unfoldment and help them express their unique capabilities through artistic, imaginative, and creative experiences." Materials may be bought separately, at lower cost, without enrolling in the school. Write for information.

SANTA FE COMMUNITY SCHOOL will help you develop your own educational program, keep records of reports you send in, record credits, send transcripts to schools or agencies at your request, and/or provide an "umbrella" service for those who want to follow their own curriculum but need legal status for state acceptance. Send a #10 SASE to: SANTA FE COMMUNITY SCHOOL, P.O.Box 2241, Santa Fe, NM 87501.

NALSAS (NATIONAL ASSOCIATION FOR THE LEGAL SUPPORT OF ALTERNATIVE SCHOOLS), P.O. Box 2823, Santa Fe, NM 87501. Information and legal service center. Several functions and services. Send a #10 SASE for information.

CALVERT SCHOOL, Tuscany Road, Baltimore, MD 21210. Correspondence school for kindergarten and grades 1 through 8, with all books and other materials supplied. Reasonable prices. Standard subjects, more or less, but with more interesting materials (such as Greek mythology in third grade) than most courses have. Children's work can be sent for evaluation and grading, if you want, for a small extra fee. Some use Calvert for a year or two, to gain confidence, then design their own studies.

STATE & PROVINCIAL
SUPPORT GROUPS & ORGANIZATIONS

Most of the following list of home-school groups and organizations was compiled by Holt Associates, Inc., 2269 Massachusetts Avenue, Cambridge, MA 02140, and is used with permission. I have gained a few additions from my own correspondence. This list is not infallible; new groups form, and older groups sometimes move or retire. Send $2.50 to Holt Associates for a copy of the annually-updated list. Ask the groups listed for your area if other groups have formed. WHEN WRITING TO ANY OF THESE ORGANIZATIONS, ALWAYS INCLUDE A #10 SASE.

U N I T E D   S T A T E S

ALABAMA
Alabama Home Educators, P.O. Box 160091, Mobile, AL 36616
Alabama Home Educators, Rt. 3 Box 360D, Montgomery, AL 36110
Alabama Home Educators, Rt. 3 Box 633, Cottondale, AL 35453
CHEAHA, P.O. Box 945, Bynum, AL 36253
Fellowship of Christian Home Educators, P.O. Box 563, Alabaster, AL 35007

Southwest Alabama Home Educators, 10641 Park Avenue East, Grand Bay, AL 36541

ALASKA
Alaska Homeschoolers Association, P.O.Box 874075, Wasilla, AK 99687
Alaska Private and Home Educators Association, P.O. Box 70, Talkeetna, AK 99676
Valley Homeschoolers Network, P.O. Box 874075, Wasilla, AK 99687

ARIZONA
Arizona Families for Home Education, P.O. Box 4661, Scottsdale, AZ 85261
Arizona Home School News, 1890 Don Carlos #1, Tempe, AZ 85281
Christian Home Educators of Arizona, 3105 S. Evergreen Road, Tempe, AZ 85282
Cochise County Families for Home Education, P.O. Box 533, St. David, AZ 85630
Parents Association of Christian Home Schools, 6166 W. Highland, Phoenix, AZ 85033
Tucson Home Education Network, P.O. Box 58176, Tucson, AZ 85732

ARKANSAS

Arkansas Christian Home Education Association, P.O. Box 501, Little Rock, AR 72201

Arkansas Christian Home Education Association, 12411 Sardis Road, Mabelvale, AR 72103

Crowley's Ridge Christian Parent Education Association, 4303 Brenda St., Jonesboro, AR 72401

CALIFORNIA

California Coalition of People for Alternative Learning Situations, P.O. Box 92, Escondido, CA 92025

Center for Educational Guidance, P.O. Box 445, N. San Juan, CA 95960

Christian Home Educators of California, P.O. Box 28644, Santa Ana, CA 92799

Christian Home Educators of Los Angeles County, P.O. Box 1888, Norwalk, CA 90651

Community Education Gazette, P.O. Box 445, North San Juan, CA 95960

Contra Costa Home Educators, 3345 Santa Paula Drive, Concord, CA 94518

Monterey County Home Learners, P.O. Box 4667, Salinas, CA 93912

North County Homeschooling Center, 1225 So. Boyle Avenue, Escondido, CA 92027

Northern California Homeschool Association, 2214 Grant Street, Berkeley, CA 94703

Parents for Home Development, 18481 Roberts Road, Riverside, CA 92504

Peninsula Homeschoolers, 2427 Grandby, San Jose, CA 95130

San Diego Homeschoolers, 3581 Mt. Aclare Avenue, San Diego, CA 92111

San Gabriel Valley Homeschoolers, 1525 Old House Road, Pasadena, CA 91107

Santa Clara Valley Homeschoolers, 795 Sheraton Drive, Sunnyvale, CA 94087

Sierra Homeschoolers, P.O. Box 74, Midpines, CA 95345

Sonoma County Homeschoolers, 8600 Templeman Road, Forestville, CA 95436

South Valley Homeschoolers Association, P.O. Box 961, San Martin, CA 95046

Yolo County Homeschoolers, P.O. Box 305, Esparto, CA 95627

COLORADO

Agape Family Schools, 5108 Edgewood Court, Loveland, CO 80538

Colorado Home Educators Association, 1616 17th Box 372, Denver, CO 80202

Colorado Homeschooling Network, 7490 West Apache, Sedalia, CO 80135

Colorado Springs Homeschoolers, 2906 Marilyn Road, Colorado Springs, CO 80909

Foothills Family Schools, 5591 Mt. Audubon Place, Longmont, CO 80501

Front Range Eclectic Homeschoolers, 12827 North Woodland Trail, Parker, CO 80209

Home Educators Resource Exchange, P.O. Box 13038, Aurora, CO 80013

Homes Offering Meaningful Education, 1015 S. Gaylord Street, Denver, CO 80209

Northern Colorado Home School Association, 4633 Skyline Drive, Fort Collins, CO 80526

North Suburban Home Schoolers, 11529 Ogden St., Northglenn, CO 80233

CONNECTICUT

Connecticut Home Educators Association, 1590 N. Benson Road, Fairfield, CT 06430

Connecticut Homeschoolers Association, 98 Bahe Road, Deep River, CT 04101

Emanuel Homestead, P.O. Box 355, South Woodstock, CT 06267

Home Education League of Parents, P.O. Box 203, Abington, CT 06230

FLORIDA

Florida Association for Schools at Home, 1000 Devil's Dip, Tallahassee, FL 32308

Florida Parent Educators Association, 1730 Vineyard Way, Tallahassee, FL 32301

West Florida Home Education Support League, 1209 Millcreek Trail, Cantonment, FL 32533

GEORGIA

Georgians for Freedom in Education, 4818 Joy Lane, Lilbum, GA 30247

Mountain Homeschoolers, Rt. 1, Box 1426, Clayton, GA 30525

Christians Concerned for Education, Rt. 3, Box 1180, Lafayette, GA 30728

HAWAII

Tropical Home Schooler, 220 Waipaiani Road, Haiku, Maui, HI 96798

IDAHO

Home Educators of Idaho, 3618 Pine Hill Drive, Coeur d'Alene, ID 83814

Idaho Home Educators/Southern Idaho, 3125 Black Hills, Boise, ID 83709

ILLINOIS

HOUSE, P.O. Box 578291, Chicago, IL 60657

Illinois Christian Home Educators, P.O. Box 261, Zion, IL 60099

INDIANA

Central Indiana Home Educators, 7262 Lakeside Drive, Indianapolis, IN 46278

Fort Wayne Area Home Schools, 4321 Mirada Drive, Fort Wayne, IN 46816

Greater Lafayette Home Educators, 926 N 19th St., Lafayette, IN 47904

Huntington County Home Educators, 1138 Byron St., Huntington, IN 46750

South Indiana Support Group, P.O. Box 388, Princeton, IN 47670

Lake County Christian Home School Association, 11202 Parrish, Cedar Lake, IN 46303

Indiana Association of Home Educators, P.O. Box 50524, Indianapolis, IN 46250

Southern Indiana Support Group, RR 1 Box 183, Patoka, IN 47666

Wabash Valley Homeschoolers Association, RR 53 Box 260, Terre Haute, IN 47805

IOWA

Iowa Families for Christian Education, RR 3 Box 143, Missouri Valley, IA 51555

Iowa Home Educators Association, P.O. Box 213, Des Moines, IA 50301

KANSAS

Kansans for Alternative Education, 19985 Renner Road, Spring Hill, KS 66083

Post Rock Home Educators, RR 1 Box 73, McCracken, KS 67556

KENTUCKY

Kentucky Christian Home School Association, 1301 Bridget Drive, Fairdale, KY 40118

Kentucky Home Education Association, P.O. Box 81, Winchester, KY 40391

Kentucky Home Schoolers, 3310 Illinois Avenue, Louisville, KY 40220

LOUISIANA
    Beauregard/Vernon Home School Association, 36 Sally Lou Lane, Leesville, LA 71446
    Christian Home Educators Fellowship of Baton Rouge, P.O. Box 14421, Baton Rouge, LA 70898
    Christian Home Educators Fellowship of Louisiana, P.O. Box 14421, Baton Rouge, LA 70898
    Louisiana Citizens for Home Education, 3404 Van Buren, Baker, LA 70714

MAINE
    Maine Homeschool Association, P.O. Box 3283, Auburn, ME 04210
    Midcoast Homeschoolers, 10 Cedar Street, Camden, ME 04843
    Talk About Learning, 25 Belmeade Road, Portland, ME 04101

MARYLAND
    Baltimore Homeschooling Contact, 2111 Eastern Avenue, Baltimore, MD 21231
    Christian Home Schools of Western Maryland, P.O. Box 564, Cumberland, MD 21502
    Fredrick County Support Group, 6521 Morningside Court, Middletown, MD 21769
    Maryland Home Education Association, 9085 Flamepool Way, Columbia, MD 21045
    Montgomery County Support Group, 26824 Howard Chapel Drive, Damascus, MD 20872
    Parents for Home Education, 13020 Blairmore St., Beltsville, MD 20705

MASSACHUSETTS
    Apple Country Homeschooling Association, P.O. Box 246, Harvard, MA 01451
    Kitchen School Group, P.O. Box 96, W. Boxford, MA 01885
    Massachusetts Home Learning Association, 16 Anderson Road, Marlboro, MA 01752
    South Shore Home Schoolers, 163 Hingham Street, Rockland, MA 02370
    Worcester Area Homeschooling Organization, 246 May St. #2, Worcester, MA 01602

MICHIGAN
    Copper County Education Coop, P.O. Box 713, Houghton, MI 49931
    Mid-Michigan Homeschoolers, 6109 Pebbleshire, Grand Blanc, MI 48439

MINNESOTA
    Families Nurturing Lifelong Learners, 2452 Southcrest Avenue, Maplewood, MN 55119
    Fargo-Moorehead Homeschool Association, 1909 8th St. S, Moorehead, MN 56560
    Minnesota Association of Christian Home Educators, Box 118, Anoka, MN 55303
    Minnesota Home School Network, 9669 E 123rd, Hastings, MN 55033

MISSISSIPPI
    Mississippi Home Schoolers Support Group, 21550 Darling Road, Pass Christian, MS 39571

MISSOURI
    Carondelet Homeschool Support Group, 6510 Morganford, St. Louis, MO 63116
    Christian Home Educators Fellowship, 601 Madison Drive, Arnold, MO 63010
    Clay-Platte Support Group, 4257 N. Drury, Kansas City, MO 64117
    Families for Home Education, Rt. 1, Box 234, Independence, MO 64050

Hill of Zion Support Group, 4646 S. Lindbergh Blvd., St. Louis, MO 63127
    Home Educators Association of Region Three, 700 SW Merritt Street, Lee's Summit, MO 64081
    Mineral Area Home Educators, Glendale Street, Flat River, MO 63601
    North County Christian Homeschooling Support Group, 236 St. Louis Avenue, Ferguson, MO 63135
    Region 4-A for Missouri Families for Home Education, RR 1, Box 8, Hughesville, MO 65334
    South-City Homeschoolers, 3727 Texas Avenue, St. Louis, MO 63118
    Springfield Area Homeschoolers, Rt. 1 Box 193, Fair Grove, MO 65648
    West County Christian Homeschoolers, 3861 Boquet Road, Pacific, MO 63069

MONTANA
    Gardiner's Homeschoolers, Box 201, Gardiner, MT 59030
    Helena Area Christian Home Educators, 1263 Bighorn Road, Helena, MT 59601
    Homeschoolers of Montana, P.O. Box 40, Billings, MT 59103
    Montana Coalition of Home Educators, P.O. Box 654, Helena, MT 59624
    Montana Homeschool News, 1702 Hwy 83 North, Seeley Lake, MT 59868
    Northern Home Educators, Box 1268, Cut Bank, MT 59868
    Seeley-Swan Homeschoolers, 1702 Hiway 83 North, Seeley Lake, MT 59868

NEBRASKA
    LEARN, 7741 E Avon Lane, Lincoln, NE 68505
    Lincoln Area Homeschoolers, 1821 Oakdale, Lincoln, NE 68506
    Nebraska Christian Home School Association, Box 1245, Columbus, NE 68601
    Nebraska Independent Homeschoolers Network, 8010 Lillibridge St., Lincoln, NE 68506
    OPEN, 7930 Raven Oaks Drive, Omaha, NE 68152

NEVADA
    Home Schools United/Vegas Valley, P.O. Box 26811, Las Vegas, NV 89109
    Nevada Home Schools, P.O. Box 21323, Reno, NV 89515

NEW HAMPSHIRE
    Christian Home Educators of New Hampshire, Box 1653, Hillsboro, NH 03244
    New Hampshire Home Education Association, 9 Mizoras Drive, Nashua, NH 03062
    New Hampshire Home Schools Newsletter, P.O. Box 97, Center Tuftonboro, NH 03816

NEW JERSEY
    Families Learning Together, 11 Bates Road, Jackson, NJ 08527
    Jersey Shore Christian Homeschoolers Association, 65 Middlesex Road, Matawwan, NJ 07747
    New Jersey Family Schools Association, RD #2 Box 236, Califon, NJ 07830
    Unschoolers Network, 2 Smith Street, Farmingdale, NJ 07727
    Unschooling Families Support Group of Central New Jersey, 40 Linden Lane, Plainsboro, NJ 08536

NEW MEXICO
    New Mexico Educators, 678 Lisbon Avenue SE, Rio Rancho, NM 87124

New Mexico Home Educators, P.O. Box 13383, Albuquerque, NM 87192

New Mexico Christian Home Education, 7417 Santa Fe Trail NW, Albuquerque, NM 87120

NEW YORK

Central New York Homeschoolers, Side Hill Springs, Becker Road, Skaneateles, NY 13152

Empire State Home Educators, Side Hill Springs, Becker Road, Skaneateles, NY 13152

Homeschoolers Exchange, RD 1 Box172E, East Chatham, NY 12060

Long Island Family Educators, P.O. Box 283, Sayville, NY 11782

New York City Home Educators Alliance, 341 East 5th Street, New York, NY 10003

New York State Homeschoolers, Rt. 1 Box 8, Ghent, NY 12075

Rochester Area Homeschoolers Association, 401 Parsells Avenue, Rochester, NY 14609

Western New York Homeschooling Netword, 85 Albany St., Buffalo, NY 14213

NORTH CAROLINA

Ed-Venturous Learning Families, 68 Lakey Creek, Franklin, NC 28734

North Carolinans for Home Education, P.O. Box 30443, Raleigh, NC 27622

Rowan County Home School Association, 13401 Culp Road, Gold Hill, NC 28071

OHIO

Christian Home Educators of Ohio, P.O. Box 1224, Kent, OH 44240

Christian Parents Education Fellowship, 310 Blue Bonnet Drive, Findlay, OH 45840

Home School Resource Center, 1444 Gurley Avenue, Akron, OH 44310

Ohio Coalition of Educational Alternatives Now, P.O. Box 094, Thompson, OH 44086

OKLAHOMA

The Family Learning Connection, P.O. Box 1938, Durant, OK 74702

Central Oklahoma Home Educators Association, P.O. Box 270601, Oklahoma City, OK 73137

Central Oklahoma Homeschoolers, P.O. Box 4, Piedmont, OK 73078

Oklahoma Christian Home Educators Association, P.O. Box 102, Jenks, OK 74037

OREGON

A.B.C. at Home, P.O. Box 460, Nehalem, OR 97131

Central Oregon Homeschoolers, 1293 NW Wall No. 1337, Bend, OR 97701

Douglas County Homeschoolers Connection, 4053 Hanna, Roseburg, OR 97470

Christian Home Education Association South East, 3619 SE Caruthers, Portland, OR 97214

East County Home Schools, 247 NE 202nd Avenue, Portland, OR 97230

Homeschoolers of Lane County, 38040 Pengra Road, Fall Creek, OR 97438

Oregon Christian Home Education Association Network, 2515 NE 37th, Portland, OR 97212

Parents Education Association, P.O. Box 1482, Beaverton, OR 97075

Portland Area Tri-County Homeschoolers, 28901 SE Davis Road, Estacada, OR 97023

PENNSYLVANIA

Home Educators of Pennsylvania, RD 2 Box 334A, Munson, PA 16860

Chester County Homeschoolers, 226 Llandovery Drive, Exton, PA 19341

Lancaster Home Educators Association, 2200 Huber Drive, Manheim, PA 17545

Parent Educators of Pennsylvania, 3334 Disston Street, Philadelphia, PA 19149

Pennsylvania Home Education Association, 1003 Arborwood Drive, Gibsonia, PA 15044

Pennsylvania Homeschoolers Association, RD 2, Box 117, Kittanning, PA 16201

RHODE ISLAND

Parent Educators of Rhode Island, P.O. Box 546, Coventry, RI 02816

Rhode Islanders for Constitutional Education, 46 E George St., Providence, RI 02906

RIGHT, 272 Pequat Avenue, Warwick, RI 02886

SOUTH CAROLINA

Carolina Family School Association, Rt 2 Box 17, St. Stephen, SC 29479

South Carolina Home Educators Association, P.O. Box 33, Goose Creek, SC 29445

SOUTH DAKOTA

South Dakota Home School Association, Rt. 2 Box 45, Garretson, SD 57030

West Dakota Christian Home Schools, 8016 Katrina Court, Rapid City, SD 57702

TENNESSEE

Home Education Association of Tennessee, 3677 Richbriar Court, Nashville, TN 37211

TEXAS

Christian Home Educators of San Antonio, 12170 New Sulphur Springs Road, Adkins, TX 78101

El Paso Homeschoolers Association, SR Box 87, Anthony, TX 79821

Family Home Educators of Dallas, P.O. Box 280584, Dallas, TX 75228

Family Educators Alliance of Southern Texas, 1400 N. Flores, San Antonio, TX 78212

Home Oriented Private Education for Texas, P.O. Box 402263, Austin, TX 78704

Texas Home Educators Newsletter, P.O. Box 835105, Richardson, TX 75083

Texas Home School Coalition, P.O. Box 140944, Dallas, TX 75214

UTAH

FCLA Utah Spice Group, 1510 W 500 N., Provo, UT 84601

Cottonwood Parent Support Group, 1399 E. 7240 South, Salt Lake City, UT 84121

Utah Christian Homeschool Association, 3190 South 4140 West, West Valley City, UT 84120

Utah Home Education Association, 657 W. 690 No., Orem, UT 84057

VERMONT

Vermont Homeschoolers, Spruce Knob Road, RR 1, Box 6680, Middletown Springs, VT 05757

VIRGINIA

Home Educators Association of Virginia, P.O. Box 1810, Front Royal, VA 22630

Home Instruction Support Group, 217 Willow Terrace, Sterling, VA 22170

Lifespan Educational and Resource Network, 2519 Buckalew Drive, Falls Church, VA 22046

North Virginia Homeschoolers Newsletter, 2519 Buckelew Drive, Falls Church, VA 22046

Northern Virginia Homeschoolers/LEARN, 3015 Fairmont Street, Falls Church, VA 22042

WASHINGTON
   Family Learning Organization, P.O. Box 7256, Spokane, WA 99207
   Families Learning Together, Box 10, Tiger Star Route, Colville, WA 99114
   FCLA West Washington Spice Group, HCR 63 Box 713, Naselle, WA 98638
   Grant County Home Educators Association, Rt. 2, 730 Road V NW, Quincy, WA 98848
   Home Educators Stanchion, 1031 SW 307, Federal Way, WA 98003
   Homeschoolers Support Association, P.O. Box 413, Maple Valley, WA 98038
   Inland Empire Home School Center, P.O. Box 980, Airway Heights, WA 99001
   Natural Learning Network, 5725 N. Elgin, Spokane, WA 99205
   Teaching Parents Association, 16109 NE 169th Place, Woodinville, WA 98072
   Trestle Homeschoolers Association, 8705 4th Place SE, Everett, WA 98208
   Washington Association of Teaching Christian Homes, P.O. Box 980, Airway Heights, WA 99001
   Washington Homeschool Organization, P.O. Box 42403, Tacoma, WA 98442

Responsible Education Achieved in the Christian Home, 20800 Hubbard Road, Lynnwood, WA 98036

WEST VIRGINIA
   Alternatives in Education, Rt. 3 Box 305, Chloe, WV 25235
   West Virginia Home Education Association, P.O. Box 266, Glenville, WV 26351
   West Virginia Home Educators Association, P.O. Box 7504, Charleston, WV 25356

WISCONSIN
   Families in Schools at Home, 4639 Conestoga Trail, Cottage Grove, WI 53527
   HOME (Madison Chapter), 5745 Bittersweet Place, Madison, WI 53705
   HOME Network New, 1428 Woodland, Eau Claire, WI 57401
   Wisconsin Parents Association, P.O. Box 2502, Madison, WI 53701

WYOMING
   Best Education System Today, Box 2197, Mills, WY 82644
   Homeschoolers of Wyoming, Box 2197, Mills, WY 82644
   Wyoming Homeschoolers, Box 1386, Lyman, WY 82937

C A N A D A

A Home Schooler's Newsletter, 268 Butler St., Woodstock, Ontario N4S 3B2
   Alberta Homeschooling Information Service, 16 Fonda Close SE, Calgary, Alberta T2A 6G3
   Canadian Alliance of Homeschoolers, 195 Markville Road, Unionville, Ontario L3R 4V8
   Home Learning Resource Centre, Box 61, Quathiaski, B.C. V0P 1N0
   Homeschoolers Association of Northern Alberta, 11415 43rd Avenue, Edmonton, Alberta T6J 0Y2

Manitoba Association for Schooling at Home, 89 Edkar Crescent, Winnipeg, Manitoba R2G 3H8
   Ontario Homeschoolers, Box 60, 260 Adelaide St. E. Toronto, Ontario M5A 1N0

Quebec Homeschooling Advisory, 4650 Acadia, Lachine, Quebec H8T 1N5
   Saskatchewan Home-Based Educators, Box 113, Neville, Sask. S0N 1T0
   Victoria Homeschoolers, 106-290 Regina, Victoria, B.C. V8Z 6S6

WITH A SYNOPSIS OF HOME-SCHOOLING LAWS

In the brief comments following each of the following addresses, I have tried to sum up the respective official attitudes toward home-schooling, according to the most recent information I have. However, laws are being changed rapidly, and individual cases often have characteristics or special aspects which don't fit the norm. Also, home-schooling is usually possible in some way even in states which are very opposed to it. For the most up-to-date information, write to Growing Without Schooling, National Homeschool Association, Home School Legal Defense Association, and/or the home-schooling organizations in your area. Be as specific in your questions as possible. Always include a #10 SASE.

UNITED STATES

ALABAMA: Private Schools Unit, Department of Education, 348 State Office Building, Montgomery, AL 36130. Mandatory school attendance, age 7 to 16. Private tutoring or church school allowed. Private tutors must be certified. Testing not required. Application must be filed.

ALASKA: Department of Education, Juneau, AK 99801. 7 to 16. Fairly liberal in interpretation of regulations allowing exemptions, including a "program of correspondence study approved by the department" or "an educational experience" approved by the school board.

ARIZONA: Department of Education, 1535 West Jefferson Street, Phoenix, AZ 85007. 8 to 16. The formal allowance for home-schooling is spelled out as instruction "at home in the subjects given in the public schools by a person passing the teachers' proficiency examination" in "basic skills."

ARKANSAS: Department of Education, State Education Building, Little Rock, AR 72201. 7 to 15, inclusive. Certification not required. Local superintendent must be notified, and children must pass an annual test.

CALIFORNIA: Department of Education, 721 Capitol Mall, Sacramento, CA 95814. 6 to 16. Not strict. A very strong home-school network has helped to bring about several favorable changes in the laws. Liberal requirements.

COLORADO: Department of Education, State Office Building, 201 East Colfax, Denver, CO 80203. 7 to 16. Liberal requirements. Testing required in some grades.

CONNECTICUT: Department of Education, Box 2219, Hartford, CT 06115. 7 to 16. Allows for the parent "to show that the child is elsewhere receiving equivalent instruction in the studies taught in the public schools." No certification or testing required.

DELAWARE: Department of Public Instruction, P.O. Box 1402, Dover, DE 19901. 6 to 16. Allows for parents to demonstrate that the child is receiving "suitable instruction elsewhere," subject to examination. Very liberal allowances for "private schools."

DISTRICT OF COLUMBIA: District of Columbia Public Schools, 415 12th St. NW, Washington, DC 20004. 7 to 16. Home instruction allowed as "private schooling" if deemed by the board of education to be "substantially equivalent."

FLORIDA: State Department of Education, Tallahassee, FL 32301. 6 to 16. Certification not required, but children must meet some test requirements.

GEORGIA: State Department of Education, Atlanta, GA 30334. 7 to 16. Parents must have high school diploma or GED. Testing required every three years.

HAWAII: Department of Education, P.O. Box 2360, Honolulu, HI 96804. 6 to 18. "Appropriate alternative educational program" approved by the superintendent; annual report of child's progress; testing in some grades.

IDAHO: Department of Education, Len B. Jordan Office Bldg., Boise, ID 83720. 7 to 16. Homeschool curriculum must be approved as "comparable instruction." Parents in some areas may have to be certified. No testing.

ILLINOIS: State Board of Education, 100 N. First St., Springfield, IL 62777. 7 to 16. Parents give local district written assurance that curriculum and attendance are comparable to those of the public schools.

INDIANA: Department of Public Instruction, Room 229, State House, Indianapolis, IN 46204. 7 to 16. "Equivalent instruction" is required -- but is not defined.

IOWA: Department of Public Instruction, Grimes State Office Bldg., Des Moines, IA 50319. 7 to 16. Approved "equivalent instruction" by a certified teacher. Exemption from required certification may be granted on religious grounds.

KANSAS: Department of Education, 120 E. 10th St., Topeka, KS 66612. 7 to 16. Registered private schools allowed. Teachers tested for "competency," but need not be certified.

KENTUCKY: Department of Education, Capital Plaza Tower, Frankfort, KY 40601. 6 to 16. Home schools may qualify as private or church schools. Certification not required.

LOUISIANA: Department of Education, P.O. Box 44064, Baton Rouge, LA 70804. 7 to 15, inclusive. Homeschooling allowed if "at least equal" to public school curriculum, and children pass annual tests.

MAINE: Department of Educational and Cultural Services, Augusta, ME 04333. 7 to 17. Home instruction allowed if "equivalent instruction" is given.

MARYLAND: State Department of Education, 200 W. Baltimore St., Baltimore, MD 21201. 6 to 16. Superintendent must approve schedule and curriculum.

MASSACHUSETTS: Department of Education, 1385 Hancock St., Quincy, MA 02169. 6 to 16. Home instruction "in a manner approved in advance" by the superintendent; fairly liberal.

MICHIGAN: Department of Education, P.O. Box 30008, Lansing, MI 48909. 6 to 16. Homeschools must be approved as private schools, with "comparable instruction" and a certified teacher in attendance for part of each school day.

MINNESOTA: State Department of Education, Capitol Square, 550 Cedar St., St. Paul, MN 55101. 7 to 16. Curriculum and progress reports must be submitted to the superintendent. Children are tested annually.

MISSISSIPPI: State Department of Education, P.O. Box 771, Jackson, MS 39205. 6 to 14. Homeschoolers must signify intent to teach at home, keep records of curriculum and their own testing, and keep samples of children's work. Testing not required.

MISSOURI: State Department of Elementary & Secondary Education, Jefferson City, MO 65101. 7 to 16. Homeschool allowed, with liberal interpretation of "suitable instruction."

MONTANA: Office of Public Instruction, State Capitol, Helena, MT 59620. 7 to 16, or to completion of 8th grade. Homeschoolers must provide a "basic educational program" defined by school board.

NEBRASKA: State Department of Education, Box 94987, Lincoln, NE 68509. 7 to 16. Homeschools may file religious objection to state requirements. Parents must show qualifications or demonstrate competency. Testing in "basic skills" required.

NEVADA: Department of Education, Capitol Complex, Carson City, NV 89701. 7 to 17. "Equivalent instruction" required. Certification, consultation with a certified teacher, or "approved" correspondence course usually required, but may be waived. Testing in several grades.

NEW HAMPSHIRE: Department of Education, 64 N. Main St., Concord, NH 03301. 6 to 16. Curriculum and parents' qualifications subject to superintendent's approval.

NEW JERSEY: Department of Education, P.O. Box 2019, Trenton, NJ 08625. 6 to 16. "Equivalent instruction" as approved by superintendent. No testing.

NEW MEXICO: Department of Education, Santa Fe, NM 87501. 8 to 16. Bachelor's degree required, but may be waived. Annual testing.

NEW YORK: State Education Department, Albany, NY 12234. 6 to 16. Curriculum submitted for approval; quarterly progress reports. Certification not required. Testing in several grades.

NORTH CAROLINA: State Department of Public Instruction, Raleigh, NC 27611. 7 to 16. High school diploma or GED required for homeschool teachers. Curriculum must be similar to that of public schools.

NORTH DAKOTA: Office of Private Education, 1310 Broadway Avenue, Fargo, ND 58102. 7 to 16. Parents must be certified teachers or have one hour supervision per week by a certified teacher. Annual testing required.

OHIO: Department of Education, Columbus, OH 43215. "Satisfactory instruction" by a "qualified" person, not necessarily certified. Testing not required.

OKLAHOMA: State Department of Education, Oklahoma City, OK 73105. 7 to 18. Homeschools not regulated; no certification or testing.

OREGON: State Department of Education, Salem, OR 97310. 7 to 18. Certification not required. Annual testing.

PENNSYLVANIA: Department of Education, Box 911, Harrisburg, PA 17108. 8 to 17. High school diploma or equivalent required of teachers. Curriculum outline and documentation, records, annual evaluation. Testing in some grades.

RHODE ISLAND: Department of Education, 22 Hayes St., Providence, RI 02908. 7 to 16. Curriculum must be approved. Certification not required. No testing.

SOUTH CAROLINA: Department of Education, Columbia, SC 29201. 7 to 16, inclusive. Homeschool may be approved if "substantially equivalent" to public schooling. High school diploma or GED required. Annual testing.

VIRGINIA: Department of Education, P.O. Box 6Q, Richmond, VA 23216. "Approved correspondence course" required unless parents have bachelor's degree or are exempted from this by local board. Annual progress reports and/or testing.

WASHINGTON: State Department of Education, Mail Stop FG-11, Olympia, WA 98504. 8 to 15. Parent-teachers must be "sufficiently qualified" or supervised by a certified teacher. Annual testing.

UTAH: State Office of Education, 250 E. 5th St., Salt Lake City, UT 84111. 6 to 18. Homeschooling allowed subject to approval of curriculum, materials, etc. Certification and testing not required.

VERMONT: Department of Education, Montpelier, VT 05602. 7 to 16. Varying requirements, generally liberal, including curriculum description, possible testing, work samples, etc.

SOUTH DAKOTA: Department of Education and Cultural Affairs, Kneip Building, Pierre, SD 57501. 7 to 16. "Competent alternative instruction" may be approved. Annual testing.

TENNESSEE: Department of Education, 142 Cordell Hull Bldg., Nashville, TN 37219. 7 to 16. High school diploma or equivalent for teaching through 8th grade; college degree or exemption for teaching through grade 12. Testing required in some grades.

TEXAS: Texas Education Agency, 201 E. 11th Street, Austin, TX 78701. 7 to 17. Homeschools allowed as private schools with public school curriculum. No certification or testing.

WEST VIRGINIA: Department of Education, Capitol Complex B-016, Charleston, WV 25305. 7 to 16. High school diploma required for teaching through 8th grade; college degree or passing score on National Teacher's Exam for teaching through 12th grade. Annual testing.

WISCONSIN: Department of Public Instruction, Box 7841, Madison, WI 53707. 6 to 18. Parents must agree to follow basic-skills curriculum and attendance requirements. Certification and testing not required.

WYOMING: State Department of Education, Hathaway Bldg., Cheyenne, WY 82002. 7 to 16. "Basic educational program" required in curriculum plan submitted annually. Certification & testing not required.

C A N A D A

For the most up-to-date information on all provinces, send $4 for a "Home Schooling Package" to CANADIAN ALLIANCE FOR HOME SCHOOLERS, 195 Markville Road, Unionville, Ontario L3R 4V8, or write (with a #10 SASE) to the home-school group nearest you.

ALBERTA: Alberta Education, 11160 Jasper Avenue, Edmonton, Alberta T5K OL2. Mandatory attendance, 6 to 16. "Efficient instruction" allowed; "efficient" including a program consistent with or comprised of Alberta public schools, approved correspondence school, "instruction by competent persons," etc. Cooperation with and by public schools encouraged.

BRITISH COLUMBIA: Ministry of Education, Parliament Buildings, Victoria, B.C. V8T 4W8. 7 to 15. Very liberal allowances for homeschooling with an "organized set of learning activities." Public schools offer free assessment, materials, etc., on request of the parents.

MANITOBA: Department of Education, Room 506, 1181 Portage Avenue, Winnipeg, Manitoba R3G OT3. 7 to 16. Homeschooling allowed, with supervision and evaluation by a ministry representative. Cooperation of local schools in providing materials is encouraged.

NEW BRUNSWICK: Department of Education, P.O. Box 6000, Fredericton, N.B. E3B 5H1. 7 to 15. "Efficient instruction elsewhere" is allowed with the minister's approval, with some supervision by a ministry representative. Usually very liberal.

NEWFOUNDLAND and LABRADOR: Department of Education, P.O. Box 4750, St. John's, Newfoundland A1C 5T7. 6 to 15. "Efficient instruction elsewhere" allowed, subject to the minister's approval.

NORTHWEST TERRITORIES: Department of Education, 3rd Floor, Arthur Laing Building, Yellowknife, N.W.T. X1A 2L9. 6 to 15. Home schooling allowed if "the child is under instruction in some other satisfactory manner" or "has reached a standard of education of the same or of a higher degree than that to be attained" in public school.

NOVA SCOTIA: Department of Education, P.O. Box 578, Halifax, N.S. B3J 2S9. 6 to 16. "Equivalent instruction elsewhere" allowed; child must pass equivalent examinations.

ONTARIO: Ministry of Education, 14th Floor, Mowat Block, Queen's Park, Toronto, Ontario M7A 1L2. 6 to 16. "Satisfactory instruction at home or elsewhere" accepted, subject to periodic visits by ministry representatives and testing.

PRINCE EDWARD ISLAND: Department of Education, Charlottetown, P.E.I. C1A 7N8. 7 to 15. "Efficient instruction elsewhere" accepted, subject to periodic monitoring by a certified teacher and progress reports to the Department of Education.

QUEBEC: Ministere de l'Education, Centre de renseignements, 1035 rue de la Chevrotiere, Quebec, P.Q. G1R 5A5. 6 to 15. "Effective instruction at home" accepted, according to "Home Instruction: The Obligation of Parents and the Obligation of the School Board (La scolarisation a domicile: le droit des parents et le droit de la commission scolaire)." Some Anglophones have difficulty in Quebec because of the complexities of church-state ties and confusing language requirements.

SASKATCHEWAN: Saskatchewan Education, 2220 College Avenue, Regina, Saskatchewan S4P 3V7. 7 to 16. A "program of instruction approved by the director or superintendent at home or elsewhere." [Note the syntax!]

YUKON: Department of Education, Whitehorse, Yukon Territory Y1A 2C6. 6 to 16. Homeschooling allowed, fairly liberal requirements.

EDUCATION
BOOKS, CASSETTE TAPES, MAGAZINES,
CORRESPONDENCE COURSES,
GENERAL RESOURCES

THE WORKS OF JOHN HOLT -- For more than 20 years, until his death from cancer in 1985, John Holt was well-regarded internationally as one of the foremost educators striving for radical reform of the public school system. Two of his earlier books -- HOW CHILDREN FAIL and HOW CHILDREN LEARN, published in the sixties -- helped Jean and me form a great deal of the educational philosophy which led us to teach at home several years before John himself turned his back on the public system. In his introduction to TEACH YOUR OWN, in which he describes his conversion to the idea of home-schooling, John seems to imply that the idea was originally his, in answer to the problems many parents had been having in trying to set up "private" schools, and makes no mention of the hundreds or thousands who had already been teaching at home for many years. Growing Without Schooling, his bimonthly magazine begun in 1977, and the publication of TEACH YOUR OWN in 1981, so easily established John as a knowledgeable thinker in the field of home education that it seems ironic that it took him so long to carry his own philosophy to its logical conclusion. However, he caught up very quickly, and soon gained almost a "cult following" which regarded all his opinions and conclusions as established fact and educational gospel -- "This is what John has been trying to tell us right along." Most of John's personal experience was with young children, and he never had children of his own, so some of his observations may not apply as well to older children. John cared very deeply about children and their rights and their happiness, but readers should remember that being a theoretician and observer, however caring, doesn't include the hopes and fears and responsibilities of full-time parenthood, 24 hours a day for several years. All of John's thoughts are worth serious consideration, but those who regard him as an infallible saint are doing a disservice to him and to the children he cared so much about. Home-schoolers will get more use from some of John's writings than from others, but will find all his writing provocative and instructive.

TEACH YOUR OWN, by John Holt (1981). Despite the many newer books now available, this is still the best "in-depth" introduction to school at home. Subjects include the reasons public schooling is bad for most kids, answers to some common objections to home schooling, how to take kids out and keep them out legally, ways of living and learning with children that are not threatening or self-defeating, learning without teaching, etc. Much of the material is taken from letters published during the first few years of Growing Without Schooling, with John's responses, and covers many different aspects of learning at home. New paperback edition, $11.95. Code BT. BROOK FARM BOOKS.

HOW CHILDREN FAIL, by John Holt (1964; revised 1982; new edition 1988). When first published, this book sparked a whole era of educational reform, and was soon accepted as a masterpiece in the field of learning. This revised edition, written from the broader perspective that John gained over the years, and in accordance with his newer home-school philosophy, discusses more deeply the ways children investigate the world, the pitfalls of classroom learning, grades, testing, trust, and authority, as well as mistakes many home-schoolers make and how to avoid them. $9.95. Code BT. BROOK FARM BOOKS.

HOW CHILDREN LEARN, by John Holt (1967; revised 1983). "Children do not need to be made to learn, told what to learn, or shown how. If we give them access to enough of the world, including our own lives and work in that world, they will see clearly what things are truly important to us and to others, and they will make for themselves a better path into that world than we could make for them." This new edition is almost twice as long as the first, with all additions and changes clearly indicated. All of John's original thoughts about the ways we learn to talk, to read, to count, and to reason have been expanded in several new chapters. Despite the title, I think much of the book could easily be applied to the ways in which anyone, of any age, learns. Whether we consider ourselves primarily learners or teachers, this book will give us an increased understanding of the learning process. $9.95. Code BT. BROOK FARM BOOKS.

INSTEAD OF EDUCATION, John Holt (1976). What real learning is; what schools are really for (or should be for); why school reform failed; what a healthy learning society might be; why learning and doing cannot be separated; and much more. The central theme of this book, which may mark the beginning of John's transition from an advocate of public school reform to a leading proponent of homeschooling, is that we learn to do things by doing them. John's proposals for more creative, practical uses of public school facilities are very sound, as are his arguments for "learning by doing" rather than "learning before doing." However, some of his suggestions, which at first glance seem surprisingly simple and practical, seem to miss the needs of many people in an increasingly complex society. His suggestion of matching skilled people with students who want to learn the same skills is an obvious choice for many; apprenticeship has been practiced around the world for centuries, and is still practiced, although much less than was once the custom. But students who haven't yet decided on a particular skill to learn, or those who want careers requiring more abstract skills and knowledge (astronomy, perhaps; or medicine; and many others) may have no option but to study and learn before doing. John gives his playing of the cello as an example of learning-by-doing,

John Holt
Instead of Education
Ways to Help People
Do Things Better

pointing out that he does not first "learn to play," and then, once that mysterious process is completed, begin "to play." He just <u>plays</u>; the learning and the doing are the same. That seems to be an important distinction, but, as John also says, "Our language gives us no other way to say it." Several years ago, I went to Mexico and began learning Spanish. When I was asked by Mexicans if I spoke Spanish, after I had learned a dozen words, it would have seemed silly to say, "Yes," when the best I could have done with the rest of the sentence would have been to hold up my thumb and forefinger half an inch apart. I learned a fair amount of the language by listening, trying out my very limited vocabulary, asking to be corrected, and so on, which is a kind of apprenticeship; but I also learned a great deal by studying books and listening to cassette tapes. Eventually, I learned enough Spanish to enable me to travel fairly freely, take part in relatively complex conversations, and understand most of the dialogue in a Mexican movie. Still, if I say, "Hablo español," I'd feel very dishonest if I did not add, "Un pocito" or "Solo se unas quantas palabras," for it is true that I speak it only a little and I know only a few words. Learning processes may be very different for different kinds of knowledge and skills, and the method which is exactly right for one may be completely wrong for another; also, some people learn better by doing, and some learn better by studying first. In our condemnation of the public schools, let's not throw the baby out with the bath water. Our disagreement with the schools' apparent insistence that everything must be learned before doing shouldn't become an equally-obstinate insistence that the opposite is always true. In learning Spanish, I learned by doing, but I also learned before doing. Undoubtedly, I could have learned Spanish only "by doing" -- that is, by listening and speaking -- but I learned more and faster by memorizing and practicing words and phrases before trying them out in conversation. I might be content to get half-price haircuts at a barber's school, where the students learn by doing; and I doubt that I'll mind, when the time comes, if my undertaker is learning by doing; but if I ever need surgery, I'll hope the surgeon has had the opportunity to practice on cadavers and plastic dummies before he practices on me. In INSTEAD OF EDUCATION, John Holt's indictment of public education is far more general and sweeping than in many of his other books, including TEACH YOUR OWN. It may be true, as John says, that compulsory education is one of the most dangerous of all mankind's social institutions, but for me it would be far down on a very long list. As much as I disapprove of most public school programs, I can't agree at all with John's statement that children are compelled to go to school simply because adults don't want them around. Unlike many of John's other books, particularly TEACH YOUR OWN and HOW CHILDREN LEARN, I think INSTEAD OF EDUCATION will be of most interest to those who are curious about the evolution of John's opinions, rather than to those who are looking for practical advice and suggestions to employ in their home schooling. The book does have many valuable thoughts and ideas, and is certainly worth reading, but, if your budget is limited, I suggest you borrow it from the library and spend your money on some of John's other books which will be of more practical use. $8.95 plus $2 postage. HOLT ASSOCIATES, 2269 Massachusetts Ave., Cambridge, MA 02140.

MORE BOOKS & OTHER WRITINGS BY JOHN HOLT -- Many other books, pamphlets, and magazine reprints by John Holt, as well as many other products and services, are available from Holt Associates.

Growing Without Schooling, 2269 Massachusetts Ave., Cambridge, MA 02140, the bimonthly magazine begun by John Holt in 1977, is primarily an informal, open forum in which home-schooling parents and children share their ideas and experiences, not as professional writers or certified experts, but simply as people who are actively involved in learning outside of school. GWS also has articles about learning and teaching, compulsory testing, and more; excerpts and reprints from John Holt's books and correspondence; current legal information; recommendations of books and other materials; and a continuing directory of readers who ask to be listed. A complete index, available for all back issues, makes GWS a gigantic encyclopedia of learning. (See also Organizations: HOLT ASSOCIATES, INC., and JOHN HOLT'S BOOK & MUSIC STORE.)

SHARING TREASURES: Book Reviews by John Holt, edited by Patrick Farenga and Jane Prest Holcomb. This book, published five years after John's death, has almost immediately become one of my favorite collections of his writings -- partly because I value his opinions (although I don't always agree with him), and partly because I enjoy good books and good reviews of good books. A good review, of course, is much more than a simple description of a book; it's a discussion of the book's ideas, balanced against the reviewer's own ideas. A good reviewer will make no attempt at "objectivity," because the reader wants his honest, personal opinion; the extent to which the reader agrees with the reviewer in general may determine whether or not he will decide to read the book. I looked right away for John's reviews of books with which I am familiar or which I particularly like, wanting to compare his opinions with mine; did he like them for the same reasons I do? Next, I read reviews of books I've heard of, but haven't read (and John's comments convinced me that I should read them soon), and then reviews of books I've never heard of (often with the same result). Subjects include Homeschooling, Tests, History and Geography, Math, Economics and Work, Health, Poetry and Literature, Music Books and Records, Art and Materials, and much more. The selections are from sources such as The New York Review of Books, Harpers, Book Week, and Growing Without Schooling. If you like books and like to read about books, and if you agree even half the time with John Holt, this book makes an ideal combination. $5.95 plus $2.50 postage. HOLT ASSOCIATES, INC., 2269 Massachusetts Avenue, Cambridge, MA 02140.

Home Education Magazine, P.O. Box 1083, Tonasket, WA 98855. Edited & published by Mark and Helen Hegener. Articles by parents, home-school leaders, and a few education "professionals"; reviews of books & other educational materials; articles about laws affecting home-schooling; letters; state and national home-schooling news; articles & features by regular columnists & many readers. (See also Organizations: HOME EDUCATION PRESS.)

THE TEACHING HOME, A Christian Magazine for Home Educators. The leading national Christian homeschool publication. All articles, features, book product reviews, etc., even advertisements, are in agreement with the magazine's statement of faith, including: Absolute infallibility of the Bible; the Holy Trinity; all men are sinners by nature and by act; salvation is only through acceptance of the sacrificial death of Jesus Christ. An article by Michael Farris (Aug/Sept 1989) says, "'Holistic education' is both humanistic and sympathetic to the New Age movement that is straight out of the pit...It is clear...that they advocate one-world globalism... the elimination of national sovereignty and religious distinctives ...[T]heir ultimate goals for education are currently being achieved by Marxist, atheistic schools in the Soviet Union..." Bimonthly; $15/year. THE TEACHING HOME, 12311 NE Brazee, Portland, OR 97230. [Michael Farris is founder and president of the Home School Legal Defense Association; see Index.]

CAUGHT'YA! Grammar with a Giggle, by Jane Bell Kiester. Probably lots of giggles, which may be one of the reasons this method of teaching grammar, spelling, punctuation, and vocabulary is so effective. The basic idea, put very simply, is that the teacher makes the mistakes (on purpose), and the students correct them. Add to that a few minutes each day of a humorous soap opera with Hairy Beast, Wilfred Warthog, Bertha Boa, and other residents at General Animal Hospital, and you certainly have grammar with a giggle. This book came too late for us to try it on our kids, but the general approach is similar to the approach we often used ourselves. Easily adapted by the teacher for several different grade levels, from third through high school. $14.95. Code MP. BROOK FARM BOOKS.

CAUGHT'YA AGAIN: More Grammar With A Giggle, by Jane Bell Kiester. More stories and lots more giggles. $14.95. Code MP. BROOK FARM BOOKS.

The Three R's
At Home

Howard & Susan Richman

1990 HOMESCHOOL
HANDBOOK

AN ANNUAL GUIDE TO HOMESCHOOLING

HOMESCHOOLING
FOR EXCELLENCE

HOW TO TAKE CHARGE OF YOUR CHILD'S
EDUCATION -- AND WHY YOU ABSOLUTELY MUST

"David and Micki Colfax teach their children at
home and send them to places like Harvard."
Tom Brokaw, NBC News

by David and Micki Colfax

THE THREE R's AT HOME, by Howard and Susan Richman.
Now and then, as new homeschooling books come out, I
have to revise my personal list of "best" books. The
Richmans have made me do it again. This one goes to
the top of my list for its detailed but informal description of a family learning and growing together.
The Richmans' approach to reading, writing, and
arithmetic -- and, through those subjects, all the
rest -- is the best example I've seen of family
learning in a semi-structured environment (and also
gives good answers to those who worry about having
too much or too little structure in their program).
The Richmans' book chronicles the discoveries of
learning in their family, from the first read-aloud
experiences, through their children's early experiments with reading, writing, and math, to increased
interest and competence. Although the Richmans are
telling the story of their own home schooling, never
overtly saying, "This is how you should do it," I
think all readers who aren't bound by ideas of rigid
structure and authoritative discipline will find
themselves in constant agreement with the Richmans'
ideas and conclusions, and will find very informative suggestions and inspirational encouragement.
For beginning homeschoolers, I think this book, better than any other, answers the questions, "But how
does home-schooling work? How do I do it?" THE
THREE R's AT HOME has no lesson plans, no step-by-
step directions, but it will help readers gain the
confidence to work out their own approach, fully as-
sured that they don't need experts and authorities.
Even if you don't think you need to learn any more
about home schooling, you'll find THE THREE R's AT
HOME is a relaxing visit with a warm, friendly family. $7.95 postpaid, from PENNSYLVANIA HOMESCHOOLERS,
RD 2, Box 117, Kittanning, PA 16201. (The Richmans
also edit and publish the quarterly 32-page newsletter Pennsylvania Homeschoolers. Send a #10 SASE for
information and current price.)

**HOMESCHOOL HANDBOOK: An Annual Guide to Homeschool-
ing.** Written, compiled, and edited by Mark and Helen
Hegener, publishers of Home Education Magazine. For
the absolute beginner or the veteran who wants a
better view of the broad range of home-schooling,
HOMESCHOOL HANDBOOK is the best concise introduction
to the many approaches to learning at home and to
the major resources available. It may also be the
best book to loan to friends or relatives who are
still skeptical. Brief but comprehensive chapters
discuss homeschooling in the national media, how
homeschooling works, early instruction, selecting
resources, homeschooling the older child, socialization, higher education, testing, legal concerns,
support groups, educational programs & curriculums,
and much more, with articles, numerous quotations, &
book excerpts representing many different approaches
to home education. $7.50 postpaid. BROOK FARM
BOOKS.

HOME SCHOOLING FOR EXCELLENCE, David and Micki Colfax. With three sons accepted by Harvard, several
television appearances, and many magazine articles
written about them, much advance publicity had already been done, so it's not too surprising that
the Colfax's self-published book was bought and released by a major publisher. Of all the homeschooling books that Warner Books might have chosen with
which to test the public market, the one selected
is a thoughtful, well-balanced description and examination of the subject. The publisher's blurb on
the back cover seems to put the cart before the
horse by referring to "a prescription for excellence -- Harvard educations for their sons..." apparently missing the point that if the excellence
hadn't come first, Harvard probably wouldn't have
come after. A Chicago Tribune review, quoted on the
cover, says the book is "a step-by-step guide,"
which also misses the mark. Readers who expect a
manual of daily instructions may be disappointed. I
think the Colfaxes deliberately avoided writing "a
step-by-step guide," recognizing that others must
work out their own approaches, according to their
own needs and resources. The Colfaxes' book gives
steady, calm assurance and answers many common (and
some not-so-common) questions about home education,
but leaves to the readers the ways of implementing
their ideas. "The educational experience is simply
much too complex, too varied, and too rich to be
reduced to a neat formula or two, or a set of pat
and trendy phrases," the authors say in their Introduction. "We did not attempt to implement a particular educational philosophy, but... attempted to
respond to the evolving needs of the children more
or less in an ad hoc fashion... [If we have a philosophy,] it is only that children will learn, will
aspire to excellence, if we recognize and respect
their different interests and abilities and give
them a chance to develop them." A very important
point, I think, is that the "ad hoc fashion" is a
definite key to homeschooling for excellence. David
and Micki list and discuss several of the materials
they feel were most useful, not to pontificate but
to suggest. Readers might use the same materials
with similar satisfaction, or they might choose entirely different materials. The diversity of the
materials listed suggests that the importance is
not in what was used, but how it was used -- with
open-minded curiosity, self-assurance, & perséver-
ance. The book isn't a blueprint for getting into
Harvard, but an encouraging sketch of how others
can find and pursue their own paths to excellence.
As the Colfaxes say, acceptance by Harvard isn't
the only "proof" of excellence in education. Their
fourth son might become a boat-builder, which probably wouldn't gain him national recognition, but,
if he's a good boat-builder, would be equal proof
of educational excellence. $8.95 plus $1 postage.
BROOK FARM BOOKS.

SCHOOLING AT HOME: Parents, Kids, and Learning, from _Mothering Magazine_, compiled & edited by Ann Pedersen and Peggy O'Mara, including articles which have appeared in _Mothering_ and many new or updated articles. Foreword by Ashley Montagu. Possibly the best of the recent "overviews" of home-schooling, presenting a clear picture of the many approaches to learning at home, dealing with authorities, and the delicate balance between too much "structure" and not enough. Contributors include Andy LePage, Ed Clark, Herbert Kohl, Thomas Armstrong, Raymond and Dorothy Moore, John Holt, Ron Miller, Nancy Wallace, Patrick Farenga, David Colfax, and Penny Barker. Several excellent articles about how children learn, which will be thought-provoking for homeschooling veterans as well as beginners. A summary of home-schooling regulations in all states, working with the public school system, the computer as a learning tool, creative approaches to reading and writing, and much more. This book would fit well on the shelf next to John Holt's TEACH YOUR OWN and Mark and Helen Hegener's HOMESCHOOL HANDBOOK. $14.95 plus $2.00 postage. BROOK FARM BOOKS.

You don't lose all the other ages you've been.
--Madelaine L'Engel

I LEARN BETTER BY TEACHING MYSELF, Agnes Leistico. Outstanding exploration of interest-directed unschooling, with lots of ideas and information for the "older" student (high school and college). 152 pages; resource list, index. $11.00 postpaid. HOME EDUCATION PRESS, PO Box 1083, Tonasket, WA 98855.

THE HOME SCHOOL READER: Perspectives on Home Schooling, edited by Mark and Helen Hegener. An anthology of more than forty articles from the first five years of _Home Education Magazine_, offering many different views on socialization, legalities, higher education, accountability, compulsory education, selecting curriculum materials, finding resources, and much more. Contributors include John Holt, Nancy Wallace, Mario Pagnoni, Susannah Sheffer, Clint Bolick, Christopher Klicka, Penny Barker, Jane Williams, Kathleen McCurdy, Donn Reed, Tom Friedlander, Mary McCarthy, Agnes Leistico, Joseph Ciano, and many others. 156 pages. $12.75 postpaid. BROOK FARM BOOKS.

WHOLE CHILD/WHOLE PARENT, by Polly Berrien Berends. "Once I had a dream," the author says in her introduction. "In the dream I was to receive a diploma as a spiritual teacher or guide of some sort... But before me there stood an enormous mountain of laundry. To receive my diploma I would first have to climb over this huge heap of laundry." Many books tell you how to clothe, feed, amuse, and educate your children; many others tell you of ways in which to indoctrinate your children with particular beliefs, or to "modify" their behavior according to your wishes. This book will lead you on an exciting path of discovery of the wholeness, the one-ness, of you and your children and of all aspects of your lives together. The usual subjects -- clothing, diaper rash, toys, books, playtime, discipline -- of most child-care books are here, but in an entirely different perspective. They are thoughtfully and lovingly considered from a viewpoint of _truth_ -- not the dogmatic "truth" of a particular creed which must be taught, but the inner essence of being which is discovered and experienced. WHOLE CHILD/WHOLE PARENT is a book to browse in frequently, to keep next to the window for rainy-day reading and on the nightstand for the last thoughts before sleeping. $12.95. Code BT. BROOK FARM BOOKS.

SUMMERHILL: A Radical Approach to Child Rearing, by A. S. Neill. The story of the remarkable school which began as an experiment and soon became a model for scores of others. Believing strongly in Freudian theory, Neill felt that social maladjustment, academic failure, and nearly all other problems were the result of artificial inhibition and repression; he therefore encouraged almost complete freedom, including deliberate violation of many of society's taboos. In a subsequent book, FREEDOM NOT LICENSE, addressed primarily to numerous objections, Neill explained that students at Summerhill learned through their interaction that real freedom includes real responsibilities. The "experiment" had much greater success at Summerhill than in its imitators, which most critics agree was because of Neill's personal influence on his students. Whether liberal or conservative, readers will probably disagree with much of what Neill advocates. At the same time, SUMMERHILL vividly demonstrates that freedom can work, although it needs guidance; that in an atmosphere of democracy and self-regulation, children can thrive, learn and grow. Disregard the Freudian view of repression; disregard the impractical consistency of total freedom for all children of all ages; still, SUMMERHILL is a refreshing, provocative book which will both challenge and encourage you. $8.95. Code BT. BROOK FARM BOOKS.

BETTER THAN SCHOOL: One Family's Declaration of Independence, by Nancy Wallace; introduction by John Holt. Ishmael Wallace, at the age of 11, was an accomplished musician and playwright; his sister Vita, 7, was also a very talented musician; they both have many other accomplishments. This book is in part the story of the Wallaces' long and difficult struggle with school authorities, and in part the story of their own "unschooling" approach to learning. One of the most important lessons in this book is not that the children accomplished so much, but that their great talents would almost certainly have been stunted by public school. However, very few 11-year-olds write symphonies, whether they are in public schools or home schools, so homeschoolers shouldn't regard the highly visible accomplishments of Ishmael and Vita as yardsticks by which to judge their own home-schooling. Nonetheless, there are many provocative and useful ideas in the book, including many excellent examples of working with a semi-structured program. $14.95 plus $2 postage from HOLT ASSOCIATES, 2269 Massachusetts Ave., Cambridge, MA 02140.

MEG JOHNSON'S BULLETINS -- For five years, Meg Johnson researched, compiled, wrote, edited, organized, and mailed quarterly bulletins with information and thoughts for homeschoolers. Meg's observations about home-schooling are among the very most valuable in the movement; new or veteran home-schoolers will enjoy and benefit from them. In September 1985, Meg discontinued her Home Education Resource Center, to enable her to spend more time with her own family. Most of the quarterly bulletins are still available; we very enthusiastically recommend all 20 of them. Subjects include "Home Schoolers -- Unity and Diversity," "Another Year -- Another Challenge," "Home Schooling -- Frustration or Accomplishment?," "The Real Reason for Home Schooling," "The Human Priority," "The Positive Picture," and "Teaching Several Children at Home." Most bulletins have 4 pages; a few early ones have 2 pages. Meg still offers her bulletins at cost, which is about 25¢ per page. For a complete list of Bulletins & other resources still available, send a #10 SASE (imperative!) to MEG JOHNSON, P.O. Box 124, Mt. Vernon, NH 03057.

TO HERALD A CHILD: The Report of the Commission of Inquiry into the Education of the Young Child, Laurier L. LaPierre, Commissioner. Ostensibly concerned with public schooling in the province of Ontario, but very applicable to public schools anywhere in North America. The Commissioner (who is also a popular TV talk show host) shocked provincial educators by recommending more family interaction with the schools, less structure, no testing or grading, buildings open to the public for recreation and community learning, and so on. Surprisingly similar to many of the views of John Holt, Ivan Illich, et al. Very useful and sensible for anyone who hopes to change public schooling. In a bilingual edition only, TO HERALD A CHILD/NOS ENFANTS, 116 pages in each language. $10 postpaid from ONTARIO PUBLIC SCHOOL MEN TEACHERS' FEDERATION, 1260 Bay Street, Toronto, Ontario M5R 2B7, Canada.

HOME GROWN KIDS, HOME SPUN SCHOOLS, BETTER LATE THAN EARLY, SCHOOL CAN WAIT, HOME-STYLE TEACHING, HOME-SCHOOL BURNOUT, and other writings by Raymond & Dorothy Moore. One of the Moores' main premises, for which they give many well-researched reasons and arguments, particularly in BETTER LATE THAN EARLY, is that children shouldn't begin formal schooling before the age of 8 or 9, or even later. "We firmly believe," they say in HOME GROWN KIDS, "that the greatest teaching talent in the world lies in the warm, responsive, and consistent parent whose love makes the needs of his children his highest concern ...Parents' daily one-to-one example amounts to master teaching at the highest level." HOME STYLE TEACHING may be most useful for specific "how-to" suggestions and examples. HOME-SCHOOL BURN-OUT suggests that many parents who become frustrated and discouraged with their home-teaching may be working too hard at it, setting impractical goals for themselves and their children, and worrying too much about achieving results which are of negligible value; many very practical suggestions are offered to increase the efficiency and pleasure of learning at home without the dangers of "burnout." The Moores are conservative Christians, but definitely not militant fundamentalists (and, in fact, are criticized by some fundamentalists for "not being Christian enough"). "...From Christianity to Judaism to Confucianism and from Taoism or Islam to Zen, the Golden Rule threads through them all. And the home is its finest nest. It is the person who understands this well who is the most able creator of a family school." Much of their philosophy is very similar to the "unschooling" (i.e., unstructured) approach of John Holt and others. Of all home-school books by conservative Christians, the Moores' books will be most useful to the less-conservative or non-Christian; they often offer a good balance between the left and right extremes, and have many ideas which will be of good use to all homeschoolers, regardless of their religious beliefs. Write for more information and prices. THE MOORE FOUNDATION, Box 1, Camas, WA 98607.

If we work upon marble, it will perish; if we work upon brass, time will efface it; if we rear temples, they will crumble into dust; but if we work upon immortal minds and instill into them just principles, we are then engraving that upon tablets which no time will efface, but will brighten and brighten to all eternity.
Daniel Webster

CHILD'S WORK: Taking Children's Choices Seriously, by Nancy Wallace; foreword by Susannah Sheffer; 1990. In many ways a sequel to BETTER THAN SCHOOL, this book is also a deeper exploration of the "unschooling" concept which some people say John Holt developed (I'll go along with that, as long as "developed" doesn't mean "originated"). If I hadn't already worked out my misgivings about BETTER THAN SCHOOL, I'd have had to go through the whole process with this book. Once again, the subject of "giftedness" is carefully brushed aside. In her foreword, Susannah Sheffer says "...some readers may think this is a story about prodigies and consider it irrelevant to their own children... If we think of Vita and Ishmael as prodigies, we avoid having to think about what helped them become as competent as they are." To a small extent, I think, she's right; despite the frequent disclaimers, it will soon be obvious to most readers that Vita and Ishmael are prodigies, and that therefore some of their story is irrelevant to most home-schoolers. So what? Do we make Mozart or Edison more "relevant" to home-schoolers by pretending they were not prodigies? Whether we use the term "prodigy" or "gifted" or whatever, we are referring to a factor which shouldn't be ignored, because its relevance to the children themselves -- in this case, Vita and Ishmael -- is obvious. I think Vita and Ishmael have achieved very great things -- in part, because their parents recognized the need to let them learn in their own ways; and, in part, because they are prodigies. If we're supposed to pretend that one factor doesn't exist, why not ignore the other factor as well? When I taught adult illiterates, one of my students had an I.Q. of 50; it would have been silly (and self-defeating) for me to pretend that this was not a serious factor in his learning. If a very low I.Q. is a factor in learning, then why isn't a very high I.Q. also a relevant factor? Although giftedness is not an acquired trait or skill, it is still the person's own; why ignore it, and try to give full credit only to the conditions under which the person is learning? I liked this book more than I liked BETTER THAN SCHOOL; I learned more from it, and I was interested in Vita and Ishmael's further development. But I also found myself disagreeing more, wanting to argue more, and (frequently) wishing Nancy would just come out and say, "Yes, my kids are prodigies, and this is how they have developed their talents, and the ways in which we have tried to help them, many of which may be useful to you, too." Vita and Ishmael had marvelous games of great complexity when they were younger (described in BETTER THAN SCHOOL), weaving fiction, fantasy, history, and politics into intricate doll societies, and I was very intrigued by Nancy's descriptions of these societies' trades and wars, but I am offended by the underlying suggestion that the children's never-fully-acknowledged giftedness had nothing to do with the complexity of their play -- because the corollary suggestion is that kids whose play is less complex are somehow deficient. If Vita and Ishmael are not "above normal," then most other kids must be "below normal," and that is not a fair implication. This was my running objection, through both of Nancy's books, interfering with my greater enjoyment of them. Most of my lesser disagreements were about "unschooling" -- how much, if any, should an adult "interfere" with a child's natural, innate learning process? Some of the problem, I think, may be that as soon as one adopts a particular philosophy, one's consistency with that philosophy will be continually tested. It's a little ironic that the unschoolers' "non-interference" with children's learning would be construed as rude condescension if applied to adults. If I interrupt my son's wood-working to show him a way to start the saw-cut without nicking a finger, then I'm interfering with his ability to learn by himself; but if I withhold the same information from an adult, and he becomes aware of it, he'll wonder why I didn't give useful advice when I could have. If someone shows me a way to get more leverage on a tire iron with less effort, I don't resent him for stunting my innate ability to learn. There are ways of using axes and saws and knives that are completely or relatively safe and there are ways of using them that cut off fingers and hands and puncture eyeballs, and I have no intention of letting my kids explore the various ways so they can learn by themselves which ways are safe and which are not. "Look, there goes Thumbless Reed. He learned all by himself to keep his thumb off the block he was splitting into kindling." Part of the idea of "unschooling" is to treat kids like adults, but this is almost constantly negated by unschoolers who consistently withhold useful or even vital help and advice from children on the theory that children should be allowed to learn at their own pace and in their own way. Waiting for the child to ask for help isn't the answer, either; if he doesn't know or suspect that there's a better way, then he has no reason to ask you to show it to him. Letting a child struggle with a task without offering advice which would make it easier is not showing him respect -- and, once he realizes that you could have helped but chose not to, probably will not increase his respect for you. Any philosophy, carried to its "logical," consistent extreme, can easily become ridiculous and indefensible. Perhaps it isn't the advice that some kids resent, but the way in which it's given. With all of these comments, and the many more pages of similar comments which I'm making myself not write, will you still believe me when I say CHILD'S WORK is informative, interesting, useful, and definitely worth reading? It is. If nothing else, it may make you explore the philosophy of unschooling more deeply than any other book now on the market -- but I think you'll find that many of Nancy's observations about learning are relevant to most children, whether they are prodigies or not. $12.95 plus $2.50 postage. HOLT ASSOCIATES, INC., 2269 Massachusetts Avenue, Cambridge, MA 02140.

CHILD'S WORK cover design by Dave Sullivan

THE Home School Manual

For parents who teach
their own children

Theodore E. Wade, Jr.
and Others

ALTERNATIVES IN EDUCATION

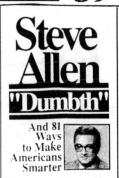

GROWING UP ABSURD

PAUL GOODMAN

Steve Allen "Dumbth"

And 81 Ways to Make Americans Smarter

THE HOME SCHOOL MANUAL: For Parents Who Teach Their Own Children, by Theodore E. Wade, Jr. Expanded, updated 5th edition, c. 500 pages. Ted and about 30 contributors discuss in detail nearly every aspect of teaching at home. Subjects range from the three R's to moral and spiritual values (from a conservative Christian viewpoint), community resources, and introducing children to art. New chapters include music, more science, phonics, and character development. Several appendices include lists of home-school organizations, publishers, schooling laws, support groups, a typical course of study, and much more, with a full index. THE **CHRISTIAN** HOME SCHOOL MANUAL would be a more accurate title, but this book has scores, perhaps hundreds, of good ideas for everyone, and a great deal of extensive information not found elsewhere. Some of my less-conservative customers and correspondents have said they disagree with the highly-structured approach, as well as the book's fundamentalism, but that they feel the wealth of ideas makes the book worthwhile, anyway. I agree. "Yes, I advocate more structure than you do," Ted has written me, "but I see it as a servant, not as master. Seeing character develop in my own children gives me confidence in certain principles." This book and the books by Raymond and Dorothy Moore are the only "conservative Christian" books I knowingly recommend to non-fundamentalists, and this is the only conservative Christian book I will sell; I wouldn't touch most of the others with a ten-foot rod or staff. If you don't agree with some of Ted's viewpoints (as I don't), I think you'll still find the book a valuable reference, worthy of a place on your home-school bookshelf. $24.95 plus $2.50 postage. BROOK FARM BOOKS.

CLUES TO WHAT? SELLING TO THE OTHER EDUCATIONAL MARKETS, by Jane Williams, is a regularly-updated guide for businesses who are interested in having their products sold or reviewed by home-school suppliers or other alternative educational businesses, and is published by Jane's company, Bluestocking Press, P.O. Box 1014, Placerville, CA 95667. (Write for a free brochure if you're interested in buying, or being listed in, this book.) Brook Farm Books is listed in the book, inviting publishers and other businesses to submit material for possible review in THE HOME SCHOOL SOURCE BOOK. We receive hundreds of books and other items, and carefully consider them all. Sometimes the decision to review or not review is difficult, but other times the material just doesn't impress us much. One such item was a 20-minute video tape (meant to sell for $24.95!) which didn't impress us at all, and it's not included in my reviews, but it gave us a little chuckle, anyway. It was titled "CLUES TO GOOD READING," and was addressed to Donna Reed, Bluestocking Press, Bridgewater, ME 04735.

ALTERNATIVES IN EDUCATION: Family Choices in Learning, Mark & Helen Hegener, publishers of Home Education Magazine. A smorgasbord of alternative education articles. Subjects include homeschooling, correspondence schools, higher education, tutoring, apprenticeships, learning exchanges, and more. Capsule introductions to the philosophies and works of Rudolph Steiner, Maria Montessori, Jean Piaget, John Dewey, Herbert Kohl, A. S. Neill, Ivan Illich, John Holt, Jonathan Kozol, James Herndon, and George Dennison; articles by Helen Hegener, Jules Archer, Ron Miller, Jane Williams, Susan Nelson, Daniel Greenberg, Catherine Johns, Judson Jerome, Thomas Kane, Pat Montgomery, Craig Conley, Sambhava Luvmour, Donn Reed, Joanne Marzioli, and Bobbie Groth. $16.75 plus $2.50 postage. BROOK FARM BOOKS.

GROWING UP ABSURD, Paul Goodman. Although not concerned only with education, per se, this book of the late 1950's was among the few which helped people begin to examine the life and education of children in our "technological paradise." Its arguments about youth and complacent America may be more pertinent today than they were then. $4.95 plus $1 shipping. WAR RESISTERS LEAGUE, 339 Lafayette St., New York, NY 10012.

"DUMBTH" by Steve Allen. Humorist, composer, author, actor, & lecturer, Steve Allen has coined the word "dumbth" as a shorthand term for the muddle-headedness he believes has become characteristic of our society -- education that fails to educate, airline mishaps, military errors, incompetence in private industry, and scores of similar cases which indicate that "the United States is suffering from a severe and worsening case of 'dumbth.'" The second half of the book is devoted to Allen's proposed solutions, beginning with the addition of "a fourth R" -- reasoning -- to the traditional reading, 'riting, and 'rithmetic. Then, he offers 81 "rules" for good thinking, arguing that thinking well is a skill like any other, that must be studied, learned, practiced, and mastered. Hardcover. $19.95. Code BT. BROOK FARM BOOKS.

HOME SCHOOLS: An Alternative, by Cheryl Gorder. Most of this book is an examination of public schooling and the reasons so many people choose to teach at home, including educational controversies; social, moral, and academic failings of schools; legal aspects; origins and development of public schooling; state laws; and so on. Many homeschool organizations and resources are listed. If you're already committed to home schooling, the facts and statistics in this book probably won't surprise you. If you're undecided, or have friends or relatives who need convincing, this book should do it. Slight conservative Christian emphasis. 200 pages. $11.95 plus $2 postage. BLUE BIRD PUBLISHING, 1713 East Broadway, Tempe, AZ 85282.

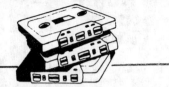

YOU ARE YOUR CHILD'S FIRST TEACHER, Rahima Baldwin. In a time when most parents are bombarded with scores of approaches to "raising" their children, this book introduces a way of insight & understanding which will be very welcome to many. Chapters include Caring for the newborn, Helping your toddler's development, The development of fantasy and creative play, Nourishing your child's imagination, Rhythm & discipline in home life; more. Black & white photographs. 320 pages. $9.95. Code TSP. BROOK FARM BOOKS. (See also Birth & Baby, SPECIAL DELIVERY, by Rahima Baldwin.)

THE CLOSING OF THE AMERICAN MIND, by Allan Bloom. "How Higher Education Has Failed Democracy and Impoverished the Souls of Today's Students." In this now-famous book, the author probes the state of American education and assesses the intellectual and moral confusions of modern students. Although Bloom has been accused by critics of "elitism," in that he seems to be writing primarily of ivy league collegiate education, I think many of his conclusions are valid, and can easily be applied to other segments of society and education, whether or not that is his intention. As home-schoolers, we certainly agree with Bloom that modern education is sadly lacking in some of the most fundamental essentials. The question is, do we agree on what is lacking, and on the possible remedies? Even if we aren't directly concerned with public education on the elementary and secondary levels, most of us would agree that many of those wishing a college education will probably go to college, which makes Bloom's indictment more relevant to us. Having withdrawn our children from an inadequate elementary school system, do we want them entering an inadequate college system? Bloom's comments and numerous historical anecdotes, tracing the educational system back to the time of Plato, are certainly worth reading, and should make us examine our own philosophies very carefully, even if we end by disagreeing completely with everything he says -- which is not likely if we are serious about education. $8.95. Code SS. BROOK FARM BOOKS.

AND THE CHILDREN PLAYED, Patricia Joudry. This has been recommended by several readers and newsletters, and I still haven't gotten around to reading it. "Funny, refreshing, personal account of ten years of home schooling with five daughters." $9.95 plus $2 postage from HOLT ASSOCIATES, 2269 Massachusetts Avenue, Cambridge, MA 02140.

THE FEELING CHILD, Arthur Janov. Jocelyn Maskerman of the Quebec Homeschooling Advisory says this book is "a must for real parenting, for real insight into how children feel." $6.50 plus $1 postage from SIMON & SCHUSTER, 1230 Avenue of the Americas, New York, NY 10020.

EDUCATION LECTURES & DISCUSSIONS ON CASSETTE TAPES --For much less than the cost of taking your family to a movie, you can invite world-famous educators into your home to share their intelligent, thought-provoking discussions. These tapes are intended primarily for an adult audience, but we think they are also very good for bright and interested high-school students, about 15 and older.

THE DESCHOOLED SOCIETY, Ivan Illich. The author of DESCHOOLING SOCIETY argues that the function of modern education is simply to produce consumers and workers in an industrial society -- not necessarily by design on the part of individual educators, but by the very structure of public education. In the process, individual autonomy is sacrificed. He challenges the concept that true learning can occur only within schools, and suggests ways of educating people more effectively than in the school system. 33 minutes. $10.95. Order by title and #729. Code JN. BROOK FARM BOOKS.

THE RIGHTS OF CHILDREN. John Holt (author of HOW CHILDREN LEARN, etc.) and psychologist Richard Farson (author of BIRTH-RIGHTS) discuss controversial changes in the treatment of children, and suggest that young people should be enfranchised. 55 minutes, recorded in 1974 (before John became a home-school advocate); from Heywood Hale Broun's "Avid Reader" Series. $12.95. Order by title and #40067. Code JN. BROOK FARM BOOKS.

CHILDHOOD. Dr. Bruno Bettelheim analyzes the modern child's difficulty in forming his own identity, as contrasted with past generations. He discusses family structure and identity formation, his own criteria for "a happy family," and the need to make schools more human institutions. Two cassettes, approximately 2 hours; recorded 1974. $31.95. Order by title and #S29622. Code JN. BROOK FARM BOOKS.

HOW PEOPLE CHANGE. Dr. Margaret Mead describes how our attitude toward change is crucial to our attitude toward the world as a whole, and what is required to effect changes in people and cultures. 25 minutes; recorded in 1962. $12.95. Order by title and #35002. Code JN. BROOK FARM BOOKS.

COMING OF AGE IN AMERICA. Dr. Margaret Mead contrasts the "shoulds" and "oughts" of traditional childhood and adult development with the realities of our present culture. Of particular interest to people interested in the cultural background of changing and alternative lifestyles. Although some statements are dated (e.g., prior to the 18-year-old vote), the emphasis on the _quality_ of life versus _quantity_ is still just as valid. This talk gives a good basic background for understanding many current social issues. A few humorous moments, too. 80 minutes; recorded in 1965. $15.95. Order by title and #35010. Code JN. BROOK FARM BOOKS.

We have to realize that for most men the right to learn is curtailed by the obligation to attend school.

Ivan Illich

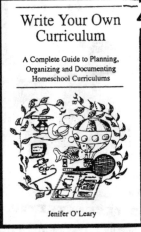

GOOD STUFF: Learning Tools for All Ages, by Rebecca Rupp. It's a little difficult for the author of a resource guide to review someone else's resource guide, unless there are major disagreements in subject matter or philosophy (as in my review of Mary Pride's BIG BOOKS OF LEARNING). "Good Stuff" is also the name of Becky Rupp's regular colum of reviews in Home Education Magazine, and this book obviously grew out of that column. I lost count several times of the items reviewed in GOOD STUFF, and can only say there are certainly many hundreds. I don't think I disagree with any of her choices, although only a few of them appear in THE HOME SCHOOL SOURCE BOOK. (That means you can consult both books with little chance of duplicated reviews.) The subjects covered include literature, writing, math, history and geography, science, languages, arts and crafts, and creative thinking. There are several short, one-paragraph reviews of many children's books; of catalogs and suppliers of cassette tapes, video tapes, tools, games, musical instruments, and periodicals in all the subjects mentioned, followed by 48 pages of publishers' and other companies' addresses, and an extensive index. Although some of our favorite subjects (conservation and ecology, religion, etc.) aren't mentioned at all, the subjects which are included are covered very comprehensively. 6"x9" paperback, 386 pages. 14.75 plus $2 postage from Home Education Press, PO Box 1083, Tonasket, WA 98855.

TAKING CHARGE THROUGH HOME SCHOOLING: Personal and Political Empowerment, M. Larry & Susan D. Kaseman. "Empowerment," say the authors, "includes identifying options and realizing that we can make choices and act on them, that we can take charge." Taking charge begins with making one's own choices about education (or anything else), which in itself is a political action; but the freedom to choose can be regained and held only by being politically active; i.e., by being aware of laws and lawmaking trends that affect home-schooling, and by taking an active part in influencing those laws. This is a very clear, comprehensive explanation of the many ways in which laws are made and how they can be influenced, and should certainly be read by anyone faced with legal or social opposition to home-schooling. Although the greater part of this book is concerned with political involvement, I think the Kasemans' suggestions regarding the everyday experience of home-schooling are just as important and useful, and make this a very valuable book even for those who don't feel ready to become politically active, or for whom just the decision to teach at home is sufficient challenge. $12.95 plus $2 shipping to: KOSHKONONG PRESS, 2545 Koshkonong Road, Stoughton, WI 53589.

WRITE YOUR OWN CURRICULUM: A COMPLETE GUIDE TO PLANNING, ORGANIZING, AND DOCUMENTING HOMESCHOOL CURRICULUMS, Jenifer O'Leary. "The most meaningful and useful education is self-directed," says the author. "Subjects overlap, spilling into each other until there is only one subject left-- LIFE! That's the way it is when the world is your classroom." Jenifer's approach to writing your own curriculum is informal and general, helping you define your goals and satisfy the school authorities, but without immersing yourself in miles of paperwork. She favors interest-directed learning and unit studies rather than a "typical" course of graded study directed by others, yet suggests ways of incorporating all essential subjects (and official requirements) into her relaxed curriculum. Her suggestions are specific enough to help you get well organized, but general enough to leave the finer details up to you. $12.95 plus $2 postage. WHOLE LIFE PUBLISHING, P.O. Box 936, Stevens Point, WI 54481.

CURRICULUM PLANNERS -- Jenifer O'Leary, author of WRITE YOUR OWN CURRICULUM (above), has also created several Curriculum Planners which will save you the time of making your own. The planners are looseleaf packets ready to insert in a 3-ring binder, and contain all the forms, charts, and instructions you need to plan, organize, & document your curriculum for a year, with monthly dividers, pages for pictures and journal entries, and an almanac to help you plan studies around special events. There are four different forms of planners: Family, Primary, Middle Grades, and High School, for $29.95 each, plus $2 postage for one item and 75¢ for each additional item. Order from WHOLE LIFE PUBLISHING (address above), or write for more information.

HOME SCHOOLING IN THE NEWS, edited by Patrick Farenga. 28 articles from 1986 to 1991 on homeschooling from a wide variety of national newspapers and magazines: TIME, etc. Not much new information for homeschoolers, but good material to show skeptical relatives and friends that establishment publications are making favorable comments about home-schooling. $6.95 plus $2.50 shipping. HOLT ASSOCIATES, INC., 2269 Massachusetts Avenue, Cambridge, MA 02140.

TEXTBOOK TIP FROM A READER -- "Some of the major textbook companies won't sell teacher's editions or answer keys to individuals, especially those without teaching certificates. I found that if I send a photocopy of the education department's letter to me, granting permission to teach at home, the companies will keep the letter on file for a year, and will sell me the teacher's editions, answer keys, etc., at school prices. I've had no trouble receiving material I wanted." [Thanks for the tip, RM.]

42

CURRICULUM -- AUDIO MAGAZINE -- FAIRY TALES

HOME SCHOOL: TAKING THE FIRST STEP, Borg Hendrickson. A very detailed, step-by-step guide to anyone planning to teach at home and not sure how to go about it, with chapters on home-schooling questions and answers (Is it legal? Will my children be too isolated?); your home-school plan (partly to satisfy school authorities, partly to keep you on track toward your own goals); key components of teaching at home (curriculum, materials, planning, records); a very extensive survey of state requirements; support groups; several pages of suggested reading material (books, periodicals, etc.) for children and adults; three appendices (teaching methods, effective teaching, and lesson planning); a glossary of terms; and several work and record sheets to photocopy. 336 pages. $16.95 plus $2 shipping from Mountain Meadow Press, P.O. Box 1170, Wrangell, AK 99929.

HOW TO WRITE A LOW COST/NO COST CURRICULUM For Your Home-School Child, Borg Hendrickson. Step-by-step ideas and suggestions for designing a very formal, detailed curriculum, with short- and long-term goals, frequent assessments, specific breakdowns of study areas and subjects for each grade, with particular attention given to keeping records which should satisfy the regulations of nearly any state, suggested reading, suggested sources of materials, a glossary, and several photocopy master sheets. $12.95 plus $2 postage from Mountain Meadow Press, P.O. Box 1170, Wrangell, AK 99929.

A GOOD USE FOR "S/HE"?

The Toronto Globe & Mail recently reported that the historical board of Genesee County, Michigan, voted to use both "he" and "she" on a courthouse plaque honoring Sarah Emma Edmonds, who fought in the Civil War disguised as a man, using the name Franklin Thompson.

DADDY'S ROOMMATE, HEATHER HAS TWO MOMMIES, & ASHA'S MUMS -- No, you won't find these titles for sale in THE HOME SCHOOL SOURCE BOOK...but you can find them in many public schools which have banned SNOWWHITE, TOM SAWYER, THE WIZARD OF OZ, and THE BIBLE.

BOOMERANG! A monthly "audio magazine," a 70-minute cassette tape with feature stories about geography, history, current events, mysteries, letters to the editor, interviews, and jokes, for kids 8-12 (more or less), professionally written from a kid's perspective and reported by kids. Each cassette is accompanied by a board game and related reading suggestions. Retail price in stores is $5.95 per issue, but an annual subscription is only $39.95, or $3.33 per tape. Credit card orders are toll-free: 1-800-333-7858; or write BOOMERANG!, 123 Townsend St., San Francisco, CA 94107 for more information.

CONSERVATION RESOURCES--Write to these organizations for information about conservation and ecology:
CHILDREN'S ALLIANCE FOR PROTECTION OF THE ENVIRONMENT, P.O. Box 307, Austin, TX 78767.
EARTH DAY USA, PO Box 470, Peterborough, NH 03458.
KIDS FOR SAVING EARTH, PO Box 47247, Plymouth, MN 55447.
THE KIDS' EARTHWORKS GROUP, 1400 Shattuck Ave., Suite 25, Berkeley, CA 94709.
NATIONAL WILDLIFE FEDERATION, 1400 Sixteenth St. NW, Washington, DC 20036.

"TYPICAL COURSE OF STUDY," a bare-bones listing of the various subjects and skills supposedly offered in public schools, divided by grade. Very general and non-specific, but maybe useful, anyway. 50¢ postage. WORLD BOOK EDUCATIONAL PRODUCTS, 101 Northwest Point Blvd., Elk Grove Village, IL 60007.

KIDS COPY, P.O. Box 42, Wyncote, PA 19095. Monthly newspaper for grades 4-8, with world and national news, features on science, sports, entertainment, health, relationships, food, and nutrition; reviews of books, games, music, and videos; puzzles & games. Write for current subscription information.

A FAIRY TALE UPDATED --
THE FOURTH LITTLE PIG, by Teresa Celsi. Yep, there is a <u>fourth</u> little pig, and SHE shows the boys that hiding and cowering is a waste of time...
THE THREE LITTLE JAVELINAS, by Susan Lowell. Three little Texican pigs, living in homes made of tumbleweeds and cactus ribs, escape the hungry wolf by hiding in their wise sister's strong adobe house...
Where would you buy these? Beats me. I didn't read that far.

THE TEENAGE LIBERATION HANDBOOK: How to Quit School and Get a Real Life and Education, Grace Llewellyn. Probably the best, most accurate review of this book was in Bloomsbury Review: "This is a very dangerous book. It contradicts all the conventional wisdom about dropouts and the importance of a formal education. It is funny and inspiring. Do not, under any circumstances, share this book with a bright, frustrated high-schooler being ground into mind-fudge by the school system. The writer cannot be responsible for the happiness and sense of personal responsibility that might come from reading this book." Grace Llewellyn has compiled a fantastic array of ideas and resources for a very comprehensive "unschooling" education, in all the standard subjects and scores of non-standard ones -- science, math, social sciences, English, languages, the arts, sports and athletics, outdoor jobs and activities, travel -- through books, personal contacts, jobs, apprenticeships and internships, volunteering, social and political activism, and more. She offers very encouraging advice throughout the book, and illustrates her arguments with dozens of real-life stories (most of them borrowed from Growing Without Schooling) of kids who have done it. Even a home-school with more structure than Grace advocates will find the numerous ideas & resources invaluable; for the truly "unschooled" teenager who is serious about doing more than watching TV, it will be an invaluable guidebook.

I have one major reservation, and a few minor ones. Like many unschoolers, Grace seems to think that any and all resources (people, places, etc.) are good -- except the child's own parents. The first thing to do after making the decision to quit school, Grace advises the teenaged reader, is "celebrate your audacity with deep chocolate ice cream," and then, step two, "consult your parents." Some parents might feel they should have something

to say about such a momentous decision, but Grace doesn't seem to have much sympathy for them. "You might get this over with after dinner tonight," she says, "or you might acclimate them slowly to the idea." At least she realizes that some old fogies may be a little slow. "Fortunately," she adds, "with a little care and planning, you will probably be able to help them see the light." Ah, yes, we remember it well -- our kids, at the age of 13 or 14, suddenly wise and mature, trying to help us see the light -- and we, stubborn and over-protective, always in the way of their freedom and happiness, trying to keep them from frying their brains or wrapping themselves around a tree. Our own "fortunately" is that they soon saw the light and grew out of this phase almost as quickly as they had grown into it, and we continued our lives together as friends and family. Over-protective or not, we still think that most kids of 13 or 14, and even some of 16 or 17, are not ready to take on the entire world on their own terms alone, with no consideration for their parents' opinions, guidance -- and, yes, even a few rules, now and then. There are exceptions, of course, but even for them there is seldom any excuse for presenting parents with ultimatums and sudden declarations of independence.

My minor reservations about the book have to do with some of Grace's recommended reading for the newly-liberated teenager. We happen to agree with most of her choices, but a few of them seem to encourage a "liberation" with which we cannot agree. Poe, Gibran, Thoreau, the Bible, Blake, Shakespeare -- excellent choices. But Grace also recommends RUBYFRUIT JUNGLE, by Rita Mae Brown, with the parenthetical note that it's "sexually explicit, offends a lot of people," which is putting it very mildly. She recommends THE COLOR PURPLE, by Alice Walker, without mentioning that it's largely about incestuous rape, sexual promiscuity, infidelity, and lesbianism. She does admit that Tom Robbins' EVEN COWGIRLS GET THE BLUES is "rated R--some sex, some drugs," but her idea of "some" is a long way from the book's nearly-total preoccupation with random promiscuity, lesbianism, and constant drug use. Grace's list of "love literature" looks okay, except "poetry by Sappho," which is explicitly lesbian. In what she calls "a short list especially tailored for searching teenagers," I think she could have made better choices than these.

These reservations are concerned with a tiny part of the book, and shouldn't keep you from buying it and using it; but keep in mind that the author has her own orientation and opinions, and you may not always agree with her. $14.95. Code LH. BROOK FARM BOOKS.

THE HBJ STUDENT THESAURUS. Especially for ages 7-12 (more or less), this easy-to-use thesaurus contains 800 main entries, with a group of two to five synonyms for each entry. An example sentence for each synonym shows how the word is distinct from others in the group, and illustrations are used to further demonstrate subtle differences among related words. Each main entry is the most common word in its synonym group, with the more precise or sophisticated words following. An index lists all 3,300 words discussed in the book. Full-color illustrations; 320 pages. $14.95. Code HBJ. BROOK FARM BOOKS.

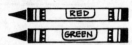

LITTLE ABC FUN SET -- Just right for kids who are beginning to learn the alphabet. 26 pressure-sensitive stickers (no licking!) of the alphabet, 26 precut alphabet stencils, 64 pages of alphabet coloring (with pictures related to the letters), and THE LITTLE ALPHABET FOLLOW-THE-DOTS BOOK. Four-booklet set (144 pages), $4.00. Code DV. BROOK FARM BOOKS.

FIRST LEARNING SERIES -- Three books written and designed to help very young children develop basic skills and knowledge in learning to read, make letters, and begin putting the letters together to form words, with several "pre-reading" and "pre-writing" exercises in letter recognition, hand control, coordination, concentration, and awareness. Suitable for age 3 and up. [For other titles in the First Learning Series, see Mathematics.]

    READY FOR READING
    READY FOR WRITING
    LETTERS
$3.50 each.   Code EDC.   BROOK FARM BOOKS.

THE ELEMENTS OF STYLE, William Strunk, Jr., & E. B. White. This thin book, about 90 pages (including the index), is a complete guide to rules of grammar, spelling, usage, and concise but expressive writing. Probably best for high school age and older, but parents can boil down its contents for their younger students. Whether writing articles, stories, essays, novels, or just letters to friends, you'll be glad to have this guide to the essentials of clear, sensible writing. $4.95. Code MAC. BROOK FARM BOOKS.

THE CHILDREN'S WORDFINDER-- This unusual dictionary in pictures contains nearly 3,000 words illustrated in full color, and helps children improve their spelling and widen their spoken and written vocabularies. $8.95. Code EDC. BROOK FARM BOOKS.

WORD DETECTIVE -- Young children increase their vocabulary and knowledge of basic grammar as well as learning the parts of speech from these humorous picture strips, in which a group of detectives -- Inspector Noun, Sergeant Verb, and Detectives Adverb, Adjective, and Pronoun -- are in pursuit of a bunch of incompetent crooks. Ages 5-12. $8.95. Code EDC. BROOK FARM BOOKS.

BOOKSTUFF -- An individualized, personal approach to beginning reading, by Patricia Reinold & Nancy Cross Aldrich. Too bad these books didn't come along until our own kids were too old for them. "My First Bookstuff" introduces kids to simple sentences composed of words, pictures, and blanks -- the blanks to be filled in with the child's own name, or the names of siblings, friends, parents, toys, pets, thus making the books really personal. The child is instructed by pictures to copy words, pictures, or answer (orally) a question. "My Second Bookstuff" continues, with slightly more difficult words & concepts. $5.95 each, plus $1 postage. Send a #10 SASE for more information and a list of other, similar publications. BOOKSTUFF, 4B SW Monroe, Box 200, Lake Oswego, OR 97034.

ENGLISH SKILLS -- In a format similar to the MATH SKILLS SERIES (See Mathematics), the activities and fortunes of a prehistoric family help children gain basic practice and skills in such an entertaining and amusing way that they won't regard the learning as a chore. Ages 7-11.

    PUNCTUATION PUZZLES
    SPELLING PUZZLES
Each book, $4.95.   Code EDC.   BROOK FARM BOOKS.

ENGLISH TRIVIA, game compiled by the Gamma chapter of the Michigan Delta Kappa Gamma Society International; 1,152 questions & answers in six categories: grammar and punctuation, spelling, research skills, literature, vocabulary, and quotations and idioms. Not-so-trivial trivia, I'd say. Level I asks, "What kind of reference book do you use to find the pronunciation of a word?" "Spell the plural of baby," and "Who wrote the Peter Rabbit books?" Level II is deeper: "Spell the words represented by the letters ESP," and "What part of a debate deals with refutation?" There are two sets of rules, competitive and noncompetitive; a score pad, and 6 achievement certificates. $14.95 plus $2.40 postage. COUNTRY CONCEPTS, c/o Pike Printing & Publishing, P.O. Box 57, Camden, MI 49232.

Really, Jean, I seen a lot of good in public schools. They learned me everything I know. Your kids won't never learn nothing at home. That's just between you and I, of course.

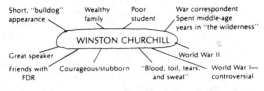

clustering Many teachers of writing now recommend a technique called "clustering." It's used during the first stage of writing, after you've chosen your topic but before you begin to write. You take the topic and write it on a sheet of paper. Then, you "cluster" around it the important facts or qualities that can be connected to it. You use this as a starting point for your paper.

| Short, "bulldog" appearance | Wealthy family | Poor student | War correspondent — Spent middle-age years in "the wilderness" |

WINSTON CHURCHILL

Great speaker — Friends with FDR — Courageous/stubborn — "Blood, toil, tears, and sweat" — World War II — World War I—controversial

PHONICS -- Our own kids all learned to read by reading, without having to learn how to read first. They picked up phonics along the way, as well as learning that many English words just aren't constructed phonetically. My personal experience has been with our own four kids and with several adult literacy classes, in English and in Spanish, which makes me just an amateur authority, not a professional. I began teaching adult illiterates with an emphasis on phonetics, as I had been taught in a special workshop at the University of Denver, and my students progressed very slowly. I switched to sight-reading of whole words -- using stories and informative articles, not lists of rhyming words -- and my students' interest and abilities leaped. Only then did I introduce the use of phonics with which to dissect troublesome words. Without exception, my adult students went from total or "functional" illiteracy to at least sixth-grade reading level in less than six months. I'm completely convinced that phonics should not be introduced until the student, of any age, has an interest in reading and has learned to sight-read at least a few words of personal interest, and even then should be used very sparingly.

> **Children don't just find their hobbies and interests. They learn of them; they are shown them; they are encouraged in various directions.**
> **--Anna Freud**

From The Daily Gleaner, Fredericton, N.B.:
    CANADIAN TIRE STORE
            NOTICE
In our advertising flyer, page 5,
  item 6, Mossberg 500 Pump Shotgun,
ILLUSTRATION NOT EXACTLY AS SHOWN.
We are sorry for any inconvenience
    this may have caused.

THE LINCOLN WRITING DICTIONARY FOR CHILDREN -- After the early childhood picture dictionaries, most kids' dictionaries aren't worth buying. Too many words are missing, too many definitions are incomplete, & the rules of grammar are ambiguous, confusing, or non-existent. This is one of the very few good kids' dictionaries, and is a useful bridge from early picture books to adult dictionaries. Besides being a clear & concise dictionary with over 35,000 entries, THE LINCOLN WRITING DICTIONARY really does have many features which will help any user, child or adult, become a better writer. 4000 examples of usages are taken from more than 500 authors, and there are 600 short essays explaining writing techniques more fully. The 700 color illustrations include drawings and photographs. Hardcover. $17.95 plus $2.50 shipping. BROOK FARM BOOKS.

THE READING REFORM FOUNDATION, 949 Market St., Tacoma, WA 98402. Several different publications, most aimed at promoting the use of phonetic teaching, with the view that the "whole word" approach is responsible for most reading problems. (I disagree.) Write for information.

PHONICS, public school textbooks. Catalog. STECK-VAUGHN CO., P.O. Box 27010, Austin, TX 78755. Specify grade level.

EASY READING KIT, a program geared to kindergarten or first grade, using a phonics approach. SASE to Mrs. Leora Stanfield, 8712 N. Ensenada Drive, Stockton, CA 95210.

PHONICS--"THE LITERACY PRIMER" and "SPELLING BOARD KIT," phonics-based technique for beginning readers. Teacher's supplement. "Homestead Series" readers. THE LITERACY PRESS, INC., 280 Pine St., Madison, GA 30650.

WORD WORKS: Why the Alphabet Is A Kid's Best Friend, by Cathryn Berger Kaye. A Brown Paper School Book. Words -- why we have them, why we need them, how we use them. Words are tools. You can build castles in the air with some highfalutin' words or craft a tiny poem for your friend's valentine. You can invent new words or find lost ones and make a record of current events to bury inside a time capsule. Words are like friends. When you're alone, you can play games with them or use them to write a letter. When you're with friends, you can use them to write and stage a play, or start your own newspaper. This very entertaining book has hundreds of suggestions and examples for doing all of these things, and much more, interwoven with fascinating facts about the growth and evolution of languages, of words, and of meanings. $9.95. Code BT. BROOK FARM BOOKS.

ON WRITING WELL: An Informal Guide to Writing Non-fiction; 4th edition, revised and enlarged, by William Zinsser. "With every rewrite," says Zinsser, "I try to make what I have written tighter, stronger, and more precise, eliminating every element that is not doing useful work, until at last I have a clean copy for the printer. Then I go over it once more, reading it aloud, and am always amazed at how much clutter can still be profitably cut." The Library Journal said this book "should be required reading for high school and college students or anyone else who plans to add to the world's store of written works." $9.95. Code HR. BROOK FARM BOOKS.

WRITING STRANDS-- A series of daily writing assignments and suggestions, Levels 1 through 8, suitable for either homeschool or classroom work. Grammar, punctuation, spelling, person, tense, etc., are all covered thoroughly. Lessons include guided practice in nearly all kinds of writing, and, if followed conscientiously, will undoubtedly result in definite writing competence. The lessons which involve observation, reporting, and discussion of things and events around the student will probably be the most useful for the development of general ideas and thinking skills as well as writing. Other lessons are "make-work" projects which will help develop knowledge and skills related to writing, but have less relevance to daily life or interests. The formal organization of these courses may make them difficult to use by home-schoolers who prefer a more relaxed approach, but I think they can be very valuable. Writing is an important skill, and doesn't come easily to most; these courses may help, even if they're not used exactly as presented. For more information, send a #10 SASE to NATIONAL WRITING INSTITUTE, 7946 Wright Road, Niles, MI 49120.

YOUNG WRITERS' CLUB, Box 216, Newburyport, MA 01950. WORDWORKS NEWSLETTER, ages 8-14; articles about writing, cartooning, rewriting, more. YOUNG WRITER'S KIT, items to encourage writing. Catalog of "intelligent gifts for children."

WRITING & GRAMMAR WORKBOOKS -- See Index, SCHOOL ZONE.

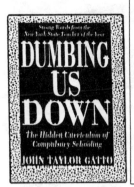

DUMBING US DOWN: The Invisible Curriculum of Compulsory Schooling, John Taylor Gatto. Several essays based on some of John's speeches about schools and education. A public school teacher for 26 years and three times named "Teacher of the Year," John's descriptions and criticisms of the public school system are wonderfully penetrating and scathing. In these essays, John doesn't speak of home-schooling, but he does advocate radical school reforms and a return to family- and community-centered learning. (His insight into the faults of public schooling is so clear, one can't help wondering why he stayed in it so long.) $9.95 plus plus $2.50 postage. NEW SOCIETY PUBLISHERS, 4527 Springfield Ave., Philadelphia, PA 19143.

HOME EDUCATION RESOURCE PACKET FOR NEW YORK STATE, by Katherine Houk. Contains complete New York state Home Instruction regulations, the laws referred to in the regulations, how to comply, resource listings, curriculum providers, support groups, recommended reading, more. $8.00 plus $1 postage. Order from: ALLPIE, P.O. Box 59, East Chatham, NY 12060.

ALLPIE -- Alliance for Parental Involvement in Education, P.O. Box 59, East Chatham, NY 12060. Nonprofit organization to assist and encourage parental involvement in education. ALLPIE offers a newsletter, referral service, workshops, book catalog, conferences, more. Send a #10 SASE for information.

CHEEZ! UNCLE SAM, Ed Nagel. "...The story of a long, brave and resourceful struggle against an indifferent and often corrupt government which all of us who care about children may have to wage one day, in one form or another." (John Holt) "...The author ignores all the rules that stipulate serious education books must be boring, over-written, and void of useful content." (The New Mexican) "...Moves fast, strikes deep, hits hard." (Jonathan Kozol) 220 pages. $8.95 postpaid from SFCS PUBLICATIONS, P.O. Box 2241, Santa Fe, NM 87501. (See also NALSAS; Santa Fe Community School; etc.)

HOW TO BEGIN HOMESCHOOLING: A Parent's Guide, by Judy Garvey. A small but very useful booklet with some of the most sensible advice and observations I've seen. Excellent thoughts about beginner's doubts, the "flushing out" of kids who have been in public school, developing a non-restrictive curriculum, much more. Highly recommended. $3.50 postpaid from: THE GENTLE WIND SCHOOL, P. O. Box 184, Surry, ME 04684.

THE KIDS CAN HELP BOOK, by Suzanne Logan. Practical, how-to information for kids concerned with helping other kids in need, the elderly, the sick, the homeless, and the environment, along with listings of the best organizations that actively involve children in their programs. $9.95. Code PB. BROOK FARM BOOKS.

LUNO -- Learning Unlimited Network of Oregon. Literate, informative, confusing, sensible, outrageous newsletter with articles, news items, word puzzles, puns, book reviews, dialogues, monologues, etc. Send $1 for a sample to: GENE LEHMAN, 31960 SE Chin St., Boring, OR 97009.

A NEED TO BE FREE: The Fight for Home Education, by Frank Turano, 8000 E. Girard Ave., Ste. 215, Denver, CO80231. The Turanos' experiences in educating their own children, including legal aspects and other information. #10 SASE for information.

LEARNING DISABILITIES -- Special section in Home Education Magazine, July-August 1992 (Vol. 9, No. 4), with essays by Peggy Nishikawa and Terri Endslen, Pat George, Pat Montgomery, and Susannah Sheffer and Patrick Farenga. "The Myth," "Symptoms," etc. $3.50 postpaid. HOME EDUCATION PRESS, P.O. Box 1083, Tonasket, WA 98855.

THE JANAN CURRICULUM, a preschool and kindergarten program, easily adapted for home use. A 200-page handbook with ideas for planning and organizing learning activities. Other items also available. Information: EDUCATIONAL BOOK DISTRIBUTORS, Box 551, San Mateo, CA 94401.

EDUCATION FOR LIFE, J. Donald Walters. The goal of education should be true maturity, not simply competent functioning in a technological society; children in public schools are overwhelmed with facts which have little to do with helping them be happy, successful people. Sensible, useful book. $9.95 plus $1.95 postage. ANANDA PUBLICATIONS, 14619 Tyler Foote Road, Nevada City, CA 95959.

EDUCATION FOR LIFE FOUNDATION, Ananda Village, 14618 Tyler Road, Nevada City, CA 95959. A school which combines the art of living with conventional education. Write for information.

INSTITUTE OF LIFETIME LEARNING, American Association of Retired Persons, 1909 K Street NW, Washington, DC 20049 offers several FREE booklets on many subjects, including art, anthropology, history, literature, philosophy, & physics, with suggestions for further study and self-tests. Write for information.

THE EMBATTLED PARENT, by Gloria Lentz. SASE. ARLINGTON HOUSE, Westport, CT 06880.

GRASSROOTS ALTERNATIVE TO SCHOOLING: Educating Your Own Child. $10 plus $1.50 postage. SASE for information. KEYS TO LEARNING, 2650 W. Trojan Place, Anaheim, CA 92804.

THE TWELVE-YEAR SENTENCE: Radical Views of Compulsory Schooling, edited by William F. Rickenbacker. SASE for information. CENTER FOR INDEPENDENT EDUCATION, 747 Front Street, San Francisco, CA 94111.

The secret of education lies in respecting the student.

Emerson

HOME EDUCATION RESOURCE GUIDE, by Don Hubbs. Updated and edited by Cheryl Gorder. Usually-brief listings of sources of legal information, correspondence courses, testing, sources of textbooks and other school supplies, educational software, publishers, Bible and Christian materials, more. The sections on "Help for the Handicapped" and "Speakers & Seminars" are more extensive than in other publications. Several pages of paid advertisements. Subtle emphasis on conservative religion and politics, although not exclusively Christian or fundamentalist. Frequently advertised as "the original resource guide," and the word "original" was deleted from my description of THE FIRST HOME-SCHOOL CATALOGUE, which was three years old when Don Hubbs listed it in his first edition. That's show biz. 128 pages, including title page, ads, index, etc. $11.95 plus $1.50 postage. BLUEBIRD PUBLISHING, 1713 East Broadway #306, Tempe, AZ 85282.

SKIPPING SCHOOL IN EARNEST, by Freda Lynn Davies. "Just Cause for Leaving a Mired System." A very thoughtful, disturbing look at current educational methods and philosophies, with strong arguments in favor of home-schooling. The emphasis is Canadian, but most of the material can be applied as well to U.S. schooling. $14.95 plus $1.25 postage (U.S. orders, use International Postal Money Order). Order from AFORE-THE-WIND, South Gillies, Ontario, Canada P0T 2V0.

MOTHER'S CHOICE, bimonthly newsletter for mothers who have chosen to stay at home with their children. Useful, interesting articles. $6/year. MOTHER'S CHOICE, 107 S. Main St., Hendersonville, NC 28739.

THE HURRIED CHILD: Growing Up Too Fast Too Soon, by David Elkind. This very disturbing book won't surprise most homeschoolers. Elkind tells how schools, media, and parents create stress-related symptoms in children today by hurrying them into adulthood -- or, worse, the semblance of it. He also gives advice on slowing the process down. Half a dozen pages about "school in the home" miss the mark entirely: Elkind thinks the main reason for teaching at home is to push children to greater heights to impress the neighbors, or to help young housewives rationalize their "guilty reluctance" to take their "proper place" in the job market. Otherwise, the book is worth reading and heeding. $8.95. Code AW. BROOK FARM BOOKS.

SCHOOL FREE: Home Based Education in Canada, by Wendy Priesnitz (founder of the Canadian Alliance of Home Schoolers). Overview & sampling of experiences of homeschoolers across Canada; basic legal information. 150 pages. $14.95 plus $1 postage in Canadian funds. (U.S. orders should be paid by International Postal Money Order, which will save about 20%, but add another dollar for the extra postage.) Order from: THE CANADIAN ALLIANCE OF HOME SCHOOLERS, 195 Markville Road, Unionville, Ont., Canada L3R 4V8.

THE BIG BOOK OF HOME LEARNING, by Mary Pride, is really four big books: 8½x11", more than 250 pages each.
Volume 1, "Getting Started," presents an overview of
various educational philosophies and a general curriculum guide. Volume 2 reviews several products for
"Preschool and Elementary." Volume 3 emphasizes courses and products for "Teen and Adult," including mail-
oder programs. Volume 4, "After-schooling & Extras,"
includes an attractive miscellany of products, including art, computers, music, etc., for all ages.

Mary has written a few other books and is a columnist for a fundamentalist home-school magazine (The
Teaching Home), but was relatively unknown to most
"secular" homeschoolers until publication of THE BIG
BOOK in 1986 (the year I published the second edition
of THE FIRST HOME-SCHOOL CATALOGUE). Blithely advertised as "the first resource guide of its kind," THE
BIG BOOK was at first reviewed very cautiously, and by
reviewers who really read it. One newsletter said it
was very good, "but you may wish Mary would get off
her soapbox." Some even ignored it, but gradually more
and more reviewers praised it very enthusiastically.

Then, like a cell dividing and re-dividing, THE
BIG BOOK was revised and expanded into two books, each
nearly as big as the first, then revised again into
four books. I received a free review copy of the first
edition, but had to buy review copies of the next two,
and there I draw the line. I'm basing this review on
the first three books, assuming that Mary's basic message hasn't changed substantially; you're welcome to
spend $60 to see if my review is accurate.

About half of the listings are very similar or identical to mine, although Mary's reviews and comments,
as you'll see, are from a very different perspective.
At least a fourth of her listings are of conventional
textbooks or materials, most of which I've ignored or
mentioned only briefly because they don't meet enough
(if any) of my criteria -- "fun, challenging, constructive, informative, and relevant to steady mental, physical, and moral growth." Many materials Mary
recommends most strongly -- for all areas of study,
including history, science, and literature -- are
judged according to a strict, literal interpretation
of the Bible. She seems to be convinced that the public schools deliberately teach and encourage drug
abuse, incest, suicide, and even cannibalism.

Mary recommends THE CHRISTIAN STUDENT DICTIONARY,
written to "reflect a Christian perspective," and a
facsimile edition of Webster's 1828 AMERICAN DICTION-
ARY OF THE ENGLISH LANGUAGE "as spoken when people believed in God and grammar."

Most of the homeschooling books Mary recommends are
by fundamentalists, who advocate strict discipline,
corporal punishment, and petty rewards such as money
and food treats for schoolwork or household chores
well done. The majority of recommended correspondence
schools and suppliers of various courses are also fundamentalist.

Mary says a study of Nature should begin with Genesis 1:1, before moving on to dinosaurs, which were
part of the six-day creation and became extinct shortly after the Flood. Next, several publications about
Creation-Science, present-day animals, biology, and
astronomy.

Complaining about African wildlife preserves for
apes, antelope, and elephants, Mary says ecology "has
become a cover for repressionist social activism."
Disregarding air and water pollution, extermination of
whole species, stripmining, interruption of the food
chain, and destruction of the rain forests which produce oxygen for the entire earth, Mary says it's an
error to think "Man is the destroyer of the planet" or
"all was fine in nature until Man came along." This,
she says, "is the famous 'It's Okay If An Elephant
Does It' doctrine. Elephants... stomp about ripping up
trees, mangling the bark, and generally wiping out
whatever range they are in... Man was told to make the
earth a garden, and insofar as man obeys God, he does
so."

"Be glad," she adds, "that African eco-freaks aren't
visiting America to help us with our problems... If we
want to see both humans and animals thriving, let the
humans own the antelopes and gorillas... Those whose
ownership interests incline them towards nonproductive
animals can set up zoos and preserves (...with their
own money)... As long as it's illegal to own hawks,
hawks will be endangered."

"Visit the wide open spaces of Iowa," Mary suggests,
for proof that overpopulation is a myth, adding that a
careful study of the RAND McNALLY FAMILY WORLD ATLAS
will show that what seems to be a problem could be
solved quite easily by dividing the world evenly and
giving 32 acres to each family of four.

Social Studies begins with several pages of Bible
study. Economics, Geography, Government, History, and
Society & Culture have more Bible-related materials.
"Worldview" ("what used to be called 'Comparative Religions,'" Mary says) includes a fundamentalist's history of Western "worldviews," a fundamentalist's analysis of Christianity being "captured by secular worldviews," a fundamentalist's exposé of New Age thought,
and a brief mention of cannibal headhunters, Baal-wor-
shippers, and "the grotesque idols in Hindu temples."

I wrote to one of the most enthusiastic reviewers
about my concern that thousands of people would gain
their first -- perhaps only -- impression of home-
schooling from this book, and received this reply:

"To be absolutely honest, I've never read any of her
books very thoroughly. I've never read the Big Book in
detail... and I apparently missed a good deal. On the
surface, her book seemed to be a wonderful resource,
[but] once I thought about it, I did recall quite a
bit of right-wing Christian bias. But we try to allow
even the [fundamentalists] their [opinions] -- to a
point -- and still felt her book was a tremendous resource."

In THE ESSENTIAL WHOLE EARTH CATALOG, Kevin Kelly
wrote, "I recommend this enormous treasure house of
tools [THE BIG BOOK, first edition] for home learners
and home teachers... It deserves kudos for honorable
work. This big book supersedes the four others we were
going to recommend." (Readers of earlier editions of
THE WHOLE EARTH CATALOG may recall another reviewer's
comment about a "Whole Earth" flag -- "the only flag I
know of that doesn't exclude someone." Who says one
species can't change into another?)

THE BIG BOOK OF HOME LEARNING, four volumes, $15
each or $60 for a boxed set. Available in Christian
bookstores or from the publisher, CROSSWAY BOOKS,
9825 West Roosevelt Road, Westchester, IL 60153.

THE CHRISTIAN HOME SCHOOL, Gregg Harris. Comprehensive fundamentalist guide. $13.95, or write for more information. CHRISTIAN LIFE WORKSHOPS, 182 S.E. Kane Road, Gresham, OR 97080.

A SURVIVOR'S GUIDE TO HOME SCHOOLING, by Luanne Shackelford & Susan White. "Children are born into the world with a sinful nature... It is hard to see a tiny baby as a sinner, but we know that it is true because the Bible says it is true... Adult sinners give birth to baby sinners." Some reviewers (not only conservative Christians) say this book is very funny, and refer to the authors as the Erma Bombecks of homeschooling. Ho ho ho. And how do we humorists deal with the little sinners we've spawned? With a "Swat Chart," to catch them in their fundamentals: Name-calling earns you 2 swats. Disrespect, 5 swats. Bad language, 10 swats. $7.95 plus $1.50 postage. CROSSWAY BOOKS, 9825 West Roosevelt Road, Westchester, IL 60153.

TEACHING YOUR CHILDREN AT HOME, by Virginia Birt Baker. Conservative Christian; setting up a curriculum, organization, schedules, discipline, socialization, books. $7 + $1.75 postage. VIRGINIA BIRT BAKER, P.O. Box 1237, Quitman, TX 75783.

OUR REEDS GROW FREE, Karl Reed (no relation to me, as far as I know). Warm, interesting, and informative story of Karl and Virginia Reed's homeschool, with suggestions, advice, and good examples. Conservative Christian, but not overly preachy. Illustrated with photos and drawings. Send a #10 SASE for information: KARL REED, P.O.Box 100, Mammoth Spring, AR 72554.

NO SCHOOL FOR MARY'S KIDS, Barrie Davey. A sweeping, ambitious novel of a family's growth and self-discovery through living and learning together. The author, now in his eighties, weaves both ordinary and dramatic incidents with dedication and understanding, portraying the satisfactions and disappointments of many people. Once a public-school teacher, Barrie says that he had planned to write a study about public versus home schooling, but decided he could add little to the already-voluminous material available, and turned to fiction instead. $7.95 plus $2 postage. (US funds for orders to the U.S.) Order from DUBORNE PRESS, Suite 408, 49 Thorncliffe Park Drive, Toronto, Ontario M4H 1J6.

AMERICAN HOME ACADEMY: The Journal of a Private Home School. SASE. Dick and Joyce Kinmont, Rt. 2, Box 106C, Brigham City, UT 84302.

THE HOW AND WHY OF HOME SCHOOLING, Ray E. Ballmann. Advice, suggestions, and arguments from a conservative Biblical perspective. Information from: CROSSWAY BOOKS, 9825 West Roosevelt Road, Westchester, IL 60153.

THE SUCCESSFUL CHRISTIAN SCHOOL, A. A. Baker. A BEKA BOOKS, 5409 Rawson Lane, Pensacola, FL 32503.

SCHOOLPROOF, by Mary Pride (author of THE BIG BOOK OF HOME LEARNING, etc. See previous page). "How to help your family beat the system and learn to love learning -- the easy, natural way." Fundamentalist Christian approach and tips to prevent educational burnout, motivate respectfully, dejunk your curriculum, more. $7.95 plus 10% postage. HOME LIFE, P.O. Box 1250, Fenton, MO 63026.

THE WAY HOME: Beyond Feminism, Back to Reality. Mary Pride's story of her journey from radical feminism to fundamentalist Christianity. Home-based living, biblical woman's role, children as a blessing, child training, family business, more. $8.95 plus 10% postage. HOME LIFE, P.O. Box 1250, Fenton, MO 63026.

STARTING A HOME SCHOOL, by J. Richard Fugate. Fundamentalist answers to "most commonly asked questions" -- Christian education, socialization, peer dependency, testing, legal problems, support groups, more. $1.50 ppd. ALPHA OMEGA PUBLICATIONS, P.O. Box 3153, Tempe, AZ 85280.

PRACTICAL HOME SCHOOLING, 1731 Smizer Mill Road, Fenton, MO 63026. Conservative Christian magazine edited and published by Mary Pride.

HOMESCHOOLING TODAY, Practical Help for Christian Families, P.O. Box 1425, Melrose, FL 32666.

SCHOOL AT HOME: Teach Your Own Child, Ingeborg U. V. Kendall. Strong arguments and reasons for teaching at home, mostly from a fundamentalist position. Methods and sources suggested, with emphasis on use of correspondence schools. Several pages of legal case histories, mostly in California, and a brief overview of other states. Small rewards (candy, pennies) are advocated for school work well-done, and the author cites the Bible to support her belief in corporal punishment. $6.95 plus $1 postage. ICER PRESS, P.O. Box 877, Claremont, CA 91711.

EDUCATION AT HOME: A Parent's Guide, Nancy Poling and Ann Blaisdel. Reasons, goals, starting, costs, college, more. Write for information, or send $9.95 to ALTERNATIVE EDUCATION SOURCES, 10506 Southshore Drive, Unionville, IN 47468.

THE CASE AGAINST GOVERNMENT SCHOOLS, Frank E. Fortkamp, Ph.D. SASE to THE CENTER FOR INDEPENDENT EDUCATION, 747 Front St., San Francisco, CA 94111.

"AN ALTERNATIVE EDUCATION, K-12," booklet. SASE. DORIE ERICKSON, Canyon Christian Academy, P.O. Box 1044, Lyons, CO 80540.

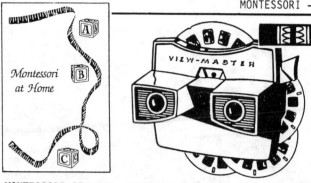

Montessori at Home

Brook Farm

MONTESSORI AT HOME, COMPLETE GUIDE TO TEACHING YOUR PRESCHOOLER AT HOME USING THE MONTESSORI METHOD, Heidi Anne Spletz. $9.95 ppd. For more information send a #10 SASE to: AMERICAN MONTESSORI CONSULTING, P.O. Box 5062, Rossmoor, CA 90721.

MONTESSORI WORLD EDUCATIONAL INSTITUTE, P.O. Box 3808, San Luis Obispo, CA 93403. Home study courses, many other programs and materials.

THE MONTESSORI OBSERVER, 912 Thayer Ave., Silver Springs, MD 20910.

VIEWMASTER -- One of the cheapest, most enjoyable teaching aids. As you probably know, each Viewmaster set contains 3 discs, each with 7 full-color stereo scenes, giving a very realistic three-dimensional view. Easily mastered, perhaps with a little help, by a 2-year-old. Most subjects are of interest to all ages, including adult. Hundreds of subjects, including classical literature, Bible stories, history, nature, science, world travel, cartoons, TV shows, many more. Most packets cost about $3.00. The individual, handheld viewer is about $4.00. With the battery-powered projector (about $20), pictures can be projected on to a screen or white cardboard for group enjoyment, although the projected picture does not have the 3-D effect. Write for catalog. WORLD-WIDE SLIDES, 7427 Washburn Ave. S., Minneapolis, MN 55423.

PERSONALIZED PENCILS -- Our kids enjoy using pencils imprinted with their own names and with "Brook Farm School." The price per pencil isn't much more than you would pay for plain, unimprinted pencils. (We usually buy them for Christmas stocking stuffers, and they last all year.) We have bought personalized pencils from both of the following companies; the prices here are recent, but you should write for a catalog with current prices before ordering.

AMSTERDAM COMPANY, Wallins Corners Road, Amsterdam, NY 12010. Set of 3 pencils, same name, 45¢ + 5¢ postage. Wooden ruler, metric & standard, name imprinted, 43¢ + 5¢. 36 pencils, all same imprint, $4.95 plus $1.40. 72 pencils, all same imprint, $11.95 + $1.70. Minimum order $5.00. Add $1 handling per order, plus the stated postage. Print personalizing instructions very clearly.

WALTER DRAKE & SONS, Drake Building, Colorado Springs, CO 80940. 12 pencils with name imprint in gold, $2.49 + $1.50 postage. Order #S854. Print name clearly.

REVIEWS OF CHILDREN'S BOOKS, TV, music, story tapes and records, toys, games, movies, video, software. Sample, $1.50. $10/year. PARENTS' CHOICE, Box 185, Waban, MA 02168.

"I LOVE MY FAMILY" -- Poster, discussion guide, lesson plans, activities promoting the importance of strong family ties, the contributions children can make to their-- Hey, how did this get back out of the waste basket?

There is nothing so stupid as an educated man, if you get him off the thing that he was educated in.

Will Rogers

You have school at home? But you look so normal!

How to Take the SAT & PSAT, by Marcia Lawrence. I'm against these things. It's bad enough to study a course with the main purpose being to pass a test about it, but this is worse: not even studying a course, but simply how to take a test. However, if you plan to go to a school which requires these tests, you may as well be prepared. Tests such as the SAT and the PSAT are very competitive; you'll be competing with thousands of others who have taken similar crash courses in how to pass tests instead of learning something useful. If you need such a course, this is one of the best. It's a complete home-study crash course in the <u>techniques</u> of test-taking, to help the student "get inside the heads of the test-makers" and thus have a better chance of determining the correct answers. "Every answer is built right into the test," says the author, who shows the student how to spot clues, how to eliminate wrong choices, and how to zero in on the right answer. In other words, how to answer correctly even if you know nothing about the subject. Any more questions about the education system? The course consists of a 372-page book and two audio cassettes to guide you through the book. $26.95 plus $2.50 shipping. BROOK FARM BOOKS.

NOT ONLY TEST PREPARATION -- We've used a number of "test preparation" guides over the years, not with any intention of preparing anyone for a test, but as comprehensive curriculum guides and basic reference works. The guides for the SAT, the SSAT, and the GED, especially, include full review and instruction in the basic subjects which are generally considered part of a good high school education. We usually ignore the tests, unless the kids want to do them to discover "weak" points, but we gain much useful information from the instructional sections.

HOW TO PREPARE FOR THE COLLEGE-LEVEL EXAMINATION PROGRAM (CLEP) GENERAL EXAM. The most comprehensive practice & review book for the CLEP, with thousands of typical questions, 20 model exams with explained answers. 640 pages. $8.95. Order "Prepare for CLEP." Code BE. BROOK FARM BOOKS.

14 DAYS TO HIGHER SAT SCORES. Includes the book BASIC TIPS ON THE SAT and two 90-minute cassettes to help develop test-taking skills. The tapes review math and verbal skills; the book contains two prep tests and a model SAT with answers. $16.95. Code BE. BROOK FARM BOOKS.

HOW TO PREPARE FOR HIGH SCHOOL ENTRANCE EXAMINATIONS (SSAT). Preparation for entrance exams required by private, parochial, and special high schools. Includes 6 diagnostic tests, 2 model SSATs, and a model Cooperative Admissions Exam. Answers explained. 544 pages. $8.95. Order "Prepare for SSAT." Code BE. BROOK FARM BOOKS.

HOW TO PREPARE FOR THE SCHOLASTIC APTITUDE TEST (SAT). Complete preparation for a major college entrance test, with 7 full-length exams modeled after the SAT. All answers explained. Extensive math and verbal reviews, and a review of the Test of Standard Written English. 608 pages. $9.95. Order "Prepare for SAT." Code BE. BROOK FARM BOOKS.

HOW TO PREPARE FOR THE HIGH SCHOOL EQUIVALENCY EXAMINATION (GED). Provides instruction and review in writing skills, social studies, sciences, reading skills, and math, in 30 lessons. Contains a diagnostic test & 3 model GED exams with explained answers, and vocabulary drill and requirements in each state. 912 pages. $8.95. Order "Prepare for GED." Code BE. BROOK FARM BOOKS.

2+2=4 / CAT ☺ TEACHER

FRANK SCHAFFER'S PRIMARY CLUB, P.O. Box 11343, Des Moines, IA 50340. Every other month, a set of 112 reproducible worksheets & idea pages covering reading readiness, phonics, science, art & holidays, social studies, a mini-book, math, and more. For grades K and 1. Each set, $11.95 plus postage. Cancel anytime; return any unwanted material; no minimum purchase required. Write for information and introductory offer (free binder, posters, etc.).

FRANK SCHAFFER'S TEACHING CLUB, P.O. Box 10175, Des Moines, IA 50340. Every other month, a set of 112 reproducible worksheets and idea pages covering science, plants and animals, language arts, social studies, study skills, reading and writing, math, seasons & holidays, & more, with posters, pictures, and stickers. For grades 2, 3, & 4. Each set is $11.95 plus postage. Cancel anytime; return any unwanted material; no minimum purchase required. Write for current information and introductory offer (free 3-ring binder, poster, etc.).

2+2=4 / CAT ☺ TEACHER

INSTRUCTOR BOOK CLUB, 3000 Cindel Drive, Delran, NJ 08075-9919. Hundreds of books for students & teachers, all levels, all subjects. Introductory offer of books totalling over $40 on 3-week trial membership. Return, cancel, & owe nothing, or accept and pay about $2, and agree to buy at least 3 selections within 24 months. Club prices average 30% discount from publishers' prices.

TEACHER BOOK CLUB, Riverside, NJ 08075. Similar to Instructor Book Club (above), but with many different selections. Generous introductory offer, trial membership, etc. Write for free information.

DESIGN-A-STUDY, by Kathryn Stout. Five very interesting guide books, with an approach similar in many ways to ours -- building studies around a unit theme. My favorite is GUIDES TO HISTORY ($7.00), which discusses the development of skills in composition, spelling, vocabulary, map reading, science, math, health, art, and music -- all through the study of history -- not with textbooks, but with independent reading and research revolving around a chosen theme. THE MAYA ($3.00) is a good model of the principles and methods outlined in GUIDES TO HISTORY. CRITICAL CONDITIONING ($7.00) helps students evaluate what they read, recognize propaganda techniques, and develop reference and study skills. NATURAL SPELLER ($20.00) is a comprehensive program for grades 1 through 8 which groups words by both sight and sound patterns, so students learn both sight reading and phonics at the same time, without being handicapped by the exclusive use of either one; it includes rules for spelling and punctuation, homophones, Greek and Latin roots, activities for dictionary use, writing, grammar, and vocabulary building. COMPREHENSIVE COMPOSITION has instructions and activities for composing paragraphs, essays, letters, outlines, reports, short stories, footnoted research papers, and bibliographies; for grades 1 through 12, and "pre-writing" skills for preschoolers. Kathryn also has a 90-minute cassette tape, "Make It Easy On Yourself" ($4.00), on which she shares ideas and resources that will save you time and money, without sacrificing quality, illustrating her assertion that "homeschooling doesn't have to drain you physically or financially." Prices as above; add 10% (minimum $1.00) for shipping. Order from: DESIGN-A-STUDY, 408 Victoria Avenue, Wilmington, DE 19804.

The direction in which education starts a man will determine his future life.
    Plato

Habit is a cable; we weave a thread of it every day, and at last we cannot break it.
    Horace Mann

The important thing is not to stop questioning.
    Albert Einstein

The desire for knowledge, the capacity for acting by oneself, the gift of observation -- all qualities children bring with them to school -- have, as a rule, at the close of the school period, disappeared.

    Ellen Key

There exists one book, which, to my taste, furnishes the happiest treatise of natural education. What then is this marvelous book? Is it Aristotle? Is it Pliny, is it Buffon? No -- it is ROBINSON CRUSOE.

    Jean Jacques Rousseau

"SAFE KIDS ARE NO ACCIDENT" -- Children's magazine about traffic safety, includes games, activities, and tips on street safety; bicycle safety & helmets, crossing streets, walking at night, telephoning in case of an emergency. FREE from: NATIONAL SAFE KIDS CAMPAIGN, 111 Michigan Ave.NW, Washington, DC 20011.

"I TAKE GOOD CARE OF ME!" Coloring book for children ages 5-10; teaches fire, water, street, and electrical safety; basic first aid; sexual assault prevention; abduction prevention; basic rescue techniques. $2.95. Teacher's guide, $3.00. Postage, $1. Order from THE CHAS. FRANKLIN PRESS, 7821 175th St. SW, Edmonds, WA 98020.

FIRE -- "Plan to Get Out Alive," a 45-minute videotape that shows the dangers of home fire, and how to escape safely. $9.95. CUSTOMER RELATIONS, McDonald's Corp., 1 McDonald Plaza, Oak Brook, IL 60521.

TOUGH TO BE FREE, educational comic book for kids 7-14 about the dangers of sniffing vapors from spray paint, glue, cleaning solvents, gasoline, other materials. One copy, FREE; more, 25¢ each. SOLVENT ABUSE FOUNDATION FOR EDUCATION (SAFE), 1500 Rhode Island Ave. NW, Washington, DC 20005.

YOUTH FOR YOUTH: Staying Free, 20-page booklet developed by a Girl Scout group in Ohio; contains activities, questions, & puzzles focusing on feelings, family, & friends to help children 6-10 learn about themselves and the dangers of drugs and alcohol. $1.00. STAYING FREE, 836 Pine St., Perrysburg, OH 43551.

HUGS ARE BETTER THAN DRUGS: A Drug Education Guide for Teens. 66-page book produced by PAR (Parental Awareness and Responsibility), describes many drugs and explains their dangers. $4.95 plus $1 postage. OPERATION PAR INC., 6613 49th St. N, Pinellas Park, FL 33565.

THROUGH TASHA'S EYES. Small book in which 9-year-old Tasha Hollingsworth tells of her uncle's death from a drug overdose. Written and illustrated as part of a Children's Writers Workshop. FREE. TROY PUBLIC LIBRARY, 100 2nd St., Troy, NY 12180.

Learning AIDS -- Comprehensive guide to more than 1,700 videos, books, pamphlets, brochures, and other educational material about AIDS; materials are reviewed critically for their value as educational tools & age appropriateness; sections for educators, parents, and administrators for grades K-12 and college. 270-page book, $24.95. Make checks payable to AmFAR. Order from: THE AMERICAN FOUNDATION FOR AIDS RESEARCH, 1515 Broadway, New York, NY 10109.

DIVORCE HAPPENS TO THE NICEST KIDS, KIDS' DIVORCE WORKBOOK, and THE DIVORCE GROUP COUNSELING PROGRAM. Divorces do happen, even to homeschoolers, and these publications really might help the kids cope with the changes and traumas. They're used in many schools, churches, and counseling programs, and have been recommended by Psychology Today Book News, Children and Teens Today, & many other periodicals. Write for full descriptions and prices: ALEGRA HOUSE PUBLISHERS, P.O. Box 1443, Warren, OH 44482.

LOVE, MEDICINE, & MIRACLES, by Bernie S. Siegel, M.D. TWO CASSETTES. Many doctors today rely increasingly on one or two of three ways of dealing with serious illness: drugs, radiation, and surgery. For many patients, none of these treatments works. Bernie Siegel tells about scores of "terminally ill" patients who gained partial or complete recovery after discovering the unity of their minds and bodies, and the understanding that allowed them to heal themselves. He discusses the ways in which anyone can achieve the same understanding and healing. This is not a "new age," faith-healing message, but a sober examination of realities which the medical establishment would rather not recognize. I read the book, enjoying it and learning from it, but hearing Dr. Siegel read on these tapes is much better. Two 90-minute cassettes. $15.95. Code HR. BROOK FARM BOOKS.

PEACE, LOVE, AND HEALING, by Bernie S. Siegel, M.D. TWO CASSETTES. Further steps in the exploration of mind-body unity which the author discussed in LOVE, MEDICINE, & MIRACLES, continuing with many examples of "self-healing," and how anyone may live better, longer, healthier without conventional medicine. Two 90-minute cassettes. $15.95. Code HR. BROOK FARM BOOKS.

"DISCIPLINE"-- A booklet with many useful, constructive ideas. FREE from MISTER ROGERS [of TV's Mister Roger's Neighborhood], c/o Daytime, Box 4019, Grand Central Station, New York, NY 10017.

BIKE SAFETY WEEK -- Bicycle fact sheet & maintenance manual for bikes, "driver's test," poster, & pamphlets. FREE. NATIONAL SAFETY COUNCIL, Community Safety Programs, 444 N Michigan Ave., Chicago, IL 60611.

ASK ME AGAIN ABOUT SOCIALIZATION -- "Schoolyard Bullying and Victimization," a 28-page booklet to help educators, parents, and students understand and respond to schoolyard bullying. $3.00. NATIONAL SCHOOL SAFETY CENTER, 16830 Ventura Blvd., Suite 200, Encino, CA 91436.

PARENTS' GUIDE TO RAISING A GIFTED CHILD: RECOGNIZ- ING AND DEVELOPING YOUR CHILD'S POTENTIAL, James Al- vino and the editors of <u>Gifted Children Monthly</u>. De- fines "giftedness" (more than just a high IQ), gives practical ideas for raising and educating gifted children from preschool to adolescence; ways to help develop critical thinking, research skills; tips on counseling; lists of recommended books and games; assesses computers. Possibly of value to parents of any child in a stimulating learning environment, whether "gifted" or not. $19.95 plus $2.50 postage. GIFTED CHILDREN MONTHLY, P.O. Box 134, Sewell, NJ 08080.

"GIFTED"-- Most kids in a free, creative environment will often seem "gifted," just as kids in restricted environments often seem stunted. In this resource guide, I've tried to weed out most of the stunting material, and have sought and emphasized the gifting material, but very little has been set aside for this "Special Education" section.

HOME EDUCATION RESOURCE GUIDE (see Index) has sever- al listings for Special Education resources.

LATEBLOOMERS, c/o Thomas Armstrong, P.O. Box 2647, Berkeley, CA 94702. One of the best sources of ideas and materials about so-called "learning-disabled," many of whom aren't.

JOHN HOLT makes several good points about the "learning-disabled" in HOW CHILDREN LEARN. See the Index.

SPECIAL NEEDS PROJECT, 1482 East Valley Rd. #A-121, Santa Barbara, CA 93108 (805-565-1914). Very exten- sive, comprehensive catalog of books and other ma- trials about children with disabilities. Free.

CHALLENGE, Box 299, Carthage, IL 62321. Magazine for gifted children.

GIFTED CHILDREN MONTHLY, P.O. Box 115, Sewell, NJ 08080. Sample, $3.

PRESENTS FOR THE PROMISING, P.O. Box 134, Sewell, NJ 08080. Catalog of about 200 items, selected by the editors of <u>GIFTED CHILDREN MONTHLY.</u>

PRISM, P.O. Box 030464, Ft. Lauderdale, FL 33303. Magazine-forum for and by gifted children; pen pals, etc.

TWO FREE NEWSLETTERS: "NEWS DIGEST" has research findings, legal issues, & services for handicapped. "TRANSITION SUMMARY" discusses roles of parents and teachers in preparing handicapped youth for future work. NATIONAL INFORMATION CENTER FOR HANDICAPPED CHILDREN AND YOUTH (NICHCY), P.O. Box 1492, Washing- ton, DC 20013.

FREE SPIRIT: News and Views on Growing Up Gifted. Bimonthly 8-page newsletter for gifted students, grades 11 & 12. Articles, interviews, information. $7.95/5 issues. Sample, $1. FREE SPIRIT PUBLISHING, 123 N. Third St., Ste. 716, Minneapolis, MN 55401.

CHALLENGE: Reaching and Teaching the Gifted Child, for parents and teachers of K-8. 64 pages. Ideas, resource, articles. $20/5 issues. Cancel after first copy if not satisfied. Order from GOOD APPLE, Box 299, Carthage, IL 62321.

CREATING FAMILIES, PO Box 218, Newcastle, ME 04553. "Creating," in this title, is an adjective, not a verb; i.e., "creative." Very interesting newsletter, published 10 times a year, with book reviews, short articles, news, and ideas about play, art, dance, & music within a creative family. $15/year.

"EASY GRAMMAR" and "DAILY GRAMS" -- A reader has recommended this as an "excellent grammar program for all ages." I haven't seen it. Write for infor- mation to: ISHA Enterprises, 5503 East Beck Lane, Scottsdale, AZ 85254.

RESOURCES FOR THE GIFTED, P.O. Box 15050, Phoenix, AZ 85060. Learning aids to develop thinking and communication skills, positive self-concepts, etc.

NATIONAL FOUNDATION FOR GIFTED & CREATIVE CHILDREN, 395 Diamond Hill Road, Warwick, RI 02886.

"TEACHING EXCEPTIONAL CHILDREN," magazine about gifted and disabled students. $15/4 issues. COUNCIL FOR EXCEPTIONAL CHILDREN, 1920 Association Drive, Reston, VA 22091.

BOOKS FOR THE GIFTED CHILD, Barbara H. Baskin and Karen H. Harris. A concise, annotated bibliography of about 150 intellectually challenging books, rang- ing from picture books to contemporary novels, for the gifted pre-reader and reader up to 12. Order #1428-1. $10.95 plus $1 postage. R. R. BOWKER CO., Box 1807, Ann Arbor, MI 48106.

Parents are slow in realizing how unimportant the learning side of school is. Children, like adults, learn what they want to learn. All prize- giving and marks and exams sidetrack proper per- sonality development... All that any child needs is the three R's; the rest should be tools and clay and sports and theater and paint and freedom.

A. S. Neill

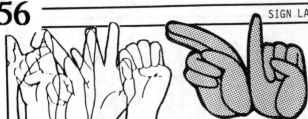

SIGN LANGUAGE -- Our three girls began studying Ameslan -- American Sign Language for the deaf -- several years ago, and frequently told each other "secrets" with it, very pleased that Jean and I didn't know what they were saying. Cathy entered a 4-H speaking contest with the subject of Nim, a chimpanzee who signs to humans and other chimpanzees, and illustrated her speech with appropriate signs. (She won 2 first prizes and 1 second.) Since then, Cathy has been in several situations in which knowledge of sign language has been an asset: counselor in a girls' summer camp, where one of the campers was deaf; working in a public library where several customers are deaf; and occasionally meeting deaf people in her travels who have been very glad to meet someone who could speak with them. More recently, Jean has studied Ameslan, and has had occasion to use it several times. Whether or not sign language will ever be of actual practical use to you or your children, it's fun to learn and to use -- and it helps one to think of what it must be like to be dependent on sign language for communication.

AMESLAN: An Introduction to American Sign Language, by Lou Fant. This is one of the first sign language books ever published for both the hearing and hearing-impaired. It has now gone through twenty printings, and is used around the world. Clear illustrations; explanations when necessary; easy to practice and learn. $13.90, including postage. JOYCE MEDIA, Box 57, Acton, CA 93510.

DEAF AND HEARING-IMPAIRED -- Many books for all ages about deafness, sign language, parents with deaf children, deaf parents, signed English dictionary, sign/word flash cards, coloring books captioned with signs, first books using signs, children's fiction about children with deafness, more. GALLAUDET UNIVERSITY PRESS, 800 Florida Avenue NE, Washington, DC 20002.

AMERICAN SIGN LANGUAGE ON VIDEO -- Learn the basics of Ameslan with dramatized video lessons which include greetings, introductions, time expressions, transportation, eating out, shopping, sports, and recreation. Each lesson has English subtitles. One 60-minute videocassette. Specify VHS or Beta. $34.95 plus $3 postage. BROOK FARM BOOKS.

SIGNING MADE EASY, by Rod R. Butterworth and Mickey Flodin. Complete program for learning sign language. Includes drills and exercises for increased comprehension and signing skill. $10.95. Code BT. BROOK FARM BOOKS.

THE PERIGEE VISUAL DICTIONARY OF SIGNING, by Rod R. Butterworth and Mickey Flodin. The most comprehensive alphabetized guide to American Sign Language available today. $9.95. Code BT. BROOK FARM BOOKS.

SIGN LANGUAGE MATERIALS -- Books, video and audio cassettes, teaching supplies, more. Free catalog. JOYCE MEDIA INC., P.O. Box 57, Acton, CA 93510.

SIGN LANGUAGE MATERIALS-- GARLIC PRESS, 100 Hillview Lane #2, Eugene, OR 97401. Catalog.

We use a lot of posters in our home. They're decorative, interesting, and informative. The kids have several on the walls of their rooms, and we have several in our school-play room. Many of them are also excellent for framing or mounting on a mat for the living room or kitchen. Besides the following listings, see History, Science, and the Index.

POSTERS AND PRINTS -- Scores of colorful prints and photos. Animals, nature, sports, travel, science, historic. Inexpensive world and country maps. 8½x11" portraits of world leaders, U.S. presidents, personalities in U.S. history and literature; 3 sets of 64, $4.99 per set. Award and certificate blanks. Much more. Large colorful brochure, free. GIANT PHOTOS, INC., P.O. Box 406, Rockford, IL 61105.

POSTERS FROM LEARNING MAGAZINE -- Dozens of inexpensive, attractive, educational posters are available from the publishers of Learning. Write for a list and prices: LEARNING MAGAZINE, P.O. Box 2031, Clinton, IA 52735.

POSTERS AND CARDS from great children's books. Free catalog. PEACEABLE KINGDOM PRESS, 2980 College Ave., Suite 2, Berkeley, CA 94705.

ANIMAL POSTERS suitable for framing. Two different of white tiger and of penguins; one each of Bengal tiger, eagle, Chincoteague pony, and orangutan; all in their natural habitats; 18x24". $4 each plus $1 postage, or full set of 8 posters for $34 ppd. SANDVED & COLEMAN, 12415 Hanger Rd., Fairfax, VA 22033.

REFERENCE WALL CHARTS -- Shapes, counting, parts of speech, arithmetic, printing & writing, metric system, more. Included in catalog from: CREATIVE TEACHING PRESS, INC., POBox 6017, Cypress, CA 90630.

BULLETIN BOARD SETS ($4.95 for several large cutouts), letters, stickers, border trim, more. Catalog. TREND ENTERPRISES, INC., P.O. Box 64073, St. Paul, MN 55164.

"CORKERS," bulletin board ideas, free booklet. EASTMAN KODAK CO., 343 State St., Rochester, NY 14650.

HOME SCHOOL BADGES -- The public schools have pins and badges, so why shouldn't home-schoolers have them, too? The badges are 2¼" in diameter, light-weight metal front and back, with plastic overlay on the front, safety-pin on the back. Your choice: THE WORLD IS MY SCHOOL (my personal favorite, and the one we sell the most of), I'M A HOME SCHOOLER, or THIS SCHOOL IS RUN ON KID POWER. $1.50 each or 4 for $5.50, postpaid. BROOK FARM BOOKS.

SCHOOL OR GROUP BADGES -- Send us a rough sketch or description of your design and the wording you want; we'll make it into a badge for you, like this one we made for the Manitoba Association for Schooling at Home. One badge, custom-made to your specifications, $3.00. Each additional badge, same design and lettering, ordered at the same time, $1.00. For 10 or more badges of the same design, write for quantity discounts, telling us how many badges you may want. BROOK FARM BOOKS.

MORE BADGES -- Send us your own artwork, magazine clipping, comic picture, even a photograph, and we'll make it into a badge for you. You or your child can design and color your own picture, decorate it, letter it. Good for unusual gifts, stocking stuffers, identification, group meetings, celebrations, I Love Grandma, or just plain fun. IMPORTANT: your original artwork or clipping should be at least <u>two and three-quarters inches</u> in diameter; the part showing on the finished badge will be two and one-quarter inches. Badges from your finished artwork, $1.50 each. Five to ten badges at one time, $1.25 each. Ten to twenty, $1.00 each. For larger quantities, write for a discounted price, telling us how many badges you may want.

DIPLOMAS, CERTIFICATES, AWARDS. Large selection. Most are in packages of 25, which you don't need, but you'll pay a lot more than $3 or $4 if you have a print shop make up just one or two. Free catalog. HAYES SCHOOL PUBLISHING CO., INC., 321 Pennwood Ave., Wilkinsburg, PA 15221.

DIPLOMAS, certificates, invitations, announcements, etc., in fine calligraphy. #10 SASE with inquiry to: MARCY MARKLIN, P.O. Box 8465, St. Louis, MO 63132.

Rubber Stamps

One of our first purchases when we began teaching at home was a rubber stamp with our school name on it. It was almost a form of magic: purchase orders with our name stamped on them often obtained sizeable discounts from school supply companies, and the Department of Education treated us more seriously. When we loan books, we stamp our school name inside the front cover, as a reminder to the borrower. A rubber stamp isn't an essential, but it's certainly a big help. The stamp we've been selling for several years is the highest quality ("hard" rubber that doesn't wear out) for the lowest price that we've found. This is approximately the actual size of the stamp:

YOUR NAME IN ALL CAPS
Your Street Address Can Go Here
Your City, State and Zip Here
Fourth Line (Optional)

The stamp doesn't have to be your name and address, of course; it can be a bank endorsement stamp, or a message stamp, with any wording you want. One year, we gave name-and-address stamps to our kids in their Christmas stockings. PRINT your name and address (or other wording) very clearly and carefully, including punctuation. Three lines, $11.00. Four lines, $13.00. POSTPAID. Order from BROOK FARM BOOKS. Please allow about three weeks for delivery.

RUBBER STAMPS of pictures from children's literature and other characters. Catalog. KIDSTAMPS, P.O. Box 18699, Cleveland Heights, OH 44118.

OFFICE SUPPLIES -- One of our favorite sources for small quantities of stationery, address labels, purchase order forms, envelopes, and other office supplies is THE BUSINESS BOOK, 1 EAST 8TH AVE., OSHKOSH, WI 54906. Not very economical for a small or medium-sized business, but very good for the smaller quantities needed by a home school.

For the larger quantities of many items -- sealing tape, heavy-duty staplers, shipping envelopes, etc. -- we've gotten the best service and lowest prices from VIKING OFFICE PRODUCTS, P.O. BOX 730, WINDSOR, CT 06095, which has discount prices on almost all items in their large catalog, & offers free shipping on all orders over $25.00.

COMMUNICATION RESOURCES, P.O.Box 2625, North Canton, OH 44720. Transfer lettering, clip art, adhesive wax sticks, lay-out forms, etc., for making newsletters, brochures, programs, etc. Primarily for churches, but could probably be of use to homeschoolers, too. Free catalog.

LETTERHEADS -- A small print shop may charge you $30 to $50 for printing letterhead stationery, and the same amount for printed envelopes. The cost per sheet or per envelope isn't high, but if you don't expect to need that many (200 to 500), you can save money by paying more per sheet for a smaller quantity. One of the best sources we've found is the mail-order catalog of MILES KIMBALL, 41 West 8th Avenue, Oshkosh, WI 54906. For about $10 plus postage, you can get a set of 100 printed stationery sheets, 50 matching plain sheets, and 100 printed envelopes. Write for the current catalog.

Handwriting

PALMER METHOD HANDWRITING -- Preferred by many. Information from MACMILLAN, Customer Service, 866 3rd Avenue, New York, NY 10022.

HANDWRITING with workbooks using art & current subjects. ZANER-BLOSER, P.O. Box 16764, Columbus, OH 43216.

HANDWRITING AND MUCH MORE -- School supplies, books, instructional aids, more. Free catalog. THE PETERSON SYSTEM, 2215, Commerce St., Dallax, TX 75201.

HANDWRITING BOOKS, including kindergarten readiness, teacher's editions, resource books. HBJ HANDWRITING, Harcourt Brace Jovanovich, Orlando, FL 32887.

CHRISTIAN HANDWRITING PROGRAM, practice with conservative Christian material. A REASON FOR WRITING, Concerned Communications, P.O. Box 700, Arroyo Grande, CA 93420.

HANDWRITING, "continuous stroke method" of early printing, supposedly eases the transition to cursive. Is it a good idea? I have no opinion. What eases "the transition" from scribbling to the continuous stroke method? Six grade levels, and "transition" book. STECK-VAUGHN CO., P.O. Box 2710, Austin, TX 78755.

ITALIC HANDWRITING -- An attractive blend of manuscript and cursive. I don't have the patience to learn this method of handwriting, but a number of readers have asked for it, saying they prefer it to standard handwriting. Wall charts, desk strips, work books, teacher's manuals. Most materials are inexpensive. If you have a school letterhead or order forms, you may qualify for a discounted price. Free brochure. PORTLAND STATE UNIVERSITY, Continuing Education, Box 1394, Portland, OR 97207.

OUR FAVORITE HANDWRITING WORKBOOKS are from SCHOOL ZONE. See the Index.

FLASH CARDS -- Presidents, states, capitols, etc. Reproducible activity books, bulletin board materials, learning games, paste, glue stick, blank flash cards, dots, stars, stickers, much more. Catalog. THE EDUCATION CENTER, INC., 1410 Mill St., Greensboro, NC 27429.

VIS-ED-- Flash cards for advanced study: languages, biology, algebra, trigonometry, calculus, computer, chemistry, verbal SAT, legal, medical, government, history, Bible verses, psychology, more. Over 80 different card sets, prices from $3.95 to $14.95. Write for catalog: VISUAL EDUCATION ASSOCIATION, P.O. Box 1666, Springfield, OH 45501.

TYPING THE EASY WAY. Helps you master basic skills in 30 days, then moves on to cover advanced techniques. Spiral-bound with an easel back, 144 pages. $8.95. Code BE. BROOK FARM BOOKS.

LEARN TOUCH-TYPING IN ONLY FOUR HOURS -- "Master Your Keyboard" is an introductory program that will teach you touch-typing in only four hours, whether you're a complete beginner or use a hunt-and-peck method. This is one of the easiest and most enjoyable typing courses we've seen, and certainly the fastest.

"Speed and Accuracy at Your Keyboard," the second volume of this series, provides twenty 30-minute exercises to give you advanced typing skills with a minimum of time and practice.

MASTER YOUR KEYBOARD, 3 cassettes, exercise book, $29.95 plus $3 shipping. BROOK FARM BOOKS.

SPEED AND ACCURACY AT YOUR KEYBOARD, 3 cassettes, exercise book, $29.95 plus $3 shipping. BROOK FARM BOOKS.

Both courses at the same time (6 cassettes, 2 exercise books), $55.00 plus $6 shipping. BROOK FARM BOOKS.

HOME SCHOOL, HOME-SCHOOL, or HOMESCHOOL? Usually I prefer "home-school," with a hyphen, although "public school" doesn't have one. I haven't thought up any impressive etymological arguments yet. I try to be consistent in spelling and punctuation, but if my word processor insists that there are only ten spaces left on the line, I usually drop the hyphen and the intervening space rather than carry six letters over to the next line. I admit that's not consistent, but it's economical. I often hear or read, "I home-school my children," but I've never heard, "I public-school my children." I think the form with the strongest support so far is "homeschool" -- one word, no hyphen. Would it surprise you to learn that some people take this problem very seriously? There are a lot of homeschoolers around, but I don't recall much reference to publicschoolers. A few people have written long arguments for one form or another, and I won't be very startled if some national organization soon puts it to a vote. The home(-)school movement may be divided by a hyphen more than by any other major issue. If you stare at the words long enough, none of them makes much sense. The same trick works with most of the arguments.

ENCYCLOPEDIAS --

Most encyclopedias will have zillions of facts and bits of information you're looking for or will find fascinating when you bump into them by accident, zillions more you don't really care much about, and at least half a zillion <u>missing</u> bits of information which will prompt you to say, "Why on earth did they leave that out?" For most research subjects, and for most general information, a set that's 20 years old will do as well as a more recent one, and can probably be found in a used book store or garage sale for ten to fifty dollars. We have a set of the Britannica, which we bought new about 20 years ago, and usually we can still find most of the information we're looking for. When we can't, we look in various other reference books we have, or go to to the public library.

If you're going to invest in a new set, your best choice is **THE ENCYCLOPEDIA BRITANNICA** or **THE WORLD BOOK ENCYCLOPEDIA.** Each has several advantages and disadvantages not shared by the other, so you'll want to compare them carefully before committing yourself. Write to the publishers, asking for a salesman -- pardon me, "representative" -- to visit you. The representatives will probably pressure you to sign up right away, but don't do it.

THE ENCYCLOPEDIA BRITANNICA has more indepth articles, many written by world-renowned scholars. THE WORLD BOOK has an easier reading style and more illustrations, and is probably suitable for a wider age-range. Both companies offer several other sets of books, such as THE BRITANNICA JUNIOR and CHILD-CRAFT, respectively. The salesman's commission on an encyclopedia sale is fairly high -- sometimes half the price of the set (several hundred dollars) -- so, to get your signature, you may be offered additional sets of books at little or no cost, which will increase the value of your purchase, and is another good reason not to make a hasty decision. Annual "yearbooks," supposedly keeping the sets up-to-date, will be offered (for about $35 each), but we found that these usually consist of windy analyses of "global trends," and have negligible value. Both companies offer monthly installment plans, with fairly low payments. Sometimes a "gift," such as a 3-volume reference set (dictionary, thesaurus, and atlas) will be given to you just for looking at the salesman's samples.

Watch out: Entries in encyclopedias are almost as likely as those in school textbooks to be "modified" to reflect current trends in political thinking, "sexism," and omission of items which may offend special interest or minority groups. For instance, whether you're Christian or not, you want the history of Christianity to be fairly accurate and truthful. Before buying, look up a few test items, such as the Pilgrims, the fall of the Roman Empire, and so on. Be prepared to accept the presence of writing attitudes you don't approve of.

ENCYCLOPEDIA BRITANNICA, INC., 310 South Michigan Avenue, Chicago, IL 60604.

WORLD BOOK, INC., Educational Services Dept., Merchandise Mart Plaza, Chicago, IL 60654.

Sometimes you'll find excellent, low-priced reference sets in catalogs from:

PUBLISHERS CENTRAL BUREAU, One Champion Avenue, Newark, NJ 07101; and

BARNES & NOBLE, 126 Fifth Avenue, New York, NY 10011. Look in their catalog for a recent edition of the one-volume THE CONCISE COLUMBIA ENCYCLOPEDIA, which has more than 15,000 capsule entries; about $15.00. I've often found information I needed in this book when I couldn't find it elsewhere.

MACMILLAN DICTIONARY FOR CHILDREN. As kids grow away from their "first" picture dictionaries, I think this is the best step up (followed closely by a concise "adult" or college dictionary). Thousands of entries, definitions, and illustrative examples. 1,100 full-color photos, illustrations, and maps. 300 highlighted word histories and language notes. More illustrative sentences per main entry than any other children's dictionary. Illustrated time line of world history. Updated atlas, maps of the world, continents, U.S., and Canada. Tables of weights and measures. $14.95. Code MAC. BROOK FARM BOOKS.

MACMILLAN VERY FIRST DICTIONARY: A Magic World of Words. Much better than most other "early" dictionaries. Definitions are clearly and simply phrased. Colorful illustrations with captions keyed to example sentences make even the most difficult or abstract words easy to understand. 1,500 words, more than 500 full-color illustrations. Very good for preschool to age 7 or 8. Large hardcover, 280 pages. $11.95. Code MAC. BROOK FARM BOOKS.

THE NEW ROGET'S THESAURUS IN DICTIONARY FORM, by Norman Lewis. If you've used Roget's Thesaurus to find just the right synonym or antonym, or to avoid excessive repetition in your writing, you know how helpful and valuable it can be. If you've used the older, original version, with words grouped by concept -- abstract, concrete, etc., etc. -- then you know how fantastically frustrating it can be; after you've searched for the word you want for twenty minutes, you decide the one you had was good enough. This new edition does away with frustration. It's fully indexed, which means you can zoom in on the words you want right away. If you use a thesaurus, or should, this is the one. $13.95. Code PG. BROOK FARM BOOKS.

DICTIONARIES AT DISCOUNT PRICES -- I had planned to offer Webster's dictionaries for sale through Brook Farm Books, but I can't beat the prices offered by WILCOX & FOLLETT, 1000 WEST WASHINGTON BLVD., CHICAGO, IL 60607, and I doubt that anyone can. W&F specializes in used, reconditioned textbooks, but these dictionaries are brand new, never used, yet at bargain prices: Elementary, $9; Intermediate, $8.20; School, $9.50; Collegiate (indexed), $11; Collegiate (w/o index), $10.50. All hardcover. Why pay more? Write for a catalog with most recent offers and prices.

MAGAZINES -- Most magazines are cheaper than an equal weight in textbooks, and many are much better. These are a few of the thousands of magazines on the market today. We read some of them all the time, some of them occasionally, and some of them never. When subscribing, we try to order magazines at different times of the year, so the renewal notices don't all show up at the same time. Fortunately, a few subscriptions have been gifts from relatives. Magazine publishers will be glad to send advertising brochures; some will send samples or enter a trial subscription.

MANY SPECIALIZED MAGAZINES (science, history, etc.) are listed in those sections.

THE THREE NATIONAL HOME-SCHOOL MAGAZINES -- Growing Without Schooling, Home Education Magazine, and The Teaching Home, are listed with books about education earlier in this chapter.

HOLISTIC EDUCATION REVIEW, 39 Pearl Street, Brandon, VT 05733. Quarterly, $26/year. Articles, reviews, letters, and reader contributions on many aspects of alternative education -- homeschooling, Montessori, Waldorf, and others. I've seen the word "holistic" on dozens of bookstore shelves and in scores of publishers' catalogs, and still don't have a firm grip on it, but it probably doesn't matter. HOLISTIC EDUCATION REVIEW is far better than the cultish New Age publications with which its name might seem to make it belong. It gives me a better grip on the aims and methods of true education, and even a little more understanding of the word. The magazine's masthead says it "aims to stimulate discussion and application of all person-centered educational ideas and methods... Explore how education can encourage the fullest possible development of human potentials and planetary consciousness. We believe that human fulfillment, global cooperation, and ecological responsibility should be the primary goals of education.." Those discussions & explorations mean that HOLISTIC EDUCATION REVIEW covers a multitude of viewpoints, and will often intrigue, inspire, inform, surprise, entertain, and occasionally irritate you. You'll frequently gain new insights, encouragement, & food for careful reflection.

SKOLE, quarterly journal of the National Coalition of Alternative Community Schools. Articles about alternatives, innovations, learning, teaching, etc. SKOLE, NCACS., RD 1, Box 378, Glenmoore, PA 19343.

CRICKET, Box 2670, Boulder, CO 80322. One of the best and most literate children's magazines, for ages 6-12, more or less. Well-known authors and artists; puzzles, crafts, readers' contributions. Sample, $1.95. $18.50/year.

CHILDHOOD: The Waldorf Perspective. Quarterly devoted to the physical, emotional, intellectual, and spiritual development of children. Painting, cooking, crafts, nature study, singing, etc., focusing on seasons and holidays. A calm, reverent, joyful approach to growing with children. Sample issue, $5.00. One year (4 issues), $20.00. CHILDHOOD, Route 2, Box 2675, Westford, VT 05494.

TURTLE, ages 2-5. **HUMPTY DUMPTY**, 4-7. **CHILDREN'S PLAYMATE**, 5-8. **JACK AND JILL**, 6-8. **CHILD LIFE**, 7-9. **CHILDREN'S DIGEST**, 8-10. **MEDICAL DETECTIVE MAGAZINE**, 10-12. All excellent magazines. Each, $9.97/year. Write for information. CHILDREN'S HEALTH PUBLICATIONS, Children's Better Health Institute, P.O. Box 567, Indianapolis, IN 46206.

LEARNING, P.O. Box 2589, Boulder, CO 80321. Our favorite "professional teacher's" magazine, intended for grade school use, but we have also been able to adapt much of it for high school use. Articles about teaching methods; frequently critical of testing, grading, etc. Strong recognition of the inadequacies of most textbooks; emphasis on hands-on approach to learning. Monthly calendar with daily bits of information about history, literature, ecology, conservation, famous people. Reproducible activity pages. News of free or almost free educational items. Letters from readers, useful advertisements. Back issues and full index available. Write for current price and introductory offer.

TEACHING K-8, P.O. Box 912, Farmingdale, NY 11737. 8 monthly issues, each with nearly 100 activities and ideas grouped by skill and grade level; pull-out file cards with bulletin board ideas; reports and news about education (seldom relevant to homeschooling), humorous anecdotes, cartoons, calendar with daily activities, reproducible activity pages, book reviews. Easily adapted to home school.

CREATIVE CLASSROOM, Box 863, Farmingdale, NY 11737. Articles, editorials, tips, suggestions, reproducible activity pages, holiday ideas & themes, useful ads, book and product reviews. Citizenship, time, writing, maps, vitamin information, shadow plays, science, minibooks, logic, games, math, plant projects, legendary heroes, more. Primary and early elementary. Written for classroom teachers, but most material is easily adapted to home school.

FAMILY LEARNING, 19 Davis Dr., Belmont, CA 94002. For parents of public school children but has ideas and articles useful for homeschoolers, too. Not as good as LEARNING MAGAZINE from the same publisher.

PRIORITY PARENTING, P.O. Box 1793, Warsaw, IN 46580. Small but very useful and interesting monthly newsletter-magazine with articles, poems, pictures, penpal listings, problems & solutions, occasional cartoons, classified ads, letters, reviews, recommendations. Good writing; good ideas. Sample, $2.00. Subscription, $14.00.

WELCOME HOME, P.O. Box 2208, Merrifield, VA 22116. Monthly magazine devoted to mothers who choose to stay at home with their families. SASE for information.

HIGHLIGHTS FOR CHILDREN, P.O. Box 269, Columbus, OH 43272. Ages 2-12. $18.95/year.

EDUCATIONAL OASIS, for teachers of grades 5-9. 64 pages of ideas and articles; 2-sided poster. 5 issues, $20. FREE sample. GOOD APPLE, Box 299, Carthage, IL 62321.

HOME SCHOOLING AT ITS BEST, 175 Gladys Ave.#7, Mountain View, CA 94043. Monthly curriculum journal with ideas, activities, & suggestions. Science, art, geography, more. 9 issues/$20.00. Write for brochure.

FESTIVALS, 160 E. Virginia St., San Jose, CA 95112. Bimonthly, $18/year. Improve your family time; celebrations for the family; folk art, legends, stories that explore the inner and outer rhythms of life; new age music; home-schooling; poems. "A network of people who are searching for alternative ways to celebrate life in the midst of the commercial diversions of popular culture."

PRACTICAL PARENTING, 18326 Minnetonka Blvd., Wayzata, MN 55391. Bimonthly newsletter offering information, ideas, resources, advice, and more on child raising. News, book reviews, letters, crafts, recipes.

WORKSHEET MAGAZINE -- Four issues each year, with nothing but interesting and informative worksheets. The pages can be used directly from the magazine, or reproduced on a photocopier for multiple copies. There are four editions, each appropriate for a certain age level. Order by number and name: R8650 Kindergarten, R8750 Grade 1, R8950 Grades 2 & 3, R8450 Grades 4 & 5. One-year subscription, $11.95. THE EDUCATION CENTER, P.O. Box 9753, Greensboro, NC 27429.

HOME SWEET SCHOOL: The Home Educators' Digest. Reprints of articles from home school publications around the country; also original articles, book reviews, etc. SASE for current price and information. HOME SWEET SCHOOL, 1919 West Melrose, Chicago, IL 60657.

THE ACORN, quarterly publication with games, stories, puppets, patterns; activities to color, cut out, assemble. Math, science, reading, writing; K-8. Recommended resources. Information from BUR OAK PRESS, 8717 Mockingbird Road, Platteville, WI 53818.

MERLYN'S PEN, magazine of artwork, plays, stories, and poems by and for students in grades 7-10. Activity guide for teachers. Subscriptions from $5.95 to $14.95. Write for information: MERLYN'S PEN, 98 Main St., East Greenwich, RI 02818.

"NOT ON THE NEWSSTANDS"-- 72-page compilation of articles from more than 100 "alternative" newsletters, magazines, and newspapers, with review information about the publications sampled. Home education, home careers, health and nutrition, child-rearing, etc. $10.00. PRIORITY PARENTING PUBLICATIONS, 104 Auditorium Lake Blvd., Winona Lake, IN 46590.

CREATIVE LEARNING MAGAZINE, Box 957, Wrightstown, NJ 08562. How-to, ideas, and information for home schoolers; articles, reviews, ads.

UTNE READER--Articles, editorials, reviews, letters, and selections from more than 1000 independent small-circulation magazines, journals, and newsletters. Offbeat, upbeat, politically aware. Bimonthly. $24/yr. New subscriber rate $18.00. Send for current information. UTNE READER, Subscriber Services, P.O. Box 1974, Marion, OH 43306.

COUNTRY KIDS. Bimonthly for and about rural children. Games, quizzes, puzzles, poems, crafts, more. $11.95/year. Write for information. REIMAN PUBLICATIONS, Box 572, Milwaukee, WI 53201.

SESAME STREET, ages 2-6. **THE ELECTRIC COMPANY,** 6-11. **3-2-1 CONTACT,** 8-14. Tied in with the TV shows of the same names. $9.95/yr each. Write for information. CHILDREN'S TELEVISION WORKSHOP, One Lincoln Plaza, New York, NY 10023.

THE FAMILY LEARNING CONNECTION, P.O.Box 12268, Oklahoma City, OK 73157. Bimonthly newsletter for home-school families. $12/year. $22/2 years. Sample, $2.

CHART YOUR COURSE, Box 6448, Mobile, AL 36660. Magazine "by and for gifted, creative, and talented children." Editorials, interviews, photos, art, poetry, reviews, essays, articles, all done by kids. $15/yr (8 issues). Sample, $2.50.

U.S. KIDS, ages 5-10. Fiction, non-fiction, puzzles, and "Kids Helping Kids" advice column. 44 pages per issue. Subscriptions, $18.95/year. Information from U.S. KIDS, P.O. Box 16687, Columbus, OH 43216.

HELP, quarterly, edited by Bill & Mary Pride (author of THE BIG BOOK OF HOME LEARNING, etc.; see Index). Home-schooling, parenting, home birth, family ministries. Conservative Christian. "Nothing New Age or occult." Ideas and personal stories from the editors and readers. $15/4 issues. Back issues available, $4 each. HOME LIFE, P.O. Box 1250, Fenton, MO 63026.

THE BLUMENFELD EDUCATION LETTER, P.O. Box 45161, Boise, ID 83711. Monthly newsletter edited by Samuel Blumenfeld, author of NEA: TROJAN HORSE IN AMERICAN EDUCATION. Right-wing critic of public schools, who believes that "death education, values clarification, and lifeboat games" prove that the "humanistic Progressives" have been deliberately leading America toward becoming a socialist society since early in this century. Many of his examples and arguments seem valid enough, but I strongly question his conclusions. Sample issue, $3.00. 12 issues, $47.80.

HOME SCHOOL DIGEST. Fundamentalist Christian homeschool magazine; quarterly. $10/year. WISDOM PUBLICATIONS, P.O. Box 3154, LaVale, MD 21502.

HAPPY TIMES, Box 902, Farmingdale, NY 11737. Development of positive values through activities, stories, games, posters. Ages 3-10. $18.95/year (10 issues). Sample $2.00.

HEART OF AMERICA REPORT, conservative Christian monthly magazine. Write for information: FAMILIES FOR HOME EDUCATION, 28103 E. Atherton Sibley Road, Sibley, MO 64088.

CHILDREN'S MAGAZINE GUIDE -- Directory of children's magazines now in print, with publishers, prices, and suggested readers' ages. $5.25 postpaid. Make check payable to IRA. Order from INTERNATIONAL READING ASSOCIATION, P.O. Box 8139, Newark, DE 19714.

AMERICAN HERITAGE, P.O. Box 977, Farmingdale, NY 11737

AMERICAN HISTORY ILLUSTRATED, P.O. Box 1776, Mt. Morris, IL 61054

AMERICA TODAY, P.O. Box 249, Louisville, NE 68037

AT HOME TOGETHER, P.O. Box 524, Makawao, HI 96768

AWAKE!, Watchtower, Wallkill, NY 12589

BIBLE PATHWAYS, P.O. Box 1515, Murfreesboro, TN 33821

BREAD FOR CHILDREN, P.O. Box 1017, Arcadia, FL 33821

CHICKADEE, very good nature magazine for preschool children. Sample, $1.50 from YOUNG NATURALIST FOUNDATION, 59 Front St. E., Toronto, Ontario M5W 1B3

DISCOVER, P.O. Box 420087, Palm Coast, FL 32142. This is our second-favorite science magazine (after SCIENCE DIGEST, listed under Science).

FUR AND FEATHERS, from THE KINDNESS CLUB, 13 Brant Avenue, Port Credit, Ontario L5G 3N9

GOOD OLD DAYS, P.O. Box 428, Seabrook, NH 03874

HERITAGE TRAILS, P.O. Box 445, Ridgewood, NJ 07451

HOMESTEADERS' NEWS, RD 2, Box 151, Addison, NY 14801. Issue #19 was devoted to home-schooling.

HORSE AND RIDER, 41919 Moreno Rd. Temecula, CA 92390

HORSE ILLUSTRATED, P.O. Box 6050, Mission Viejo, CA 92690

THE HUMANIST, P.O. Box 146, Amherst, NY 14226

THE MOTHER EARTH NEWS, P.O. Box 70, Hendersonville, NC 28791

NATURE FRIEND MAGAZINE, P.O. Box 73, Goshen, IN 46526

NATURE STUDY, RR 1, Homer, NY 13077

NURTURING, The Journal of Motherhood, 20 Paperbirch Drive, Don Mills, Ontario M3C 2E7

OWL, good children's nature magazine, from THE YOUNG NATURALIST FOUNDATION, 59 Front St. E., Toronto, Ontario M5W 1B3

READER'S DIGEST, Pleasantville, NY 10570 or 215 Redfern Avenue, Montreal, Quebec H3Z 9Z9. Our kids have spent more time with this magazine than with any other.

SPACE WORLD, P.O. Box 7535, Ben Franklin Station, Washington, DC 20044

SPIRITUAL MOTHERING JOURNAL, Box 128, Dover, NH 03820

WESTERN HORSEMAN, P.O. Box 7980, Colorado Springs, CO 80933

MAGAZINES AT DISCOUNT PRICES -- Companies offering up to 50% off the regular prices, sometimes more, of most popular kids' and adults' magazines.

AMERICAN FAMILY PUBLISHERS, P.O.Box 8210, Chicago, IL 60680.

MAGAZINES AT DISCOUNT, P.O. Box 601, Broomall, PA 19008.

MAGAZINE BUYERS' SERVICE, 669 S. 3rd Ave., Mt. Vernon, NY 10559.

AMERICAN EDUCATIONAL SERVICE, University House, 419 Lentz Court, Lansing, MI 48917. Use school letterhead, if possible.

PUBLISHERS CLEARING HOUSE, 382 Channel Drive, Port Washington, NY 11050.

SMC PUBLICATIONS MARKETING GROUP, 310 Madison Avenue, New York, NY 10017.

UNIVERSITY SUBSCRIPTION SERVICE, 1213 Butterfield Road, Downers Grove, IL 60515.

CATALOGS OF TEACHING AIDS & OTHER MATERIALS

Catalogs which feature items primarily for one particular subject or area of interest are listed in the appropriate sections (Art, Math, Science, etc.). This section has catalogs which are more general, with materials in many different fields. Many specific items and subjects can be found in the index; for others, be adventurous; browse and explore.

THE ARK, 4242 Crestline Ave., Fair Oaks, CA 95628. Toys, dolls, books, art & craft supplies.

ABC SCHOOL SUPPLY, INC., P.O. Box 4750, Norcross, GA 30071. Catalog of toys, books, etc.

ASHLEY'S HOME TUTOR KITS, P.O. Box 566, Byhalia, MS 38611.

AMERICAN MONTESSORI SOCIETY, 150 Fifth Avenue, New York, NY 10011. SASE for a list of books and other information about the Montessori method & materials.

THE ANTHROPOSOPHIC PRESS, RR 4 Box 94 A-1, Hudson, NY 12534. Waldorf and other education books.

BIRTH AND LIFE BOOKSTORE, P.O. Box 70625, Seattle, WA 98107. Books by mail, for children and parents.

BRAIN STORMS, 7851 East Lake Road, Erie, PA 16511. Various materials for hands-on learning; non-competitive games; more.

CARDS OF KNOWLEDGE, Box 1778, Middelsex, NJ 08846. Study cards, various topics.

CHILDCRAFT, 20 Kilmer Road, Edison, NJ 08818. Free catalog of toys, games, craft materials, musical supplies, costumes (flapper, astronaut, ladybug, penguin, etc.), magnetic marbles, more. Very good.

CHILDREN'S BOOK AND MUSIC CENTER, P.O. Box 1130, Santa Monica, CA 90406. Books, records, cassettes. Family relationships, emotions, health, safety, art, math, science, physical education, much more.

CHILDREN'S RECORDINGS, P.O. Box 1343, Eugene, OR 97440. Songs and stories on records and cassettes from many publishers.

CHINABERRY BOOK SERVICE, 3160 Ivy St., San Diego, CA 92104. $1 (refundable) for catalog of excellent children's books.

CHRISTIAN LIGHT PUBLICATIONS, P.O. Box 1126, Harrisonburg, VA 22801. Books and other materials, Bible-oriented curriculum for grades 1-12.

CONSTRUCTIVE PLAYTHINGS, 1227 E 119th St., Grandview, MO 64030.

CONSUMER INFORMATION CENTER, Box 100, Pueblo, CO 81002. About 200 titles, some of them free. Categories include careers, child care, early education, high school and beyond, federal benefits, food, nutrition, medical problems, weight control, mental health, housing, money management, small business, travel, hobbies, much more. Free catalog.

CREATIVE EDUCATIONAL MATERIALS, P.O. Box 18344, West St. Paul, MN 55118. Books, work and activity sheets, stickers, note pads, certificates, bulletin board material, more.

CREATIVE PUBLICATIONS, P.O. Box 10328, Palo Alto, CA 94303. Math toys and games.

CREATIVE TEACHING PRESS, INC., P.O. Box 6017, Cypress, CA 90630. K-8. Maps, bookmarks, awards, stickers, posters, reference charts, reproducible activities, much more.

CRESTWOOD HOUSE, INC., Box 3427, Hwy. 66 South, Mankato, MN 56002. High interest, low vocabulary books. Also many cassette tapes for "reluctant readers." #10 SASE for catalog.

DALE SEYMOUR PUBLICATIONS, Box 10888, Palo Alto, CA 94303. Large selection, K-8. Math, thinking skills, calculators, science, language arts, gifted, art and graphics.

T. S. DENISON AND COMPANY, INC., 9601 Newton Ave. S., Minneapolis, MN 55431. Preschool and elementary teaching resources, whole language, story telling, flannel boards, reading, science, math, library skills, bulletin boards, art, awards, daycare, plan books, finger plays, more.

DEVELOPMENTAL LEARNING MATERIALS, 7440 Natchez Ave., Niles, IL 60648. Catalog of books and educational aids.

DUKANE CORPORATION, Audio Visual Division, 2900 Dukane Drive, St. Charles, IL 60174. Filmstrip projectors, from simple and inexpensive to very complex and expensive.

EDUCAT PUBLICATIONS, Box 2158, Berkeley, CA 94702. Several different catalogs in many subject areas.

EDUCATIONAL ACTIVITIES, P.O. Box 392, Freeport, NY 11520. Software, videos, records, filmstrips, cassettes, workbooks.

EDUCATIONAL FUN GAMES, INC., P.O.Box 56, Winnetka, IL 60093. Mostly math games. SASE for information.

EDUCATIONAL INSIGHTS, 19560 Rancho Way, Dominguez Hills, CA 90220. Many very good, unusual materials for learning & playing with art, arithmetic, alphabet and reading, science, etc.

THE EDUCATION CENTER, 1410 Mill St., Greensboro, NC 27408. Large catalog of calendars, awards, bookmarks, clocks, bulletin boards, banners, duplicating masters, construction materials, flash cards, games, globes, videos, software, records, pencils, posters, stencils, much more.

EDUCATORS PUBLISHING SERVICE, INC., 75 Moulton St., Cambridge, MA 02238. #10 SASE for information about materials in reading, spelling, vocabulary, grammar, composition; handwriting, math, history.

EDUCATOR SUPPLIES, 105 Falcon St., London, Ontario N5W 5H2.

ESP PUBLISHERS, Box 5080, Jonesboro, AR 72403. Basic skills workbooks; some are mediocre at best; others, very interesting & useful. Choose carefully. Over 200 titles, only $1.98 each, minimum order 10 titles. Free sample and catalog.

GARDEN GATE KINDER COLLEGE, P.O. Box 15094, Salt Lake City, UT 84115. Pre-school program for children at home.

GEODE EDUCATIONAL OPTIONS, P.O.Box 106, West Chester, PA 19381. Exceptional books, tapes, games, puzzles, stuffed animals, puppets, and other resources for learning.

GOOD MORNING FARM, P.O. Box 135, Church Hill, MD 21623. Catalog of books, toys, other family items.

G. K. HALL, 70 Lincoln St., Boston, MA 02111. Good source of large-print books on many subjects, fiction and nonfiction.

HISTORICAL PRODUCTS, PO Box 604, Barre, VT 05641. Literary T-shirts & musical T-shirts. I don't think I want to wear someone else's portrait in public, but I've toyed with the idea of getting a couple of these for night shirts. Or maybe barn shirts, and see what Mrs. Montgomery thinks of them. (Mrs. Montgomery is our Jersey cow.) Famous people, real and fictional, such as Bach, Einstein, Darwin, Newton, Twain, Verdi, Marx Brothers, Cheshire Cat, Bogart, Hemingway, Michelangelo, Thoreau, many more. Or wear a quotation ("Common sense is not so common" -- Voltaire) or a musical selection from Bach, Beethoven, or Mozart. The same designs are also available on linen calendars, aprons, totebags, & sweatshirts.

HOME SCHOOL HORIZONS, predominately conservative Christian. Character building, "scientific creationism." A poster of the sixth day of creation, with various flora and fauna including Adam, an elephant, an ibex, and a dinosaur. Some interesting and useful non-Bible materials -- craft tools, paint sets, science kits. ALPHA OMEGA PUBLICATIONS, Box 3153, Tempe, AZ 85280.

HOMESCHOOL MARKETPLACE, bimonthly newsletter-catalog for Christian homeschoolers. HERITAGE SCHOOLHOUSE, 12311 NE Brazee, Portland, OR 97230.

HOME SCHOOL SUPPLY HOUSE, 3254 E Mitchell, Petoskey, MI 49770. 24-page catalog of many useful items -- books, workbooks, science tools, creative thinking, math, more.

IDEAL SCHOOL SUPPLY COMPANY CATALOG-- Large selection of learning materials for age 3 and up. Early learning, language arts, math, science, social studies, teacher resources. Mostly good materials, but stay from pigeon-holers such as Structural Analysis and Gross Motor Skills. Offered by several companies, including J. L. HAMMETT CO., P.O. Box 545, Braintree, MA 02184.

JOHNSON SMITH CO., 4514 19th Court East, Bradenton, FL 34203. Request "Novelty Catalog." Scan as quickly as you can past the idiotic junk, such as itching powder, squirting camera, safety pin through your nose, dribble glass, rubber cockroaches, and other "practical jokes," and watch for the relatively sane and useful things -- an Indian bead set, ant farm, 1000 mini-magnets for $2.95, replica of a Civil War muzzle-loading pistol, Davy Crockett cap, foreign coins, gemstone & mineral set, reproductions of early U.S. money, toy rockets, crystal radio kit, miniature steam engine that really works, more.

JUDY/INSTRUCTO EDUCATIONAL MATERIALS, 4325 Hiawatha Ave. S, Minneapolis, MN 55406. Wooden puzzles, floor puzzles, math materials, science and social studies kits, craft books, more.

KEY CURRICULUM PROJECT, P.O. Box 2304, Berkeley, CA 94702. Math materials, text/workbooks, grades 4-12.

KIMBO EDUCATIONAL, Box 477E, Long Branch, NJ 07740. Educational videos, filmstrips, records, cassettes, real-alongs.

LAKESHORE CURRICULUM MATERIALS CO., 2695 E. Dominguez St., Carson, CA 90749. Many hundred items for preschool through adult education. Arts and crafts, toys, computer supplies, science materials, more.

LEARNING AT HOME, Box 270, Honaunau, HI 96726. Home school guides, workbooks, grade level programs, test preparation guides, art, science, math, more.

LEARNING EVERY DAY, Rte. 1, Box 5, Fairfield, WA 99012. Many items for home schoolers.

LEARNING WELL, 200 So. Service Road, Roslyn Hts., NY 11577. Boardgames, kits, books, cassettes, video and filmstrips, computer software, reproducible work books in reading skills, vocabulary, grammar, spelling, writing, phonics & "word attack," early learning, thinking skills, more.

THE LEARNING WORKS, P.O. Box 6187, Santa Barbara, CA 93160. Inexpensive and very useful reproducible activity books for grades K-12 in reading, math, grammar and language, creative writing, research and study skills, handwriting, bulletin boards, holiday and art ideas, enrichment and gifted, science and computers, health, and preschool. Free catalog. (See also Art, "Clip Art Carousel," and Science, "Reproducible Science Series.")

LEARNING WORLD, 500 Westlake Ave., Seattle, WA 98109. Workbooks, posters, maps, books, games, art and craft materials, science, music, toys, more.

THE LONDON MONTESSORI CENTRE, P.O. Box 9, Marlborough, Wilts, England. Correspondence courses for Montessori teachers; nursery, primary, and advanced level modern courses in child education and development. Diploma.

METROPOLITAN MUSEUM OF ART, 225 Gracie Stn., New York, NY 10028. Ask to have your name added to the mailing list for catalogs of books, gifts, art work, calendars, etc.

MICHAEL OLAF, The Montessori Shop, 4284 Gilbert St., Oakland, CA 94611. Books, supplies, toys, tapes, models, geography, history, games, music, art, writing, language, math, etc., including Montessori material. Catalog $1.00.

MILES KIMBALL, 152 Bond St., Oshkosh, WI 54906. Large, colorful catalog of gifts, worthless gadgets, and other miscellany -- but also, here and there, educational toys, name-and-address labels, inexpensive stationery, etc.

MILLIKEN PUBLISHING COMPANY, P.O. Box 21579, St. Louis, MO 63132. Reproducible activities, awards, readiness, reading, spelling, handwriting, vocabulary, grammar, games, puzzles, creative writing, math, science, social studies, study skills, more.

MONICA FOLTZER, St. Ursula Academy, 1339 E. McMillan St., Cincinnati, OH 45206. Phonics manual, flash cards, etc.

NATIONAL BOOK COMPANY, 333 SW Park Ave., Portland, OR 97205. Recorded instructional programs in many subjects.

NATIONAL TEACHING AIDS, INC., New Hyde Park, NY 11040. Free catalog. Great materials for elementary and high school levels in science and health education. Very low prices.

NEW ENGLAND SCHOOL SUPPLY, P.O. Box 1581, Springfield, MA 01101.

NIENHUIS MONTESSORI, 320 Pioneer Ave., Mountain View, CA 94041.

OFFICIAL STICKER CATALOG, 348 N. 30th Road, Box 802, La Salle, IL 61301. Stickers of scores of items and animals; books, stationery, club membership, much more.

ORANGE CAT BOOKS, 442 Church St., Garberville, CA 95440. Mail-order books for kids and parents.

THE PETERSON SYSTEM, 2215 Commerce St., Dallas, TX 75201. Free catalog of school supplies, biographies, work books, etc.

PIED PIPER, Box 11408, Phoenix, AZ 85061. Good selection of toys, books, science kits, games, more.

PLAY FAIR TOYS, 1690 28th St., Boulder, CO 80301. Fairly large selection of toys, crafts, games, etc., some not found elsewhere; some a little more expensive than elsewhere. "Nonsexist," says the catalog, "because all children are created equal.," which is illustrated by a picture of a boy playing with a dollhouse and a girl playing with a train set. If they traded activities, it would be sexist and discriminatory. Our girls used to play with cars and trains, and Derek played with dolls. The girls put the cars and trains in blankets and nursed them or sang lullabies to them. Derek pushed dolls across the floor and made motor noises. Nice catalog; just be sure you don't buy the wrong toy for your equal boy/girl.

PLAYING FOR KNOWLEDGE, INC., 4 Poplar Run, East Windsor, NJ 08520. Enrichment materials, manipulative math, resources for gifted, preschool, etc.

PLAYTHINKS, P.O. Box 2628, Setauket, NY 11733. Educational toys.

PSYCAN, 101 Amber St., Markham, Ontario L3R 3B2. Miscellaneous educational materials.

PUBLIC ARCHIVES OF CANADA, 395 Wellington St., Ottawa, Ontario, Canada K1A ON3. Public and private records, films, photographs, maps. Ask about public use.

THE READING TUTORIUM, 9121-A Centreville Rd., Manassas, VA 22110. Assistance for parents, especially of gifted children.

RECORDED BOOKS, INC., P.O. Box 79, Carlotte Hill, MD 20622. Unabridged recordings of books on cassettes, for monthly rent or purchase, prices based on number of cassettes per title (many titles have 20 hours or more). We prefer to do our own reading when we want the unabridged version of a book; for recorded books, we prefer abridged versions (listed elsewhere; see the Index), which are usually between two and three hours, are carefully edited so the original story and style are well preserved, and are much less likely to put us to sleep.

SCHOOL ZONE PUBLISHING CO., 1819 Industrial Drive, Grand Haven, MI 49417. This company has some of the very few workbooks of which we thoroughly approve. They're clear and easy to understand, they stick to basic principles and explain them well, and they present exercises which make learning fairly easy and even fun. The books are graded, but most of the materials can be used without regard for the grade level intended by the publisher. Workbooks are available in Math, Grammar, Spelling, Reading, Phonics, Handwriting, Reading and Number Readiness, and several Preschool Activities. Prices are reasonable, and the service is prompt and efficient.

C CAT D DOG

SELECTIVE EDUCATIONAL EQUIPMENT, 3 Bridge St., Newton, MA 02195.

SENTINEL TEACHERS SUPPLY, 1200 W. Evans, Denver, CO 80223. Elementary grades, large selection.

SCHOOL SUPPLY, P.O. Box 660, Belton, TX 76513.

SHOP TALK, 5737 64th St., Lubbock, TX 79424. "Family Market Cards," a package of advertising cards sent quarterly, with products and services related to homeschooling, home business, parenting. Free.

SOCIAL STUDIES SCHOOL SERVICE, P.O. Box 802, Culver City, CA 90232. This is one of our favorite companies from which to buy books, pamphlets, posters, and many other materials. Several catalogs, including Geography, Social Studies, Psychology, Writing, Home Economics, World History, American History. Request the general catalog, which lists all the special catalogs.

ST. THOMAS PRESS, P.O. Box 35096, Houston, TX 77235. Books primarily with conservative Christian viewpoint, related to morality, theology, economics, government, etc.

RUDOLPH STEINER: Educating the mind, body, & soul; emphasizing the beautiful and creative nature of the individual. Important parts of Steiner's method are art, movement, music play, story-telling. Books by & about Steiner and his work are available from Rudolf Steiner College Publications, 9200 Fair Oaks Blvd., Fair Oaks, CA 95628.

STAMP COLLECTING: Monthly newsletter "Stamp News," FREE from BENJAMIN FRANKLIN STAMP CLUB, Box 23506, Washington, DC 20024.

SUNBURST COMMUNICATIONS, 39 Washington Avenue, Pleasantville, NY 10570. Writing, math, library skills, science, problem solving, basic forms, work books, literature, a few videos. Grades 3-9.

SUNDANCE PUBLISHERS, Newtown Road, Littleton, Ma 01460. Two catalogs (grades 1-6 and 6-12) of scores of low-priced children's books; many subject areas.

SUPERINTENDENT OF DOCUMENTS, Washington, DC 20402. More than 1000 books, pamphlets, and posters available from the U.S. government printing office; many subjects, some free. Free catalog.

THE SYCAMORE TREE, INC., 2179 Meyer Place, Costa Mesa, CA 92627. Catalog of 2500 educational items, many Bible-oriented, $3, refundable. Correspondence courses, guidance services, lesson plans, assistance in finding Bible-oriented material.

TELLTALES, P.O. Box 614, Bath, ME 04530. Books for ages 6 months to 12 years.

THE TIMBERDOODLE, E. 1610 Spencer Lake Road, Shelton, WA 98584. Books, stickers, coloring books, puzzles, building sets, workbooks, more. Very good.

TOAD'S TOOLS, P.O. Box 173, Oberlin, OH 44074. High-quality, child-size, real tools: screwdrivers, saws, vises, hammers, etc. Catalog, $1, refundable.

TOTLINE BOOKS, P.O. Box 2255, Everett, WA 98203. Holiday song books, celebrations, folktales, story songs for pre-schoolers. The Totline Newsletter, bimonthly, 24 pages, preschool activities. Free brochure.

THE TOY SOLDIER, 8 McIntosh Lane, Clifton Park, NY 12065. Very extensive collection of antique and modern paper dolls, soldiers, trains, cars, planes, famous buildings, and more, more, more. Catalog, $3. Worth it.

"TOYS TO GROW ON," 30+ page catalog of wooden toys, outdoor equipment, sand and water play, furniture, art supplies, craft kits, board games, math puzzles, building toys, teaching machines, science projects, books. Catalog 50¢. UNSCHOOLERS NETWORK, 2 Smith St., Farmingdale, NJ 07727.

TOYS TO GROW ON, Box 17, Long Beach, CA 90801. Educational toys and just plain toys.

UPSTART, Box 889, Hagerstown, MD 21741. More than 240 products to promote reading for fun-- bookmarks, bulletin boards, posters, mobiles, shirts, buttons, gifts.

WORKSHOP FOR LEARNING THINGS, 5 Bridge St., Watertown, MA 02172. Catalog.

ZEPHYR PRESS, P.O. Box 13448-A, Tucson, AZ 85732. One of the best sources of material for bright, inquiring students, from kindergarten through 12 (and older, including adult), with outstanding materials in arts and humanities, social studies, science, math, global awareness, philosophy, books for adults on teaching and parenting, early learning, more.

I am convinced that it is of prime importance to learn more every year than the year before. After all, what is education but a process by which a person begins to learn how to learn?

Peter Ustinov

Nothing in education is so astonishing as the amount of ignorance it accumulates in the form of inert facts.

Henry Brooks Adams

A teacher who is attempting to teach without inspiring the pupil with a desire to learn is hammering on cold iron.

Horace Mann

Our highest endeavor must be to develop free human beings, who are able of themselves to impart purpose and direction to their lives.

Rudolph Steiner

Soap and education are not as sudden as a massacre, but they are more deadly in the long run.

Mark Twain

Derek sure is lucky to have school at home, Mom. This morning he did barn chores with the cow and calf and goats and ducks and hens. Then he read stories about some people called Alexander the Great and King Henry and Marco Polo. Then he drew pictures of a rocket ship with a ruler and a tropractor, and watched a TV show about 'stinct animals and heard a story tape about the Pilgirns, and read his Ranger Rick magazine, and looked at the sky to see what the weather will be.

He didn't have to learn a single thing, all day long!

Having concluded before we started teaching at home that the loosely-structured approach is definitely best, we were sometimes dismayed to find that it wasn't working, and it's hard to find an instruction manual for something that isn't supposed to have instructions. Until the kids were about six or seven, they were certainly eager to learn anything and everything around them. After that, sometimes they were eager to learn, and sometimes they'd go out to lunch for two or three weeks. We watched and waited, and told each other that they'd soon get tired of old Donald Duck comics or television and would return to doing something productive. Maybe they just needed a break. Usually, they did tire of their early retirement, and began reading, thinking, drawing, making things, and asking us twenty questions a minute about anything at all, but occasionally it looked as if they'd settled down for a long winter's nap.

"Hey, look, kids," we'd say, "we're having school at home. That means you're supposed to be learning something."

"Okay, Dad. What do you want us to learn?"

"What causes gravity? What makes the Aurora Borealis light up? Why was Mona Lisa smiling? What does x represent if five times x to the fourth power equals eighteen? How do you drive a nail without mashing your thumb? How can you collect a dozen eggs in the barn and deliver twelve

eggs to the house? How high is up? Things like that."

"Dad, have you read this story about when Donald Duck and his nephews went to Yellowstone Park and--"

"Okay, then, where is Yellowstone Park?"

"You mean there really is a Yellowstone Park?"

"That's all, folks. Back to the drawing board. Notebooks, pens, pencils, eager minds and smiling faces. Nine o'clock tomorrow morning. All drinks of water, toilet trips, and forgotten books to be remembered before then."

"Really? Okay, Dad! We were wondering if you were going to help us learn any more, or if you were too busy."

"That's what I thought you were wondering. Is that about the time the Beagle Boys think Donald Duck has a buried treasure under a geyser? Let me borrow it when you're done with it."

So our unschool would become a home-school again, and we'd have fairly regular hours, and lots of discussions, and real Assignments For Tomorrow, and after a while we'd try the unschooling again. After all, how can I write a book about how well unschooling works for us if it doesn't? The kids just never realized what a responsibility they had to my readers.

School, as we all know, is a box or series of boxes in which children are required to sit for several hours a day, while government-inspected teachers attempt to transfer information out of books into the children's heads.

Home-school was around a long time before school, and often consisted of nothing more than a borrowed book and the light from a fireplace. Sometimes, just the fireplace. Some people did quite well with this arrangement, and went on to become president or to invent the phonograph. At that time, most of the unschools were not different from the nonschools. Instead of spending years in preparing to learn how to make a living, people went out to make a living. Or stayed at home to make a living.

The industrial revolution reduced the number of job opportunities, so a different kind of child labor had to be invented. School was the answer. The government told parents they were too stupid and ignorant to teach their children anything, and the parents were too stupid and ignorant to realize the government was wrong, so the children tucked baked potatoes into their pockets and trotted off to school. A few people still became presidents and a few still invented things, and everyone had a piece of paper certifying that he had spent a lot of time behind a desk, so schools were considered to be Good Things.

Gradually the parents got smarter and noticed that their children were getting dumber. Although some were still growing up to be presidents or to invent things, most of the presidents were stupider, and so were the inventions; so a few parents re-invented home-schools. The children were taken out of school to be taught at home. Unfortunately, the parents had been taught in schools and thought school methods were the only methods, so the home-schools were not much different from the schools, except that fewer students were smoking dope or getting pregnant or both. They still learned to be almost as stupid and uninventive as they had in the public schools.

Most home-schools had a structure as rigid as that of most public schools, with the entire day planned in detail -- so many minutes for spelling, so many for math, so many for standing in line, so many for getting out your books and sharpening your pencils, hold up two fingers when you have to go to the bathroom, and so on -- with regular testing, grading, and even "home-work" to be done in the evenings.

Many of the new home-schoolers were fundamentalists, who were usually very concerned with authority and obedience, which they felt couldn't be maintained without a rigid teaching structure and lots of what they called strict discipline. The fundamentalists frequently recommended an intricate system of rewards, bribes, punishments,

and psychological games -- not only for school work, but even for such daily chores as making the bed. Punishments included spanking, forfeiture of meals, and withholding of play privileges; rewards included food treats, games, special trips, and even money. The fundamentalists didn't realize that such rewards and punishments not only undermined their goal of discipline, but usually indicated that discipline had already broken down. Or maybe it was too late, because now they had to try to maintain control over children who had unwittingly been taught that everything has its price. It must be discouraging to know that sinfulness has been a dominant characteristic on both sides of your family ever since Adam and Eve ate the fruit of the tree of knowledge.

A few public schoolers and a few homeschoolers, who had read ROBINSON CRUSOE or MOWGLI OF THE WOLVES and had heard of Jean Jacques Rousseau, decided to chuck the whole works and have unschools. The unschools had no lesson plans, no assigned subjects, no guided study, and the students could go to the bathroom without raising their hands. The unstudents unlearned several of the things they had learned in the schools and home-schools, and were allowed to sit at desks if they wanted to, to read books if they wanted to, and to get jobs as construction workers or hairdressers or magazine editors if they wanted to.

Sometimes unschooling is referred to as the invited learning approach. I think the idea is that when the kids decide they want to know something, they invite someone to teach them. Otherwise, they are protected by the First Amendment from any obligation to learn anything. Adults have no moral right to intrude on children's lives without invitation.

In New York City, parents don't have any legal control over their children who have reached the age of sixteen, but they are responsible for all contracts and crimes of their children who have not reached the age of eighteen. Many parents have found that this creates some very interesting situations.

Back to unschooling. The prefix "un" was meant to communicate the unschooling parents' rejection of stiff structures and canned curricula. The term "unschool" has the drawback of saying what it is not, but not saying what it is. "Unhorsed" gives the impression of an impromptu flight from the back of a horse, but it doesn't say if the un-rider is walking, dazed, or dead; only that he is no longer on the horse. When I stand up, am I unchaired?

Most home-schoolers are somewhere between these extremes, not requiring the students to hold up two fingers or sit still with their backs straight and listen, but also realizing that not all kids will learn reading, writing, arithmetic, history, geography, home economics, and penmanship just from sitting in the woods with a screwdriver and a pile of books.

Some people credit Thomas Mann with starting public schooling in America. Others blame him for it. John Holt, very liberal, says public school is not a good idea gone wrong, but was a bad idea from the very start. Samuel Blumenfeld, very conservative and a fundamentalist, says we never needed schools at all. I went to school for twelve years, and often tried to convince my parents I didn't need it, but some of my history lessons were about people two or three hundred years ago who surely could have used a little of it, whether they actually needed it or not.

There were books about schools before Moses left Egypt, and many more have been published since then. Now, there are also many books about home-schools, and even a few about unschools. Books about schools and schooling are usually cataloged under the heading of Education, which, considering that a government agency does the cataloging, makes unexpected sense. When they began cataloging books about home-school, they could have used the heading "Home education," but apparently "home" was considered too homey, so they chose to call it "Domestic Education." Look on the back of the title page of any home-school book which has Cataloging in Publication Data, which is information supplied by the Library of Congress or the Library of Canada to tell librarians that TEACH YOUR OWN does not belong with the books on farming or plumbing.

Was the term devised as a smokescreen? Home-schools (and unschools, although authorities seldom see any difference) are not often applauded by officialdom, so perhaps the cataloging officials sought to camouflage their existence with a pedantic euphemism. If you were searching the card files in your local library for books about home-schooling, would you think (before I told you) to riffle through the **D** section? There might be two dozen books on the subject, and you could

April 8, 1991

Dear Donn,
  Just received your delightful book today. I'm really enjoying it, but please correct [p.69]. It's Horace Mann, not Thomas. Thomas was the great (greatest?) German novelist -- Horace was the "father of the American public school system" -- essentially to train the labor force of an industrial capitalist society. And the Socratic method [p.70] is essentially the teaching of absolute syllogisms -- it is only the appearance of conversation. A close and exhaustive reading of Plato (Yuk -- I was a philosophy student and teacher) demonstrates that. But your book is great!

                [M. E.]
                NYC

Apparently, M.E. is one of those who blame him, but she's absolutely right that it was Horace, not Thomas. I'm still blushing. **DR**

Dad, the Library of Congress and the Library of Canada list books about home-schooling as "domestic education." According to the dictionary, "domestic" is the opposite of "wild." That doesn't say much for public schools, does it?

easily miss them all.

Another possibility is that the term was invented by a public school official. School officials seldom speak English; they speak Educationese, as when the district superintendent wrote, "Please enlighten me with respect to your intentions relative to the education of your children for the approaching year." I divided both sides of the equation by the number of superintendents it takes to change a light bulb and reduced it to "Please tell me your plans for the year."

Educationese is one of the two foreign languages in which I have a little fluency, and sometimes I practice it when I correspond with school officials. Usually, however, Educationese is a lot like maple sap: it needs to be boiled down a great deal before it is of much use to human beings.

In my dictionaries, there are several definitions of "school" which don't refer to the formal institutions with which we usually associate the word. The problem, then, is not in the word, but in our associations with it. "A source of knowledge" is one of the definitions which I think would be acceptable to even the most dedicated unschooler. But our conditioning is strong: when someone says "school," we automatically think of report cards and corridors reeking of antiseptic. The word is lightened somewhat by the addition of "home," but some stigma remains. "Unschooling" has the disadvantage of adding a negative prefix to an already stigmatized word.

It's probably too late to coin a better term. "Home-learning" is used by some, especially those who want to make it plain that adults also can learn outside of school, but really is just as restrictive: it implies that learning takes place primarily in the home, which is little better than the conventional assumption that learning takes place only in school.

Home-schoolers and unschoolers are well aware that a great deal of learning takes place outside of both home and school -- in the streets, in the woods and fields; in fact, in any situation in which we're participants or spectators. Being alive is learning, and the extent of our learning may depend upon the extent to which we are really living.

John Holt's advocacy of a very loose structure, and even of no structure at all, isn't new with his one home-school book, TEACH YOUR OWN. Many similar ideas and arguments were presented in his HOW CHILDREN LEARN and HOW CHILDREN FAIL in the early sixties. A few years earlier, A. S. Neill's SUMMERHILL carried a similar message -- if you leave kids alone, and let them study what and when they want to, they'll educate themselves. It worked for Mowgli and for Tarzan, and sometimes it has worked for us. Other times we've wondered why so few of the great educators have children of their own.

John Dewey, father of the "progressive education" movement of the first half of this century, encouraged teachers to be co-workers with their students rather than taskmasters, and to build their lessons around the students' natural interests. That was a compromise between schooling, which almost everybody had by then, and unschooling, which a lot of people had but didn't particularly want.

Before Dewey, Leo Tolstoy and Henry David Thoreau both felt that as much could be learned in the woods and fields as in the classroom. I don't think they meant that a walk in the woods would teach you the three R's, or that people didn't need the three R's; just that there's a lot to learn in the world besides the three R's, and some of it comes from doing and observing and thinking instead of listening to someone talk. Socrates and Confucius, nearly contemporaries in the fifth century B.C., both used conversation as a learning aid, with the goals of discovering truth rather than teaching beliefs, and of developing each pupil to his own highest potential. The approach of the modern schools differs only in that the teacher does most of the talking, and then asks questions about something else, and nobody cares about silly abstractions such as truth and highest potential.

The rigid approach to teaching is repeatedly condemned by Maria Montessori, Ashley Montagu, Ivan Illich, Herbert Kohl, Paul Goodman, George Dennison, and many other knowledgeable educators, still including John Holt. Some of them have kids of their own, and some practice on other people's kids. Learning Magazine frequently features articles questioning or attacking the concepts and practices of testing, grading, rigid structure, and a tight curriculum. A lot of teachers read Learning. I don't know if any of them are allowed by their school boards to pay attention to it.

Among the growing number of books about home-schooling, the ones with a fundamentalist orientation are strongest in their recommendation of a strict curriculum. Ted Wade's THE HOME SCHOOL MANUAL argues strongly for a planned structure, although he has written me, "Free time and exploring are important, [but] I feel it's important to work from a plan and to choose on the basis of goals rather than by what seems fun at the moment."

Most of the home-schoolers who argue against

loose structure actually consider it to be synonymous with "what seems fun at the moment," and seem to rest their case primarily on a puritanical assumption that anything that is fun is automatically suspect, and is probably bad.

Advocates of loose structure repeatedly assert and sometimes demonstrate that most children are eager to learn, anything and everything; and, if not stunted by educational malpractice, will follow their own interests and curiosity into ever-expanding fields of knowledge and skills. No child will prefer a steady diet of comic books anymore than he will choose a constant diet of candy and cookies, although a child's appetite for junk food, both intestinal and cranial, can sometimes amaze even the most imaginative adult. Before long -- that's "long" by his standards -- he will have a craving for real nutrition, whether in food or knowledge. Many of those who favor rigidity are basing their arguments on observations of children who have never learned in a loosely-structured situation. For the sake of argument, perhaps, they "try it" for a few days or weeks, and then announce that it doesn't work. Part of the problem is that they're dealing with children who are accustomed to having some form of knowledge or opinion poured into funnels which have been stuck in their heads, and part of the problem is that sometimes that's the only way to find out if the kids are awake. Like the parents and the teachers, the kids have come to believe that this is the only way to "learn," and will sit around waiting for someone to teach them

something. Sometimes, it's quite a revelation to them that they can learn something by themselves.

Ironically, the proverb that "Virtue is its own reward" is promoted more by the so-called secular humanists than by many fundamentalists, who make virtue synonymous with obedience, and offer material rewards for both.

Perhaps a rigid structure depends upon such rewards and punishments. The more authority is asserted, the more it will be resented and tested, and the more it must be enforced, either by coercion or by bribery. It seems axiomatic that any program needing constant enforcement -- whether with subtle bribes, rewards, threats, fear, punishment, or psychological games -- must have several inherent weaknesses.

"Hey, Mom, I'll be good if you give me a dime."
"Now, son, why can't you be good for nothing, like your father?"

We have never used any form of punishment with our children, and they have never given us any "discipline" problems that couldn't be resolved with discussion. They do their share of our daily work -- barn chores, housework, firewood, etc. -- and spend each day learning hundreds of things. We often share a bowl of popcorn, a pot of cocoa, a game of cards or pingpong, but never as rewards for obedience or accomplishment. Such pleasures are ordinary parts of our daily life.

Loosely-structured learning isn't necessarily "what seems fun at the moment," but usually what is fun for a child (or an adult) in a creative

environment will be interesting, provocative, and broadening -- in other words, educational.

Another misconception of loose structure which is firmly held by many of its opponents is that there is little or no contribution by adults. The opposite is closer to the fact. With a loose structure, children and adults interact more often without regard for artificial barriers such as age differences, school walls, and honorific formalities. The parent plays several roles, the least of which is "teacher." The parent suggests, guides, converses, questions, supports, praises, encourages, and helps to obtain material. The parent is friend, mentor, confidante, and fellow student.

Throughout <u>Growing Without Schooling</u> are scores of readers' letters recounting their experiences with loosely-structured learning. The factor most common to them all is interaction between adults and children in real-life situations, in which the children learn real skills and gain real knowledge. At an age when most kids are still working on how much Sally spent for three oranges if the price is 6 for $1.00, some homeschool kids are earning money, putting it into their own checking accounts, and writing their own checks.

The parents whose kids are less precocious, and even dislike studying and thinking, don't often write books or articles, although they sometimes write letters asking what's wrong with them or what are they doing wrong. The answer to both questions is "nothing." Wait a while, and try again. Some kids just don't like studying and thinking, whether they're in public school, home school, or unschool. But they can sure fix cars or build birdhouses or catch fish. I know a lot of very nice people who fix cars and couldn't tell a noun from a nun. They have expensive homes and go to Florida for two weeks every winter.

Nancy Wallace, in BETTER THAN SCHOOL, tells of frequently chauffeuring her children to and from music and language lessons, and of the many hours she and her husband often spent reading to their children. The Wallaces' home-school program was as far from being only "what seems fun at the moment" as it was from the rigid structure of the public schools.

The older our kids got, the longer their lunch breaks became. Jean and I compared notes and concluded that the two who had had the most contact with other kids at an early age were the quickest to lose interest in learning or creating. So much for the values of socialization.

Sometimes all four scurried through the day, learning and creating and discussing ideas, and sometimes one or two would sort of fade out and need a little jiggle, and sometimes all of them would just run down. After what we felt was a suitable break from straining their brains, we'd

wind them up again.

By the time the kids were doing sixth and seventh grade work, we discovered a few flaws in Rousseau's, or whoever's, ideas about plunking a kid in the woods with a screwdriver and a pile of books. The biggest flaw was, then what? Once the kids have mastered the basics of language and arithmetic and nail pounding and cake making, will they go on to write and then discuss The Great Books and The History of Civilization all by themselves, or could they use a little more input from those who have gone before?

Does "invited learning" mean we shouldn't occasionally try to lead them into areas of which they aren't yet aware, and therefore can't invite us to help them in? Does "invited learning" mean the same kind of choppy, incomplete, fragmented learning that's going on in the public schools?

We never really figured out exactly what "invited learning" does mean, but we decided we couldn't always wait to be invited. Sometimes we just crashed the party, and amazed ourselves with the structure and organization we could devise. "Let's hope John Holt never sees this," we'd say to each other. "He'll stop selling our books." But the kids became so interested in Alexander the Great or the Renaissance or Martin Luther and the papal bulls that they forgot all about Donald Duck. They learned psychology and economics and world history and geography and where Yellowstone National Park is. They even began inviting us to introduce more subjects, or help them with the ones they were on, and then we began feeling safe again. We always felt a little like renegades when we taught something without having been invited to do so.

When we were having unschool, the kids mostly set their own unschedules. When we were having home-school, it often went something like this--

6:45 - Jean and Donn get up with the alarm, feed fires, dress, etc. Feed dog, then let her out. Two cats in, growling at each other. Jean wakes Derek. Donn cleans and sharpens chain saw on pingpong table.

7:30 - Jean wakes Cathy or Karen or Susan, who take turns daily setting the table, getting breakfast, and tending fires. Jean and Derek go to the barn, feed and water the pig, cow, calf, and 25 hens; clean the gutter; milk the cow; collect eggs. Donn puts fuel in chain saw, then goes out to cut firewood. The one on breakfast duty calls the others, who are usually already awake and reading in bed.

8:15 - Breakfast: Hot cereal, whole wheat toast from home-made bread, home-made butter and apple jelly, honey, fresh milk, fresh eggs, peanut butter. Coffee for Jean and Donn.

9:00 - Jean and two girls clear the table, do dishes, put away. One girl sweeps house, straightens odds and ends. Girls rotate these chores daily. Every fourth day, Derek sweeps. Donn goes out to split firewood.

9:30 - Derek and Susan or Cathy and Karen bring water, one dipping buckets into the brook (six feet from the corner of the house) and passing them in, the other carrying them to the kitchen and filling the 50-gallon can, stove reservoir, and large kettle on the stove. In warm weather, the pipes aren't frozen, and this chore is eliminated.

9:45 - Official school time, morning session, at the kitchen-dining table. Donn leading (or

being led). (Jean listens, comments, sews, mends, plans meals, does laundry, plans her afternoon school work, tends fires, bakes bread, etc.) Discussion of daily offering of Word-A-Day calendar ("saprogenic") and Quote-A-Day calendar ("A sharp tongue is the only edge tool that grows keener with constant use" - Washington Irving.) We pull the legs and wings off the words, examining roots, derivations, associations, usages, sometimes using the dictionary. We discuss the quotation and its author: Do you agree? Why or why not? What is his most-famous story? Does anyone know when he lived?

10:00 (this and other times given in Official School Time are approximate; we have no schedule) - Word play, dictionary and encyclopedia assignments from yesterday. Cathy: Tass, tacit, taciturn, apocrypha, anarchy, anachronism. Karen: cosmos, cosmic, wax, wane, flat, flatulent. Susan: awesome, awful, offal, neapolitan, obese, obeisance. Derek: auk, gross, grosbeak, eject, elect. Words for tomorrow: faker, fakir, guild, gild, microcosm, macrocosm, zenith, nadir, anathema, spike, bolt, sally, dally. Each student gives definitions, uses the words in sentences; others take notes, discuss uses and usefulness, often making puns and other bad jokes.

10:30 - Yesterday's Detective Assignment, for encyclopedia and general book shelf research. True or false? Support your answers. Cathy: The Lutheran Church was founded by Martin Luther King, Jr. Karen: George Fox was an American Indian. Susan: Betsy Ross was a famous opera singer. Derek: "Doctor Livingstone, I presume?" was said by Sherlock Holmes. Students discuss and take notes on each other's research.

10:45 - Research assignment, to be worked on individually or together, your choice. Problem: A man lost in the woods can find no food except rabbits, which are plentiful and easy to snare. He has all he wants of rabbit meat, yet a few weeks later is found dead of starvation. Why? (Students had to consult several cooking and nutrition books before finding even a hint, and then had to brainstorm their findings to arrive at the answer.)

10:50 - Poetry: Read aloud the selection you found and practiced yesterday. Cathy: Ogden Nash. Karen: Carl Sandburg. Susan: Edna St. Vincent Millay. Derek: Robert Louis Stevenson. Tomorrow, bring one of your own choosing; practice reading aloud beforehand.

11:15 - Writing assignment: Discussion of more articles for our family newsletter, who will write what. To be done on your own time and submitted for discussion and refinement tomorrow.

11:20 - Self-image: Design and draw a button or T-shirt which would express The Real You.

11:40 - Discussion of ethics. How can we know what is "right"? Do values change as society wants them to, or is there a constant right-and-wrong for all people and all times? How can we

"It's just amazing, the way you can spend so many hours teaching your children, and still do your housework — cooking, cleaning, dishwashing, laundry, sweeping, making butter, and all that. How in the world do you do it?"

"It's easy. The kids all do a lot of it. We call it our Home Economics course."

know? What is "conscience"?

12:00 - Donn reads excerpts from biographies, to be discussed.

12:30 - Research assignment for tomorrow: Find and read the story of the Prodigal Son. What does "prodigal" mean? What does "gospel" mean? Which are the "synoptic" gospels, and why?

12:35 - Discussion: Where do we get the common expression, "I wash my hands of it." What does it mean? From last night's readings, what are some of the similarities in Christianity and Buddhism?

12:50 - History Simulation. Karen, you are a prosecuting attorney at the Nuremberg Trials; your position is that anyone who contributed in any way to the persecution and murder of Jews should be punished very severely. Cathy, you are Franz Gruber; you were 17 years old, a railroad guard 60 miles from Auschwitz; you knew that Jews were in the train cars, but you had your orders; besides, you had been taught that Jews were a threat to your country. Susan and Derek, you are judges; you listen to each side as the defendant and the prosecutor argue their cases, then decide if Franz Gruber is guilty of 'crimes against humanity,' and, if so, what the sentence should be. Explain your decisions. (The students ad lib, with no attempt at drama or entertainment.)

1:30 - Lunch: sandwiches, milk, carrot sticks, etc. Free reading, pingpong, walks outside.

2:15 - Official school time, afternoon session, Jean leading. (Donn works on business orders and correspondence, or writing.) First aid, instruction and practice. Music, theory and practice; guitar, flute, clarinet, recorder; singing. Nutrition and health. Work on individual electives, with help when wanted or needed. Cathy: Spanish, typing, history, literature, counseling, geography. Karen: French, typing, psychology. Susan: math, history, spelling, civics, French. Derek: math, handwriting, history, typing, art, Spanish, spelling.

3:30 - Official Time is over. The kids often continue working by themselves on their own electives or on morning assignments. Some go skiing or hiking. All four bring in firewood, usually five or six armloads each. The two who didn't haul water in the morning do so now. Reading; pingpong. Visiting friends. Begin supper, sharing and rotating jobs.

6:00 - Donn goes to the barn for evening chores: milk cow, feed animals, etc.

6:30 - Supper.

7:15 - Supper clean-up shared and rotated. Baking cookies, cakes, pies. Sometimes TV (powered by a car battery). Reading books and magazines. The girls sew, knit, tat, and crochet. Derek builds models of planes and spaceships. The girls have each made several articles of clothing -- dresses, blouses, sweaters, etc. Small personal laundry. Letter writing, churning butter, square dancing (in town), skating, 4-H meetings, board games. Popcorn; maybe ice cream. Donn works in his office. Jean reads or plays guitar.

10:30 - Bedtime. Cats out. Fires fed and shut down. All lights out. Goodnight!

One of my favorite recent dictionaries, the Oxford American, mentions several uses of the word "home" (as a noun, an adjective, a verb, and an adverb), but between "home-room" and "home-sick," where "home-school" should be, there is nothing. Even the third edition of THE RANDOM HOUSE DICTIONARY OF THE ENGLISH LANGUAGE, which weighs twelve pounds and is the most recent unabridged dictionary, with thousands of words I don't know and thousands more I don't care to know, somehow missed all references to home-education, by that or any other name, when its compilers were combing the oceans of print in search of serendipitous fillers.

Nonetheless, I think "home-school" is becoming well-established in the language, just as it is in society, and future lexicographers will have to make note of it.

Ironically, "unschooled" _is_ offered by dictionaries, which claim it means "untrained, uneducated." Hardly accurate, of course, but I haven't time to write my own dictionary. Maybe next year.

In the meantime, we should recall the words of Shakespeare:

"What's in a name?
That which we call a home-school
By any other name would teach as well."

Not to mention the warning of Abraham Lincoln: "You can school some of the people all of the time, and all of the people some of the time, but you can't school all of the people all of the time."

The practice of referring to children as kids is thought by some to have begun as a tax dodge employed by slavers in the 1700's. Rather than declare their valuable and highly-dutiable cargo, the righteous captains would insist they were importing goats and their kids, which even zealous customs officers admitted to be of little value.

Our daughter Karen would certainly agree with the customs officers, if not with the slave importers. Karen is a good kid and a great kidder, but she kids you not when she suggests that goats are not overly bright.

When one of our neighbors recently liquidated much of his barnyard stock, some of the flow ended up in our barn in the forms of five goats, four of whom keep our cow company and provide healthy exercise for our children's fingers and Karen's vocabulary.

(Digressing a little: we "water the cow," meaning we give water to her, and we "milk the cow," meaning we take milk away from her, and still we think English is a language which even young children can understand. Water and milk are both liquids, at least in their most common and desirable states, so could we say, in either case, that we have liquidated the stock?

(Digressing still further: Our little brook, central to our farm and our aspirations, is certainly a liquid asset, although financial reports usually reserve that term for money, as in "cash flow," as if even money might come from a spring up on the hill. Not our spring on our hill, I can assure them with satisfaction; what would our cow do with a bucket of money?)

Anyway, back to the goats. Derek cares for Shawna and Jingle, two young does who have not yet learned how to make milk. Susan milks Heidi and Karen milks Buffy, and they both care for their goats, although, playing with definitions, sometimes they say they don't very much.

The buck, we were told, was named Keyops by his parents, but a previous caretaker kept forgetting the name and decided to call him Fred. Fred went to live with a man named Fred who called him Tyler. Then Tyler stayed with George who continued to call him Tyler. Then Tyler moved in with us. His proud bearing, majestic horns, and strong odor reminded us of Egyptian mummies and other ancient artifacts, so we restored his earlier name, with the proper spelling of Cheops.

At first, Karen and Susan and Heidi and Buffy took turns amusing each other when the former two attempted to extract milk from the latter two, and the entire operation was a splashing success. Heidi soon settled down and eventually gave Susan

less trouble than milk, but Buffy continued to think milking time was circus time, and Karen developed very strong opinions about Buffy's intelligence.

Whenever Karen touched the faucets, Buffy became a rodeo queen -- kicking, bucking, prancing, somersaulting, standing on her head, and sitting in the milk bucket. Karen was very impressed, and said so.

"Dumb goat," she muttered, over and over, as she tried to milk. At night, she had no need to count sheep jumping fences. "Dumb goat," we heard her mutter in her sleep.

I raided my tool box and made a few quick installations in the goat pen.

"Observe," I instructed Karen and Susan. "This rope, with the loop in one end, attaches quickly to the goat's collar. The free end then goes through the eye-screw, down here, six inches from the floor. Notice how Buffy's head goes down as I pull the rope up. Now her collar is snug against the post, and so is her neck, and she is reluctant to practice gymnastics of any kind."

Karen and Susan nodded solemnly.

"Now," I continued, "Buffy is quite happy to wait patiently while you tie the remainder of the rope up here, to this long screw. I recommend a clove hitch, which is made so -- a loop, another loop, and pull it tight. Some people call it a double half-hitch, but it's stronger if you call it a clove hitch. Any questions?"

"No," said Karen, "but you forgot two things."

"Two things?" I echoed. I looked over the entire arrangement -- the taut rope, the perfect clove hitch which I had learned in the Boy Scouts, the waiting milk bucket, and the immobilized goat. "What did I forget?"

"A lever on the wall," Karen said grimly, "and a trapdoor under the goat."

As I've said elsewhere, we have never used any form of punishment with our children, and they have never given us any "discipline" problems which couldn't be resolved with discussion.

Our children are honest, respectful of people and things, polite, and usually very well-behaved.

"If you don't punish your children, how do you discipline them?"

In one 1957 dictionary, "punishment" is not one of the definitions of discipline, although it's mentioned as a colloquial synonym. A 1973 dictionary lists "punishment" as the eighth definition, and in a 1980 dictionary it's third. The word has come a long way, baby.

"Discipline" is still used to mean "a branch of instruction or learning, such as 'an academic discipline,'" but that definition, once the first (and not really very long ago), is now fourth -- coming after the meaning of "punishment given to correct a person or enforce obedience."

In verb form, "discipline" means, first, "to train to be obedient and orderly"; and, second, "to punish."

When we watch other parents with their children, we think that we may have many more rules of conduct than most -- advice and suggestions and instructions covering nearly every situation -- but our rules of conduct are more like social customs than laws; and nearly all of them could easily be expressed by the Golden Rule or a close parallel.

When our children begin crawling and exploring, we place limits only for their own protection or the protection of things which might be damaged by inexperienced handling. In our own home, we keep fragile or dangerous items out of reach. Our house has always been arranged for the presence of the kids. When visiting in other homes which haven't been "child-proofed," we watch our kids closely, but interfere with their movements, either physically or verbally, only when really necessary. We describe and explain the limits as briefly and clearly as possible. If the kids are curious about a fragile or dangerous item, we hold the item for inspection and discussion, and then set it out of reach. We never say, "Don't touch that; you might break it." Instead, we say, "Be very careful with this, because it's very fragile, and might break if it falls," or, "I'll help you hold this, to make it easier for you to see." When prescribing limits, we stick to the facts, without exaggeration or threats.

Our kids always know that we expect only good behavior from them -- not because of bribes or threats, but because we know they have no natural desire to break or lie or cheat or steal. Children, like adults, want to do what is right. They want to be liked, loved, and respected. They want to respect themselves. Whenever one of our kids does something wrong or has made a mistake in judgement, we are quick to sympathize, to understand, and to forgive. Our expectation of goodness always includes the knowledge that mistakes will be made, and that they don't diminish the child's inherent goodness.

A young child understands much of what is said to him, long before he can talk. When he is big enough to hold an object, he is old enough to understand directions about holding it.

The child is always more important than the object, even if his actions toward it must be limited, and he must never be made to think otherwise.

In the relatively rare instances of "bad" behavior, we do our best to make it very clear that it's the behavior which is being rejected, not the child. We know parents who put their offending child out of the room, even out of the house, saying, "You're welcome to come back in when you're ready to behave the way you should." I don't think the child will make the desired distinction; no matter what the parent says, the child will feel personally rejected. Separation from the group or situation is often very effective, but if it's used as a punishment it just fosters resentment. "I'm not punishing you," says the parent, "I'm putting you outside to think it over." The child doesn't believe it. All he will think over is that he has been rejected, he is alone, he didn't mean to misbehave, and he's not big enough or strong enough to put his mother and father outside to think it over when they misbehave. He shouldn't be put outside; he should be taken out, and held closely, and not lectured.

For a young child, even with the most loving and understanding parents, the world is very often a frightening and incomprehensible maze of people and objects and rules. A parent who really tries to understand the child's feelings from the child's own point of view will be a much more positive influence on him than will a distant judge. We try to put ourselves in our children's places; really try to understand the situation as they do. We try to remember our own childhood, the times we misbehaved, perhaps in the same way or worse; how we felt about the people around us, how we felt about the ways we were punished.

We don't try to exact promises from our children

"How many times have I told you not to hit your brother? I'll have to spank you, to help you remember that hitting is wrong."

such as, "Now, we'll go back inside if you think you can be nice." We talk about the problem, explaining why it is a problem, not expecting to reach solutions that will cover all future problems, and then drop it, perhaps even changing the subject. The situation may come up again, and we will deal with it in the same way, but the child never feels unloved or rejected. He doesn't resent us or feel a need to retaliate. Wilful misbehavior was, and is, very rare. We are sure our children know we love them whatever they do.

We have never punished our children, in any way, for anything. We don't withhold privileges, or spank them, or send them to bed without supper. We don't threaten them with any kind of pain or suffering or deprivation. If there's a problem in action or behavior, we discuss it; we consider it our problem. No one is "to blame"; it isn't "your fault" or "his fault." Fault and blame are irrelevant. Nearly every conflict between people is one of misunderstanding or lack of communication or an unfulfilled need. We discuss the problem -- what led to it, how it might be avoided in the future. If something different should have been done or said, we discuss it, not to assign blame, but always to seek a better relationship in the future.

We don't reward our children for good behavior, or for obedience, or for doing their work. We give praise for jobs well done, conflicts dealt with creatively and positively, or problems solved intelligently, but not as a reward. Such achievements deserve honest recognition.

Our children aren't paragons of peacefulness and harmony, but there is no physical violence between them, with the exception of occasional light slaps or pokes when they're very angry. They argue, complain, bicker, and sometimes call each other names. It's interesting that the kids who have had the most contact with public school kids at early ages are the ones most prone to name-calling and petty bickering.

In working to help the kids resolve their problems and conflicts with each other or with us, Jean and I sometimes lose our tempers right along with them. They shout at us; we shout back. When it's all over, we apologize to them for our having lost our tempers, and they learn from our example that even loving parents can get angry, can lose their tempers, and can apologize. They learn to apologize to us and to each other. They learn to accept apologies.

In examining disagreements, we search for the roots -- away from issues of personality, always trying to avoid the concepts of fault and blame. The questions is not who is wrong, but what is wrong, and what can be done to correct the present situation and to avoid its reoccurrence.

Peaceful conflict resolution isn't easy. It takes far more time and effort, more introspection, more discussion, than would be taken by establishing blame and meting out punishment. But it works, and is well worth the effort. It also puts more responsibility on the kids for monitoring and controlling their own behavior, by not "releasing" them from past actions through having "paid" for them by receiving punishment. As the kids get older, we see them searching more and more for peaceful solutions.

The dual concepts of blame and punishment are rooted deeply throughout our culture -- in its religions, its government, and its family life. The courts and churches insist that if you have done something wrong, you must pay for it. This belief has its roots in the pre-Mosaic code of "an eye for an eye," which may have acted as a deterrent, but hardly worked as a correction, any more than such punishments do today. Jesus tried to overturn this rule, but with little success, even within "his" churches. His doctrine of forgiveness is often preached, but seldom practiced.

Parents who punish their children, either physically or psychologically, are using fear and coercion to manipulate behavior. A child may not repeat an act for which he has been punished, but it's usually only because he fears the consequences; not because he understands the wrongness of what he has done. An ancient Hebrew said that the man who does not beat his son must hate him, and his cynical observation is taken by millions of parents to be a divine injunction to spank their children. Jesus didn't threaten children or adults with either a spanking or hellfire; he promised love and forgiveness. His lessons appeal to the conscience -- realize what you have done, he said, and feel sorry about it, and don't do it anymore.

In our family, we strive for discipline from within. We want our children to know and understand the difference between right and wrong, good and bad, and to choose rightness and goodness because they want to; not because they're afraid of any external consequences or punishments.

The development of the conscience is sometimes difficult. Most of the people and institutions of our society are against it, although they often pretend otherwise.

Behavior codes are relaxing and eroding around the world, which is one of the proofs that morality cannot be enforced by laws or fear. It can only come from within each individual, from strong convictions about what is right and good, and the desire to live by those convictions. It comes from the strength and courage to go against the current -- to do what is right because it is right, not because of hope of reward or fear of punishment. Those convictions and that strength constitute the only discipline, moral or social, that is lasting and real. We can't force it on to our children, or even give it to them. We can only try to help them find and develop it within themselves.

OBEDIENCE TRAINING vs. "INVITED LEARNING"

or, HOME-SCHOOLING GOES TO THE DOGS

"Invited Learning," as I understand it -- and I'm sure some home-school theorists will be quick to say I don't -- seems to mean that children intuitively know what they need to learn and when they need to learn it, and no one should presume to offer them information about anything at all until they ask for it. If they ask for it, of course, it's really Invited <u>Teaching</u>, but more people than you might suppose (unless you're one of them) get purple in the face over this, insisting that "teaching" is <u>doing something TO someone else</u>, and is therefore a form of aggression -- unless the students ask for it, and then it's okay, because then we can call it Invited <u>Learning</u>.

To Jean and me, the entire debate is slightly more exciting than the afternoon soaps or taking out the garbage, but "Invited Learning" is an intriguing concept, whether we understand it or not, and sometimes we like to play around with it and see what we can discover about it.

One of the things we've discovered about Invited Learning is that it often results in excessive barking, muddy paw prints on the sofa, missing or mangled shoes, and late-night festivities involving a mouthful of porcupine quills and a pair of pliers. With dogs, that is. Invited Learning with children is another story, most of which can be told in polite language, but which isn't a part of this report.

We've had a few smart dogs over the years (usually one at a time), but we've never given much thought to leading them into any sort of Higher Education. Or even Lower Education. With our dogs, as with our children, we lean (not too firmly, I admit) toward a sort of Invited Learning, the biggest difference being that with the children it's usually more from conviction than laziness.

With dogs, it usually seems easier to brush mud off the sofa before sitting than to teach them to wipe their feet at the door, so we tend to excuse their poor manners by muttering, "Dogs will be dogs" (just as people used to say, "Boys will be boys" -- another truism which, according to recent news magazines, is no longer the certainty we once thought it was; but that is also another story).

About a year and a half ago, Gus came to live with us, and almost immediately began challenging

many of our favorite educational theories and convictions, including our smug assumption that dogs will be dogs.

Gus is about ninety percent German Shepherd and ten percent something else. We found him (or vice versa) in January, at the SPCA sixty miles away, where he was being held in solitary confinement as a vagrant. He was a puppy, only eight months old, but already weighed 62 pounds, and it cost us more than a dollar a pound to spring him. When I brought him home, sitting beside me in our '84 pickup, he had the familiar dazed look of most ex-cons who have been in stir too long, and didn't say much, but several times he expressed his gratitude by cleaning my right ear very thoroughly. He also made a few mechanical adjustments when my attention was elsewhere, and I finally had to explain to him -- after the truck suddenly lost its oomph and nearly coasted to a stop before I found the cause of its unusual behavior -- that he could move the rearview mirror all he liked but I would be in charge of the gear shift. He apologized by cleaning my ear again, and we got home with no more surprises.

Jean and I showed Gus the doors that connect Inside to Outside, and he signified his understanding by testing them all. We showed him his food and water dishes in the little nook in the hallway, and he tested them, too, giving no indication that the arrangement was less than satisfactory. We introduced him to Big Guy, our ferocious feline mouse-killer, and said we hoped they would be friends. Gus, very pleased, offered to clean Big Guy's ears. Big Guy, who had once been chased up a very small tree by a very large dog, offered to clean Gus's clock, then ran upstairs to hide in the rafters until spring. (That turned out to be another lesson in Invited Learning because for the next three months, at least once a day, we had to risk being torn to shreds by inviting Big Guy to go for a little walk outside, dog or no dog, and he soon learned to hide from us in places we couldn't reach.)

One evening about three weeks after he had come to live with us, Gus barked at the door, then at me, then again at the door. Making a natural assumption, I opened the door for him, but he stood and barked at me again. He wanted me to go outside to play toss-and-chase with his empty plastic milk jug.

"You're out of your mind," I told him. "It's ten below zero out there, with two feet of snow."

He still refused to go out by himself, so I shut the door and went back to my book and chair beside the wood stove, pretending to ignore the disgusted look he was giving me.

Just when I thought he had given up, Gus went to the hall closet and ran back with one of my snow boots in his teeth. He dropped it beside me, then returned to the closet for the second boot, which he dropped next to the first one.

"Gus," I managed to say, "dogs do this only in movies."

He put a paw on one of the boots and barked at me.

"Okay, okay," I said, pushing my foot into one of the boots. "You've made your point. But you should know that real dogs don't do this."

Putting the other boot on, I said to Jean, "Did you see what Gus just did? He's really smart!"

"It's a good thing one of you is," she said, as I went to the closet for my jacket and mittens.

Women tend to say things like that sometimes, so I pretended I hadn't heard her; but on the way out the door, I whispered to Gus, "See what I'm up against? You don't have to make it worse."

A squeaky rubber football, about six inches long, became Gus's favorite indoor toy. Sometimes he just chews on it, enjoying its squeak. Sometimes he steps on it, daring it to squeak, then grabs it in his teeth and flips it into the air, then runs after it. Occasionally he loses it, and then spends twenty minutes or more searching for it -- behind furniture, under pillows, down the

hall, wherever a tricky rubber ball might be hiding. Usually he finds it, but sometimes he gives up, and barks at Jean or me to find it for him -- which eventually gave us the brilliant idea that he was Inviting us to help him Learn something.

I called him to the end of the hall, then told him to sit and count to ten while I hid the ball. "Ten" is a very large number for a young dog, but I managed to get the ball behind a sofa cushion before Gus came galloping after me into the living room.

"<u>Find</u> the ball," I said, in that tricky way parents have of enlarging their children's vocabulary. "<u>Find</u> it."

Gus sniffed the air, which didn't help, then began searching, pushing chairs, poking his nose under magazines and into armpits, and flipping cushions around until he finally found the ball. He tossed it into the air, jumped and caught it, then dropped it in front of me and barked. This time, there was no doubt: he was definitely <u>Inviting</u> me to help him <u>Learn</u> something. (Some people might say he was inviting <u>me</u> to learn something, and others might say he was just inviting me to play a game, but I know better.)

We did it several times that evening, and it became a daily game. I hid the ball in different places each time, and Gus always kept searching until he found it. At the same time, his vocabulary grew. Besides <u>find</u> and <u>ball</u>, he soon learned <u>sit</u>, <u>wait</u>, <u>stay</u>, <u>come</u>, <u>sofa</u>, <u>other sofa</u>, <u>chair</u>, <u>bed</u>, <u>wrong way</u>, <u>down</u>, <u>higher</u>, and <u>behind the pillows</u>. Some of the concepts seemed pretty abstract to us, but <u>abstract</u> was one of the words Gus hadn't learned.

One day Gus took his ball into our bedroom (which is downstairs, near the kitchen), stayed a few moments, then came out without it and barked at me. It had been quite a while since I had dismissed Gus's barking as mere random noise. If he was bright enough to tell me something but I wasn't bright enough to understand him, I'd have to fake it.

Stalling for time, I asked, "Lost your ball?"

"Woof," he said, wagging his tail.

"Is it in the bedroom?" I asked.

"Woof," he said again, still wagging.

"Can you find it?" I asked.

His tail stopped wagging. Gently but firmly, he took my hand in his mouth and pulled me toward the bedroom door. Releasing my hand, he said, "Rrowrrf!" and waited expectantly. Sometimes he seems to think I'm Learning Disabled.

Searching my mind for possibilities, I made a wild guess. "You want <u>me</u> to find the ball?" I asked him, not really believing it.

"Rowf!" Gus exclaimed, wagging his tail again.

Feeling ridiculous, I went into the bedroom to look for the ball, which I quickly found on the floor beside the bed. Gus grabbed the ball from my hand and raced excitedly down the hall, then back to the living room, then back into the bedroom. He came out -- no ball -- and barked at me.

"Right," I said, still not believing; "Gotcha." I found the ball in the same place beside the bed. Gus grabbed it, ran around with it to celebrate, then hid it in the bedroom again. We went through the whole thing several times, and Gus looked at me with approval each time I found the ball. I hoped he could see that I may be slow sometimes but I'm not Learning Disabled.

"Jean," I said, "is this possible? Is Gus really hiding the ball for me to find?"

"You said he's smart," she reminded me.

"Lucky for me," I said, "he's not smart enough to put the ball in different places. He always hides it in the same place."

I shouldn't have said it when Gus was listening. The next time he told me to look for the ball, it wasn't there. I finally found it on the bed, under my pillow. The next time, it was under Jean's pillow. "Gus," I told him, "this Invited Learning is going to your head. You're forgetting you're just a dog." It's hard to tell with dogs, but I think he laughed at me.

Gus likes Flavor Snacks -- crunchy, bone-shaped dog biscuits -- which I keep on the back of my desk so I can bribe him to go away when I'm working and he wants me to play with him. As usual, he's a step ahead of me. Bounding into my office, he bumps my elbow with his nose and says, "If you give me three Flavor Snacks, I won't bother you for a while." I don't know why he wants three. If I give him two, he demands another. If I give him four, he accepts them, but doesn't care much about the fourth one. So I give him three, and he goes away.

"Impossible," I told myself the first few times it happened. "Numbers are too abstract for a dog. Even a smart one. I'm going to prove it."

I broke a Flavor Snack in half, held one piece up for Gus to see, and asked him, "How many?"

He woofed, once, but that didn't prove anything because in Dog Talk "woof" is a homonym; like many English words, its meaning must be deduced from its context. It can mean "Please" or "I want to go out" or "I'm hungry." I wasn't convinced that it could also mean "one."

I gave Gus the Flavor Snack, then held up two pieces, one in each hand, and asked him, "How many?"

"Woof," he said, eyeing the piece in my right hand. When I didn't give it to him, he looked at the piece in my left hand and said, "Woof."

"Coincidence," I said, giving him both pieces. "Accident." Holding up one, I asked him how many.

"Woof," he said. I waited. He waited. We both waited. Finally, suspecting that his attention span might be longer than mine, I gave him the Flavor Snack, and waited for him to eat it -- crunch-glumph, like a boa constrictor. Then I held up two pieces, one in each hand, and asked, "How many?"

He woofed at the one in my right hand, then at the one in my left hand. I gave them to him. We did it again and again that evening, and several times in the next few days, always with the same result: a woof for each hand. I still didn't know if Gus was counting them or had only decided that I wanted him to woof for each one.

About a week later, when I held up two Flavor Snacks and asked Gus, "How many?" he hesitated.

He looked at one, then the other; then at the first again, then back to the second. Back and forth, several times. Then he looked at me and very distinctly said, "Woof-woof." Two syllables; one word.

Had he finally said "two"? We did it several times, sometimes with one, sometimes with two -- and he answered correctly every time. He wasn't as certain, at first, about "two" as he was about "one" -- he always took time to consider very carefully before saying "two" ("woof-woof") -- but he obviously knew the difference. Gus could count!

So far, he hasn't mastered "three," a quantity which often excites him to the point of saying, "Nine! Fourteen! Six!" although he is always insistent on exactly three Flavor Snacks. Apparently he knows the quantity of three, but doesn't have a word for it. I've read of an aboriginal jungle tribe, purportedly unchanged since the Stone Age, whose entire numerical system is "One, two, three, plenty," meaning that any quantity over three is too much to count separately. Gus's numerical system -- "One, two, plenty" -- is only one digit short of Stone Age man's.

Since then, we've continued to be impressed by Gus's intelligence, but we're seldom surprised by it. When he's hungry, he brings his food dish into the kitchen. If he wants one of us to go out with him, he brings our boots (dirty sneakers, in the summertime), and then goes back to the closet to pull a jacket (usually the right one) off the hanger. If he wants his chest scratched, he pulls someone's hand down and leans against it. If we ask him to whisper, he makes a very soft, barely audible, <u>huff</u> sound. When he's riding in the truck and sees a <u>Stop</u> sign or hears the click of the turn signal, he sits down and braces his front legs.

Early one spring, a sign in town announced registration for Obedience Training, bringing us face-to-face with the unexpected question of formal education. We discussed it. We hadn't wanted it for any of our kids, and all four of them have done very well without it, but maybe it would be different for Gus. "Different how?" we asked ourselves. Well, socialization, for one thing; he'd get to meet other dogs, learn to interact meaningfully with his peers. Broaden his cultural horizons by showing him part of the world beyond our rural homestead.

Gus said he wasn't sure what we meant by "obedience" or "socialization," but anything involving a ride in the truck was okay with him.

We still weren't sure. Having devoted so much of our lives to home-schooling, it just didn't seem right to enroll our dog in public school.

On the other hand, we home-schoolers are a strange, perverse lot. I don't mean "we" meaning <u>us</u>, Jean and Donn Reed, personally; I mean we home-schoolers in general; generic home-schoolers or the home-schooling masses. We reject the standards and methods and results of public schools. We say we don't want our kids to meet public-school standards, because those standards are empty and false. We say the world would be better off if public schools had never been invented.

And then whom do we choose as our homeschool heroes? John Taylor Gatto, honored as "Teacher of the Year" three times before he quit the public school system after twenty-six years. David Colfax, described on another author's book jacket as "father of three homeschooled Harvard graduates" -- not even mentioning his fourth son who was also homeschooled but hasn't gone to Harvard. Grace Llewellyn, described on the cover of her book as "a former middle school English teacher." We're like dying atheists asking a priest for absolution -- not really believing in it, but hedging our bets, not taking any chances. A stamp of approval from professional teachers who have quit the public schools after ten or twenty years seems to mean more to us than the opinions of people who got out before they got in -- that is, who never got involved in public schools at all.

Perverse or not, Gus and I registered for the course. Each Tuesday evening, for eight weeks, we drove to the community recreation center and, along with about 30 other dogs and their owners, received instruction from a member of the American Kennel Club. Every day, at home, Gus and I diligently did our homework, most of which he thought was dumb and boring, but he was a good pupil, and more than willing to put up with such nonsense if it meant being outdoors with me. He even brought my boots and jacket to me two or three times a day, plainly inviting me to help him learn more.

We learned to Heel on Leash, which included Stopping or Starting on Command, Right- and Left-angle Turns, About Face, and promptly Sitting (Gus; not me) without command at each Stop. Gus didn't see the point of it, but he mastered it quickly and didn't argue about it.

Then came Heeling on Leash in a Figure 8, which Gus thought was one of the stupidest exercises he had ever heard of. At school, he wanted to make it a Figure 6 or 99 or 54, anything but Figure 8; and when we practiced at home during the week, he wrapped his paws around my ankle and chewed my foot.

The Long Sit (sitting and staying in place with minimal movement for at least a minute) and Long Down (lying down and staying in place for three minutes) were easy because he had already learned them at home when he was waiting for me to hide his rubber football.

Recall -- sitting, staying, then coming on command -- was also easy, for the same reason.

The final lesson, in preparation for exam night, was Stand for Inspection, and Gus thought it was dumber than the Figure 8. The idea was that he would sit beside me in Heel position, I would tell him to stand, and he would promptly stand; then I would walk away to the end of the leash, and he would stay, still standing, while the instructor walked up to him, ran a hand along his back, and walked away; and would remain there until I returned to his side. The whole exercise was a snap for him -- all except the first part.

Gus refused to stand on command. I had to nudge his belly with my toe, tug forward on his leash, and repeat the command several times, and then Gus would very reluctantly stand. Once he was standing, he did the rest of the entire exercise without a hitch, but after two weeks of practice he still refused to stand on command.

Graduation Night arrived. Gus and I discussed our test-taking strategy, and I told Jean before we left not to expect too much. Neither Gus nor I had taken the course very seriously, and I honestly expected us to score about 28th in a class of 30.

We started off with 100 points. On the Heel on Leash, we lost 3 points out of 20, for holding the leash too tight. On the Figure 8, we lost 1 point out of 10, for the same reason. On the Long Sit, no points lost, out of 20. On the Long Down, no points lost, out of 20. On Recall, 1 point lost out of 15, for "handler error" (I tugged on the leash once when I shouldn't have). Gus was nonchalant, and I was amazed. But the worst was yet to come, and I knew it would be our downfall.

"Stand your dog for inspection," the judge said. "Stand," I commanded, knowing he wouldn't, and getting ready to sneak my toe under him. He stood immediately, without a nudge, and didn't move as I walked away from him. The judge walked up to him, ran his hand along Gus's back, then walked away, and Gus stood still as I returned to him. No points lost, out of 15.

Total points lost, 5. Final score, 95. <u>Second place!</u>

The next day, at home, I asked Gus to Stand. He yawned at me. I made it a command, and he chewed my foot.

There's a lesson in there somewhere, but I'm not sure what it is. Probably Gus was way ahead of us again, and just wanted to make a point about learning. Maybe about Invited Learning.

Gus has interrupted me several times while I've been writing this. He hid his football in the bedroom, then came to my office and told me to look for it. I knew he wouldn't leave me alone until I did, so I went to the bedroom. It wasn't beside the bed. Not under the pillows, which he had rearranged (probably just to mislead me). I finally found it under the covers, which he had pulled back, then pulled up over the ball. I told him to stay on the bed and count to 10 while I hid the ball. He's still not very good at numbers over 3, but I got the ball hidden under a pile of sofa pillows before he came charging after me. He pushed pillows all over until he found the ball, then went to hide it again. Came to tell me to look for it. I went. Nowhere in the bedroom this time. I finally found it down the hall, just inside the bathroom door. Gus was laughing at me. Smart alecky dog. My turn; I hid the ball under a folded blanket on the other sofa. Gus flipped pillows around with his nose, then checked the other sofa, lifted the blanket with his nose, and got the ball. Hid it in the bedroom again, told me to look for it. I told him I'm busy writing a serious article about education. He sighed and looked out the window and woofed.

"Not now," I said. "Maybe later."

He woofed at the box of Flavor Snacks on the back of my desk. I took two out of the box and showed them to him. He counted them, then looked at the box and growled softly. I got another. He accepted all three, one at a time, and cleaned up the crumbs on the floor.

I went back to work. Gus jumped up on one of the sofas, rearranged the pillows, then lay down and looked at Jean, who was playing De Visée's "Suite in D Minor" on her guitar. I don't even know what D Minor means, but Gus does, and he doesn't like it. He always growls -- a very low rumble deep in his throat -- whenever Jean plays anything in D minor. He growled and muttered, so Jean switched to Bach's "Gavotte in A Minor." Gus sighed contentedly, and went to sleep.

He sure is smart.

It's a good thing one of us is.

READING, WRITING, and SPELLING

A reader wrote to say that she and her husband (a math teacher) were disappointed by my comments about math. "Math literacy" -- the understanding and enjoyment of all levels of math -- are as important, she said, as reading literacy.

I wrote her a long letter, emphasizing that it certainly is not the study of mathematics which I oppose, but the mandatory studying of math without enjoyment or purpose. I realize there are many people who really need math, and I'm even a little envious of those who enjoy it.

Our culture -- in philosophy, history, and myth -- is communicated much more through literature than through math, so I can't agree that a lack of "math-literacy" is equal to a lack of reading literacy. A person who is well-read but non-mathematical will have a greater awareness and understanding of the world than a mathematician whose reading has been confined to mathematics. That doesn't preclude the possible desirability of being well-educated in both fields; but, if I have to make a choice, I'll choose literature.

All four of our kids read a great deal, but none of them seems to have a natural bent for writing, so it's as unlikely that they'll be journalists as it is that they'll be astronomers. With writing, therefore, as with math, we encourage a general, basic competency which will be of use to them in the areas which they probably will pursue, and in the most "real-life" situations: various styles of letters, basic reports (which may or may not be useful, but are easy to master and will probably be of good use someday), simplified research notes, and so on, along with basic spelling skills, grammar, sentence structure, and a few handshakes with parts of speech. If they ever need more advanced writing (or more advanced math), they have solid foundations on which to build.

The essential purpose of language -- whether it consists of animal grunts and growls, human speech, mathematical equations, or computer symbols -- is the communication of information and ideas. As the subject of this chapter, I'll consider writing and reading to be human speech on paper. Its basic purpose is still the communica-

tion of information and ideas. Spelling is little more than a standardized system of encoding sounds and their meanings, to facilitate that communication.

There's an old story, which you've probably heard, about a little boy who scribbled laboriously on a piece of paper and proudly told his mother, "Look, I'm writing."

"How nice," said his mother. "What does it say?"

"I don't know," the boy replied. "I haven't learned how to read yet."

Like many apocryphal stories, this one may have some basis in fact, but most of us learn to read before we learn to write.

Ideally, however -- except in modern schools which try to teach how to read without offering reading material of any substance, and how to write without asking that the writing be about anything of substance -- the two processes soon overlap, each one contributing to the other. Spelling, principal parts of speech, and basic grammar are all learned at the same time. The reading will be about subjects which interest the kids, and they will write about things or events which interest them. The formation of letters is also learned at the same time, as well as the extension of meanings by the use of suffixes and prefixes, by different tenses, etc.

READING

We never taught our children to read.

When they were very young, we read to them. When they were three months old, they gurgled happily as we read nursery rhymes, poetry, and even captions of "first interest" animal books. At six months, they smiled and pointed at interesting shapes and colors. When they were a year old, we read books with them, discussing the pictures and answering millions of questions. We often asked each other, "Where is the truck?" "Can you put your finger on the nose?" "Which flower is red?" and similar questions. The kids weren't reading words yet, but even picture books with no words involved verbal communication and a growing vocabulary, including concepts of space, size, color, action, and direction.

Between eighteen months and two years, each of them spent many hours each day with books, not yet recognizing many words, but studying the pictures. Despite the kids' early interest in books, we never pushed reading. It was unimportant to us if they learned to read at the age of two or six or ten. It wasn't long before the questions were about the letters and words as often as about the pictures. The kids were fascinated by the idea that the story was not only in the pictures, and were eager to decode the words. They asked us to identify specific words, especially nouns with which they were familiar (cow, horse, car, tree) and verbs, especially of movement (run, jump, fall). They'd point at a word (sometimes at random, sometimes deliberately) and ask "'Cow'?" If, by chance, the "choice" was correct, the child felt such pride and delight that the word might never be forgotten. When the random choice was incorrect, we moved the pointing finger to the right word, saying, "Here's 'cow.'" If the child then returned to the first choice, wanting to know what it was, then we'd tell him; otherwise, we ignored it.

Their own curiosity about the pictures and the accompanying words which we read to them taught them to read.

Frequent positive reinforcement and absolute avoidance of negative corrections encouraged the kids, and they learned rapidly. None of them ever said, "I can't get it. It's too hard," because we never asked them to "get" anything. There was never any pressure to do something which they hadn't yet learned to do.

All four kids could identify and read several words before they knew the sounds of individual letters. We never had a definite plan of "how to teach reading," except to be sure it was always fun and interesting, so there didn't seem much point in interrupting their reading to teach them how to read.

As it turned out, phonics and grammar grew naturally with the kids' learning to write.

We let the kids lead the way. Once the partial similarity of COW to CAR was noticed and questioned, it was very natural for us to discuss the alphabet and the different sounds of letters. Being able to "sound out" words phonetically is important, but it's just as important to be able to read entire words and even whole phrases without having to dissect them.

The conventional "sounding out" of "baby" is buh-ay-buh-ee. Once the child can point to the letters in turn and make these sounds, we are

supposed to say, "Very good! Now say the sounds faster; run them together." We are supposed to demonstrate the method, slowly and ponderously saying, "BUHay-BUHee," over and over, until the child finally hears -- or guesses -- the word "baby." "Now you do it," we say, with the reminder, "Sound out each letter, then run the sounds together -- and you have the word!"

It doesn't really work that way. For most beginning readers, it still comes out as buh-ay-buh-ee, but speeded up -- "buhaybuhee." The sounds trip over each other, but are not "run together." The trick is to condense four syllables into two -- but then it's no longer a strictly phonetic approach; it's sight reading of syllables. The transition from four separate letter-sounds to two syllables is less a matter of logic than of intuition. The conclusion may be accepted, but there is no logical transition to be understood.

Later, when we began using school readers, we made the mistake of also using the tests of "comprehension and retention" which invariably followed each story. We still hadn't learned to reject the methods of the "experts." Luckily, we soon realized that our kids' lessening interest in reading was the direct result of having to answer dumb questions about their reading, but it took us longer than it should have. We should have known better without even trying it.

I was reminded of those dumb questions many years later when I read Longfellow's "The Courtship of Miles Standish" to the family. It was in a book prepared for classroom use, and the poem was followed by about fifty questions, such as, "The Pilgrims came to America on the (a) Atlantic (b) Mayflower (c) Titanic (d) Damascus." Like many test questions in the public schools, some of these were not only ridiculous, but intentionally tricky. Even if the student has been asleep throughout the entire poem, he isn't likely to answer either "Titanic" or "Damascus," even if he doesn't know what they are. But a conscientious student might easily suspect a trick in the first two choices. The Pilgrims came to America on the Mayflower, but they also came on the Atlantic. The teacher has the answer key and knows that the correct answer is b, which is what most students will answer. Does that mean that a is incorrect? The student who answers "the Atlantic" will be laughed at. The teacher, smiling condescendingly, will say, "The question is about the name of the ship." "But," the student might argue, "the question didn't say 'ship.' 'Damascus' isn't a ship's name." The teacher smiles tolerantly at the student's stupidity. The other students snicker -- even those who answered "Titanic."

When Derek was nine, he became interested in sharks, and quickly exhausted the small amount of material we have on the subject. He borrowed books from the public library, and requested more through inter-library loans. Relatives sent him books about sharks; he searched back issues of The National Geographic. Except for helping him find material, we left him alone. We didn't try to direct his studies, or tie them in with any other subject, or test his "comprehension and retention." We knew that if he didn't understand the books, he wouldn't have chosen to read them. Soon he scoffed at popularized images of sharks, such as the movie "Jaws," and could point out, in detail, the errors in them -- not to impress anyone with his knowledge, but because he felt that both sharks and people were being wronged by the misconceptions and misrepresentations. His "retention," apparently, was excellent.

When Derek first showed an interest in sharks, we might have thought, "Ah ha! Here's our chance. We can direct his study, so that it will include history, geography, oceanography, other aquatic life forms, sociology, anthropology, and psychology. We can expand his vocabulary."

We didn't; the thought never occurred to us. Had we assigned readings, followed by tests for comprehension and retention, I'm sure he would have lost interest in the subject very quickly. Such an approach to any subject is one of the quickest ways to kill interest in it. Derek studied sharks for two years because he wanted to, and learned a great deal about history, geography, oceanography, other aquatic life forms, sociology, anthropology, and psychology. His vocabulary certainly expanded.

Books have always been a prominent part of our lives. When Jean and I aren't busy with building, gardening, barn chores, housework, teaching, and writing, we read. There are books in every room

of our house; we surround ourselves with books. In providing books for our children, from the time they could first focus their eyes on a picture, we've always treated books as sources of pleasure, adventure, information, and discovery. Reading should never be a tedious chore; it should always be exciting and rewarding -- as it will be, if we don't try to harness it, control it, pen it up, or direct it for our own purposes.

Educational distributors now offer innumerable books for "the reluctant reader." Because most children spend so many hours watching movies and television, publishers and teachers offer them countless books with "TV tie-ins" -- i.e., stories based on popular shows and characters -- with the hope that the tie-in will lead the kids from their mania for TV to a mania for reading; then, once hooked, they'll move on to better material.

Does it work? I doubt it. Early Christians, seeking to convert the heathens, incorporated non-Christian rituals, symbols, and even dates into some of their holidays (holy days) in an attempt to make conversion more palatable. Celebration of the springtime birth of Jesus was moved to more-nearly coincide with the winter solstice. Painted eggs, chicks, and baby rabbits -- once parts of pre-Christian fertility rites -- are now popular parts of the Easter observance of many Christians. Who was converted -- the pagans or the Christians?

Meaningless trivia on a movie or TV screen is not likely to become more meaningful or less trivial in a book. Why yield to the uneducated choices of the lowest common denominator? Are the antics of television soap operas and cartoons and sitcoms really more exciting and more meaningful than the writings of Dickens, London, Stevenson, Poe, Pyle, even Shakespeare? Granted that millions of high school students are still struggling with a third-grade reading ability; they have been deprived, by an incompetent school system, of the pleasures of reading.

The concerned teacher can read to them, helping them to feel the magic of words in books such as A TALE OF TWO CITIES, THE THREE MUSKETEERS, LOST HORIZON, and SHANE. Such books read, not for instruction, but for the mutual enjoyment of both teacher and students, and without tests afterward for comprehension and retention, might in time overshadow the TV tie-ins. Maybe not; maybe it's too late. But if the students can be helped to realize that the pleasure is worth the effort -- that is, once they want to read -- they will do so, just as much younger children can begin reading B-A-B-Y.

When I have taught adult illiterates, this approach has been successful in every case, as the basis for both reading and writing.

If the students will ever be led to better reading, it will be through the introduction of better literature; certainly not through low-vocabulary books about dirt bikes, teen romance, and the selfish cynicism of Garfield.

Teachers say, "My students will never be interested in the great authors, but at least they're reading. It's better to read about television characters than to read nothing at all."

Is it?

Is it better to write verses in restrooms than to write nothing at all? Is it better to listen to punk rock and thrash metal than to hear no music at all?

Whether the book is by an ancient great or a modern unknown, if it doesn't make at least a small positive contribution to the reader's life -- his values, his knowledge, his understanding, his growth as a human being, enjoyment of life -- then it's not worth the time of reading. As an avid reader, I feel that illiteracy is a very sad handicap; but the cynicism, narcissism, and hedonism promoted by most television shows and their literary tie-ins, as well as a huge portion of other popular publications, are much greater handicaps.

It's hard for me to imagine my own life without books, but I know many people who don't read, yet are happy and successful -- good neighbors, caring parents, and hard workers. Why should they clutter up their lives with books about puerile, melodramatic electronic images?

Just as Gandhi, probably the world's greatest proponent and practitioner of non-violence, said that violence is preferable to cowardice, I am sure that illiteracy is preferable to the exclusive reading of debasing or condescending trivia.

WRITING

I think we taught our kids a little more about how to write than we did about how to read. Their writing, like their reading, seemed to grow by itself, with only a little help from us. We showed them how to make letters, what sounds the letters represent, and so on. In the beginning, we tried to follow standard school books, but we soon found that most of them followed logical sequences as much as the beginning readers did. Very little, that is.

Although a few school books are fairly good, we were soon much happier with the various activity books sometimes sold in toy departments, drug stores, and grocery stores. These books include dot-to-dot pictures (which, besides being fun, teach number recognition and sequence), math and reading readiness, writing preparation, colors, shapes, sizes, and so on. Many are very good primers in natural science. Perhaps because these books are prepared and designed to appeal to parents rather than to school boards, they are often more attractive and interesting than school books. Future sales are largely dependent on the purchasers' satisfaction, so the books are both educational, which pleases the parents, and fun, which pleases the children.

We put printed alphabet cards on the kitchen wall, where they could easily be seen and copied. We showed the kids how to print their names -- always the first thing a child wants to be able to write -- and their favorite words, names of friends and relatives and pets, and two more favorite words: YES and NO. Besides pencil or crayons and paper, we used a wall-mounted chalkboard, magnetic letters on the refrigerator, and individual letters printed on cardboard. The kids sometimes spent hours printing letters, words, names, and eventually short sentences. Jean and I printed short messages to them on the chalkboard, and the kids printed answers. We arranged the magnetic letters into words; the kids rearranged them into different words.

We agree wholeheartedly with John Holt's recommendation, in HOW CHILDREN LEARN, that very young children be given access to a typewriter. As John points out, the kids will be fascinated by the machine's inner workings; they'll also want to learn correct spelling, capitalization, and punctuation -- perhaps because typewritten material looks so official, so permanent, and so real. Just touch a key and see how many different things move, and the letter you want is printed right beside the previous letter. A good, reconditioned, used typewriter can usually be gotten for fifty dollars or less at an office supply store. Yard and garage sales frequently have very good typewriters for $10 to $25. Most typewriters sold in toy departments, Christmas catalogs, and even by some educational suppliers, although they look solid enough and sell for as much as $150, aren't worth shelf space. They are too flimsy for the rough handling a child will sometimes give them; the parts, including the ribbons, are often a special size or brand which you can't find anywhere; and, if there happens to be a breakdown or defect covered by the very limited warranty, the only "authorized service center" is ten thousand miles away and receives mail only by Camel Express.

Crossword puzzles for children, found in book and toy stores, increase spelling and vocabulary. The girls enjoyed them; Derek didn't.

The best preparation for writing is reading, anything and everything. The child (or adult) who gets little pleasure from reading will seldom see much purpose in writing.

When Derek was nine, he began reading the Tarzan novels, by Edgar Rice Burroughs. The first of these books was written in 1929, and Burroughs' style is very formal and often pedantic, as was the style of most writers in those days; the sentences are occasionally ponderous, with several subordinate clauses. The vocabulary is sometimes just as imposing: a friendly ape may be referred to as an amiable anthropoid. Try getting all that into the local school's curriculum! I read all of the Tarzan books (more than twenty) several times when I was a kid, and I still read them occasionally, so I knew Derek was starting out in pretty deep water. He asked help with a few words, but soon figured most of them out from their context, and was soon sailing smoothly. Within two years, he had read all the books at least once, and some of them many times.

When he was ten, Derek started writing his own stories of Tarzan and his son Korak, with enthusiastic and bloodthirsty imitation of Burroughs' own style--

KORAK, MAN OR BEAST?
by Derek Reed

He swung silently through the lower branches of the trees. He stopped now and again to sniff the air. Now he stopped, thirty feet off the ground, for he was hunting, a beast among beasts, for this is Korak, son of Tarzan, and he is in Africa, the Dark Continent. You're probably wondering what he is hunting. Well, no matter, for you shall find out. For now, he swings into a natural clearing and sees what he has been tracking for

about half an hour, but he does not know this. For he carries no watch, he just knows that he is terribly hungry and he is but a scarce eight feet from Bara the deer. He but broke upon the clearing when he launched himself full upon the buck's back. He fastened his teeth in Bara's neck and sunk his knife into his heart. Bara gave a little quiver and lay still. At that moment a wounded lion came upon them. He headed straight for Korak. Korak leaped high in the air, turned around in mid-air and came down upon the lion's back.

One bronze arm encircled the throat, while the two legs locked under the belly. The free arm drew the knife and drove it home into that savage heart. Again, he drives the knife home. Three times he drives it home. He feels the giant muscles relax. The body quivers and lays still. Korak leaps up, places his foot on the lion's neck and screams forth the victory cry of the bull ape twice. Once for Bara and once for Numa. He went back to Bara and cut a hole in his neck, this is so he will bleed and not be so messy. As he cuts a juicy steak, he finds himself wondering about his friends and if they could see him now naked except for a G-string. "I am a man" thought Korak, "but I act like a beast." And then he took his kill to a tree and finding a comfortable place, fell asleep.

THE END

Derek usually disliked assigned writing topics, but seemed to be developing adequate writing skills without them, so we gave him very few. A thank-you note for a birthday or Christmas gift might take several weeks, unless we just lay down the law. But if he's writing about a subject which interests him personally and deeply -- horses, sharks, Tarzan -- he can fill pages in a very short time.

Cathy, Karen, and Susan have always enjoyed writing long, newsy letters to friends and relatives. When asked, we have helped them edit their spelling and punctuation. When Cathy was elected club reporter for her 4-H club, it was her job to write about club activities for a regional 4-H newsletter and for two local newspapers. Two years later, Karen received the job of 4-H club reporter. Having their articles in print, with their own bylines, was rewarding, and gave them incentive for steady improvement. Both girls developed an easy writing fluency, and wrote several papers for us on research subjects such as existentialism, William Penn, and a comparison of Leonardo da Vinci and Buckminster Fuller.

When Susan was eight, we let her attend a public school for the entire year, mostly because she enjoyed the social life so much. Her teacher

was a screaming bully, and we saw several potential problems, but Susan never complained about the teacher, and we somehow convinced ourselves that any harm being done was superficial, and could be corrected easily. Early in the year, Susan lost all interest in reading to herself. When reading aloud, which she had been able to do smoothly and competently, she stuttered, coughed, covered her mouth, mumbled, mispronounced simple words, juxtaposed words, and missed words completely. Her spelling became so literally phonetic that it was almost incomprehensible: "Th tcher sed tak ot yr boke. i opnd it and b gen tu red." Her spelling hadn't been that bad since she was five. But she still seemed happy in school and did well in most other subjects. Her reading problems, we told ourselves, were superficial, and we could straighten them out next year.

We were very wrong. It took us years to correct the damage, to rebuild the reading and writing skills which that third grade teacher had nearly destroyed in just a few months. Although Susan now reads avidly, for both pleasure and information, and can write and spell quite well, I'm sure that neither her reading nor her writing is as good as it would be if we had had the sense and courage to take her out of school when we saw the problems beginning. Susan's self-confidence took much longer to rebuild. "I can't do it, I just know I can't," was her standard response to any suggestion of writing. We continued to encourage her.

In April 1983, Highlights for Children Magazine printed a prose-poem Susan had submitted a year earlier, when she was eleven:

"The Beauty of a Tree

"Can anyone see the beauty of a tree? The colors of light and dark in the summer? The leaves falling in the fall? What about the icicles hanging from the trees in the winter? Or the buds starting to grow in the spring? Some people may think a tree is just a thing to be used for firewood and building things, but it's not. A tree should be cared for, for just a square inch cut from the bark could end its life. What is the beauty of a tree? The beauty of a tree is life itself."

Her self-confidence leaped. Later that spring, she entered a 4-H club essay-writing contest, and in July 1983 two local papers, The Woodstock Bugle and The Hartland Observer, carried this story:

"Knowlesville Girl
Wins Kings Landing Trip

"Susan Reed of Knowlesville is one of two winners in a province-wide 4-H Essay Contest, writing on the topic 'Why I Would Like to Live at Kings Landing.' Her prize: five days as a 'Visiting Cousin' at Kings Landing.

"Each year, 4-H Club members of New Brunswick are invited to submit essays about why they would like to live at Kings Landing. Only two entries are selected as winners -- one in French, and one in English. The winners are each awarded five days as a Visiting Cousin at Kings Landing Historical Settlement, with all expenses paid.

"Susan, twelve years old, is a member of the Glassville Co-Eds 4-H Club. She and her brother and two sisters attend school at home, taught by their parents.

"'I'm very excited about the trip,' Susan says. 'It will be like going in a time machine to the past.'

"This will be the second time Susan's writing has gained public recognition. In April, 'Highlights for Children' Magazine published a poem Susan had submitted last fall.

"Susan will begin her visit at Kings Landing July 12, and return home July 16 -- her 13th birthday."

"That's quite a plug for home-schooling," some friends told us.

Yes, we agreed, it was. But it was also much more. They would never know what a long, tedious, often frustrating journey it had been for Susan, and for Jean and me. They wouldn't know our fears and feelings of guilt about Susan's year in third grade; fears that were finally erased by Susan's achievement.

In September of that year, Susan wrote about her trip for our family newsletter:

"My trip back in time began at the Education Building, where I was fitted in a costume of 1840 and learned a little about the program I would take part in through the next week. I was assigned to the Killeen House, a square log cabin of an Irish immigrant. Besides cooking, eating, and other activities in 'my own' home, I spent time in several other homes and buildings, learn-

ing to make soap, candles, noodles, straw hats, crackers, and butter (which I already knew). I visited the blacksmith shop, spun flax, hooked a rug, learned about furniture making, and went to a quilting bee. Each day, I went to school with the other Visiting Cousins; at recess time, we played games of the 1840's. On Friday, I baked a crumb cake in the coals of the fireplace (we didn't have a stove for cooking), and on Saturday my cake and many others were served to the parents of the Visiting Cousins.

"I had a wonderful time and made many new friends."

Yes, it was definitely a plug for homeschooling. But, far more importantly, it was a plug for Susan, who had worked harder to reach that point than anyone outside our family would ever know.

It was also a strong lesson for us, although not a new one. It reinforced our conviction that children's learning should not be pushed. It can be encouraged, and should be, but always with care and patience and understanding.

It took me fifteen years to discover that I had no talent for writing, but I couldn't give it up because by that time I was too famous.
Robert Benchley

Writing is easy. All you do is stare at a blank sheet of paper until drops of blood form on your forehead.

Gene Fowler

For the things we have to learn before we can do them, we learn by doing them.
Aristotle

My desire is... that mine adversary had written a book.

Book of Job

ABCDEFGHIJKLMNOPQRSTUVWXYZ

SPELLING

"I before E, except after C, or when sounded as A, as in neighbor and weigh."

"Silent E on the end of a word makes the preceding vowel long."

"A single vowel before a double consonant is short."

Rules such as these seem to be of some help to beginning spellers and readers, and sometimes we have tacked them up somewhere in the house. We never teach such rules, however, without a reminder that there are often exceptions to them.

The first, for instance, has at least one weird exception. The second rule makes me cringe. The third rule is another form of grossness.

Try the word, we say, applying the rule; if it doesn't seem to work, then try the reverse of the rule. "When adding 'ing' to a verb that ends in 'e,' drop the 'e.' Oddly enough, that rule works for 'cringe,' but not for 'singe.' "Oddly enough" is a phrase that helps the kids accept the idiosyncrasies of English. An attempt to learn spelling only by the rules will result in constant perplexity and frustration.

"That's the exception that proves the rule," some of my teachers used to say. I wondered where they had dug up such an illogical saying, and why they thought it meant anything. Years later, looking at reproductions of old English printing,

I realized that some medieval monk must have forgotten his glasses when he was copying a manuscript. In some calligraphic lettering styles, the 'b' still resembles a 'v.' The exception that <u>probes</u> the rule, not <u>proves</u> it.

What makes a good speller? Why can some people spell correctly so easily, while others are forever turning to the dictionary (or should be)? I asked Jean. She is well-educated, and has an above-average intelligence, but before she mails a letter to a friend or relative, she has me look it over for spelling mistakes. There won't be many, but it's seldom that I don't find at least one. Her weekly shopping lists usually have at least one word misspelled, often one which is consistently misspelled week after week. She doesn't know why, nor do I. (I love her anyway.)

When I was in school, I usually got A+ for my spelling, and I almost always won school-wide spelling bees. Why?

I used to think that the ability to spell was nurtured most by reading, but Jean reads as much as I do.

I have a theory, which you're welcome to take or leave: I think that good spellers have, to some degree, photographic memories. Not to the extent that they could Amaze Their Friends With Astounding Feats of Memory Magic; not the kind, which a gifted few actually have, which enables them to read, from memory, a page which has been briefly scanned. In most things, I have as much and as little difficulty in remembering as most people have -- names, dates, numbers, lists, and so on. But, when I'm in doubt about the spelling of a word, I close my eyes and try to visualize it; the word, usually printed, seems to float inside my eyelids. Have I called it up from a forgotten memory? If I can't visualize it that way, I write down several possible spellings; one will just "look right" to me, and it's almost always the correct one. Neither method is infallible, but usually one or the other works for me. Both methods work for Jean, too, but not as often.

I think it's related to sight-reading. The sooner a person learns to read whole syllables and words instead of "sounding out" the words letter-by-letter, the better his spelling will be. Maybe. That's my theory.

We used to have the kids study lists of words, and then we tested them, just as the public schools do. The older the kids were, and the more reading they had done, the easier the spelling was. We discarded that approach, and then discarded all approaches. It made no difference in the kids' spelling abilities. When they wrote letters or essays, they sometimes asked us how to spell a word. If the word was short, we spelled it for them; if it was long, or didn't follow a neat rule, we wrote it down for them. Sometimes we'd suggest they look in the dictionary, but this was usually such an interruption of their train of thought that we didn't do it often. We didn't want to discourage their trying unfamiliar words by making the words a tedious chore. As they got older, they consulted the dictionary more often without our suggestion. If there was a catchy rule that might help them remember the word in the future, we'd give it to them. ("Write" ends with "e"; the paper we write on is stationery.)

If the word had interesting homonyms, derivations, or second cousins, we often mentioned them, either at the time or later in general discussion. We helped the kids break words down, pull the wings off, tickle them, play with them. This builds vocabulary, spelling, perspective, and humor. Puns are excellent learning aids. (Is Sirius the only star that doesn't tell any jokes? Is that because dogs can't laugh?)

Reading, writing, and spelling (and even talking) are so closely related that trying to separate them is impractical and nearly impossible.

Another device we all enjoy is Tom Swifties. Remember them? They were a small fad in the 50's and 60's, parodies of the writing style of the Tom Swift series of boys' books popular in the 20's and 30's -- TOM SWIFT AND HIS ELECTRIC SUBMARINE, etc.

"I like camping in the rain," he said intently.

"I won't eat ham," he said pigheadedly.

"I won't be there," he said absently.

"I can't find the light," he said darkly.

"There's a hole in the tire," he said flatly.

It may take the kids a while to catch on to the kind of pun involved. The adverb must be related to the statement and it must be appropriate to the implied situation, and it must be a pun. The basic statement can be almost anything; the punch is in the adverb.

I was writing about spelling, and got sidetracked on to reading, writing, parts of speech, and vocabulary. Or is it a side-track?

"Does that make you feel like a dunce?" Jean asked pointedly.

"It's my typewriter's fault," I said mechanically.

"What are you driving at?" she asked automatically.

"It's gone with the wind," I answered rhetorically.

As you probably know, the worse a pun is (like my last one), the better it is; the proper response is a groan -- unless you can top the pun with a better (worse) one. Once you get the hang of them, Tom Swifties are sort of like peanuts: you don't want to stop with just one.

* See my **P.S.** at the end of this chapter for more about "Tom Swifties."

A man who could make so vile a pun would not scruple to pick a pocket.
—— John Dennis ——

2+2=4 / CAT ☼ TEACHER \ ↑↓ ▱

Back to spelling. Like all other learning, it can't be forced, but I have no doubt that a lot of reading will help it grow. Positive reinforcement definitely helps. When we're asked for the spelling of a word, we don't say, "Try to sound it out," unless the word really is phonetic and we think it can be sounded out easily. If we're not sure, either, we admit it freely, and get the dictionary.

When we spell a polysyllabic word for the kids, we do it by syllables -- sometimes repeating each syllable as we go, then spelling it, then saying the whole word and spelling it all at once. Sometimes we ask to have the word spelled back to us -- but only after the child has written it down. This helps to set the visual image. I think.

Trying to sound out a word which isn't fully phonetic results only in confusion, frustration, and random guessing, all of which can only reinforce incorrect spelling and lack of confidence.

Can you sound out GHOTI?

It's "fish," of course. GH as in "tough," O as in "women," and TI as in "nation."

Probably there are some spelling books that will help, but if one doesn't read a lot and

write a lot, memorization of rules won't do much good.

Here is a letter I received several years ago:

"Der Don rede how ar you gud I hop. I am fin to. I hop I gettig ot frum thagt insttushn sun nd yu to. I m lrng rdng nd rtng pred gud. thank yu fr techng me to red nd rte. yur frend, ------ -------."

The writer was twenty-two years old, serving three years in a federal prison for interstate car theft. When he joined my class for adult illiterates, six weeks before he wrote me that letter, he didn't know how to write his name.

I think he was lrng pred gud.

Of making many books there is no end; and much study is a weariness of the flesh.

Ecclesiastes

A child educated only at school is an uneducated child.

George Santayana

P.S. More about "Tom Swifties"
and a few other miscellaneous notes
of equal importance

In the spring of 1992, Teri Palazzolo, a customer and occasional correspondent in Italy, sent me a photocopied entry form for an international "adverb contest" from Practical English Teaching, a British teachers' magazine. Teri said she was going to enter and hoped to win an unabridged LONGMAN DICTIONARY OF THE ENGLISH LANGUAGE, which was offered for both the first and second prizes. The "adverb contest" consisted of what we have always called "Tom Swifties," so I revised one of my earlier favorites -- "'Has he gone with the wind?' Scarlett asked rhetorically'" -- and mailed it off to England. The following November, long after I'd forgotten the contest, I received a letter of congratulations and a large, heavy package -- second prize, an unabridged Longman dictionary, sent by Air Mail (which cost 18 pounds sterling, or about $40.00). Naturally, the dictionary had British spellings and usages -- kerb instead of curb, truck meaning barter, and so on (not to mention being on queer street, which in the Mother Country means being financially embarrassed) -- so it wasn't of much real worth to me. Since Teri had sent me the entry form which had given me this brief moment of fame, I wrote to her, offering to give the dictionary to her if she would pay the postage (only $6 by surface mail). She accepted, and wrote me that she had been a runner-up in the Adverb Competition. How's that for irony and poetic (in)justice?

I don't subscribe to Practical English Teaching, and Teri hasn't sent me any more entry forms, but I'm preparing for the next contest by building my stock of Tom Swifties, usually in the middle of the night when Gus wakes me up to let him out. Rather than return to bed and be almost asleep when he woofs to come back in, I exercise my mind while I wait for him. As you probably know, some of one's greatest thoughts may come when one isn't quite awake. So far, Gus's untimely excursions have helped me produce the following:

"I can't think of the letter that comes after U," the boy said vehemently.

"Thanks for loaning me your pickup, Joe," he said truculently.

"I finally went to an exorcist for help," he said dispiritedly.

"That Kelly girl was delicious," the cannibal said gracefully.

"Oy, I don't think this food is kosher," the rabbi said judiciously.

"If I were a man, I wouldn't be a queen," Elizabeth said achingly.

"I'll show you the evidence again," the lawyer said reprovingly.

"I have to go home before sunrise," Dracula said cryptically.

THE QUESTION IS, WHICH HALF?

An official in the Department of Education told me one day that a certain school district was retiring 1.3 teachers. Another district would have no change in staff, but was hiring two new teachers. In another district, there would be 3.5 new teachers.

I scratched my head and murmured, "Pardon me?"

He said it all again, which didn't help, and I tried to visualize 3.5 teachers coming to work in the morning, but that didn't help, either.

It reminded me of the stage magician who asked another magician, "Who was that lady I sawed with you last night?"

"Oh, that was no lady," the second magician replied. "That was my half-sister."

I asked the official if he meant an average of 3.5 teachers. Say, two in one district and five in another. The average would be...

"No," he said, "not an average." He spoke slowly, to help me understand. "Three point five teachers."

In plain English, spelled out, that's three and a half teachers. Isn't it?

I'm still working on it. Just give me a little more time.

GENERALLY SPEAKING--

Exciting news from Newsweek: "There's a new way to get children buzzing at the very thought of reading. Tune in to **Mrs. Bush's Story Time** on the ABC Radio Networks. You'll hear favorite children's stories, with special guests including Bugs Bunny, Big Bird, and Norman Schwarzkopf."

And more exciting news from a Music Club flyer: "General H. Norman Schwarzkopf and conductor Leonard Slatkin team up for a stirring performance of Copland's Lincoln Portrait."

Everyone else my age is an adult, whereas I am merely in disguise.

--Margaret Atwood

Without education, we are in a horrible and deadly danger of taking educated people seriously.

--G. K. Chesterton

NEW TRANSLATOR WANTED

Received in the mail, for $3.99:
ELECTRONIC MOSQUITO REPELLER
*Use special frequency and waveform
to repell the mostquito away
*No harm to human beings and pets
*Simple and, safe operation
*Only one UM-3 battery
*Effective distance: about 4 meters
Experiments Report
Mosquitos frequently infect you place in Summer, especially at night, They are extemely irritating as they disturbed our sleep and the most annoying of all is the difficulty in getting rid of the itch & soreness. After, ordinary mosquito increase or "Electrified Mosquito Killer" are used. However, the odour is unbearable and the abuse of some of them may become dangerous. In order to do away with the above nuisance, "Electronic Mosquito Repeller" has now been produced. According to the research of insect ecology, most of biting mosquitos are female ones in spawning period. A Spawning female mosquito is very disgusted at the approaching of male mosquito. Therefore, the frequency of Repel-It' is made to imitate the sound signal of male mosquitos to repell female mosquitos away.
MADE IN HONG KONG

MATHEMATICS

When I was a high school junior, in Brattleboro, Vermont, I wanted to take a course in auto mechanics.

"You can't," the guidance director told me. "That isn't part of the college prep course."

"But I don't plan to go to college," I said. "I plan to travel and work and study."

He chuckled. We argued. The guidance director had the final word, of course: "Your IQ and your aptitude tests indicate that you belong in the college prep program. I'm sure you'll come to your senses about college when the time comes."

Although I think college is fine for those who want or need it, I didn't change my mind. I traveled and I worked, and I have never attended college (except a brief summer workshop at the University of Denver). When another institution asked for my high school transcript, the same guidance director wrote in the margin, "Too much a noncomformist to ever be happy." The split infinitive was his. I concluded that he knew as much about English as I knew about auto mechanics. The difference was that he was employed as an English teacher as well as a guidance director, and I have never been employed as an auto mechanic. I can change a tire, but I didn't learn how to in high school.

I did learn in school that a quadrilateral is a parallelogram if the diagonals bisect each other. I also learned how to find FH and DF if AB, CD, EF, and GH are parallel and AC and CE and EG and BD each equal 3. I've read that everything we ever learn or experience is tucked away somewhere in a dusty corner of the mind, and I don't doubt it, but you may be surprised to learn that since I graduated from high school I have had neither reason nor desire to find FH and DF. Most of the quadrilaterals I've encountered since then have been school officials, and their purposes are usually perpendicular to mine.

So much for at least half of the math I learned in twelve years of schooling. Hypnosis might revive my memory of it, just as it could help me remember the first time I fell off a bike, but I'm content to leave both memories buried in cobwebs.

If you like math, or expect to have a good use for it, then study it. We all use math in our daily lives, directly and personally; without it, our lives would be very different and probably difficult. We need math to bake a cake, plan a shopping list, or balance a checkbook. Jean and the kids and I built our own house, doing all the work ourselves, and we did a lot of measuring and calculating, both in building the house and in

I planted a tree that was 8 inches tall. At the end of the first year it was 12 inches tall; at the end of the second year it was 18 inches tall; and at the end of the third year it was 27 inches tall. How tall was it at the end of the fourth year?

buying materials for it.

Most of the math we used, however, and most of that which I use daily, is no more advanced than simple long division, which is usually mastered in the fifth grade. I use a little plane geometry and, occasionally, some very elementary solid geometry (how big a hay loft do I need to hold three tons of hay?).

If I were suddenly confronted with a need to find FH and DF, I'm sure I could learn quickly how to do so, even if I had never once learned it. The desire to learn is the greatest incentive.

Most school students, if asked why they study math (or most other subjects), will answer, "It's required" or "So I can pass the exams." Neither reason is enough. Over a twelve-year period, first grade through high school, most students will spend an hour a day, including homework, for about two hundred days of the year, trying to learn various forms of arithmetic and mathematics. That's 2,400 hours out of a lifetime. (See how easily I figured that out?) Will the information studied be used half that many hours after school? It's not a bad exchange if the information and skills are of real interest or use. Some people enjoy math, just as others enjoy word puzzles; others may not enjoy it, but know or expect that it will be of practical use to them in a chosen career, such as chemistry, astronomy, or architecture. I have no argument against studying advanced math for those who like it or need it; but to spend a hundred 24-hour days studying something only to pass a series of tests is a ridiculous waste of time and energy.

A common argument in favor of math, with or without practical application, is that "it develops skills of reasoning" -- that is, a logical approach to problem solving. That's undoubtedly true, but is it the only exercise -- or even the best -- which develops reasoning? Mathematicians have no monopoly on the ability to perceive, consider, compare, evaluate, extrapolate, hypothesize, and reach conclusions. These processes are frequently related to math, but never limited to it.

Author Henry Miller once wrote, "Anyone can write; a writer can't do anything else." The same might be said of math and mathematicians. For those of us who need and use math only occasionally, just a few basics are necessary. If I need to calculate the stress of a certain weight on a ten-foot 2"x4", I can easily find the appropriate formula, or even a chart or graph with the answer already given. An understanding of elementary mathematics is very desirable, perhaps necessary, in daily life; but tedious memorization of principles and facts which I'll probably never use, and in which I have no interest, is neither reasonable nor logical.

For many years, we tried several standard math textbooks, at all grade levels, and found partial satisfaction only after two of our children had grown up and left home. Most math books seem to have been written by people who know a great deal about mathematics but very little about children or about the learning process. Before we found the few existing books which make math enjoyable, understandable, and useful, we tortured our kids and ourselves with the same textbooks used in the public schools. Like most parents (and teachers), we believed that math was a necessary evil; that, no matter how unpleasant it might be, it must be mastered -- "because someday you'll need it." The standard textbooks -- being unpleasant, illogical, and monotonous -- reinforced that belief.

For more years than I want to admit, we didn't stop to realize that the only use Jean and I had for most of the math we had learned in school was to try to teach it to our kids. In the normal scheme of things, they would someday pass it on to their own kids, and so on. The sins of the fathers are visited upon the children.

I don't know why it took us so much longer to break away from conventional study of math than from most other forms of conventional study. Like many other home-schoolers, we believed the public system was wrong or inadequate, but we lacked enough confidence in ourselves to reject it; we were afraid that if our kids didn't measure up to the standards of the public schools, they would be at a disadvantage in later life. Gradually, we realized that just the opposite is true. By adhering to public school standards (not only in math), we were holding our kids back. We directed so much of their energy into the study of ordinary math -- "to develop skills of reasoning" -- that real reasoning skills were being stunted or warped.

"Laziness in doing a stupid thing," said the High Lama of Shangri-La in James Hilton's LOST HORIZON, "can be a virtue."

Sometimes, the study of math became so frustrating and unpleasant, for all of us, that we just dropped it for a few days, or even weeks, and spent the time with other studies. We noticed that the kids were still using math frequently -- in cooking, drawing spaceships, feeding the hens and cow, making dresses, calculating their babysitting earnings, or buying material for a new blouse. We stopped worrying.

Still, we thought, the basics of the math they were using had been learned very painfully, by being beaten over the head daily with standard textbooks. There must be a better way. Once we were open to better approaches, we found several -- the best of which is the use of tools and materials of ordinary daily life.

The first step to a better approach was a change of attitude. We had to realize that a child's age has no bearing on the level or degree of math (or reading, or writing) which he can or should master. If it doesn't come easily, there is no need to push and no need to worry; it will come sometime.

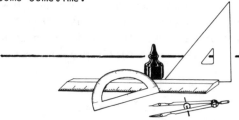

At age nine, Derek was bored and angered by his fourth grade arithmetic book. We gave him a math kit -- protractor, compass, ruler -- and turned him loose with a high school plane geometry book. He asked a few questions and we helped him sort out a few beginning principles. He drew spaceships, inside and out, with wonderful complexity and precision. Although he continued to bristle at the thought of the fourth grade math, he could measure angles, bisect lines, and correctly construct complex geometric designs. He could also read and follow a cooking recipe, measure the pigs' grain, and draw accurate plans of his room. We didn't push him, and we didn't worry. We knew that Derek might not go back to simple multiplication and division for many years, or he might return to them a week later. When he felt a need of them, he would study them, and learning them would be like learning to fry an egg after mastering soufflé. It was a number of years before he went back to the "beginning" and filled in the missing gaps. What was lost?

Suppose walking or talking were taught in the same way math and reading are usually taught:

"Dear Parent, Your son/daughter is not achieving the level of Walking Competency which is expected for his/her age. He/she is now 13.8 months old and should have completed Level 7.9, but still crawls on level 5.4. I am sorry to report that he/she may be Walking Disabled. I will place him/her in the Bluebird Section for Slow Walkers, but I think he/she may need Special Assistance. Sincerely, His/Her Teacher."

Children begin counting very early. They like to count -- fingers, toes, cars, leaves, spoons, stones, steps, anything. By the age of three or four, most children will have gained several mathematical skills, and will enjoy using them. By the age of six, if they go to public schools, or if they are pushed too much at home, they will have lost much of their skill and all of their interest.

At 16, Cathy was taking a high school correspondence course, besides working with our own materials. She worked at her own speed, sending completed lessons for grading. When she began algebra, it was clear sailing at first, but less than halfway through the course, it became increasingly difficult. Dad to the rescue! -- Confident that he could recall enough from years ago to smooth out the wrinkles. Looking through her textbook, I quickly realized that this was an entirely different animal from the one I had struggled with for two years before moving on to struggle for another two years with plane and solid geometry. I passed all four courses, and that was back in the days when students didn't pass unless they actually earned passing grades, but it was more through the patience and hard work of my teachers than through any great understanding on my part. Cathy's dislike of math was not acquired; it was in my genes, and she inherited it from me. (I studied biology, too!) It didn't help me that her book was titled MODERN ALGEBRA. What was wrong with the old algebra? I put myself through a quick refresher course, from the beginning, skimming and sorting until I felt I could handle it -- with a lot of luck. Cathy and I worked together on the lessons and problems. It was still very difficult, for both of us. We weren't enjoying it, and were doing it only because it was a required subject in the college prep course. Cathy and I were both frustrated and bored by this modern algebra. One of the simpler problems ran something like this:

$$\frac{3a^3b^2 + 15a^3b^2}{2ab^2} + \frac{4a^6b^3 - 10a^6b^3}{2a^4b^3} = ?$$

I'm sure it's easy for some, and I'm even willing to admit that some people might enjoy playing with it. I'd rather split wood or shovel manure. If Cathy or we could anticipate any need for such math in her future, we would have continued struggling with it, but we knew she was very unlikely to pursue a career or way of life requiring the use of a subject which was so distasteful to her. Why waste so much time and energy? The only reason seemed to be that it was required as part of the college prep course; it was required because many colleges required it; and many colleges required it because they had always required it; or just because, that's why.

Math stretches the brain and gives you new reasoning skills. With the new reasoning skills I gained from this course, I came up with a brilliant solution: ask the school to change Cathy's course from College Prep to General High School. It was done, and with no arguments from the guidance director. In place of algebra, to obtain the necessary credits, Cathy chose general math, more of the physical and social sciences, and more literature. She enjoyed them all. We both kept our sanity. It was an excellent exchange.

My mathematical aptitudes and attitudes embarrass me a little (but not very much). I think it's obvious that the universe and nearly all things in it (the exceptions include most math books) are constructed and governed by very precise principles, all of which can be or someday will be expressed in mathematical terms -- which is, perhaps, a step toward understanding. However, I think it is just as true that mathematics is only one of many ways to view and understand the universe. A poet or a mystic may understand

I think Dad just made an administrative decision about my algebra book.

HALF OF $1.99 IS... WELL, $1.99 DIVIDED BY 12 IS... NO, WAIT A MINUTE...

99

as much as a mathematician; the biggest difference may be that it's easier for the mathematician to communicate what he has learned -- but with the significant drawback that only other mathematicians can understand what he's saying.

There are a few fortunate exceptions.

Stephen Hawking, perhaps the most brilliant physicist and mathematician in the world's history, insists that even the most profound discoveries and theories about the universe can be expressed in non-mathematical terms. His book, A BRIEF HISTORY OF TIME (see Science) seems to be evidence of this.

We have found several basic arithmetic and math books which not only develop necessary skills and knowledge, but which are actually fun to read and use, thus removing most of the drudgery. Unfortunately, a few things -- e.g., basic multiplication tables, and deciding which procedures to use in solving word problems -- may still need to be learned through boring repetition, but once they are learned, most of the rest will be clear and easy sailing, at least for all that's really necessary. Approaching math through a side door, THE I HATE MATHEMATICS! BOOK and MATH FOR SMARTY PANTS fool you into thinking math is fun, ha ha.

There are numerous toys, games, and puzzles to help learn most levels of math without too much pain, and many of them really are fun.

Fun or not, math seems to be here to stay. Waiting patiently while the cashier tries to figure the cost of half a dozen doughnuts if the price of a dozen is $1.99 has led me to realize that a little math won't hurt anyone, so we have come full circle to the point of telling our kids that they have to learn some of it whether it hurts or not. The important thing is to know when to stop. Let's consider carefully before we spend too much of our time or our children's time trying to learn facts and gain skills which will probably have little or no use in life. If the study is easy, fun, or has a probable use, then carry on. If running headfirst into a brick wall would be more fun, force yourselves through SURVIVAL MATHEMATICS (below), then go for a walk or read a book or shovel manure.

SAXON MATH -- John Saxon's now-famous math books may be the only ones making full use of an "incremental" approach to learning -- the introduction of topics in bits and pieces, which permits complete assimilation of one facet of a concept before the next is introduced, along with continuous review of all material learned previously.

An article in Newsweek (3/1/93) said that over 2.3 million of Saxon's math books have been sold. Saxon claims that his method produces better results, faster, than any other. Many other educators insist that this claim can't be substantiated, and only twelve states recommend one or more of his books to the schools in their districts.

We first learned of "the Saxon method" in 1985 from an article in Reader's Digest. We bought a copy of ALGEBRA 1/2, tried it, and were very favorably impressed. Since then, we have also used Saxon's MATH 76 and ALGEBRA I, with fairly remarkable results. Two of our four children, who had seemed to have almost no mathematical aptitudes, gained a basic understanding (and even a little interest) in a very short time. On the other hand, the only "advanced" math studied by our daughter Karen, the only one of our children ever to be officially tested, was in an out-dated, out-of-print copy of HIGH SCHOOL SUBJECTS SELF TAUGHT, and a year later she scored very high in the national SSAT (and was accepted by a college with no high school diploma and no other "official" credentials).

We have watched the evolution of the Saxon books since 1985. In 1986, the student editions had answers in the back to only half the problems, so we recommended (and used) the teacher's editions, which had answers in the back to all the problems. (Cheating, in a home-school setting, seemed unlikely; besides, the problems still had to be worked out to arrive at an answer, so copying wouldn't do any good even if it were done.) Separate tests and answers were available, but we didn't recommend or sell them, because we felt progress (or lack of it) would be self-evident in a home-school situation.

More books in the series were published, and the publishers began printing the teacher editions with the answers to all the problems, in red, beside the problems, rather than in the back of the books, thus making the books completely useless by themselves to home-schoolers, who then had to buy both the student and teacher editions. Of course, two books cost twice as much as one, which didn't hurt Saxon Publishers. By then, the publishers were targeting home-schools as well as public schools, but home-schoolers said that two books cost too much.

Saxon Publishers offered a compromise: "Homeschool Kits," comprised of the student edition, an answer key, and a test booklet, with a price about halfway between two books.

In 1986, the ALGEBRA 1/2 textbook cost $20.45.

Today, eight years later, the textbook has been replaced by a homeschool kit which costs $42.00 (maybe more when you read this). We expect prices to increase from year to year, but I don't know of any other books which have more than doubled in cost in that period. You can get the student edition alone for $36, but it has answers to only half the problems. The answer key and tests, in a separate booklet, cost $16.50.

With Saxon's books, as with soap and cars, every time a new, improved version is announced, the cost goes up and the quality seems to go down.

Fundamentalist home-schoolers complained to Saxon about his playful allusions to mythical beasts, pagan gods, and other "Satanic" images in his word problems -- so Saxon either removed or rewrote the offending passages (which seems to indicate, to me at least, that the books are for sale in more ways than one).

For mastering advanced math, especially if it will have application in sciences such as chemistry (which is emphasized in some Saxon books), of if you're going to need a lot of math to get into college, Saxon's method may be the best -- but many people are mastering math without ever seeing a Saxon book. Most people don't need advanced math, anyway. Our daughter Karen became fairly proficient in algebra and geometry, and is now a freelance business consultant, with very little need for more math than she needs to pay her bills, keep her accounts, and prepare tax returns (with the help of her computer). Cathy, a reluctant but fairly competent math student (with Saxon books), worked for several years as a librarian, was manager of a four-state team of fund-raisers for volunteer service organizations, and is now an assistant administrator in a small school -- and has had no need of advanced math. Derek never got over his intense dislike for math, and resisted it at every turn; today, he trains horses and teaches riding, and pays a CPA a few dollars each year to figure his income tax (although I'm sure he could it himself if he wanted to). Before spending $50 a year or more for a math textbook, we should consider where we want to go and what we need to get there. A $12 book that covers all the basic math principles, with enough drill and practice to know whether or not you're going to be a nuclear physicist, may be sufficient; it's a lot easier on the wallet, and may be a lot easier on the student.

Saxon's K-3 program was developed "especially for classroom use," and is very difficult to adapt to individual use. The textbooks cost about $35, and the corresponding teacher's manual -- which you're required to buy -- costs $125.00. The programs make extensive use of "manipulatives," to be bought separately; the set recommended by Saxon Publishers costs over $100.00. Now that is math in action.

We no longer recommend, or sell, the Saxon math books. If the weekly news magazines have convinced you of the need for your child to compete with the Russians or the Japanese or Martians, and if you have more money than you need, write to Saxon Publishers, Inc., 1320 West Lindsay, Norman, OK 73069, and ask for the "Homeschooling Catalog."

If you just want your children to be reasonably competent in arithmetic (and reasonably happy with their studies), then let's pursue a more realistic course.

Making or finding "manipulatives" is no problem, and doesn't require the spending of a hundred dollars or more. You and your child can work together to make a cardboard clock face with movable hands. You can make paper or cardboard play money, or buy a set of Monopoly money in a toy store. Your kitchen has measuring containers. Ordinary dominoes make excellent counters. Working together to find and make these items will even be a part of your learning together -- measuring, drawing, cutting, sorting, and so on.

For the more "structured" aspects of arithmetic, which may be a necessary evil in today's world, we think you'll find most of what you need in the math sections of the "Core Knowledge Series" (WHAT YOUR 1ST GRADER NEEDS TO KNOW, etc.), reviewed a little later on, along with several of the other books listed on these pages.

Looking ahead, by the time your student has finished fifth or sixth grade math, you can move on to ARITHMETIC MADE SIMPLE or SURVIVAL MATHEMATICS (which has more daily-life applications).

THE FIRST BOOK OF NUMBERS. Brilliantly-illustrated introduction for kids 4 to 8 years old. How numbers were developed, how they relate to time and measurement, and many other fascinating facts. Puzzles and tricks extend the grasp of basic number concepts, including sets, sequence, shapes, size, and a world without numbers. $8.95. Code EDC. BROOK FARM BOOKS.

HELP YOUR CHILD LEARN NUMBER SKILLS. Lots of very good ideas for using materials in your home to help your child learn basic math. Well illustrated. $6.95. Code EDC. BROOK FARM BOOKS.

BUILDING MATH SKILLS -- Two books which help kids 7 to 11 (more or less) develop basic math skills. Following the fortunes of a prehistoric family, these books bring math into amusing everyday situations that help children absorb the rules of math in a way that clearly demonstrates their usefulness.
ADDING & SUBTRACTING PUZZLES
MULTIPLYING PUZZLES
Each book, $4.95. Code EDC. BROOK FARM BOOKS.

FIRST LEARNING SERIES -- With a handful of crayons and an adult's playful guidance, these books introduce young children to various mathematical concepts. Several titles, all useful (not all of these are math books): LETTERS -- NUMBERS -- STARTING TO MEASURE -- COLOR -- SHAPES -- STARTING TO ADD -- STARTING TO SUBTRACT -- READY FOR READING -- SIZES -- TIME -- ODD ONE OUT -- STARTING TO COUNT -- COUNTING -- READY FOR WRITING. $3.50 each. Code EDC. BROOK FARM BOOKS.

BRAINBENDERS -- Full-color puzzle books, full of spot-the-mistake puzzles, exciting mazes, humorous mixed-up pictures, and lots of number puzzles based on simple arithmetic. Age 8 and up. Three titles: NUMBER PUZZLES, BRAIN PUZZLES, and PICTURE PUZZLES, $4.50 each OR all three for $12.00. Code EDC. BROOK FARM BOOKS.

If it takes two men a day to dig a hole, it will take four men two days, because they'll get in each other's way. If the men are over ninety, the hole should be six feet deep.

ARITHMETIC MADE SIMPLE, A. P. Sperling & Samuel D. Levison. A complete guide to all the functions of arithmetic, beginning with the basic use of numbers and working through addition, subtraction, multiplication, division, fractions, decimals, percentages, money, measurement, simple plane and solid geometry, ratio and proportion, graphs, signed numbers, and use of a calculator. Although the book begins with the simplest of arithmetic terms and usages, it's written for teens or adults who need to review (or learn for the first time), and isn't suitable for the use of young children. However, with an adult's patient help, it could probably be adapted to the use of children about 10 or so. (For younger children, we recommend the math sections of the "Core Knowledge" Series. See Index.) 173 pages, including answers to all problems and an index. $12.00. Code DD. BROOK FARM BOOKS.

THE I HATE MATHEMATICS! BOOK, by Marilyn Burns. What does mathematics have to do with schemes to get rich quick, games called "Creep," "Pig," and "Poison," or getting a vest off your grandfather without removing his coat? Are you a permutation ice cream cone eater or a combination ice cream cone eater? What offers you many new riddles, sidewalk games, things to do when you have the flu, and a sneaky away around drying the dishes? Answer: this book, which is about changing from a mathematical weakling to a mathematical heavyweight. Does it use tricks? Fancy talk? Threats? Fun and games? Yes! But there's a secret to it: you are a mathematical genius in disguise! $9.95. Code LB. BROOK FARM BOOKS.

LAUGH WITH MATH, by Martin Weissman & Keith Monse. 94 pages of cartoon strips about a wacky classroom of students, with nearly 500 algebraic problems presented, explained, and solved. For junior high through adult. Funny enough to be interesting even if you have no intention of learning algebra. Regular price, $19.95. Special, $9.95 plus $3.95. LAUGH AND LEARN, RD 1 Box 2232, Lafayette, NJ 07848. Write for free information.

SURVIVAL MATHEMATICS -- All the practical math skills and basic concepts most people will ever find useful or essential in everyday life, with a minimum of "abstract" math; with emphasis on skills and knowledge needed in bank transactions, stores, restaurants, tax forms, etc., and a full introduction to fractions, percentages, simple graphs, and elementary algebra. An excellent alternative to standard textbooks, and more useful in daily applications even if you plan to study advanced math, too. Grade 7 or 8 through high school and adult. 320 pages, 8½x11". $11.95. Code BE. BROOK FARM BOOKS.

MATH FOR SMARTY PANTS, by Marilyn Burns. Are you a mathematical whiz? If you answer "No," this book has a surprise for you; you may be smarter than you think. If you said "Yes," the book may still surprise you. You may be smarter than you think and not so smart, too -- because being smart at math doesn't mean being able to multiply fractions in your head at the speed of light. Numbers are only a part of math. Some people see shapes better than others; some can figure out logical problems better than others. There are many ways to be smart when it comes to mathematics, and this book will tell you about all of them. $9.95. Code LB. BROOK FARM BOOKS.

Mom, what is $(6x^2 + x^2 - 2x + 17)$ divided by $(2x + 3)$ times $(12y^3 - 17y^2 + 21y - 8)$ divided by $(3y-2)$?

CHILDREN'S MATHEMATICS CALENDAR. Very intriguing daily math problems whose solution is that days's date; activities, puzzles, etc. Grades 4-8. $6.95. MATH AIDS, Box 64, San Carlos, CA 94070.

HANDS-ON EQUATIONS -- When Alison Purdon, one of my readers, recommended this system of learning algebra, telling me it was both fun and easy, even for young children, I was skeptical but intrigued. I trust my readers' judgement, so I asked Dr. Henry Borenson, inventor of the system, for a review copy. With our four kids spread around the country at the moment, I had to be my own guinea pig. As you have inferred by now, I am happily innumerate, and of the firm opinion that algebra won't be fun for me, even if it is for the rest of the world. When the package arrived, I began to see that Dr. Borenson might change my thinking a little. There was a pack of game pieces -- white pawns, blue pawns, and red and green cubes similar to dice but with numbers instead of dots. Very easy-to-understand manuals for three levels, with each step carefully illustrated. A laminated picture of a balance scale on which to place the pawns and cubes. The object, of course, is to make the scale "balance" by keeping equal "weights" (or values) on each side. If two blue pawns on one side equal a "1" and a "5" on the other side, then one blue pawn ("x") must equal "3." And so on, building in complexity, through positive and negative integers, removing equal amounts from each side of the scale to simplify the problem, and checking solutions. I skipped around in all three levels, and discovered that I actually understood what I was doing. If I can master basic algebra with this method, surely any third grader can. Yes, it's meant for third graders, and up, including adults like me who don't think algebra can be fun or understood. About $35 for the whole works. Write for more information and prices: BORENSON AND ASSOCIATES, P.O. Box 3328, Allentown, PA 18106.

CUISENAIRE COMPANY OF AMERICA, 12 Church Street, New Rochelle, NY 10805. Books, games, tiles, calculators, pattern blocks, many more math-related materials; especially the well-known Cuisenaire Rods, colorful teaching aids which help develop many mathematical concepts long before formal lessons are introduced. Write for a catalog.

KEY CURRICULUM PROJECT, Box 2304, Berkeley, CA 94702. "Non-threatening" workbooks in fractions, decimals, geometry, algebra. Catalog.

SKILL-BUILDING GAMES, creative puzzles, books, computer software, hands-on materials, much more. Catalog. NASCO MATH, Fort Atkinson, WI 53538 or Modesto, CA 95352.

MATH-A-FACT-- Six basic math card games. Information from MARGWEN PRODUCTS, 382 34th St. SE, Cedar Rapids, IA 52403.

EXCELLENT WORKBOOKS in math and other subjects. See Index, SCHOOL ZONE.

WONDERFUL IDEAS, P.O. Box 64691, Burlington, VT 05406. A math newsletter filled with activities, puzzles, games, worksheets, & other ideas for teachers of elementary and middle grades. Eight monthly issues through the school year, $24.00.

PIG OUT ON MATH, A Catalog of Materials for Math Maniacs. Definitely what it says. Manipulatives, measuring tools, models, books for all levels of math, puzzles, games, origami, much more. INSTITUTE FOR MATH MANIA, P.O. Box 910, Montpelier, VT 05601 (802-223-5871).

MATH PRODUCTS PLUS, PO Box 64, San Carlos, CA 94070. A lot more math products than you might think there could be -- T-shirts, calendars, resource books, enrichment books, reference books, math diversions, math history, computer books, puzzles, postcards, hats & visors, stationery, manipulatives, magnets, games, jewelry, posters, and more, more, more. Free catalog.

HOME SCHOOLING & "CULTURAL LITERACY"

Reflections on **CULTURAL LITERACY: What Every American Needs to Know,** by E. D. Hirsch, Jr.

I went to school in southern Vermont in the 1940's and 1950's, and Jean went to school in suburban Illinois and a private high school in Colorado, just five years behind me. Three of our children -- Cathy, Karen, and Derek -- stayed at home with us through most or all of their "high school" education, and therefore have similar, if not superior, backgrounds. When we discuss key events in history or major works of literature, we usually understand each other very quickly; we learned the same basic information, and don't need to give each other long parenthetical explanations of our reference points before continuing a general discussion.

Our daughter Susan attended The Meeting School, a supposedly-Quaker "alternative" boarding high school in southern New Hampshire, for two years. At least, it was founded by Quakers. She and I visited the school before her enrollment, and were very impressed by the informality, the large library, and the spacious grounds. The expectations Jean and I had of "alternative education" were that it would encompass most standard subjects, such as English, math, history, science, etc., but taught in a non-standard manner: i.e., without rote learning of dead facts without reflection, without quarterly exams, without grading of papers and performance, and so on. We soon realized, after Susan felt well-established in the school and happy with many new friends, that the school's definition of "alternative," especially in some subjects, was very different from ours, and often depended largely on what the students felt like studying. Theoretically, that's the basis of "invited learning," and in theory I'm all for it. In practice, I need to see it working; if it isn't, I favor a little uninvited learning.

In one U.S. history course, Susan chose to concentrate on the role of women in U.S. history, which we thought was fine. A study of the important, but largely forgotten or ignored, roles of women in U.S. history should certainly give the student new perspectives on old concepts. Susan's final term paper on the subject, prepared with regular advice from a faculty advisor, and awarded an A+, was an emotional defense of "rising feminism" through the ages, hardly touching any "historical" issues except that women have always been mistreated by a male-dominated society. Another student chose to study American history through

its music, which we thought was a good idea; we suggested (through Susan) that he begin with Alan Lomax's FOLK SONGS OF NORTH AMERICA, which is almost a history course in itself. He began his "study" with Bob Dylan's later, "electrified" rock music, decided it was too tame, and devoted the rest of his time, including a four-week intercession, to being a Grateful Dead groupie, following the rock group from city to city, sleeping in his car and skipping meals so he could pay for rock concert tickets. And so on. All the students chose what we thought would be excellent behind-the-scenes approaches to history, and ended with little or no knowledge at all of even the most basic facts of U.S. history, such as the causes of the Civil War or of the two world wars, the significance or even the existence of the Monroe Doctrine, and relations between the United States and other countries. To the question, "Did you study U.S. history in school?" all the students will answer, "Yes," but their various impressions are more faulty and incomplete than those of the six blind men trying to determine what an elephant is.

And there are two very good examples of the importance of Hirsch's message -- that being "culturally literate" is to possess a large amount of "shared knowledge" of "basic information" about our world and our culture. Without that shared knowledge, says Hirsch, communications fail, and then the undertakings; and that, he adds, is the moral of the story of the Tower of Babel.

Shared knowledge is neither more nor less than a kind of language which has evolved in our culture over many, many years, and provides a short-cut to effective communication.

If our family is sitting around the TV discussing a news item about some U.S. activity in the mid-East, someone may comment that it seems to be in violation of the Monroe Doctrine; for all of us, except Susan -- through absolutely no fault of her own -- many years of U.S. history and policy-making are summed up in that one reference, including many of the problems preceding Monroe's administration as well as more recent activities such as the never-declared Korean War. For someone unfamiliar with the Monroe Doctrine, a lengthy explanation may be necessary to make it relevant to the present discussion, and by that time everyone else has wandered off to play pingpong.

The second example is my allusion to the six blind men. For most children of my generation, it's a familiar story; for many children growing up in the seventies and eighties, it draws a mental blank. If you know the story, my point is made quickly and picturesquely with less than a dozen words; if you don't know the story, I must either tell it to you, or use ten times as many words to communicate my thought to you.

Hirsch blames much of our society's decreasing "shared knowledge" on Jean Jacques Rousseau and John Dewey, although he concedes that their ideas may have been carried to unreasonable extremes by their adherents. Until about 1960 or a little earlier, children's stories, literary heroes, and school subjects across the country were very similar, as were basic courses in secondary schools and universities, and such "short-cuts" in communication as I've described were easy and common. Then, many leading educators decided that children were being made to memorize too many "facts" without being taught how to think about them. Public education changed almost overnight to emphasize "thinking skills" and "communication skills." At first, this seemed to be an important advance, but gradually people began to see that although children may have been learning how to think, they had nothing to think about. Publishers and teachers, not wanting to be accused of teaching dead facts, reduced history and science and literature to the bland consistency of vanilla pudding. Magazine articles complained that Johnny and Janie couldn't read, but no one seemed to realize that Johnny and Janie no longer <u>cared</u> about reading because their story books and textbooks were as exciting as yesterday's oatmeal. Today's students are still being taught "how to think," but are still being given very few facts or ideas to think about. They're

absorbing their cultural knowledge from television and rock music groups because no one else is telling them anything of interest. There is very little on television about the Monroe Doctrine, and rock groups seldom sing about the Renaissance or the Reformation. Hollywood no longer makes movies about Joan of Arc or King Arthur or Lewis and Clark or Alexander Graham Bell or the Oklahoma Land Run. The people and events of the past which were a part of our everyday lives -- in books, movies, radio programs, and even early television programs -- are no more than blank faces and meaningless dates to most children today.

A friend in New Jersey wrote, "I told my husband I thought 'cultural literacy' was just what everybody knows. He just looked at me, and didn't say anything." That, of course, is the point: "cultural literacy" <u>used to be</u> what everyone knew. Each day now, fewer and fewer people know the same things. "We have ignored cultural literacy in thinking about education," says Hirsch, "precisely because it was something we have been able to take for granted. We ignore the air we breathe until it is thin or foul."

Since reading Hirsch's book, I encounter constant reminders of its truth:

In discussing our model of the solar system with a neighbor, an intelligent adult who finished the ninth grade of school, I discover that he doesn't know the planets go around the sun. Pointing at the model's sun, he thinks it's the moon.

Adult acquaintances in Vermont, learning that we once lived in British Columbia, say, "Really? Why did you go all the way to South America?"

Hirsch has been most seriously criticized for his book's 63-page appendix, an alphabetical listing of words, phrases, book and song titles, historical and geographical references, aphorisms, and quotations which Hirsch says "literate Americans know." Critics ignore Hirsch's own disclaimer that the list is meant to be suggestive rather than definitive. Not every literate person, Hirsch says, is familiar with every item in his list; and, although he and two colleagues worked hard to make their list as complete as they could, Hirsch invites interested readers to suggest amendments and additions to the list. Although I haven't tried to "score" myself on his list -- hardly his purpose in presenting it -- I've looked it over, testing myself at random, and would guess that I am completely familiar with about half, somewhat familiar with another fourth, and completely ignorant of the other fourth. I can easily come up with several references I think he missed (or perhaps chose not to include). Conversations and correspondence among educated, "literate" people are rife with references and allusions which often convey paragraphs or even volumes of meaning in a few well-chosen words. Much more than idle whim directs many authors to borrow from the Bible, Shakespeare, and other great literary works for their titles. Readers are given extra measures of meaning in the books if they are familiar with the chosen phrases in their original contexts. Derek recently wrote a very good book review of John Steinbeck's OF MICE AND MEN, not knowing that the title had been borrowed from a poem by Robert Burns. I sent Derek to Bartlett's FAMILIAR QUOTATIONS, in which he read the words in their original context; he then re-wrote his review, having quickly reinterpreted Steinbeck's book in light of his new understanding of the title. EAST OF EDEN is another Steinbeck title which comes to mind; a very good book, even if one doesn't recognize the origin of the title -- but how much more meaning will be found by the reader who realizes that Steinbeck is drawing a loose parallel with the banishment of Adam and Eve from the Garden of Eden, along with the implicit implications of toil and shame and sorrow?

"Learning without thought is labor lost," said Confucius, seemingly in agreement with Rousseau and Dewey; but, he added, "thought without learning is perilous," which I think is Hirsch's contention. We want our children to know "how to think," of course; but without the lessons of history, the examples of good literature, knowledge of other peoples and cultures, and basic information about the physical world around them, their ability to think won't help them emerge from a personal repetition of the Dark Ages. We don't want to teach our children <u>what</u> to think, but <u>how</u> to think; and, to do that, we must help them find facts and information and ideas to <u>think about.</u> Word games and puzzles in logic are no substitute for information and ideas about the "real world" of the past and present and -- if we're ready -- the future.

In our home school, we've tried to cover everything. It's a star we'll never reach, of course, but still worth aiming for. Just a few of the subjects we've entertained at Brook Farm School are reading, 'riting, 'rithmetic, geography, history, science, art, music, mythology, literature, languages, psychology, ethics, religion, philosophy, humor, home economics, physical education, civics, politics, government, citizenship, commitment, integrity, self-reliance, sympathy, empathy, responsibility, map reading, typing, biology, and physiology. We also toss in a little astronomy, physics, chemistry, botany, and woodworking. We discuss and evaluate astrology, palmistry, dream

interpretation, and telepathy. We talk about marriage and divorce, birth and death, abortion, the death penalty, drugs, alcohol, and the world's health and hunger problem.

We occasionally refer to our home-schooling as "elementary and secondary education in the liberal arts." As immigrants to Canada, but not forgetting our American background, and with two of our children born in each of the two countries, our home-schooling has included the history, literature, and culture of both countries, which are, after all, very similar, and in many ways inseparable, having both sprung from Western Europe, bringing with them shared laws, history, literature, and tradition. As E. D. Hirsch makes us look back over the years, wondering if we have helped our children acquire "cultural literacy," we realize that his newly-coined phrase is a more concise way of saying what we've been saying right along. Our children have, and are continuing to acquire, much of the "basic information" which used to be "shared knowledge," and which E. D. Hirsch hopes will be restored not only to everyone's formal education, but also to everyone's thinking and communication.

One important omission, which Hirsch could not have foreseen, in his list of "what literate Americans know," is the phrase "cultural literacy." Besides conveying a meaning far beyond a basic competency in reading and writing, the phrase now represents a new way of looking at education. In discussing educational theories and practices with other educators, I feel the conversation would be as difficult without a shared knowledge of Hirsch's ideas as it would be without a shared knowledge of the basic ideas of Rousseau, Dewey, and John Holt. "Cultural literacy" has become an important part of cultural literacy.

CULTURAL LITERACY: What Every American Needs to Know, by E. D. Hirsch, Jr. (Reviewed on the previous pages.) $9.95. Code RH. BROOK FARM BOOKS.

THE DICTIONARY OF CULTURAL LITERACY: What Every American Needs to Know, by E. D. Hirsch, Jr., Joseph Kett, and James Trefil. Expanding and augmenting the controversial list of "what literate Americans know" from the book CULTURAL LITERACY, this book identifies the people, places, sayings, and ideas that form the common heritage of American culture. 23 alphabetically-arranged sections address major categories of knowledge with hundreds of entries that discuss ideas, events, and individuals, explaining their significance in our culture and placing them in context. Features 300 maps, charts, and illustrations. This book isn't a course in "instant cultural literacy," nor is it intended to be, but it will be a very useful skeleton guide to enjoyable, productive reading and study: with the collection of ideas and information in this book as jumping-off points, the reader can become acquainted (or re-acquainted) with vast areas of knowledge which may have been vague or missing. $19.95. Code HM. BROOK FARM BOOKS.

A FIRST DICTIONARY OF CULTURAL LITERACY: What Our Children Need to Know, E. D. Hirsch, Jr. This book is even more controversial than Hirsch's other two, but I think those who object that "Hirsch is telling us what to teach our kids" are like medieval kings who beheaded messengers who brought bad news. Public educators agree more and more with the opinion homeschoolers have had for years, that today's kids are not being educated. Taking them out of school is no solution if they aren't being educated. This book presents Hirsch's concept of the core body of knowledge that has been (and should be) the framework of American society and culture, particularly for children through the sixth grade. More than 2,000 concise, understandable entries are presented in 21 sections, ranging from the Bible and mythology to geography, history, and mathematics; the sciences, health, and technology. Richly-illustrated with photographs, drawings, charts, and maps. Like the lists in CULTURAL LITERACY and THE DICTIONARY OF CULTURAL LITERACY, this one is meant to be suggestive, not definitive, and readers can easily adapt it to their use. We think it's a very useful skeleton for all parents and teachers -- especially homeschoolers -- to use as a basic reference in designing a curriculum, in stocking a home library, or in choosing books to read aloud to the family, both before and after the children have learned to read. The suggestions in this book give children many things to think about while they're learning to think. $14.95. Code HM. BROOK FARM BOOKS.

N E W !
THE "CORE KNOWLEDGE" SERIES
edited by E. D. Hirsch, Jr.

There are six books in this series -- WHAT YOUR 1st [2nd, 3rd, 4th, 5th, or 6th] GRADER NEEDS TO KNOW, sub-titled "Fundamentals of a Good 1st [2nd, 3rd, etc.] Grade Education." Each book is a very comprehensive, almost-encyclopedic outline of basic information for each respective grade level in Language Arts, Fine Arts, History, Geography, Mathematics, Science, and Technology. The mathematics sections don't have "lessons," as such, but their very detailed summaries of all the basic facts, information, and skills which are most desirable will serve as excellent skeletons (or "cores," as the series' title suggests) around which to build your materials and activities. All the other subjects -- such as nursery rhymes and Aesop's fables in 1st GRADER through stories and poems and more advanced literature selections in the higher grades -- are very good, but will need to be supplemented with other similar materials; e.g., more literature, more biographies, etc. The series seems to be similar in some ways to Saxon's approach to math -- i.e., using an incremental method of teaching, presenting very basic information at first, and then slowly building on that information, year by year, to give a more complete picture, without bombarding the child with so much information that it can't be remembered or used. We have reservations about a few details, but in general we're very favorably impressed by the books. If they had been published when we were still teaching young kids, they would have made it much easier for us to design our own curricula. The arithmetic and math sections of these books -- supplemented with some of the other early-learning books we recommend -- can easily be all that's necessary to prepare for SURVIVAL MATHEMATICS (or Saxon's MATH 76, if you prefer a more academic program), with no need for the monotonous drill in standard school textbooks.

Each book in the series is $22.50. As I write this, the first two are also also in paperback for $10.95 each; I assume the others will be published in paperback, too, probably for the same price, but I don't know when. Unless you prefer the hardcover, we'll send you the paperback _if it's available_ and refund the difference in price. Code DD. Brook Farm Books.

BUT--

Having praised and recommended the "Core Knowledge Series," I have to remind you that the books were not <u>written</u> by E. D. Hirsch, Jr., but were <u>edited</u> by him, and I sometimes wonder if he was watching Sesame Street at the same time. Most of the books in the series are well done and need no apology, but the first, WHAT YOUR 1st GRADER NEEDS TO KNOW, is one of the most poorly-written books of its type that I have ever read. As I read through the book, I scribbled out 8 pages of notes, of which I'll give you a little sampling:

Many sentences are not properly punctuated; commas, in particular, are often missing. Throughout the book, many sentences begin with conjunctions (and, but), apparently to "simplify" the reading by dividing one sentence into two. The writer frequently jumps from third person to second person, then back again.

Several words and phrases need explanation; e.g., in a story about "Brer Tiger," the apostrophe is missing from "Br'er," and there is no explanation that the word is a colloquial abbreviation of "brother." There is no pronunciation guide for non-Hispanics of "Medio Pollito" (MAY-de-o po-YEE-to). There are several inane statements such as, "A written sentence starts out with a capital letter that says, 'Hey, a new sentence is starting'" and "A paragraph is made of several sentences <u>that talk</u> about the same thing" (my emphasis). <u>Rhyming words</u> are referred to as <u>rhyme words</u>.

"Since it is a northern country, Canada is cold in the winter," says the book, ignoring the fact that many parts of Canada are warmer than some parts of the United States. Should the reader infer that Antarctica is warm because it's a southern continent?

World religions are tossed around as if they were cute nursery stories, with no mention of their place in world history, and with no regard for their real substance. Buddha "sat beneath a tree for 98 days! Don't you think that is a long time to keep quiet?"

People crossed from Asia to North America on a "bridge," the book says, with no explanation of a <u>land bridge</u> and how it differs from a man-made bridge.

"It may seem strange to you, but for thousands of years only a few ships from Europe had 'bumped into' North or South America." Most small children will take "bumped into" literally, like bumping into a table. Why not "found" or "discovered"?

"Some [of the Native Americans] wanted so much to be thought brave that they clashed [?] with the men of other tribes. They called it 'going on the warpath.'" Is that a direct translation from an Indian language? An old John Wayne movie?

"One reason that [sic] Mozart was so good [sic] at music was that his father's job was teaching music, so you might say that music was in Mozart's family." Does this idiocy need a comment?

In The World of Plants, "a seed is a little plant in a box with its lunch..." "Let's pretend you are a tree, to see how a plant works." Sure; and then let's pretend you're a typewriter, to see how an editor works.

"The Pilgrims were very religious people," says the book, and I don't disagree, but what does "very religious" mean to the average six-year-old? "They came to <u>our country</u> [my emphasis] to worship in a way that was not allowed in England." What way? Why not allowed?

"Even though [Washington] would have preferred to be at his home, Mount Vernon, with his wife, Martha, he agreed to become President and was in office for eight years. This is why he is called the Father of His Country." Whups, lost me again. Because he left his wife for eight years? Because he was in his office for eight years?

Supposedly this book was written <u>for</u> first-graders and not <u>by</u> them, but how can you tell? If there were some other book I could recommend in its place, I'd do so, but I don't know of any. I still think it's a good core for a first grade curriculum, but don't be surprised if you sometimes feel like throwing it on the floor and jumping on it.

HISTORY, BIOGRAPHY, & GEOGRAPHY

There is properly no history, only biography.
Ralph Waldo Emerson

Biography is the only true history.
Thomas Carlyle

I want to know what were the steps by which man passed from barbarism to civilization.
Voltaire

Human history is in essence a history of ideas.
H. G. Wells

Yesterday, we played the cassette tape of an Old Radio program called "Battle Hymn of the Republic," which tells the dramatic story of Julia Ward Howe writing the words to go with the popular tune of "John Brown's Body." This morning, we started another tape, with a script written by Stephen Vincent Benét. We didn't get past the introduction. (We'll probably try again tomorrow.)

"That name sounds familiar," one of the kids said. "Don't we have some books by him?"

I stopped the tape and waited, as the kids looked at each other, searching their memories.

Seeing that they were all drawing blanks, I prompted. "It was mentioned briefly in the tape we heard yesterday," I said. "That is, something of the same name. A long poem, book-length."

"Hiawatha?" someone suggested, knowing better.

"What was the song in the story?" I asked.

"Battle Hymn! Of the Republic!"

"Right," I said. "Where did the tune come from?"

"Someone wrote it." (Always a wise guy.)

"Who?"

"Stephen Vincent Benét?" "Longfellow?" "John Brown?"

"John Brown's Body! Nobody knows who wrote it!"

"You win again. Perhaps it just grew, as people repeated the song. Who was John Brown? Did people really sing about his body?"

And so on. Sometimes the kids know the answers, or can brainstorm the answers. Sometimes we jog their memories with hints, riddles, puns, jokes, and related tidbits of information. Sometimes the subject or concept is new to them, and we tell them of our own ideas and experiences, books we've read, places we've seen. We bring out maps, posters, magazine articles, more books. We help them collect miscellaneous pieces of information and ideas and tie them together -- to relate the facts and ideas to each other, to the world, and to themselves.

This morning, John Brown led to State's rights, the Declaration of Independence, the Constitution, the Gettysburg Address, slavery, the Fugitive Slave Act, Thoreau, the Boston Tea Party, the Mexican War, democracy, UNCLE TOM'S CABIN, and several versions and usages of the word "yankee." The discussion which was interwoven with all these subjects was lively, with quick exchanges of ideas and opinions, and spiced with several puns, jokes, and wisecracks.

We like history, but there are very few history books we like. Browse through a public school's history books; notice how much they are concerned with wars. Not big wars, fought for principle, good against evil, but petty wars, fought for greed, money, power, and territory. See how little attention is given to the great thinkers, to inventions and discoveries, works of art, music, philosophy, and medicine.

I received passing grades when I was in school, so I suppose I must have learned the answers to at least half the questions, such as, Who fought the battle of Kickme? On what date did the commanding general lose his suspenders, and why? How did anteaters affect the outcome? Why was this battle important to the development of the fur trade in colonial Chicago? I have long since forgotten most of the answers, and I doubt that remembering them would contribute very greatly to my happiness or my worth as a person.

We learn more from historical novels than from textbooks. We listen to dramatized historical events on cassette tapes; we put up facsimiles of historical posters; we assemble models of historical buildings and castles and towns; we color pictures of great events and great people; cut out and arrange paper dolls of great people; and we talk, talk, talk. We use history books, but seldom as intended by the authors and editors. Sometimes we immerse ourselves in an event or a period, collecting information about it from as many different sources as possible. Other times, we skip and bounce, skim and dive, reading aloud, discussing what we find, and relating it to other times and other events. We show the kids how to search out the highlights and the hidden undercurrents. We look for truly significant happenings in the development of humanity and human society. We look for "human interest" -- unusual or humorous facts which demonstrate that the people of the past were real people, like us, not just shadows or silhouettes, who ate, slept, loved, feared, and hoped just as we do. We use maps -- regional, national, historical, and the world -- and a globe. We point; we let our fingers do the walking over continents and over centuries...

Some scientists say humanity began here... Biblical scholars say it began here... Here is where agriculture is believed to have started... Here, glaciers swept the continent... How did people survive?... Here was the first man to proclaim there is only one God... Here, a new thought in philosophy... government... science... medicine... architecture...

We look for the forerunners of democracy. We trace the evolution of human government -- family patriarchs or matriarchs, tribal chiefs, religious leaders; monarchy, oligarchy. We discuss "good" kings and "bad" kings -- what made them so, and what influence did they have on society's growth? We often brush over the names and usually settle for an approximate time, such as "about a thousand years ago." For our purposes, it seldom matters if an event occurred in the year 1169 or

1269. As the gap narrows, as the event is closer to us in time, we make finer distinctions.

Many facts of history stand by themselves; they have significance regardless of the time in which they occurred. Taking the history of mankind as a whole, very few individual names, dates, or happenings have any great significance. There is no reason to memorize most of them just for the sake of "knowing" them. For centuries, the little kingdoms and countries of western Europe were embroiled in countless wars, with heads of state shifting as fast as boundaries. Stevenson's THE BLACK ARROW gives us a vivid picture of shifting alliances in medieval Britain. We can read about one or two "representative" wars, and imagine the rest; there's no need to memorize dates and principals.

Other facts seem meaningless until they are put into perspective by relating them to their own time, their own place, their own circumstances. Pivotal points and key figures in society's growth deserve a closer look. We have Old Radio programs on cassettes that take us back to Alexander's conquest of Asia, to Julius Caesar's victories and defeats, and to the signing of the Magna Carta, giving us front row seats at some of the most significant events in history.

Besides knowing that Alexander the Great conquered a vast part of the world known to him, it's interesting and probably significant to know that he was taught by Aristotle, who was taught by Plato, whose teacher was Socrates. Was Alexander only seeking territory and power, or did he intend to promote a better form of government? What's the evidence? What would our society be like today if Caesar had not crossed the Rubicon? If Constantine, after pledging to spread Christianity if he won the next day's battle, had lost?

We feel it's important to have an understanding of the broad sweep of history -- the long journey people have made from the caves and swamps to the moon. We believe it's important to know that we of today are not the first real people; that a hundred years ago, a thousand, ten thousand, people got dressed and ate breakfast and worked for a living and taught their children; they laughed and cried; when a boy of ancient Rome skinned his knee, it hurt and bled just as it would today.

We are not so greatly removed from our ancestors as we often think. Despite today's great advantages (and many disadvantages) in technology, industry, and medicine, we have changed very little over the centuries. That which makes us human -- whether it's the size of our brain, the opposable thumb, or a share of divinity -- is unchanged.

We marvel at the scientific discoveries and advances of the last hundred years. Technologically, why did mankind crawl for so long, and then suddenly walk, run, and fly? We marvel at our humanity, our self-healing bodies, our hopes and fears. The men who have walked on the moon have the same flesh as did the students of Socrates.

As we draw our fingers over the globe or map, and scan the centuries with our talk and our hands, we can back off into space for a broad overview or zoom in closely for a detailed picture. This big ball has been spinning through space for a long time, warmed and lighted by one of the dimmest stars... Down here a woman is preparing breakfast for her family. Is it charred mammoth, or corn flakes and toast? Here is a man digging a hole. A pitfall for a tiger? A hiding place for pirates' treasure? A city sewage line?

Men and women have always been concerned with good and bad, right and wrong. They have always strived for truth, for a good life, and for good government. Most of the best ideas in today's governments had their roots in very ancient times. Our social growth has not kept pace with our technological growth, but we are still advancing, moving from various forms of tyranny toward total emancipation.

A very few, here and there, such as the Hopi Indians of Arizona and the traditional Society of Friends, are models of what all humanity may one day achieve. Democracy, as visualized by Paine, Washington, Jefferson and other architects of the U.S. government, and by Lincoln -- "government of the people, by the people, and for the people" -- is the highest form of government yet achieved by any large society; but it's just a stepping stone. Majority rule is better than dictatorship, but the majority is not always right, and the minority may still be misused and wronged. We wait, and strive, for the next development.

The next step in social government will be consensus and general agreement. Each member will seek what is right and good for all members, not only what is right for himself, or what is desirable for the majority, or for those with the most influence and power. There will be no lobbying or filibustering or voting; only calm consideration and discussion until unanimity of opinion is reached.

"But that would take too long," many object. "People can never agree that much. Nothing would ever get done."

That's true, of course. As most of us are now, democracy is the best we can hope for. A thousand years ago, democracy was considered an impractical dream, when it was considered at all. A thousand years from now -- who knows?

Our descendants will be living then, and we like to think that their society's conscience and spirit will have begun to catch up to the spaceships and computers. We hope the study of our yesterdays will help them have better tomorrows.

THE USBORNE BOOK OF WORLD HISTORY. This book, combining six titles, presents a concise but very comprehensive outline of the development of mankind from the Stone Age to World War I, covering great scientific discoveries, evolution of the arts, the founding and spreading of the major religions, colonization, major revolutions, and the development of several civilizations. THE FIRST CIVILIZATIONS, from 10,000 B.C. to 1500 B.C.; artwork, myths, religion, architecture, daily life of the Sumerians, ancient Egyptians, Cretans, Babylonians; children's games, cosmetics, cuneiform writing, bread and wine making, much more. WARRIORS & SEAFARERS, 1500 B.C. to 500 B.C. (approximate time of the Old Testament), a time of invaders, explorers, & conquerors in the ancient world, with details of the culture, battles, maps, & architecture of the Hittite, Mycenaean, Canaanite, Phoenician, & ancient Chinese. EMPIRES & BARBARIANS, 500 B.C. to 600 A.D., the Greeks, Romans, Chinese, Mongols, Celts, and Persians, with maps & detailed drawings of life in China, northern Europe, Africa, South America, Athens, & Rome; the Great Wall of China, Pompeii, Alexander the Great. CRUSADERS, AZTECS & SAMURAI, 600 A.D. to 1450 A.D., the Dark and Middle Ages in Europe, rise of Islam, life in Asia, Vikings, life in Europe (village life, the Church, knights, castles), Genghis Khan & the Mongols, trade with China, Samurai of Japan, life in Africa and the Americas. EXPLORATION & DISCOVERY, 1450 A.D. to 1750 A.D.; exploration, conquest, & settlement of the New World; artists, scientists, explorers; Renaissance & Reformation in Europe; Elizabethan England; Hapsburg & Romanov Empires; life in Japan, Muslim Empires, & the Mogul Empire in India. THE AGE OF REVOLUTIONS, 1750 A.D. to 1914 A.D.; effects of the agricultural and industrial revolutions; highlights of the French & American revolutions; the colonization of Africa, India, & Australia; Commodore Perry in Japan; impact of newly-invented cars, steam locomotives, and airplanes.

For age 8 and up, including adults, who will find it more fascinating and informative than any school textbook on the same subject. 195 pages. $21.95. Code EDC. BROOK FARM BOOKS.

ILLUSTRATED WORLD HISTORY DATES: From Stone Age to Computer Age. An easy-to-read, profusely-illustrated reference that combines detailed date charts with features on important themes in world history, such as The First Farmers, The Provincial Wars in Japan, The Rise of the Manchu Dynasty, and The Great Depression. Colorful maps, diagrams, and very detailed drawings on every page. Age 10 up, including teens. $12.95. Code EDC. BROOK FARM BOOKS.

FIRST HISTORY -- LIVING IN PREHISTORIC TIMES, LIVING IN ROMAN TIMES, and LIVING IN CASTLE TIMES. A fascinating introduction to history for age 7 and up, including adult. Each book focuses on one central character to give a vivid picture of life in the different periods. Very detailed. colorful pictures. 3 books in one volume, $9.95. Code EDC. BROOK FARM BOOKS.

ILLUSTRATED HANDBOOK OF INVENTION AND DISCOVERY. The most important inventions and discoveries marking the progress of the human race, from the Stone Age to the Space Age. Arranged thematically under general topics, the book tells when and by whom something was invented or discovered, what improvements were made, and what the most recent version is. General topics include transportation, communication, warfare, scientific instruments, and domestic appliances. Detailed, full-color illustrations throughout. $9.95. Code EDC. BROOK FARM BOOKS.

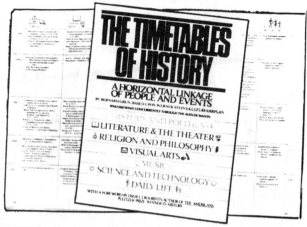

THE USBORNE TIME TRAVELLER'S OMNIBUS, combining four titles in one volume, takes readers back in time for a very detailed introduction to fascinating aspects of daily life in four major periods. Colorful, detailed, well-researched drawings show the houses, social life, clothing, weapons, cooking utensils, farm equipment, schools, shops, markets, battles, feasts, religious rites. PHARAOHS & PYRAMIDS shows construction of a pyramid, elaborate burial rites, court of the pharaoh, an Egyptian temple with explanations of beliefs about the spirit world and afterlife; feasts, household structure, life on the Nile; hieroglyphics. ROME AND ROMANS shows a typical home, public baths, shops, markets, Colosseum, temples, forums, aqueducts, gladiators, charioteers, a Roman feast; life in the city, country, at school, in the army. KNIGHTS & CASTLES shows foot soldiers, serfs, squires, and stewards at work and play; detailed drawings of the castle courtyard, keep, other buildings; outfitting a knight; jousting; and an attack on the castle. VIKING RAIDERS shows the steps in building the famous Viking warships, preparing for a raid on an Irish monastery, journeys to Iceland and the Shetlands, life in a longhouse, winter festival of games, sports, and feasting.

Packed with very detailed, accurate illustrations and lively, imaginative text. Age 8 and up, definitely including adults, who will find it much more interesting and informative than any school book on the subject. $18.95. Code EDC. BROOK FARM BOOKS.

THE TIMETABLES OF HISTORY: A Horizontal Linkage of People and Events, by Bernard Grun; based on Verner Stein's KULTURFAHRPLAN. One of the most unusual books published, and one of our favorites. Look up any year from 4241 B.C. to the present and read in brief synopsis the major events and accomplishments in seven areas: History and Politics, Literature and the Theatre, Religion and Philosophy, the Visual Arts, Music, Science and Technology, and Daily Life. For instance, in 1853, Franklin Pierce became U.S. president, the Crimean War began, Hawthorne published TANGLEWOOD TALES, Vincent van Gogh was born, Wagner completed the text for "The Ring," and Samuel Colt revolutionized the manufacture of guns. 676 pages, fully indexed. $20.00. Code SS. BROOK FARM BOOKS.

ESSENTIALS OF WORLD HISTORY, by Jean Reeder Smith and Lucey Baldwin Smith. A concise reference book, with brief articles which outline ancient, medieval, and modern periods of major world areas: the Middle East, Europe, Russia, North America, Latin America, India and Southwest Asia, China, Japan, Southeast Asia, and sub-Sahara Africa. Bibliography and index. Very useful, but with definite limitations. In keeping with modern publishers' fear of controversy, ESSENTIALS OF WORLD HISTORY presents very bare facts with little mention of the political or sociological causes and effects, particularly if those causes or effects border on religion. For instance, the story of the Pilgrims being persecuted in England and eventually emigrating to America is told -- but with no mention whatsoever of _why_ they were persecuted or why they felt it necessary to emigrate. An excellent example of "neutrality" as defined by a U.S. Appeals Court (see Omission of Religion from Textbooks). Despite this serious shortcoming, ESSENTIALS OF WORLD HISTORY can serve as an excellent skeleton upon which to build a good study program, simply by using the entries as guides to further research. $11.95. Code BE. BROOK FARM BOOKS.

THE STORY OF A CASTLE, John S. Goodall. Beautiful illustrations, without words, of the evolution of a part of English social history. The castle was built by Norman conquerors, unsuccessfully defended against the Roundheads in the 17th century, refurbished for the festive lifestyles of the 18th and 19th centuries, became a hospital during World War II, was the site of celebrations of the coronation of Elizabeth II, and opened to the public in 1970. 60 pages. All ages. $14.95. Code MAC. BROOK FARM BOOKS.

THE GOLDEN AGE OF ATHENS

POP-UP BOOKS TO MAKE YOURSELF -- We didn't discover these until the kids were too old for them, but I'm still young enough to work with them, and I ordered a few right away. I'm working on the Storming of the Bastille, now. Most of the pop-ups are easy enough for children about 9 or 10; a little help might be needed on the small cuts and folds of a few pieces. Besides learning about the subject in each book, you have the fun of learning about the engineering in a pop-up book, and the satisfaction of making it yourself. Each book contains six main scenes, with a number of mini-pop-ups built in, and brief text with interesting information and ideas.

POP-UP PARIS. Famous buildings: Notre Dame; Arc de Triomphe; Monmartre; the Pompidou Centre; the storming of the Bastille. Text is in English and French.

POP-UP LONDON. The Tower of London; St. Paul's Cathedral; Trafalgar Square; the House of Parliament; Buckingham Palace; a visitor's tour.

THE EGYPTIANS POP-UP. Black Land, Red Land; Kamak; the Great Pyramid; Tutankhamun; Abu Simbel; Cleopatra and the Romans.

THE MAYA, AZTECS, & INCAS POP-UP. Takai; human sacrifice; Teochtitlian; the struggle between the Aztecs and the Conquistadors; the Inca Empire; the Golden Enclosure.

THE ROMANS POP-UP. City of Rome; the Forum; the Roman house; the army; gladiators; Ostia, the port of Rome.

THE GREEKS POP-UP. Knossos; Mycenae; the Battle of Salamis; the Golden Age of Athens; the theatre; Alexander the Great.

Each "Pop-up Book to Make Yourself," $7.95. Code PW. BROOK FARM BOOKS.

FORT CUSTER

EASY-TO-MAKE HISTORICAL TOYS AND MODELS--

PLAINS INDIANS TEEPEE VILLAGE. Five decorated teepees, 20 action figures (riding horses, cooking, hunting, dancing, playing lacrosse, more. Age 5 up.

WESTERN FRONTIER FORT. Stockade fence encompassing three buildings; 17 soldiers on horseback, bugling, aiming rifles, walking, etc. Age 5 up.

COLUMBUS DISCOVERS AMERICA PANORAMA. Sturdy full-color model, 25" long, includes paper models of Columbus' three ships, painted representations of crew, natives, thatched huts, animals, more. Age 6 up.

PLAYTIME VILLAGE. Full-color, sturdy model of small American town; houses, church, schoolhouse, firehouse, general store, more. Age 6 up.

PLAYTIME FARM. Full-color rural homestead, including barn, farmhouse, toolshed, well, chicken coop, farm animals, more. Age 4 up.

PLAYTIME CASTLE. Full-color, three-dimensional model of medieval fortress. Instructions, diagrams. Age 6 up.

EASY-TO-MAKE HISTORICAL TOYS AND MODELS, $3.95 each. Code DV. BROOK FARM BOOKS.

COBBLESTONE, The History Magazine for Young People. American history presented in a unique and exciting way -- through original firsthand accounts, biographies, poems, maps, games, puzzles, cartoons, songs, and recipes. Each 48-page issue focuses on a single theme drawing from the political, business, scientific, artistic, and literary areas of life in the period covered. Ages 10 up. Annual subscription (12 issues), $22.95. More than 125 back issues always available, $3.95 each. Annual sets (12 back issues, slipcase, and index to all previously-published issues, $44.95. Write for catalog and list of back issues, which includes The Alamo, Alexander Hamilton, Buffalo, Eleanor Roosevelt, Great Debates, Immigrants, Old-Time Schools, Transcendentalism, many more. COBBLESTONE PUBLISHING, INC., 30 Grove St., Peterborough, NH 03458.

CALLIOPE, World History for Young People -- Very interesting and informative magazine about the myths, legends, history, and cultures from ancient civilizations through the Middle Ages and the Renaissance, for ages 10 and up. Excellent introduction to many of the roots of present-day civilization and the many ways in which modern society has grown from the thoughts and customs of older societies. 1 year (5 issues), $17.95. Back issues available. COBBLESTONE PUBLISHING, INC., 30 Grove Street, Peterborough, NH 03458. (See also Global Awareness, "Faces.")

HISTORY COLORING BOOKS -- Detailed, authentic illustrations of many historical periods, people, and events, with informative captions. Very interesting & educational, even if you don't want to color them. We've found that colored art pencils work best; crayons are too clumsy, and it's difficult to get gentle shades with felt markers.

FROM ANTIETAM TO GETTYSBURG COLORING BOOK. 45 precise illustrations which document the battlefield action & many personalities of the Civil War. $2.75.

COLUMBUS DISCOVERS AMERICA COLORING BOOK--41 drawings of shipboard life, the Spanish monarchs, storms at sea, arrival in the New World; etc. $2.95.

STORY OF THE VIKINGS COLORING BOOK -- 38 detailed illustrations of the Viking saga; European raids, American and Russian presence, ship construction, weapons, art, literature, more. $2.95.

LEWIS AND CLARK EXPEDITION COLORING BOOK-- 45 historically accurate illustrations of the highpoints of the expedition, with captions identifying the action and providing background information. $2.75.

ABRAHAM LINCOLN COLORING BOOK-- 40 detailed scenes from Lincoln's life: log cabin birthplace, debating Douglas, Gettysburg Address, etc. $2.75.

COWBOYS OF THE OLD WEST COLORING BOOK. 37 detailed illustrations and informative captions about these symbols of the American spirit. $2.75.

PLAINS INDIANS COLORING BOOK -- 40 line drawings accurately depict the costumes and culture of the Apache, Pawnee, Blackfoot, Crow, and other Plains Indians. $2.75.

NORTHWEST COAST INDIANS--33 accurate line drawings of the costumes and lifestyle of Northwest Coast Indians from the 18th to 20th centuries. $2.75.

STORY OF THE CALIFORNIA GOLD RUSH COLORING BOOK -- 40 scenes, including Sutter's Mill in 1848, mining camps and boomtowns, old San Francisco, prospectors panning for gold, more. $2.95.

PIRATES & BUCCANEERS COLORING BOOK. Morgan, Blackbeard, Anne Bonny, Mary Read, others; 44 accurate illustrations. $2.75.

CASTLES OF THE WORLD COLORING BOOK -- 31 medieval castles around the world, including Austria, France, Britain, Germany, Italy, Syria, Japan. $2.75.

KNIGHTS AND ARMOR COLORING BOOK -- Historically accurate depictions of knights in armor: Vikings, Crusaders, jousters, foot soldiers, Henry VIII, more. Introduction, glossary. $2.75.

THE MIDDLE AGES COLORING BOOK-- More than 50 woodcuts from German incunabular ("before 1501," my dictionary says) sources: knights, jousts, ships, maidens, medieval towns, battles, labors, incredible beasts. $2.75.

STATUE OF LIBERTY AND ELLIS ISLAND COLORING BOOK-- 45 illustrations adapted from historic photographs & engravings detail Liberty's history, immigration at Ellis Island, etc. $2.75.

EARLY AMERICAN TRADES COLORING BOOK -- Wigmakers, glassblowers, hatters, and 19 other craftsmen, accompanied on facing pages by their tools & products. $2.75.

STORY OF THE AMERICAN REVOLUTION COLORING BOOK -- 40 finely-drawn scenes of the Boston Massacre, Paul Revere's ride, execution of Nathan Hale, much more. $2.95.

UNIFORMS OF THE AMERICAN REVOLUTION COLORING BOOK -- 31 panoramas of military attire, with complete instructions for accurate coloring. $2.75.

EVERYDAY DRESS OF THE AMERICAN COLONIAL PERIOD COLORING BOOK. Broomseller, farmer, wagoner, sailor, etc., accurately depicted with 14 color examples on covers. $2.75.

CIVIL WAR UNIFORMS COLORING BOOK-- 21 Confederate, 24 Union uniforms, different ranks, states, units; historical figures, Grant, Lee, Farragut, etc.; in color on covers. $2.95.

WORLD WAR I UNIFORMS COLORING BOOK -- A Romanian infantry colonel, German flying ace, U.S. Marine corporal, more. $2.95.

UNIFORMS OF THE NAPOLEONIC WARS COLORING BOOK-- 45 full-page illustrations of combatants. $2.50.

FOLK COSTUMES OF EUROPE COLORING BOOK--130 authentic costumes, male and female, in 45 pictures, from Italy, Spain, Central Europe, Balkans, Russia, etc. $2.75.

HISTORY OF FLIGHT COLORING BOOK -- 47 accurate drawings of the most important flying achievements, including 18th-century balloons, 19th-century dirigibles, Spirit of St. Louis, fighters, bombers, the Concorde, and the space shuttle. $2.75.

ALL THE ABOVE "HISTORY COLORING BOOKS," prices as indicated. Code DV. BROOK FARM BOOKS.

HISTORY COLORING BOOKS & ACTIVITY BOOKS -- Based on the art, sculpture, architecture, and costumes of the times, authentically reproduced, with explanatory text and captions. I didn't think I had much interest in old castles until I built the Chateau Gaillard of King Richard the Lion-Heart a couple of years ago, and then I became the family's Castle Authority. I even impressed a few visiting neighbors with my, ahem, model-building skills. Derek built several airplanes, and the girls brightened the clothing and surroundings of people through the ages and around the world. Jean's enjoyment of these books, so far, has been largely vicarious. I don't mean anything in particular by that; it's just a fact.

ANCIENT CHINA COLORING BOOK--An excursion into Chinese art, from earliest paintings and ancient bronze animals to the famous painters of priceless scrolls; and famous emperors and empresses. $3.50.

A COLORING BOOK OF JAPAN -- A history of Japanese art, from the most ancient to Ho-kusai and Utamaro. Warriors, actors, dancers, children playing, and animals. $3.50.

THE ANCIENT NEAR EAST -- The art of 3,000 B.C. from Ur to that of the Babylonians, Assyrians, and Persians. Gods, goddesses, and great rulers. $2.95.

A COLORING BOOK OF ANCIENT EGYPT -- Art from the earliest king through 3,000 years to Cleopatra. Animals at play, gods and goddesses, ships, dancers, scenes of Egyptians at work and sport. $3.50.

A COLORING BOOK OF ANCIENT GREECE-- All the Olympian gods and goddesses. Many scenes of daily life: music making, dance, chariot and foot races; more. Art from the finest ancient vase painters. $3.50.

A COLORING BOOK OF ROME--All the Caesars, from Julius to Septimius Severus, chariot races, and more, are in this collection of art from Imperial Rome, with text in both English and Latin. $3.50.

A COLORING BOOK OF THE OLYMPICS -- The story is told by a boy at the games in 468 B.C., and the events illustrated are taken from beautiful ancient sources. $3.50.

A COLORING BOOK OF ANCIENT HAWAII--An art history of Hawaii, including temple images, drawings by explorers, and portraits of early kings; some cutouts also. $2.50.

ALEXANDER THE GREAT COLORING BOOK-- The monuments of Alexander's life are illustrated, along with the golden relics of the people he conquered. $3.50.

A COLORING BOOK OF ANCIENT AFRICA -- From the art of Benin, showing the Oba, his warriors, and their costumes; his palace, and a noble Queen of Benin. Some of the world's greatest portraits. $1.50.

A COLORING BOOK OF ANCIENT IRELAND -- A child's history of ancient Irish art, with amusing Celtic people and animals woven into ancient mazes & patterns. From 8th and 9th century artifacts and the Books of Durrow and Kells. $3.50.

ANCIENT FACES TO CUT OUT AND WEAR-- Eight different masks, printed in full, authentic color, patterned after ancient relics in the Metropolitan Museum of Art. $4.95.

MYTHS & LEGENDS OF THE VIKINGS COLORING BOOK -- Pictures of the heroes of Norse sagas, taken from ancient art. $2.95.

VIKING SHIPS TO ASSEMBLE--Oseberg, Gokstad, Skuldelev ships printed in full color on heavy stock, with very authentic detail. Ready to be cut out and put together. $4.95.

PAPER SOLDIERS OF THE AMERICAN REVOLUTION -- A small army, complete with cannon, ready to color and cut out. Each soldier is on a stand which identifies his regiment. $3.50.

A COLORING BOOK OF THE MIDDLE AGES -- Little marginal figures of medieval manuscripts and full-size pictures of King Arthur, Sir Lancelot, Charlemagne, William the Conqueror, Richard the Lion-Hearted, more. $2.95.

A COLORING BOOK OF THE RENAISSANCE -- Fascinating scenes and people, including Cesare Borgia and his sister Lucretia. $3.50.

A COLORING BOOK OF KINGS AND QUEENS OF ENGLAND -- From the most ancient to the present queen, clothed in elegant garb requiring only to be brightly colored. $3.50.

CASTLES TO CUT OUT & PUT TOGETHER -- The Tower of London and King Richard the Lion-Heart's Chateau Gaillard, authentically drawn to scale, with full informative text. $3.50.

CASTLES OF SCOTLAND TO CUT OUT & PUT TOGETHER -- The greatest of Scots fortresses, with their exciting history. $3.50.

PAPER SOLDIERS OF THE MIDDLE AGES--Authentic figures representing several different stations in the middle ages, ready to color, cut out, assemble, and attack someone's castle. $3.50.

A MEDIEVAL ALPHABET TO ILLUMINATE-- The intricate letters of medieval manuscripts are beautiful and elegant, and frequently contain the excellent humor of the 12th-century monks who labored on them for days at a time. $2.95.

QUEEN ELIZABETH I: PAPER DOLLS TO COLOR -- The queen & her gowns, Sir Walter Raleigh & his armor, with text by the Queen. $3.50.

HENRY VIII & HIS WIVES: PAPER DOLLS TO COLOR -- Beautiful suits of armor, rich damasks, glittering jewelery, with full stories. $3.50.

A SHAKESPEARE COLORING BOOK-- A history of Shakespearean illustration, from the very old Peacham drawing to illustrations of Richard Burton as Henry V, Orson Welles as Othello, and more. $2.95.

All "HISTORY COLORING BOOKS & ACTIVITY BOOKS," prices as indicated. Code BB. BROOK FARM BOOKS.

HEROES OF THE AMERICAN REVOLUTION COLORING BOOK-- Pictures taken from old portrait engravings, with stories of the heroes who founded the United States. $2.95.

SHIPS OF THE AMERICAN REVOLUTION COLORING BOOK -- Many ships, their captains, and their stories. $3.50.

A COLORING BOOK OF THE CIVIL WAR--The interesting uniforms of different units were far more colorful than just blue and gray. $2.95.

CIVIL WAR FLAGS TO COLOR -- Both sides had intricate, colorful banners. $1.50.

A COLORING BOOK OF INCAS, AZTECS & MAYAS -- Some of the finest art of these pre-Columbian civilizations: ballplayers, dancers, calendars, counting devices, and gods. $3.50.

GREAT WOMEN PAPER DOLLS-- Sappho, Cleopatra, Joan of Arc, Pocahontas, Susan B. Anthony, Florence Nightingale, Golda Meir, & others, each with appropriate costumes and a speech for her cause. $3.50.

INFAMOUS WOMEN PAPER DOLLS TO COLOR -- Messalina, Agrippina, Lucrezia Borgia, the Empress Wu, Catherine the Great, Catherine de Medici, Mata Hari, and many others, with their histories. $3.50.

A COLORING BOOK OF GREAT EXPLORERS -- Columbus, Balboa, Cortez, the Cabots, and many more. $3.50.

13 COLONIES COLORING BOOK-- With stories of their earliest settling, and their flags and emblems to color. $3.50.

A COLORING BOOK OF THE AMERICAN REVOLUTION -- Political cartoons and caricatures from the age of the Revolution, offering an unusual glimpse at early American history. $2.95.

NEW ENGLAND SOLDIERS OF THE AMERICAN REVOLUTION-- A coloring book of the beautiful and complex uniforms of some of the Yankee soldiers, some of which never got beyond the designing stage. $3.50.

GREAT INDIAN CHIEFS COLORING BOOK -- 50 portraits and brief biographies of Powhatan and Pocahontas, Hiawatha, Sitting Bull, Crazy Horse, Chief Joseph, and many more. $2.95.

A COLORING BOOK OF AMERICAN INDIANS--Many different areas of American Indian art, and scenes by white men of Indians using their art, from prehistory to the present. Also, masks to wear. $2.95.

GREAT INDIANS OF CALIFORNIA COLORING BOOK -- Very different cultures from the better-known Plains Indians, and just as dedicated in trying to preserve them. $3.50.

GREAT LAWYERS COLORING BOOK -- Hammurabi, Moses, Demosthenes, Cicero, Portia, Coke, Blackstone, Marshall, Webster, Lincoln, Holmes, Darrow, and many more. Interesting introduction to the law. $3.50.

AMELIA EARHART COLORING BOOK-- Full-page pictures of Amelia Earhart, with text by her sister, Muriel Earhart Morrisey. $3.50.

GREAT AMERICAN AIRPLANES TO FLY -- The Wright Brothers' plane, Lindberg's Spirit of St. Louis, the Bell XS-1 (breaker of the sound barrier), Amelia Earhart's Lockheed Vega; to color, cut out, and glue together. $3.50.

ACES & AIRPLANES OF WORLD WAR I -- The earliest flying flivvers to the advanced planes at the end of the war, with the stories of Great Aces of both sides. $2.95.

FAMOUS FIGHTERS TO COLOR, CUT OUT, & FLY -- They really do fly well (with a careful thrust of the arm), but I recommend a soft lawn for the landing field, or you'll have some extensive repair work to do. The P40, the Spitfire, the Zero, the Messerschmitt 109, and more, very accurately drawn, and somewhat challenging to assemble. $3.50.

MODERN FIGHTERS TO COLOR, CUT OUT, & FLY -- Accurate scale models of the F-15A, the F-16, the MiG 25, the Sea Harrier, the British Jaguar, ready to color, cut out, and glue together. $3.50.

GREAT DOGS COLORING BOOK-- Heroic feats performed by dogs and their famous owners, in nearly every period of history and literature. $2.95.

COWGIRLS COLORING BOOK -- From the earliest working cow women to those of Buffalo Bill's troop to movie queens and rodeo stars to Wild Horse Annie, who worked to save the wild mustangs. $3.50.

COWBOYS COLORING BOOK-- From earliest vaqueros to the great settlers of the ranges, from Buffalo Bill to Hoot Gibson and Roy Rogers, each in his most magnificent garb. $3.50.

THE STORY OF EARLY CALIFORNIA & HER FLAGS TO COLOR -- From Queen Califia, Cabrillo, Drake, Portola, Padre Serra, Anza to the rule of Mexico, the Bear Flag Republic to the Civil War to the Suffragettes. $3.50.

CALIFORNIA MISSIONS COLORING BOOK -- The earliest series of views made in 1856 of California's grand Spanish missions. $3.95.

THE DECORATION OF THE CALIFORNIA MISSIONS COLORING BOOK-- Wall paintings and patterns, and a guide to all the missions; with some colored pictures included. $5.95.

DOS CALIFORNIOS COLORING BOOK-- A story about the 1818 pirate raid on the California coast, and how a young Californio and his old sea otter thwart the evildoers. Text in English and Spanish. $2.95.

ROSIE AND THE BEAR FLAG COLORING BOOK -- In the early days of California, young Rosalie Leese becomes involved in the strange events of the wild Bear Flag bash. This is also a complete book of California flags. $3.50.

All "HISTORY COLORING BOOKS & ACTIVITY BOOKS," prices as indicated. Code BB. BROOK FARM BOOKS.

CUT & ASSEMBLE HISTORIC MODELS. Our only problem with these is finding a place to display them all when they're done, so we usually rotate our displays according to how we feel and what we're studying. These models are fun, challenging, educational, and attractive. With scissors, a hobby knife, a straight-edge ruler, and some white glue, you can construct authentic replicas of historic buildings, villages, and ways of life. Except with the "Easy-to-Make" titles, some of the small cuts and folds are a little tricky, and may be best for ages 10 or 12 and up, definitely including adult.

AN OLD-FASHIONED TRAIN IN FULL COLOR. Meticulously rendered replica includes locomotive, passenger car, caboose, station, more, with complete instructions. $4.95.

A CRUSADER CASTLE IN FULL COLOR: The Krak des Chevaliers in Syria. A detailed three-dimensional model of one of the most powerful and imposing crusader castles, built in the 12th and 13th centuries on a towering precipice in Syria. $4.95.

A MEDIEVAL CASTLE: Authentic, full-color model of Caenarvon Castle in Wales. $4.95.

AN EARLY NEW ENGLAND VILLAGE. 12 authentic buildings in H-O scale: Adams' home in Quincy, Mass., Oliver Wright house in Sturbridge, smithy, store, church, and seven others. $4.95.

A WESTERN FRONTIER TOWN. Ten authentic full-color buildings in H-O scale: Opera house, sheriff's office, jail, Wells Fargo office, saloon, etc. $4.95.

A SOUTHERN PLANTATION -- An H-O scale model of an antebellum Southern plantation, with authentic buildings and outbuildings. $5.95.

A VICTORIAN SEASIDE RESORT. Nine easy-to-make buildings in H-O scale: ice-cream stand, bandstand, bathhouse and boardwalk, life-saving station, four cottages, and a tower. $4.95.

MAIN STREET. Nine full-color buildings of a small Southern town in the 1930's. $4.95.

HISTORIC BUILDINGS AT GREENFIELD VILLAGE. Full-color models of Henry Ford's Bagley Avenue Shop, Edison's Menlo Park Labaratory, William McGuffey's birthplace, Wright Brothers' Cycle Shop, many more. $4.95.

AN OLD-FASHIONED FARM. Nine full-color buildings in H-O scale: Farmhouse, barn, piggery, machine shed, smokehouse, more. $4.95.

AN EARLY AMERICAN SEAPORT. Eleven easy-to-make, full-color buildings in H-O scale. Lighthouse, cooper's shop, ship chandlery, tavern, seven more. $4.95.

AN OLD ENGLISH VILLAGE. Twelve H-O scale buildings and structures of a typical village in the south of England, including a church, vicarage, an inn, three cottages, telephone box, lych-gate, gravestones, war memorial, more. $4.95.

NEW YORK HARBOR. Beautifully illustrated, expertly designed panorama includes Brooklyn Bridge, Statue of Liberty, skyscrapers, tugboats, Staten Island Ferry, rivers, bay, much more. $4.95.

THE MAYFLOWER. Detailed, full-color 17" model of the reconstructed Mayflower at Plimoth Plantation. Challenging. $5.95.

DINOSAUR DIORAMAS. Two easy-to-assemble, three-dimensional dioramas in full color, with 31 animal and plant cut-outs. $4.50.

CAVEMAN DIORAMAS. Two full-color, 3-dimensional dioramas of human life 30,000 years ago --one of Cro-Magnon, one of Neanderthal-- with many cut-out figures. $4.50.

PLAINS INDIANS DIORAMA. Two dioramas, a buffalo hunt & a small camp, with many cut-out figures illustrating the lost culture of the Plains Indians. $4.95.

MAYA DIORAMAS. Two pre-Columbian cities, Chichén Itza & Tulum, complete with temples, broad plazas, cut-out figures of slaves, priests, children, traders, weavers, more. $5.95.

ALL "CUT & ASSEMBLE HISTORIC MODELS." prices as indicated. Code DV. BROOK FARM BOOKS.

TIME LINES -- Decorative, interesting, informative. Transportation, Inventions, Building a Nation, Civil Rights in America, Explorers, and Famous Scientists. Each set contains eight 8x22" colorful panels. About $6.95 each, plus shipping. Correlated reproducible books available, $2.95 each. Included in catalog from: CREATIVE TEACHING PRESS, INC., P.O. Box 6017, Cypress, CA 90630.

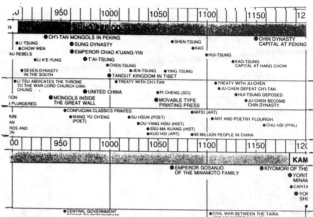

THE HISTORY CHART -- 34" high, 8 feet long. A 6,000-year chronology of the world's people and events. (The history of the United States takes up only two inches of the eight feet!). People & events covered include politics, literature, theology, mythology, and archaeology. $19.95 plus $5 shipping. Add $15 if you want plastic-lamination. INTERNATIONAL TIMELINE, 2565 Chain Bridge Road, Vienna, VA 22180.

THE VILLAGE OF BLUE STONE, Stephen Trimble. More than three centuries before the Europeans explored North America, a highly-developed civilization of the people we call the Anasazi flourished in the area where Utah, Colorado, New Mexico, and Arizona meet. They are the ancestors of the Pueblo Indians, who preserve many of their ways. In words and pictures, THE VILLAGE OF BLUE STONE describes a year in the life of an Anasazi community. Beginning with the winter solstice, carefully calculated by painstaking astronomical observation, the reader follows members of the different clans in the village through their work and festivals, learning about their methods of agriculture, hunting, pottery making, child rearing, and religion. All ages. Hardcover. $12.95. Code MAC. BROOK FARM BOOKS.

YESTERDAY'S HEADLINES, TODAY'S HISTORY -- Original radio broadcasts of world news events, including Lindbergh welcomed home, the crash of the Hindenburg, the Dempsey-Tunney fight, the Pearl Harbor invasion, the fall of Corregidor, the D-Day invasion, Truman announcing the dropping of the A- Bomb, MacArthur at the Japanese surrender, the Nuremberg trials, the assassination of JFK, much more. One cassette. $10.95. Code JN. BROOK FARM BOOKS.

VOICES FROM THE PAST-- Actual voices of more than 40 famous people of history, including Florence Nightingale, Thomas Edison, P. T. Barnum, Enrico Caruso, Teddy Roosevelt, Woodrow Wilson, V. I. Lenin, Will Rogers, Billy Sunday, W.C. Fields, Calvin Coolidge, Herbert Hoover, Mahatma Gandhi, Albert Einstein, and many others. One cassette. $10.95. Code JN. BROOK FARM BOOKS.

THE ANCIENT MEDITERRANEAN VIEW OF MAN. Arnold Toynbee analyzes man's knowledge of ancient Greek life, especially the contributions of the city states to art, poetry, science, philosophy, and war. ONE CASSETTE. $10.95. Code JN. BROOK FARM BOOKS.

THE DELIGHT MAKERS, Adolf F. Bandelier. A fictional reconstruction of prehistoric Indian culture in the American Southwest, by a 19th-century archaeologist. $10.95. Code HBJ. BROOK FARM BOOKS.

HISTORICAL EVENTS AND NOVELS ON VIDEO -- Movies and other dramatizations of literature, history, plays, mythology, more. Steinbeck, Dickens, Shakespeare, Melville, Cooper, Twain, Crane, Bradbury, et al. Some about $27, but most are higher, probably too expensive for most homeschoolers, but homeschool groups might be able to share costs. (If some entrepreneur begins a mail-order rental service with these videos, we'll be steady customers!) Catalog: ZENGER VIDEO, P.O. Box 802, Culver City, CA 90232.

GREAT IDEAS THAT HAVE SHAPED OUR WORLD -- The works of classic thinkers throughout history are sometimes referred to as "The Great Conversation," because the authors respond to each other's ideas, although they may have lived thousands of miles or hundreds of years apart; and because, in various ways, they all address the most important and enduring questions and problems of humanity -- What is truth? What is happiness? What is human nature? What principles should guide our actions? What authorities deserve our allegiance? These questions are as new -- and as old -- for us today as they were for Plato. The "Great Ideas" or "The Great Conversation" are not the useless ponderings of ancient, abstract philosophers. If we consider them in their historical contexts, we gain a better understanding of the past; if we apply them to our own time, they become powerful tools to help us better understand these times, our real nature, and our rights and responsibilities as human beings. Most of the Great Ideas were developed within the context of particular events of the past, and studying them will give us a better understanding of those events; but a higher value is that the basic principles are applicable to any period and circumstance, including our own.

When I first saw this cassette program advertised, I was very skeptical, expecting it to be no more than readings of condensed classics, which would be interesting and valuable, but of limited use. I requested a sample (CIVIL DISOBEDIENCE, by Henry David Thoreau, because I am especially interested in Thoreau's life and philosophy). I was very agreeably surprised and impressed.

The cassette tapes of GREAT IDEAS THAT SHAPED OUR WORLD are dramatized, with multiple voices portraying the author, contemporary observers, and critics, drawing on actual writings and quotations of the time, with an overview presented by a narrator. Each tape is about 90 minutes long, divided into shorter segments (about 20 minutes each) for more convenient study. The social and historical background of each work is presented, as well as the effects, both immediate and long-term, which the work had on contemporary and future society. There are numerous references to other works and historical events, demonstrating the continuing influence of the author's ideas.

The knowledge and understanding to be gained from each cassette program is easily equivalent to several hours of reading or high-school and college-level lecturing. These tapes won't take the place of the books presented, but they are very comprehensive introductions, and will definitely increase one's enjoyment and understanding of those works. For those who don't have the time or inclination to read the original works, these programs will make a very adequate substitute. After our complete satisfaction with our first tape, we bought several more, and are steadily adding titles to our library. We have listened to them several times, not only for "study," but for repeated enjoyment, just as we often browse through the Great Ideas in books.

SET 1. COMMON SENSE, by Thomas Paine. The little pamphlet which swept through the American colonies, converting thousands to the idea of independence. THE DECLARATION OF INDEPENDENCE, the announcement to the world of a new republic and the reasons for its inception.

SET 2. CIVIL DISOBEDIENCE, by Henry David Thoreau, one of the most influential essays in history, written after Thoreau was jailed for his opposition to slavery and the Mexican War, raising essential questions about law, conscience, and morality, and arguing that being _a person_ must always come before being _a citizen_. THE LIBERATOR, the most outspoken abolitionist newspaper, edited by William Lloyd Garrison.

SET 3. WEALTH OF NATIONS, by Adam Smith, Part 1. In 1776, a shy professor from Scotland published this masterpiece on economics which changed forever what people thought of the role of government in the economy. Smith is suspicious of businessmen who say "a balance of trade" is in the national interest; such a proposal, he says, is motivated by a desire to restrict competition.

SET 4. WEALTH OF NATIONS, by Adam Smith, Part 2. Continuing the discussions of Part 1, covering such themes as unplanned economic order (the "invisible hand"), the division of labor, the theory of value, and the role of free trade in economic prosperity. (Sets 3 and 4 may be used separately, but contain the best representation of Smith's ideas if used together.)

SET 5. ON LIBERTY, by John Stuart Mill, a strong and well-reasoned defense of individual rights against the state. VINDICATION OF THE RIGHTS OF WO-MAN, by Mary Wollstonecraft, considered by many to be the first declaration of "women's rights," written in 19th century England, when women were excluded from universities and many professions, and could not bring a lawsuit, sign a contract, or vote.

SET 6. THE PRINCE, by Niccolo Machiavelli. A master politician who wanted to expand government power discusses the pros and cons of telling the truth, arguing that the end usually justifies the means. DISCOURSE ON VOLUNTARY SERVITUDE, by Etienne de la Boetie, who sought to limit government's power. The nearly opposite views of these two thinkers present an excellent dialogue of ideas.

SET 7. THE COMMUNIST MANIFESTO, by Karl Marx and Frederick Engels, one of the most famous, most misunderstood, and most misused documents in history, arguing that the best interests of the individual derive from merging with the greater social good, much of its reasoning based on the economic struggle between the poor working class and the wealthy owners. THE SOCIAL CONTRACT, by Jean Jacques Rousseau. Arguing more from a concern for civil rights and liberties than for economic or ownership status, Rousseau arrived at startlingly similar views about the precedence which "the greater good" should have over the individual.

SET 8. REFLECTIONS ON THE REVOLUTION IN FRANCE, by Edmund Burke, a heated condemnation of the French Revolution, and a passing criticism of Thomas Paine's roles in both the American and French Revolutions. THE RIGHTS OF MAN, by Thomas Paine, written in rebuttal of Burke's attack, argued further for the inherent rights of all individuals. The "debate" between these men produced two of the best-selling books of the 18th century.

SET 9. THE FEDERALIST PAPERS, by Alexander Hamilton, James Madison, and John Jay. During the bitter debate over the ratification of the U.S. Constitution, these articles were published in various newspapers as part of a campaign to swing the pivotal state of New York, and formed the basis of many aspects of the Constitution as it is today.

SET 10. LEVIATHAN, by Thomas Hobbes. Some of the most compelling arguments ever set forth in favor of a strong, centralized government. Although condemned by many political theorists, this powerful book continues to be fascinating, and some of its ideas will be found in even the most "liberal" of today's democracies.

SET 11. TWO TREATISES OF GOVERNMENT, by John Locke. Locke's ideas on individual liberty, government by consent, and the right of revolution helped set the stage for the English Revolution of 1688, the American Revolution of 1776, and the French Revolution of 1789.

SET 12. DEMOCRACY IN AMERICA, by Alexis de Tocqueville. Although written in the 1830's, this book is still considered by many to be the best examination of American democracy and the American character, and contains many provocative insights to help us evaluate democracy as perceived and practiced in today's America, and to see that many of our national concepts have changed radically, although we may use the same words.

EACH SET (two cassettes, approximately 3 hours), $15.95. Postage: $2.00 for the first set, and $1.00 for each additional set. Specify "Great Ideas," set number, & first title in the set (e.g.: "Great Ideas #5, On Liberty"). Order from BROOK FARM BOOKS.

YOUNG DISCOVERY LIBRARY -- Compact, comprehensive introductions to many fascinating facts and periods of history. Each book has 40 pages, hardcover, with brief but very informative text and more than 50 brilliant, detailed pictures throughout. There are many helpful diagrams and charts, and many suggested activities to involve the readers more directly in each subject. Authors and illustrators work in collaboration with specialist advisors to ensure accuracy in both the text and illustrations. Especially suitable for ages 5 to 10, but very interesting for older kids and adults, too.

AUSTRALIA: ON THE OTHER SIDE OF THE WORLD. A land of perpetual fascination -- Aborigines, the Outback, kangaroos, wallabees; cities, children, and history.

THE BARBARIANS. A complete introduction to the tribes that came to conquer and stayed to settle Europe in the Middle Ages, featuring pictures and descriptions of Attila, the Vikings, Charlemagne, and many others; their ways of life, dress, weapons, and travel.

CATHEDRALS: STONE UPON STONE. Stained glass, flying buttresses, gargoyles introduce the beautiful cathedrals of Europe from the 11th century to the 15th; how they were built, how they were used, and the part they played in history.

FOLLOWING INDIAN TRAILS. How native Americans came to this land, acquired horses, built villages, taught their children, and protected their lands. Many surprising facts not often found in children's books.

GOING WEST: COWBOYS AND PIONEERS. Adventures of the pioneers, including details of a two-month trip across the Great Plains, life during the Gold Rush, settling a new town, the Pony Express, and everyday life in the old west.

JAPAN: LAND OF SAMURAI AND ROBOTS. A colorful introduction to the traditions and modern growth of the land which is comprised of 1,042 islands; Tokyo and its huge suburbs; calligraphy, haiku, flower arranging, origami, much more.

LIVING IN ANCIENT ROME. Daily life in Rome, art, schools, architecture, battles, and language over 1000 years of history.

LIVING IN INDIA. Fascinating details on the clothing, foods, language, religion, schools, and many more aspects of life in one of the world's most populated lands, with beautiful pictures of ceremonies and festivals.

LIVING ON A TROPICAL ISLAND. A portrait of the island of Nossy-Bé near Madagascar tells the story of what it's like to live in the tropics -- how to climb a coconut tree, spot a lemur, recognize hibiscus, grow crops, fish, and much more.

LIVING WITH THE ESKIMOS. Everyday life in an Eskimo community, including how kayaks are made, dogs are trained, igloos are built, and sharks are caught by the Inuit, Laplanders, and other Arctic peoples.

LONG AGO IN A CASTLE. Realistic illustrations of many castles across Europe, with facts about castle communities of the Middle Ages, and information on building techniques, home life, feasts, knights, and lords.

ON THE BANKS OF THE PHARAOH'S NILE. Depicts life in Ancient Egypt through 322 B.C. -- why the Nile River was important, what the Pharaoh actually did, children's toys, making of a mummy, hieroglyphics.

Each YOUNG DISCOVERY LIBRARY title, $4.95. Code YD. BROOK FARM BOOKS. (For more books in this series, see Science and Music.)

● ● ●

LIFE IN ANCIENT EGYPT COLORING BOOK -- 44 detailed and authentic drawings of ancient Egypt, from about 3000 B.C. to the Roman conquest in 30 B.C., with full-page illustrations of the pyramids, the Sphinx, gigantic temples, Cleopatra, Ramses II, Akhenaten, & many of the daily activities of the Egyptians, including arts & crafts, funerary practices, religion, architecture, warfare, and much more. $2.95. Code DV. BROOK FARM BOOKS.

THE GREAT WALL OF CHINA, Leonard Everett Fisher. The story behind the building of the Great Wall of China, told with brief text and very impressive pictures -- buildings, people, and animals seem almost three-dimensional in the large, colorful paintings. Ages 8 and up. Hardcover, 8½x11", 32 pages. $12.95. Code MAC. BROOK FARM BOOKS.

THE MYSTERY OF THE ANCIENT MAYA, Carolyn Meyer and Charles Gallencamp. The excitement of the early explorers who discovered the jungle-shrouded ruins of what had been a wonderful civilization, with fascinating details of the culture and the people. Illustrated with charts, diagrams, and photographs. Age 10 and up. $12.95. Code MAC. BROOK FARM BOOKS.

There is no king who has not had a slave among his ancestors, and no slave who has not had a king among his.

Helen Keller

JOHNNY TREMAIN, by Esther Forbes. A young apprentice silversmith in revolutionary Boston becomes involved with Paul Revere, John Hancock, Sam Adams, and other rebelling colonists. While revolution takes shape around him, Johnny also learns important lessons about friendship, love, responsibility, and growing up. I first read this book when I was in the eighth grade, and it is still one of my favorite historical novels. Age 12 to adult. $12.95. Code HM. BROOK FARM BOOKS.

THE RED BADGE OF COURAGE, by Stephen Crane. Two cassettes, approx. 2 hours, read by Dick Cavett. Set against the background of the Civil War, this stunning psychological portrait of a young Union soldier who learns the meaning of cowardice and true heroism was one of the first realistic treatments of modern warfare. $15.95. Code LFP. BROOK FARM BOOKS.

JEREMIAH MARTIN, Robert H. Fowler. An intricately-plotted historical novel which follows Jeremiah Martin, a black-sheep Virginia aristocrat, through almost every aspect of the Revolutionary War on land & at sea. Jeremiah serves as an American spy, from the battle at Lexington, through the siege of Boston and the battle of Bunker Hill, then with Washington at Brandywine and Germantown, the dismal winter at Valley Forge, and on privateers that sail to Philadelphia, Barbados, London, and France. The author's thorough research makes this an accurate portrayal of the period as well as an exciting, enjoyable, and enlightening tour of the Revolutionary War. 352 pages. $18.95. Code STM. BROOK FARM BOOKS.

1787, fiction by Joan Anderson. In the historic summer of 1787, young Jared Mifflin works as an aide to James Madison, and learns a great deal about politics, friendship, and romance. Age 10 up. Hardcover, 176 pages, illustrated. $14.95. Code HBJ. BROOK FARM BOOKS.

THE THOMAS PAINE READER--Tom Paine was the first man to use the phrase "the United States of America," and, had it not been for him and his little booklet "Common Sense," there might never have been such a country. He was born in Thetford, England, in 1737. When he emigrated to the American colonies in 1774, his only asset was a letter of introduction and recommendation from Benjamin Franklin, whom he had met in London. Paine's life had been marked with constant failure and setback; Franklin had suggested that Paine try his luck in America.. Soon after his arrival in Philadelphia, Paine became editor of the newly-established "Pennsylvania Magazine," and in that position he began crusading -- against slavery, advocating equal rights for women, suggesting international copyright laws, condemning cruelty to animals, criticizing the practice of dueling, and asking for the end of war as a means of settling international disputes. Following the battles of Concord, Lexington, and Bunker Hill in 1775, opinions through the colonies were still strongly divided between loyalty to the King and a feeling that war and separation were both necessary and inevitable. Sam Adams and John Hancock favored separation; Washington, Franklin, and Jefferson remained loyal to England. Paine spent the fall of 1775 writing down his thoughts; Dr. Benjamin Rush suggested the title, "Common Sense," and Robert Bell of Philadelphia published the booklet.

COMMON SENSE began selling on January 10, 1776 -- 47 pages, for two shillings. The price was high, because the printer didn't expect many copies to be sold, and was afraid he wouldn't even break even on the cost of printing 500 copies. In three months, 120,000 copies had sold; total sales reached over half a million in less than six months. Tradesmen, farmers, soldiers, and politicians carried copies in their pockets, and discussed the booklet's ideas heatedly and excitedly. Opinions changed rapidly, and on July 4, 1776, the Continental Congress proclaimed the independence of the United States of America.

This book includes COMMON SENSE, excerpts from THE RIGHTS OF MAN, THE AMERICAN CRISIS, and THE AGE OF REASON. $8.95. Code BT. BROOK FARM BOOKS.

DEMOCRACY -- The highest form of government to which most societies have yet attained. We give it a lot of thought at Brook Farm, for ourselves and for the world: how to achieve it, how to preserve it, how to keep it truly democratic. Democracy, after all, does not come from a government; "demos" means people. It's up to us, and our children.

EASY BIOGRAPHIES-- An amazing amount of interesting information is packed into the short texts of these books, which concentrate on the childhood and early adulthood of several famous men and women. Although they're written for young readers, they'll be of interest to older ones, too.

ABE LINCOLN, The Young Years -- AMELIA EARHART, Adventure in the Sky -- ANDREW JACKSON, Frontier Patriot -- BABE RUTH, Home Run Hero-- CLARA BARTON, Angel of the Battlefield -- COURAGE OF HELEN KELLER -- DANIEL BOONE, Frontier Adventures -- DAVY CROCKETT, Young Pioneer-- ELIZABETH BLACKWELL, The First Woman Doctor -- GANDHI -- GEORGE WASHINGTON, Young Leader -- THE GREAT HOUDINI, Daring Escape Artist --HARRIET TUBMAN, The Road to Freedom -- JAMES MONROE, Young Patriot -- JESSE OWENS, Olympic Hero -- JIM THORPE, Young Athlete -- JOHN ADAMS, Brave Patriot -- JOHN PAUL JONES, Hero of the Seas -- LAFAYETTE, Hero of Two Nations -- LOU GEHRIG, Pride of the Yankees -- LOUIS PASTEUR, Young Scientist -- LOUISA MAY ALCOTT, Young Writer -- MARIE CURIE, Brave Scientist -- MOZART, Young Music Genius -- NARCISSA WHITMAN, Brave Pioneer -- PATRICK HENRY, Voice of American Revolution -- PAUL REVERE, Son of Liberty -- ROBERT E. LEE, Brave Leader -- TEDDY ROOSEVELT, Rough Rider -- THOMAS ALVA EDISON, Young Inventor -- WILBUR AND ORVILLE WRIGHT, The Flight to Adventure -- WILLIE MAYS, Young Superstar -- YOUNG ALBERT EINSTEIN -- YOUNG BEN FRANKLIN -- YOUNG ELEANOR ROOSEVELT-- YOUNG FREDERICK DOUGLASS, Fight for Freedom -- YOUNG MARK TWAIN -- YOUNG QUEEN ELIZABETH -- YOUNG THOMAS JEFFERSON

Age 8 and up. Each book, 7x9", 48 pages, black & white illustrations. Specify "Easy Biographies" and title. $3.50 each. Code TRL. BROOK FARM BOOKS.

ILLUSTRATED BIOGRAPHIES-- Twelve 64-page books with clear black-and-white drawings and easy text (about 4th or 5th grade), fully researched for historical accuracy and background information. Each book has the biographies of two people (or groups).

Charles Lindberg & Amelia Earhart
Houdini & Walt Disney
Davy Crockett & Danial Boone
Elvis Presley & The Beatles
Benjamin Franklin & Martin Luther King, Jr.
Abraham Lincoln & Franklin D. Roosevelt
George Washington & Thomas Jefferson
Madame Curie & Albert Einstein
Thomas Edison & Alexander Graham Bell
Vince Lombardi & Pelé
Babe Ruth & Jackie Robinson
Jim Thorpe & Althea Gibson

FULL SET OF 12 BOOKS, $36.00 plus $3 shipping. (Individual titles may be ordered if combined with Illustrated Classics, Illustrated Shakespeare, or Illustrated U.S. History, for a <u>minimum of 12 books</u>.) BROOK FARM BOOKS.

POSTERS OF THE PAST -- History on your wall or in your hands. Authentic reproductions of posters, handbills, broadsides, prints, and advertisements, tracing the political and social history of America from very early times to the recent past. We've used them for years, and have found they often create more interest in history than most textbooks can, as well as giving unusual insights into events of the past. We also have several of these posters matted and on walls around the house as interesting "decorations." There are posters and other material from the early American colonies, the Revolutionary War, the New Nation, Slavery, the Civil War, through the later 1800's. Most cost less than $1.00 each. Write for a catalog: BUCK HILL ASSOCIATES, Box 501, North Creek, NY 12853.

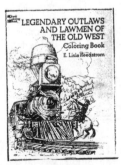

LEGENDARY OUTLAWS & LAWMEN OF THE OLD WEST COLORING BOOK-- 45 authentic scenes of good guys (Bat Masterson, Wyatt Earp, more) and bad guys (Billy the Kid, Jesse James, more), with biographical captions. $2.95. Code DV. BROOK FARM BOOKS.

LANDMARK BOOKS -- I think I had at least thirty of the Landmark Books when I was a kid, and re-read them often. They were exciting, dramatic, and informative. Several titles are once again available, in paperbacks. Each book relates an important event in history with a lively, well-documented text featuring character portraits and anecdotes. Most volumes are illustrated with photographs and maps. For some reason, a few titles available just two or three years ago are out of print again, but new titles have been added to the list. Keeping my fingers crossed, these are the ones now available:

THE LANDING OF THE PILGRIMS, by James Dougherty. Excellent account of the Pilgrims' search for religious freedom, dangerous ocean voyage, & hardships in establishing a colony. $4.95.

THE WITCHCRAFT OF SALEM VILLAGE, by Shirley Jackson. The terrible time in the Massachusetts Bay Colony when pious villagers accused each other of devil worship. $2.95.

BEN FRANKLIN OF OLD PHILADELPHIA, by Margaret Cousins. Lively record of Franklin's patriotic public life as statesman, advisor, ambassador, diplomat, inventor, printer, writer, and editor. $4.95.

THE AMERICAN REVOLUTION, by Bruce Bliven. Detailed account and examination of the major causes of the Revolutionary War, historic events, and battles from Lexington to Yorktown, with portraits in words of Washington, Howe, Greene, Cornwallis, and others. Many maps and photographs. $3.95.

OUR INDEPENDENCE AND THE CONSTITUTION, by Dorothy Canfield Fisher. Through the eyes of a Philadelphia family, this book describes the early days of freedom, the Founding Fathers, and their work toward a constitution that would satisfy each state. $2.95.

THE CALIFORNIA GOLD RUSH, by May McNeer. Dramatic anecdotes about fabulous strikes & legendary characters of the mining camps. $2.95.

ABE LINCOLN: LOG CABIN TO WHITE HOUSE, by Sterling North. Lincoln's early years in Kentucky & Indiana, his frontier education, and his various jobs, from Mississippi flatboatman, farming, and carpentry to state assemblyman, lawyer, and President. $2.95.

GETTYSBURG, by MacKinlay Kantor. The bitter three-day Civil War battle; portraits of many brigades, townspeople, and generals. Maps and the text of Lincoln's Gettysburg Address. $2.95.

THE PIONEERS GO WEST, by George R. Stewart. Encounters with Indians and buffalo, near-starvation, disasters encountered by an eleven-wagon train from Iowa in 1844. Many maps. $2.95.

YOUNG MARK TWAIN AND THE MISSISSIPPI, by Harnett T. Kane. Based on Twain's own remembrances of his boyhood in Hannibal, Missouri; his river education, days on the farm, big city experiences in St. Louis, and journeys as a cub steamboat pilot. $2.95.

CUSTER'S LAST STAND, by Quentin Reynolds. Vivid history of the Little Bighorn battle, and the controversial West Point cadet, Civil War hero, 25-year-old general, and Indian fighter. $2.95.

THE STORY OF D-DAY: JUNE 6, 1944, by Bruce Bliven. Dramatic, factual, eyewitness account of the Allied invasion of Normandy, which began the end of World War II. Photographs and maps. $2.95.

THE PHARAOHS OF ANCIENT EGYPT, by Elizabeth Payne. A clear and dramatic account of 3000 years of Egyptian history, and of the soldiers, scholars, and graverobbers who rediscovered the ancient civilization's buried treasures. $4.95.

THE WRIGHT BROTHERS, Quentin Reynolds. The boyhood and early experiments of the pioneers of aviation, who tinkered with sleds, bicycles, printing presses -- but their dream was to fly. $3.95.

THE VIKINGS, by Elizabeth Janeway. Semi-fictional account based on Norse sagas records Eric the Red's discovery of Greenland and his son Leif's voyages to North America 500 years before Columbus. $4.95.

Prices as indicated. Specify "Landmark" and title. Code RH. BROOK FARM BOOKS.

OLD-FASHIONED FARM LIFE COLORING BOOK -- The daily 19th-century activities on the Firestone Farm at Greenfield Village in Dearborn, Michigan. Finely-detailed illustrations include churning butter, shearing sheep, plowing, making maple syrup, mowing hay, planting, caring for livestock, and many other activities. $2.95. Code DV. BROOK FARM BOOKS.

ABE LINCOLN GROWS UP, by Carl Sandburg. The chapters on Lincoln's boyhood, from Sandburg's monumental ABRAHAM LINCOLN: THE PRAIRIE YEARS. 222 pages, 59 line drawings. Ages 12 and up. $16.95. Code HBJ. BROOK FARM BOOKS.

ABRAHAM LINCOLN: THE PRAIRIE YEARS & THE WAR YEARS, by Carl Sandburg. A one-volume edition containing the essence of the author's acclaimed six-volume biography. 762 pages. [Published in hardcover for $49.95.] Paperback, $14.95. Code HBJ. BROOK FARM BOOKS.

THE AMERICAN SONGBAG, edited by Carl Sandburg. A collection of 280 songs, ballads, and ditties which people have sung in the making of America. Piano accompaniments. 495 pages. $12.95. Code HBJ. BROOK FARM BOOKS.

DRAMATIZED
HISTORY & BIOGRAPHY
FROM "OLD TIME RADIO"

Old radio programs are among our favorite learning tools. Besides being very entertaining, they give us a feeling of "being there" which is almost as good as actually being able to go back in time.

"Old Radio" has become so popular with many of our readers that we've recently added several new titles to our listing. These programs were produced on old radio's finest shows -- Lux Radio Theatre, Hallmark Hall of Fame, Screen Director's Playhouse, Favorite Story, Cavalcade of America, CBS's "You Are There," Mercury Theatre, and many others. Most are carefully-researched dramatizations of actual events; others are historical fiction, interwoven with an authentic historical background. All have appropriate sound effects and musical background. Most of them have excellent sound, although a few are slightly muffled in places (due to the recording techniques then used). Some school suppliers offer a few (about 10) of these programs, for $12 or more per hour; we sell them for half that price.

The following sets are each <u>one hour</u>, with either two 30-minute shows or one 60-minute show.

#1. THE LAST DAY OF POMPEII. THE FALL OF TROY.
#2. ALEXANDER: THE PEACE OFFER FROM PERSIA. ALEXANDER: THE BATTLE FOR ASIA.
#3. ALEXANDER: MUTINY IN INDIA. JOAN OF ARC.
#4. CAESAR CROSSES THE RUBICON. ASSASSINATION OF CAESAR.
#5. THE SIGNING OF THE MAGNA CARTA. THE EXECUTION CAPTAIN KIDD.
#6. DEATH OF MONTEZUMA. SAILING OF THE MAYFLOWER.
#7. THE COUNT OF MONTE CRISTO.
#8. PHILADELPHIA, JULY 4, 1776. RATIFICATION OF THE CONSTITUTION.
#9. A TALE OF TWO CITIES.
#10. LES MISERABLES (Ronald Colman, Debra Paget).
#11. NAPOLEON RETURNS FROM EXILE. IRELAND SEPARATES FROM ENGLAND.
#12. 1781: MUTINY IN WASHINGTON'S ARMY. BETRAYAL OF TOUSSAINT L'OUVERTURE.
#13. COLONEL JOHNSON EATS THE LOVE APPLE. THE TRIAL OF JOHN PETER ZENGER.
#14. SENTENCING OF CHARLES I. FALL OF SAVONAROLA.
#15. BATTLE OF HASTINGS. HANGING OF ROBERT EMMENT.
#16. EXECUTION OF MARY, QUEEN OF SCOTS. THE DREYFUS CASE.
#17. SIEGE OF LEIDEN. TRIAL OF SAMUEL CHASE.
#18. LEWIS & CLARK. (Parts are muffled; still good.)
#19. SWANEE RIVER (biography of Stephen Foster).

"MR. PRESIDENT" SERIES. Each 30-minute program dramatizes an important but little-known event or circumstance in the administration of one of the U.S. presidents.

#20. GEORGE WASHINGTON AND THOMAS JEFFERSON.
#21. JOHN QUINCY ADAMS and ZACHARY TAYLOR.
#22. ANDREW JACKSON - 2 separate episodes.
#23. JOHN TYLER - 2 separate episodes.
#24. MILLARD FILLMORE and FRANKLIN PEARCE.
#25. ABRAHAM LINCOLN. LAST DAYS OF LINCOLN'S LIFE.
#26. ULYSSES S. GRANT - 2 separate episodes.
#27. GROVER CLEVELAND and WOODROW WILSON.

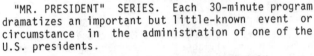

#28. IMPEACHMENT OF ANDREW JOHNSON. TRIAL OF AARON BURR.
#29. ANNA KARENINA.
#30. LIFE ON THE MISSISSIPPI, Mark Twain's youth on a riverboat. THE BALLAD OF THE IRON HORSE.
#31. HUCKLEBERRY FINN.
#32. ABRAHAM LINCOLN (played by Orson Welles).
#33. JOHN BROWN. THE MONITOR AND THE MERRIMAC.
#34. THE PRAIRIE YEARS (Sandburg's biography of Lincoln, played by Gregory Peck). THE BATTLE HYMN OF THE REPUBLIC.
#35. BATTLE OF LEXINGTON. I, MARY PEABODY.
#36. THE RED BADGE OF COURAGE.
#37. BATTLE OF GETTYSBURG. LEE SURRENDERS TO GRANT.
#38. MR. LINCOLN GOES TO THE PLAY. THE CAPTURE OF JOHN WILKES BOOTH.
#39. THE VIRGINIAN (Gary Cooper).
#40. VIVA ZAPATA! (Charlton Heston).
#41. BROKEN ARROW (one of the few Westerns sympathetic to both white and Indian sides).
#42. SURRENDER OF SITTING BULL. OKLAHOMA LAND RUN.
#43. SHANE (Alan Ladd, Van Heflin).
#44. GREELEY OF THE TRIBUNE. PEARY AT THE NORTH POLE.
#45. THE SHIP THE NAZIS HAD TO GET (carrying tanks to head off Rommel; great suspense!). CBS IS THERE, highlights of early radio--war news, abdication of King Edward, sports, more.
#46. "I CAN HEAR IT NOW," the history of an era, 1933-1945, with the voices and actual sounds of the time: Roosevelt, Truman, Hitler, Mussolini, Stalin, newscasters; narrated by Edward R. Murrow.
#47. THE GRAPES OF WRATH (Steinbeck's novel of the Depression; with Henry Fonda).
#48. ALEXANDER GRAHAM BELL.
#49. YOUNG TOM EDISON (Mickey Rooney).
#50. MADAME CURIE (Greer Garson, Walter Pidgeon).

Order by NUMBER and FULL TITLE. Each one-hour tape, $6.00. POSTAGE: $1.50 for one tape, 25¢ for each additional tape. 20 or more tapes at one time, $5 each, postpaid (cannot be combined with other discounts). Order from BROOK FARM BOOKS.

ILLUSTRATED HISTORY OF AMERICA -- Major events of American history from 1500 to 1981 are portrayed through their impact on ordinary families in twelve 64-page paperback books, with an easy-to-read text and black-and-white line drawings, both based on careful research. The reading level is for age 10 and up, but we've found the illustrations very useful for all ages, and of as much interest to adults as to children. <u>Seeing</u> the people, architecture, transportation, clothing, weapons, and general scenery is much more interesting and informative than just reading about them. I think the books are over-priced; they could be sold for half the price, and the publishers would still make a fair profit. Just the same, I think the information and excellent illustrations are worth buying, even if the price should be lower. The set includes:

THE NEW WORLD, 1500-1750. Columbus, French explorers, English settlements, the development of the New England and Southern colonies, and the emergence of an "American spirit." THE FIGHT FOR FREEDOM, 1750-

1783. The French and Indian War, political organization of the colonies, Revolutionary War. THE UNITED STATES EMERGES, 1783-1800. Economic problems after the Revolution, opening the West, the Constitutional Convention, the administrations of Washington and Adams. PROBLEMS OF THE NEW NATION, 1800-1830. Jefferson's administration, the War of 1812, the Monroe Doctrine, administrations of John Quincy Adams and Andrew Jackson. AMERICANS MOVE WESTWARD, 1830-1850. The movement west, the Louisiana Purchase, roads and canals, missionaries, pioneers across the prairies, & the Oregon territory. BEFORE THE CIVIL WAR, 1830-1860. American move into northern Mexico, Mormon migration, Mexican-American War, Indian removal, the women's rights movement, economic expansion, and the growing problems of slavery. THE CIVIL WAR, 1850-1876. Unrest among the slaves, abolitionism, Lincoln's election, the war, beginning of Reconstruction. THE INDUSTRIAL ERA, 1865-1915. 19th century immigration, growth of large corporations, building of the railroads, Indian resistance in the West, the fight in the South for black rights, the beginnings of labor unions. AMERICA BECOMES A WORLD POWER, 1890-1920. American expansion in the Pacific, the opening of Japan, the Spanish-American War, American activity in Puerto Rico and the Philippines, Teddy Roosevelt's administration, World War I. THE ROARING TWENTIES & THE GREAT DEPRESSION, 1920-1940. Changes in American values, Henry Ford's cheap automobiles, stock market crash, Depression, the New Deal. WORLD WAR II, 1940-1945. Rise to power of dictators in Europe, beginnings of World War II in Europe, Japan attacks Pearl Harbor, events of the war, the United Nations. AMERICA TODAY, 1945-1981. Growth of the Civil Rights movement, Kennedy and King assassinations, moon landings, Vietnam, Watergate, Iran hostage crisis, beginning of the Reagan administration.

SET OF TWELVE BOOKS, "Illustrated U.S. History," $36.00 plus $3 postage. BROOK FARM BOOKS.

LOUISIANA PURCHASE: An American Story, John Chase. Beginning with the United States' desire to expand its borders, the book covers the many facets of the great land deal, such as the roles of Daniel Boone, Thomas Jefferson, & Sacajawa. Originally published in 1953 as a nationally-syndicated <u>comic strip</u>. 96 pages, 8½x11". $8.95. Code PEL. BROOK FARM BOOKS.

DON'T KNOW MUCH ABOUT HISTORY: Everything You Need to Know About American History But Never Learned, Kenneth C. Davis. What did Franklin Delano Roosevelt know about an impending Japanese attack, and when did he know it? What was "voodoo economics"? Using an easy-to-follow question-and-answer format, sometimes irreverent but well-researched, this book explores the myths, landmark events, controversial issues, & colorful people of American history from the voyages of Columbus through the Reagan presidency. The book also has several mini-biographies, excerpts from notable speeches & writings, and informative chronologies. Not really "everything you need to know," but very interesting and informative anyway. A good supplement to other readings in U.S. history. High school and adult. $11.00. Code CR. BROOK FARM BOOKS.

AMERICAN ADVENTURES: True Stories from America's Past, by Morrie Greenberg. "Moving North," "The Good Old Days of Medicine," "The Man Who Jumped to Fame," "The Orphan Train," "Camels of the Old West, "The Three Hundred Dollar Baby," and more -- 15 stories of unusual and fascinating people and events between 1770 and 1870. Each story is preceded by a brief timeline and a summary of "What else was happening" (good), and followed by writing & discussion activities (too schoolish, but you may not mind them). Black and white illustrations. Ages 10 & up. $9.95. Code BR. BROOK FARM BOOKS.

 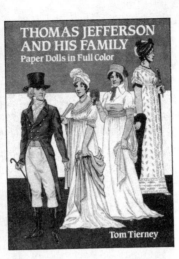

THE LIFE AND SELECTED WRITINGS OF THOMAS JEFFERSON.
At a dinner honoring Nobel Prize recipients, John F. Kennedy remarked that his guests were "the most extraordinary collection of talent, of human knowledge, that has ever been gathered at the White House, with the possible exception of when Thomas Jefferson dined alone." Jefferson was a statesman, architect, scientist, naturalist, educator, and public servant; he was the main author of the Declaration of Independence and the Virginia Statute on Religious Freedoms; governor of Virginia, Secretary of State, ambassador to France, vice-president and third president of the United States. This 800-page volume is a comprehensive collection of his travel journals, biographical sketches of some of his notable contemporaries, important public papers, and a large selection of his letters on both public and private matters. $12.00. Code RH. BROOK FARM BOOKS.

THOMAS JEFFERSON AND HIS FAMILY PAPER DOLLS in Full Color --
With several different, authentic costumes showing Jefferson and his family in various activities. $3.95. Code DV. BROOK FARM BOOKS.

"WE'RE FREE" -- Two-sided wall poster. A simplified but accurate version of the Declaration of Independence. On the other side, "Who needs freedom?" -- a picture essay raising questions about what our daily lives might be like without the Bill of Rights. $2.20. PITMAN LEARNING, INC., P.O. Box 2688, Clinton, IA 52735.

"WE THE PEOPLE" CALENDAR. $3.00. CONSUMER INFORMATION CENTER, Pueblo, CO 81009.

U.S. CONSTITUTION: copy of the original. FREE from THE CONSTITUTION, Citicorp, P.O.Box 1787, New York, NY 10001.

CONSTITUTION CURRICULUM PACKAGE, FREE from NATIONAL CONFERENCE OF CHRISTIANS AND JEWS, 71 Fifth Ave., New York, NY 10003.

THE BILL OF RIGHTS, FREE copy from VETERANS OF FOREIGN WARS, Americanism Dept., Broadway at 34th St., Kansas City, MO 64111.

MAGNA CARTA TO THE CONSTITUTION: Liberty Under the Law. 64-page book tracing the development of Anglo-American principles of democracy; excellent reproductions of relevant paintings. $7.95. OFFICE FOR THE BICENTENNIAL OF THE U.S. CONSTITUTION, Maryland State Archives, 350 Rowe Blvd., Annapolis MD 21401.

HISTORIC WALL CHARTS -- Declaration of Independence, Preamble, Bill of Rights, Gettysburg Address, Emancipation Proclamation, Pledge of Allegiance, Star Spangled Banner, Black Americans. About $2 each, plus postage. Included in catalog from: CREATIVE TEACHING PRESS, INC., POBox 6017, Cypress, CA 90630.

THE LITTLE RED, WHITE, AND BLUE BOOK. Quick-reference, 132-page book with the Declaration of Independence, Constitution, articles on their origins & background, excerpts from other writings & speeches and a chronology of important U.S. history dates. $5.95. PHAROS BOOKS, 200 Park Ave., New York, NY 10166.

"HELPING CHILDREN UNDERSTAND THE U.S. CONSTITUTION" booklet, $2.00. AMERICAN BAR ASSOCIATION, 750 North Lake Shore Drive, Chicago, IL 60611.

WE THE PEOPLE, Doris and Harold Faber. The story of the U.S. Constitution, from its inception in 1787 through the arguments about slavery, income tax, and women's suffrage, to the present day. Many pertinent quotations. Emphasis is on the Constitution as a "living document" that has evolved gradually, with much thought and debate, in response to the nation's changing social and political mores. Ages 12 and up. Hardcover, 256 pages. $13.95. Code MAC. BROOK FARM BOOKS.

"SIGNERS OF THE CONSTITUTION," poster. $3.25 to: SIGNERS OF THE CONSTITUTION, P.O. Box 41950, Kansas City, MO 64111.

HISTORIC DOCUMENTS-- Large colorful prints (24x36") of Gettysburg Address, Bill of Rights, presidents, etc. 8½x11 prints of U.S. and world leaders and other personalities, authors, etc. Inexpensive. Free brochure. GIANT PHOTOS, INC., P.O. Box 406, Rockford, IL 61105.

CONSTITUTION: FREE "EDUCATION PACKET" includes an illustrated calendar of historic sites and events, each date with an historical fact from 1788 related to the ratification; a pocket edition of the Constitution, a ratification brochure, and a newsletter. Write to: THE COMMISSION ON THE BICENTENNIAL OF THE U. S. CONSTITUTION, 808 17th St. NW, Washington, DC 20006.

THE LITTLE HOUSE BOOKS, by Laura Ingalls Wilder. Pictures by Garth Williams. These warm and moving stories of one family's move westward mirror the growth of the nation. The Ingalls, a close and happy family, struggle at times for survival as they move west during the 1870's & 1880's, but their troubles only make them closer. The first book, in which the story's children are quite young, is written on an easy reading level; the reading level becomes higher through each succeeding book, as the children grow older. Whether you and your children read these books as entertainment or as biography and history, you'll feel a closeness to the Ingalls family as well as a deeper understanding of the time in which they lived.

LITTLE HOUSE IN THE BIG WOODS. The Ingalls family is snug in their Wisconsin cabin, in spite of blizzards, wolves, and the big forest.

LITTLE HOUSE ON THE PRAIRIE. Laura and her family journey west by covered wagon, only to find they are in Indian territory and must move again.

FARMER BOY. The boyhood of Almanzo Wilder, the future husband of Laura, on his father's farm in upper New York state.

ON THE BANKS OF PLUM CREEK. After moving to Minnesota, the Ingalls family encounters a terrible blizzard and a grasshopper plague.

BY THE SHORES OF SILVER LAKE. In Dakota Territory, Pa has a job in a railroad building camp, and Laura is now 13.

THE LONG WINTER. Almanzo makes a dangerous trip to secure wheat to save the village from starvation during the terrible winter of 1880-81.

LITTLE TOWN ON THE PRAIRIE. The little settlement becomes a frontier town, and Laura, at 15, receives a certificate to teach school.

THESE HAPPY GOLDEN YEARS. Laura is courted by Almanzo; they marry, and move to their own little house on a homestead claim.

THE FIRST FOUR YEARS. This 9th book of the series tells of Laura and Almanzo's Dakota homesteading in the 1880's, and of the birth of their daughter Rose. EACH TITLE, $3.95. Code HR. BROOK FARM BOOKS.

SPECIAL: All nine "Little House" books in a Boxed Gift Edition, only $35.50, plus $3 postage. BROOK FARM BOOKS.

STEVEN CANEY'S KIDS' AMERICA, Steven Caney. Kids 4 to 14 and older explore American history through fascinating stories, anecdotes, toys, games, photographs, crafts, silly autograph sayings, and much more. A huge collection of fun and learning. Younger kids will enjoy the fun; older kids will enjoy participating in history. $11.95. Code BT. BROOK FARM BOOKS. (See also Art, STEVEN CANEY'S TOYBOOK and STEVEN CANEY'S PLAY BOOK; also Science, STEVEN CANEY'S INVENTION BOOK).

HOME LIFE IN COLONIAL AMERICA, Alice Morse Earle. Comprehensive account of how early Americans lived, worked, built their homes and villages. Travel, meals, housewares, dress, planting, industry, and tools. 470 pages, illustrated. Catalog #118. $5.95 plus $1 postage. OLD MAIN BOOKS, P.O. Box 2353, Mechanicsburg, PA 17055.

LET'S BE EARLY SETTLERS WITH DANIEL BOONE, Peggy Parish. Easy-to-follow instructions in a simplified introduction to make-it-yourself pioneer life, with clear directions for making a complete costume with accessories: model tools, log cabins, flatboats, covered wagons, etc., & dioramas of life in a frontier outpost. I wish I'd had this book when I was a kid. In between being a knight, a cowboy, and a spaceman, I was a pretty good pioneer, but this book would have helped me be a better one. Age 6 up. $12.95. Code HR. BROOK FARM BOOKS.

A POCKETFUL OF COLONIAL GAMES. Small, 32-page booklet describes 12 simple games of colonial children. $2.00. ROSALIND L. SCHILDER, P.O.Box 153, Plymouth Meeting, PA 19462.

MADE FOR TRADE, A Game of Early American Life. Take on the role of such characters as Eliza Oglethorpe, tavern maid; Makepeace Middleton, the continental soldier; or Christian Fairhill, the wealthy ship-owner-merchant. Within your role, you try to earn shillings & trade for goods in the town shops after you've escaped from indentured service. You and your fellow players will try to avoid customs and other taxes of the time while obeying the dictates of historical events cited on the 60 Events Cards. The player who accumulates the most wealth in objects purchased and shillings saved is the winner. (Times haven't changed much, have they?) Contents include a colorful board, 8 illustrated character cards with stands, 8 inventory lists, 40 object cards, 60 Event cards, 60 plastic replicas of 1652 shillings, one pair dice. Ages 8 to adult; 2 to 4 players; 4 levels of play. $22.00 plus $3 shipping. BROOK FARM BOOKS.

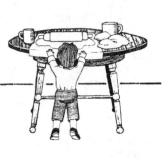

HISTORIC AND HOLIDAY COSTUME PATTERNS -- Die-cut patterns, ready to trace onto construction paper (some parts onto heavy felt for more realism). Costumes can be glued or stapled together. Lincoln hat and beard, Washington hat, Pilgrim girl's cap and apron, Pilgrim boy's hat and collar, leprechaun hat, mortarboard, leaf collar, Halloween, Christmas, much more. Included in catalog from: CREATIVE TEACHING PRESS, INC., P.O. Box 6017, Cypress, CA 90630.

PATTERNS FOR HISTORIC CLOTHING, Western tools, Indian crafts. Catalog $2. CRAZY COW TRADING POST, Box 314, Denison, TX 75020.

DAILY LIFE IN THE CONSTITUTION PERIOD -- Many excellent books & other publications about early American daily life. Resource Packets about school, family, recreation, and work, containing facsimile documents such as diaries, letters, accounts, and inventories. Craft activity cards; historical reproductions for "hands-on" learning; more. Free catalog. OLD STURBRIDGE VILLAGE, Mail Order Dept., 1 Old Sturbridge Road, Sturbridge, MA 01566.

DRAMATIZED AMERICAN HISTORY, by Kenneth Bruce. Relive yesterday's events through exciting dramatizations, narrated by a master storyteller and historian, with sound effects, music, and multiple-voice recordings.

#1. PATHWAY TO INDEPENDENCE, THE AMERICAN REVOLUTION, JOHN ADAMS AND UNDECLARED WAR WITH FRANCE.

#2. THE CHESAPEAKE AFFAIR, DISCOVERY OF THE COLUMBIA RIVER, DISCOVERY & SETTLEMENT OF CALIFORNIA.

#3. THE LOUISIANA PURCHASE, THE ERA OF GOOD FEELING, THE LONE STAR REPUBLIC.

#4. THE LEWIS AND CLARK EXPEDITION, THE ERA OF MOUNTAIN MEN, MANIFEST DESTINY, THE OREGON TRAIL.

#5. THE RISE OF SECTIONALISM AND THE MONROE DOCTRINE, THE AGE OF JACKSON, PATHWAY TO DESTRUCTION.

#6. THE CIVIL WAR, THE MAXIMILLIAN AFFAIR.

#7. THE SAN FRANCISCO EARTHQUAKE AND FIRE, THE RACE TO THE POLE BY HANSON AND PEARY, THE TITANIC DISASTER.

#8. THE BUILDING OF THE PANAMA CANAL, THE AROUND-THE-WORLD AUTOMOBILE RACE, THE FLIGHT OF THE SPIRIT OF ST. LOUIS.

#9. PRELUDE TO WORLD WAR I, THE STRUGGLE TO REMAIN NEUTRAL.

#10. THE LAST VOYAGE OF THE LUSITANIA, THE UNITED STATES IN WORLD WAR I.

#11. BACKGROUND TO WORLD WAR II IN THE PACIFIC, PRELUDE TO PEARL HARBOR.

#12. DAY OF INFAMY, THE BAY OF PIGS.

#13. THE CUBAN MISSILE CRISIS.

Each cassette, $10.95. Code JN. BROOK FARM BOOKS.

AMERICAN INDIAN BIOGRAPHIES -- Ten famous Indian leaders and their struggle to protect their land and freedom, with many details about the customs, beliefs, and cultures of the various tribes, and how the tribes were affected by coming of the European settlers. Full-color illustrations.

BLACK HAWK, Frontier Warrior --CHIEF JOSEPH, Leader of Destiny -- OSCEOLA, Seminole Warrior -- POCAHONTAS, Girl of Jamestown -- PONTIAC, Chief of the Ottawas -- SACAJAWEA, Wilderness Guide -- SEQUOYAH, Cherokee Hero -- SITTING BULL, Warrior of the Sioux -- SQUANTO, the Pilgrim Adventure -- TECUMSEH, Shawnee War Chief.

Each 48-page book, $3.50. Code TRL. BROOK FARM BOOKS.

QUANAH PARKER, by Len Hilts. Son of a Comanche chief & a white woman, Quanah Parker became a great chief who valiantly led his people in an attempt to save their homeland. Both feared and respected by those whom he fought, he became a symbol of the Comanches. Photographs and map. Ages 10 and up. Hard- cover, 96 pages. $12.95. Code HBJ. BROOK FARM BOOKS.

MUSEUM OF THE AMERICAN INDIAN, 3753 Broadway, New York, NY 10032. Catalogs of many different kinds of material about American Indians.

CUT AND MAKE AMERICAN INDIAN MASKS--Eight full-size, full-color masks based on authentic North American Indian designs, including bird and raven masks of the Makah Indians of British Columbia, two Eskimo masks, a Hopi corn man, a Kwakiutl human-bear mask, Iroquois false-face mask, and an Aztec mask. $2.95. Code DV. BROOK FARM BOOKS.

CIVIL WAR PAPER SOLDIERS IN FULL COLOR. 100 authentic, free-standing Union and Confederate figures -- foot soldiers, commanders on horseback, cannons, campfires, more. $4.50. Code DV. BROOK FARM BOOKS.

ILLUSTRATED CATALOG OF CIVIL WAR MILITARY GOODS. Unabridged reproduction of a rare 1864 catalog, brimming with detailed descriptions of hats, coats, "trowsers," boots, tents, swords, horse "furniture," tables of military pay, more. 160 pages; 9x12", 226 illustrations. $9.95. Code DV. BROOK FARM BOOKS.

CADDIE WOODLAWN, by Carol Ryrie Brink. Wisconsin frontier life in the 1860's, through the eyes of Caddie (the author's grandmother) and her family and friends. Realistic portrayal of work, attitudes, and relationships, with interesting characters. Pen-and-ink drawings by Trina Schart Hyman, one of the best illustrators of children's books. Ages 10 and up. Hardcover, 288 pages. $13.95. Code MAC. BROOK FARM BOOKS.

A GATHERING OF DAYS: A New England Girl's Journal, 1830-1832, by Joan Blos. A novel in the form of a diary kept by 14-year-old Catherine Cabot Hill, of New England, recording in succinct journal entries the friendships, relationships with parents, and changes and activities of daily life. Almost like short personal notes from a close friend. Hardcover, 144 pages. Ages 10 and up. $12.95. Code MAC. BROOK FARM BOOKS.

THE COURAGE OF SARAH NOBLE, Alice Dalgliesh. Sarah and her father leave their family to build a home in the wilderness of colonial America. When they finish, Sarah's father goes away to bring the rest of the family, telling Sarah that "to be afraid and to be brave is the best courage of all." Sarah proves her courage while she waits in the care of an Indian family. A simple, dignified, realistic, and moving story. Hardcover; illustrated. $12.95. Code MAC. BROOK FARM BOOKS.

CALICO BUSH, Rachel Field. A moving novel of an orphaned French girl "bound out" in service to a family of settlers on the Maine coast in the 1740's. A close look at an aspect of pioneer life often neglected. Age 12 and up. $12.95. Code MAC. BROOK FARM BOOKS.

ANOTHER SHORE, Nancy Bond. 17-year-old Lyn, working in a reconstructed Nova Scotia village, is suddenly transported in time back to the original French settlement, becoming enmeshed in questions of identity, loyalty, and choice in the 18th-century port village. A well-researched story, with a very powerful ending. Age 12 and up. Hardcover, 320 pages. $14.95. Code MAC. BROOK FARM BOOKS.

THE LAST OF THE MOHICANS, James Fenimore Cooper. During the French & Indian War, adventure and tragedy befall two sisters as they travel through the wilderness near Lake Champlain to join their father, the British commander of Fort William Henry. Illustrated with several beautiful full-color paintings by illustrator N. C. Wyeth. Hardcover, 376 pages. $23.95. Code MAC. Specify N.C. WYETH EDITION, along with the title. BROOK FARM BOOKS.

RELIGION IN HISTORY -- LEARNING MAGAZINE reported in November 1987 that the Association for Supervision and Curriculum Development encourages teachers to return to the inclusion of religion in their courses about history and society. LEARNING said the ASCD's report, "Religion in the Curriculum," complained that "public-school children aren't learning enough about the importance of religion in American history and society because educators and textbook publishers fear controversy." LEARNING then quoted the report directly: "'Teachers must understand that although religion is a sensitive issue, it is not too hot for them to handle in an informal, descriptive, and impartial way.'"

OMISSION OF RELIGION FROM TEXTBOOKS--U.S. District Court Judge W. Brevard Hand ruled on March 4, 1987 that 39 history and social studies texts and six home economics texts used in Alabama's 129 school systems "discriminate against the very concept of religion and theistic religions in particular, by omissions so serious that a student learning history from them would not be apprised of relevant facts about America's history...References to religion are isolated and the integration of religion in the history of American society is ignored."

The various textbooks include the WINDOWS ON OUR WORLD SERIES (published by Houghton Mifflin), OUR AMERICAN HERITAGE (Silver Burdett), HISTORY OF A FREE PEOPLE (Macmillan), AMERICA IS (Merrill), TODAY'S TEEN (Bennett), UNDERSTANDING THE SOCIAL SCIENCES (Laidlaw), STECK VAUGHN SOCIAL STUDIES (Steck Vaughn), A HISTORY OF OUR AMERICAN REPUBLIC (Laidlaw), CARING, DECIDING AND GROWING (Ginn), HOMEMAKING: SKILLS FOR EVERYDAY LIVING (Goodheart-Wilcox), PEOPLE AND OUR COUNTRY (Holt Rinehart), THESE UNITED STATES (Houghton Mifflin), THE AMERICAN DREAM (Scott Foresman), SOCIAL STUDIES SERIES (Scott, Foresman), and RISE OF THE AMERICAN NATION (Harcourt Brace Jovanovich).

On August 26, 1987, the U.S. Court of Appeals for the Eleventh Circuit unanimously overturned Judge Hand's decision by ruling that the information in the books was **"essentially neutral in its religious content."** The fact that the texts <u>omitted references to religion</u> was "not an advancement of secular humanism or an active hostility toward theistic religion." Superior courts refused to hear further appeals.

This information is from the American Library Association's BANNED BOOKS WEEK '89: A RESOURCE BOOK, published for the use of booksellers in promoting the freedom to read. The American Library Association, American Booksellers Association, and other sponsors of Banned Book Week considered Judge Hand's ruling against the books to be an act of censorship, in that the charge of "promoting secular humanism" had been brought by fundamentalists; but the ruling which overturned Judge Hand's ruling was regarded as a righteous blow struck for freedom of the press.

The members of that Court of Appeals should be reminded that fictional history is not the same as historical fiction. Whether or not the omission of references to religion constitutes "active hostility toward religion," it certainly seems to indicate a disdain for truth and accuracy in history. Religion, Christianity in particular, was of unimpeachable importance in the founding and growth of the United States; the deliberate omission of that fact from school text books, along with supporting references throughout, is hardly "neutral." Such "neutrality" constitutes a censorship far more real and more malignant than Judge Hand's ruling against it.

Mark Twain said that God made a fool for practice, and then made school boards. I'd say that was for further practice; then God made the U.S. Court of Appeals which overturned Judge Hand's efforts to remove fictional history from the schools of Alabama.

Code for Smoke Signals

I am lost. Help!

All come to Council

TWO LITTLE SAVAGES, by Ernest Thompson Seton. When I was about 12, I borrowed this book from the public library and took it camping with me in my grand-father's back woodlot. Rain seeped into my tent, the book got wet, and the cover came off. The library charged my father a dollar and let us keep the book. In the next few years I probably read it fifty times. It's the story of Yan and Sam, two farmboys at the turn of the century, who "play Indian" when-ever they're given a short holiday from farm chores. With the help of an old hermit, they (and the read-er) learn to make authentic Indian clothing, drums, weapons, and a tepee, along with many bits of useful and interesting woods lore. Many illustrations. $5.95. Code DV. BROOK FARM BOOKS.

REPLICAS OF HISTORIC WEAPONS -- "Toy" replicas pat-terned after rifles, muskets, and pistols that had important parts in U.S. history -- Revolutionary War, Civil War, Kentucky long rifle, blunderbuss pistol, etc. Excepting a few carbine cork-shooters (called "pop-guns," when I was a kid), these guns cannot fire any kind of ammunition or projectile. As you will have gathered, I don't favor militarism, in reality or in play, but I think a few of these rep-licas might have a place in a family "hands-on" his-tory study; perhaps a display. Wars <u>did</u> happen, for good or bad, and some have actually been fought for good purposes, even if we may wish those purposes might have been achieved peaceably. When I was a kid, my heroes included Roy Rogers, Gene Autry, Kit Carson, Daniel Boone, and others like them who were always presented in movies, comic books, radio pro-grams, and television shows as "the good guys" who never shot first, never shot to kill, and always protected the weak. Sometimes I reenacted various historic wars, always with the aim of defending freedom, and always with the principle that "good guys never shoot first." However inaccurate this may be, historically, it was a good principle to grow up with. The only modern gun-toting "heroes" seem to be Rambo-like psychopaths, so maybe there isn't any way for kids to play wholesome, moral games with guns anymore. Catalog. PARRIS MFG. CO., P.O. Box 338, Savannah, TN 38372.

THE BEST OF ENEMIES, Nancy Bond. In Concord, Massa-chusetts, as the annual Patriots' Day approaches, Charlotte is looking forward to being one of the ac-tors who will reenact the beginning of the Revolu-tionary War... then learns of a band of Englishmen who plan to sabotage the celebration. An intriguing story within a story, combining historic lore with a vivid portrayal of Concord's present-day physical and social atmosphere. Realistic characters and dia-logue. Hardcover, 276 pages. Ages 10 and up. $13.95. Code MAC. BROOK FARM BOOKS.

MY BROTHER SAM IS DEAD, James Lincoln Collier and Christopher Collier. Fictional reconstruction of how the Revolutionary War affects a nonpartisan family in the Tory town of Redding, Connecticut. Gives readers a sobering, mature view of history and of war. Ages 12 and up. Hardcover, 224 pages. $13.95. Code MAC. BROOK FARM BOOKS.

THE BLOODY COUNTRY, James Lincoln Collier & Christo-pher Collier. The narrator of this novel is caught in the struggle between Connecticut farms along the Susquehanna River and the Native Pennsylvanians who are determined to drive them out. An intense, power-ful story of the Revolutionary War period. Ages 12 and up. Hardcover, $12.95. Code MAC. BROOK FARM BOOKS.

THE WINTER HERO, James Lincoln Collier and Christo-pher Collier. Historically accurate novel about 14-year-old Justin Conkey and the Shays' Rebellion of 1786-87, the farmers' fight against oppressive taxes. Ages 12 and up. Hardcover, 160 pages. $11.95. Code MAC. BROOK FARM BOOKS.

LAFITTE THE PIRATE, Lyle Saxon. Jean Lafitte was a romantic rogue whose den of pirates at Barataria Bay near New Orleans made him a terror throughout the Gulf of Mexico and the Caribbean. His battles with the law were legendary. When Louisiana Gover-nor Claiborne offered a reward for his capture, La-fitte offered a larger reward for the capture of Claiborne. But when the British landed in Louisiana and threatened New Orleans, the pirate became a pa-triot and joined his band of outlaws with the army of Andrew Jackson to win the Battle of New Orleans. Age 10 to adult. 352 pages; illustrated; bibliogra-phy. First published in 1930. $10.95. Code PEL. BROOK FARM BOOKS.

THE PEOPLE, YES, by Carl Sandburg. An epic poem uti-lizing the myths, legends, tall tales, and popular sayings of America to create a beautifully unique cultural history. 286 pages. $10.95. Code HBJ. BROOK FARM BOOKS.

THE FIRST WORLD WAR IN POSTERS, Joseph Darracott. 75 posters (48 in full color) from the Imperial War Museum in London. Works by Christy, Steinlen, Brangwyn, Hohlwein, 61 others. 80 pages, 9x12". $9.95. Code DV. BROOK FARM BOOKS.

ON WINGS OF EAGLES, by Ken Follett. Two cassettes, approx. 2 hours, read by Barry Morse. The suspenseful, real-life story about the rescue of two American executives imprisoned in a Tehran fortress. Ross Perot, powerful chairman of a Dallas-based corporation, enlists a former Green Beret to mastermind their escape. $15.95. Code LFP. BROOK FARM BOOKS.

PROFILES IN COURAGE. John F. Kennedy, Jr., reads from his father's Pulitzer Prize-winning portraits of great Americans, with profiles of Daniel Webster, John Quincy Adams, and Sam Houston. Two cassettes (3 hours). $15.95. Code BT. BROOK FARM BOOKS.

CHILDREN OF STRANGERS, Lyle Saxon. This masterpiece of historical fiction, first published over 60 years ago, tells the powerful story of life on a Louisiana plantation during the early decades of this century, and the interactions among the plantation-owning whites, the black sharecroppers, and the half-breed mulattoes. Famie, the heroine of the story, is a mulatto girl descended from free black slave-owners, who once rivaled the white planters in wealth and culture before the Civil War. Her dream is that her son Joel may someday escape the stigma of his black ancestry and be accepted by the whites. 312 pages. Age 12 to adult. $10.95. Code PEL. BROOK FARM BOOKS.

WAR AND PEACE, Leo Tolstoy. See Literature, "Modern Library."

✳◉✳◎✳◉✳◉✳◎✳◉✳◎✳

PROBING BEHIND THE EVENTS--Very detailed discussions and analyses of such subjects as Kennedy's assassination, mind control, the CIA and narcotics traffic, Iran-Contragate, life in Germany during the rise of Hitler, many more. Radio programs (from Radio Free Europe, Dave Emory, and others) on cassette tapes. Inexpensive -- about $7 for two 90-minute tapes. Send a #10 SASE and ask for list of Dave Emory Archive Tapes. ARCHIVES ON AUDIO, P.O. Box 170023, San Francisco, CA 94117.

THE INCREDIBLE SIXTIES: The Stormy Years That Changed America, by Jules Archer. Captivating retrospective of the social, intellectual, and political events in a decade that changed much of American society and culture. 240 pp., approximately 40 photographs. Ages 12 and up. $17.95. BROOK FARM BOOKS.

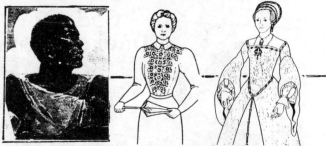

BLACK HEROES OF THE AMERICAN REVOLUTION, by Burke Davis. The black soldiers, sailors, spies, guides, and wagoners who participated in the fight for American independence. Prints and portraits of the period. Bibliography, index. Age 10 and up. Hardcover, 80 pages. $12.95. Code HBJ. BROOK FARM BOOKS.

MY BONDAGE AND MY FREEDOM, Frederick Douglas. Autobiography of a man born into slavery and later freed who became an outspoken force in the anti-slavery movement before the Civil War. Many detailed descriptions of slave life. $6.95. Code DV. BROOK FARM BOOKS.

LEADING THE WAY, page-long biographies of 22 black people including George Washington Carver and Stevie Wonder, with a page of questions for each, grades 2 and 3. MEETING THE CHALLENGE, grades 4+, has thirty people, including most of those in the lower-grade workbook. 4-page teacher's guide. $5.95 plus $1.25 for each one. CONTINENTAL PRESS, 520 E. Bainbridge St., Elizabethtown, PA 17022.

BLACK HISTORY CALENDAR, 16x22", biographies of 12 black achievers with color portraits, with daily notations of black achievements in science, politics, education, sports, and arts. $2.00. BLACK HISTORY CALENDAR, Aetna Life & Casualty, 151 Farmington Ave., Hartford, CT 06156.

MARTIN LUTHER KING, JR. -- Photos; complete "I have a dream" speech; lesson plans (all grade levels), & a booklet. FREE; request on a postcard. AFT, HUMAN RIGHTS DEPT., 555 New Jersey Ave. NW, Washington, DC 20001.

MARTIN LUTHER KING, JR. -- Poster of King with excerpts from "I have a dream" speech; 17x22". $4.50. RESOURCE CENTER FOR NONVIOLENCE, 515 Broadway, Santa Cruz, CA 95060.

MARTIN LUTHER KING, JR. -- 15x23" poster; booklet of ideas for observing King's birthday & Black History Month. $4.00. AMERICAN LIBRARY ASSOCIATION, Public Information Office (King), 50 E. Huron St., Chicago, IL 60611.

✳◉✳◎✳◉✳◉✳◎✳◉✳◎✳

WOMEN IN HISTORY. Books, posters, videos, tapes, games, & more, emphasizing women in history. Grades K-12. Catalog. NATIONAL WOMEN'S HISTORY PROJECT, P.O. Box 3716, Santa Rosa, CA 95402.

GOOD MEDICINE BOOKS, Box 844, Skoookumchuck, B.C., Canada VOB 2EO. Several excellent titles about Indian history, crafts, and culture by Beverly and Adolf Hungry Wolf. Also books about old trains. Free catalog.

A YOUNG GIRL'S NEEDLEWORK TREASURY-- See Crafts.

PAPER DOLLS OF HISTORIC PEOPLE-- Our neighbors sometimes think parts of our lifestyle are a little strange, but so far no one has caught me playing with paper dolls. Don't be silly; I'm not playing with them, I'm arranging them in groups to illustrate the periods of history we're studying. It's very serious work. (How will I explain it after the kids have all grown up and moved away?) Oh, yeah, I guess I should mention that our kids like these paper dolls, too.

The dolls and their clothing are printed in full color, with authentic clothing and accessories; many of the books also have informative text.

GREAT EMPRESSES AND QUEENS -- Sixteen of history's most intriguing women. $3.95.

AMERICAN FAMILY OF THE PILGRIM PERIOD--Eight dolls and 28 costumes -- suits, busks, jerkins, shifts, capes, etc. $3.95.

AMERICAN FAMILY OF THE COLONIAL ERA -- A family of eight, spanning three generations, is shown in period clothing in a variety of situations. $3.95.

AMERICAN FAMILY OF THE EARLY REPUBLIC-- Nine dolls and 46 detailed costumes of the Federal Period, for work at home, on the land, excursions into town, a family wedding, more. $3.95.

AMERICAN FAMILY OF THE CIVIL WAR ERA -- Nine paper dolls & 36 authentic Civil War era costumes. $3.95.

AMERICAN FAMILY OF THE VICTORIAN ERA--Nine members of 3 generations of a typical middle-class family, with 36 everyday fashions of America in the 1870's and 1880's. $3.95.

AMERICAN FAMILY OF THE 1920's--Eleven dolls and 47 outfits (rompers, knickers, wool tweed knicker suit, lacy chemises, fur-trimmed coats; more), and informative notes. $3.95.

FAMOUS AMERICAN WOMEN -- 16 dolls, 32 authentic, detailed costumes of Amelia Earhart, Clara Barton, Mary Pickford, and 13 more. Text. $3.95.

GEORGE WASHINGTON AND HIS FAMILY-- Martha, George, and the four Custis grandchildren, with 32 costumes (silk taffeta gown, knee breeches, embroidered waistcoats, black velvet suit, gold satin gown, more). $3.95.

FASHIONS OF THE OLD SOUTH-- Two beautiful Southern belles of the pre-Civil War era, with 12 detailed costumes; 6 children with period clothing, two Confederate Army soldiers, and a civilian man. $3.95.

THEODORE ROOSEVELT AND HIS FAMILY--Teddy, his wife Edith, and their 6 children, with 33 costumes & accessories (including family pets). $3.95.

ABRAHAM LINCOLN & HIS FAMILY PAPER DOLLS-- 5 dolls and 32 detailed costumes for Lincoln, his wife, and three sons; frock coats, stovepipe hats, evening gowns, more. $3.95.

ALL "PAPER DOLLS OF HISTORIC PEOPLE," prices as indicated. Code DV. BROOK FARM BOOKS.

THE HUMAN COMEDY, by William Saroyan. An amusing, wise, engrossing story of the home front during World War II. Homer McCauley, 14, gets a job as "the fastest messenger boy in town" in San Joaquin, California, and learns about the joys of love, the pain of faraway death, and the modest greatness of ordinary human beings. High school and adult. $14.95. Code HBJ. BROOK FARM BOOKS.

DIARY OF A YOUNG GIRL, Anne Frank. See Literature, "Modern Library."

EDUCATIONAL SPECTRUMS CATALOG-- Very wide selection of U.S. history books, timelines, tapes, and other materials; extensive list of books by and about Laura Ingalls Wilder (author of "The Little House" books); economics; government; many other subjects. Catalog, $1.00. BLUESTOCKING PRESS, P.O. Box 1014, Placerville, CA 95667-1014.

HISTORICAL NOVELS, Indians, etc., with excellent drawings and photographs, for children of varying ages. Prices $5.95 to $8.95. Catalog. POCAHONTAS PRESS, 2805 Wellesley Court, Blacksburg, VA 24060.

ILLUSTRATED HISTORICAL NOVELS -- See Literature, "Illustrated Classics," especially titles marked with an asterisk.

THE WORLD'S GREAT SPEECHES, edited by Lewis Copeland and Lawrence W. Lamm. This wide-ranging collection of 278 speeches from the early Greeks to 1970 presents a powerful, unique look at history. $11.95. Code DV. BROOK FARM BOOKS.

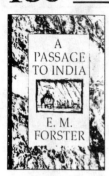

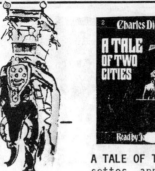

A PASSAGE TO INDIA, E. M. Forster. This historical novel examines both sides of the clash between Eastern and Western cultures during the British rule in India, and is an authentic, very moving depiction of the last days when "the sun never set on the British Empire." High school and adult. $14.95. Code HBJ. BROOK FARM BOOKS.

THE LAST OF THE MOHICANS, by James Fenimore Cooper. Exciting historical fiction about the flight of a small group of Americans fleeing before the British and their Indian allies in the French and Indian Wars. Read by Theodore Bikel. Two cassettes. $16.95. Code LFP. BROOK FARM BOOKS.

THE ADVENTURES OF HUCKLEBERRY FINN, Mark Twain. Two cassettes, approx. 2 hours, read by Dick Cavett. Young Huck fakes his own death and, with runaway slave Jim, escapes to freedom and adventure on a raft down the Mississippi. Huck faces the world's cruelty and greed with simple honesty and faith in right and wrong. $15.95. Code LFP. BROOK FARM BOOKS.

THE ADVENTURES OF TOM SAWYER, Mark Twain. Two cassettes, approx. 2 hours, read by Robby Benson. Tom and his friends, Huck Finn and Becky Thatcher, begin by playing pranks, but their sense of adventure leads to real danger as they discover a den of thieves and must use ingenuity to survive. $15.95. Code LFP. BROOK FARM BOOKS.

TREASURE ISLAND, Robert Louis Stevenson. Two cassettes, approx. 2 hours; read by Keir Dullea. The rousing tale of adventure on the high seas, in which young Jim Hawkins finds a treasure map but must elude the dreaded pirate, Long John Silver. $15.95. Code LFP. BROOK FARM BOOKS.

A TALE OF TWO CITIES, by Charles Dickens. Two cassettes, approx. 3 hours, read by Tom Baker. The French Revolution; Charles Darnay, who must guard the secret of his aristocratic birth with his life; his look-alike Sydney Carton; and Lucie, the woman they both love. "It was the best of times, it was the worst of times..." This is one of my favorite historical novels, and this reading of it is superb. $15.95. Code LFP. BROOK FARM BOOKS.

OLIVER TWIST, by Charles Dickens. Two cassettes, approx. 2½ hours, read by Dick Cavett. An orphan boy flees the wretched conditions of the workhouse and joins a band of desperate thieves, led by the master criminal Fagin. Only the sinister Monks knows the secret of Oliver's birth. $15.95. Code LFP. BROOK FARM BOOKS.

DAVID COPPERFIELD, by Charles Dickens. 2 cassettes, approx. 2 hours, read by Simon Callow. The story of David Copperfield was Dickens' own favorite of his novels, and closely mirrored his own life. $15.95. Code LFP. BROOK FARM BOOKS.

LITTLE WOMEN, Louisa May Alcott. Two cassettes, approx. 3 hours; read by Jean Smart. The popular novel about the four March sisters, Meg, Beth, Jo, & Amy, which is still loved for its warm scenes of family life in the 1800's. $15.95. Code LFP. BROOK FARM BOOKS.

THE THREE MUSKETEERS, Alexander Dumas. 2 cassettes, approx. 2 hours; read by Louis Jordan. The exciting story of young Gascon D'Artagnan, whose charm, wit, and skill at arms prove insufficient, and his faithful friends, the Three Musketeers, save the day. $15.95. Code LFP. BROOK FARM BOOKS.

SHANE, Jack Schaefer. 2 cassettes, approx. 2 hours; read by Dick Cavett. A thoughtful, engrossing reading of the western classic in which a mysterious stranger rescues the homesteaders from a greedy land baron. $15.95. Code LFP. BROOK FARM BOOKS.

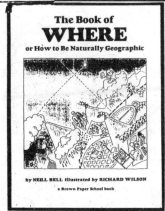

THE SCARLET PIMPERNEL, by Baroness Orczy. Two cassettes, approx. 2½ hours, read by Simon Williams. Paris, 1792. At the height of "The Terror" -- the aftermath of the French Revolution -- the guillotine claims a hundred aristocrats each day -- old men, young women, and even tiny babies. But working in ever-changing disguises, the Scarlet Pimpernel and his "band of meddlesome Englishmen" are helping a large number to escape, often right under the noses of Parisian guards, and to reach England in safety. While French soldiers and English sympathizers wonder at his identity and search for him everywhere, he continues to slip through their fingers, leaving behind a little picture of the pretty English flower, the Scarlet Pimpernel. $15.95. Code LFP. BROOK FARM BOOKS.

THE BOOK OF WHERE: How To Be Naturally Geographic, by Neill Bell (A Brown Paper School Book). Where in the world are you anyway? You may think you know the answer, but don't be too sure. "Sitting on the floor at the foot of my bed next to my sneakers" is only part of the answer. The world is a pretty big place, and if you don't know where most of its parts are, then can't possibly be sure of your own location. If you think that the Philippines is a rock group or the name of an all-you-can-eat vegetarian restaurant, then you need to look inside this book. If you aren't sure where the Andes are (or even what they are), look inside this book. And if you don't know that most of us live on big hunks of earth that move around like dinner plates, look in this book. It's a trip around the world in 119 pages. $8.95. Code LB. BROOK FARM BOOKS.

THE LITTLE HOUSE COOKBOOK: Frontier Foods from Laura Ingalls Wilder's Classic Stories, by Barbara Walker; pictures by Garth Wiliams. More than 100 recipes introduce the foods and cooking of the pioneer childhood in the Little House books. Each recipe is prefaced by a short, well-researched essay on its origins, development, and characteristics. A lot of fun to read and look at, even if you don't try the recipes -- but you will. $14.95. Code HR. BROOK FARM BOOKS.

MY BACKYARD HISTORY BOOK, David Weltzman. History surrounds us in attics, on street corners, and in people's memories. Hundreds of projects, stories, and activities plunge readers into becoming personally involved with history rather than being wedged between dates & facts in a textbook. "Out on a Limb of the Family Tree," "Whatshis name," and "Friday Night at Grandma's" are a few of the chapters that will challenge readers to explore history around them. Age 10 up. $9.95. Code LB. BROOK FARM BOOKS.

HISTORY SET TO MUSIC -- See Music, FOLK SONGS OF NORTH AMERICA.

LUST FOR LIFE, by Irving Stone. Two cassettes, approx. 3 hours, read by Sam Waterston. The unforgettable story, masterfully read, of Vincent Van Gogh, whose life was a constant struggle against poverty, madness, and despair, yet whose art reflects a clear and powerful vision and love of humanity. $15.95. Code LFP. BROOK FARM BOOKS.

"HISTORIC BOOK ARTS PROJECTS," a portfolio of 35 book-making projects, including binding, papermaking, calligraphy, paper marbling, etching, more; plans for a wooden press; time line chart, highlighting important dates in the development of books. Very useful and unusual. Preschool through high school. $15.00. PALACE PRINT SHOP, Museum of New Mexico, P.O. Box 2087, Santa Fe, NM 87504.

AMERICAN HISTORY, P.O. Box 977, Farmingdale, NY 11737. Monthly magazine.

THE HISTORY BOOK CLUB, Box 790, Stamford, CT 06904. Discounts of 30% or more on many history books. Write for information and introductory offer.

HISTORY OF TRANSPORTATION-- A cartoon scrapbook FREE from UNITED TRANSPORTATION UNION, Public Relations Dept., 14600 Detroit Ave., Cleveland, OH 44107.

HISTORICAL QUOTATIONS -- See BARTLETT'S FAMILIAR QUOTATIONS, under Literature.

DRAMATIZED RECORDINGS of biographies of inventors, pioneers, and explorers. Free catalog. THE MIND'S EYE, Box 6727, San Francisco, CA 94101.

"KNOWLEDGE IS TRUMP"-- a card game which teaches about 80 famous people. Information from S.L.L. ASSOCIATES, P.O. Box 212, New Hope, PA 18938.

ABRAHAM LINCOLN. See Literature, "Modern Library."

LIFE & SELECTED WRITING OF THOMAS JEFFERSON. See Literature, "Modern Library."

PLUTARCH'S LIVES. See Literature, "Modern Library."

THE STORIES OF KING ARTHUR--
In 1902, Howard Pyle undertook the retelling of the old Arthurian tales and eventually produced four volumes, which were published from 1903 to 1910. Other books have been written about King Arthur, but Pyle's works are the enduring classics, usually preferred over all others. The stories are packed with action, adventure, loyalty, bravery, romance, and heroism. Historians generally agree that King Arthur is fictional, but these stories can still be read as "historical fiction" because they portray fairly accurately the attitudes, beliefs, and political and religious issues of a short period of English history, many of which have carried over into our present society's legal and moral culture. Like millions of others, I grew up with these stories; we passed them on to our children, and we certainly hope our grandchildren will have them, too. Whether the stories are historically accurate or not, most of their ideas and values will always be valid and desirable.

   KING ARTHUR AND HIS KNIGHTS
   SIR LAUNCELOT AND HIS COMPANIONS
   THE CHAMPIONS OF THE ROUND TABLE
   THE STORY OF THE GRAIL & THE PASSING OF ARTHUR
All four books are written & illustrated by Howard Pyle. Hardcover, 340 to 360 pages each. $17.95 each, except THE STORY OF THE GRAIL which is $14.95. Code MAC. BROOK FARM BOOKS.

A CONNECTICUT YANKEE IN KING ARTHUR'S COURT, by Mark Twain. A blow on the head sends this practical Yankee, the superintendent of an arms factory, back to the time of King Arthur's court in medieval England, where his Yankee ingenuity and knowledge of scientific invention startle the Knights of the Round Table. Read by Richard Kiley. Two cassettes. $16.95. Code LFP. BROOK FARM BOOKS.

THE MERRY ADVENTURES OF ROBIN HOOD, by Howard Pyle. Facsimile of original 1883 edition, with 23 illustrations by Pyle. $5.95. Code DV. BROOK FARM BOOKS.

THE STORY OF KING ARTHUR AND HIS KNIGHTS, Howard Pyle. Perhaps the best version of the life of King Arthur. 48 illustrations by Pyle. $6.50. Code DV. BROOK FARM BOOKS.

THE STORY OF THE CHAMPIONS OF THE ROUND TABLE, Howard Pyle. The second volume in Pyle's definitive version of the Arthurian legend, including the adventures of Sir Tristram, Sir Launcelot, Sir Percival, etc. 50 illustrations. $6.95. Code DV. BROOK FARM BOOKS.

THE ADVENTURES OF ROBIN HOOD, by Patricia Leitch. Two cassettes, approx. 2 hours, read by Keith Barron. The immortal story of the Merry Men of Sherwood Forest, the lovely Maid Marian, and Robin Hood's many adventures, his rise to legendary stature, and his final days. $15.95. Code LFP. BROOK FARM BOOKS.

THE BLACK ARROW: A Tale of Two Roses, by Robert Louis Stevenson. I read this book (for the first time, I admit) just a few weeks ago, and was fascinated by its vivid depiction of fifteenth-century Britain's conflicts -- in this case, between York and Lancaster, in the 30-year War of the Roses. Besides being a tale of adventure and romance amid the country's shifting alliances, THE BLACK ARROW is also a dramatic portrayal of the suffering which war inflicts on all sides. Stevenson's recreation of 15th-century English gives an insight into the evolution of our language. Originally published in 1888. This is a reprint of the 1916 edition, with 14 beautiful paintings by famed illustrator N.C. Wyeth. Hardcover gift edition, 336 pages. $23.95. Code MAC. Specify N. C. WYETH EDITION, along with the title. BROOK FARM BOOKS.

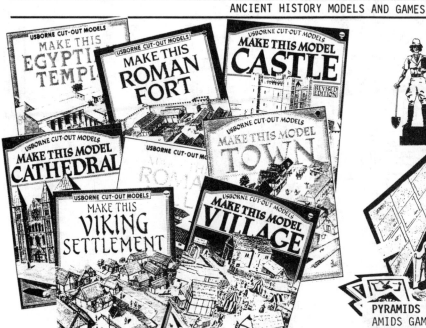

CUT-OUT MODELS -- A tube of glue and a pair of scissors or a craft knife are all that are required to turn these books into superb models. Each model has been carefully checked for historical accuracy. The baseboards of the village, town, cathedral, & castle have been especially designed so they can be fitted together to make one large model. Over 40 cut-out figures are included in each book. The models are compatible with the OO/HO scale, so extra figures and accessories of the same scale are available in most hobby stores. Each book is 9½x12", 32 pages. Suitable for ages 8 or 9 and up. Fun for adults, too, and the finished models are very satisfying to display.

   MAKE THIS EGYPTIAN TEMPLE
   MAKE THIS ROMAN VILLA
   MAKE THIS VIKING SETTLEMENT
   MAKE THIS ROMAN FORT
   MAKE THIS MODEL TOWN
   MAKE THIS MODEL CATHEDRAL
   MAKE THIS MODEL CASTLE
   MAKE THIS MODEL VILLAGE

Each Cut-out Model Book, **$9.95.** Code EDC. BROOK FARM BOOKS.

PYRAMIDS AND MUMMIES: Two Games in One. In THE PYRAMIDS GAME, players age 7 & up cooperate to decipher messages in cryptic rebus writing and work together to build a pyramid. The game board opens to reveal the inside of a Pyramid and the setting for THE MUMMY GAME. Players 8 and up compete, following the hieroglyphic path, interpreting rebuses as they race to the Mummy Chamber. Lots of excitement, along with bits of ancient Egyptian lore. Contents: two-way board, a dome, 2 decks of cards, 4 playing pieces, a hieroglyphic die, coins, & instructions. Older kids and adults enjoy the game, too. 2 to 4 players. $32.00 plus $3 shipping. BROOK FARM BOOKS.

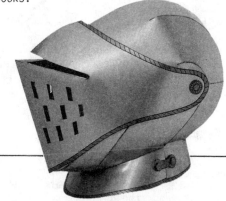

CUT AND MAKE A KNIGHT'S HELMET-- With just scissors and glue, kids can assemble this <u>full-size</u>, authentic, silver-and-gold replica of an armet, a type of closed-visor helmet worn in the Middle Ages, about 1450-1500. Clear instructions with diagrams. $3.95. Code DV. BROOK FARM BOOKS.

CUT-OUT MODELS FROM THE BRITISH MUSEUM -- Full-color heavy-paper models to cut out and glue together, based on artifacts in the British Museum. Historical information, cultural background, with full instructions for assembly. Age 8 or 9, and up -- including adults!

   EGYPTIAN FUNERAL BOAT
   EGYPTIAN MUMMY CASE
   VIKING SHIP
   ANGLO-SAXON HELMET

Each model, $6.95. Code PW. BROOK FARM BOOKS.

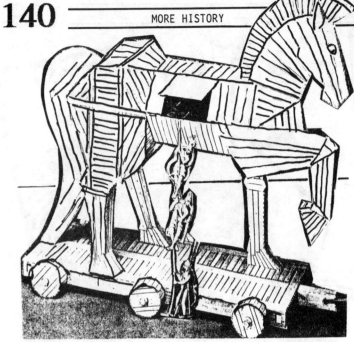

MAKE THIS MODEL TROJAN HORSE -- You need only glue and a pair of scissors or a craft knife to build this model of the legendary Trojan Horse, with wheels that turn and a hatch that opens to reveal the secret interior where Greek soldiers were hidden in the exciting conclusion to the Trojan War. The horse is 13" high. The backdrop, 26½ long, shows the city of Troy by both day and night so the whole story can be recreated. There are several figures of people to attack -- or defend -- the city. $9.95. Code EDC. BROOK FARM BOOKS.

WORLD HISTORY DATES: From Stone Age to Computer Age. An easy-to-read, illustrated reference that combines detailed date charts with features on important themes in world history. Displaying colorful maps, diagrams, & drawings on every page, this book introduces readers to important dates in world history and briefly illuminates such topics as "The First Farmers," "The Provincial Wars in Japan," "The Rise of the Manchu Dynasty," & "The Great Depression." Age 12 up. $12.95. Code EDC. BROOK FARM BOOKS.

OLD NEWS, 400 Stackstown Road, Marietta, PA 17547. Tabloid-size "newspaper" featuring items from history, with period photos and illustrations. My sample issue contains "Crewman Describes Wreck of the Titanic," "Presidential Candidate's Wife Accused of Bigamy," "Sitting Bull Predicts Victory," "First Shot Fired in American Civil War," and more. Eleven issues per year, $15.00.

LIFE IN ANCIENT GREECE COLORING BOOK-- 41 illustrations depict life in Athens in the 5th and 4th century B.C. Introduction & detailed captions describe Greek civilization of the period and the individual scenes showing art, culture, government, costumes, daily life and activities, historical events, more. $2.95. Code DV. BROOK FARM BOOKS.

HISTORY QUIZBOOK, by Alastair Smith. How long did it take to build a pyramid? What people built their capital city in the middle of a lake? Using a question-and-answer format, this colorful book engages the reader's curiosity on a variety of topics, from the age of the dinosaurs to the 20th century, including a coverage of ancient Egypt, the Vikings, the Aztecs and Incas, inventions and discoveries, and cars, trains, and planes. Full-color illustrations on every page enhance the information in the text. Age 8-12. $6.95. Code EDC. BROOK FARM BOOKS.

EGYPTIAN PUNCH-OUT MUMMY CASE -- Simple directions and diagrams explain how to assemble a handsome model of a mummy case that once held the remains of a royal architect who lived during the reign of Ramses II (1304-1237 B.C.) Approximately 11" long, 3½" wide, and 4" deep, the brightly colored and ornamented sarcophagus, decorated with hieroglyphics, emblems of gods, and other artwork, comes complete with a removable lid and a gauze-shrouded figure inside the case. No scissors needed; just punch out the pieces on perforated lines, fold, and glue. $3.95. Code DV. BROOK FARM BOOKS.

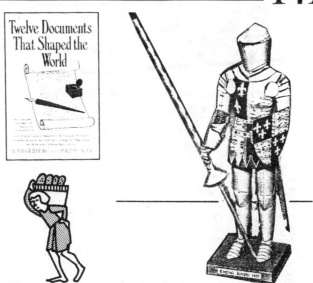

THE LIVING HISTORY SERIES--Breathtaking photographs and a fact-filled text almost bring history to life in these new books. This series re-creates scenes from various historical periods using an innovative computer technique combining photographs of real locations with artifacts, costumed actors, and detailed miniature models. The books are edited by John D. Clare, an historian and teacher who has pioneered in the use of computers in the teaching of history. To ensure accuracy, museum curators and historians have checked every detail of the text & photographs. Each book also has maps, timelines, & an index. Ages 8-12 and up.

   KNIGHTS IN ARMOR
   PYRAMIDS OF ANCIENT EGYPT
   THE VIKINGS
   THE VOYAGES OF CHRISTOPHER COLUMBUS
   FOURTEENTH-CENTURY TOWNS
   CLASSICAL ROME
Each book, $16.95. Code HBJ. BROOK FARM BOOKS.

CUT AND MAKE A KNIGHT IN ARMOR -- A full-color reproduction of a full suit of armor worn by King Henry V of England, about 1415. Includes all the components: helmet, breast- and backplates, shield and sword, etc. 13½" high. $3.95. Code DV. BROOK FARM BOOKS.

TWELVE DOCUMENTS THAT SHAPED THE WORLD, by Mort Gerberg and Jerome Agel. Texts, commentaries, and illustrations of 12 of the most important social and political documents of the world. $6.95. Code PG. BROOK FARM BOOKS.

PRESS-OUT MODEL CASTLE -- This is the easiest-to-assemble model castle we've found, requiring no scissors to put together. Just punch out the pieces and fold, then glue together. Vines grow over the large stones of the walls, which are made of sturdy cardboard printed on both sides. There are 17 knights and other figures, and even a dragon for those who want to mix fantasy with history. $6.95. Code TRL. BROOK FARM BOOKS.

KNIGHTS AND CASTLES: The Adventure-in-Chivalry Game. The first to arrive at home castle wins! Begin as a page, but don't stop there. You'll earn the ranks of squire, then knight, as you travel along the questing trail. Answer knightly questions, build impassable blockades and joust with worthy opponents as you progress. A timeline helps put it all into perspective. Wonderful illustrations and multi-level play make KNIGHTS AND CASTLES an adventure in fun. 2 to 4 players, age 6 and up. $25.00 plus $3.00 postage. BROOK FARM BOOKS.

CORNERSTONES OF FREEDOM -- These books explore several important events and people in United States history. Many full-color photos and black-and-white engravings, with clear text, almost give readers a sense of witnessing history in the making. Each book is 8"x9½", 32 pages; reading level about 4th grade, interest level ages 8 to 12 or so.

ADMIRAL PEARY AT THE NORTH POLE
THE ALAMO
THE BATTLE OF BULL RUN
THE BATTLE OF SHILOH
THE BILL OF RIGHTS
BOOKER T. WASHINGTON
THE BOSTON TEA PARTY
THE CHICAGO FIRE
CLARA BARTON
CHRISTOPHER COLUMBUS
THE CONSTITUTION
D-DAY
THE DECLARATION OF INDEPENDENCE
THE ELECTION OF ABRAHAM LINCOLN
ELLIS ISLAND
THE SALEM WITCH TRIALS
SHERMAN'S MARCH TO THE SEA
THE SPIRIT OF ST. LOUIS
THE STAR-SPANGLED BANNER

THE EMPIRE STATE BUILDING
THE ERIE CANAL
FORD'S THEATER AND THE DEATH OF LINCOLN
GERONIMO
THE GETTYSBURG ADDRESS
HARRIET BEECHER STOWE
HENRY FORD AND THE AUTOMOBILE
JANE ADDAMS AND HULL HOUSE
JOHN BROWN'S RAID ON HARPER'S FERRY
THE JOHNSTOWN FLOOD
JONAS SALK AND THE DISCOVERY OF THE POLIO VACCINE
THE LEWIS AND CLARK EXPEDITION
LEXINGTON AND CONCORD
THE LITTLE BIGHORN
THE LONE STAR REPUBLIC
THE MAYFLOWER COMPACT
MISSISSIPPI STEAMBOATS
THE MONITOR AND THE MERRIMAC
THE MONTGOMERY BUS BOYCOTT
THE NEW YORK STOCK EXCHANGE
OLD IRONSIDES
THE OREGON TRAIL
THE PEACE CORPS
THE POWERS OF CONGRESS
PRESIDENTIAL ELECTIONS
RACHEL CARSON & THE ENVIRONMENTAL MOVEMENT
THE ROUGH RIDERS
THE STATUE OF LIBERTY
THE SURRENDER AT APPOMATTOX COURT HOUSE
THE SURRENDER AT YORKTOWN
THE TEAPOT DOME SCANDAL
THE TRAIL OF TEARS
THE UNDERGROUND RAILROAD
THE UNIFICATION OF GERMANY
THE U.S.S. ARIZONA
WILLIAMSBURG
WOMEN WHO SHAPED THE WEST
WOUNDED KNEE

Each book, $3.95. Order "Cornerstones of Freedom" and title. Code CP. BROOK FARM BOOKS.

LAND HO! ¡TIERRA TIERRA! The Voyage to America Game in Spanish and English. Set sail with Columbus on the Niña, Pinta, or Santa Maria on a voyage that changed the world. Navigate your course through the perils of the 15th-century ocean, watch out for sea monsters and unfriendly winds, and be the first ship to arrive in the New World and you win. Completely bilingual, LAND HO! can be played in Spanish, English, or both, for a quick game of fun and learning. The cards and the ship's log provide fascinating historical details. 2 or 3 players or teams, age 8 up. $22.00 plus $3.00 postage. BROOK FARM BOOKS.

AROUND THE WORLD IN 100 YEARS: From Henry the Navigator to Magellan, by Jean Fritz; maps and illustrations by Anthony Bacon Venti. In the 15th century, people believed that just off the west coast of Africa the oceans boiled, the air was poisonous, and ships caught fire. This book tells of the dangers, real and imaginary, faced by explorers who ventured into the Unknown, and chronicles the achievements of ten men -- Henry the Navigator, Bartholomew Diaz, Christopher Columbus, Vasco da Gama, Pedro Alvares Cabral, John Cabot, Amerigo Vespucci, Juan Ponce de Leon, Vasco Nuñez de Balboa, and Ferdinand Magellan -- who voyaged to India, Africa, the Americas, and eventually around the world. Ages 7-12. $17.95. Code PG. BROOK FARM BOOKS.

FIRST HOUSES: Native American Homes & Sacred Structures, by Jean Guard Monroe and Ray A. Williamson; black-and-white illustrations by Susan Johnston Carlson. Native American creation myths include stories about the legendary "first houses" that the tribes used as patterns for their own homes and ritual structures. Many Native Americans considered their buildings -- from the Iroquois longhouse to the Navajo hogan -- be be constructed on cosmic patterns given by the gods. Their mythology is filled with exciting tales of the first houses and the beings that created them. Ages 9-15. $14.95. Code HM. BROOK FARM BOOKS.

FROM THE EARTH TO BEYOND THE SKY: Native American Medicine, by Evelyn Wolfson; black-and-white illustrations by Jennifer Hewitson. In 1535, French explorer Jacques Cartier and his crew were marooned on the frozen St. Lawrence River. Twenty-five men had died, and the rest were close to death when native Americans restored them to life with hemlock or pine-needle tea. It was 150 years later when Europeans realized the men had been dying from a lack of vitamin C, which is contained in the leaves and bark of those two trees. This is only one of the interesting things to be discovered in this account of the lore of native American medicine men who, from earliest times, had lived close to nature and learned many of its secrets. Ages 9-15. $14.95. Code HM. BROOK FARM BOOKS.

THE EARLIEST AMERICANS, by Helen Roney Sattler; illustrated by Jean Zallinger. Convincing evidence of the most widely-accepted theories about the origins of civilization in the Western Hemisphere. Ages 9-15. $16.95. Code HM. BROOK FARM BOOKS.

WHEN THE GREAT CANOES CAME, Mary Louise Clifford. 75 years after the settlement of Jamestown, Cockacoeske, the queen of the Pamunkey Indians, tells the adolescents of her tribe about the people, places, and episodes which were a part of American history before the Europeans arrived. This speculative fiction is based on tribal legends, history, and artifacts. Illustrated; with a map, chronology, genealogical chart, and bibliography. $12.95. Code PEL. BROOK FARM BOOKS.

THE CHARM OF THE BEAR CLAW NECKLACE, Margaret Zehmer Searcy. Redwolf and Windyway are two Stone Age Indian siblings living in what is now the Southeastern United States. Because they have no permanent shelter, camping is a part of everyday life. The children must constantly be aware of the danger presented by wild animals and tempestuous weather. Age 10 up. $6.95. Code PEL. BROOK FARM BOOKS.

IKWA OF THE MOUND-BUILDER INDIANS, Margaret Zahmer Searcy. Ikwa is a young Indian girl living in what is now the Southeastern United States before colonization. One day, as she carries an offering up the temple mound to the priest of the sun god, she sees two crows and a hawk flying toward the Alligator Village -- a sign that a strange visitor will come soon. Age 10 up. Photos, illustrations, maps. $6.95. Code PEL. BROOK FARM BOOKS.

QUANAH PARKER: COMANCHE CHIEF, Rosemary Kissinger. A son born to a white mother and a Comanche father, Quanah became one of the greatest Comanche leaders. He fought the encroachment onto Indian Lands, but was forced to the reservation by the severe lack of food, clothing, and housing brought about by the slaughter of the buffalo herds. He was the last Indian chief to surrender. Named chief of all the Comanches, he worked for a peaceful coexistence between the red and white races, lobbying for Indian rights until his death in 1911. Teen & adult. Photos; bibiliography. $12.95. Code PEL. BROOK FARM BOOKS.

EASY-TO-MAKE PUEBLO VILLAGE-- Detailed but easy-to-cut and assemble model of a typical pueblo village, the communal home of many Southwestern Indians for centuries. Populate the village with several two-sided free-standing figures of Indians engaged in day-to-day activities, games, and rituals. Scissors and glue are required. $2.95. Code DV. BROOK FARM BOOKS.

NORTHWEST COAST PUNCH-OUT INDIAN VILLAGE-- Complete with totem poles, dugout canoe, cedar plank house, carvings of gods and ancestors, several Indians in authentic dress and activities. No scissors needed. Just punch out, fold, and glue. $2.95. Code DV. BROOK FARM BOOKS.

PLAINS INDIANS PUNCH-OUT PANORAMA-- No scissors required to assemble and glue this early western scene of a tepee village and several figures, with a mountainous background. $2.95. Code DV. BROOK FARM BOOKS.

GREAT PLAINS INDIAN ACTION SET -- 24 pages of full-color, punch-out figures and a three-dimensional backdrop scene with amazingly realistic detail. Easy to assemble; for play or display. Age 6 up. $5.95. Code PG. BROOK FARM BOOKS. [See also Science: ANIMAL ACTION SETS and DINOSAURS.]

INDIAN BOYHOOD, Charles Eastman. A vivid and detailed account of a mid-19th-century Indian upbringing, including training for the hunt, woodlore, and much more. $4.50. Code DV. BROOK FARM BOOKS.

CHRISTOPHER COLUMBUS Paper Dolls in Full Color -- Columbus and his family and other important figures in his voyage, with many authentic costumes. $3.95.
COLUMBUS DISCOVERS AMERICA Coloring Book, $2.95.
Cut and Assemble COLUMBUS' "SANTA MARIA," in full color. A detailed, accurately-scaled model. $5.95.
EXPLORATION OF NORTH AMERICA Coloring Book. The story, in text and detailed pictures, of the first Europeans in North America. $2.95.
All titles, Code DV. BROOK FARM BOOKS.

TRUTH IS A BRIGHT STAR: A Hopi Adventure, by Joan Price. This gripping tale of courage, based on a real historical event, tells the story of Loma, one of 14 children captured by Spanish soldiers from a peaceful Hopi village in 1832. How 12-year-old Loma copes with a completely foreign way of life makes this a thought-provoking story about growing understanding between people of different cultures. 156 pages; bibliography, glossary. Ages 8-12. $8.95. Code TSP. BROOK FARM BOOKS.

Slave Catchers and runaway slave from "THE UNDERGROUND RAILROAD"

A 1903 Packard from "OLD PACIFIC"

AMERICAN ADVENTURE GAMES are among the least expensive, yet most informative and most enjoyable, historical games available. They let you become a part of American history... Imagine yourself in a whaleboat or riding with Paul Revere... Follow the North Star to freedom as a "passenger" on the Underground Railroad, or command the ironclad warship <u>Monitor</u> in battle. Journey with the Pilgrims or travel the Erie Canal. Each game has an 11"x17" game board, printed in three colors. Game pieces are cut out by you; some are folded to create playing pieces. A spinner or die comes with each game, along with complete rules for playing. The rules provide interpretive information to help players understand the event portrayed in the game. Many of the games also include a historical essay and educator's notes along with other background information about the period.

AMERICA'S CHALLENGE -- Recreates the 1851 race that began yachting's most enduring tradition.

THE BATTLE OF BUNKER HILL -- Based on the 18th-century game "Asalto," players attack or defend the redoubt on Breed's Hill.

DON'T GIVE UP THE SHIP! -- American and British fleets clash on Lake Erie, September 10, 1813.

THE ERIE CANAL -- Travel the 1830's Erie Canal with a boat full of cargo or passengers.

FRIGATES! -- Walk the quarterdeck of the U.S.S. Constitution or the U.S.S. Constellation as they sail into battle.

THE MONITOR AND THE MERRIMACK -- One of the most famous naval combats in American history is recreated in this game of dueling warships.

THE "OLD PACIFIC" -- Take the driver's seat in the Packard that made a spectacular transcontinental trip in 1903 from California to New York.

THE REDCOATS ARE COMING! -- Ride with Paul Revere and William Dawes on April 18, 1775, as they ride through the dark Massachusetts countryside to warn patriots of advancing British troops.

THAR SHE BLOWS! -- Take command of a whaling ship in the 1820's and sail the icy, fogbound waters off Greenland.

THE UNDERGROUND RAILROAD -- As a fugitive runaway slave, surrounded by spies and slave catchers, make the perilous journey north from slavery to freedom.

THE VOYAGE OF THE MAYFLOWER -- Sail with the Pilgrims on their hazardous 1620 voyage to an uncertain future in the New World.

THE WRIGHT BROTHERS--Travel the path of discovery and invention that led the Wright Brothers to succeed where so many had failed, in the development of a heavier-than-air "flying machine."

Prices: ONE GAME, $9.95. ANY TWO GAMES, $8.95 EACH. ANY THREE GAMES, $7.95 EACH. FOUR OR MORE GAMES, $6.95 EACH. Code RT. BROOK FARM BOOKS.

Special: THE UNDERGROUND RAILROAD is also available as a GAME & MUSIC SET, with the game as described above accompanied by a 35-minute cassette of powerful music associated with the Underground Railroad, performed in the context of narrative passages. $16.95 if ordered alone; $14.95 if ordered with one or more of the other games. Code RT. BROOK FARM BOOKS.

HISTORY ALIVE! THROUGH MUSIC -- Rediscover American history with these book-and-tape sets of music, historic art, and stories.

AMERICA: This is a chronological overview of America from the Revolutionary War to the transcontinental railroad through songs & stories, including "Old Dan Tucker," "Erie Canal," "Sweet Betsy from Pike," and "Yankee Doodle." The accompanying 8.5"x11" book has authentic period illustrations and stories.

WESTWARD HO! Going West with the settlers, the cowboys, and the California gold diggers of 1849, you'll relive the past with such songs as "Little Old Sod Shanty on My Claim," "Home on the Range," and "The San Juan Pig War." (It's a fact! In 1853, America and England nearly went to war over a pig.) Fourteen songs and stories in all.

MUSICAL MEMORIES OF LAURA INGALLS WILDER. In her "Little House" books, Laura Ingalls Wilder often tells of listening to her Pa play such tunes as "Pop! Goes the Weasel!" and "Oft in the Stilly Night" on his fiddle. The tape in this set has 13 songs, performed by a quartet specializing in pioneer music. The companion book features color photos of many of the things and places Laura wrote about, with black-and-white historic pictures from the late 1800's. Musical scores for guitar and words are given for all the songs.

Each set, $19.95. Code HL. BROOK FARM BOOKS.

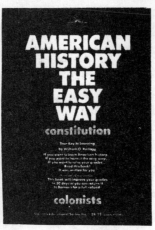

AMERICAN HISTORY MADE SIMPLE, Jack C. Estrin and Marilyn Miller. Written and presented in a clear, comprehensive format, this revised edition outlines the historical, social, and political events that have shaped the United States. A chronological study of American history from the discovery & settlement of America to the Bush administration includes major figures, dates, and events, and their impact on society. Includes a timeline of major historical events. Grade 7 up. 336 pages. $12.00. Code DD. BROOK FARM BOOKS.

AMERICAN HISTORY THE EASY WAY, William O. Kellogg. The full sweep of American history is presented in clearly-written narrative, covering events, trends, landmarks, and personalities from the arrival of aboriginal tribes across the Bering Strait through the Persian Gulf War. Discussion of each historical period is divided into brief sections that feature a summary of key points, quizzes, review material, and "links from the past to the present." Chapters begin with a discussion of historians' methods of gathering information to present a mosaic of the past. Grades 8 & up. Index; illustrated with maps, charts, and editorial cartoons. 8x11", 346 pages. $10.95. Code BE. BROOK FARM BOOKS.

A PEOPLE'S HISTORY OF THE UNITED STATES, by Howard Zinn. The Library Journal says this is "A brilliant and moving history of the American people from the point of view of those who have been exploited politically and economically and whose plight has been largely omitted from most histories. An excellent antidote to establishment history. Stories of blacks, women, Indians, poor laborers, and war resisters of all nationalities." Since the "establishment" history books are unbalanced in the other direction, skipping over most of the exploitation and broken treaties in U.S. history, an "antidote" such as this is probably needed, but no one should regard it as a complete history in itself. It was used as the <u>main</u> <u>textbook</u> in one of Susan's U.S. History courses in the "alternative" school she went to for two years, and she came out of the course with justified sympathy for our society's underdogs, but draws a blank on most key events and people of U.S. history, such as the Federalist Papers, Paine, Jefferson, and most of the <u>positive</u> things in U.S. history. Unbalance is unbalance, regardless of its direction. 614 pages. $12.00. Code RH. BROOK FARM BOOKS.

LOOKING AT HISTORY: A Review of Major U.S. History Texts, a disturbing, informative study of the very significant omissions and distortions in school history books -- but this is a very liberal organization, so omissions and distortions of interest to conservatives may be omitted or somewhat distorted. $8.95. PEOPLE FOR THE AMERICAN WAY, Suite 601, 1424 16th Street N.W., Washington, DC 20036.

THE POWER OF THE PEOPLE: ACTIVE NONVIOLENCE IN THE UNITED STATES, edited by Robert Cooney and Hellen Michalowski. A very comprehensive pictorial encyclopedia of struggles in the U.S. of men & women working for peace and social justice through nonviolent action, from 1650 to the present. 300 photos & illustrations. Not leftist propaganda, but a legitimate part of U.S. history usually ignored or forgotten. Lots of photographs. Large paperback, 272 pages. $22.95. Code IN. BROOK FARM BOOKS.

THE FIRST THANKSGIVING, by Jean Craighead George; illustrated in full color by Thomas Locker. The hero in this story of the first Thanksgiving is Squanto, who saved the Pilgrims by sharing with them his people's knowledge of the land and the animals around them. The text is for age 4 and up, but the beautiful paintings will be appreciated and admired by all ages, including adults. Hardcover, 32 pages. $15.95. Code PG. BROOK FARM BOOKS.

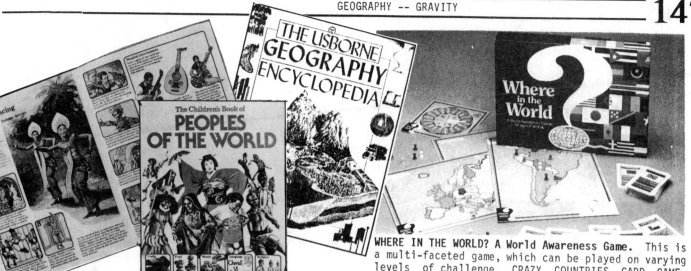

WHERE IN THE WORLD? A World Awareness Game. This is a multi-faceted game, which can be played on varying levels of challenge. CRAZY COUNTRIES CARD GAME, played like Crazy Eights, introduces players to the countries of each continent. STATESMAN, DIPLOMAT and AMBASSADOR Board Games acquaint players with the geographical locations as well as cultural and economic information about all the countries of the world. Several variations, from easy to difficult, may be chosen. Experts and novices can play the same game at levels of individual challenge. Contents include 6 Region boards, 174 country cards, 1 category spinner, 120 playing pieces, and instructions for four games of graduated difficulty. Ages 8 to adult; 2 to 6 players. After you've played a few times you'll know where in the world you are, no matter where in the world you are. $35 plus $4 shipping. BROOK FARM BOOKS.

PEOPLES OF THE WORLD, Roma Trundle. Colorful introduction to the customs, traditions, languages, and beliefs of different cultures around the world. Topics include foods, crafts, folk dances, and celebrations. Detailed illustrations throughout, with many specific examples of customs, such as the Japanese bow of greeting, the body paint of the Nuba tribe, Indonesian batik, and how to wrap a sari. The major religions of the world are described in simple terms. Age 8 up. $6.95. Code EDC. BROOK FARM BOOKS.

GEOGRAPHY ENCYCLOPEDIA -- Hundreds of full-color drawings, along with charts, graphs, maps, and diagrams illustrate clear explanations of important geographical concepts. Topics covered are mapping, rocks and landscapes, water, weather and climate, people, settlements, land use, transport & communication, and the environment. Sidebars furnish fascinating facts, and cross references clarify relationships of topics. A colorful atlas section in the back of the book includes maps, facts, & flags. Age 10 up. Glossary. $12.95. Code EDC. BROOK FARM BOOKS.

Meow?

WHY DON'T WE FALL OFF?

The roundness of the world is a difficult concept for young children, and is a fascinating subject to consider and explore in many ways. We compare the land mass with the immensity of the waters. Using a flashlight and a baseball, we demonstrate the relationship of sun, moon, and earth -- sunrise, sunset, eclipses, quarters of the moon; earth's orbit around the sun, and the moon's orbit around the earth. When we begin working with maps, which are also fascinating, we show the relationship of the two-dimensional plane to the three-dimensional ball. What is "down"? Why don't we fall off? The earth is spinning rapidly, and the law of centrifugal force says we should be thrown off by the spin, yet we're not. "Gravity"? What is gravity? Scientists tell us it's the force that pulls objects toward the center of the earth -- but that doesn't explain what it is, or how it works, or why; just that it does. Certainly there is not enough "magnetic attraction" between earth, wood, flesh, and water to counter the force and speed of our earth's movement through space. We introduce the mystery, and we never pretend it isn't a mystery.

THE USBORNE BOOK OF WORLD GEOGRAPHY. Large annotated scenes, picture strips, and bright, pictorial maps explain the basic facts of geography and give a detailed & very interesting introduction to our earth, the seas, people of the world, and houses and homes. 160 pages. Age 8 up. Very interesting and informative for all ages, including adults. $19.95. Code EDC. BROOK FARM BOOKS.

INFLATABLE GLOBE, 33"-diameter. Earth's surface, countries, cities, mountain ranges, rivers, lakes, oceans. Very heavy material, suitable for hard play or easy looking. Information: SPORTIME WORLD BALL, 2905-E Amwiler Road, Atlanta, GA 30360.

A WORLD OF FUN

"Right here is where your Grandma Betty lives," I told the kids as my finger dropped halfway to the equator on our world globe. "This is called Florida."

"Why is it green?" asked Karen, who was six years old.

"Because it's carpeted with money," I told her, firmly believing in telling children the truth. "This is Canada, where we live." I pointed. "And over here is Vermont, where we used to live."

"Wow," exclaimed Cathy, who was eight. "It sure took us a long time to drive just from here to here!"

"It's a lot farther than it looks on this globe, Cathy. You know the earth is like a ball. This globe is a little map of the world. Even a big city wouldn't--"

Derek, two years old, interrupted me. "Daddy, can I turn this ball?"

"Uh... just a little, Derek. A big city, Cathy, would be smaller than a tiny dot on this globe. Even a city with millions of--"

"Can I turn it more, Daddy?"

"Not now, Derek, please. Even a city with millions of people would be--"

"Daddy, I want to turn the ball!"

"Where was I? Oh, yes; even a city with--"

"Do people live on the earth, Daddy?" asked four-year-old Susan.

"Sure they do. We live on the earth, and everybody--"

"But, Daddy, I don't see any people!"

"There aren't any people on this globe. This is a--"

"But, Daddy, you just said--"

"Daddy! I want to turn this ball!"

"Dad, where's our house on this globe?"

"Remember, Karen, Dad just said a million people--"

"Member-shmember! Dad said we live here, so our house must be here. But I don't see it! Dad, how come--"

"Whoa, kids, back up! Wait a minute! The real earth is much larger than this. This is just a... a toy. No, I don't mean a toy, not a toy to play with. I mean this is a pretend earth. Not real. Look, these big blue spaces are the oceans. This is Russia, here's Africa, here's Australia--"

"Dad," asked Cathy, "is this the place Columbus was looking for?"

"You mean India? Yes, you're right. He was looking for India. And China. But he found America instead. That's why the people he found were called Indians."

"You mean because they were in America?"

"No, I mean because Columbus thought he'd gotten to India."

"Too bad he doesn't have a globe like this," Karen said scornfully. "Then he wouldn't get losted like that if he did. Right, Dad?"

"Ah... right."

Cathy put her finger on India and asked, "You mean Columbus wanted to get here, Dad?"

"Right," I said again. "He was looking for a new way to the East."

Cathy nodded solemnly. "So he took his boat west. Isn't that a little strange, Dad?"

"He didn't know there was a big island in the way," I explained.

"Even so," Cathy said, "that would sure be a new way, all right, going west to get east. Are the people in America really called Indians?"

"Well, no, not most of them. Just the ones Columbus found when he first got there."

Karen's eyes got big. "You mean they're still alive?"

"No, no," I said quickly. "Not the same ones. I mean--"

"I know, Dad!" Susan said excitedly. "This is where we used to live, right?"

"Uh... right."

"And this is where Grandma Mary lives?"

"Right, Susan! Very good! You're really catching on."

Susan's eyes twinkled. She put her finger on Mexico and said, "I bet I know what this is!"

"Sure you do," I said proudly. "Tell us, then. What is it?"

She grinned, with pride matching mine, and said happily, "Our driveway!"

"Uh..."

"Daddy, can I please play with this ball now?"

✦✦✦✦✦✦✦✦✦✦

It's a good thing our ancestors found their way to America, because today 24 million American adults -- one in seven -- can't even find the United States on a map of the world.
                    Gilbert Grosvenor (President,
                    National Geographic Society)

THE BEST WORLD GLOBES -- After comparing the globes from several different manufacturers, we have chosen those made by Replogle, the world's largest manufacturer of globes, as being best in quality, attractiveness, durability, accuracy, & price. They all have sturdy bases. All but The Gemini have clear maps and easy-to-read place names. All but The Gemini and The Moon have mountains in raised relief.

THE ATLANTIS -- A new globe, replacing The Pioneer as our favorite. Both raised and indented geographical relief enhance the globe's geographical features. The political boundaries and names are clear and easy to read, but the colors are lighter & more subtle, blending in with the realistic coloration of land & water areas, including deserts, mountain ranges, forests, and undersea physical features. Except for The Gemini (which has no political markings), The Atlantis most resembles the earth as it appears from space. 12" globe, 17" high, double-meridian gyrosphere mounting. $38.95 plus $4.00 shipping. BROOK FARM BOOKS.

THE GEMINI, with <u>no political markings</u>, is our most beautiful -- and unusual -- world globe. Wispy traces of clouds seem to float over the Earth's vast expanses of vegetation, deserts, mountains, rivers, islands, and oceans, which are depicted in vivid, realistic colors, giving a rare view of the Earth as seen from beyond our atmosphere. The globe can be removed from its mounting for direct viewing of all areas. 12" globe, 15" high on a solid hardwood base. $65.00 plus $4.00 shipping. BROOK FARM BOOKS.

THE PIONEER has a full meridian with double-action gyrosphere mounting (which means you can turn the globe a full 360 degrees in any direction for easy viewing of any region). The 12" globe is 17" high, including the polished base. Full-numbered meridian ring, 3500 place names, brightly contrasting map colors. $38.00 + $4.00 shipping. BROOK FARM BOOKS.

THE EXPLORER -- Very similar to The Pioneer, but with semi-meridian mounting (rotates on the earth's axis). Clear place names and country boundaries; blue ocean. 12" globe, 16" high on a metal goldtone base. $27.95 plus $4.00 shipping. BROOK FARM BOOKS.

THE FRANKLIN -- Identical to The Explorer, except that the oceans are "antique" (light tan parchment) instead of blue. $27.95 plus $4.00 shipping. BROOK FARM BOOKS.

THE MOON-- Accurately depicts the geographical features of Earth's moon, including craters, "seas," and mountain ranges. The first Apollo landing site is highlighted. Approved by NASA. 12" globe, 15" high on stand. $37.00 plus $4.00 shipping. BROOK FARM BOOKS.

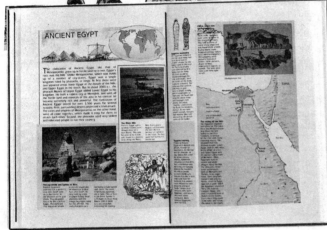

MY WORLD & GLOBE -- An 18-inch inflatable globe is combined with a fully-illustrated 64-page book which surveys all the continents, oceans, major islands and rivers; where they are and how they were formed; the weather, people, and animals there. The globe is printed with only the most basic features -- water, land masses, and equator. Using a magic marker and over 100 colorful stickers featuring people, places, cities, and blanks to fill in, kids make their own world of personalized knowledge. They can draw in boundaries, label the oceans, name the countries, and put the "I live here" arrow exactly where it belongs. Ages 5 and up. $12.95. Code WKM. BROOK FARM BOOKS.

CONFUSING DESCRIPTIONS?

"Dear Donn,

"One problem I had with your reviews was that I had a hard time ascertaining if some books were appropriate for my son's age level, and ended up with several expensive and unusable books. It was confusing to have some of the books described as 'x-years to adult' and 'lavishly illustrated' and then find that I had ordered basically a picture book. In the future, will you please advise me if you think I'm ordering books that are too 'young'?"

I'm sorry I've confused you! In general, books which I describe as suitable for "age 10 to adult" are primarily for kids (say, 10 to 12 or 14), but will still be of interest to older kids and adults. If you want high school or college books, don't order anything which I recommend for young kids, even if I say it will also be of interest to older kids and adults. Books for young kids usually have more pictures than text, so the meaning of "lavishly illustrated" may depend on the age level for which the book is recommended. Books which I recommend only for "older teens" or "high school and adult" will probably be either too difficult or of little interest to younger kids. I often recommend books which are written primarily for young kids to older kids and adults as well because their descriptions and explanations of basic facts and principles (in Science, for instance) are usually much clearer than similar "introductions" intended for older readers; the accompanying illustrations increase the readers' understanding. Many books can be enjoyed and understood at different levels, and are therefore suitable for a great range of ages. Anyway, tell me your child's age and the level of materials you want, and I'll be glad to advise you as you ask.

The Reader's Digest CHILDREN'S ATLAS OF WORLD HISTORY. The rise of the Roman Empire, great dynasties of China, Viking invasions, kingdoms of Africa, the age of exploration... Every key period in the history of the world is vividly portrayed in this beautifully-illustrated atlas. Young readers are taken inside all the great moments of the past -- from the very first civilization in Mesopotamia through the Middle Ages, the world's great empires, and the age of industry and revolution -- all the way up to the wars and scientific advances of the 20th century. Each important historic period is given its own two-page spread, with an easy-to-read introduction providing an overview of the time and putting it into context. A complete world map for each section shows major empires, centers of civilization, and nations of that time, & also includes such important information as trade routes, invasion paths, and voyages. A time chart puts major events into context; boxed features cover key people, places, and events; everyday life throughout history is shown in photographs of art and other illustrations. Special "Who's Who in History" and "The World Today" sections and a comprehensive glossary enhance the value of the atlas. Ages 7-14. 128 pages, hardcover, full-color illustrations. $20.00. Code RH. BROOK FARM BOOKS.

THE DAILY GEOGRAPHY & ANALOGIES SERIES -- Recommended by a reader. I haven't seen it. Write for information to McDougal Littell & Co., P.O. Box 8000, St. Charles, IL 60174.

PADDLE-TO-THE-SEA, Holling Clancy Holling. A young Indian boy carves a small canoe, names it Paddle-to-the-Sea, and sets it off on a long journey. With brief text and large, wonderfully-detailed, colorful pictures, the reader follows Paddle-to-the-Sea through the Great Lakes, down the Saint Lawrence, into the Atlantic. Great art, geography, history. Very enjoyable for almost any age, preschool through adult. A reader of my first edition recommended this book to us, and even sent her own copy (published in the 1940's) on loan, to convince me that it should be in my Catalogue. I agreed immediately, and was glad to find that it's still in print, now in a large, inexpensive paperback. $5.95. Code HM. BROOK FARM BOOKS.

LEARNING BASIC SKILLS WITH U.S. GEOGRAPHY. Grades 4-6. Use of maps to identify location, topography, etc.; contrast various sections of the U.S.; much more. #24074. $2.35 plus $1 postage. WEEKLY READER SKILLS BOOKS, P.O. Box 16607, Columbus, OH 43272.

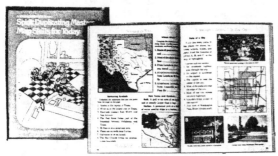

MAP SKILLS FOR TODAY. Very good introduction to the use and understanding of maps. Each of these books is intended for a certain grade (1 to 6), but the information presented is useful regardless of grade or age. I recommend use of the entire set, beginning with grade 1, and progressing as far and as fast as the student's interest and ability allow. These are basic map skills useful or necessary to older kids, too. (And adults.) Each of 6 books, about $2.00. For more information, ask about "Map Skills for Today." WEEKLY READER SKILLS BOOKS, P.O.Box 16607, Columbus, OH 43272.

MAP OF EXPLORERS' ROUTES -- 18x25" reproduction of a 1907 map showing all journeys between 1501 and 1844 important to defining North American boundaries, including Lewis and Clark, Fremont, etc. $2.40 plus $1 postage. Make check payable to: Dept. of the Interior, USGS. Order Item #8-A (05365), "Map of the Conterminous United States Showing Routes of the Principal Explorers." Order from: U.S. GEOLOGICAL SURVEY, Map Distribution, Federal Center, Bldg. 41, Box 25286, Denver, CO 80225.

WORLD BIOGEOGRAPHICAL PROVINCES MAP -- The world of plants and animals is divided differently than the world of humans. This beautiful and scientific map shows how the world is divided by nature rather than by politics. 22x39", mailed in a tube, with a descriptive brochure. Our wall space seldom allows more than one large map at a time, and I'm always reluctant to take this one down when it's time to check the world's political divisions again. Apparently, the price has gone up a whole dollar since we bought our copy several years ago. $5 postpaid from WHOLE EARTH ACCESS, 2950 7th Street, Berkeley, CA 94710.

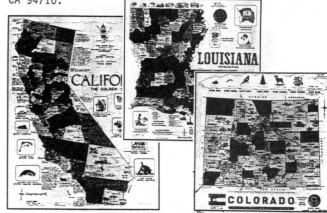

PUZZLE MAPS--100-piece puzzles of Arkansas, California, Colorado, Connecticut, Illinois, Iowa, Kansas, Louisiana, Massachusetts, Minnesota, Missouri, Nebraska, New Jersey, New Mexico, New York, Oklahoma, Pennsylvania, Texas, Washington, and Wisconsin; other states in production (write for information if your state isn't named here). $9.95 each plus $2 shipping. Puzzle map of the USA, each state 1 piece, $12.95 plus $2 shipping. THE GLOBE PEQUOT PRESS, Box Q, Chester, CT 06412.

GEOGRAPHY AND EDUCATION: Through the Souls of Our Feet, Kieran O'Mahoney. A study of geographic illiteracy in the classroom: a "lost" generation. $24.95 plus 10% shipping. EDUCARE PRESS INC., P.O. Box 31511, Seattle, WA 98103.

INTERNATIONAL TRAVEL VIDEO COLLECTION. Historical, educational, enjoyable "tours" of many cities, regions, and countries, on VHS video tapes. Cruise the Rhine River past historic cities, towns, castles, & vineyards. Ski down the Swiss Alps; tour the Louvre; see the Bolshoi Theatre, the Kremlin, and many other attractions of Moscow. Mexico, Hawaii, the Caribbean, Guatemala, China, Japan, and more. Hundreds of titles. Free catalog. HOUSE OF TYROL, P.O. Box 909, Gateway Plaza, Cleveland, GA 30528.

NATIONAL GEOGRAPHIC-- Anthropological travels around the world, visiting peoples, cities, cultures, climates, animals and their habitats, and the wonders of natural science with beautiful photographs. Subscription information: NATIONAL GEOGRAPHIC SOCIETY, Washington, DC 20036.

NATIONAL GEOGRAPHIC WORLD, Box 2330, Washington, DC 20077. Ages 8-14. $10.95/yr.

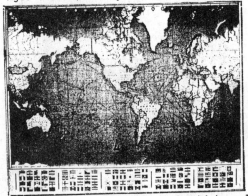

MAPS -- The best buy we've found, for high quality and low price. World, continent, and country maps, 50x38", only $2.75 each. Also many other posters and prints. Large, color brochure, free. GIANT PHOTOS, INC., P.O. Box 406, Rockford, IL 61105.

MAPS OF NORTH AMERICA -- 3-map set: Canada, U.S., Mexico. $6.00 plus shipping. Included in catalog from: CREATIVE TEACHING PRESS, INC., P.O. Box 6017, Cypress, CA 90630.

MAPS -- HUBBARD COMPANY, P.O. Box 104, Northbrook, IL 60062. (Also science materials.)

MORE MAPS, GEOGRAPHIC BOOKS, ETC.--
 AMERICAN MAP CORPORATION, 46-35 54th Road, Maspeth, NY 11378.
 HAMMOND, INC., 515 Valley St., Maplewood, NJ 07040.
 HUBBARD COMPANY, P.O. Box 104, Northbrook, IL 60062.
 NATIONAL GEOGRAPHIC SOCIETY, P.O. Box 2330, Washington, DC 20013.
 RAND McNALLY & CO., P.O. Box 7600, Chicago, IL 60680.

MATCH-EM. U.S. geography card game. 50 cards with pictures of the states, 50 cards with the state capitals; two-color map of the U.S. Plays like rummy; any number of players, age 6 to adult. One set, $7 ppd.; 2 sets, $11 ppd. ROY BRIDGES CO., INC., 253 West Allen Ave., San Dimas, CA 91773.

USA TRIP 50 -- Geographic card game, similar to rummy, but faster, more exciting, and more informative. Players choose "take-off" states from the cards dealt them, then draw, pick up, and discard until one player connects all his cards in a continuous chain of states. Players learn locations and relationships of states, and a few principal facts about each one. 62 cards, 8 small reference maps. Instructions for four different games. Order #1200, USA TRIP 50; $5.95 plus $1.95 shipping for any number of items (see WORLD 7, below). Delivery is by UPS only; give your street address. In Ohio, add 6% tax. PAL PRODUCTIONS, INC., 7825 North Dixie Drive, Dayton, OH 45414.

WORLD 7-- Card game similar to rummy that challenges players from 8 to adult to discover the countries and continents of the world. Players choose "take-off" countries from first cards dealt, then draw, pick up, and discard until one player connects all his cards in a continuous chain of countries, at the same time hoping to avoid the "kicker" cards, such as Wild Airplanes, Lost Luggage, and Jet Lag. Order #1600 WORLD 7 CARD GAME, $5.95 plus $1.95 shipping for any number of items (see USA TRIP 50, above). Delivery is by UPS only; give your street address. In Ohio, add 6% tax. PAL PRODUCTIONS, INC., 7825 North Dixie Drive, Dayton, OH 45414.

The Reader's Digest CHILDREN'S WORLD ATLAS -- Completely revised and updated to reflect the most recent political changes in the world. Far more than just a collection of maps and color photos, this atlas's colorful text creates a lasting picture of the character & culture of the world's continents, countries, & regions, and provides valuable information on every country's capital, largest city, currency, language, and chief products. Besides providing fascinating information, this atlas gives excellent preparation for the complexity of an "adult" atlas. Age 7-15. Hardcover, 128 pages, profusely illustrated throughout. $20.00. Code RH. BROOK FARM BOOKS.

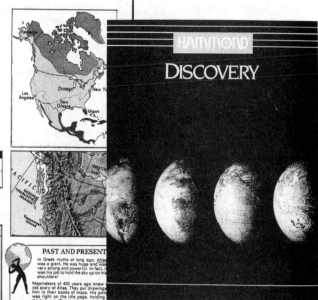

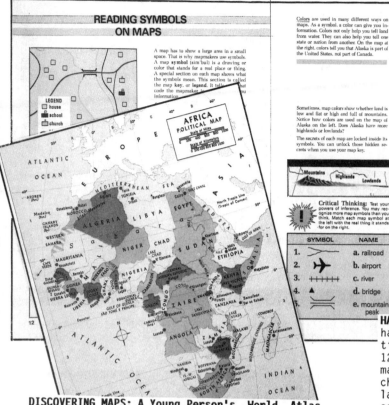

HAMMOND DISCOVERY WORLD ATLAS -- The best low-priced hardcover "family" atlas we've found. 16-page section of "sculptured" physical maps of world regions, 128-page foreign map section, 46 pages of state maps, special interest maps highlighting dominant characteristics of particular regions; major flags, languages, religions, and monetary units for all countries; same-page indexes accompanying all foreign maps; comprehensive A-Z master index at the back of the book; a gazetteer-index of the world; 32 pages of thematic world maps, tables, and diagrams; and a special section covering the Ice Ages, the Geologic Record, Life Support Cycles, and more. 224 pages. $19.95. Code HMD. BROOK FARM BOOKS.

DISCOVERING MAPS: A Young Person's World Atlas -- This unique book is intended for children up to the age of 12 or so, but is an excellent introduction to maps and other atlas features for students of any age, including adults. The first section contains descriptive explanations of symbols, scale, latitude, longitude, map indexes, projections, and time zones, using clear text, diagrams, maps, and full-color illustrations. The second section is a complete world atlas, with full-color political, physical, and special maps of the world, continents, Canada, and the United States. The third section has 16 pages of miscellaneous but very interesting facts and "trivia" about the world and its people, arranged in colorful chart form with many illustrations, followed by a glossary of important geographic terms and a digest of world statistics. 8½x11", 80 pages, hardcover. $10.95. Code HMD. BROOK FARM BOOKS.

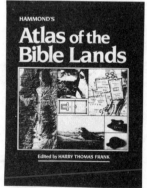

ATLAS OF THE BIBLE LANDS, edited by Harry Thomas Frank. A collection of 43 terrain maps (28 in natural vegetation colors), 15 city plans (6 of Jerusalem), and more than 80 illustrations in color and black-and-white on important Biblical sites, archaeological excavations, and artifacts. Hardcover, 48 pages, 9x12". $12.95. Code HMD. BROOK FARM BOOKS.

UNITED STATES HISTORY ATLAS -- The ecologic, social, demographic, and economic factors that have molded American history are shown in more than 100 maps, diagrams, and inset maps that range in topic from exploration, expansion, wars, growth, and the economy to modern urban problems. Full index. 9½x12½", 72 pages, hardcover. $11.95. Code HMD. BROOK FARM BOOKS.

ATLAS OF WORLD HISTORY. Revised, expanded edition. The tremendous sweep of world history is vividly pictured in this atlas, which shows the many great changes brought about in civilization through exploration, wars, migrations, and other historic factors. This new edition includes coverage of African, Asian, & other non-western civilizations; 118 full-color world maps arranged chronologically, and an 8-page time chart. 9x12", 72 pages, hardcover. $12.95. Code HMD. BROOK FARM BOOKS.

FREE MAPS, POSTERS, LEAFLETS, BOOKLETS, AND OTHER SOURCES OF INFORMATION--These agencies and organizations have a variety of material, much of which is free upon request. Be as specific as possible when writing; mention the kind of information you need, and the age level(s) for which it is intended.

> Dear Sir or Madam,
>   My fifth and seventh grade geography classes are currently studying the American Southwest. We would appreciate very much receiving any information you can send us about your state or region. Thank you very much for your help.
>   Yours truly,
>   Jean Reed

UNITED STATES--

ALABAMA
Bureau of Tourism and Travel, 532 South Perry St., Montgomery, AL 36104.
Birmingham Convention & Visitors Bureau, 2027 First Avenue, N. Birmingham, AL 35203.

ALASKA
Division of Tourism, State Office Bldg., P.O. Box E, Juneau, AK 99811.

ARIZONA
Office of Tourism, Office of the Governor, 1480 E. Bethany Home Road, Phoenix, AZ 85014.
Arizona Highways Magazine, 2039 West Lewis Avenue, Phoenix, AZ 85009.

ARKANSAS
Department of Parks and Tourism, 1 Capitol Mall, Little Rock, AR 72201.

CALIFORNIA
Office of Tourism, Department of Commerce, 1121 L St., Suite 103, Sacramento, CA 95814.
Palm Springs Convention & Visitors Bureau, Municipal Airport Terminal, Palm Springs, CA 92262.
San Diego Convention & Visitors Bureau, 1200 Third Avenue, Suite 824, San Diego, CA 92101.

COLORADO
Colorado Tourism Board, 5500 S. Syracuse Circle, Suite 267, Englewood, CO 80111.

CONNECTICUT
Tourism Division, Dept. of Economic Development, 210 Washington Street, Hartford, CT 06106.
Mystic Seaport, Tourist Information, Mystic, CT 06355.

DELAWARE
Delaware State Travel Service, Executive Office of the Governor, P.O. Box 1401, Dover, DE 19903.

DISTRICT OF COLUMBIA
Executive Office of the Mayor, 210 District Bldg., 1350 Pennsylvania Avenue NW, Washington, DC 20004.

FLORIDA
Division of Tourism, 505 Collins Bldg., 107 W. Gaines St., Tallahassee, FL 32301.

GEORGIA
Tourist Division, Department of Industry and Trade, P.O. Box 1776, Atlanta, GA 30301.

HAWAII
Office of Tourism, Kamamalu Bldg., P.O. Box 2359, Honolulu, HI 96804.
Hawaii Visitor's Bureau, 441 Lexington Ave., New York, NY 10017.
Hawaii Visitor's Bureau, 3440 Wilshire Blvd., Ste. 203, Los Angeles, CA 90010.

IDAHO
Idaho Department of Commerce, 108 State Capitol Bldg., 700 W. Jefferson St., Boise, ID 83720.

ILLINOIS
Tourism Office, Department of Commerce, 620 East Adams St., Springfield, IL 62701.
Illinois Travel Information Center, 208 N. Michigan Avenue, Chicago, IL 60601.
Chicago Convention & Tourism Bureau, McCormick Place on the Lake, Chicago, IL 60616.

INDIANA
Indiana Tourism Division, One N. Capitol St., Suite 700, Indianapolis, IN 46204.

IOWA
Visitors and Tourism Division, 600 E. Court Avenue, Des Moines, IA 50309.

KANSAS
Travel and Tourism Division, 400 W. 8th Street, 5th Floor, Topeka, KS 66603.

KENTUCKY
Travel, Capital Plaza Tower, Frankfort, KY 40601.

LOUISIANA
Office of Tourism, P.O. Box 94291, Baton Rouge, LA 70804.

MAINE
Division of Tourism, State House, Station 59, Augusta, ME 04333.
Maine Publicity Bureau, 142 Free St., Portland, ME 04102.

MARYLAND
Office of Tourist Development, 45 Calvert Street, Annapolis, MD 21401.

MASSACHUSETTS
Division of Tourism, 100 Cambridge Street, 13th Floor, Boston, MA 02202.

MICHIGAN
Michigan Travel Bureau, 333 S. Capitol Ave., Lansing, MI 48909.

MINNESOTA
Minnesota Office of Tourism, 240 Bremer Bldg., 419 N. Robert St., St. Paul, MN 55101.

MISSISSIPPI
Division of Tourism, P.O. Box 849, Jackson, MS 39205.

MISSOURI
Division of Tourism, P.O. Box 1055, Jefferson City, MO 65102.

MONTANA
Montana Promotion Division, 1424 9th Avenue, Helena, MT 59620.

NEBRASKA
   Division of Travel and Tourism, P.O. Box 94666, Lincoln, NE 68509.

NEVADA
   Commission on Tourism, 600 E. Williams St., Suite 207, Carson City, NV 89710.

NEW HAMPSHIRE
   New Hampshire Office of Vacation Travel, P.O. Box 856, Concord, NH 03301.

NEW JERSEY
   Division of Travel & Tourism, New Jersey National Bank Bldg., 1 W. State St., Trenton, NJ 08625.

NEW MEXICO
   Tourism & Travel Division, Bataan Memorial Bldg., Santa Fe, NM 87503.

NEW YORK
   Division of Tourism, One Commerce Plaza, 99 Washington Avenue, Albany, NY 12245.
   I Love New York Vacations, Box 808204, Latham, NY 12110.
   Empire State Building Observatory, 350 Fifth Ave., New York, NY 10001.

NORTH CAROLINA
   Travel and Tourism Division, 430 N. Salisbury St., Raleigh, NC 27611.

NORTH DAKOTA
   North Dakota Tourism Promotion, Liberty Memorial Bldg., State Capitol Grounds, Bismark, ND 58505.

OHIO
   Office of Travel and Tourism, P.O. Box 1001, Columbus, OH 43216.

OKLAHOMA
   Tourism and Recreation Dept., 500 Will Rogers Bldg., Oklahoma City, OK 73205.

OREGON
   Tourism Division, 595 Cottage Street NE, Salem, OR 97310.

PENNSYLVANIA
   Bureau of Travel Development, 416 Forum Bldg., Walnut St. & Commonwealth Ave., Harrisburg, PA 17120.
   Bureau of Forestry, P.O. Box 1467, Harrisburg, PA 17120.
   Pennsylvania Dutch Tourist Bureau, 1799 Hempstead Road, Lancaster, PA 17601.

RHODE ISLAND
   Tourist Promotion Division, 7 Jackson Walkway, Providence, RI 02903.

SOUTH CAROLINA
   Division of Tourism, Edgar A. Brown Bldg., 1205 Pendleton Street, Columbia, SC 29201.

SOUTH DAKOTA
   Division of Tourism, P.O. Box 6000, Pierre, SD 57501.

TENNESSEE
   Department of Tourist Development, P.O. Box 23170, Nashville, TN 37202.

TEXAS
   Tourist Development Agency, P.O. Box 12008, Capitol Stn., Austin, TX 78711.

UTAH
   Utah Travel Council, Capitol Hall, Salt Lake City, UT 84114.

VERMONT
   Vermont Travel Division, 134 State Street, Montpelier, VT 05602.

VIRGINIA
   Virginia Division of Tourism, 202 N. 9th Street, Suite 500, Richmond, VA 23219.
   Bush Gardens, Williamsburg, VA 23185.

WASHINGTON
   Tourism Development Division, 101 General Admin. Bldg., 11th Ave. & Columbia St., Olympia, WA 98504.

WEST VIRGINIA
   Department of Commerce, 1900 Washington St. E, Charleston, WV 25305.

WISCONSIN
   Division of Tourism, P.O. Box 7970, Madison, WI 53707.

WYOMING
   Wyoming Travel Commission, I-25 at Etchepare Circle, Cheyenne, WY 82002.

CANADA--

   Canadian Government Office of Tourism, Ottawa, Ontario, Canada K1A OH6.
   Canadian Consulate General, 1251 Avenue of the Americas, New York, NY 10020.
   Alberta Government Travel Bureau, 331 Highways Bldg., Edmondston, Alberta, Canada.
   British Columbia Government Travel Bureau, Parliament Bldg., Victoria, British Columbia, Canada.
   Tourist Development Branch, Dept. of Industry and Commerce, Winnipeg, Manitoba, Canada.
   New Brunswick Travel Bureau, 796 Queen St., Fredericton, New Brunswick, Canada.
   Newfoundland Tourist Development Office, St. Johns, Newfoundland, Canada.
   Nova Scotia Travel Bureau, Dept. of Trade & Industry, Halifax, Nova Scotia, Canada.
   Ontario Dept. of Tourism & Information, 67 College St., Toronto, Ontario, Canada.
   Prince Edward Island Travel Bureau, P.O. Box 1087, Charlottetown, P.E.I., Canada.
   Department of Tourism, Fish, & Game, 12 Rue St. Anne, Quebec, Quebec, Canada.
   Tourist Development Branch, Power Bldg., Regina, Saskatchewan, Canada.
   Ontario Ministry of Tourism, Queens Park, Toronto, Ontario, Canada.

AROUND THE WORLD--

   Department of Information & Public Affairs, Organization of American States, Washington, DC 20006.
   Argentina Embassy, 1600 New Hampshire Ave., Washington, DC 20009.
   Aruba Tourist Bureau, 1270 Avenue of the Americas, New York, NY 10020.
   Australian Tourist Commission Distribution Center, P.O. Box A-1, 132012, Addison, IL 60101.

Austrian National Tourist Office, 545 Fifth Ave., New York, NY 10017.

Barbados Board of Tourism, 800 Second Ave., New York, NY 10017.

Belgian National Tourist Office, 745 Fifth Ave., New York, NY 10169.

Brazilian Tourism Authority, 230 Park Ave., New York, NY 10169.

British Tourist Authority, 680 Fifth Avenue, New York, NY 10019.

BritRail, Travel International, 630 Third Avenue, New York, NY 10017.

Bermuda Dept. of Tourism, 630 Fifth Avenue, New York, NY 10020.

Caribbean Tourism Association, 20 East 46th St., New York, NY 10017.

Ceylon Tourist Board, 609 Fifth Avenue, New York, NY 10017.

China International Travel Service, 60 E. 42nd St., New York, NY 10165.

Egyptian Government Travel Office, 630 Fifth Ave., New York, NY 10111.

French Government Travel Office, 610 Fifth Avenue, New York, NY 10020.

Air France, 1350 Avenue of the Americas, New York, NY 10019.

Lufthansa German Airlines, 1640 Hempstead Turnpike, East Meadow, NY 11554.

German National Tourist Office, 747 Third Avenue, New York, NY 10017.

GermanRail, 747 Third Avenue, New York, NY 10017.

Greek National Tourist Organization, Olympic Tower, 645 Fifth Ave., New York, NY 10022.

Haiti Government Tourist Bureau, 7100 Biscayne Blvd., Suite 310, Miami, FL 33138.

Tourist Services, Kim Royal Dutch Airlines, 437 Madison Avenue, New York, NY 10022.

Consulate General of Hungarian People's Republic, 8 E. 75th St., New York, NY 10021.

Information Service of India, Embassy of India, Washington, DC 20008.

Consulate General of Indonesia, Information Section, 5 E. 68th St., New York, NY 10022.

Irish Tourist Board, 590 Fifth Avenue, New York, NY 10036.

Israel Government Tourist Office, 350 Fifth Ave., New York, NY 10118.

Ivory Coast Embassy, 2424 Massachusetts Avenue NW, Washington, DC 20008.

Jamaica Tourist Board, 3750 NW 28th St., Bay 111, Miami, FL 33142.

Japanese Tourist Organization, 630 Fifth Avenue, New York, NY 10111.

Japan Air Lines, 655 Fifth Avenue, New York, NY 10022.

Malaysia Tourist Information Center, Transamerica Pyramid, 600 Montgomery St., San Francisco, CA 94111.

Mexican National Tourist Council, 405 Park Avenue, New York, NY 10022.

New Zealand Consulate General, Suite 530, 630 Fifth Avenue, New York, NY 10020.

Royal Air Maroc, 680 Fifth Avenue, New York, NY 10019.

Royal Norwegian Embassy, 2720 34th St. NW, Washington, DC 20008.

Paradise Island Promotion Board, 255 Alhambra Circle, Coral Gables, FL 33134.

Portuguese National Tourist Office, 548 Fifth Ave., New York, NY 10036.

Commonwealth of Puerto Rico, 1290 Avenue of the Americas, New York, NY 10104.

Romanian Embassy, Washington, DC 10021.

Russia Intourist, 630 Fifth Avenue, New York, NY 10111.

Scandinavian National Tourist Office, 75 Rockefeller Plaza, New York, NY 10019.

Singapore Tourist Board, 251 Post St., San Francisco, CA 94108.

South African Tourist Corp., 610 Fifth Ave., New York, NY 10020.

Spanish National Tourist Office, 685 Fifth Ave., New York, NY 10022.

Iberia, 97-77 Queens Blvd., Rego Park, NY 11374.

Swiss National Tourist Office, 608 Fifth Avenue, New York, NY 10020.

U.S. Virgin Islands Tourism, 1270 Avenue of the Americas, New York, NY 10020.

Zambia National Tourist Office, 235 E. 52nd St., New York, NY 10155.

EARLY READING, CLASSICS, NOVELS, CASSETTE TAPES

COMMIT NO NUISANCE

MANY TITLES YOU WOULD EXPECT to find in this section aren't, because I have put them with History or Government or some other section which I think is just as appropriate. As author, I put historical fiction under Literature. As my own editor, I put it with the History. As editor, after all, I have the final word. As author, I must go along with the editor's decisions, and ask you to do the same.

HELP YOUR CHILD LEARN TO READ, by Betty Root. This is the only book of this kind I'd recommend. Most "help your child to read" books advocate impossible phonics, boring repetition of uninteresting words, and daily "practice." If you have any of these, throw them out the window or line the canary cage with them. This book has lots of sensible, practical suggestions and ideas which really will help you to help your child learn to read, without taking any of the fun out of it, for either of you. When to talk, when not to; what kinds of reading material to have on hand, and how to use it. Interesting illustrations and a wealth of good ideas. $6.95. Code EDC. BROOK FARM BOOKS.

BEGINNING TO READ -- These are some of the books our kids read over and over and requested from us over and over, as they were learning to read without lessons in how to read.

HOP ON POP, by Dr. Seuss. Sort of a combination of sight-reading and incidental phonics. Possibly the very first book the kids could read all the way through by themselves.

ARE YOU MY MOTHER? by P. D. Eastman. A long-time favorite. A funny but meaningful introduction to relationships and perceptions.

GREEN EGGS AND HAM, by Dr. Seuss. Tickles children's funny bones, and helps them learn to read.

FOX IN SOX, by Dr. Seuss. Outrageous, fantastic tongue-twisters. The kids may not read much of it for a while, but they'll try, and they'll be in hysterics as you try to read it to them without tongling your tangue.

Each, $6.95. Code RH. BROOK FARM BOOKS.

THE USBORNE ALPHABET BOOK -- Learning the letters of the alphabet and their sounds will be an enjoyable experience with this book, which is illustrated with amusing and colorful people, animals, and common objects. Each letter has a clear picture of a variety of things beginning with that letter, and a nonsense rhyme to make repetition of the sounds fun and to reinforce the learning. There are many things to identify and talk about, making this a great book for children and adults to browse in together. I recommend using this book along with THE FIRST HUNDRED WORDS or a similar "word book," to mix sight-reading with basic phonics. Age 2 and up. Hardcover. $11.95. Code EDC. BROOK FARM BOOKS.

THE FIRST HUNDRED WORDS -- This picture book gives very young children (about 2 and up) pictures of objects, actions, and situations along with the words naming or describing them. Humorous illustrations and bold print soon give kids mastery of these common words -- ball, boot, cat, etc. -- and use at the same of a book such as THE USBORNE ALPHABET BOOK or a similar "beginning letter" book will provide an effective blend of sight-reading and basic phonics. $7.95. Code EDC. BROOK FARM BOOKS.

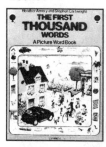

THE FIRST THOUSAND WORDS -- Three levels of fun with words: "talk-about" words and pictures for very young children just beginning to speak and recognize pictures; simple word books for beginning readers; and a source of ideas and spelling practice for those starting to write. Ages 2 to ? 8? 10? $10.95. Code EDC. BROOK FARM BOOKS.

THE ANIMAL PICTURE WORD BOOK -- Similar to THE FIRST THOUSAND WORDS (above), but, as the title says, about animals -- big, small, tame, wild, well-known and rare. $10.95. Code EDC. BROOK FARM BOOKS.

THE ROUND THE WORLD PICTURE WORD BOOK -- Similar to THE FIRST THOUSAND WORDS (above), but presenting a tour of the world's people and places in detailed, colorful illustrations and 1000 basic words. A good introduction to geography as well as a beginning reader. $10.95. Code EDC. BROOK FARM BOOKS.

GOODNIGHT MOON, by Margaret Wise Brown; pictures by Clement Hurd. We began to get tired of some books after the first 1000 requests, but not this one, which is still absolutely, positively one of our favorites. Warm, friendly pictures gradually darken as the little rabbit child prepares to go to sleep, saying goodnight to all the familiar things in his room. <u>He</u> doesn't notice the tiny mouse, but you and your child will. Whoops -- where did he go? There he is, on the window sill! Age 2 and up. If your child is 5, it may not be too late. If he's older, have him read it with someone younger; or get it for yourself, and save it for your grandchildren. The book is available in a thin paperback, which we have tried, but it didn't last. We prefer and recommend the hardcovered edition, because it will surely get a lot of use. $9.95. Code HR. BROOK FARM BOOKS.

CHILDREN'S CLASSICS ON CASSETTE TAPES -- Ten children's classics, carefully read for young listeners.
  THE WIND IN THE WILLOWS, Kenneth Grahame
  JUNGLE BOOKS, Volume I: MOWGLI'S BROTHERS and RIKKI-TIKKI-TAVI, by Rudyard Kipling
  JUNGLE BOOKS, Volume II: TIGER! TIGER! and TOOMAI OF THE ELEPHANTS, by Rudyard Kipling
  AN ANTHOLOGY OF POETRY FOR CHILDREN: 31 perennial favorites
  ALICE IN WONDERLAND & THROUGH THE LOOKING GLASS: Excerpts and poems, by Lewis Carroll
  THE ADVENTURES OF TOM SAWYER, by Mark Twain
  THE ADVENTURES OF HUCKLEBERRY FINN, by Mark Twain
  A CHRISTMAS CAROL, by Charles Dickens
  GULLIVER'S TRAVELS, by Jonathan Swift
Each cassette, $10.95. Code SPO. BROOK FARM BOOKS.

OLD MOTHER WEST WIND STORIES on cassette--The first 16 Old Mother West Wind stories, on two cassettes, <u>unabridged</u>. $21.90. Code SPO. BROOK FARM BOOKS.

ADVENTURE CLASSICS ON CASSETTES -- Ten stories of adventure, fully dramatized with a full cast of actors, sound effects, and musical background.
  ROBINSON CRUSOE, by Daniel Defoe
  CAPTAINS COURAGEOUS, by Rudyard Kipling
  TREASURE ISLAND, by Robert Louis Stevenson
  20,000 LEAGUES UNDER THE SEA, by Jules Verne
  KIDNAPPED, by Robert Louis Stevenson
  THE SWISS FAMILY ROBINSON, by Johann Wyss
  KIM, by Rudyard Kipling
  AROUND THE WORLD IN 80 DAYS, by Jules Verne
  THE TIME MACHINE, by H. G. Wells
  THE LOST WORLD, by Sir Arthur Conan Doyle
Each cassette, $10.95. Code SPO. BROOK FARM BOOKS.

CHILDREN'S BOOKS OF THE YEAR. Annotated book list of more than 400 books chosen from over 2000 published during the current year. $3 postpaid from CHILD STUDY CHILDREN'S BOOK COMMITTEE, Bank Street College, 610 W. 112th Street, New York, NY 10025.

CHILDREN'S CLASSICS -- I don't want to get into a long tirade about cultural literacy for toddlers (not here, anyway), so I'll just say I'm glad most of these stories were a part of my early childhood, and, of course, we made sure not to deprive our own children of them. Each book is 32 pages, 7½x9", and has large, colorful illustrations. Ideal for reading aloud, pointing at things, and talking over details in the pictures. Age 3, 4, 5 -- ?
  Adventures of Tom Thumb -- Aladdin and the Wonderful Lamp -- Beauty and the Beast -- Brave Little Tailor -- Bremen Town Musicians -- Christmas Carol -- Cinderella -- Dick Whittington -- Elves and the Shoemaker -- Emperor & the Nightingale -- Emperor's New Clothes -- Fisherman and His Wife -- Frog Prince -- Gingerbread Boy -- Golden Goose -- Goldilocks and the Three Bears -- Hare and the Tortoise -- Henny Penny -- House That Jack Built -- Jack and the Beanstalk -- Jorinda and Joringel -- King of the Golden Mountain -- Lazy Jack -- Lion and the Mouse -- Little Red Riding Hood -- The Nutcracker -- Peter and the Wolf -- Puss in Boots -- Rapunzel -- Reluctant Dragon -- Rumpelstiltskin -- Snow White and Rose Red -- Sorcerer's Apprentice -- Stone Soup -- Story of the Christmas Rose -- Tale of Benjamin Bunny -- Tale of Peter Rabbit -- Three Billy Goats Gruff -- Three Little Pigs -- Three Sillies -- Three Wishes -- Thumbelina -- Town Mouse and Country Mouse -- Twelve Dancing Princesses -- Twelve Days of Christmas -- Ugly Duckling -- The Velveteen Rabbit -- Wild Swans -- Wolf and Seven Kids
  Each book, $1.95. Specify "Children's Classics" and title. Code TRL. BROOK FARM BOOKS.

THE LITTLE HOUSE BOOKS. See History (or Index).

RAINBOW IN THE SKY, edited by Louis Untermeyer. Golden Anniversary Edition of a classic collection of timeless poems, for ages 8 and up, compiled by one of the most distinguished anthologists in the field of children's literature. 528 pages, 100 illustrations. $19.95. Code HBJ. BROOK FARM BOOKS.

There is no money in poetry, but then there is no poetry in money, either.
                                        Robert Graves

CHILDREN'S CLASSICS FOR ONLY $1.00 -- Favorite children's stories, poems, and fairy tales, complete and unabridged (unless otherwise noted), in attractive, illustrated editions with easy-to-read type for young readers. All books about 5"x8".

LITTLE MERMAID and Other Fairy Tales, Anderson
THE UGLY DUCKLING and Other Fairy Tales, Anderson
STORY OF PETER PAN, Barrie & O'Connor
ADVENTURES OF BUSTER BEAR, Thornton W. Burgess
ADVENTURES OF CHATTERER THE SQUIRREL, Burgess
ADVENTURES OF DANNY MEADOW MOUSE, Burgess
ADVENTURES OF GRANDFATHER FROG, Burgess
ADVENTURES OF JERRY MUSKRAT, Burgess
ADVENTURES OF PETER COTTONTAIL, Burgess
ADVENTURES OF POOR MRS. QUACK, Burgess
ADVENTURES OF REDDY FOX, Burgess
ADVENTURES OF JIMMY SKUNK, Burgess
PICTURE FOLK TALES
SLEEPING BEAUTY and Other Fairy Tales, Grimm
ELEPHANT'S CHILD and Other Stories, Kipling
HOW THE LEOPARD GOT HIS SPOTS, Kipling
A DOG OF FLANDERS, Ouida
PETER RABBIT and 11 Other Favorite Tales, Potter
BLACK BEAUTY (Abridged), Anna Sewell
ALADDIN and Other Favorite Arabian Nights Stories
FAVORITE NORTH AMERICAN INDIAN LEGENDS
FAVORITE POEMS OF CHILDHOOD
IRISH FAIRY TALES
JAPANESE FAIRY TALES
ROBIN HOOD, Philip Smith (ed.)
CHILD'S GARDEN OF VERSES, Robert Louis Stevenson
THE HAPPY PRINCE & Other Fairy Tales, Oscar Wilde
AESOP'S FABLES, Aesop
3 BILLY GOATS GRUFF and Other Read-Aloud Stories
THE SECRET GARDEN, Frances Hodgson Burnett
THE STORY OF POCAHONTAS, Brian Doherty (ed.)
MOWGLI STORIES from The Jungle Book, Kipling
NONSENSE POEMS, Edward Lear
BEAUTY AND THE BEAST and Other Fairy Tales

ALL TITLES, ONLY $1.00 EACH. Code DV. BROOK FARM BOOKS. [IMPORTANT: See the note about special postage rates for these books under "Classic Literature for only $1.00."]

🌸🌸🌸🌸🌸🌸🌸🌸🌸🌸🌸

THE FAMILY ALBUM OF FAVORITE POEMS, edited by P. Edward Ernest. A collection of more than 500 poems and verses by Milton, Keats, Blake, Wordsworth, Shakespeare, Kipling, Longfellow, Whitman, Eliot, Frost, Poe, Cummings, and many more. $17.95. Code PG. BROOK FARM BOOKS.

EARLY AMERICAN WRITING, edited by Giles Gunn. Drawing material from journals and diaries, political documents and religious sermons, this panoramic survey of early American life & literature includes such writings as Cherokee, Hopi, and other Amerindian genesis legends, narratives of discovery by Columbus and Vespucci, & selections by John Smith, Anne Hutchinson, Chief Powhatan, Chief Tecumseh, Thomas Jefferson, Abigail Adams, and Phyllis Wheatley. 720 pages. $12.95. Code VP. BROOK FARM BOOKS.

LEGENDS OF THE WORLD -- Very artistic illustrations and unusual stories from around the world. For ages 7-12.

CLAMSHELL BOY, A Makah Legend
DANCING DRUM, A Cherokee Legend
KA-HA-SI AND THE LOON, An Eskimo Legend
LITTLE FIREFLY, An Algonquian Legend
QUILLWORKER, A Cheyenne Legend
TURQUOISE BOY, A Navajo Legend
THE LAMA'S SECRET, A Peruvian Legend
OPOSSUM & THE GREAT FIREMAKER, A Mexican Legend
THE SEA SERPENT'S DAUGHTER, A Brazilian Legend
THE HUMMINGBIRD KING, A Guatemalan Legend
SPIDER AND THE SKY GOD, An Akan Legend
TALK, TALK, An Ashanti Legend
GIFT OF THE NILE, An Egyptian Legend
THE PRINCESS WHO LOST HER HAIR, An Akamba Legend
THE GOLDEN SLIPPER, A Vietnamese Legend

THE MAGIC AMBER, A Korean Legend
PEACH BOY, A Japanese Legend
THE SEVENTH SISTER, A Chinese Legend
Each book, $3.95. Code TRL. BROOK FARM BOOKS.

160

GREAT EXPECTATIONS, by Charles Dickens. 2 cassettes, approx. 2 hours; read by Tom Baker. The story of Pip and his mysterious rise from ill-used orphan to gentleman; Magwitch, the brutal convict; withered Miss Havisham, still wearing her yellowed wedding gown; the heartless and beautiful Estella; and many other unforgettable characters. $16.95. Code LFP. BROOK FARM BOOKS.

FOUR CLASSICS ON CASSETTE -- Excellent readings of four favorite children's stories. Each tape is 60 minutes long.
　PETER PAN, J. M. Barrie
　ALICE'S ADVENTURES IN WONDERLAND, Lewis Carroll
　TREASURE ISLAND, Robert Louis Stevenson
　THE SECRET GARDEN, Frances Hodgson Burnett
Each tape, $11.00. Code RH. BROOK FARM BOOKS.

MOBY DICK, by Herman Melville. 2 cassettes, approx. 2 hours, read by George Kennedy. Captain Ahab maniacally hunts the great White Whale across the seven oceans and through a sea of philosophical dilemma. Packed with lore and legend, Melville's deep existential adventure is also an exciting sea story. $16.95. Code LFP. BROOK FARM BOOKS.

BLACK BEAUTY, by Anna Sewell. 2 cassettes, approx. 2 hours; read by Frances Sternhagen. A sleek and aristocratic horse in his youth, Black Beauty passes from owner to owner and faces an old age of hardship and abuse. This fictional plea against cruelty to animals was very influential in law reform, and continues to be a favorite children's story. $16.95. Code LFP. BROOK FARM BOOKS.

CALL OF THE WILD, by Jack London. Two cassettes, approx. 2 hours; read by Theodore Bikel. Buck, a huge and cunning California-bred dog, is shipped to Alaska in the days of the gold rush. His reputation as a sled-dog grows throughout the territory; but despite his love for his master, his primitive instincts quicken when he hears the call of the wolves. $16.95. Code LFP. BROOK FARM BOOKS.

GREAT LITERATURE AND OTHER STORIES related by Jim Weiss, an award-winning storyteller. Jim doesn't just _read_ the stories on these cassette tapes, but tells them as exciting stories, and easily captivates the imaginations of his listeners, especially from ages 4 or 5 to about 12, but many older children and adults, too.

SHERLOCK HOLMES FOR CHILDREN. Brings the world of the great detective to life for young children. Four stories.

GOOD NIGHT. Bedtime tape with six vignettes that take the listener into scenes bring about feelings of safety and love. A minute of gentle music follows each vignette.

KING ARTHUR AND HIS KNIGHTS. Seven stories of the fabled king and his Knights of the Round Table.

THE THREE MUSKETEERS and ROBIN HOOD. Violence is down-played, and the characters in these 7 swashbuckling stories are portrayed as humans with feelings and thoughts.

GREEK MYTHS. Makes Hercules, King Midas, and Perseus and Medusa understandable to children, with a strong emphasis on character over violence.

TALES FROM CULTURES NEAR AND FAR. Six stories which convey the message that, whatever the source -- the wisdom of the Orient, wildly funny Native American and Spanish tales, or an African romance -- the human beings who tell them are related.

SHE & HE: ADVENTURES IN MYTHOLOGY. Addresses the equality of the sexes and the value of love and honor in the stories of Pygmalion, Narcissus, Baucis, Philemon, and Atalanta and the Golden Apples.

ANIMAL TALES. Nine classic fables from Aesop, the Brothers Grimm, and Chaucer.

ARABIAN NIGHTS. Scheherazade, who first spun the tales, leads the listener into the magical world of "Ali Baba & the 40 Thieves" and three other tales.

RIP VAN WINKLE and GULLIVER'S TRAVELS. From the sly humor of Rip to the adventures of Gulliver among the tiny Lilliputians, and on through a wise Jewish folk tale, the best motives and clearest thoughts of the characters always shine through.

TALES FROM THE OLD TESTAMENT. A non-denominational portrayal of biblical people as understandable, caring humans facing extraordinary situations.

MYSTERY! MYSTERY! FOR CHILDREN. Three of the most popular mysteries of all time, featuring Sherlock Holmes, Auguste Dupin, and Father Brown.

FAIRYTALE FAVORITES IN SONG & STORY. Stone Soup, Puss in Boots, Shoemaker & the Elves, and Rapunzel.
　Each tape, $9.95. Code GH. BROOK FARM BOOKS.

CHARLOTTE'S WEB and two other classics by E. B. White. CHARLOTTE'S WEB is the wonderful blend of fantasy and reality in which Wilbur, a loveable and terrific pig, is rescued from a cruel and certain fate by a beautiful, intelligent spider named Charlotte. STUART LITTLE, an adventurous and heroic little mouse with very human qualities, searches for his lost friend, the lovely bird Margalo. Full of wit, wisdom, and amusement. THE TRUMPET OF THE SWAN, the eventful life of Louis, a voiceless trumpeter swan, from hatching to contented fatherhood. Wonderful humor and beautiful depiction of nature, beauty, relationships, and the passing of time. Kids and adults! BOXED GIFT SET of all three titles, $11.95. Code HR. BROOK FARM BOOKS.

CHARLOTTE'S WEB IN LATIN! See Languages, "Tela Charlottae."

THE CHRONICLES OF NARNIA, C. S. Lewis. Great entertainment, and philosophy. Our kids have read and reread these books many times. Seven titles: THE LION, THE WITCH, AND THE WARDROBE; THE MAGICIAN'S NEPHEW; THE HORSE AND HIS BOY; PRINCE CASPIAN; THE SILVER CHAIR; THE VOYAGE OF THE "DAWN TREADER"; & THE LAST BATTLE. Illustrated by Pauline Baynes. Age 10 up. BOXED SET $19.95. Code MAC. BROOK FARM BOOKS.

GREAT HORSE STORIES BY MARGUERITE HENRY -- More than "just horse stories," these books have themes relevant in many ways to everyday life, with interesting history, geography, nature, and animal lore woven into the stories. All four of our kids have read these books several times.

BRIGHTY OF THE GRAND CANYON. A story based on fact about a little burro who helped to catch a criminal.

JUSTIN MORGAN HAD A HORSE. The true story of the first Morgan colt.

KING OF THE WIND. Newberry Medal Winner about the legendary Godolphin Aragon, forefather of Man O' War and other great thoroughbreds.

MISTY OF CHINCOTEAGUE. An exciting horse story set in the picturesque islands off Virginia.

BLACK GOLD
BORN TO TROT
MUSTANG, WILD SPIRIT OF THE WEST
SAN DOMINGO, THE MEDICINE HAT STALLION
SEA STAR, ORPHAN OF CHINCOTEAGUE
STORMY, MISTY'S FOAL

$4.95 each. Specify title and "Marguerite Henry." Code MAC. BROOK FARM BOOKS

THE ADVENTURES OF TINTIN, by Hergé. Humor, excitement, and touches of history and geography with Tintin, the world-famous boy reporter, and his dog Snowy, as they face international bad guys of all kinds--pirates, jewel thieves, smugglers, and spies. Large colorful cartoons, with wonderful dialogue. For children (about 10 up) and adults. They're comical books -- but they're not "comic books." They're literate, intelligent, and imaginative.

TINTIN AND THE BLACK ISLAND
TINTIN AND THE BROKEN EAR
TINTIN AND THE SHOOTING STAR
TINTIN IN TIBET
TINTIN AND FLIGHT 714
TINTIN AND THE RED SEA SHARKS
TINTIN IN AMERICA
TINTIN AND THE CIGARS OF THE PHARAOH
TINTIN AND THE PICAROS
TINTIN AND THE CALCULUS AFFAIR
TINTIN AND THE LAND OF BLACK GOLD
TINTIN: DESTINATION MOON
TINTIN: EXPLORERS ON THE MOON
TINTIN AND KING OTTOKAR'S SCEPTRE
TINTIN AND THE CASTAFIORE EMERALD
TINTIN AND THE PRISONERS OF THE SUN
TINTIN AND RED RACKHAM'S TREASURE
TINTIN AND THE SECRET OF THE UNICORN
TINTIN: CRAB WITH THE GOLDEN CLAWS
TINTIN AND THE SEVEN CRYSTAL BALLS

Each title, $6.95. Code LB. BROOK FARM BOOKS.

GREAT CLASSICS, LOW PRICES -- These are the best editions of these classics I've found for such a low price -- most at only $2.50, and a few at $2.95. The books are unabridged, and the print is clear and large enough to read easily. The covers have attractive paintings. We try to get copies of our favorites in hardcover, when we can afford them, but in the meantime, and for ones we want to read but which aren't favorites, we'll gladly settle for these inexpensive paperbacks. The books are listed alphabetically by title. Those in **bold print** have particular social or historical significance (many are described in more detail elsewhere).

1. ****ADVENTURES OF HUCKLEBERRY FINN,** Twain
2. ADVENTURES OF PINOCCHIO, Collodi
3. ADVENTURES OF SHERLOCK HOLMES, Doyle
4. **ADVENTURES OF TOM SAWYER,** Twain
5. AESOP'S FABLES, Aesop
6. ALICE'S ADVENTURES IN WONDERLAND, Carroll
7. ANNE OF AVONLEA, Montgomery
8. ANNE OF GREEN GABLES, Montgomery
9. AROUND THE WORLD IN 80 DAYS, Verne
10. AT BACK OF THE NORTH WIND, MacDonald
11. BEST-LOVED SHORT STORIES
12. BEST OF SHERLOCK HOLMES, Doyle
13. BIRDS' CHRISTMAS CAROL, Wiggin
14. **THE BLACK ARROW,** Stevenson
15. BLACK BEAUTY, Sewell
16. BOB, SON OF BATTLE, Ollivant
17. BOOK OF DRAGONS, Nesbit
18. CALL OF THE WILD, London
19. **CAPTAINS COURAGEOUS,** Kipling
20. CHRISTMAS CAROL, Dickens
21. CONN. YANKEE IN KING ARTHUR'S COURT, Twain
22. DADDY LONG-LEGS, Webster
23. DOROTHY AND THE WIZARD OF OZ, Baum
24. DRACULA, Stoker
25. EIGHT COUSINS, Alcott
26. EMERALD CITY OF OZ, Baum
27. FAMOUS GHOST STORIES
28. FAMOUS TALES OF MYSTERY & HORROR
29. FAMOUS TALES OF TERROR
30. FIVE CHILDREN AND IT, Nesbit
31. FIVE LITTLE PEPPERS & HOW THEY GREW, Sidney
32. FIVE LITTLE PEPPERS MIDWAY, Sidney
33. FRANKENSTEIN, Shelley
34. GREAT ADVENTURE STORIES
35. GREAT AMERICAN SHORT STORIES
36. GREAT DETECTIVE STORIES
37. ****GREAT EXPECTATIONS,** Dickens
38. GREAT GHOST STORIES
39. GREAT TALES OF SUSPENSE
40. GREAT TALES OF TERROR, Poe
41. GULLIVER'S TRAVELS, Swift
42. **HANS BRINKER,** Dodge
43. ****HARD TIMES,** Dickens
44. **HEIDI,** Spyri
45. **HELEN KELLER: STORY OF MY LIFE**
46. HOUND OF THE BASKERVILLES, Doyle
47. **HOUSE OF THE SEVEN GABLES,** Hawthorne
48. IN THE DAYS OF THE COMET, Wells
49. INVISIBLE MAN, Wells
50. ****JANE EYRE,** Bronte
51. JOURNEY TO THE CENTER OF THE EARTH, Verne
52. JUNGLE BOOK, Kipling

53. JUST SO STORIES, Kipling
54. **KIDNAPPED,** Stevenson
55. **KIM,** Kipling
56. LAND OF OZ, Baum
57. LEGEND OF SLEEPY HOLLOW, Irving
58. LITTLE LAME PRINCE, Craik
59. LITTLE LORD FAUNTLEROY, Burnett
60. ****LITTLE MEN,** Alcott
61. LITTLE PRINCESS, Burnett
62. **LITTLE WOMEN,** Alcott
63. **MASTER OF BALLANTRAE,** Stevenson
64. MASTER OF THE WORLD, Verne
65. MIDNIGHT FRIGHT: GHOST STORIES
66. ****MOBY DICK,** Melville
67. MOONFLEET, Falkner
68. ****MYSTERIOUS ISLAND,** Verne
69. ****OLD-FASHIONED GIRL,** Alcott
70. **OLIVER TWIST,** Dickens
71. OUTCASTS OF POKER FLAT, Harte
72. OZMA OF OZ, Baum
73. PATCHWORK GIRL OF OZ, Baum
74. PETER PAN, Barrie
75. PHOENIX AND THE CARPET, Nesbit
76. PICTURE OF DORIAN GRAY, Wilde
77. POLLYANNA, Porter
78. ****PRIDE AND PREJUDICE,** Austen
79. **PRINCE AND THE PAUPER,** Twain
80. PRINCESS AND CURDIE, MacDonald
81. PRINCESS AND THE GOBLIN, MacDonald
82. **PRISONER OF ZENDA,** Hope
83. RAILWAY CHILDREN, Nesbit
84. REBECCA OF SUNNYBROOK FARM, Wiggin
85. **RED BADGE OF COURAGE,** Crane
86. ROAD TO OZ, Baum
87. ROBINSON CRUSOE, Defoe
88. **SCARLET LETTER,** Hawthorne
89. **SCARLET PIMPERNEL,** Orczy
90. SEA WOLF, London
91. SECRET GARDEN, Burnett
92. SIGN OF FOUR, Doyle
93. **SILAS MARNER,** Eliot
94. DR. JEKYLL & MR. HYDE, Stevenson
95. STRANGE STORIES OF THE SUPERNATURAL
96. STUDY IN SCARLET, Doyle
97. SWISS FAMILY ROBINSON, Wyss
98. ****TALE OF TWO CITIES,** Dickens
99. TIME MACHINE, Wells
100. ****TOM BROWN'S SCHOOL DAYS,** Hughes
101. TOM SAWYER ABROAD, Twain
102. TOM SAWYER, DETECTIVE, Twain
103. **TREASURE ISLAND,** Stevenson
104. 20,000 LEAGUES UNDER THE SEA, Verne
105. UNDER THE LILACS, Alcott
106. ****THE VIRGINIAN,** Wister
107. WAR OF THE WORLDS, Wells
108. WHITE FANG, London
109. WIND IN THE WILLOWS, Grahame
110. WONDERFUL WIZARD OF OZ, Baum
111. WUTHERING HEIGHTS, Bronte

Titles preceded by a double asterisk (**) are $2.95 each. All others are $2.50 each. Specify "Great Classics," number, and title. Code TRL. BROOK FARM BOOKS.

ILLUSTRATED CLASSICS --

Don't dismiss them because they're adaptations of the originals. Unlike most other "illustrated classics," such as those sometimes sold in stores along with other "comics," this series has very skillful abridgements of the original texts; the artwork is not obscured by fat speech balloons; and the text is not lettered by hand, but is printed in eleven-point upper and lower cases. They'll never replace the originals, of course -- at least, we hope they won't -- but they're good introductions and companions to the world's great literature, for adults as well as for children. For those who don't always have the time or inclination to read the originals, it's certainly better to read these illustrated, abridged versions than to dismiss them as "children's books" or "comic books," and continue through life without having much more than a vague idea of what the books are about. The artwork in the books is based on extensive research into the period and locale. Because so many of the classic stories take place in periods and places with which most of us have little familiarity, it's often difficult to visualize the proper settings, no matter how skillfully the authors may have presented them; and, of course, many facets of everyday life were taken for granted at the time of writing, but have since become nearly forgotten. The artwork in these books gives us accurate images, adding a great deal to our understanding and enjoyment, not only of these abridged versions, but also of the originals when we read them later. The pictures are black-and-white line drawings, on heavy opaque paper. Each book is about 64 pages, with a colorful cover, and has a short biographical note about the author. The reading level is approximately fifth grade, but our kids began reading them when they were about 8 years old, and still (many years later) enjoy reading them occasionally. Jean and I read them, too, and aren't offended by the simplified text. After all, at least eighty percent of the vocabulary most of us use daily is probably "fifth grade." (And how many of these books have you been planning to read, and just haven't gotten around to it?) I have put an asterisk (*) in front of the titles which most particularly may be considered historical novels, whether or not they are based on actual incidents.

PRIDE AND PREJUDICE, Jane Austen
WUTHERING HEIGHTS, Emily Bronte
JANE EYRE, Charlotte Bronte
DON QUIXOTE, Miguel de Cervantes
LORD JIM, Joseph Conrad
* THE LAST OF THE MOHICANS, James Fenimore Cooper
* THE RED BADGE OF COURAGE, Stephen Crane
TWO YEARS BEFORE THE MAST, Richard Henry Dana
ROBINSON CRUSOE, Daniel Defoe

A CHRISTMAS CAROL, Charles Dickens
* GREAT EXPECTATIONS, Charles Dickens
* OLIVER TWIST, Charles Dickens
* A TALE OF TWO CITIES, Charles Dickens
CRIME AND PUNISHMENT, Dostoevsky
SHERLOCK HOLMES, Sir Arthur Conan Doyle
THE HOUND OF THE BASKERVILLES, Doyle
* THE MAN IN THE IRON MASK, Alexander Dumas
* THE THREE MUSKETEERS, Alexander Dumas
MUTINY ON BOARD THE HMS BOUNTY, Hall & Nordhoff
RETURN OF THE NATIVE, Thomas Hardy
* THE SCARLET LETTER, Nathaniel Hawthorne
* THE HOUSE OF THE SEVEN GABLES, Hawthorne
THE PRISONER OF ZENDA, Anthony Hope
* THE ILIAD, Homer
* THE ODYSSEY, Homer
* THE HUNCHBACK OF NOTRE DAME, Victor Hugo
THE TURN OF THE SCREW, Henry James
* THE STORY OF MY LIFE, Helen Keller
CAPTAINS COURAGEOUS, Rudyard Kipling
THE CALL OF THE WILD, Jack London
THE SEA WOLF, Jack London
WHITE FANG, Jack London
BILLY BUDD, Herman Melville
MOBY DICK, Herman Melville
* THE SCARLET PIMPERNEL, Baroness Orczy
THE BEST OF EDGAR ALLEN POE
THE BEST OF O. HENRY, William S. Porter
* IVANHOE, Sir Walter Scott
BLACK BEAUTY, Anna Sewell
FRANKENSTEIN, Mary Shelley
HEIDI, Johanna Spyri
DR. JEKYLL AND MR. HYDE, Robert Louis Stevenson
* KIDNAPPED, Robert Louis Stevenson
* TREASURE ISLAND, Robert Louis Stevenson
DRACULA, Bram Stoker
GULLIVER'S TRAVELS, Jonathan Swift
* THE ADVENTURES OF HUCKLEBERRY FINN, Mark Twain
* THE ADVENTURES OF TOM SAWYER, Mark Twain
CONNECTICUT YANKEE IN KING ARTHUR'S COURT, Twain
THE PRINCE AND THE PAUPER, Mark Twain
* AROUND THE WORLD IN EIGHTY DAYS, Jules Verne
JOURNEY TO THE CENTER OF THE EARTH, Jules Verne
MYSTERIOUS ISLAND, Jules Verne
20,000 LEAGUES UNDER THE SEA, Jules Verne
* BEN HUR, Lew Wallace
FOOD OF THE GODS, H. G. Wells
THE TIME MACHINE, H. G. Wells
THE INVISIBLE MAN, H. G. Wells
THE WAR OF THE WORLDS, H. G. Wells
SWISS FAMILY ROBINSON, Johann Wyss

ILLUSTRATED CLASSICS -- $3.00 each. Minimum order, 12 titles (may be combined with Illustrated Biographies, Illustrated U.S. History, or Illustrated Shakespeare for a minimum of 12 titles). Postage, $3 for any size order. BROOK FARM BOOKS.

THE BOY'S
KING ARTHUR

Illustrated by N.C. WYETH

GREAT CLASSIC LITERATURE ILLUSTRATED BY N.C. WYETH.
These familiar classics are all wonderful reading,
and deserve places in every family's home simply on
their own merits as literature (and, sometimes, as
historical fiction). The handsome bindings and
beautiful paintings by famed illustrator N. C.
Wyeth (1882-1945) in this series make these books
handsome, enjoyable additions to any home library,
as well as excellent holiday and birthday gifts.
They're a little expensive, but everyone in our
family -- including Mom and Dad -- has read them at
least twice and has browsed in them several times,
making them worthwhile investments in lasting enjoyment, and I'm sure the books will be passed on
to our grandchildren with great mutual pleasure.
(Incidentally, older editions, identical in every
way except the date of publication, now sell in
rare book stores for as much as $50 or $60.)

   THE BOY'S KING ARTHUR, edited by Sidney Lanier
from Laory's MORTE D'ARTHUR.
   ROBIN HOOD, by Paul Creswick.
   ROBINSON CRUSOE, by Daniel Defoe.
   THE YEARLING, by Marjorie Kinnan Rawlings
   KIDNAPPED, by Robert Louis Stevenson.
   TREASURE ISLAND, by Robert Louis Stevenson.
   THE MYSTERIOUS ISLAND, by Jules Verne.
EACH TITLE, $24.95. Code MAC. Specify N. C. WYETH
EDITION along with the title. BROOK FARM BOOKS.
(See also History: THE LAST OF THE MOHICANS and THE
BLACK ARROW.)

THE CLASSICS -- FOR CHILDREN ONLY? It's interesting
and curious that most of the books usually thought
of today as "children's classics" were not written
for children. Many, in fact, although enjoyable
for children, are better suited to older readers,
because the experience of younger readers is not
yet great enough to help them understand many circumstances and situations. W. H. Auden, referring
to ALICE'S ADVENTURES IN WONDERLAND as an example,
said, "There are good books which are only for
adults because comprehension presupposes adult experiences, but there are no good books which are
only for children." A few years ago, I read ALICE'S
ADVENTURES aloud to the family, in daily installments, and Jean and I enjoyed it at least as much
as the kids did. Not long ago, I re-read THE THREE
MUSKETEERS, and enjoyed it more than I did when I
was 12; perhaps not "more," but in a different way,
and on many more levels. I can read A TALE OF TWO
CITIES every five or six years, and browse in it
occasionally, each time with a little more enjoyment, as if each reading earns compound interest.
Classics are those books which endure, sometimes
for centuries, not only because they tell exciting
stories, or acquaint us with times and people of
the past -- and they are very valuable for doing
that -- but, more especially, because they tell us
something of ourselves. Clifton Fadiman suggests
that we don't get more from a book each time we re-
read it, as much as we get more from ourselves. At
the age of twelve, I enjoyed the excitement and in-
trigue of THE THREE MUSKETEERS; a decade later, I
could better appreciate the more subtle verbal exchanges; after another decade, I could also admire
the writer's artistry and wit. Each time I read the
book, I am able to receive more from it because I'm
able to take more to it. Each time I read it, I
bounce myself against it and come back amplified,
like an echo rebounding in a canyon. Children will
enjoy the classics, but their parents may enjoy
them even more.

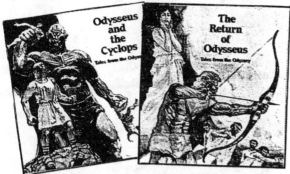

CLASSICS FROM ANCIENT TIMES. Dream-like impressionistic watercolor art and lively adaptations capture the danger, suspense, and heroism of these ancient stories and legends. Ages 9 and up.

ADVENTURES OF EROS AND PSYCHE-- ADVENTURES OF HERCULES -- DEMETER AND PERSEPHONE-- JASON AND THE GOLDEN FLEECE -- PEGASUS, THE WINGED HORSE -- PERSEUS AND MEDUSA -- PROMETHEUS AND THE STORY OF FIRE -- THESEUS AND THE MINOTAUR -- THE WOODEN HORSE -- THE VOYAGE OF ODYSSEUS -- ODYSSEUS AND THE CYCLOPS -- ODYSSEUS AND THE GIANTS -- ODYSSEUS AND THE MAGIC OF CIRCE -- ODYSSEUS AND THE GREAT CHALLENGE -- THE RETURN OF ODYSSEUS.

Each 32-page book, $2.95. Code TRL. BROOK FARM BOOKS.

BY JOVE, A Game and A Book of Classical Adventure. Players travel the beautifully illustrated board as mere mortals risking the perils of adventure, the whims of unpredictable Gods, and the decrees of Oracles. By escaping the Labyrinth and voyaging with Jason on the Quest of the Golden Fleece, players compete to be the first to collect gold coins and Adventure Awards to become Game Hero or Heroine, and win. BY JOVE STORIES is a 64-page book telling of all the mythological characters in the game, with a pronunciation guide and index. Game contents include a board, dice, 8 hero cards with stands, 16 potluck cards, 50 adventure awards, 12 Minotaur/Labyrinth Awards, 60 plastic replicas of ancient Roman coins, 40 oracle cards, and BY JOVE STORIES book. Ages 10 to adult, 2 to 6 players. $22.00 plus $3 shipping. BROOK FARM BOOKS.

◁▷ ◁▷ ◁▷ ◁▷ ◁▷ ◁▷ ◁▷ ◁▷

THE BOOK OF LEGENDS. The Greek legends of Ulysses, Hercules, and Jason are told with simplicity and gentle humor & colorful, interesting illustrations. Age 7 up. $10.95. Code EDC. BROOK FARM BOOKS.

THE BOOK OF GREEK & NORSE LEGENDS. The best-known gods, heroes, and fantasy creatures, brilliantly illustrated, with invaluable reference information. 112 pages. Ages 10 up. $12.95. Code EDC. BROOK FARM BOOKS.

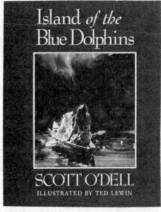

MORE THAN HUMAN, by Theodore Sturgeon. We recommend this novel to our kids as they reach the age of 16 or 17 -- not just as a great story (which it is), but also for its moral and ethical implications. Homo gestalt seems to be the next step in human evolution, but is still in its infancy: a small group of social misfits, each with a certain psychic ability or power, including orphaned twins who can't talk but can disappear at will; the village idiot, whose strength seems to be in his eyes; a young girl who can move things with her mind; and a Mongoloid baby, whose computer-like brain holds them together; and together they are more powerful than any other being on earth -- but, so far, Homo gestalt lacks the most human attribute... a conscience. NOW OUT OF PRINT, BUT LOOK FOR IT IN USED BOOK STORES.

A book, shut tight, is but a block of paper.
From a Salada tea bag

ISLAND OF THE BLUE DOLPHINS, by Scott O'Dell. A young Indian girl, stranded on a rocky Pacific island for eighteen years, learns the art of survival -- and more. This book was a winner of the 1960 Newbery Medal, and continues to attract fan mail thanking the author for the story. This thirtieth-anniversary edition is illustrated with 14 beautiful watercolor paintings. Exciting, inspiring, and thought-provoking for children and adults. $18.95. Code HM. BROOK FARM BOOKS.

JULIE OF THE WOLVES, by Jean Craighead George. A moving and realistic story of an Eskimo girl lost on the North Slope of Alaska who is befriended by a pack of wolves. $3.95. Code HR. BROOK FARM BOOKS.

In literature, as in love, we are astonished at what is chosen by others.

André Maurois

TARZAN -- If you've seen Tarzan in movies or Saturday morning cartoons, but haven't read any of the original books by Edgar Rice Burroughs, then you don't know Tarzan. When Derek was ten, he wrote this review:

"The books about Tarzan are very good. I like the idea of a baby growing up with a tribe of apes and learning to swing through the trees. There is a big difference between the Tarzan in the books and in the cartoons. In the cartoons they make him look like an uneducated man. In the books he is very intelligent, and he can speak other languages besides that of the apes and English. His real name is John Clayton. Tarzan means Whiteskin in Ape language. The adventures he has are very exciting. He finds lots of lost civilizations, and sometimes he gets caught and has to figure out a way to escape. Sometimes he finds other people who want to escape too, and he helps them, unless they are burglars or something like that; then he just leaves them there."

Derek has enjoyed Tarzan as much as I did when I was a boy, and a few of our Tarzan books are ones which were my father's when he was a boy. I've re-read a few of them recently, and I still enjoy them. The author never visited Africa, so you won't learn many "facts" from these books, but you'll enjoy the drama and adventure.

Titles, in sequence of writing and of Tarzan's own chronology, are:

TARZAN OF THE APES (his origin)
THE RETURN OF TARZAN
THE BEASTS OF TARZAN
THE SON OF TARZAN
TARZAN AND THE JEWELS OF OPAR
JUNGLE TALES OF TARZAN
TARZAN THE UNTAMED
TARZAN THE TERRIBLE
TARZAN AND THE GOLDEN LION
TARZAN AND THE ANT MEN
TARZAN, LORD OF THE JUNGLE
TARZAN AND THE LOST EMPIRE
TARZAN AT THE EARTH'S CORE
TARZAN THE INVINCIBLE
TARZAN THE TRIUMPHANT
TARZAN AND THE CITY OF GOLD
TARZAN AND THE LION MAN
TARZAN AND THE LEOPARD MAN
TARZAN'S QUEST
TARZAN AND THE FORBIDDEN CITY
TARZAN THE MAGNIFICENT
TARZAN AND THE FOREIGN LEGION
TARZAN AND THE CASTAWAYS

Ages 10 to adult. Each title, $3.95. Code HR. BROOK FARM BOOKS.

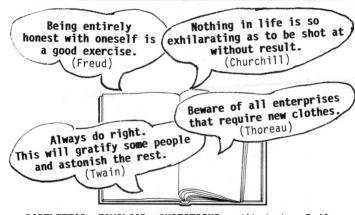

BARTLETT'S FAMILIAR QUOTATIONS, edited by Emily Morison Beck. This is much more than a collection of miscellaneous quotations; it's a distillation of humanity's thoughts through the centuries; a well of ideas which never runs dry; a favorite book for browsing when you can't settle on anything else to read, and the first book to take from the shelf when you want to know "Who said that?" or "What did so-and-so say about that?" Skimming this book or being guided through it by the index of authors is also a good way to become familiar with thousands of writers, thinkers, and statesmen whom you might otherwise never meet. This 16th edition of BART-LETT'S is revised and updated, with more than 2500 new quotations on such topics as science, the women's movement, and recent political history. There are quotations from authors as current as Eudora Welty and as historically important as Pythagoras; more translations from non-English works, and fresh translations of some quotations that were in previous editions; expanded Biblical, Shakespearean, and classical sections; selections from the Koran, and from Buddhist and Sanskrit writings. Each quotation has a number, keyed to the index, so it can easily be found. All authors are listed alphabetically. Hardcover; 22,500 quotations on 1,540 pages. $39.95. Code LB. BROOK FARM BOOKS.

I hate quotations.

Ralph Waldo Emerson

GREAT IDEAS THAT HAVE SHAPED OUR WORLD -- Excellent cassette programs presenting the ideas of Paine, Jefferson, Thoreau, Garrison, Adam Smith, Mill, Burke, Hamilton, Hobbes, Locke, de Tocqueville, and others. See this title under History.

There is no worse robber than a bad book.
Italian proverb

THE LIFETIME READING PLAN, by Clifton Fadiman. Brief introductions to suggested readings of some of the best of the world's literature, from Homer to the present day. "The books here discussed," says the author, "may take you fifty years to finish. They can of course be read in a much shorter time. The point is that they are intended to occupy an important part of a whole life, no matter what your present age may be. Many of them happen to be more entertaining than the latest best-seller. Still, it is not on the entertainment level that they are most profitably read. What they offer is of larger dimensions. It is rather like what is offered by loving and marrying, having and rearing children, carving out a career, creating a home. They can be ...a source of continuous internal growth. Hence the word _Lifetime_. These authors are life companions. Once part of you, they work in and on and with you until you die. They should not be read in a hurry, any more than friends are made in a hurry." Revised edition, $7.95. Code HR. BROOK FARM BOOKS.

When you re-read a classic you do not see more in the book than you did before; you see more in _you_ than there was before.
Clifton Fadiman

LITERARY POSTERS-- A series of 12 literary maps that plot, annotate, and illustrate the locales mentioned in the works of famous authors, including The John Steinbeck Map of America, The Sherlock Holmes Mystery Map, The Ernest Hemingway Adventure Map of the World, The Jane Austen Map of England, The Ian Fleming Thriller Map, The Raymond Chandler Mystery Map, and other literary maps of New York, Los Angeles, Latin America, Paris, and South America. $5.75 folded or $9.00 rolled, postpaid. Write for a complete list. AARON BLAKE PUBLISHERS, 1800 S. Robertson Blvd., Los Angeles, CA 90035.

[A classic is] a book which people praise and don't read.
Mark Twain

How many a man has dated a new era in his life from the reading of a book!
Henry David Thoreau

Some books are to be tasted, others to be swallowed, and some few to be chewed and digested.
Francis Bacon

I don't know which is more discouraging, literature or chickens.
E. B. White

CLASSIC LITERATURE FOR ONLY $1.00 -- Complete and unabridged, new editions of fiction, poetry, plays, and essays, attractively bound, approximately 5x8", 64-160 pages, with clear print.

FICTION

ADVENTURES OF HUCKLEBERRY FINN, Mark Twain
ALICE'S ADVENTURES IN WONDERLAND, Lewis Carroll
BARTLEBY AND BENITO CERONO, Herman Melville
THE BEAST IN THE JUNGLE and Other Stories, James
BEOWULF, Beowulf
THE CALL OF THE WILD, Jack London
CANDIDE, Voltaire
A CHRISTMAS CAROL, Charles Dickens
THE CRICKET ON THE HEARTH & Other Christmas Stor-
    ies, Charles Dickens
DR. JEKYLL AND MR. HYDE, Robert Louis Stevenson
FAVORITE FATHER BROWN STORIES, G. K. Chesterton
FIVE GREAT SHORT STORIES, Anton Chekhov
FIVE GREAT SHORT STORIES, Jack London
FLATLAND, Abbot
GIFT OF THE MAGI and Other Stories, O. Henry
THE GOLD BUG and Other Tales, Edgar Allen Poe
GREAT GHOST STORIES, Grafton (ed.)
SIX GREAT SHERLOCK HOLMES STORIES, Doyle
THE INVISIBLE MAN, H. G. Wells
THE LUCK OF ROARING CAMP and Other Short Stories,
    Bret Harte
THE MYSTERIOUS STRANGER and Other Stories, Twain
THE NECKLACE and Other Stories, Guy de Maupassant
NOTES FROM THE UNDERGROUND, Fyodor Dostoyevsky
THE OPEN BOAT and Other Stories, Steven Crane
O PIONEERS! Willa Cather
THE RED BADGE OF COURAGE, Steven Crane
THE SCARLET LETTER, Nathaniel Hawthorne
STORIES, Ambrose Bierce
TREASURE ISLAND, Robert Louis Stevenson
WHITE FANG, Jack London
YOUNG GOODMAN BROWN and Other Stories, Hawthorne

NON-FICTION

CIVIL DISOBEDIENCE, Henry David Thoreau
THE DEVIL'S DICTIONARY, Ambrose Bierce
GREAT SPEECHES, Abraham Lincoln
THE PRINCE, Machiavelli
SELF-RELIANCE and Other Essays, R. W. Emerson
THE SOULS OF BLACK FOLK, DuBois
SYMPOSIUM and PHAEDRUS, Plato
THE THEORY OF THE LEISURE CLASS, Thorsten Veblen
THE TRIAL AND DEATH OF SOCRATES, Plato

POETRY

THE BHAGAVADGITA (Hindu Sacred Literature)
THE BOOK OF PSALMS, King James Bible
A BOY'S WILL and NORTH OF BOSTON, Robert Frost
CHICAGO and Other Poems, Carl Sandburg
CHRISTMAS CAROLS, Weller (ed.)
COMPLETE SONGS FROM PLAYS, William Shakespeare
COMPLETE SONNETS, William Shakespeare
EARLY POEMS, William Butler Yeats
ESSAY ON MAN and Other Poems, Alexander Pope
FAVORITE POEMS, Henry Wadsworth Longfellow
FAVORITE POEMS, William Wordsworth
GREAT LOVE POEMS, Weller (ed.)
GREAT SONNETS, Negri (ed.)
GUNGA DIN and Other Poems, Rudyard Kipling
LYRIC POEMS, John Keats
MY LAST DUCHESS and Other Poems, Browning
POEMS AND SONGS, Robert Burns
THE RAVEN and Other Poems, Edgar Allen Poe
RENASCENCE & Other Poems, Edna St. Vincent Millay
THE RIME OF THE ANCIENT MARINER and Other Poems,
    Samuel Coleridge
THE ROAD NOT TAKEN and Other Poems, Robert Frost
THE RUBAIYAT OF OMAR KHAYYAM, Edward FitzGerald
SELECTED POEMS, Byron
SELECTED POEMS, Emily Dickinson
SELECTED POEMS, John Donne
SELECTED POEMS, John Milton
SELECTED POEMS, Percy Bysshe Shelley
SELECTED POEMS, Alfred Lord Tennyson
SELECTED POEMS, Walt Whitman
THE SHOOTING OF DAN McGREW and Other Poems,
    Robert W. Service
SONGS OF INNOCENCE and SONGS OF EXPERIENCE,
    William Blake
SONNETS FROM THE PORTUGUESE and Other Poems,
    Elizabeth Barret Browning
SPOON RIVER ANTHOLOGY, Edgar Lee Masters

PLAYS

ANTIGONE, Sophocles
ARMS AND THE MAN, George Bernard Shaw
THE CHERRY ORCHARD, Anton Chekhov
A DOLL'S HOUSE, Henrik Ibsen
FAUST, Part I, Goethe
HAMLET, William Shakespeare
THE IMPORTANCE OF BEING EARNEST, Oscar Wilde
JULIUS CAESAR, William Shakespeare
KING LEAR, William Shakespeare
MACBETH, William Shakespeare
MEDEA, Euripides
A MIDSUMMER NIGHT'S DREAM, William Shakespeare
THE MIKADO, Gilbert
THE MISANTHROPE, Moliere
OEDIPUS REX, Sophocles
ROMEO AND JULIET, William Shakespeare

ALL TITLES, ONLY $1.00 EACH. Code DV. BROOK FARM BOOKS. [IMPORTANT: If you're ordering $1.00 Classics AND other books in the "Code DV" group at the same time, use our regular postage rates (see "Ordering Instructions" in the back of the book); however, if you're ordering only 5 or more $1.00 Classics in the "Code DV" Group, count the first FIVE titles as ONE BOOK, then count all others individually, and then calculate the postage accordingly. I.e., $2.50 for the first five $1.00 Classics, and 25¢ for each additional title. THESE SPECIAL POSTAGE RATES APPLY ONLY TO 5 or more $1.00 CLASSICS, and only when you're not ordering other books in the "Code DV" Group at the same time.]

MODERN LIBRARY -- Several selections of classic literature in well-made, attractive, hardcover books at reasonable prices:

ABRAHAM LINCOLN: A BIOGRAPHY, Thomas $13.95
ADVENTURES OF HUCKLEBERRY FINN, Twain $15.50
ANNA KARENINA, Tolstoy $20.00
BASIC WRITINGS OF SIGMUND FREUD $19.95
BASIC WRITINGS OF C. G. JUNG $17.00
BASIC WRITINGS OF FRIEDRICH NIETZSCHE $20.00
BEST SHORT STORIES OF O. HENRY $12.00
THE BROTHERS KARAMAZOV, Dostoyevsky $17.00
BULLFINCH'S MYTHOLOGY $20.00
CANDIDE & PHILOSOPHICAL LETTERS, Voltaire $13.50
THE CITY OF GOD, St. Augustine $19.00
COLLECTED WORKS OF LEWIS CARROLL $20.00
COMPLETE NOVELS & SELECTED TALES, Hawthorne
    Vol. I, $18.00. Vol. II, $19.00
COMPLETE POETRY & SELECTED PROSE, Donne $17.00
COMPLETE TALES & POEMS, Poe $20.00
DECLINE AND FALL OF THE ROMAN EMPIRE, Gibbon. Vols.
    I, II, and III, $20.00 each
DIARY OF A YOUNG GIRL, Frank $12.00
ENGLISH PHILOSOPHERS FROM BACON TO MILL $17.95
EUROPEAN PHILOSOPHERS: DESCARTES TO NIETZCHE $20
FRANKENSTEIN, Mary Shelley $13.50
GREAT CLASSICAL MYTHS, Godolphin $15.00
I, CLAUDIUS, Graves $15.00
INTERPRETATION OF DREAMS, Freud $12.00
INTRODUCTION TO ARISTOTLE $18.50
JANE EYRE, Bronte $17.50
LEAVES OF GRASS, Whitman $16.50
LES MISERABLES, Hugo $21.00
LIFE & SELECTED WRITINGS OF THOMAS JEFFERSON $19
THE MAGIC MOUNTAIN, Thomas Mann $19.00
MOBY DICK, Melville $20.00
ORIGIN OF SPECIES & DESCENT OF MAN, Darwin $19.00
PHILOSOPHY OF EMANUEL KANT $18.00
RED BADGE OF COURAGE, Crane $13.50
THE REPUBLIC, Plato $10.95
SELECTED WRITINGS OF RALPH WALDO EMERSON $20.00
TE-TAO CHING, Lao Tzu $13.50
THUS SPAKE ZARATHUSTRA, Nietzsche $11.95
UNCLE TOM'S CABIN, Stowe $17.50
VARIETIES OF RELIGIOUS EXPERIENCE, James $17.50
WALDEN & OTHER WRITINGS, Thoreau $18.50
WAR AND PEACE, Tolstoy $19.00
WEALTH OF NATIONS, Smith $21.00
WISDOM OF CONFUCIUS $8.95
WISDOM OF LAO TSE $10.00
WUTHERING HEIGHTS, Bronte $12.95
When ordering, specify "Modern Library" and full title. Code RH. BROOK FARM BOOKS.

FIRST WORDS, 305 E. Washington, Delavan, WI 53115. Books for infants, toddlers, and pre-schoolers, chosen for their appeal to the parents as well as the kids. Free catalog.

BOOKS AT DISCOUNT OR VERY LOW PRICES --

THE STRAND BOOKSTORE, 828 Broadway, New York, NY 10003. Up to 80% off all books, all subjects, including out-of-print books. Request catalogs on postcard, not a letter.

EDWARD R. HAMILTON, Falls Village, CT 06031. Free catalog of publishers' overstocks, bargain books. 2000 titles, many subjects.

DOVER PUBLICATIONS, INC., 180 Varick Street, New York, NY 10014. Without a doubt, one of the world's best sources of very good, inexpensive books -- some original publications, many reprints of otherwise out-of-print books. Thousands of titles; most of them $6 or less. Free general catalog of over 3000 titles.

BARNES & NOBLE, 126 Fifth Avenue, New York, NY 10011. Discounts up to 90% on books, records, tapes; nearly all subjects.

MARBORO BOOKS, 205 Moonachie Road, Moonachie, NJ 07074. Free catalog of publishers' remainders, hardcover and paperback; all categories.

PUBLISHERS CENTRAL BUREAU, 1 Champion Avenue, Avenel, NJ 07131. Up to 83% discount on books, tapes, records. Catalog.

ADAMS BOOK COMPANY, 537 Sackett Street, Brooklyn, NY 11217.

WILCOX & FOLLETT BOOK CO., 1000 W. Washington Blvd., Chicago, IL 60607. Used textbooks, all subjects, all levels, reconditioned, guaranteed 80% as good as the original, for one fourth to one half less than the new price. New, unused Webster dictionaries, all levels, discount prices. Free catalog.

HORIZON BOOK PROMOTIONS, 230 Fifth Avenue, Suite 1907, New York, NY 10001. Publishers' remainders. Catalog.

QUALITY PAPERBACK BOOK CLUB, Middletown, PA 17057. Our favorite book club. Begin by buying 3 books for $1 each plus postage. No other purchases required, ever. Prices are about 10% less than publishers' prices. Each purchase earns bonus points which may be used for the full purchase price of future orders. Write for free information.

WHO READS WHAT WHEN: Literature Selections for Children Ages Three Through Thirteen, Jane Williams. Recommended reading list and guide to 500+ titles, indexed by age level, author, and title. Even 5,000 titles wouldn't be a complete list, but these 500 selections are good suggestions, and are suggestive of further related reading. $5.45 ppd. BLUE STOCKING PRESS, P.O. Box 1014, Placerville, CA 95667.

ILLUSTRATED SHAKESPEARE --

These twelve plays have been edited and illustrated in a format similar to that of the Illustrated Classics, and are excellent introductions to Shakespeare not only for children, but also for adults who don't have time or inclination to read the originals, and for all who think Shakespeare is boring or too complicated to enjoy. The reading level is about fifth grade; but, as with the Classics, we find the excellent black-and-white drawings easily make up for the simplified text. Besides vividly showing the settings and costumes of the characters and their background, the illustrations help to clarify situations which are somewhat vague in the text, and will be appreciated even by those who enjoy reading the original plays in their entirety.

   AS YOU LIKE IT
   HAMLET
   JULIUS CAESAR
   KING LEAR
   MACBETH
   THE MERCHANT OF VENICE
   A MIDSUMMER NIGHT'S DREAM
   OTHELLO
   ROMEO AND JULIET
   THE TAMING OF THE SHREW
   THE TEMPEST
   TWELFTH NIGHT

ILLUSTRATED SHAKESPEARE -- Set of 12 plays, $36.00 plus $3 shipping. (Individual titles may be combined with Illustrated U.S. History, Illustrated Biographies, or Illustrated Classics for a minimum of 12 titles.) BROOK FARM BOOKS.

SHAKESPEARE MADE EASY SERIES -- Twelve of Shakespeare's major plays, presented complete with original text on each left-hand page and modern translation on the facing right-hand page. There are also discussion questions and background material. Good companions to Shakespeare on tape and the Illustrated Shakespeare.

   HAMLET -- HENRY IV, PART I -- JULIUS CAESAR -- KING LEAR -- MACBETH -- MERCHANT OF VENICE -- MIDSUMMER NIGHT'S DREAM -- ROMEO AND JULIET -- THE TEMPEST -- TWELFTH NIGHT.

   Each book, 224 to 288 pages, $6.95. Order "Shakespeare Made Easy" and title. Code BE. BROOK FARM BOOKS.

THE COMPLETE WORKS OF SHAKESPEARE -- All of Shakespeare's plays, poems, and sonnets in an attractive hardcover volume. $24.95. Code DD. BROOK FARM BOOKS.

A SHAKESPEARE COLORING BOOK -- This is a history of Shakespearean illustration from the very old Peacham drawing to Ronald Searle's illustrations of Richard Burton as Henry V, and Orson Welles as Othello. A good companion to any reading of Shakespeare. $3.50. Code BB. BROOK FARM BOOKS.

SHAKESPEARE'S PLAYS ON CASSETTES -- Full-cast performances of Shakespeare's plays, by Dublin Gate Theatre Productions, Folio Theatre Players, or Swan Theatre Players. Carefully abridged to preserve all important story points, characters, and historical references. Each tape, approximately 50-60 minutes.

   OTHELLO
   ROMEO AND JULIET
   TROILUS AND CRESSIDA
   AS YOU LIKE IT
   A COMEDY OF ERRORS
   THE MERCHANT OF VENICE
   A MIDSUMMER NIGHT'S DREAM
   MUCH ADO ABOUT NOTHING
   THE TAMING OF THE SHREW
   THE TEMPEST
   TWELFTH NIGHT
   TWO GENTLEMEN OF VERONA
   THE WINTER'S TALE
   HENRY IV, Part I
   HENRY IV, Part II
   HENRY V
   HENRY VIII
   RICHARD II
   RICHARD III

Each cassette tape, $10.95. Code SPO. BROOK FARM BOOKS.

HOW TO STOCK A QUALITY HOME LIBRARY INEXPENSIVELY,
by Jane A. Williams. First of all, I have to say I
object to "quality" as an adjective, meaning "high
quality" as opposed to "low quality," but such usage
is all the rage these days, having begun with advertising writers who were short on space, either on
paper or between their ears. With that out of the
way, I'll say that this is a very useful little
book, listing 22 sources of discount books, mail order book suppliers, and remainder dealers. Jane also
suggests many other sources of inexpensive books,
such as used book sales (where to find them, what to
look for), and ways of accumulating money to spend
on books. The book's price makes it possible for you
to add it to your own home library inexpensively,
and it's a good investment. $4.95 plus $1.25 postage. BLUESTOCKING PRESS, Box 1014, Placerville, CA
95667.

This will never be a civilized country until we
expend more money for books than we do for chewing
gum.

Elbert Hubbard

BUYING BOOKS CHEAPLY WITHOUT BEING CHEAP -- Our home
has thousands of books, and our car -- I mean, our
pickup, now that the girls have all moved out and
Derek has his own car -- is trained to stop at all
lawn & garage sales, right next to the book tables.
We usually live well below the poverty level, sub-
sisting on a very small business income, occasional
outside jobs, and our own home-raised food, so we're
always alert for bargains. However, one of the
reasons we're so poor in other kinds of material
wealth is that we're rich in books. Mixed in with
our 25¢ bargains are many books which have cost $10,
$20, or $30, and a few at twice that price. If we
see a book we want but wince at the price, we can:
a) wait for it to come out in paperback, and hope we
still want it by then; 2) borrow it from the public
library and return it in two weeks; 3) go without;
or, 4) cut financial corners on something else and
buy the book. Sometimes the corners have already
been cut for some other purpose, but usually we're
able to discover the money somewhere. Our kids have
read and re-read hundreds of books we own partly because they had easy access to them, and partly because they, too, enjoy ownership of books. Just seeing a familiar, favorite book on the shelf can bring
back memories of enjoyment. The classics with illustrations by N. C. Wyeth (see Literature and History)
cost $20 to $25, and are good examples of our occasional extravagant purchases. They make great gifts,
and are far more enjoyable than their cheaper coun-
terparts. If you find one of these books in a garage
sale, consider yourself lucky. My brother, who buys
and sells antiques and rare books, easily sells older copies of them for $40 or more. The value of many
things, including books, is often beyond price. We
look for bargains, and try to buy what we want as
cheaply as we can, but we don't want to become so
fanatic about saving money that we miss the enjoyment or information in a few expensive books now and
then.

SCIENCE

THE UNIVERSE
PREHISTORY - THE HUMAN BODY
NATURAL SCIENCE: THE EARTH
SPACE: ASTRONOMY & SPACE TRAVEL
GENERAL SCIENCE: PHYSICS, CHEMISTRY,
BIOLOGY, INVENTIONS, & EXPERIMENTS
SUPPLIERS OF SCIENCE MATERIALS

EINSTEIN AND THE BUDDHA -- Dr. Fritjof Capra, lecturer & researcher at the Lawrence Berkeley Laboratories in California and author of THE TAO OF PHYSICS, talking with Jocelyn Ryder-Smith, discussing parallels between modern particle physics and Eastern mysticism, proposes that the two themes -- fundamental unity and interpendence of all phenomena; and the intrinsically dynamic nature of reality -- are common to both views. He also suggests that physics and mysticism have much to offer to the fields of medicine, economics, & politics. (I think it may be significant that Eastern "mystics" might be more likely to say that physics and mysticism are not only parallel, but very probably the same phenomena expressed in different vocabularies. As physicists probe deeper into the mysteries of physical matter, they realize increasingly that material effects are influenced, and perhaps governed, by consciousness. The mystics have known this for centuries.) ONE CASSETTE. $10.95. Code JN. BROOK FARM BOOKS.

SECRETS OF THE UNIVERSE, Paul Fleisher. Simplified but very detailed descriptions & clear explanations of natural law, including certain basic laws of physics such as Archimedes' principle, planetary motion, Pascal's law, relativity, and quantum mechanics. Everyday examples of each principle in application, with some experiments for testing them. Concise but informative. Useful for adults who want a basic understanding without lengthy study, as well as for kids, ages 12 and up. Hardcover, 224 pages. $18.95. Code MAC. BROOK FARM BOOKS.

gy=c -- If you agree with Albert Einstein's opinion that God does not play dice with the universe, you may be interested in this equation, which I found in GODWHALE, a science fiction novel (now out of print) by J. G. Ballard. The letters stand for "gravity times a year equals the speed of light." The kids and I spent several hours one morning playing with it, trying to prove or disprove it. Sure enough: the rate of gravity (32 feet per second per second) times the seconds in a year equals the speed of light (expressed in seconds). Try it. The speed of light is the one absolute constant fact throughout the universe. Does this have any real significance -- or is it just the roll of the dice? A "coincidence" -- or God's signature?

That the universe was formed by a fortuitous concourse of atoms, I will no more believe than that the accidental jumbling of the alphabet would fall into a most ingenious treatise of philosophy.

Jonathan Swift

ONE MILLION GALAXIES-- A computer photo-map of the galaxies brighter than 19th magnitude visible from the northern hemisphere. Detailed border pictures of several different galaxies (mere dots in the photo-map) to help put things in perspective as we remember that our solar system is a mere dot in our galaxy. And this is only a <u>suggestion</u> of the immensity of the universe. Listen to the first five minutes of Straus's <u>Also Sprach Zarathustra</u> while gazing at this picture, and then check the foundations of your philosophy -- whatever it is. 39x47", rolled, mailed in a tube. $5 postpaid. (Worth more; if the price has gone up, pay it.) WHOLE EARTH ACCESS, 2990 Seventh St., Berkeley, CA 94710.

FROM QUARKS TO QUASARS: A Tour of the Universe, by James Jespersen & Jane Fitz-Randolph. Engrossing account of how more than fifty great philosophers and scientists have thought about the universe, how it works, and where our planet fits in. Closely-reasoned, clear descriptions of Newton's theories, Einstein's doubts about some of Newton's conclusions, and new directions in cosmological and sub-atomic research. A good introduction for ages 12 and up, including adults. Hardcover, 224 pages. $16.95. Code MAC. BROOK FARM BOOKS.

FIRST GUIDE TO THE UNIVERSE-- Exciting pictures with brief text presenting a wealth of information about the earth, moon, planets, sun, rockets, and spaceflight. Age 7 up. $10.95. Code EDC. BROOK FARM BOOKS.

POWERS OF TEN: About the Relative Size of Things in the Universe, by Philip Morrison, Phylis Morrison, and the Office of Charles and Ray Eames. A fascinating, mind-boggling excursion through the universe, from the very smallest sub-atomic particles known, to the farthest limits of space yet discovered, moving in forty-two orders of magnitude, taking us one jump at a time to give us a breathtaking sense of the relative sizes within us and around us. A book to browse in, over and over, very slowly, with awe and wonder. 164 pages, 312 illustrations. $19.95. Code WHF. BROOK FARM BOOKS.

COSMOS, Carl Sagan. Based on the COSMOS television series, this book was on the New York _Times_ bestseller list for 70 weeks. With over 250 full-color illustrations & several in black-and-white, COSMOS is about science in its broadest context, tracing the growth together of science and civilization. The book explores spacecraft missions of discovery of the nearby planets, research in the library of ancient Alexandria, the human brain, Egyptian hieroglyphics, the origin of life, death of the Sun, the evolution of galaxies & the origins of matter, suns, and worlds. Sagan retraces the fifteen billion years of cosmic evolution that have transformed matter into life and consciousness, enabling the Cosmos to wonder about itself. He considers the latest findings about life elsewhere & how we might communicate with the beings of other worlds. COSMOS is the story of our long journey of discovery & the forces and people who helped shape modern science, including Democritus, Hypatia, Kepler, Newton, Huygens, Champollion, Lowell, and Humason. Sagan looks at our earth from an extraterrestrial vantage point & sees a blue jewellike world, inhabited by a lifeform that is just beginning to discover its own unity and to venture into the vast ocean of space. A beautiful, informative, exciting, reverent book. $29.95. (Also available in a smaller paperback, without all the photographs, for $6.95.) Code RH. BROOK FARM BOOKS.

A BRIEF HISTORY OF TIME, Stephen W. Hawking. Large paperback. $9.95. Code BT. BROOK FARM BOOKS.

A BRIEF HISTORY OF TIME, by Stephen W. Hawking -- AUDIOCASSETTES. "[When] I decided to ... write a popular book about space and time... there were already a considerable number of books about the early universe and black holes... I felt that none of them really addressed the questions that had led me to do research in cosmology and quantum theory. Where did the universe come from? How and why did it begin? Will it come to an end, and if so, how? ...Modern science has become so technical that only a very small number of specialists are able to master the mathematics used to describe them. Yet the basic ideas about the origin and fate of the universe can be stated without mathematics in a form that people without a scientific education can understand. This is what I have attempted to do..." If you've read my comments about math, you may be surprised that I'd read a book by the man who is considered by many to be the most brilliant physicist in the history of the world, and even more surprised that I understand it enough to enjoy it. I'll admit I've taken some of it in very small doses and I do a lot of ruminating, but it hasn't been as tedious for me as you might think. _Time_ said of Hawking, "Even as he sits helpless in his wheelchair, his mind seems to soar ever more brilliantly across the vastness of space and time to unlock the secrets of the universe." _Astronomy_ wrote: "The work of Stephen Hawking will be writ large in the annals of science." _Vanity Fair:_ "Stephen Hawking has overcome a crippling disease to become the supernova of world physics... He is leaping beyond relativity, beyond quantum mechanics, beyond the big bang, to the 'dance of geometry' that created the universe." Listening to this clear reading of Hawking's book is even better than reading it myself; I can close my eyes and imagine that Hawking is leading me through veils of human knowledge, a little closer to the nature of the universe. FOUR CASSETTES -- SIX HOURS. Special price, $19.95. Code BT. BROOK FARM BOOKS.

The world embarrasses me, and I cannot dream
That this watch exists and has no watchmaker.
Voltaire

PREHISTORY -- Three books that form a brilliantly-visual, continuous account of our world through the beginnings of early man. They have been prepared with the help of experts in each period of history, and are written and illustrated with great attention to detail and accuracy. DINOSAURS, from the beginning of the world to the age of dinosaurs. PREHISTORIC MAMMALS, our world after the dinosaurs became extinct. EARLY MAN, the story of the first people on earth.

Age 8 up, to adult. Each book, $6.95; or all 3 in a combined volume, PREHISTORIC LIFE, for only $12.95 (save $7.90). Code EDC. BROOK FARM BOOKS.

USBORNE SCIENCE & NATURE GUIDES -- Written and fully illustrated to introduce the complete beginner to the basic knowledge and skills of each subject, from choosing and using equipment to increased understanding and enjoyment. Lots of interesting background information, many helpful hints and tips. Age 10 and up.

  THE YOUNG ASTRONOMER
  THE YOUNG NATURALIST
  UNDERSTANDING & COLLECTING ROCKS & FOSSILS
Each book, $6.95. Code EDC. BROOK FARM BOOKS.

FOSSIL SETS -- 15 different fossils from all of the different geological time periods are identified in individual packets noting the type, what time period they're from, and where the fossils were found. Set, $5.00. Individual fossils such as gastropods and trilobites also available. 100% money-back guarantee. JIM AND MARY SHAFFER, 15398 Beatty St., San Leandro, CA 94579.

TOWER OF TIME, a beautiful poster with a mural-like pictorial time line showing evolution of 700 million years, from the single cell to man. One of our favorite posters. The other side has a lifesize (30") Compsognathus. $2.30. LEARNING, P.O. Box 2580, Boulder, CO 80322.

ARCHAEOLOGY, POBox 385, Martinsville, NJ 08836. Bimonthly magazine with news, articles, photographs, book reviews, more.

ORIGIN OF SPECIES & THE DESCENT OF MAN, by Charles Darwin. See Literature, "Modern Library."

THE BIG BEAST BOOK: Dinosaurs and How They Got That Way, Jerry Booth. A Brown Paper School Book. Exciting, thought-provoking experiments, puzzles, projects, and activities about dinosaurs. Great. $9.95. Code LB. BROOK FARM BOOKS.

THE EVOLUTION BOOK, by Sara Stein. Books such as this (one of the best) should be read, and perhaps discussed, with at least a little skepticism now and then, tempered with reason. Evolution within a species is obvious, even in the limited time and space of a barnyard. Evolution of one species to another is still without evidence of any kind. The missing link is still missing. This book offers scores of projects from preserving sea stars to making seaweed pudding, has hundreds of drawings and photographs, and attempts to answer several important questions, such as How did life begin? What makes the continents move? The answers to such questions, says the author, can be discovered by reading the ancient messages left on the earth. Like Voltaire, I can't believe "the watch has no watchmaker," so I don't swallow the entire evolutionary theory, but neither do I believe "the watchmaker" is a white-bearded egomaniac playing with mudpies. Movement of continents is a measurable phenomenon. The beginning of life, supposedly from a chance collision of cosmic debris, is only a "scientific" doctrine, with no more to support it than corresponding religious doctrines. Most of this book deals with demonstrable facts, presenting them in very informative and interesting ways. The attempts to describe and define the greater mysteries, such as the beginning of life and consciousness, should be recognized as no more than current theory, with as little foundation as the divine creation theory. Age 10 and up, including adults. $12.95. Code BT. BROOK FARM BOOKS.

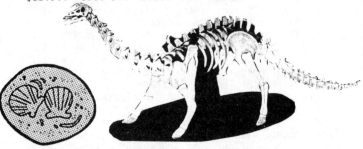

EASY-TO-MAKE APATOSAURUS SKELETON -- Step-by-step instructions with easy-to-follow diagrams will help children about 7 or 8 and older, with little or no adult help, to assemble this sturdy paper model, which is 20 inches long and 8 inches high. 16 pages of fully-colored parts, easily cut out and put together. $2.95. Code DV. BROOK FARM BOOKS.

CAVE ART TRANSCRIPTS-- Free booklet. GALLERY OF PREHISTORIC PAINTINGS, 25-60 49th St., 2nd Floor, Astoria, NY 11103.

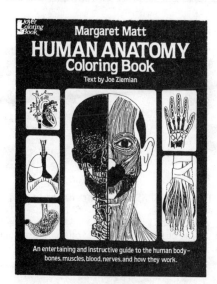

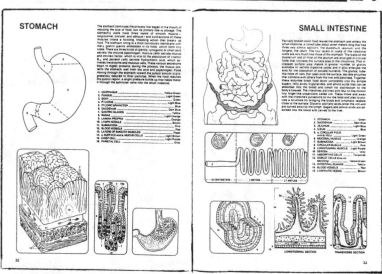

HUMAN ANATOMY COLORING BOOK, by Margaret Matt and Joe Ziemian. This book won't prepare you to take a medical exam tomorrow, but it's the best book we've found for beginners of any age (about 10 to adult), and will give you a very comprehensive understanding of the basics of human anatomy. Forty-three scientifically-accurate pictures of the body's organs and major systems, with numerous views, cross-sections, diagrams, clear explanatory text, and suggestions for coloring. Because the body's struc-

tures can't be understood independently of what they do, the functions as well as shape and location of body parts and systems are described and explained, as well as their relationships to each other. You'll need a set of good "pencil crayons," with at least a dozen different colors. Jean began working in one of these books a few days ago, spending about an hour each evening reading about the body's innards and then coloring them, and she doesn't hear me when I speak to her. $2.95. Code DV. BROOK FARM BOOKS.

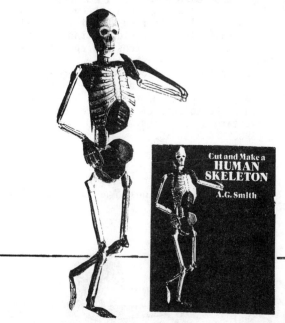

CUT AND MAKE A HUMAN SKELETON -- Pre-teens, teens, and adults can make a three-dimensional model 16½" high which accurately represents the full human skeletal structure. All parts are printed on heavy stock (some parts on both sides), in appropriate colors, and can easily be assembled using scissors, glue, a hobby knife for a few small tricky pieces, and a needle and thread for connecting some of the joints. Diagrams, introduction, and instructions include information about the skeleton and the medical terminology of its components. When completed, the skeleton can be mounted on a base, and can be positioned in "lifelike" poses. $3.95. Code DV. BROOK FARM BOOKS.

THE HUMAN BODY: AN ACTION BOOK, by Jonathan Miller & David Pelham. Six double-spread "pop-up" figures in full color and amazing, accurate detail. Each set is a three-dimensional action study of parts of the human body, translating the intracacies & wonders of the body into models that really "work," with sections that move, slide, fold, or expand. Kids and adults will turn the pages with awe and respect for the wonderful complexity and economy of design in the human body. $22.50. Code SS. BROOK FARM BOOKS. BOOKS.

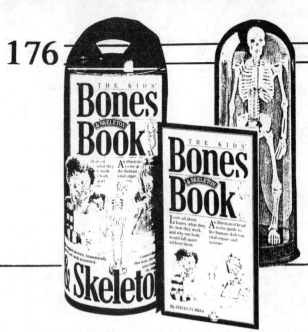

LEARN ABOUT THE SENSES -- Interesting and useful facts about HEARING, SEEING, SMELLING, TASTING, TOUCHING, and, yes, THINKING. Six 24-page books, 8x8", with full-color illustrations. Ages 7 and up. $1.95 each. Code TRL. BROOK FARM BOOKS.

THE BONES BOOK and SKELETON, by Stephen Cumbaa; illustrated by Kim La Fave. Shake those bones and become an anatomist! Then put them all together to get a good look at how your amazing bones form one of nature's most successful inventions -- the skeleton. From maxilla and mandible to pelvis and patella, THE BONES BOOK is a lively and informative head-to-toe account of how bones grow, fit, flex, and sometimes break. Learn how bones make blood; why people shrink during the day and grow again at night; and what the shape of bones may be in the future. THE BONES BOOK also describes all the vital parts which bones protect in the body, including the brain, digestive tract, and circulatory system. The accompanying plastic skeleton is the most accurate model available for children on the market today, sculpted by a professional prothesisist to the standards set by GRAY'S ANATOMY. The skeleton's joints simulate the connections of real bones and move the way actual skeletons move. The 21-piece skeleton parts come unassembled in a clear plastic cylinder which may be used to display the assembled 11½" skeleton. $12.95. Code WKM. BROOK FARM BOOKS.

THE BODY BOOK, by Sara Stein. DNA, chromosomes, and genes; how one sandwich can feed 40 trillion cells; the biggest brain in the world and thoughts that travel 250 miles per hour; tonsils, appendix, and the remnants of a tail; how the little bits of iron that color your blood red also flowed through the veins of dinosaurs; and hundreds of other facts, statistics, explanations, and fascinating illustrations that turn the science of the human body into a series of exciting discoveries. Age 10 up. $11.95. Code WKM. BROOK FARM BOOKS.

FOOD, FITNESS, AND HEALTH -- Packed with facts and information about health, eating habits, food additives, diets, allergies, exercise, and keeping fit. Colorful, detailed illustrations. Age 10 up. $11.95. Code EDC. BROOK FARM BOOKS.

GOOD FOR ME! All About Food in 32 Bites. Marilyn Burns (a Brown Paper School Book). You have holes in your head. In one of them, you put plants and animal parts, you pour water and other liquids, and sometimes you chew on things too fierce to mention. We call that eating. If you have ever wondered why you eat things and what happens when you do, this is a book for you. You'll learn why you should drink that glass of milk, and why that triple-dip-cream-filled-nutcrunch-winko might just gum up your works. You'll get acquainted with your pals, the vitamins and minerals. You'll learn what's good for you and why, and also what isn't; how the hot dog got its name, and about a man named Diamond Jim Brady, who some folks say ate himself to death. When you're through reading this book, you'll be the food expert in your home. All that in 32 bites! $9.95. Code LB. BROOK FARM BOOKS.

BLOOD AND GUTS, A Working Guide to Your Own Insides --By Linda Allison (A Brown Paper School Book). You are many things -- miles of blood vessels, hundreds of muscles, many thousands of hairs. You are a furnace, filters, and a fancy computer with a huge memory bank. You are a finely tuned organism with more parts than there are people in New York. This book will help you explore the amazing territory inside the bag you call your skin. It will show you experiments to try, tests to take, and tools to make that will help you see and feel and hear what is going on inside. You'll amaze yourself. $9.95. Code LB. BROOK FARM BOOKS.

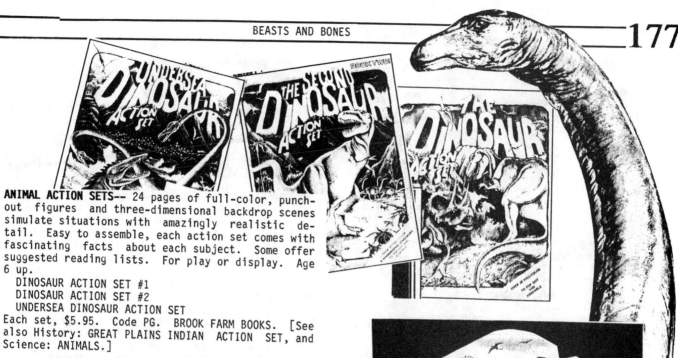

ANIMAL ACTION SETS-- 24 pages of full-color, punch-out figures and three-dimensional backdrop scenes simulate situations with amazingly realistic detail. Easy to assemble, each action set comes with fascinating facts about each subject. Some offer suggested reading lists. For play or display. Age 6 up.
  DINOSAUR ACTION SET #1
  DINOSAUR ACTION SET #2
  UNDERSEA DINOSAUR ACTION SET
Each set, $5.95. Code PG. BROOK FARM BOOKS. [See also History: GREAT PLAINS INDIAN ACTION SET, and Science: ANIMALS.]

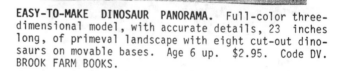

EASY-TO-MAKE DINOSAUR PANORAMA. Full-color three-dimensional model, with accurate details, 23 inches long, of primeval landscape with eight cut-out dinosaurs on movable bases. Age 6 up. $2.95. Code DV. BROOK FARM BOOKS.

THE BONES AND SKELETON GAMEBOOK, by Stephen Cumbaa and Karen C. Anderson. A step beyond the fun and science of THE BONES BOOK & SKELETON, this workbook is a heavily-illustrated, large-size collection of activities, quizzes, paper games, puzzles, and experiments to help kids (or adults!) learn even more about the human body & how it works. Kids can solve mysteries of the body: make a working model of a lung with balloons, rubber bands, and a bottle. Play "Meet Me at the Joint" to name the intersection of Humerus and Scapula streets; discover a trick to expand long-term memory; crack the Genetic Codes; and perform Aristotle's Illusion (suddenly, you have two noses!). $7.95. Code WK. BROOK FARM BOOKS.

DINOSAUR T-SHIRTS, fossil replicas, books, more. Free catalog. SAURUS, 530 South 4th East, Centerville, UT 84014.

DINOSAUR CLUB OF AMERICA. Certificate, membership kit, newsletter, T-shirt, more. $14.95 or write for information. ROCKETT GRAPHICS, Box 600, Clinton, MD 20735.

DINOSAURS AND THINGS, From Beginning to End -- A Board Game. Travel through the geological ages of prehistory, learning about the various forms of life and when they lived. There are two levels of play -- an easy one for preschoolers and a more-challenging one for early readers. Contents include puzzle game board depicting prehistoric environment, 36 creature cutouts, 9 creature question cards, 4 fossil feet playing pieces, a 6-colored die, and instructions for two levels of play. Also included are a museum guide of dinosaur exhibits in the U.S. and Canada, and a bibliography of dinosaur books. Age 4 to 10 (and up). 2 to 4 players. $22.00 plus $3 shipping. BROOK FARM BOOKS.

SOME BODY: The Human Anatomy Game. Four different games, 2 different levels of play. Younger children will use the Some Body as a puzzle activity; older ones can cooperate or compete in the games. All will learn to name body parts and their functions while they play. Contents: 4 Some Body boards, 4 Body Parts sheets, 2 decks of cards, instructions for 4 games. Ages 6 to 10 (more or less). 1 to 4 players. $20.00 plus $3 postage. BROOK FARM BOOKS.

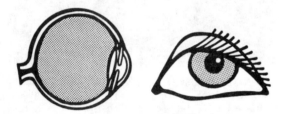

THE HUMAN EYE -- "Challenge Me," a science kit for ages 6-12. Experiments, activities, learning cards help children discover the mysteries of the eye. $9.50. TEAM TEACH. 1815 East Front, Traverse City, MI 49684.

MEDICAL MONOPOLY -- Each player gets $500 to spend on a pharmacy, an operating room, or on organ parts such as a heart, liver, or kidney. When landing on "office visit," each doctor must correctly diagnose and treat the symptoms to admit the patient. Each player races to be the first to fill up his hospital with patients. "An ideal gift for all medical enthusiasts young and old," says the catalog. I think it's a realistic look at the mercenary attitudes of many doctors. (Did you know that the United States is the only "developed" nation that doesn't have free medicare for everyone, regardless of age?) The price of this game could buy something really worthwhile, but if you're determined to have it, send $19.95 for Item #30200 to MEDICAL ARTS PRESS, 3440 Winnetka Avenue North, Minneapolis, MN 55427.

THE ORGANIC PUPPET THEATRE -- Easy-to-make puppets show children (and their puppet-show audiences) how various bodily organs work, and the importance of good eating habits and exercise. THE ORGANIC PUPPET THEATRE is a 92-page book, 8½x11", on heavy durable paper, with puppet patterns for the stomach, lungs, teeth, skull, skeletal hand, kidneys, bladder, and heart; with lesson plans for each puppet, including basic facts about each organ (color, shape, size, location, & function), a complete puppet show script and a shorter skit script, three songs about the body, and suggestions for more activities. Puppets are made with common household items, such as tape, sandwich bags, crayons, etc. These activities were developed at the Mayo Medical Museum in Rochester, Minnesota, and presentations have been offered in schools, hospitals, and conferences in Europe, the U.S., and Canada. $15.95 plus $1.50 shipping. NIGHT OWL PRESS, 1997 Stillwater Street, White Bear Lake, MN 55110.

SCIENCE BY MAIL, Museum of Science, Science Park, Boston, MA 02114. National pen-pal program which pairs scientists with kids in grades 4-9. Kids receive three "challenge packets" in the mail during the course of a school year. The packets contain hands-on experiments and materials that prepare the students for the "three Big Challenges." Kids send their solutions to their pen-pal scientists, who then respond with encouraging comments. Previous packets have included activities such as kite and glider design, a mechanical toy, building a crystal radio, and making a pinhole camera. Family membership, up to 4 children, costs $49 per year.

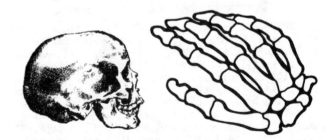

ANATOMICAL PRODUCTS, professional & student medical books, charts, health education products, training models, patient simulators, much more. Mostly for professionals or graduate-level schools. Very high prices for non-professionals (life-size skeleton, $430; human skull, $150). A few cheaper items for intensive health and medical studies, & a few home-school-size anatomical models and charts, with reasonable prices. Catalog. ANATOMICAL CHART CO., 7124 N. Clark St., Chicago, IL 60626.

PLASTIC ANATOMY KITS & many other science materials. (Also maps.) HUBBARD COMPANY, P.O. Box 104, Northbrook, IL 60062.

NATURE COLORING BOOKS FOR KIDS AND ADULTS -- Attractive, authentic drawings with informative captions. Many of the books have the subjects in full color on the covers. Interesting reading and browsing, even when you're not in a coloring mood.

BIRDS OF PREY COLORING BOOK -- 42 species from around the world -- bald eagle, great horned owl, Andean condor, common black hawk, osprey, many more. $2.95.

AUDOBON'S BIRDS OF AMERICA COLORING BOOK --45 of John James Audobon's illustrations: red-winged blackbird, painted bunting, great blue heron, wood duck, ruby-throated humming-bird, more. $2.75.

FIFTY FAVORITE BIRDS COLORING BOOK -- Accurate drawings of 50 favorite birds, including the myrtle warbler and ruby-throated hummingbird; scientific names and other information. $2.75.

TROPICAL BIRDS COLORING BOOK -- Accurate line drawings of 44 species: greentailed sylph, bird of paradise, scarletibis, rhinoceros hornbill, mandarin duck, regal sunbird, many others. $2.95.

SEASHORE LIFE COLORING BOOK -- 46 scenes of more than 150 forms of marine life in typical habitats. Fish, sea urchins, marine algae, coral, starfish, abalone, crabs, jellyfish, shrimp, mollusks, barnacles, more. $2.95.

SHELLS OF THE WORLD COLORING BOOK -- 45 drawings; more than 100 shells (all in full color on the covers). $2.95.

TROPICAL FISH COLORING BOOK-- 41 different species of fish and 26 species of marine plants, including ten double-page spreads. $2.50.

WILD ANIMALS COLORING BOOK -- Accurate, detailed drawings of 47 species: snow leopard, giraffe, tiger, rhinoceros, reindeer, gorilla, giant panda, elephant, kangaroo, many more. $2.75.

FAVORITE DOGS COLORING BOOK -- 42 popular dogs, including poodle, collie, dachshund, more. Detailed drawings, brief histories, more. $2.75.

HORSES OF THE WORLD COLORING BOOK -- 42 accurate illustrations of horses in authentic settings around the world. $2.95.

WILD CATS OF THE WORLD COLORING BOOK-- 41 drawings of lion, tiger, ocelot, Spanish lynx, and other species. $2.75.

MONKEYS AND APES COLORING BOOK-- 42 realistic pictures: chimpanzee, gibbon, orangutan, gorilla, lemur, mandrill, bushbaby, Barbary ape, tarsier, others. $2.95.

FAVORITE ROSES COLORING BOOK -- 46 varieties of hybrid tea roses, grandiflora, floribunda, climbers, miniatures, historic roses. $2.95.

AMERICAN WILD FLOWERS COLORING BOOK -- 46 species: lady's slipper, bird's foot violet, cardinal flower, pitcher plant, trout lily, others. Botanical identifications, common names, and habitat. $2.75.

GARDEN FLOWERS COLORING BOOK -- 40 flowers: tulip, peony, daffodil, petunia, zinnia, dahlia, delphinium, iris, fox-glove, snapdragon, more; common and scientific names, colors, seasons, etc. $2.75.

TROPICAL FLOWERS OF THE WORLD COLORING BOOK -- 45 exotic flowers: cannonball tree of Brazil and Trinidad, bird-of-paradise flower of South Africa, sausage tree of Africa, and 42 others. $2.75.

FLORAL ALPHABET COLORING BOOK -- 26 attractive designs (one for each letter) contain flowers & plants beginning with the letter it decorates -- apples and artichokes to zucchini and zinnias. $2.50.

SMALL ANIMALS OF NORTH AMERICA COLORING BOOK -- 46 accurate drawings of armadillo, badger, peccary, kangaroo rat, bobcat, pika and many more. $2.95.

Idaho — Mockorange — Mountain Bluebird

BIRDS OF PREY Coloring Book — John Green

WILD CATS OF THE WORLD Coloring Book — John Green

Audubon's Birds of America Coloring Book

John Green MONKEYS AND APES Coloring Book

Lisa Bonforte FIFTY FAVORITE BIRDS Coloring Book

Favorite Roses Coloring Book

TROPICAL BIRDS Coloring Book

SEASHORE LIFE COLORING BOOK

American Wild Flowers

STEFEN BERNATH GARDEN FLOWERS COLORING BOOK

Lucia de Leiris SHELLS OF THE WORLD Coloring Book

Lynda E. Chandler TROPICAL FLOWERS of the

FLORAL ALPHABET Coloring Book

Stefen Bernath TROPICAL FISH COLORING BOOK

SMALL ANIMALS of North America Coloring Book

WILD ANIMALS Coloring Book — John Green

Thomas C. Quirk, Jr. REPTILES AND AMPHIBIANS Coloring Book

REPTILES AND AMPHIBIANS COLORING BOOK -- Over 70 alligators, snakes, lizards, frogs, toads, etc., in 44 illustrations. $2.95.

ABOVE "NATURE COLORING BOOKS," prices as indicated. Code DV. BROOK FARM BOOKS.

THE NATURE OF THE SEASHORE, DRIFTWOOD, & DOES ANYONE KNOW WHERE A HERMIT CRAB GOES? Three very interesting booklets for young children by Michael Glaser, creator of THE DISCOVERY CREW Science Club. $3.95 each. Send a #10 SASE for full descriptions and ordering information. KNICKERBOCKER PUBLISHING CO., P.O. Box 113, Fiskdale, MA 01518.

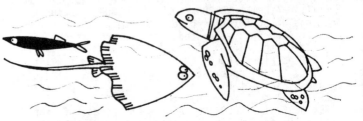

LEARN ABOUT NATURE SERIES -- Very colorful, scientifically-accurate illustrations with short text.
AMAZING WORLD OF ANTS, AMAZING WORLD OF BIRDS, AMAZING WORLD OF BUTTERFLIES AND MOTHS, AMAZING WORLD OF DINOSAURS, AMAZING WORLD OF NIGHT CREATURES, AMAZING WORLD OF SPIDERS, DISCOVERING EARTHQUAKES & VOLCANOES, DISCOVERING ELECTRICITY, DISCOVERING PREHISTORIC ANIMALS, DISCOVERING REPTILES AND AMPHIBIANS, DISCOVERING THE STARS, DISCOVERING TREES, DISCOVERING WHALES & DOLPHINS, WHAT MAKES IT RAIN, WHAT MAKES THE WIND, WONDERS OF PLANTS AND FLOWERS, WONDERS OF RIVERS, WONDERS OF SWAMPS AND MARSHES, WONDERS OF THE DESERT, WONDERS OF THE FOREST, WONDERS OF THE POND, WONDERS OF THE RAIN FOREST, WONDERS OF THE SEA, WONDERS OF THE SEASONS
Age 6 up. Each book, 8x9½", 32 pages, fully illustrated. Specify "Learn About Nature" and title. $2.95 each. Code TRL. BROOK FARM BOOKS.

MARINE EDUCATION, a quarterly publication about marine life, for students and teachers. Write for information: SEA GRANT COLLEGE PROGRAM, Texas A&M University, College Station, TX 77943.

SuperScience, monthly science magazines for public schools but also available by individual subscription; two levels, grades 1-3 and 4-6. Lots of pictures, experiments, & interesting articles. Write for information to SCHOLASTIC, INC., 730 Broadway, New York, NY 10003.

"THE LANGUAGE AND MUSIC OF THE WOLVES." Thrilling harmony and talking of wolves, narrated by Robert Redford, on audio cassette, with notes. We used to live in the mountains of British Columbia's Central Interior, and often heard wolves howling to each other -- an eery, hairlifting, but beautiful sound, very unlike the cacaphony of coyotes or dogs. This tape is the next best thing, and you won't have to stand outside when it's forty below zero. About $10 plus postage. Write for information. AMERICAN MUSEUM OF NATURAL HISTORY, Central Park West at 79th St., New York, NY 10024.

LIVING THINGS -- Attractive, detailed, colorful illustrations and clear, explanatory text describe many of the earth's different forms of life, how they interact, and why they are all important to each other. Basic concepts are demonstrated by easy experiments. Age 7 up. $8.95. Code EDC. BROOK FARM BOOKS.

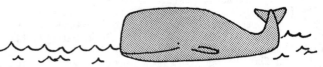

ADOPT A WHALE. The International Wildlife Coalition is sponsoring a Whale Adoption Project which provides several materials to "foster parents": an official Protector Certificate, a photo and biography of the adopted whale, a whale calendar, and a map of whale migratory routes. Teachers receive free teaching kits with lessons in math, biology, and geography, featuring whales. There is a $15 adopting fee, which is used for expanded protection, research, and educational programs. For more information, write: THE WHALE ADOPTION PROJECT, 70 East Falmouth Highway, East Falmouth, MA 02536.

ENDANGERED ANIMALS -- Realistic, handheld face masks of several different animals, some endangered, for use in story telling, plays, or just to decorate a wall. Coloring books, cassettes, posters, mazes, plays, and more. All excellent materials, and very inexpensive. Catalog. SPIZZIRRI PUBLISHING INC., P.O. Box 9397, Rapid City, SD 57709.

THE DOLPHIN LOG, ages 6-16. $10/year. THE COSTEAU SOCIETY, 8140 Santa Monica Blvd., Los Angeles, CA 90069.

REPRODUCIBLE SCIENCE SERIES-- Detailed illustrations of animals accompanied by interesting facts and follow-up activities that include research projects, math, creative writing, vocabulary, art, coloring, games, and puzzles. Ages 5 and up. Five books: #265 Dinosaurs, #266 Birds, #267 Mammals, #268 Fishes, & #269 Reptiles. Each book, $3.95. Minimum postage, $2 for any quantity. Order from: THE LEARNING WORKS, P.O. Box 6187, Santa Barbara, CA 93160. (See also Art, "Clip Art Carousel," and Teaching Aids, "The Learning Works.")

ZOOBOOKS, P.O. Box 85271, San Diego, CA 92138. Outstanding, inexpensive wildlife books, beautiful art work, detailed information. Catalog.

NATIONAL AUDOBON SOCIETY, RFD 1, Box 149B, Lubec, ME 14652.

WILDBIRD, P.O. Box 6040, Mission Viejo, CA 92690. Monthly magazine; birdwatching, field tips, equipment, news, more.

YOUNG NATURALIST, 614 East 5th St., Newton, KS 67114. Free catalog of nature-oriented gifts, games, toys.

NATURAL SCIENCE BOOK CLUB, Riverside, NJ 08075. Club discounts, bonus book plan, large selection of titles. Ask for information and introductory offer.

YOUR BIG BACKYARD, ages 3-5, $8.50/yr. **RANGER RICK'S NATURE MAGAZINE,** 6-12, $12/year. Nature, conservation, ecology; puzzles, games, stories, articles. NATIONAL WILDLIFE FEDERATION, 1412 16th Street, Washington, DC 20036.

NATURESCOPE -- Science information for elementary level in magazine format. Each 64-page issue focuses on a single theme, with accurate and interesting information presented with hands-on activities, games, puzzles, craft ideas, and exercise pages to photocopy. Subjects include dinosaurs, weather, deserts, insects, wetlands, mammals, birds, trees, astronomy, geology, endangered species, and more. For more information, write to: NATIONAL WILDLIFE FEDERATION, 1412 Sixteenth Street NW, Washington, DC 20036.

NATIONAL WILDLIFE WEEK: 4 posters, teaching guide with reproducible pages, 36 stamps with different wildlife facts; catalog of other educational materials. FREE. WILDLIFE WEEK KIT, National Wildlife Federation, Leesburg Pike, Vienna, VA 22184.

THE BIG GOOD WOLF, by Honey Loring; illustrated by Nicholas Deutsch. Captivating, informative wolf-shaped book for young children which dispels the myth of wolves as dangerous to humans. For more information and price, write to GONE TO THE DOGS, RR 1, Box 958, Putney, VT 05346, or phone 802-387-5673.

CHICKADEE, ages 4-8. **OWL,** 8-12. Very good nature magazines for kids. $15/yr each. Write for information. YOUNG NATURALIST FOUNDATION, 59 Front Street East, Toronto, Ontario, Canada M5E 1B3.

THE NATURE STORE, 15 W. Bay Road, Osterville, MA 02655. Unusual and interesting science materials.

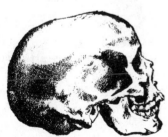

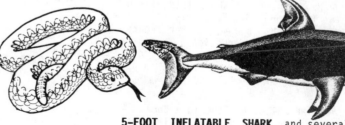

SKULLS-- Realistic, museum-quality reproductions for displays. Grizzly, sabertooth tiger, gorilla, human, lion, etc. Interesting catalog for $1.00. Prices may be high for just a casual interest. SKULLDUGGERY, P.O. Box 1021, Brea, CA 92621.

5-FOOT INFLATABLE SHARK and several other cuddly critters, including an 8-foot pteranodon, 6-foot iguana, 5-foot stegosaurus, and others. Shirts, jewelry, paperweights, realistic inflatable snakes, neckties that resemble fish (!), and more and more. Catalog: THE NATURE COMPANY, P.O. Box 2310, Berkeley, CA 94702.

QUESTION AND ANSWER SCIENCE LIBRARY -- These are some of the very best general introductions to science I've found, with very detailed, full-color drawings and short text, covering many different aspects of the subjects.

AIR, AIR, AIR -- ALL ABOUT ANIMAL MIGRATIONS -- ALL ABOUT DESERTS -- ALL ABOUT ISLANDS -- ALL ABOUT THE MOON -- ALL ABOUT MOUNTAINS & VOLCANOES -- ALL ABOUT PONDS -- ALL ABOUT RIVERS -- ALL ABOUT SOUND -- ALL ABOUT THE STARS -- ALL ABOUT TREES -- AMAZING MAGNETS -- AMAZING WORLD OF ANIMALS -- AMAZING WORLD OF PLANTS -- DISCOVERING FOSSILS -- OUR AMAZING OCEAN -- OUR AMAZING SUN -- OUR WONDERFUL SEASONS -- OUR WONDERFUL SOLAR SEASON -- ROCKS AND MINERALS -- WONDERS OF ENERGY -- WONDERS OF WATER -- WORLD OF WEATHER

Each book, 7½x10", 32 pages, full color. Ages 8 and up (adults, too!). Specify "Q and A Science," & title. $2.95 each. Code TRL. BROOK FARM BOOKS.

PLANET EARTH: A Pop-up Guide. In three dimensions and vivid color, this spectacular pop-up book shows the shifting continents, what causes earthquakes, how mountains are formed and volcanoes erupt, and takes the reader into the center of the earth. Five double-page pop-ups include a double globe showing the structure of the earth, an exploding volcano, and a deep-sea submarine. The informative text and numerous illustrations explain how geological forces have combined to build the world around us, and describe the latest technology for exploring and measuring the planet. Large hardcover book, full-color illustrations throughout. $14.95. Code SS. BROOK FARM BOOKS.

THE WEATHER POP-UP BOOK. All the intricacies of weather in simple text and outstandingly graphic pop-up art. Pull the tabs to move weather fronts, jet streams, and atmospheric depressions; watch a hurricane and cyclone build; and much, much more. Fascinating and very informative. Age 8 and up. $13.95. Code SS. BROOK FARM BOOKS.

THE POP-UP ATLAS OF THE WORLD: A Globe in a Book. A unique atlas that opens up to reveal 3 full-color, three-dimensional globes. Lots of interesting maps and fascinating facts about the world. Ages 7 and up. $13.95. Code SS. BROOK FARM BOOKS.

Speak to the earth, and it shall teach thee.
Book of Job

TO THE TOP OF THE WORLD: Adventures with Arctic Wolves, by Jim Brandenburg. Beautiful and enlightening photographs taken by the author during 2 months of living with an Arctic wolf pack, with comments about the wolves' nature and society. Ages 8 up. $16.95. Code WA. BROOK FARM BOOKS.

WOLF SONG OF ALASKA, P.O. Box 110309, Anchorage, AK 99511. Non-profit organization dedicated to awareness and protection of wolves. Free catalog <u>for teachers</u> (use a letterhead, if possible) of wolf-related gifts and educational materials. Newsletter.

ECOLOGY, by R. Spurgeon & K. Chan. Experiments, projects, and activities. 48 large-format pages, profusely illustrated. Ages 10-16. $7.95. Code EDC. BROOK FARM BOOKS.

THE REASONS FOR SEASONS: The Great Cosmic Megagalactic Trip Without Moving from Your Chair, Linda Allison (a Brown Paper School Book). This is a book about the trip the earth makes around the sun. It explains the reasons for seasons, and a lot more. Inside it are things to make, things to do, ideas to think about, stories to read, and things to inspect, collect, and give away. Most of this book is about our home, the Earth. Some of it's about time and space, the invisible world, The Big Out There. All of it is in a kind of order -- the kind that comes with seasons. When you read this book and think about it some, you'll know that the order of life on earth is seasonal, too. $9.95. Code LB. BROOK FARM BOOKS.

FACTS & LISTS. Facts about weather, space, the earth, & countries of the world. Packed with facts, records, and lists. Very interesting for browsing or steady reading. Colorful illustrations. Age 8 up. $12.95. Code EDC. BROOK FARM BOOKS.

OKLAHOMA TWISTER: "pet tornado" in a bottle. Shake it a few seconds, then watch a miniature twister that swirls inside the bottle like a real tornado. Good demonstration of a tornado's appearance and immense power. $4 plus $1 postage. McCOY PRODUCTIONS, 1305 S. Rock Island, El Reno, OK 73036.

HURRICANES -- THE BIG BIRD GET READY FOR HURRICANES KIT. 16-page booklet, recording of the song "Hurricane Blues," and "Hurricane Force" board game. $2.25. CHILDREN'S TELEVISION WORKSHOP, One Lincoln Plaza, New York, NY 10023.

SILENT SPRING, by Rachel Carson. Two cassettes, approx. 2½ hours, read by Ellen Burstyn. This is the book that began to awaken Americans to the dangers of pesticide pollution. Rachel Carson eloquently evokes the specter of a barren land in which all of the familiar voices of spring have been silenced, and documents the immediacy of the threat with shocking case histories. Far more important today than when it was written. $15.95. Code LFP. BROOK FARM BOOKS.

"WE ALL NEED TREES," 17x22" poster of many products made from trees. The other side, "Tree Trivia," lists 23 interesting (and not really trivial) facts about trees. $1.00. PLT POSTER, American Forest Council, 1250 Conn. Ave. NW, Washington, DC 20036.

WATER EDUCATION. Grades K-6. 166-page guide to teaching about water; its physical & chemical make-up, its importance, more; background information, lessons, activities. $3.00 including postage. PUBLICATIONS, International Office for Water Education, Utah Water Research Laboratory, Logan, UT 84322.

"CONSERVATION ACTIVITIES FOR THE CLASSROOM," 2-page list of activities involving various forms of energy, conservation techniques, solutions to an energy crisis, discussion of a society fueled only by renewable energy. FREE from: CONSERVATION AND RENEWABLE ENERGY INQUIRY AND REFERRAL SERVICE, P.O. Box 8900, Silver Spring, MD 20907.

"BACKYARD RESEARCH" -- Science fun & education with garden experiments. Write: SOIL & HEALTH SOCIETY, 33 E. Minor St., Emmaus, PA 18049.

A child's world is fresh and new and beautiful, full of wonder and excitement. It is our misfortune that for most of us that clear-eyed vision, that true instinct for what is beautiful and awe-inspiring, is dimmed and even lost before we reach adulthood.

Rachel Carson

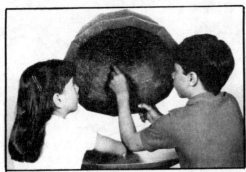

ASTRODOME -- Create a miniature planetarium with the pre-cut pages of this 40-page book. Easy-to-follow instructions lead to an attractive three-dimensional dome, 20 inches in diameter. The inside of the dome shows the major stars and constellations as seen from the Northern Hemisphere. The stars glow in the dark. Includes a 24-page booklet explaining the history, myths, and most prominent stars of the major constellations. $10.95 plus $1.50 postage. BROOK FARM BOOKS.

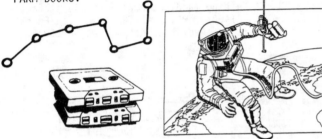

TAPES OF THE NIGHT SKY--Great idea! Instead of shining your flashlight on your star map, then looking up at the sky and wondering what happened to your night vision, you listen to this audio-cassette guided tour of the heavens, which teaches you to locate and identify the major stars & constellations. The program includes two cassettes, which contain four half-hour tours (one for each season of the year), with clear instructions and brief pauses to give you time to get oriented; four star maps for additional reference, a suggested reading list, and an illustrated booklet. $19.95. Code JN. BROOK FARM BOOKS.

HISTORY OF SPACE EXPLORATION COLORING BOOK. Major milestones in space exploration, from the launching of the first liquid-fuel rocket in 1926 to the Challenger tragedy; Sputnik, first man in space, first U.S. space walk, first space rendezvous, much more. $2.95. Code DV. BROOK FARM BOOKS.

THE SPACE SHUTTLE ACTION BOOK, Patrick Moore and Tom Stimson. Combines solid information with the fun and inventiveness of 3-dimensional pages with moveable parts. The "pop-up" illustrations are detailed, colorful, and carefully keyed to clear explanations, showing the whole process of a typical shuttle mission. Age 7 up, including adult. $15.95. Code RH. BROOK FARM BOOKS.

THE NIGHT SKY BOOK: An Everyday Guide to Every Night by Jamie Jobb (A Brown Paper School Book). Learn the wonders of the night sky; get to know Pegasus, Hercules, Bootes, and many other fascinating constellations; learn how for centuries people have used stars as signposts; make a cross-staff or nadir-zenith finder; learn about meteors, auroras, zodiacal light, counterglow, and much more. This book will keep you up at night! $9.95. Code LB. BROOK FARM BOOKS.

ASTRONOMY POSTERS -- Five beautiful posters from the Lick Observatory: Orion Nebula (central region), Orion Nebula (long exposure), Crab Nebula, Dumbbell Nebula, Full Moon. Full color, 22x29", suitable for framing; rolled for mailing. All five, $10 postpaid. Also available, set of 12 colored postcards including views named above and other deep-space scenes, $2.00. Catalog, $1. Foreign orders, pay in US funds and add $2 for postage. Check or money order to: HANSEN PLANETARIUM, 15 South State St., Salt Lake City, UT 84111.

TELESCOPE MAKING. Build your own telescope, observatory, etc. $12/yr(4 issues). ASTROMEDIA PUBLICATIONS, 1027 N. 7th St., Milwaukee, WI 53233.

ORION TELESCOPE CENTER, P.O. Box 1158, Santa Cruz, CA 95061. Specializes in telescopes and other astronomy materials. Large selection. Catalog.

METEORITES. Display specimens, jewelry, books. Catalog $2, refundable. BETHANY TRADING, Box 3726, New Haven, CT 06525.

SPACE MISSION VIDEOTAPES: Apollo, Lunar, Shuttle, planets, etc. Low prices. Free catalog. SPECTRUM VIDEO, P.O. Box 3698, Ontario, CA 91761.

This whole earth which we inhabit is but a point in space.

Henry David Thoreau

  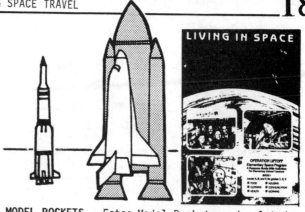

ODYSSEY, P.O. Box 92788, Milwaukee, WI 53202. Children's magazine about astronomy & outer space; many illustrations. Games, crafts, puzzles, cartoons, articles. Sample, $2. $16/year.

ASTRONOMY, "World's most popular & beautiful astronomy magazine." $21/12 issues. ASTROMEDIA PUBLICATIONS, 1027 N. 7th St., Milwaukee, WI 53233.

DEEP SKY. Magazine of galaxies, nebulae, star clusters, double stars, distant mysterious objects... $12/yr (4 issues). ASTROMEDIA PUBLICATIONS, 1027 N. 7th Street, Milwaukee, WI 53233.

AIR & SPACE, bimonthly magazine; past, present, and future of air and space travel; history, culture, & technology of flight. $18/year. SMITHSONIAN, P.O. Box 51244, Boulder, CO 80321.

NATIONAL AIR AND SPACE MUSEUM, Smithsonian Institution, Washington, DC 20560. Request FREE MATERIALS information.

SOLAR SYSTEM POSTER, 38x26". Chart of information, including relative sizes, distances, and characteristics of each planet. $7.95 plus $3 postage. Also request catalog of posters, software, calendars, games, etc. (If sending for the catalog only, send 2 first-class stamps.) ASTRONOMICAL SOCIETY OF THE PACIFIC, 390 Ashton Ave., San Francisco, CA 94112.

THE SPACE PRIMER--Booklet describing the development of satellites, rockets, shuttles, orbiting, life in space, more. FREE from THE AEROSPACE CORPORATION, Box 92957, Los Angeles, CA 90009.

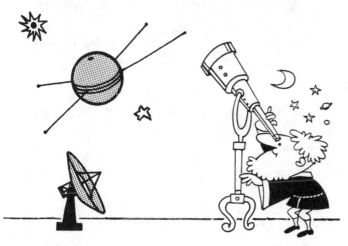

THE PLANETARY SOCIETY, 65 North Catalina Avenue, Pasadena, CA 91106. Carl Sagan, president. Seeks to promote space exploration, search for extra-terrestrial life. Members receive The Planetary Report and several other benefits. Write for information.

MODEL ROCKETS. Estes Model Rockets and related materials, with more than 100 flying rockets. Scale models of real rockets, space shuttle, gliders, more. Large color catalog, $1.00. ESTES INDUSTRIES, Penrose, CO 81240.

LIVING IN SPACE, from NASA, has easy, hands-on science experiments in six categories: food, clothing, health, housing, communication, and working. Each category has background information and experiments. Subjects include dehydration, various math problems, graphing and charting, and nutrition. Unbound, 3-hole punched book (provide your own binder). Request Book 1 for grades 1-3 or Book 2 for grades 4-6. $4.75 each. SUPERINTENDENT OF DOCUMENTS, U.S. Government Printing Office, Washington, DC 20402.

NASA TEACHING MATERIALS -- 30-minute videotapes, $16.00. Filmstrip and slide programs, $6 to $12. Free catalog; request on a school letterhead. NASA CORE, Lorain County JVS, 15181 Route 58 S, Oberlin, OH 44074.

THE UNIVERSE IN THE CLASSROOM: A NEWSLETTER ON TEACHING ASTRONOMY. Each issue of this quarterly newsletter features a different topic, and includes a student activity and list of additional resources. FREE to teachers of grades 3 to 12 and librarians. You MUST use school stationery, and indicate the grade(s) you teach. Write to: ASTRONOMICAL SOCIETY OF THE PACIFIC, Teacher's Newsletter, 1290 24th Avenue, San Francisco, CA 94122.

ASTRONOMY BOOK CLUB, Riverside, NJ 08075. Write for information. Introductory offer may include over $60 worth of books for about $5.00.

FIRST SCIENCE BOOKS -- Very exciting books with brightly colored pictures of entertaining monsters who illustrate and explain basic scientific ideas. Completely safe experiments using everyday household materials and utensils.

   SCIENCE SURPRISES
   SCIENCE TRICKS & MAGIC
Age 7 and up. $3.95 each.   Code EDC.   BROOK FARM BOOKS.

SIMPLE SCIENCE BOOKS --

   LIVING THINGS presents questions such as "Why don't fish drown?" and "Do plants breathe?" and stimulates active observation of plants and animals.

   HOW THINGS WORK and SIMPLE SCIENCE clearly explain the basic principles of physics which can be seen in the natural world around us and those on which machines work.

   Age 8 and up. $10.95 each. Code EDC. BROOK FARM BOOKS.

THE USBORNE ILLUSTRATED DICTIONARY OF SCIENCE, including Biology, Chemistry, and Physics. Profusely illustrated guides to the key terms and concepts of each subject. The book is arranged thematically, so the words are explained in context, and each definition is supported by detailed pictures and diagrams. The words are arranged in a way that is logical to the subject, and definitions are in clear, easy language. Age 10 & up. The basic information and clear explanations make this book excellent for beginning students of any age, including adults. $23.95. Code EDC. BROOK FARM BOOKS.

THE USBORNE SCIENCE ENCYCLOPEDIA, 128 pages; ages 9-12. A very comprehensive young readers' encyclopedia, answering many of the questions children have about the world. $12.95. Code EDC. BROOK FARM BOOKS.

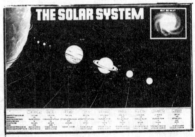

LARGE POSTERS (24x36") of animals, fish, solar system, many non-science subjects. Inexpensive. Free brochure. GIANT PHOTOS, INC., P.O. Box 406, Rockford, IL 61105.

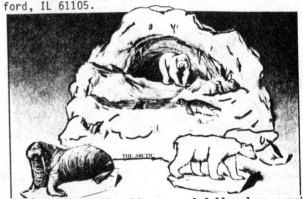

ANIMAL ACTION SETS-- 24 pages of full-color, punch-out figures and three-dimensional backdrop scenes simulate situations with amazingly realistic detail. Easy to assemble, each action set comes with fascinating facts about each subject. Some offer suggested reading lists. For play or display. Age 6 up.

   ZOO ANIMALS #1
   ZOO ANIMALS #2
   DOLPHINS AND WHALES
Each set, $5.95. Code PG. BROOK FARM BOOKS. [See also History: GREAT PLAINS INDIAN ACTION SET and Science: DINOSAURS.]

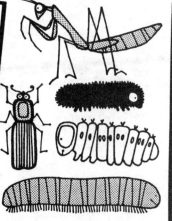

ONLY HUMAN: Why We Are the Way We Are, by Neill Bell (a Brown Paper School Book). What we used to be several million years ago, the ways in which we have changed -- and the ways in which we haven't changed very much -- and why. $9.95. Code LB. BROOK FARM BOOKS.

GEE, WIZ! How to Mix Art and Science, or the Art of Thinking Scientifically, by Linda Allison and David Katz (a Brown Paper School Book). This book is about science. It's also about Art. Inside you'll find the Wizard (also known as Professor Bumble) and the Lizard (who is the Wizard's reptilian side-kick). You'll learn that science is more than test tubes, lab coats, and microscopes. Science is a way of thinking about the world. It's a way of finding out what you don't know by figuring out what you do know. This book will show you that scientists and artists share one very important trait -- imagination. The absentminded scientist, Wiz, and his efficient, curious assistant, Art, will lead you to new answers to some old questions. One of the best things about science is that you don't need experts or books or magical hocus-pocus to get answers. All you need is a question and enough curiosity to find an answer. $9.95. Code LB. BROOK FARM BOOKS.

The gift of fantasy has meant more to me than my talent for absorbing positive knowledge.
Albert Einstein

THINGS OF SCIENCE, P.O. Box 579, Sarasota, FL 34230. For a small annual subscription fee (about $20), you receive a Science Surprise Kit each month, containing instructions for demonstrations & experiments, a booklet with background information, & all necessary materials. Topics include seed growth, optical illusions, aerodynamics, magnetism, reflections, skin senses, computation, color, fossils, a sextant, a sundial, and much more. Write for current prices and information.

BEASTLY NEIGHBORS, or Why Earwigs Make Good Mothers (a Brown Paper School Book). The little creatures hiding under your sink, under the back steps, or in your flower garden, have very complex and interesting lives, and aren't always the slithery intruders we think they are. After reading this book, you probably still won't want to invite them into your home for tea and cookies, but you'll have a greater appreciation of them -- and maybe they'll appreciate you a little more, too (although it's hard for them to show it). $9.95. Code LB. BROOK FARM BOOKS.

THIS BOOK IS ABOUT TIME, by Marilyn Burns (a Brown Paper School Book). Time to read, time to think, time to do, time to wonder about time and you. When did people start measuring time? Why did they do it at all? What did they use to measure time? What does time have to with flowers, birds, bees, and the fiddler crab? Besides telling you the whole story, this book's activities will help you perk up your time sense, make a timepiece or two, understand time zones, and look at your own biological clock. When you learn about time, you learn about history, biology, biorhythms, and more -- the Mayas, the ancient Egyptians, jet lag, and the Roman calendar. And you'll have the time of your life. $9.95. Code LB. BROOK FARM BOOKS.

THE USBORNE BOOK OF KNOWLEDGE -- A thoroughly illustrated book explaining how things work, how things began, and how creatures live. Clear text, very detailed pictures. Five titles combined in one volume: HOW YOUR BODY WORKS, HOW MACHINES WORK, HOW THINGS BEGAN, HOW BIRDS LIVE, and HOW ANIMALS LIFE. Very good introductions for children age 7 & up. $24.95. Code EDC. BROOK FARM BOOKS.

CUP AND SAUCER CHEMISTRY -- 38 safe experiments for ages 7 and up, using common household items such as aspirin, paper towels, and vinegar. Easy instructions, illustrated. $3.95. Code DV. BROOK FARM BOOKS.

SCIENCE RESEARCH EXPERIMENTS FOR YOUNG PEOPLE, by George Barr. Illustrated collection of 40 experiments in electricity and magnetism, transportation, sound and light, the human body, weather, water, distance, insects, plants, time, & "Science in Your Home." Age 10 up. $3.95. Code DV. BROOK FARM BOOKS.

47 EASY-TO-DO CLASSIC SCIENCE EXPERIMENTS -- Experiments performed with common household materials teach the principles of light, elasticity, perspective, gravity, air pressure, optics, more. $3.50. Code DV. BROOK FARM BOOKS.

SAFE AND SIMPLE ELECTRICAL EXPERIMENTS -- 101 entertaining projects and experiments which teach basic principles of electricity. All ages, including adult. $4.50. Code DV. BROOK FARM BOOKS.

THE STORY OF ELECTRICITY, by George deLucenay Leon. The chronicle of significant discoveries in electricity and magnetism over 2500 years, and instructions for repeating 20 famous experiments. Age 10 and up. $4.95. Code DV. BROOK FARM BOOKS.

SCIENCE EXPERIMENTS AND AMUSEMENTS FOR CHILDREN -- 73 safe, easy experiments requiring only household materials such as candles, coins, steel wool, etc., illustrate basic phenomena and simple chemical reactions. $2.95. Code DV. BROOK FARM BOOKS.

PHYSICS EXPERIMENTS FOR CHILDREN -- 103 projects demonstrate composition of objects, how substances are affected by various forms of energy, such as heat, light, sound, electricity, etc. $2.75. Code DV. BROOK FARM BOOKS.

BIOLOGY EXPERIMENTS FOR CHILDREN -- 77 experiments involve growing protozoa, bacteria, building a terrarium, growing seeds in a sponge, studying spider web formation, much more. Over 100 illustrations. $2.95. Code DV. BROOK FARM BOOKS.

HUMAN ANATOMY FOR CHILDREN -- Organs, body areas, major systems in straight-forward, non-technical language, with several references and explanations of familiar, puzzling phenomena such as sneezing, curly hair, and more. $2.75. Code DV. BROOK FARM BOOKS.

ENTERTAINING SCIENCE EXPERIMENTS WITH EVERYDAY OBJECTS, by Martin Gardner. 100 amusing tricks and experiments delight you and your children while teaching the elements of astronomy, chemistry, mathematics, mechanics, geometry, and more. $2.75. Code DV. BROOK FARM BOOKS.

STEVEN CANEY'S INVENTION BOOK, Steven Caney. Bursting with ideas, illustrations, diagrams, and photographs, this is almost the ultimate book for the young inventor. The author covers everything from setting up a workshop and building the prototype to naming the creation, applying for a patent, and even marketing the final product -- but it isn't as serious as it sounds. It's a great introduction to the world of inventing, and suggests how to get into an inventing frame of mind, with 20 projects (from fly catchers to back-scratchers) to concoct from household items. Caney also tells the stories behind 35 landmark American inventions, and lists hundreds of invention possibilities. Ages 8 to 15 and up. 208 pages. $11.95. Code BT. BROOK FARM BOOKS. (See also Art, STEVEN CANEY'S TOYBOOK and STEVEN CANEY'S PLAY BOOK; also History, STEVEN CANEY'S KIDS' AMERICA.)

THE SCIENCE BOOK, Sara Stein. Why pets and pests and people behave as they do; why bedbugs bite and moths circle light bulbs; why you can put your finger through jam but not through a rock; what it's like inside a kidney. This is a book of doing as well as of reading, with many experiments & activities to demonstrate scientific principles and facts. 288 pages, with lots of line art and photographs. Age 8+. $9.95. Code BT. BROOK FARM BOOKS.

INTRODUCTIONS TO SCIENCE -- How the stagecoach got its name, where cave people lived in summer, why the moon seems to change shape, how a telephone works, why ships float, how a skyscraper is built, where bananas come from, what gears are for, how glass is made, how big the earth is, why food is frozen, what plastic is made of, how planes fly, and much, much more. Superb introductions to science for ages 7 and up.

   LIVING LONG AGO -- Food and eating, Houses and Homes, Clothes and Fashion, Travel and Transport.

   WHERE THINGS COME FROM AND HOW THINGS ARE MADE

   FINDING OUT ABOUT WINGS, WHEELS, AND WATER: A First Book of Transport

   FIRST GUIDE TO THE UNIVERSE: The sun, moon, and planets; Our earth; Rockets and spaceflight.

   EVERYDAY THINGS -- Things that go, things at home, and things outdoors.

   Each book, $10.95. Code EDC. BROOK FARM BOOKS.

THE WAY THINGS WORK, From Levers to Lasers, Cars to Computers--A Visual Guide to the World of Machines, by David Macaulay. Intricate full color illustrations and clear explanatory text give fascinating depiction of how machines do what they do, from the simplest lever to the space shuttle, including the building of the pyramids and many "simple" gadgets we use daily without thinking of them as machines, such as zippers. Difficult concepts are made easy, and common bits of technology we usually take for granted are shown to have greater significance. If this were no more than a textbook, to be skimmed or studied and then forgotten, I'd balk at the price; but it's a book that will draw readers' back for frequent browsing, each time giving added knowledge and understanding of many key inventions that shape our lives. Children and adults, all ages. Absolutely worth the price. $29.95 plus $3 postage. BROOK FARM BOOKS.

THE WORLD OF THE MICROSCOPE. Encourages readers to make their own observations and perform simple but effective experiments to reinforce the learning. Very clear text, detailed & colorful illustrations. An excellent introduction to the microscope for all ages, 8 and up. $7.95. Code EDC. BROOK FARM BOOKS.

ADVENTURES WITH A MICROSCOPE, Richard Headstrom. Recommended by several readers. Suggestions for specific microscope work. 231 pages, 142 illustrations. $4.50 plus $1 postage. THE TEACHER'S LABORATORY, INC., P.O. Box 6480, Brattleboro, VT 05301.

THE WORLD OF ELECTRONICS. An up-to-date exploration and explanation of contemporary electronic technology, covering TV and video, audio and radio, films, & special effects. Profusely illustrated with clear, colorful drawings & diagrams, describing the latest equipment and how it works, and explaining much of the confusing jargon used in the electronics industry. Age 10 and up. A very good introduction to the subject for beginners of any age. $6.95. Code EDC. BROOK FARM BOOKS.

AC/DC ELECTRIC CIRCUIT GAME-- Sort of like dominoes, but more complicated, more interesting, and more educational. Various components of an electric system are printed on cards, which must be placed together to form a circuit that delivers the current where it should go, and doesn't short out or give the player a shock. Good introduction to electricity for all ages, including adults. $7.95 plus $1.50 postage. AMPERSAND PRESS, 691 26th St., Oakland, CA 94612.

ELECTRONICS BOOK CLUB, P.O. Box 10, Blue Ridge Summit, PA 17214. 20% to 75% discount on selected books; bonus books. Write for current information & introductory offer (up to $130 worth of books for about $5).

GOOD DETECTIVE GUIDES -- CLUES & SUSPECTS, CATCHING CROOKS, and FAKES AND FORGERIES. Three light-hearted guides follow a team of intrepid sleuths as they try to spot clues, find hidden loot, check alibis, and find evidence. Each book contains mysteries to unravel & directions for making equipment. 3 books in one volume. $8.95. Code EDC. BROOK FARM BOOKS.

Give me a lever long enough and a prop strong enough, I can single-handed move the world.
Archimedes

YOUNG DISCOVERY LIBRARY -- Compact, comprehensive introductions to many fascinating facts about animals, nature, and the physical sciences. Each book has 40 pages, hardcover, with brief but very informative text and more than 50 brilliant, detailed pictures throughout. There are many helpful diagrams and charts, and many suggested activities to involve the readers more directly in each subject. Authors and illustrators work in collaboration with specialist advisors to ensure accuracy in both the text and illustrations. Especially suitable for ages 5 to 10, but very interesting for older kids and adults, too.

All About Wool

The Blue Planet: Seas & Oceans

From Oil to Plastic

Crocodiles and Alligators

ALL ABOUT WOOL. How fleece becomes a sweater, why shepherds need sheepdogs, what people wore before they used wool, how looms work; many more interesting facts in the story of wool from ancient times.

ANIMALS IN WINTER. Weasels turn white (and are then called ermine), ducks fly south, fish burrow into mud, and other creatures all adapt in their own ways to the cold.

ANIMALS UNDERGROUND. The lives and habitats of ants, earthworms, millipedes, rabbits, mice, moles, and many other creatures are "uncovered" in this book.

BEARS, BIG AND LITTLE. Beautifully illustrated descriptions of eight bear species and their habitats, with interesting facts about what they eat, how they raise their cubs, and much more.

THE BLUE PLANET: SEAS AND OCEANS. All about the oceans -- how they got their names, why they are important to us, what lives far below the surface, how waves are formed, and much more.

CROCODILES AND ALLIGATORS. The daily lives, evolution, eggs, babies, and other natural history of the big reptiles from the time they were worshipped in ancient Egypt to today.

ELEPHANTS: BIG, STRONG, AND WISE. Baby elephants suck their trunks, adults shower themselves with dust, Indian elephants are different in many ways from those in Africa, and in some places elephants are dressed for ceremonies.

FROM OIL TO PLASTIC. The whole story of plastic, from its beginning as oil brought up from under the sea; life on an oil rig, how plastic is used in rockets, the impact of plastic on the environment.

GRAINS OF SALT. A book full of scientific facts and folklore about salt -- how we get it from sea and land, why it was especially precious in ancient times, how it is used today, why our bodies need it, and more, along with some projects using salt.

METALS: BORN OF EARTH AND FIRE. What metal is, how people first discovered how to smelt, what makes rust, what ancient alchemists attempted, how metal is mined on land and under the sea, more.

MONKEYS, APES, AND OTHER PRIMATES. Dozens of species in realistic, entertaining pictures and informative text; why lemurs stay up all night; why gorillas are strong; how gibbons "fly"; why primates have thumbs; more.

THE STORY OF PAPER. Where and when paper was invented, what it is made of, what people used before paper was invented, how trees become paper, how so many different kinds of paper are made; more.

UNDERSEA GIANTS. Poetry, lore, and authoritative illustrations and text introduce the world of whales, seals, dolphins, and other sea mammals, with facts about their communication, reproduction, and protection of the species.

Each YOUNG DISCOVERY LIBRARY title, $4.95. Code YD. BROOK FARM BOOKS. (For more books in this series, see History and Music.)

SCIENCE IS... Here, in one book, are enough exciting and informative activities to help your child (maybe even you) learn the basics in nearly all areas of earth science, under headings such as Science Olympics, Matter & Energy, Humans, Environmental Awareness, Rocks, Plants, Living Creatures, Weather, The Heavens, and Applying Science. Learn how to do a bee dance, learn about animal yoga, the impossible-to-straighten cord, cookie concerns, soap bubble derby, shadow creatures, and the plane truth. Suitable for age 7 to 14, more or less, working by themselves; also enjoyable for older kids, and for kids and **adults working together.** Over 500 pages in a sturdy 3-ring binder. The book is divided into three major sections: QUICKIES, short activities requiring few or no materials; MAKE TIME, a little planning and a few inexpensive materials; and ONE LEADS TO ANOTHER, a series of related activities. Interesting tidbits of information are scattered through the book in "Fact and Fun Circles." (E.g., "Are clouds really light?" A mid-sized cloud can have the mass of five elephants!) <u>SCIENCE IS...</u> was written by Susan V. Bosak, working with the Youth Science Foundation, and is absolutely one of the best science books you'll find. $29.95. Code SCH. BROOK FARM BOOKS.

THE BACKYARD SCIENTIST, by Jane Hoffman. Safe and easy science experiments children can perform around the house & yard, using common household materials, with step-by-step instructions; designed specifically for home schoolers age 4-12. Teaches critical thinking as well as scientific principles of chemistry and physics. Several books in the series. Send a #10 SASE for information. BACKYARD SCIENTIST, P.O. Box 16966, Irvine, CA 92713.

LEARN WHILE YOU SCRUB: Science in the Tub, by James Lewis. 55 experiments for ages 5-10 to learn while bathing: how a pump works, why water evaporates, what causes a whirlpool, how air pressure works, how water changes an object's weight, why water magnifies objects, more. #0-671-68999-1. $5.95 plus $1 postage. MEADOWBROOK PRESS, 18318 Minnetonka Blvd., Deephaven, MN 55391.

"WHY IS A CARTON OF MILK LIKE A BANANA?" Poster, teacher's guide, four reproducible activity sheets. FREE. Ask for "Milk: A Great Food in a Great Package." From: MILK INFORMATION, 1101 Vermont Ave. NW, Suite 411, Washington, DC 20005.

HOW PAPER CAME TO AMERICA, wall chart illustrates various ways paper was first made and its arrival in America. "How You Can Make Paper" brochure with step-by-step directions for making paper using ordinary household utensils and materials. Both, FREE. AMERICAN PAPER INSTITUTE, 260 Madison Ave., New York, NY 10016.

SCIENCE CALENDAR: Smithsonian Family Learning Activities. Illustrated; monthly activities; updated each year. $13.45 ppd. Also request information about "Smithsonian Science Activity Books." GALISON BOOKS, 25 West 43rd St., New York, NY 10036.

GREAT SCIENCE EXPERIMENTS-- The Edison Teaching Kit, a series of eight illustrated booklets full of science experiments, written for use at different grade levels. Magnetism and electricity, the environment, energy conservation, energy for the future, alternative energy sources, and nuclear energy. A small charge is made to cover postage. Request information from CHARLES EDISON FUND, 101 S Harrison St., East Orange, NJ 07018.

SCIENCELAND, 501 Fifth Ave. #2102, New York, NY 10017. Monthly; for primary grades. Write for information.

CAPSELA CONSTRUCTION SYSTEMS-- Kits of varying sizes and comlexity which give clear understanding of several principles of physics, such as electricity, mechanical relationships, bouyancy, etc. Capselas are clear plastic, interlocking capsules; some with gears, some with clutches, some with motors. They can be combined to build boats, submarines, a working vacuum cleaner, a dune buggy, and many other mechanical toys. Capselas have been exhibited at the Museum of Modern Art in New York and the Smithsonian in Washington. Prices range from $11.95 to $119.95. Sold in many toy and department stores and by Sears; or write to: PLAYJOUR, INC., 200 Fifth Ave., Suite 1024, New York, NY 10010.

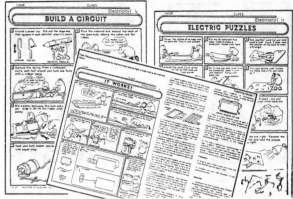

TOPS LEARNING SYSTEMS, 10978 S. Mulino Road, Canby, OR 97013. Very well-developed lesson-activities for various ages in electricity, measurement, balance, magnetism, heat, pressure, sound, motion, light, machines, etc. "Task cards," reproducible activity sheets, guide for teaching. SASE for current information.

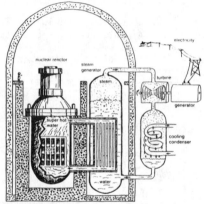

UNDERSTANDING RADIOACTIVITY, Lorus J. and Margery Milne. Earth's core, X-rays, carbon dating, and the sun have one thing in common -- radioactivity. Beginning to understand radioactivity has led scientists to develop X-rays, nuclear power plants, fusion bombs, & nuclear waste. This book's clear text explains what radioactivity is and how it affects our everyday lives, for better and for worse. Detailed graphs & line drawings help clarify difficult concepts such as atomic decay. Glossary, bibliography, and index. Age 10 and up. $12.95. Code MAC. BROOK FARM BOOKS.

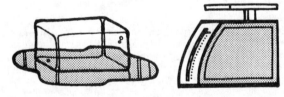

WONDERSCIENCE--An 8-page comic book with activities for children and adults to do together using household products, to learn the wonders of everyday science. $4/year. AMERICAN CHEMICAL SOCIETY, 1155 Sixteenth St. NW, Washington, DC 20036.

WONDER SCIENCE POSTERS: Three 17x22-inch, two-sided posters with explanations and activities about acid-base indicators, color, and polymers. Grade 3 & up. $3 each, or all three for $8, including shipping. WONDER SCIENCE POSTERS, American Chemical Society, P.O. Box 57136, West End Station, Washington, DC 20037.

CURRENT SCIENCE -- An excellent school periodical, which not only reports and discusses recent science findings and developments, but gives information to help readers understand how the news in science and technology affects their own lives and futures. Frequently reports new developments before major "adult" publications mention them. Each issue has a teacher's guide with extra background information, "skillmaster" worksheets, and a summary of important articles. Reading & interest levels are appropriate for ages 12 and up, including high school and adult. 18 issues through the school year, about $11.00 for a single subscription. Write for current information: CURRENT SCIENCE, WEEKLY READER SECONDARY PERIODICALS, P.O. Box 16686, Columbus, OH 43216.

EDUCATIONAL TOYS INC., P.O. Box 630685, Miami, FL 33163-9950. Free catalog. Realistic scale models of animals, reptiles, dinosaurs, etc. (such as a 3' crocodile that will keep salesmen away from your door!), craft kits, educational (and enjoyable) card games, fossil replicas, microscope kit, mineral collections, much more.

SCIENCE WEEKLY, P.O. Box 70154, Washington, DC 20088. Biweekly (despite its name) children's magazine that introduces and explains science and mathematics. Ask for free sample; specify grade level, K through 8.

SIMPLY SCIENCE, newsletter for preschool & primary instructors, with activities, experiment ideas, children's science literature, monthly science calendar, instructions for making science equipment, reviews, reproducible science sheet. $8/10 issues. THE SCIENCE EYE, Box 11440, Pittsburgh, PA 15238.

THE BEST INTRODUCTIONS TO SCIENCE are books written for young children. They explain terms and concepts much more completely than do the books for older readers, without assuming prior knowledge which the reader may not have, and they always have lots of clear diagrams and pictures.

EYEWITNESS VISUAL DICTIONARIES -- The only full-color, photographic dictionaries available, this series of reference books is without parallel for authority, clarity, and beauty. After depicting whole objects, the format "explodes" them, detailing the most minute features with labels and annotations that build up to a 3,500-word scientific vocabulary. Each photographic spread is previewed by introductory text. Books are 10x12", 64 pages, laminated softcover, with over 750 full-color photographs throughout. All ages.

THE VISUAL DICTIONARY OF--
    THE UNIVERSE
    THE EARTH
    ANIMALS
    EVERYDAY THINGS
    THE HUMAN BODY
    SHIPS AND SAILING
    CARS
    PLANTS
    MILITARY UNIFORMS
    FLIGHT
    BUILDINGS
    DINOSAURS

Each title, $14.95.   Code HM.   BROOK FARM BOOKS.

EYEWITNESS SCIENCE -- Clear, informative text -- written in consultation with The Science Museum of London -- and sharp, seemingly three-dimensional photographs and intricate drawings make complex scientific principles and issues clear and fascinating to children and adults without oversimplifying them. A hands-on approach includes actual landmark experiments. Each book is 64 pages, 8½x11", hardcover, with more than 300 full-color illustrations.

    ECOLOGY
    HUMAN BODY
    ELECTRONICS
    MATTER
    CHEMISTRY
    ELECTRICITY
    ENERGY
    LIGHT
    EVOLUTION
    FORCE & MOTION

Each title, $15.95.   Code HM.   BROOK FARM BOOKS.

THE MACMILLAN BOOK OF HOW THINGS WORK, Michael and Marcia Folsom. Clear explanations of more than 100 everyday objects, each with a 1- or 2-page section with attractive, colorful diagrams. Useful and interesting to adults as well as to children. Ages 10 and up. Hardcover, 8½x11", 80 pages. $15.95. Code MAC. BROOK FARM BOOKS.

AEROSPACE EXPLORER, 1516 W. Lake St., Minneapolis, MN 55408. 8-page student quarterly covering space and other science topics. Age 10 up. $2.00.

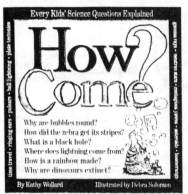

Every Kids' Science Questions Explained

How Come?

Why are bubbles round?
How did the zebra get its stripes?
What is a black hole?
Where does lightning come from?
How is a rainbow made?
Why are dinosaurs extinct?

By Kathy Wollard   Illustrated by Debra Solomon

HOW COME? by Kathy Wollard; illustrated by Debra Solomon. Why are bubbles round? Where does lightning come from? Why do stars twinkle? What are hiccups? Why can cats survive high falls? Why is yawning so contagious? Why is the sky blue? For every kid who really wants to know -- and for every exasperated parent who <u>almost</u> knows, but doesn't really -- here is a gathering of explanations of more than 100 frequently-asked kids' questions. 256 pages; ages 8-14. $9.95. Code WKM. BROOK FARM BOOKS.

MORSE CODE IN 25 MINUTES -- Jerry Mintz (publisher of <u>Aero-Gramme</u>) has developed a technique for learning Morse Code in 25 minutes or less. The technique is demonstrated on a videotape of two 12-year-olds learning the method in less than 20 minutes. A letter to Jerry said, "My daughter learned the entire alphabet and all the numbers in a single sitting, then started sending me code faster than I could take it down." Order "Code Crash," $20 plus $2.00 shipping from: Jerry Mintz, 417 Roslyn Road, Roslyn Heights, NY 11577.

KIDS DISCOVER, P.O. Box 54205, Boulder, CO 80322. Science magazine for ages 6-12. Each issue is devoted to one topic with several articles and photos; also puzzles, word games, and things to make or do. Write for current subscription information.

DON'T BREATHE IN THE SUMMER -- Our daughter Karen sent us this item from a Boston newspaper:

AIR QUALITY
    Because fall and winter air tends to be less polluted than at other times of the year, the Massachusetts Department of Environmental Protection has suspended air quality reports until April.

SCOTTS VALLEY BOOKS, P.O. Box 67241, Scotts Valley, CA 95067. Science and nature books for kids. Small catalog, good selections.

LABORATORY SUPPLIES AND EQUIPMENT -- AVES SCIENCE KIT CO., P.O. Box 229, Peru, ME 04290. Several different kits, especially for homeschoolers.

CLOCK -- Every school room needs an "old-fashioned" face clock! With a face clock, it's easy to convey the divisions of the day into hours, hours into minutes, and minutes into seconds. If you must have a digital clock or watch, show how the numbers relate to positions of the hands on a face clock. A digital clock may tell what time it is, but it won't give any sense of time.

AQUA QWOCK, a clock which gets its power from ordinary water. An instruction booklet explains that the clock's copper electrode absorbs electrons which have been released by the zinc electrode; the electron flow powers the clock for up to six weeks before new water is needed. $15.00. Order from SKIL-CRAFT, 8601 Waukegan Road, Morton Grove, IL 60053.

HOW TO MAKE AND USE A PINHOLE CAMERA from a tin can or small cardboard box; 12-page booklet, FREE from EASTMAN KODAK COMPANY, Photo Information Dept., 343 State Street, Rochester, NY 14650.

ANTHRO NOTES, free natural history newsletter, three issues per year. Request from: Public Information Office, Dept. of Anthropology, Smithsonian Institution, Washington, DC 20560.

CORK: NATURE'S ANSWER is an 8-page booklet about the characteristics of cork (lighter than water, more elastic than plastic) and its use in bridge joints, fishing equipment, shoes, and space shuttles. FREE from: CORK INSTITUTE OF AMERICA, P.O. Box 1297, Lancaster, PA 17603.

RAINBOW GLASSES-- Cardboard spectacles with plastic lenses which change any light -- sunshine, light bulb, TV screen -- into brilliant flashes of rainbow colors. Fun and fascinating for all ages. Pamphlet with scientific explanation. Very inexpensive. Write for prices and information about related materials. MR. RAINBOWS, P.O.Box 27056, Philadelphia, PA 19118.

SCIENTIFIC AMERICAN, P.O. Box 970, Farmingdale, NY 11737. New ideas and discoveries in all sciences for "intelligent, educated" people; "not edited for mass readership"; no "warmed-over, popularized pap." Definitely worthwhile, although I can also learn a lot from warmed-over, popularized pap (hoping that's no reflection on my education or intelligence). Write for information, which may include a trial subscription offer.

SUNPRINTS. All you need is sun, water, simple materials, and imagination to make photograph-like images without a camera; no chemicals. Catalog: DISCOVERY CORNER, Lawrence Hall of Science, University of California, Berkeley, CA 94720.

AG IN THE CLASSROOM--Set of booklets, guides, a poster, and reproducible information sheets about farming. You will also be put on a mailing list for "Ag in the Classroom Notes," a bimonthly newsletter. Request must be on school stationery. AG IN THE CLASSROOM, U.S. Dept. of Agriculture, Office of the Secretary, Washington, DC 20250.

THE TEACHER'S LABORATORY--Large and excellent selection of magnifiers, microscopes, kits, charts, posters, motors, books, and more. Activities in measuring, weighing, magnifying, natural science, math resources, robotics, electricity, earth science, health, and simple machines. Advertised "for grades K-8," but why stop there? Great for all ages, including adults. One of the best places to start looking for good materials and reasonable prices. Colorful catalog. THE TEACHER'S LABORATORY, P.O. Box 6480, Brattleboro, VT 05301.

DISCOUNT SCIENCE EQUIPMENT -- Brand-new $260 telescope for $99, and many other similar bargains. Factory close-outs, surplus purchases, etc. Free catalog. COMB DIRECT MARKETING CORP., 1405 Xenium Lane N., Minneapolis, MN 55441.

NORRIS SCIENCE LABS AND KITS, 4561 Sacks Drive, Las Vegas, NV 89122. Science labs for all grade levels, including "Mini-Lab," designed especially for home educators, with complete tools & materials for many experiments, such as making a thermometer, a friction scale, a steam turbine engine, glass making, and making a fuse. Write for more information; a first class stamp (not an SASE) will be appreciated.

DISCOVERY CORNER, Lawrence Hall of Science, University of California, Berkeley, CA 74720. Science learning materials, books, toys; solar energy kit, moon & universe maps, telescopes, microscopes, more.

EDMUND SCIENTIFIC EDUCATIONAL/INDUSTRIAL CATALOG. Microscopes, telescopes, science kits, magnets, chemistry equipment, weather instruments, much more. Catalog. EDMUND SCIENTIFIC, 101 East Gloucester Pike, Barrington, NJ 08007.

FRANZ CARL WEBER, Pro Juventute, Zentralsekretariat, 8022 Zurich, Switzerland. Very good learning & play materials for all ages from birth through adult. Electronic, optical, chemical, and model supplies.

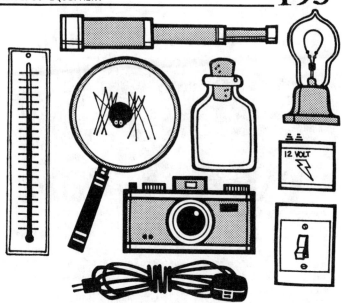

KITS, MODELS, much more. Free Elementary Science & Math Materials Catalog. CAROLINA BIOLOGICAL SUPPLY CO., 2700 York Road, Burlington, NC 27215. (This is a large, expensive catalog, for serious use by institutions, and should not be requested just out of curiosity.)

FREY SCIENTIFIC CO., P.O. Box 8101, Mansfield, OH 44905. Free 176-page catalog of school science materials.

NASCO, 901 Janesville Ave., Fort Atkinson, WI 53538.

ANT FARM from NASCO, in which ants sow, reap, and harvest their own food. Or you might like an Ant City, with skyscrapers, transparent subway tunnels, and no smog.

ELEMENTARY SCIENCE ACTIVITIES GUIDE AND CATALOG. A catalog that includes several "magazine" features: hands-on activities, miniposter, section on general science, more. FREE from SARGENT-WELCH SCIENTIFIC CO., P.O. Box 1026, Skokie, IL 60077. (Meant for public school teachers, so a letterhead and formal request will help.)

NATIONAL TEACHING AIDS, INC., 120 Fulton Ave., Garden City Park, NY 11040. Catalog of excellent materials for elementary age through high school science and health education. Inexpensive study-slides, Science-Made-Easy Kits, chemistry, genetics and much more.

MORE SCIENCE SUPPLIES--
Don't overlook SEARS, RADIO SHACK, and other local and/or mail-order stores. The prices are often lower than those of school suppliers, and their products are usually as good or better.

AMERICAN SCIENCE & SURPLUS, 3605 Howard St., Skokie, IL 60076. A cornucopia of bits, pieces, gears, gadgets, lights, switches, alarms, hinges, containers of all sizes and shapes, unidentified technical artifacts, and thousands of other miscellaneous items for "teachers, labs, tinkerers, small manufacturers," and so on. Catalog $1. Well worth it, even if you're just a browser. The catalog listings are written with great humor, and there's a chance you'll see at least one item you've always wanted but didn't know it.

CURRENT EVENTS
TODAY'S HEADLINES, TOMORROW'S HISTORY

"NEWS" MAGAZINES -- I don't think there's any really objective news magazine being published today. The news articles are riddled with opinions, pontifical analyses, and biased writing. I've almost learned to tolerate it with radio weather forecasts, so I don't mutter too loudly when the "meteorologist" says, "Well, folks, it's going to be another miserable day tomorrow, with lots of rain all day." Why should it be assumed that rain will make the day miserable for me? Perhaps my garden needs water, or maybe I like to walk in the rain. It's worse when the "reporting" is of national or international events. Just tell me what's going on, without what you and your team of experts think it "means." We'd like to boycott all the news magazines, but, for all their fluff and biases, they do tell us a little of current events, so we grit our teeth and try to read between the lines. We assume that half of the truth isn't being told and that half of what is being told isn't true or is being told in a slanted, misleading manner. If a magazine has a four-page car advertisement, costing thousands of dollars per inch, we don't expect the magazine to say much about the safety hazards of automobiles. If the magazine receives support from major oil companies, we don't expect it to dig very deeply into the causes of oil spills or the failures of oil companies to clean up their messes. If the magazine's demographic surveys show that 76% of its readers are suspicious of what the Russians are up to now, we don't expect it to risk six million cancelled subscriptions by telling the truth when the Russians actually do something good and right. We try to balance our understanding of the news by reading publications such as The Nation and The Washington Spectator which don't depend on big corporations for their revenue. Since most of them tend to be somewhat or very leftwing, we don't believe all they say either, but at least their biases are more open and honest. We read both viewpoints, divide by the number of starving children in the world, multiply by the number of politicians it takes to change a lightbulb, and hope thereby to arrive at some measure of the truth.

We tried TIME, NEWSWEEK, and U.S. NEWS & WORLD REPORT, all at one time, comparing them for a full year. U.S. NEWS claims to have a higher percentage of "hard" news than the other two, but I think its extra margin is concerned primarily with the stock market. TIME and NEWSWEEK were neck-and-neck, but TIME kept billing us for our subscription long after we had paid for it, so for several years we've subscribed only to NEWSWEEK, and don't feel any great loss. You can't judge any of the magazines by their cover stories, which will be about real news one week (politics, wars, elections) and popular culture the next week (the latest movie craze or why Americans like to go to the beach). Inside, the magazine will always be the same mishmash of news and garbage and expert analyses of both. Lumping all such publications under one representative name, Thoreau said, "Read not the Times; read the eternities." Reader's Digest recently printed an anecdote about a vacationer in the woods of Wisconsin who told his guide, "It'll be interesting when I get back home to read the papers and see what's been happening in the real world." The guide replied, "I thought that was why you came out here."

THE WASHINGTON SPECTATOR, edited by Tristam Coffin. A very informative, politically-aware 4-page newsletter, published 22 times a year. Each issue usually focuses on a particular political, social, or environmental situation, with information, excerpts, and editorial comment from many different sources, such as Washington Post, Christian Science Monitor, Los Angeles Times, recent books, and legislators. Background to many news items, frequently ignored by the mass media as too controversial and/or objectionable to corporate advertisers, is often disclosed in The Spectator. Each issue has half a page of "FYI, Items of Interest from Spectator Files," such as the following note: "The Houston Post has dug up a new angle on the savings and loan scandal. Four major borrowers of a Colorado S & L that failed also made deals with individuals and savings and loans that did business with organized crime or the CIA. Apparently, the Colorado S & L was used for money-laundering." No matter what other publications we read, or how many, we feel we're getting only half the news until we read The Spectator. One year (22 issues), only $10 (a bargain at twice the price) or 2 years for $18. Seniors and students, $9 and $17. Send payment with your name and address to: THE PUBLIC CONCERN FOUNDATION, INC., P.O. Box 20065, London Terrace Station, New York, NY 10011.

THE NATION, 72 Fifth Avenue, New York, NY 10011. This monthly magazine is a very close second to The Washington Spectator as a publication without which we would feel we were missing at least half the news of the world, regardless of how many others we read. Somewhat leftwing, sometimes, but not radical or rabble-rousing. Pokes sharp needles of inquiry into the pomposity of politicians, social incongruities, and the mass media. Uncovers hidden facts and motives behind the headlines. Write for current subscription rates.

WEEKLY READER, P.O. Box 16730, Columbus, OH 43216. Student newspapers, different edition for each level from preschool through sixth grade. Varied subject matter, as appropriate to the grade level -- news, science, global issues, etc. Our kids have always looked forward to receiving this newspaper, and I remember enjoying it when I was in school. Write for current subscription rates.

CURRENT EVENTS-- Student newspaper, 26 issues during the school year. Very impressive in its thorough reporting of key issues, usually with photographs, helpful graphs, tables, and maps. Nine mini-study units each year, focusing on events or places of particular importance in world news. Reproducible tests, vocabulary lists of names and places in the news, a crossword puzzle based on current news. Surprisingly objective -- more so than Newsweek or Time. Reading level, about 6th grade (but that's the level of most "adult" periodicals). We've subscribed to Current Events for several years, using it in high school studies to help pinpoint issues reported in the larger news magazines, and often giving less-slanted, more-reliable reporting. About $11 per year, which is hard to beat. Write for information: WEEKLY READER SECONDARY LEVEL PERIODICALS, P.O. Box 16626, Columbus, OH 43216.

WORLD MONITOR -- News magazine from The Christian Science Monitor. World news, editorials, analyses of the news; articles on art, music, film, education, science, technology, and more. Photographs, charts, maps. Edited somewhat from a global viewpoint, rather than that of a particular nation or region, but the view is still basically Western. Although I'm sometimes disturbed by The Monitor's subtle (sometimes, not so subtle) slanting of the news and by editorial comment woven into the reporting, the news coverage tends to be more objective than in most major news magazines, and more of the content is given to real news rather than trivial fillers on pop culture. Just the same, I'm disappointed that the magazine isn't as much better as it could be. Monthly. $14.97/year. WORLD MONITOR, P.O. Box 11267, Des Moines, IA 50347.

WORLD PRESS REVIEW, P.O. Box 1997, Marion, OH 43306-2097. Articles, editorials, political cartoons, and news from newspapers and magazines around the world -- Russia, Japan, China, Germany, France, Spain, Italy, England, Australia, Brazil, everywhere; both liberal and conservative selections. It's very interesting and useful to know what "others" are saying and thinking without having their views filtered through the eyes and biases of our own media. Easily worth the full price of $25 or more, but an introductory subscription (12 monthly issues) is $18 or less. Write for current information.

"RESOURCES FOR SUCCESS," a series of teaching aids based on each current issue of Newsweek, for high school and college. Print materials, filmstrips, software, videotapes, more. Write to: NEWSWEEK EDUCATION DIVISION, Box 414, Livingston, NJ 07039 or phone 1-800-526-2595 (in NJ, 1-800-962-1201).

TIME EDUCATION PROGRAM, fact sheets, quizzes, vocabulary boosters, more; sent each week to coincide with the current issue of Time Magazine. High school and college. Write: TIME EDUCATION PROGRAM, 10 No. Main St., Yardley, PA 19067 or phone 1-800-345-3496 (in PA, 1-800-637-8509).

MULTINEWSPAPERS, Box DE, Dana Point, CA 92629. Newspapers from many different countries; varying subscriptions available. Free information.

THE MIDDLE EAST: Understanding the News. Grades 6-9. Hostage-taking, terrorism, Persian Gulf fighting, etc.; how and why these conditions began; how the US is affected. Maps, charts, graphs, tables; climate, topography, directions, population, political divisions, more. Religions of the Middle East; ancient & modern history; resources, languages, population, oil, land use, manufacturing. Order #25074. $2.35 plus $1 postage. WEEKLY READER SKILLS BOOKS, P.O. Box 16607, Columbus, OH 43272.

STRUCTURE, PURPOSE, FUNCTION, POLITICS, CITIZENSHIP, BENEFITS, DANGERS, CENSORSHIP & CONSPIRACIES

INTRODUCTION TO POLITICS & GOVERNMENT-- Very clear, detailed, <u>unbiased</u> descriptions of various forms of government, how they compare and how they relate to each other, with historic and modern examples, including dictatorships, fascism, elections, republics, democracy, Marxism, diplomacy, and summit meetings. Very well-illustrated with detailed, colorful drawings. Age 10 to adult. $5.95. Code EDC. BROOK FARM BOOKS.

"IF I WERE PRESIDENT, WHAT WOULD I DO?" Board game for 2 to 4 people, age 10 and up. Players are candidates for the presidency, and advance toward the Oval Office by answering true-false questions on U.S. history, and by receiving votes from other players for their responses to questions concerning foreign policy, education, crime, the economy, etc. Complete with playing cards, die, and markers. $6 plus $2.50 shipping. SULCORP INC., P.O. Box 8902, Pembroke Pines, FL 33024.

HAIL TO THE CHIEF: The Presidential Election Game. Players compete to become elected President of the United States. First, they must achieve candidacy by answering historical and constitutional questions about the Presidency. Then, on the campaign trail, they travel from state to state to win electoral votes by answering questions on the history and geography of the 50 states. (No mention is made of political promises, party fund-raising or TV advertising, but players will learn a lot about U.S. history and geography anyway, as well as the <u>theory</u> of how presidents are elected.) Contents: U.S. map gameboard, 84 president cards (624 historical and Constitutional questions about the presidency), 36 campaign cards, 84 state cards (336 historical and geographical questions about the U.S.), 2 dice, 4 playing pieces, instruction booklet, and coupons for free updates. Age 10 and up, 2 to 4 players. $25.00 plus $3 shipping. BROOK FARM BOOKS.

PERILS OF DEMOCRACY -- Who should know better than an elected public servant what dangers there are in a democracy? In July 1989, the Los Angeles <u>Times</u> noted that California State Senator Bill Craven was worried about "the rise in citizen's initiatives, in which people sign petitions to enact changes in laws," and quoted Craven as saying, "[If we legislators] don't watch our respective tails, the <u>people</u> are going to be running the government."

The strength of the Constitution lies entirely in the determination of each citizen to defend it. Only if every single citizen feels duty bound to do his share in this defense are the constitutional rights secure.

Albert Einstein

VICE-PRESIDENTIAL WIT & WISDOM -- Responding to charges that he sometimes says what he doesn't mean, Dan Quayle said, "I stand by all the misstatements." (Reported in NEWSWEEK.)

Addressing members of the United Negro College Fund, trying to quote the UNCF slogan, <u>A mind is a terrible thing to waste</u>, Dan Quayle said, "What a waste it is to lose one's mind -- or not to have a mind. How true that is." (Reported in NEWSWEEK.)

A politician thinks of the next election; a statesman, of the next generation.

James Freeman Clarke

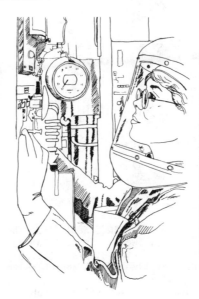

1984, by George Orwell. When the year 1984 came and went, popular pundits looked around at modern society and smugly announced that Orwell was wrong, both in his predictions and in the date. They were completely mistaken on both counts. **1984** was not meant as a prediction, but as a warning, and the message is more pertinent today than it was when the book was written, or even in the year 1984. In the novel, the government's Ministry of Truth continually rewrites history, manipulating society's opinions and attitudes through Newspeak, a form of word-garbling that increasingly makes free and independent thinking impossible, and popularizes slogans such as "War is Peace" and "Freedom is Slavery." In our "real world" of today, literature and history books are being rewritten to reflect the desires of scores of minority pressure groups as well as current governmental policies, and the government bombards us daily with phrases such as "negative benefits" and "first strike defense," while telling us that "our" unbelievable military buildup -- using more than fifty percent of the entire federal budget -- is "to preserve world peace." The message of **1984** should be read and considered very seriously. The more we allow the meanings of words to become vague & cloudy, the more difficult true communication becomes; and the more easily our attitudes and beliefs will be manipulated by corporations, governments, or religious demagogues using repetitive slogans and doctrinal affirmations. No high school or college study of democracy and censorship is complete without a thoughtful reading of this book. We can't afford to look around complacently and say, "Well, it hasn't happened yet." If we don't move immediately to reverse the trend, it _will_ happen -- and its beginnings are already all around us. $12.95. Code HBJ. BROOK FARM BOOKS.

DOUBLE-SPEAK, William Lutz. Exploring how everyday use of deceptive, evasive, confusing, euphemistic, or self-contradictory language has become increasingly common, this book emphasizes that doublespeak is not simply a slip of the tongue, but rather very conscious use of language as a weapon of power, exploitation, and oppression. Chronicling such terms as "inoperative statements" (lies) and "terminate with extreme prejudice" (kill), the book examines champion doublespeakers in advertising, government, business, and even food labels. Alarming, disturbing, and eye-opening. Older teens & adults. $8.95. Code HR. BROOK FARM BOOKS.

ANIMAL FARM, George Orwell. An amusing, biting satire on totalitarianism -- and the dangers to democracy when it isn't carefully guarded. "We're all created equal, but some are more equal than others." A very funny, very serious, very disturbing book. New edition, illustrated with 37 line drawings. $12.95. Code HBJ. BROOK FARM BOOKS.

BRAVE NEW WORLD. One-hour old-radio program on cassette, with Richard Widmark. Based on the novel by Aldous Huxley about a society of genetic manipulation, in which the words "mother" and "father" are considered obscene. Read the news, and say it won't happen. $6.00 plus $2 postage. (May be combined with "History & Biography from Old Radio" cassette tapes for quantity discount and lower postage.) BROOK FARM BOOKS.

FAHRENHEIT 451, Ray Bradbury. In a not-too-distant evolution of our society, in which most people spend the day conversing with their fictional television families, Montag is a fireman -- not a firefighter, but a professional bookburner, working for an authoritarian state which endeavors to banish all printed material, and, by implication, all freedom of thought. When Montag accidentally reads some of the books he is supposed to burn, he begins to question... first, his job; then, the state. Unlike **1984** and BRAVE NEW WORLD, this disturbing picture of total censorship ends with a hopeful note -- which, however, shouldn't weaken its implicit warning. Older teens and adults. $6.95. Code RH. BROOK FARM BOOKS.

A SMALL CIVIL WAR, John Neufeld. Two young people challenge the injustice of a book-burning crusade in a small town. Fiction; teen and older. $2.50 plus $2 postage. Order by title and No. XB80909. THE PERFECTION FORM COMPANY, 1000 North Second Ave., Logan, IA 51546.

Rebellion to tyrants is obedience to God.
Motto on Thomas Jefferson's seal.

PROTECTING PRIVACY IN SURVEILLANCE SOCIETIES: The Federal Republic of Germany, Sweden, France, Canada, and the United States, by David H. Flaherty. Big Brother pops up again, this time not in apprehensive fiction but in a critical analysis of present-day realities. As individuals are increasingly subject to surveillance by government and corporate data bases, concern for the protection of personal privacy has become a very important issue. Let's not be sidetracked by myths of Soviet "thought-police." The author examines the passage, revision, and implementation (or lack of it) of privacy and data protection laws at the national and state levels in five countries -- Germany, Sweden, France, and Canada, where formal agencies are charged with protecting privacy, and the United States, where the administration of privacy laws is in the hands of, ahem, civil servants. "There is a battle being fought in every technologically advanced country," says U.S. Congressman Glenn English, "between the individual's right to privacy and the surveillance needs of government. Flaherty has written a guidebook to that battle. I enthusiastically recommend the book to legislators, policymakers, scholars, and concerned citizens throughout the world." Hardcover, 480 pages. $45.00, plus $3.00 postage. BROOK FARM BOOKS. (A hefty price. If your local library doesn't have it, it can probably be gotten through an intra-library loan.)

THE DAY THEY CAME TO ARREST THE BOOK, Nat Hentoff. Who would have believed THE ADVENTURES OF HUCKLEBERRY FINN could cause the worst crisis in the history of George Mason High School? Certainly not Barney Roth, editor of the school paper. But when a small but vocal group of students and parents decide that the book is racist, sexist, and immoral-- and should be removed from reading lists and the school library -- Barney takes matters into his own hands. As the HUCK FINN issue comes up for a hearing, Barney decides to write a story about previous censorship efforts at school. He's sure that investigative reporting and publicity can help the cause. But is he too late to turn the tide of censorship? This intelligent novel for teens and adults is entertaining and thought-provoking. Publishers Weekly called it "an outstanding work, given added value by the author's honest, comprehensive coverage of all sides of the argument over 'dangerous freedoms.'" $10.95. Code DD. BROOK FARM BOOKS.

"It's mighty hard to figure, Jim. When Mark Twain first wrote about us, most everyone thought I should be in school. Nowadays, half the schools don't even want to let me in. Black folks don't like to read about us 'cause in the old days you was called a 'nigger,' an' thought nothin' of it, an' white folks don't want to read about us 'cause I'd rather go to Hell than send a man back into slavery, an' what neither of them wants for theirselves, they don't want no one else to have neither. I tell you, Jim, I just can't figure it."

IF THE PRESS DIDN'T TELL US, WHO WOULD? Brochure about the value of a free press, and how citizens' rights are protected by the press. FREE. FIRST AMENDMENT CENTER, National Press Bldg., Washington, DC 20045.

"ATTACKS ON THE FREEDOM TO LEARN: The 1987- 1988 Report," a 60-page report documenting 157 incidents of "certain special interest groups to pressure public schools into accepting their agendas." Leftwing view which apparently doesn't feel the omission of important information from school books is also an attack on the freedom to learn. $6.95 postpaid. PEOPLE FOR THE AMERICAN WAY, 2000 M St. NW, Suite 400, Washington, DC 20036.

LORD OF THE FLIES, by William Golding. Fiction. This is one of the books frequently targeted for removal from schools; I've forgotten why, but I think it's because of a few mild cuss words. I wouldn't worry about them. There are far more disturbing things in the book -- ideas. According to Rousseau, Burroughs, and many others, a child will develop a healthy and mature perspective naturally, without being taught or trained. This novel explores the concept with a group of boys marooned in the wilderness, faced with the need to establish some sort of basic government for their mutual survival. Those of us who take democracy for granted consider its benefits obvious, but Golding's story is a reminder that democracy has taken thousands of years to develop, and may not be as "natural" as we would like to think. LORD OF THE FLIES is also, in many ways, an "answer" to A. S. Neill (author of SUMMERHILL) and others who advocate the enfranchising of children: without a knowledge of history, without an understanding of the democratic process, without an acquired sense of fairness and justice, can we expect anyone -- child or adult -- to have an inherent desire for society's greatest good, and to leap over centuries of slow social evolution to an enlightened democracy? Golding's answer is not definitive; but it is certainly provocative. Older teens and adults. $5.95. Code BT. BROOK FARM BOOKS.

NATIONAL COALITION AGAINST CENSORSHIP, 132 W. 43rd St., New York, NY 10036. Publications, information about censorship; suggestions for forming a local review committee.

NATIONAL COUNCIL OF TEACHERS OF ENGLISH, 1111 Kenyon Rd., Urbana, IL 61801. Publications and information about censorship.

LAISSEZ FAIRE BOOKS, 206 Mercer St., New York, NY 10012. Catalog of books about free market principles and the principle of liberty. Free catalog.

You can only protect your liberties in this world by protecting the other man's freedom. You can only be free if I am free.

Clarence Darrow

CONSCIENCE VERSUS LAW: Case Studies in the American Experience, Bernard Feder. Using both modern and historical examples, this well-illustrated book examines social and political change through confrontation, both peaceful and violent, leading the reader to compare both the efficacy and the "rightness" of each. Dramatic drawings, prints, & photographs, both historic and modern, illustrate such events as Thoreau's tax boycott, Abolitionist demonstrations, and the Mississippi lunch counter sit-ins. These peaceful demonstrations are contrasted with the violence of John Brown's raid at Harper's Ferry and the race riots of the 1960's. Each chapter concludes with questions for thought and discussion, all addressing the central question: Is violent confrontation with one's own society or government ever justified -- or even the most effective way of bringing change? We've gotten the best use of this book through group readings and discussions. The writing is for kids about 10 to 15, but the ideas are pertinent for all ages. $4.50 plus $2 postage. Order #GLB-567-13. SOCIAL STUDIES SCHOOL SERVICE, 10000 Culver Blvd., Culver City, CA 90230.

RIGHT vs. LEFT--
The Washington Spectator (see index) quotes some of "the true differences between Democrats and Republicans" from a newsletter called "Unconventional Wisdom":

"Democrats eat the fish they catch. Republicans mount them on the wall.

"Democrats buy most of the books that have been banned somewhere. Republicans form censorship committees and read them as a group.

"Republicans tend to keep the shades drawn, although there is seldom any reason why they should. Democrats ought to, but don't.

"Republican boys date Democrat girls. They plan to marry Republicans, but they feel entitled to a little fun first.

"Democrats have chapped hands and headaches. Republicans have tennis elbow and gout."

Quoted in Newsweek: Robert Carroll, spokesman for Pratt and Whitney, explaining why his company charged the Air Force $999 for a single pair of pliers, said, "They're multipurpose; not only do they put the clips on but they take them off."

CENSORSHIP & CONSPIRACIES -- Which came first, the right-wing censorship or the left-wing conspiracies? The extreme right complains that the schools are teaching secular humanism, and the extreme left complains that its First Amendment rights are being violated if children are told anything at all about religion. The right-wing arguments are based primarily on a strict, literal interpretation of the Bible; the left-wing arguments are based on a strict, literal interpretation of the U.S. Constitution. Education, caught in the middle and pulled by both groups in a tug-of-war, has stretched and snapped and gotten lost in the shuffle.

It's sadly true that public schools don't include much about religion, even in history courses. It's also sadly true that they don't include much about anything. Sometimes both sides seem to have some very valid, reasonable arguments and examples, and sometimes they both just bounce off the walls. The complaints and threats of both sides have scared textbook publishers, whose main desire (second to making money, of course) is to avoid offending anyone. Since someone, somewhere, either left or right, will be offended by anything at all, the publishers have thought it prudent to publish books that don't say anything, and find it very discouraging that some people are offended even by that. At present, despite a Republican administration* and the growth spurt of fundmentalism, the left-wingers seem to be gaining ground in the schools and in the courts. Perhaps the irresponsible "rights" demanded by the far left will eventually result in an even greater reaction from the far right, which might result, for a while at least, in a more reasonable balance between the two. Probably neither side will be satisfied with a balance, but will continue to fight for increasing control, so the scales will continue to teeter-totter. Both extremes, the far-right fundamentalists and the far-left "secular humanists," are loud minorities. Jerry Falwell's "Moral Majority" was nothing more than a splinter of the right-wing minority, but there is a real moral majority -- the great number of people who are not fundamentalists but disapprove of flag-burning and pornography; who don't believe the universe was created in six days, but who do believe that homosexuality and hate-music are wrong. This real majority, out-shouted by the left-right extremists, is too intimidated by both groups to speak up in favor of a return to sound, "old-fashioned" moral values, academic competence, and common sense education.

Let the far left return to being consenting adults in the privacy of their own homes, and let the far right teach Scientific Creationism in the privacy of their own homes and churches.

For far-left complaints, sometimes valid, about the far-right, read publications of the American Civil Liberties Union, the War Resisters League (not to be lumped with other pacifist groups), Planned Parenthood, and anything you can handle by radical feminists, homosexuals (who, I understand, don't like to be called that), and Madalyn Murray O'Hair, who publishes THE ATHEIST MAGAZINE.

For far-right complaints, sometimes valid, about the far-left, read **WHAT ARE THEY TEACHING OUR CHILDREN?** by Mel & Norma Gabler ($5.95 + $1.50 postage, MEL AND NORMA GABLER, Box 7518, Longview, TX 75607); **CHANGE AGENTS IN THE SCHOOLS,** by Barbara Morris ($9.95 plus $1.50 postage, BARBARA MORRIS, P.O. Box 2166, Carlsbad, CA 92008); **CHILD ABUSE IN THE CLASSROOM,** by Phyllis Schlafly ($5.95 plus $1.50 postage, CROSSWAY BOOKS, 9825 W. Roosevelt Road, Westchester, IL 60153); **CENSORSHIP: Evidence of Bias in Our Chil-**

dren's **Textbooks,** by Paul Vitz ($6.95 plus $1.50, SERVANT BOOKS, P.O. Box 7455, Ann Arbor, MI 48107, and several passages in Mary Pride's **THE BIG BOOK OF HOME LEARNING** (listed elsewhere in this book).

Don't expect great intellectual feats from either side. Left-wingers take the Bible from schools, claiming that exposure to a religious book is an infringement of their First Amendment rights. Right-wingers remove CHARLOTTE'S WEB and PETER RABBIT from many schools because animals can't really talk, and HUCKLEBERRY FINN because Huck would rather go to Hell than betray an escaped slave. Joseph Scheidler, director of the ultra-right Pro-Life Action League, says "contraception is disgusting -- people using each other for pleasure." Planned Parenthood, determined to match Scheidler's ignorance and stupidity, quotes his pious complaint to support its claim that making abortion illegal will "return women to a position of subservience." Both sides act as if their brains had been aborted.

I'm not a fundamentalist, as you've probably inferred by now, and I don't usually consider myself a right-winger in much of anything, but it seems to me that many of the arguments of the right-wing are more valid than those of the left-wing. I don't think "Bible Science" should be taught in schools, but neither do I think that the recognition of Thanksgiving and Christmas as religious holidays will threaten anyone's liberty.

My brother says the older we get, the more conservative we get. I think I'm still as "liberal" as I've ever been, but the far-left keeps moving so much further left that my liberalism seems increasingly conservative.

Kahlil Gibran tells of three frogs on a floating log, arguing about whether the log is moving, or the river is moving, or their movement is only in their thoughts. A fourth frog, who has stayed out of the argument, finally says, "All three of you are right. The river is moving, the log is moving, and we move in our thoughts." The first three frogs stare at the fourth for a moment; then, all together, rush at him and push him off the log.

Splash.

* This was written during George Bush's reign of error.

SPACESHIP EARTH, HUMANITY AS ONE FAMILY, PEACE & WAR, ECOLOGY, CONSERVATION, MEDIA MONOPOLIES

The world is shrinking--

Figuratively, because of the speed of modern transportation and communication;

And literally, because some of the earth's substance is dissipating into space in the form of gas and some of the earth's substance is settling and becoming more compacted.

Although codes of behavior vary from culture to culture, there are some standards which have always existed in nearly all of them. Among these is the law that it's wrong to hurt another member of one's own group, whether the group is a family, a tribe, or a nation. Murder or theft within one's own group is a punishable offense everywhere, even among those people whose highest awards and honor are for such actions if the victims are from another group.

As the world shrinks, the boundaries of our groups blend and overlap. We can no longer pretend, as we have for centuries, that humanity is not all one family, regardless of color or religion or place of birth.

"Am I my brother's keeper?" Cain asked God, but God knew Cain was being sarcastic, and didn't answer. The shrinking of our world is his answer now.

Most of the materials in this book relate, in one way or another, to global awareness -- i.e., awareness that we occupy this planet with billions of other beings and life-forms, with whom we share the

responsibility of preserving the health of the earth and its creatures; and, to do so, we need at least basic information about our fellow beings, and about both the good and the bad directions our species seems to be going. Entries in this section are those which most specifically address the subject.

GAMES AROUND THE WORLD--40 ball games, string games, stick games, board games, brain teasers, running games, marble games, stone games, response games, & handicrafts from children of Nigeria, Thailand, Ghana, Philippines, Egypt, Sri Lanka, Korea, and several other developing nations. The games require no expensive or elaborate materials, and can be played almost anywhere. They're best for young children (about 12 and under), but older children will find them interesting, too. Each 8½x11" game sheet has photos, instructions, & one or two little-known facts about the country from which the game comes. $3.50 plus $1 postage. U.S. COMMITTEE FOR UNICEF, 331 E. 38th St., New York, NY 10016 or UNICEF CANADA, 443 Mt. Pleasant Rd., Toronto, Ont., M4S 2L8.

FRIENDS AROUND THE WORLD: A Game of World Peace, by Joan Walsh Anglund. A cooperative game, in which players race to get 16 International Friends to World Peace ahead of the Blob. If the Friends arrive first, everyone wins! Contents: a game board, 2 decks of cards, 16 International Friends with biographical sketches, 16 stands, dice, a map showing the homelands of the Friends, and instructions for two levels of play. Age 5 and up; 2 to 4 players. $20.00 plus $3 postage. BROOK FARM BOOKS.

To see what is right and not to do it is want of courage.

Confucius

Our country is the world, our countrymen are all mankind.

William Lloyd Garrison

SO, ALL TOGETHER, THEY WROTE A DOCUMENT. IN THIS DOCUMENT THEY TRIED TO MAKE A LIST OF THE RIGHTS THAT EVERY HUMAN BEING HAS, AND THAT EVERYONE ELSE SHOULD RESPECT.

THE UNIVERSAL DECLARATION OF HUMAN RIGHTS: An Adaptation for Children, by Ruth Rocha and Octavio Roth. Especially for ages 5 to 12, but interesting and informative for all ages. Based on the 1948 Universal Declaration of Human Rights, beautifully illustrated, this book is an excellent introduction to the concept of human rights, and to the efforts being made by the United Nations to help countries around the world develop and protect human rights. Order #E.89.I.19-h. $9.95 postpaid. Checks should be made out to "UN Publications." Order from UNITED NATIONS PUBLICATIONS, Sales Section, Rm. DC2-853, Dept. 202, New York, NY 10017.

BLUE AND BEAUTIFUL: PLANET EARTH, OUR HOME, by Ruth Rocha and Otavio Roth. Beautifully illustrated book to help children of all ages understand the role each of us needs to play to keep our planet "blue and beautiful" for ourselves and for future generations. Based on the 1972 Stockholm Declaration on Human Environment. Order #E.90.I.15. $9.95 postpaid. Checks should be made out to "UN Publications." Order from UNITED NATIONS PUBLICATIONS, Sales Section, Rm. DC2-853, Dept. 202, New York, NY 10017.

I would no more teach children military training than teach them arson, robbery, or assassination.
Eugene Victor Debs

SKIPPING STONES: A Multi-ethnic Children's Forum. By and for children of all ages, all countries, all languages (translated to English for this edition); stories, interviews, memories, art, photographs, activities, poems, penpals, recipes, letters, more. Ages 7-12, more or less. $15/year. Sample, $4.00. APPROVECHO INSTITUTE, 80574 Hazelton Road, Cottage Grove, OR. 97424.

STONE SOUP, The Magazine by Children. Powerful, thoughtful writing and artwork by children around the world from seven to thirteen years old. Very impressive. Sample, $3.75. $18/yr (5 issues). STONE SOUP, Children's Art Foundation, P.O. Box 83, Santa Cruz, CA 95063.

 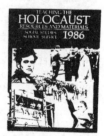

FACES -- Magazine of world culture from the publishers of Cobblestone History Magazine and the American Museum of Natural History, for age 10 up. Societies and individuals around the world, how they live, their customs, prejudices, fears, and beliefs. Each issue centers on one theme -- Asante World, Becoming Human, Coming of Age, Hands, Migration, etc. -- with articles, puzzles, recipes, maps, and photo essays. 1 year (9 issues), $17.95. Back issues available. COBBLESTONE PUBLISHING, INC., 30 Grove Street, Peterborough, NH 03458. (See also History, "Cobblestone" and "Calliope.")

PENPALS -- THE INTERNATIONAL FRIENDSHIP LEAGUE, 22 Batterymarch St., Boston, MA 02109. Penpal exchange, operating in more than 100 countries. Write for application.

SOCIAL STUDIES SCHOOL SERVICE, Box 802, Culver City, CA 90230. Several catalogs of school materials in nearly every field. The best single source for books and other materials about human rights, global education, social studies, history, and many other subjects, from scores of publishers. (Many titles reflect current trends in laissez faire morality, so choose carefully). Very reasonable prices. Ask for one copy each of all catalogs. Use a letterhead, if possible.

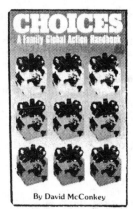

THE GLOBAL ECOLOGY HANDBOOK, by The Global Tomorrow Coalition. Every day we become more aware of the destruction of our natural environment. We are also gradually realizing that our national problems can't be solved apart from the problems of the world as a whole. This book documents the current state of the world and gives information about the many groups & individuals working toward solutions to the problems -- population growth, waste, tropical forests, air & water pollution, energy, species extinction, etc.-- and offers concrete suggestions for making our own lifestyles less destructive to the earth, along with names and addresses of specific interest groups, and a list of books for further reading. 240 pages, photographs. $12.95. Code HR. BROOK FARM BOOKS.

INVEST YOURSELF, a catalogue of volunteer opportunities from The Commission on Voluntary Service & Action (CVSA). Photos, articles, and listings of more than 40,000 opportunities for summer and full-time volunteers throughout North America and the world in a very broad range of programs -- working with the aged; agriculture; arts, drama, and recreation; children and youth; community service; construction and trades; counseling; teaching; environment and natural science; health care; legal; mentally or physically handicapped; religious service; organizing; and more. Most programs provide room and board; some also give a small spending allowance. Some provide transportation cost to and from the volunteer's home. A great way to travel, learn, and help others, for a few months, a few years, or a lifetime. $7.50 ppd. from CVSA, P.O. Box 117, New York, NY 10009.

CHOICES: A Family Global Action Handbook, by David McConkey. Thought-provoking articles, ideas, and practical suggestions to help families live and work in ways that promote global peace and understanding; peaceful parenting, nonviolent conflict resolution. Very good, very useful. $5 plus $1 postage. THE MARQUIS PROJECT, 107 7th St. #200, Brandon, Manitoba R7A 3S5, Canada.

GLOBAL THOUGHTS, LOCAL ACTIONS, by David McConkey. What can we, as individuals, do in our daily lives to improve conditions and relationships around the world? David McConkey is a homeschooler and is active in international development education. What we do -- or don't do -- can make a difference, and David gives scores of practical suggestions to show how we can contribute to a better world without leaving home. Although written primarily for adults, this book is suitable for high school students, and for discussion ideas in helping younger children gain global awareness. $4.50 postpaid from THE MARQUIS PROJECT, 220 8th St., Brandon, Manitoba, Canada R7A 3X3.

TRANET, "a quarterly newsletter-directory of, by, and for people who are changing the world by changing their own lives -- people who are adopting alternative technologies." TRANET, not quite an acronym, is derived from "Transnational Network for Appropriate/Alternative Technologies." (Readers will recognize "appropriate technology" as the concept explored by E. F. Schumacher in SMALL IS BEAUTIFUL, which refers to the development of technology appropriate to the region in which it is being used; i.e., on a scale within the limits of the resources it has. The idea is repugnant to the big corporation that want to tear down Paradise to put in a parking lot.) TRANET carries brief news items, announcements, book and product reviews, lists of resources (including homeschooling), legal advances and setbacks, etc., from all over the world. Categories include Food & Agriculture, Environment & Resources, Housing & Habitat, Water & Sanitation, Health Care, Technology, Energy, Communications, Transportation, Economics, Green Politics, Law, Family, Philosophy & Religion, Youth and Learning, and Cultural Tourism. Individual subscription, $30 (which also pays for a subscription to someone in the Third World). Make check payable to: TRANET, P.O. Box 567, Rangeley, ME 04970.

SMALL ENERGY SOURCES: Choices That Work, by Augusta Goldin. Zeroing in on the abundant potential of small, renewable energy sources, this book points the way to an abundant and affordable global supply of energy. Ages 12 and up. Hardcover, 176 pages. $17.95. Code HBJ. BROOK FARM BOOKS.

TREES -- "One tree has the cooling effect of five air conditioners... One acre of growing trees will scrub clean the air polluted by eight automobiles operated for twelve hours." (From The Washington Spectator, quoting the Maryland Forest Service.)

With greatly increased offensive and defensive preparations the United States could hold casualties in a nuclear war to 20 million, a level compatible with survival and recovery.

Colin Gray
State Department consultant

NUCLEAR WAR EDUCATION-- Write to these organizations for information about programs and materials for teaching about nuclear war, probable consequences, & what can be done to avoid it. Not meant to be scary, but to offer practical ways of dealing with present-day realities.

EDUCATORS FOR SOCIAL RESPONSIBILITY, 639 Massachusetts Avenue, Cambridge, MA 02139.

JOBS FOR PEACE TASK FORCE, Room 111, 77 Summer Street, Boston, MA 02110.

NATIONAL EDUCATION ASSOCIATION, Professional Library, P.O.Box 509, West Haven, CT 06516.

CALIFORNIA FEDERATION OF TEACHERS, 2412 West Magnolia Blvd., Burbank, CA 91506.

ORGANIZATIONS FOR PEACE: These are a few of the organizations which oppose war and actively work for nonviolent alternatives, both on a personal level and a global level. Most of these groups have religious motivation, but are non-denominational & non-doctrinal. Most of them publish newsletters or other periodicals & books, which will be valuable springboards for family discussions, even if you don't always agree with their views.

AMERICAN FRIENDS SERVICE COMMITTEE, 1501 Cherry St., Philadelphia, PA 19102.

CATHOLIC PEACE FELLOWSHIP, 339 Lafayette St., New York, NY 10012.

CCCO: An Agency for Military and Draft Counseling, 2208 South St., Philadelphia, PA 19146.

FELLOWSHIP OF RECONCILIATION, Box 271, Nyack, NY 10960.

MENNONITE CENTRAL COMMITTEE, 21 South 12th St., Akron, PA 17501.

PEACEMAKERS, P.O. Box 627, Garberville, CA 95440.

SOUTHERN CHRISTIAN LEADERSHIP CONFERENCE, 334 Auburn Avenue NE, Atlanta, GA 303030.

WAR RESISTERS LEAGUE, 339 Lafayette St., New York, NY 10012.

VETERANS FOR PEACE, INC., P.O. Box 3881, Portland, ME 04104. The Washington Spectator reported 4/15/90 that this is the fastest-growing veterans' organization in the U.S. Its president is retired Marine Corps Col. John Barr, who says, "There is a myth that military personnel are war lovers; in 30 years of service, I met no one who was genuinely fond of war." The aims of Veterans for Peace are to increase public knowledge of the human costs of war, restrain the government from military intervention abroad, end the arms race, and eliminate war as an instrument of foreign policy.

HANDBOOK FOR CONSCIENTIOUS OBJECTORS, Robert A. Seeley. Clearly answers questions about CO status, preparing CO claims, draft registration, methods of resisting registration, & alternative service (civilian or non-combatant). The definitive guide to draft regulations, war resistance in various forms, and the court system. Excellent not only for those facing decisions about registration, but also for anyone concerned about the military's role in today's society. 218 pages. $3.00 plus $1 postage. WAR RESISTERS LEAGUE, 339 Lafayette Street, New York, NY 10012.

"CONFLICT: What's It All About?" Wall poster, featuring a gallery of photos which will stimulate discussion of many varieties of conflict, from sports to war, strikes to classroom disputes. On the other side, "Peace Challenge," a board game which gives young children a chance to practice peace-making skills. Simple but provocative, even for older kids; younger kids (5-10) may get the most from it. $2.20 postpaid. PITMAN LEARNING, INC., P.O.Box 2031, Clinton, IA 52735.

"A DAY OF DIALOGUE," planning and resource guide for teachers who want to introduce discussion of nuclear issues. $10.00. EDUCATORS FOR SOCIAL RESPONSIBILITY, 639 Massachusetts Ave., Cambridge, MA 02139.

CHOICES: A UNIT ON CONFLICT AND NUCLEAR WAR -- $9.95 from THE NATIONAL EDUCATION ASSOCIATION, Professional Library, P.O. Box 509, West Haven, CT 06516.

AIN'T GONNA STUDY WAR NO MORE, by Milton Meltzer. Well-documented stories of individuals and groups who have risked reputation, livelihood, and even life to protest war and violence. From the Colonial Wars and the American Revolution to the Vietnam War and the peace movement of the 1980s, the book tells the experiences and often severe consequences of following conscience rather than civil authority. Grades 4 and up. $12.95. Code HR. BROOK FARM BOOKS.

The pioneers of a warless world are the young men who refuse military service.

Albert Einstein

40,000 AMERICAN SOLDIERS DIED in Vietnam during ten years of war. In the poor countries of the world, 40,000 children under the age of 5 die of malnutrition, dehydration, or disease <u>every day</u>. Our family lives very simply, usually on the edge of poverty by North American standards, but we are healthy, educated, well-fed, and live in a comfortable home. We are never so poor that we cannot send at least a small financial token to UNICEF, the United Nations Children's Fund, which is trying to combat the economic, cultural, political, and natural enemies of these children. During UNICEF's annual Halloween campaign, we place collection boxes in local stores and the public library. We put UNICEF posters in store windows, and write letters about UNICEF to the local papers. We hang a collection box on our dining room wall and put odd pieces of change into it whenever we pass, and then add our own small donation to those we collect, and mail a check to UNICEF, wishing we could do much more. The largest killer of children is simply dehydration caused by severe diarrhea; but a simple packet of oral rehydration salts can save the life of a child just hours from death. Two hundred children's lives can be saved by a donation of only $20.00. Enough measles vaccine to save 235 children's lives costs only $35.00. We can't think of a better use for our money -- or a better way to go trick-or-treating at Halloween. For information on how your family can help in similar ways, at Halloween or anytime, write: United States Committee for UNICEF, 333 East 38th St., New York, NY 10016.

The greatest evil today is <u>indifference</u>. To know and not to act is a way of consenting to these injustices. The planet has become a very small place. What happens in other countries affects us.

Elie Wiesel

"TEACHABLE MOMENTS," 2-page teaching guides mailed biweekly during the school year, exploring hunger, poverty, competition, gender roles, etc., around the world. FREE. THE STANLEY FOUNDATION, 420 E. Third St., Muscatine, IA 52761.

PULLING TOGETHER: A Program for America in the United Nations. 71-page 1988 report from the United Nations Association of the United States, suggesting an agenda for multinational actions in health, environment, arms control, etc. $7.50. Or send for the "Pulling Together" Brochure, a 16-page brochure summarizing the report; 50¢. UNA PUBLICATIONS DEPT., 485 Fifth Ave. 2nd Floor, New York, NY 10017.

FAMILY ACTION TOWARD PEACE AND UNDERSTANDING. Ecumenical and interfaith organization offering several services and publications throughout the U.S. and Canada. Send a #10 SASE to: PARENTING FOR PEACE AND JUSTICE NETWORK, Institute for Peace and Justice, 4144 Lindell Blvd., Room 122, St. Louis, MO 63108.

AMNESTY INTERNATIONAL -- A worldwide organization, independent of any government, political group, ideology, economic interest, or religious creed, which seeks the release of men and women detained in prison anywhere for their beliefs, color, sex, ethnic origin, language or religion, provided they have neither used nor advocated violence. Amnesty International advocates fair and early trials for all political prisoners; it opposes the death penalty and torture or other cruel or degrading treatment of all prisoners. It acts on the basis of the United Nations Universal Declaration of Human Rights & other international instruments. Members are asked to contribute modestly to help support AI, and to participate in several supportive activities, including letter writing in support of prisoners of conscience, which has been found to be very effective in helping to gain the release of hundreds of prisoners around the world. Home-schooling families may find that participation in Amnesty International is a rewarding way to contribute to human rights around the world. We can't afford large donations to the various organizations which we believe are helping to keep the world alive and somewhat sane, but writing three or four letters each month doesn't take much time or effort, and really does make a significant difference. Write for information to: AMNESTY INTERNATIONAL USA, 304 West 58th St., New York, NY 10019 or AMNESTY INTERNATIONAL, 294 Albert St., Suite 204, Ottawa, Ontario K1P 6E6.

In Germany they first came for the Communists and I didn't speak up because I wasn't a communist. Then they came for the Jews, and I didn't speak up because I wasn't a Jew. Then they came for the trade unionists, and I didn't speak up because I wasn't a trade unionist. Then they came for the Catholics, and I didn't speak up because I was a Protestant. Then they came for me -- and by that time no one was left to speak up.

Pastor Martin Niemoller

INTERNATIONAL WORKCAMPS -- Work and travel in 36 countries in Western and Eastern Europe, North and Central America, and North West Africa, living in small "family" groups of 10 to 20 people from at least four different countries, participating in two- or three-week construction, restoration, environmental, social, agricultural, & maintenance workcamps. Anyone age 18 and older may participate; there are limited openings for ages 15-18. Volunteers frequently register for multiple workcamps in the same or neighboring countries, to extend the experience. Volunteers contribute $75-$90 per workcamp, and pay for their own transportation to the workcamp site. All meals and accommodation are provided by workcamp hosts. All participating organizations are sanctioned by the United Nations. Although some foreign language may be desirable, none is required. Write for a free copy of "The International Workcamper," the annual newsletter of VOLUNTEERS FOR PEACE, Tiffany Road, Belmont, VT 05730. The newsletter contains much more information, and a listing of other publications, including detailed lists of workcamps and programs.

CHANGE JOBS, CHANGE THE WORLD. "Community Jobs," monthly publication listing hundreds of jobs and internships in socially responsible organizations across the country, in peace and justice work, environment, women's issues, social service, alternative media, more. Jobs available; duties, requirements; how to apply. 12 issues, $15; 6 issues, $12. COMMUNITY JOBS, 1516 P St. NW, Washington, DC 20005.

INTERNATIONAL EXCHANGE STUDENTS-- Live with a family in another country for 10 months or invite a student from another country to your home for 10 months. 23 countries on 5 continents participate. This program seems to be aimed at families of students in conventional schooling situations, but homeschoolers might qualify. For more information, write to: EDUCATIONAL FOUNDATION FOR FOREIGN STUDY, One Memorial Dr., Cambridge, MA 02142 or EF FOUNDATION, 1425 Chapala St., Santa Barbara, CA 93101.

RAIN: Journal of Appropriate Technology, 2270 NW Irving, Portland, OR 97210.

PEACE LINKS, 747 Eighth St.SE, Washington, DC 20003. Kit of ideas and materials for children up to 10 years old about peace; 5-day lesson plan using books, games, songs, & art; plan a Peace Day; plant a pine tree for peace; booklet. $4.00.

NEW SOCIETY PUBLISHERS, P.O. Box 582, Santa Cruz, CA 95061. Non-profit publisher of select titles about peace, environmental studies (and cures), human rights, third world, etc. Many books for all ages. Not left-wing rabble-rousers, but considered studies and proposals for working with present-day problems for a better tomorrow. Catalog.

THE LORDS OF THE GLOBAL VILLAGE, Ben H. Bagdikian. This lead article in a special issue of The Nation assesses the alarming growth of the communications corporation, the shrinking of the media universe, and the consequent threat to freedom and diversity in global news, information, and culture. Meet a gallery of media barons such as Rupert Murdoch and Reinhard Mohn, who amass, homogenize, dominate, and devour media corporations around the world. "A handful of mammoth private organizations have begun to dominate the world's mass media," says the article. "Most of them confidently announce that...they -- five to ten corporate giants -- will control most of the world's important newspapers, magazines, books, broadcast stations, movies, recordings, and videocassettes. Moreover, each of these planetary corporations plans to gather under its control every step in the information process, from creation of 'the product' to all the various means by which modern technology delivers media messages to the public -- news, information, ideas, entertainment, and public culture..." Very scary and thought-provoking. Essential reading if you're concerned about freedom of communication and ideas. Order by title. $3.00 postpaid. NATION REPRINTS, 72 Fifth Avenue, New York, NY 10011.

> The path of civilization is paved with tin cans.
> Elbert Hubbard

"THE RIGHT TO KNOW," list of resources related to global issues, FREE. CALIFORNIA FEDERATION OF TEACHERS, 2412 W. Magnolia Blvd., Burbank, CA 91506.

FAMILY SPIRIT, P.O. Box 82503, Albuquerque, NM 87198. Quarterly. "For parents interested in developing a peaceful humanity and fostering the family as an integral part of world peace. The journal provides a forum to inspire and support parents in the noble work of raising children as spiritual beings." 4 issues, $14.00. Sample, $4.00.

SOVIET LIFE MAGAZINE, P.O. Box 578, Fredericksburg, VA 22404. Beautiful photographs and informative articles about the more than 100 different nationalities living in the Soviet Union -- artists, doctors, farmers, scientists, dancers, sailors, cosmonauts; theater, circus, opera, comedy; landmarks, shrines. Introductory offer, $15/12 issues (regular $27).

If a thousand... were not to pay their tax bills this year, that would not be a violent and bloody measure, as it would be to pay them, and enable the State to commit violence and shed innocent blood. This is, in fact, the definition of a peaceable revolution.

Henry David Thoreau

THE POWER OF NONVIOLENCE, Richard B. Gregg. This book, first published in 1935, revised and expanded in 1966, continues to be a modern classic on the subject; not so much about the tactic of nonviolence (which is often accompanied by great psychological violence; e.g., when used to coerce one's opponent through feelings of guilt, etc.) but about the nonviolent spirit, true feelings of love & brotherhood which really can influence others (and oneself) in a positive way. I've heard students of social action say, "Let's go do some civil disobedience," as if its primary purpose were to get in someone's way and be arrested for it. Their use of "nonviolence" is very violent psychologically, and shows a complete misunderstanding of the principles of nonviolence. This book might help. $7.50 + $1.50 shipping. WAR RESISTERS LEAGUE, 339 Lafayette Street, New York, NY 10012.

PEACE AND WAR BOOKS -- Many titles about disarmament and the nuclear threat, draft resistance, conscientious objection, ecology & the environment, Gandhi, the Middle East, Latin America, militarism, pacifism and nonviolent action, prisons and capital punishment, socialism and philosophical anarchism, Third World, and more. GROWING UP ABSURD, by Paul Goodman; HUMAN SCALE, by Kirkpatrick Sale; HANDBOOK FOR CONSCIENTIOUS OBJECTORS (the definitive resource on draft regulations); many more, including some super-leftist and/or feminist and/or "gay" manifestoes which I mostly ignore. Send for general information and a literature list. You'll be invited to join and to donate money, but you don't need to be a member to order books. WAR RESISTERS LEAGUE, 339 Lafayette Street, New York, NY 10012.

Nobody made a greater mistake than he who did nothing because he could only do a little.

Edmund Burke

WRITINGS ON CIVIL DISOBEDIENCE AND NONVIOLENCE, by Leo Tolstoy. A collection of Tolstoy's major writings on conscience, with the main premise that peace begins only with the individual's refusal to participate in state-organized killing, and that we must seek ways to end our moral complicity and cooperation with the economic, social, and political processes which lead to war. Foreword by George Zbelka, the military chaplain who became a pacifist after blessing the pilots of the planes which dropped atomic bombs on Hiroshima and Nagasaki. $12.95 plus $1.50 shipping. BROOK FARM BOOKS.

HUMAN SCALE, Kirkpatrick Sale. Schools, factories, businesses, and governments get out of hand when they are no longer scaled to humans -- that is, when they become so big that humans become less important than the institutions which were intended to serve them. This is a thoroughly documented study of where and why things go wrong in nearly every facet of society, and what could be done about it. The chapter on education may be of particular interest to homeschoolers, although the entire book is fascinating, horrifying, and -- if we're smart enough -- hopeful. $5.00 plus $1 shipping. Order from WAR RESISTERS LEAGUE, 339 Lafayette St., New York, NY 10012.

CIA WARFARE MANUAL: Operaciones Sicologicas en Guerra de Guerrillas (Psychological Operations in Guerrilla Warfare). This little 48-page book (published, ironically, in 1984), tells a little of how we good guys preserve the world from the bad guys. It was prepared by the CIA for use by the Nicaraguan contras, and offers enough directions in psychological manipulation, "selective murders," and "implicit terror" to help you put down any democratic revolution in your own neighborhood. $3.50 plus $1 postage. Don't order it from the CIA unless you live in Latin America. Order from: WAR RESISTERS LEAGUE, 339 Lafayette Street, New York, NY 10012.

HANDGUNS, The number of people killed by, in 1985:
Great Britain, 8
Sweden, 21
Switzerland, 34
West Germany, 42
Japan, 48
Canada, 52
Israel, 58
United States, 10,728

LAWYERS COMMITTEE FOR HUMAN RIGHTS, 330 7th Avenue, New York, NY 10001. Publisher of books and reports about human rights conditions and systems of justice around the world; immigration training manuals used by private attorneys and law clinics; reports & manuals for people seeking political asylum. Catalog.

AKWESASNE NOTES, Mohawk Nation, via Rooseveltown, NY 13683. This official publication of the Mohawk Nation at Kanawake has informative & intriguing news, articles, letters, & editorials by and about Indians of today. When writing for subscription information, ask also about Akwesasne Notes Posters & the Native American Calendar.

The conquest of the earth, which mostly means the taking it away from those who have a different complexion or slightly flatter noses than ourselves, is not a pretty thing when you look into it.

Joseph Conrad

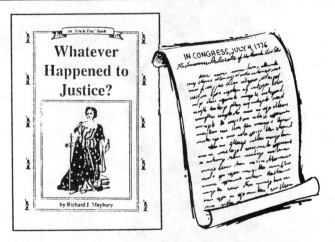

THE KID'S GUIDE TO SOCIAL ACTION, by Barbara A. Lewis. "How to solve the social problems you choose -- and turn creative thinking into positive action." Here's everything kids need to take social action: step-by-step directions for letter-writing, interviewing, speechmaking, fund-raising, media coverage, and more; petitions, proclamations, and news releases; addresses and phone numbers for government offices, other social action groups, and awards programs; and inspiring true stories about real kids accomplishing great things. This is the most comprehensive guide available for kids who want to make a difference in the world, written by a teacher whose own students' efforts have resulted in the cleanup of a hazardous waste site and the passage of two new laws. Ages 12 and up. 208 pages, paperback, with black-and-white photos and illustrations. $14.95. Code FS. BROOK FARM BOOKS.

WHATEVER HAPPENED TO JUSTICE? by Richard J. Maybury. A brief but clear and comprehensive examination of the ways in which the concept of "law" has changed from that of America's Founders, who believed, says the author, that "all proposed legislation must be measured against the principles of Higher Law." Age 12 up; adults, too, will find it very interesting and informative. $14.95 plus $2 postage. BLUESTOCKING PRESS, P.O. Box 1014, Placerville, CA 95667.

※ ▨ ◉ ❀ ✳

IN A NUTSHELL-- "Omit needless words," is one of the rules for clear writing in Strunk and White's THE ELEMENTS OF STYLE. The Lord's Prayer has 56 words. The Gettysburg Address has 266 words. The Ten Commandments have 297 words. The Declaration of Independence has 300 words. A U.S. Government directive on setting the price of cabbage has 29,611 words.

PLEASE– *DON'T* COLOR MY WORLD

Fools rush in where angels fear to tread.
     --Alexander Pope.

"But the emperor has no clothes!" the little boy cried.

     --Hans Christian Anderson

I find it interesting, but not alarming, that a Jewish home-school group and a Muslim home-school group are included in a published list of groups which excludes all "exclusivist" Christian groups -- that is, which accept as members only those who profess certain religious tenets. There are also Catholic and Mormon groups, presumably (although I don't know why) not so exclusivist as the Protestants.

In case you're qualified to join one of these, and because I haven't listed them elsewhere, they are:

JEWISH HOME EDUCATOR'S NETWORK, 2 Webb Road, Sharon, MA 02067

ISLAMIC HOMESCHOOL ASSOCIATION OF NORTH AMERICA, 1312 Plymouth Court, Raleigh, NC 27610;

NATIONAL ASSOCIATION OF CATHOLIC HOME EDUCATORS, P.O. Box 420225, San Diego, CA 94142; and

NATIONAL ASSOCIATION FOR MORMON HOME EDUCATORS, 2770 S. 1000 West, Perry, UT 84302.

Interesting, because it seems inconsistent; but I'm frequently inconsistent, too, so I don't mind allowing others the same privilege. Not alarming, because the fundamentalist Christians have their own national network, and are in no danger of being unnoticed by anyone who is qualified to join. It seems to be true that birds of a feather flock together, but I think it's a narrow way of thinking when the "feather" is a particular religious belief; however, I don't think these groups pose any threat to other home-schoolers -- certainly not to me -- so I don't find their existence any more alarming than their presence on a list which excludes other exclusivist groups.

I am very alarmed, however, by a different kind of exclusivist thinking which is growing rapidly, not only in general society, but also within the home-school movement: racism.

I would be among the very first to denounce any "all-white" home-school group or publication, and I don't see any difference between that and an "all non-white" group or publication.

UMOJA-UNIDAD-UNITED (5621 S Lakeshore Drive, Idlewild, MI 49642) is "A Newsletter for Homeschoolers of Color," and invites as subscribers "both Latina/o and Black homeschoolers... and anyone else out there who identifies themselves as a person/family of color, regardless of nationality, percentage of color, language, religion, or any of the other factors that sometimes keep us apart." Unless you're white, that is, with no "percentage of color."

THE DRINKING GOURD (P.O. Box 2557, Redmond, WA 98073) is a "Multicultural Home Education Magazine" that focuses "on the issues and concerns of People of color -- Black, Latino/a, Indian, Asian American and anyone else who identifies themselves or their families to be 'of color.'"

An advertisement for UMOJA-UNIDAD-UNITY says it was started "because we, as homeschoolers of color, have often felt isolated from and ignored by the larger home schooling community."

The editor of THE DRINKING GOURD wrote to HOME EDUCATION MAGAZINE that, "It is time we created our own theories on the development of our children, for they are not like everybody else's children." (And is her magazine's sub-title, "The Multicultural Home Education Magazine," meant to imply that Mark and Helen Hegener's magazine is _not_ multi-cultural?)

To the best of my knowledge, I have no "percentage of color" -- but I have known several blacks, two of whom were very close friends; and I have visited the Hopi village of Hotevilla in Arizona for several days, and I have taught blacks and Indians (along with whites) to read and write English, and Mexicans to read and write Spanish (although I am far from fluent in the language), and was once a librarian with an Indian assistant. I have known people of many races and ethnic backgrounds, in a variety of circumstances, and have gotten to know them all fairly well. We were not "colored" and "white" to each other, but just _people_. We all laughed and cried and bled in the same color, and I absolutely do not believe that their children "are not like everybody else's children."

In saying "our children," the editor means all children "of color," as distinguished from children who are white. In other words, she is saying that the needs and concerns of children "of color" are different from the needs and concerns of white children. Turn it around, and you have the bigoted argument with which white supremacists have justified their actions for centuries -- that "colored" people don't have the same needs and concerns that white people have.

APRICOT

MAHOGANY

Have you seen Crayola's new "multicultural" crayons, pencils, modeling clay, and washable paints and markers? Apricot, burnt sienna, mahogany, peach, sepia, tan, plus black and white for blending -- "to help build skills and self-esteem," say the ads.

Of course, it's nicer to talk about "culture" than "race," but you won't convince me that those colors refer to culture. They refer to skin color, which is one of the factors often differentiating races. There is no such thing as a "black culture" or "red culture" -- or "apricot" or "mahogany culture" -- any more than there is a "white culture." All races have had as many differences among themselves as with each other. Some people of each race have built castles or pyramids while others of the same race were building mud huts.

I'm not against the skin-colored crayons. In fact, I think they're a good idea. I remember the frustration of trying to find a good skin-colored crayon -- my skin, that is, or so-called "white" -- when I was a kid. Light pink didn't work, and white was anemic albino. The larger crayon sets had "flesh," which was closest -- but why, even then, didn't they just call it "skin"?

Maybe the people "of color" want to think their needs are different because it was the white Europeans who enslaved or slaughtered their ancestors (and to some extent are still doing so, either literally or symbolically), but the Europeans were not alone in their guilt. Quite often they didn't even have to leave their ships to kidnap a cargo of Africans -- because the people of some tribes were quite happy to sell the people of other tribes once they realized it was more profitable than enslaving them or eating them. Africans had been enslaving each other long before the whites came along to buy slaves, just as earlier Europeans had enslaved each other, and just as many American Indians enslaved those of other tribes. The sins and crimes of white Europeans have been truly terrible, but they are not unique. With the possible exception of the Hopis and the Kalahari bushmen, there has probably been no society in human history that hasn't practiced its own full quota of atrocities on someone.

The Chinese invented gunpowder, but the Europeans discovered how effective it was in killing people -- just other Europeans, at first, but eventually it proved to be just as effective when used on blacks, reds, browns, and other non-whites. I don't think history would have been much different if the power of gunpowder had been discovered first by people of some other race; only the names (and colors) would be changed.

While we're remembering unpleasant facts, let's not forget that some of the rich and powerful plantation owners in the antebellum Southern states were free blacks, who bought and sold other blacks at the same auctions attended by the whites. The bad guys haven't always been white.

White Europeans and their descendants have certainly wreaked havoc around the world, but they have also produced some of the world's greatest philosophies, scientific advances, and humanitarian impulses -- including the American ideals of "life, liberty, and the pursuit of happiness" for all people; and the premise that "all men are created equal."

Because those ideals have been only partially realized is certainly no reason to discard them and revert to ethnic tribalism. We have made greater advances toward achieving them in the last two decades than in the previous two centuries. Newsletters and organizations exclusively for people "of color" threaten to undermine all the advances which were begun by Rosa Parks and Martin Luther King, Jr, just as surely as a "whites-only" policy would. They are not "celebrating diversity," as they claim, but merely emphasizing racial differences and turning their backs on the greater similarities of people, regardless of race.

This is not multi-culturism, but racial tribalism, which has been around since before people climbed out of trees to live in caves. It probably began when Og and his mate Ooga discovered that a single mastodon wasn't enough to feed their entire village and all the people from the next valley, too. Homo wasn't very sapiens then, so Og said, "I know, let's just feed the people who look like us." Ooga said, "That's logical," and they began throwing rocks at the people with different hair, eyes, clothing, and skin color.

Only recently, at least ten thousand years later, have we begun to find ways of living without throwing rocks at each other, and now some of those who have been stoned the most want to revive the attitudes that led to the rock-throwing in the first place.

We don't have to be identical to communicate with each other, nor do we need to have the same skin color to understand each other. Both magazines say the needs of people "of color" have not been met by other home-school publications. I have read copies of both magazines very carefully, trying -- without success -- to learn exactly what those different needs are. The editor of THE DRINKING GOURD said in her letter to HOME EDUCATION MAGAZINE (using "she" as the new generic pronoun), "...when you deny a person her ethnicity, you are removing her reason to survive, and helping to create a goal of self destruction. Once the person loses herself... her family will not matter, her body will not matter, and her soul will be denied."

"Denying" her ethnicity? "Denying" her <u>soul</u>?

Come, now. Just because North American society doesn't revolve around the cultures of ancient Africa or China or pre-Columbian America doesn't mean that people whose ancestors lived there are being denied the right to identify with any ethnicity they choose. Not many have had the advantage of an Alex Haley to trace their roots for them, so it really is a choice, and the choices must often be fairly general and made at random. Africa is a very large continent, and the people who lived there before the whites arrived were just as diversified in their cultures -- not to mention many aspects of stature and physiognomy -- as European whites were. After so many centuries, so much intermingling of various tribes, so much interracial mixing, how does one decide which ancestors to claim?

I think M. B. Tolson had at least part of the best answer: "I, as a black poet, have absorbed the Great Ideas of the Great White World, and interpreted them in the melting-pot idiom of my people. <u>My roots are in Africa, Europe, and America.</u>"

Having grown up in the United States, but living now in Canada, Jean and I still prefer to celebrate the American Thanksgiving in November rather than the Canadian Thanksgiving in mid-October. We still "feel" American, and continue to identify more with American history and heritage than Canadian. Our Canadian neighbors don't share our preferences, or several other family and cultural traditions which we have, but that doesn't mean they are trying in any way to deny our ethnicity, nor do they think we are interfering with theirs. We accept each other and get along well. Occasionally, we compare some of the differences in our backgrounds, but our similarities -- working for a living, raising a family, trying to stay sane and healthy in an increasingly complex world -- are far more important than our differences.

UMOJA-UNIDAD-UNITY and THE DRINKING GOURD seem to be saying, as are people "of color" throughout society, that if the prevalent histories and popular culture don't reflect <u>their</u> roots and viewpoints,

then their ethnicity is being denied. To a large extent, this has certainly been true in the past, but modern society had begun rectifying the injustice even before the current fad of decrying the absence in history books (and in literature in general) of blacks, Indians, Hispanics, women, and other minority groups. (I've always assumed that women comprised about half of the world's population, give or take a few thousand, but lately many of them seem to feel they're in a minority, a large percentage of which are Black Belts in karate, so who am I to argue? You open a door for one of them and get a thumb in the eye for your trouble.)

The victors usually write the histories, along with their own rationalizations and self-justifications, which certainly promotes a certain degree of inaccuracy, but I doubt that the history books would be any more objective or accurate if they were written by the vanquished.

Most North American history in the last four hundred years has involved descendants of Western Europeans more than people from other places around the world, so it seems natural, even if not "right," for history to have been written from their viewpoint.

The treatment by the whites of the blacks, browns, reds, and yellows has certainly been despicable, but it's still a fact, whether "right" or "wrong," that the whites have usually been pretty much in charge of things. Scores of minorities, religious and philosophical as well as racial and cultural (and even including many with various sexual aberrations), want the history books re-written from <u>their</u> viewpoints, and insist that books not written from their viewpoints are discriminatory and racist. The societies of Canada and the United States have become much more diverse, racially and ethnically, but their legal and cultural backgrounds are still mostly derived from Western Europe, so most of the histories will probably continue to be written from that viewpoint, although many recent publications have made a serious effort to include experiences and viewpoints of the minorities.

The changes aren't being made fast enough to suit the minorities, however, so they're writing their own history books -- but instead of writing new histories with a more-balanced picture of life as it

really was, with a sincere attempt at objectivity, they're writing specialized black, red, Hispanic, and women's histories, to be studied separately, or even exclusively. Black students may now choose to study black history only -- which may help them know and appreciate their own ancestral heritage, but will hardly give them a realistic picture of their actual roles in world history.

Women study women; Indians study Indians; and so on. Each special-interest group thinks it is studying the hub of history, rather than an important but rather small spoke.

Our history books should include the many achievements -- in the arts, politics, science, sports, music, education, etc. -- of minority peoples who have been skipped in most history books of the past, but without emphasis, or even undue mention, of the color or race of the achiever unless it was a significant factor in the achievement. It's significant that Jackie Robinson was the first black player in Major League baseball, but the race or color of players since then has been much less significant. To concentrate exclusively on the achievements of any special interest group -- as in Black History Month -- is even more false and deceptive than the abridged histories which have been in use. Studying any subject out of context greatly reduces its meaning. Such "studies" are often intended to increase the "self-esteem" of the minority peoples who have been too much ignored -- but anyone whose self-esteem is dependent on being submerged in a larger entity, whether it's a race, a nation, a religion, or a place of birth, needs a different kind of therapy than fictional history will give.

I don't need to wear my hair as my ancestors did, or worship the same gods or dance around the same fires, to know that I have a place in the universe. It pleases me to know that I had two ancestors who fought in the Civil War and five ancestors on the Mayflower, but that knowledge isn't a matter of "pride" for me anymore than the hanging of another ancestor as a horse-thief is a matter of shame. My ancestors came from Europe, but I don't consider myself a "European-American"; simply "American."

If the term "Afro-American" is used to identify blacks, what do we call a white person whose ances-

tors lived in Africa? Some American Indians -- Native Americans -- referred to blacks as "black white men," because they seemed so much alike except in skin color.

As more and more students study only fragments of history, based on their own race, nationality, religion, or gender, the more society becomes like scattered pieces of several jigsaw puzzles, growing steadily away from the American ideal of a cultural "melting pot" or the Canadian ideal of a cultural "mosaic." It will take more than all the king's horses and all the king's men to put the pieces together again.

Separating into groups based on race or religion won't put the pieces together again, either.

I fully realize that racial minorities have problems with poverty, education, and health which much of the white population doesn't have -- but those problems will never be solved by a renewed emphasis on racial and cultural differences. It was exactly that kind of paranoia and exclusionary thinking -- on the part of many races and cultures -- which led to the problems in the first place.

If "people of color" really want to be included in the larger home-school community, they certainly won't achieve it by withdrawing into self-conscious shells, or by wearing placards proclaiming, "We're different" and "Nobody understands us." They'll achieve it, and be warmly welcomed, when they realize that we are all different in many ways, but the goals and values which we, as parents and as homeschoolers, have in common -- happy, well-educated children -- are far more important than superficial differences such as skin color or racial origins.

FREE (OR ALMOST FREE) TEACHING & LEARNING AIDS

Scores of educational items free or almost free, just for the cost of a postcard, a postage stamp and an envelope, or sometimes a small fee. Suggestions: Be reasonable; don't request items you don't really want or need; when possible, be specific in your requests. Although many of the following items are not necessarily intended for school use, it will often be helpful if you mention the age or grade level for which the material is intended. Many items can be requested on a postcard; others should be requested in letters written in standard business form, by the teacher (not the students), preferably on a school letterhead. Usually, you can tell by the item listed which form of request will be appropriate. If an SASE (self-addressed, stamped envelope) is requested, be sure to include it; a #10 (business size) envelope is usually best.

I have tried to be sure that all offers are current and that the sources and other information are correct, but I can't guarantee either. Offers and prices change; companies move or, occasionally, go

out of business. If an offer has been withdrawn, usually the company will send or offer another in its place. For all items no longer offered, and for all requests returned to you as "not forwardable," I apologize.

The following sample letter is a good model, to be adapted to your own particular situation:

> (Address)
> (Date)
>
> National Society for the
>   Prevention of Blindness
> 79 Madison Avenue
> New York, NY 10016
>   Dear Sir or Madam:
>   My sixth grade health class is studying the care and anatomy of the human eye. I would like to request your HOME EYE TEST, and a list of any other charts or publications which you feel would be of interest to us.
>   Thank you very much for your assistance.
>   Sincerely yours,
>   (Mrs.) Jean Reed

NOTE: All the following items are completely FREE unless otherwise noted -- i.e., a small charge (usually less than $2), or SASE, or other requirement).

SOURCE DIRECTORY OF INDIAN, ESKIMO, AND ALEUT ARTS AND CRAFTS BUSINESSES. Indian Arts and Crafts Board, U.S. Dept. of the Interior, Washington, DC 20240.

INDIAN INFORMATION PACKAGE. U.S. Dept. of the Interior, Bureau of Indian Affairs, Washington, DC 20242.

"ABOUT INDIANS" catalog of 1450 books about Indians, with descriptions, full-color reproductions of native art work. Department of Indian Affairs, Ottawa, Ontario, Canada.

FIRST AID GUIDE wall chart; "Childhood Diseases"; many others. The Prudential Insurance Co. of America, Public Relations Dept., Box 141, Prudential Center, Boston, MA 02199.

FIRST AID GUIDE & WALL CHART. Johnson & Johnson, New Brunswick, NJ 08903.

POCKET-SIZED FIRST AID GUIDE, health record, rescue breathing card. International Brotherhood of Electrical Workers, 1125 15th Street NW, Washington, DC 20005.

PERSONAL HEALTH RECORD; Child Safety; First Aid for the Family. Brochures and posters. List of other materials, too. Postcard request. Health & Safety Education Division, Metropolitan Life Insurance Co., One Madison Avenue, New York, NY 10010.

FIRST AID CHART and other health & safety materials and booklets; list, free educational materials. Health & Welfare Div., Metropolitan Life Insurance Co., One Madison Avenue, New York, NY 10010.

"HOW WE SEE," poster. 50¢ and SASE. National Society to Prevent Blindness, 79 Madison Avenue, New York, NY 10016.

"YOUR MIRACULOUS EYES" & "A Schematic Chart of the Human Eye." SASE. American Optometric Association, Education Dept., 243 N. Lindbergh, St. Louis, MO 63141.

HUMAN EYE FOLDER. SASE. American Optometric Assn., Education Dept., 243 N. Lindbrgh, St. Louis, MO 63141.

INFORMATION ABOUT BLINDNESS. The Seeing Eye, Inc., Morristown, NJ 07960.

"WHAT DO YOU DO WHEN YOU SEE A BLIND PERSON?" pamphlet. Request on letterhead, with your reason for requesting. American Foundation for the Blind, 15 West 16th St., New York, NY 10011.

GLOSSARY OF OPTICAL and mechanical terms. Bausch & Lomb, Education Dept., Rochester, NY 14602.

"HOW A BABY GROWS" chart. Johnson & Johnson, Baby Products Co., Grandview Road, Skillman, NJ 08854.

"HOW CHILDREN GROW." From fertilized egg through puberty. Postcard request. Department of Health & Human Service, Bethesda, MD 20205.

"THE STORY OF BLOOD," "History of the Red Cross," "Blood as medicine," other books and posters. American Red Cross, 17th and "D" Streets NW, Washington, DC 20006.

LIST OF FREE MATERIALS. American Lung Association, 1740 Broadway, New York, NY 10019.

"THE BREATH OF LIFE," artificial respiration; etc. Education Dept., Aetna Life Affiliated Companies, 151 Farmington Ave., Hartford, CT 06115.

PHYSICAL FITNESS GUIDE and exercise program. Tea Council of the USA, 230 Park Avenue, New York, NY 10017.

"THE CARE AND SAFETY OF YOUNG CHILDREN" & "Child's Mind, Child's Body." Council on Family Health, 420 Lexington Avenue, New York, NY 10017.

"THE SUPER SITTER," babysitting booklet. U.S. Consumer Product Safety Commission, Washington, DC 20207. Booklet #052-011-00114-7.

"WHEN YOU HAVE A CHILD IN DAY CARE," by Fred Rogers (of TV's Mister Rogers Neighborhood). SASE. Day Care, c/o Mister Rogers, 4802 Fifth Avenue, Pittsburgh, PA 15213.

"YOUR BODY AND HOW IT WORKS," ages 6-9. American Medical Association, Dept. of Health Education, 5350 North Dearborn Street, Chicago, IL 60610.

CLEAN TEETH CLUB Chart. Postcard request. Lever Brothers Co., Education Dept., 390 Park Avenue, New York, NY 10022.

"NUTRITION LADDER" booklet, cut-out toy ladder, etc. Florida Citrus Commission, POBox 148, Lakeland, FL 33802.

"HOW TO ACHIEVE A DANCER'S BODY THROUGH DANCE EXERCISE." Ballet Makers, One Campus Road, Totowa, NJ 07512.

"YOUR HEART AND HOW IT WORKS" chart, and others. Jigsaw puzzle "How the heart works." American Heart Association, 205 East 42nd St., New York, NY 10017.

FACTS ABOUT DRUGS AND ALCOHOL. SASE. Do It Now Foundation, Box 5115, Phoenix, AZ 85010.

"IF YOUR CHILD STUTTERS: A Guide for Parents." $2.00. Speech Foundation of America, P.O. Box 11749, Memphis, TN 38111.

METRIC HEIGHT CHART. Publications Section, Community Affairs and Education Branch, N.A.S.A., 400 Maryland Avenue SW, Washington, DC 20546.

SIX-FOOT GROWING RULE with vegetable design, for charting child's growth, 50¢ postage. Del Monte Kitchens, POBox 7758, San Francisco, CA 94119.

"YES, YOU CAN!" booklet about Thomas Edison, Albert Einstein, Beethoven, Pasteur, and Rodin, who were "learning disabled." $2.00. The National Easter Seal Society, 2023 W. Ogden Avenue, Chicago, IL 60612.

POISON IVY, oak, sumac, 11x14" poster FOR TEACHERS ONLY (letterhead or rubber stamp!). Ivy Corp., Box 596, West Caldwell, NJ 07006.

"THE GREAT VITAMIN MYSTERY." 75¢. Order Dept., National Dairy Council, 6300 N. River Road, Rosemont, IL 60018.

"A FIVE-MINUTE COURSE IN NEW-TRITION." 25¢. Center for Science in the Public Interest, 1501 Sixteenth Street NW, Washington, DC 20036.

"LET THERE BE BREAD," booklet. The UN Food & Agriculture Bureau, 1325 "C" St. SW, Washington, DC 20437.

"FREEDOM FROM HUNGER" wall poster. UN Food & Agriculture Bureau, 1325 "C" St. SW, Washington, DC 20437.

"DAILY GUIDE TO GOOD EATING." Public Relations, Ralston Purina Co., Checkerboard Square, St. Louis, MO 63164.

FOODS COLORING BOOK. Information, Food and Nutrition Service, S-51 12th St.SE #764, Washington, DC 20250.

"STORY OF HONEY PRODUCTION." Dadant & Sons, Inc., Hamilton, IL 62341.

"I LOVE HONEY." California Honey Advisory Board, P.O. Box 265, Sonoma, CA 95476.

"MR. PEANUT'S GUIDE TO NUTRITION." Educational Services, Standard Brands, Inc., PO Box 2695, Grand Central Stn., New York, NY 10017.

"PEANUTS FOR THE GOOD & HEALTHY LIFE." How peanuts grow, and why they're good for you. SASE. Georgia Peanut Commission, Box 967, Tifton, GA 31794.

"PEANUTS, THE FUN FOOD," 4-page coloring book. Send 1st class stamp. Growers Peanut Food Promotions, P.O. Box 1709, Rocky Mount, NC 27802.

"KIDS ARE COOKS TOO." Ragu Family Tradition, 415 Madison Avenue, New York, NY 10017.

"WHY DO YOU NEED VITAMIN C?" Postcard. Florida Department of Citrus, Box 148, Lakeland, FL 33802.

"ALL ABOUT CORN." Corn Refiners Association, 1001 Connecticut Avenue NW, Washington, DC 20036.

"THE STORY OF COLUMBIAN COFFEE," "A Sketch of Columbia," "Columbia Today." Columbia Information Service, 140 E. 57th St., New York, NY 10022.

"A WEEK OF FAST FOOD THAT WON'T SLOW YOU DOWN" poster. Castle & Cooke Foods, Box 7757, San Francisco, CA 94120.

HISTORY OF SPICES FROM 50,000 B.C. 25¢ postage. American Spice Trade Assn., Education Dept., 580 Sylvan Avenue, Englewood Cliffs, NJ 07632.

"SHERLOCK HOG" poster, about pork. Sherlock Poster, National Pork Council, Box 10370, Des Moines, IA 50306.

AVOCADO SEED GROWING, booklet, 25¢. Seed Growing, Box 19159, Irvine, CA 92713.

SCRATCH 'N' SNIFF APRICOT STICKERS. California Apricot Advisory Board, 1280 Blvd. Way, Walnut Creek, CA 94595.

"THE HANDBOOK OF MILKING." De Laval Separator Co., Poughkeepsie, NY 12602.

"RAISINLAND USA," descriptive folder, how raisins are made, history, suggestions for projects. The California Raisin Advisory Board, 2240 North Angus, Fresno, CA 93703.

"THE F.A.O. INFORMATION PACKAGE," how the Food & Agricultural Organization of the UN is trying to eliminate world hunger. Food & Agricultural Organization of the U.N., Liaison Office, 1776 F Street NW, Washington, DC 20437.

"STORY OF CHOCOLATE AND COCOA" and others. Request list. The Hershey Chocolate Corp., Education Dept., 19 East Chocolate Avenue, Hershey, PA 17033.

"HISTORY OF COCOA AND CHOCOLATE." The Nestle Co., 100 Bloomingdale Road, White Plains, NY 10605.

BICYCLE SAFETY TIPS. SASE. National Easter Seal Society, 2023 Ogden Ave., Chicago, IL 60612.

"BICYCLE SAFETY." Aetna, 151 Farmington Ave., Hartford, CT 06156.

BIKE SAFETY, traffic safety, and other posters. Postcard request. Employers Insurance of Wausau, Box 150, Wausau, WI 54401.

BICYCLE SAFETY KIT, bike license, poster, tips on safety, membership card, 25¢ postage. Bicycle Mfgrs. Assn., 1101 15th Street NW, Washington, DC 20005.

BICYCLE SAFETY POSTERS, U.S. Consumer Product Safety Commission, Washington, DC 20207.

"HI, BIKE PILOTS," bike safety rules folder. Safety Div., Public Affairs Dept., Allstate Insurance Co., 7447 Skokie Blvd., Skokie, IL 60078.

TIPS FOR TEENAGE DRIVERS. Firestone Tire & Rubber Co., Educational Services Bureau, Akron, OH 44317.

HOW TO READ FASTER, How to Use a Library, How to Read a Newspaper, How to Enjoy the Classics, How to Enjoy Poetry, How to Encourage Your Child to Read, How to Write Clearly, How to Write With Style, How to Improve Your Vocabulary, How to Spell, How to Punctuate. One-page essays by well-known writers and others. Request by title. Power of the Printed Word, International Paper Co., P.O. Box 954, Madison Square Stn., New York, NY 10010.

"GROWING UP WITH BOOKS," "Growing up with science" -- recommended bibliography. R.R. Bowker Co., 1180 Avenue of the Americas, New York, NY 10036.

CATALOG OF STANDARDIZED TESTS. USE LETTERHEAD, IF POSSIBLE; if not, use a rubber stamp. Bureau of Education Measurements, Emphoria State University, 1200 Commercial, Emphoria, KS 66810.

EARTHBOOKS LENDING LIBRARY, Mountainburg, AR 72946. SASE for catalog.

"GETTING SKILLED: A Guide to Private Trade and Technical Schools." $1.50. National Association of Trade and Technical Schools, 2251 Wisconsin Avenue NW, Washington, DC 20007.

"TIPS ON TRADE AND TECHNICAL SCHOOLS" (#24-190). Council of Better Business Bureaus, 1515 Wilson Blvd., Arlington, VA 22209.

"TIPS 'N' TITLES," bimonthly newsletter of book reviews for grades K-8. Send 5 #10 SASE's. TNT, Graduate Division, University of Santa Clara, Santa Clara, CA 95053.

"HOW TO HELP YOUR CHILD BECOME A BETTER WRITER." SASE. National Council of Teachers of English, 1111 Kenyon Road, Urbana, IL 61801.

"A WAY OF TEACHING VALUES IN THE SCHOOLS." SASE. The Language Press, Box 342, Whitewater, WI 53190.

"TIPS ON HOME STUDY SCHOOLS" (#311-02229). Council of Better Business Bureaus, 1515 Wilson Blvd., Arlington, VA 22209.

"COLLEGE EDUCATION FOR ADULTS" (#546). $1.00. Public Affairs Pamphlets, 381 Park Avenue South, New York, NY 10016.

"STUDENT WORK, STUDY, TRAVEL CATALOG" (living and working in other countries). Council on International Educational Exchange, 205 East 42nd Street, New York, NY 10017.

"COLLEGE PROSPECTING" booklet. SASE. Office of University Communications, University of Rochester, Rochester, NY 14627.

"TYPICAL COURSE OF STUDY, K-12," curriculum guide. 29¢ postage. World Book Educational Products, 101 Northwest Point Blvd., Elk Grove Village, IL 60007.

❋◉❋◉❋◉❋◉❋

WRITE BEAUTIFUL LETTERS with lettering charts: Gothic, Roman, Old English, etc. Ask on a postcard for "Hunt Lettering Charts." Hunt Manufacturing Co., Speedball Road, Statesville, NC 28677.

12 ILLUSTRATED POSTCARDS (manufacturer's overstock). Ask for Postcard Offer. 50¢. IMC Management, Inc., P.O. Box 11, Garnerville, NY 10923.

12 LITTLE LETTERS -- mailable note cards with 12 seals. $1.00. IMC Management, Inc., P.O. Box 11, Garnerville, NY 10923.

STATUE OF LIBERTY NEEDLEPOINT KIT. $2.00. The NeedleCraft Club of America, 352 Route 59, Monsey, NY 10952.

BABY QUILT PATTERN. 50¢ and SASE. Emily Ann Creations, 303 South 34th Street, Tacoma, WA 98408.

"HOW TO MAKE PAPER BY HAND." 50¢. Hammermill Papers Group, P.O. Box 1440, Erie, PA 16533.

HOW-TO GUIDES, including steel brushes, linoleum block carving and printing, pen lettering guide, pen drawing. The Hunt Mfg. Co., Speedball Road, Statesville, NC 28677.

EGGORY'S EGG CRAFT IDEAS, $2.00. Eggory, Georgia Egg Commission, State Farmer's Market, Forest Park, GA 30050.

"COPPER HANDICRAFT," booklet of basic techniques, etc. Postcard request. Copper Development Association, Greenwich Office Park 2, Box 1840, Greenwich, CT 06836.

"HOW TO MAKE PLAY CLAY." Make decorations, gifts, and jewelry. Request on postcard. Play Clay, Arm & Hammer, P.O. Box 369, Piscataway, NJ 08854.

NEEDLECRAFT catalog & more than 100 yarn samples. Wool Design, 8916 York Road, Charlotte. NC 28224.

CANDLECRAFT catalog. Barker Enterprises, Inc., 15106 10th Avenue SW, Seattle, WA 98166.

"COLORFUN PROJECT IDEAS," coloring book. Crayola Products Div., Binney & Smith, Inc., P.O. Box 431, Easton, PA 18042.

"BY THE DOZENS," "Halloween masks & party favors," "Christmas ideas." All 3, 50¢ postage. "Can Do" Elmer's, POBox 157, Hilliard, OH 43026.

"MODELING WITH CLAY," "FINGER PAINTING," and several other booklets. Milton Bradley Co., 74 Park St., Springfield, MA 01102.

BASKETRY, WOODWORKING, stitchery, macrame, most materials and equipment. 48-page catalog of craft kits and projects. Discounts 20% to 50% from retail; no minimum. The Craft Basket, Colchester, CT 06415.

"FAMILY CRAFTS BOUTIQUE" booklet, many ideas for house, holidays, parties. SASE. Borden Consumer Products, Information Center, Box 157, Hilliard, OH 43026.

"EASY TO MAKE GIFTS FOR THE SMALL BUDGET," others. Consumer Education Dept., Johnson Wax, Racine, WI 53403.

CRAFT MAGIC BOOKLET, many projects. Dow Chemical Co., Consumer Products Dept., Midland, MI 48640.

"FUN WITH STA-FLO STARCH" ideas for finger-painting, string art, hand puppets, stenciling, etc. A.E. Staley Mfg., 2222 Kensington Ct., Oak Brook, IL 60521.

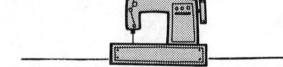

6" PLASTIC RULER; tape measure. Union Label Dept., ILGWU, 275 Seventh Avenue, New York, NY 10001.

FREE SCISSORS SHARPENER, 25¢ postage. Fabric Cut Aways, POBox 424, Arcadia, SC 29320.

"THE BEAR FACTS" & "COPING WITH TRAIL BUGS OF THE NORTHEAST," two brochures, 25¢ and SASE. Adirondack Mountain Club, Inc., 172 Ridge St., Glens Falls, NY 12801.

"BEARS OF PENNSYLVANIA" poster. Pennsylvania Game Commission, P.O. Box 1567, Harrisburg, PA 17120.

"OUR NATIONAL PARK SYSTEM." The Garden Club of America, 598 Madison Avenue, New York, NY 10022.

KEEP AMERICA BEAUTIFUL Information Kit." Keep America Beautiful, 99 Park Avenue, New York, NY 10016.

"MICHAEL RECYCLE" comic book tells kids how to collect aluminum soda cans, etc., and sell them back to the Reynolds Company. "Michael Recycle," Reynolds Aluminum Co., Box 27003, Richmond, VA 23261.

"RECYCLING," educational reprint. National Wildlife Federation, 1412 16th St. NW, Washington, DC 20036.

"THE AMERICAN BUFFALO" booklet. U.S. Dept. of the Interior, Fish & Wildlife Service, Washington, DC 20240.

"ENDANGERED SPECIES" (#589P). Consumer Information Center, P.O. Box 100, Pueblo, CO 81002.

"ANIMALS... It's Their World Too!" Bumper sticker. 50¢. The Humane Society of the United States, 2100 L Street N.W., Washington, DC 20037.

"OTTO OTTER FOR SAFE WATER" coloring book. Office of Public Affairs, Water & Power Resources Service, Dept. of the Interior, Washington, DC 20240.

"NATIONAL WILDLIFE REFUGES: A Visitor's Guide" (#149P). $1.00. Consumer Information Center, P.O. Box 100, Pueblo, CO 81002.

NATURE BADGES, STICKERS, & fire prevention information. Smokey Bear Hdqrts., Washington, DC 20252.

NATIONAL WILDLIFE WEEK: 4 posters, teaching guide with reproducible pages, 36 stamps with different wildlife facts; catalog of other educational materials. FREE. Wildlife Week Kit, National Wildlife Federation, Leesburg Pike, Vienna, VA 22184.

"HOW TO START A NATURE CLUB." National Wildlife Federation, 1412 16th Street NW, Washington, DC 20036.

THE WOODSY OWL POLLUTION FIGHTER PACKAGE; member card, posters to color, bookmark, sticker, song sheet. Woodsy Owl, Forest Service, P.O. Box 2417, Washington, DC 20013.

WOODSY OWL POSTER and folder about hiking, camping, and the woods. USDA Forest Service, P.O. Box 2417, Washington, DC 20013.

"WILDLIFE SANCTUARY" reprint. National Wildlife Federation, 1412 16th St. NW, Washington, DC 20036.

"ENVIRONMENTAL EDUCATION PACKET." Garden Club of America, 598 Madison Avenue, New York, NY 10022.

"BIRDWATCHING," booklet. National Wildlife Federation, 1412 16th Street NW, Washington, DC 20036.

"BIRDS." "Attracting & feeding birds." U.S. Dept. of the Interior, Fish & Wildlife Service, Washington, DC 20240.

BIRD POSTER. Environmental Protection Agency, Office of Public Awareness, 401 M St. NW, Gallery 2, Washington, DC 20460.

MAP OF MOUNT ST. HELENS and vicinity showing area affected by 1980 eruption; photos of area before eruption. $1.00. U. S. Geological Survey, Box 25286, Denver, CO 80225.

VOLCANIC ASH FROM MOUNT ST. HELENS from May 18, 1980 eruption. 50¢ postage. Dean Foster Nurseries, Dept. "ASH," Rt. 2, Hartford, MI 49057.

HOW TO FORECAST WEATHER booklet. Gudebrod Brothers Silk Co., 12 South 12th St., Philadelphia, PA 19107.

GUIDE TO THE WEATHER. Wolf's Head Oil Refining Co., Oil City, PA 16301.

"STORY OF GRANITE." Barre Granite Assn., Box 481, Barre, VT.

"LET'S COLLECT SHELLS AND ROCKS." Shell Oil Co., Public Affairs, P.O. Box 2463, Houston, TX 77001.

STONE MOUNTAIN PARK teaching aids: color brochure, pamphlet on mountain carving and geology, color photo, and order form for educational books and filmstrips. Stone Mountain Park, P.O. Box 778, Stone Mountain, GA 30086.

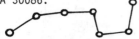

"STARS IN YOUR EYES: A Guide to the Northern Skies" (#150P). $1.50. Consumer Information Center, P.O. Box 100, Pueblo, CO 81002.

BLACK HOLES PACKET; non-technical articles. $2.00. Black Holes Packet, Astronomical Society of the Pacific, 1290 24th Ave., San Francisco, CA 94122.

"QUASARS ARE FAR OUT," "Interstellar Matter is a Gas," "Astronomy is Looking Up." Bumper (or wall) stickers. $1.00 each. Astronomical Society of the Pacific, 1290 24th Avenue, San Francisco, CA 94122.

"TONIGHT'S ASTEROIDS." SASE. Asteroids, 1411 N. Magnum St., Durham, NC 27701.

"COMETS," "METEORITES," "LIFE IN THE UNIVERSE." Public Affairs Office, Harvard Smithsonian Center for Astrophysics, 60 Garden St., Cambridge, MA 02138.

"STEPS TO THE MOON." U.S. Dept. of the Interior, Geological Survey, 604 South Picket Street, Alexandria, VA 22304.

SPACE SHUTTLE FACTS. Public Affairs Office, JFK Space Center, Cape Canaveral, FL 32899.

NASA PUBLICATIONS, including "What's New on the Moon?" "U.S. Space Shuttle Glider," etc. Use letterhead or rubber stamp if possible. Educational Programs Officer, NASA Ames Research Center, Moffett Field, CA 94035.

"SKY & TELESCOPE" magazine, sample. Sky Publishing Corp., 49 Bay Street Road, Cambridge, MA 02138.

"GEORGE WASHINGTON AND THE AMERICAN REVOLUTION." Washington National Insurance Co., Evanston, IL 60201.

"THE DECLARATION OF INDEPENDENCE" and "The U.S. Constitution," booklets. Phillips Petroleum Co., Public Affairs, 16 PB, Bartlesville, OK 74004.

FLAG FOLDERS. The Star-Spangled Banner Assn., 844 E. Pratt Street, Baltimore, MD 21202.

DECLARATION OF INDEPENDENCE & BILL OF RIGHTS on aged parchment-like paper. $1.00. Historical Documents Co., 8 N. Preston St., Philadelphia, PA 19104.

"HOW TO RESPECT & DISPLAY OUR FLAG." Publications, U.S. Marine Corps, Dept. of the Navy, Washington, DC 20380.

"THE BILL OF RIGHTS TODAY" (#489A). $1.00. Public Affairs Pamphlets, 381 Park Avenue South, New York, NY 10016.

"PHOTO TOUR OF THE WHITE HOUSE." The White House, Washington, DC 20500.

LINCOLN'S BIRTHPLACE folder. Lincoln Birthplace National Historic Site, Rte. 1, Hodgenville, KY 42748.

STAR SPANGLED BANNER, TAUNTON, GRAND UNION, three flag posters, with their histories and notes. $1.50 and a self-addressed mailing label. National Flag Foundation, Flag Plaza, Pittsburgh, PA 15219.

U.S. PRESIDENTS & HISTORY OF AMERICAN FLAGS. Posters. $1.00. Historical Documents Co., 8 N. Preston St., Philadelphia, PA 19104.

"THIS LAND OF OURS." Greyhound Bus Lines, Public Relations Dept., Clark & Randolph Sts., Chicago, IL 60601.

"FAMOUS JEWISH-AMERICAN PATRIOTS," 50¢ postage. Jewish-American Patriots, Box 4488, Grand Central Stn., New York, NY 10017.

"WOMEN IN AMERICA" booklet on achievements of American women in history, arts, science, etc. Sperry & Hutchinson, Consumer Services Dept., 2900 West Seminary Drive, Fort Worth, TX 76133.

BILLY THE KID & JESSE JAMES reward posters. $1.00 each. Historical Documents Co., 8 N. Preston St., Philadelphia, PA 19104.

"THE OUTLINE OF THE HISTORY OF CHEMISTRY," chart. Mallinckrodt Chemical Works, 2nd & Mallinckrodt Streets, St. Louis, MO.

"CHEMISTRY ADDS DIMENSION TO YOUR LIFE," decorative polygon (14 sides!). American Chemical Society, 1155 Sixteenth St. NW, Washington, DC 20036.

CHEMISTRY PROJECTS and science fairs, booklet. Manufacturing Chemists Assn., Education Dept., 1825 Connecticut Ave. NW, Washington, DC 20009.

"THE STORY OF FERMENTATION." Education Services Dept., Pfizer International, Inc., 235 East 42nd Street, New York, 10017.

"THE CHEMICAL FACTS OF LIFE." Monsanto Co., 800 N. Lindberg Blvd., St. Louis, MO 63166.

NATURAL GAS -- Inquire about several free materials and activities for teaching about natural gas and its uses. Educational Programs, American Gas Association, 1515 Wilson Blvd., Arlington, VA 22209.

"EXCEPTIONAL BLACK SCIENTISTS," set of posters. Consumer Relations, CIBA-GEIGY Corp., Ardsley, NY 10502.

BOOKLETS ON RAILROADS. Public Relations Dept., Santa Fe System Lines, 80 East Jackson Blvd., Chicago, IL 60604.

RAILROAD MAP OF THE USA and other educational material. The Union Pacific Railroad Co., 1416 Dodge St., Omaha, NE 68102.

"THE STORY OF HARNESS RACING." The U.S. Trotting Association, 750 Michigan Ave., Columbus, OH 43215.

"THE HARNESS RACING PUZZLE BOOK." The U.S. Trotting Association, 750 Michigan Ave., Columbus, OH 43215.

AMERICAN QUARTER HORSE POSTERS. American Quarter Horse Association, Amarillo, TX 79168.

"AMERICAN ENTERPRISE TEACHING NOTES" newsletter with economic activities for all grade levels. Playback Associates, 708 3rd Avenue, New York, NY 10017.

"WHAT IS THE CHAMBER OF COMMERCE?" Chamber of Commerce of the U.S., 1615 H Street NW, Washington, DC 20062.

MICKEY MOUSE & GOOFY EXPLORE BUSINESS comic book-- Exxon, Public Affairs, Box 2180, Houston, TX 77001.

REPLICA OF REVOLUTIONARY DICE, copied from originals made by soldiers who pounded lead bullets in rough cubes, then poked holes with bayonet tips. $1.00. Historical Documents Co., 8 N. Preston St., Philadelphia, PA 19104.

COLONIAL MONEY; replicas of 14 bank notes issued by the Continental Congress. $1.00. Historical Documents Co., 8 N. Preston St., Philadelphia, PA 19104.

CONFEDERATE MONEY, replicas of various bills issued under the Confederate States of America. Two different sets. $1.00 each. Historical Documents Co., 8 N. Preston St., Philadelphia, PA 19104.

"THE STORY OF MONEY," comic-book format. Federal Reserve Bank of New York, Public Information Dept., 33 Liberty St., New York, NY 10045.

"THE STORY OF CHECKS AND ELECTRONIC PAYMENTS." History in comic-book format. Federal Reserve Bank of New York, Public Information Dept., 33 Liberty St., New York, NY 10045.

"FUNDAMENTAL FACTS ABOUT U.S. MONEY." Federal Reserve Bank of Atlanta, Atlanta, GA 30303.

"THE STORY OF INFLATION." Federal Reserve Bank of New York, Public Information Dept., 33 Liberty St., New York, NY 10045.

"THE STORY OF BANKS." Federal Reserve Bank of New York, Public Information Dept., 33 Liberty St., New York, NY 10045.

"THE STORY OF FOREIGN TRADE AND EXCHANGE." Federal Reserve Bank of New York, Public Information Dept., 33 Liberty St., New York, NY 10045.

"MONEY: MASTER OR SERVANT?" Public Information Department, Federal Reserve Bank, 33 Liberty St., New York, NY 10045.

"COINS AND CURRENCY." Public Information Dept., Federal Reserve Bank, 33 Liberty St., New York, NY 10045.

"A DAY AT THE FED" (how banking works). Public Information Dept., Federal Reserve Bank, 33 Liberty St., New York, NY 10045.

OLD MONEY: 3 coins at least 75 years old. $2.00. Jolie Coins, P.O. Box 68 US, Roslyn Hts., NY 11577.

"JOURNEY THROUGH A STOCK EXCHANGE." American Stock Exchange, Publications Dept., 86 Trinity Place, New York, NY 10006.

"CBA BANK FACTS." The Canadian Bankers Association, Box 282, Toronto Dominion Centre, Toronto, Ontario M5K 1K2.

1840 BANK NOTES, catalog and sample reproduction. 50¢ postage. The Fun House, POBox 1225, Newark, NJ 07101.

HISTORY & POWER OF GOLD, literature and booklets. The Gold Information Center, 645 Fifth Avenue, New York, NY 10022.

"A PRIMER ON MONEY" and how the system works. Committee on Banking, House of Representatives, Washington, DC 20515.

SILVER VALUE CHART for U.S. and Canadian coins. Numismatic News Weekly, Iola, WI 54945.

"COINS AND CURRENCY," 22-page booklet tracing money from its origin as trinkets, then bartered goods and services, to present-day form. FREE. Federal Reserve Bank of New York, Public Information Dept., 33 Liberty St., New York, NY 10045.

GUIDE TO RECOGNIZING COUNTERFEIT MONEY. United States Secret Service, 1800 G Street NW, Washington, DC 20226.

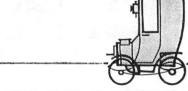

"THE WORLD MAKES AN AUTOMOBILE" chart and other free books and posters. The Automobile Manufacturers Assn., 320 New Center Building, Detroit, MI 48202.

"THE MAKING OF A CAR" activity sheets, teacher's guide, wall poster. Request on postcard, using rubber stamp address if possible. The Making Of A Car, POBox 14312, Dayton, OH 45414.

BASIC AUTOMOTIVE IGNITION SYSTEM, chart. Champion Spark Plug Co., Technical Service Dept., P.O. Box 910, Toledo, OH 43601.

RUBBER, seed to finished product. Ask for "Firestone in Liberia." Firestone Tire & Rubber, Public Relations Dept., Akron, OH 44317.

"THE STORY OF OIL," "The Story of Geothermal Energy," posters. Geothermal Energy booklet. Corporate Communications, Union Oil of California, P.O. Box 7600, Los Angeles, CA 90051.

STORY OF OIL IN CALIFORNIA, chart on formation of oil. Public Relations Dept., Union Oil Co. of California, P.O. Box 7600, Los Angeles, CA 90054.

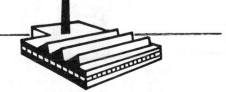

"STEEL: A PICTURE STORY." Bethlehem Steel Corp., Bethlehem, PA 18016.

"THE STORY OF LEAD." Lead Industry Association, 292 Madison Avenue, New York, NY 10017.

"COAL FACTS." National Coal Association, Education Dept., Coal Bldg., 1130 17th Street NW, Washington, DC 20036.

"STORY OF ALUMINUM AND ALCOA." Alcoa, 1501 Alcoa Bldg., Pittsburgh, PA 15219.

"LEATHER IN OUR LIVES." Leather Industries of America, 411 Fifth Ave., New York, NY 10016.

"THE STORY OF MEAT ANIMALS," "The story of soil," many other educational materials. Swift & Co., Education Supply Dept., 41st & South Laflin Station, Chicago, IL 60609.

LIST OF MEAT PRODUCTIONS, FOLDERS, POSTERS, MANUALS, streamers, signs, wall charts, etc. National Livestock and Meat Board, 444 North Michigan Avenue, Chicago, IL 60611.

"THE STORY OF COTTON," poster. National Cotton Council, P.O. Box 12285, Memphis, TN 38112.

TREES, how they are planted, nurtured, and processed. Posters. Educational Services, Georgia Pacific Corporation, 133 Peachtree St. NW, Atlanta, GA 30303.

"FROM FOREST TREE TO FINE PAPER" illustrated booklet, tour of a large paper plant. Educational Services Dept., Hammermill Papers, Erie, PA 16512.

MAKING PAPER FROM TREES, folder. Forest Service, U.S. Dept. of Agriculture, Washington, DC 20250.

USES OF WOOD AND WOOD CONSTRUCTION. National Forest Products Assn., Educational Services, 1619 Massachusetts Avenue NW, Washington, DC 20036.

"OUR REDWOOD HERITAGE." Service Library, California Redwood Association, 591 Redwood Highway, Mill Valley, CA 94941.

"ForesTalk RESOURCE MAGAZINE," glossy magazine about British Columbia's forests, photos & articles. ForesTalk, Ministry of Forests, Information Services Branch, 1450 Government St., Victoria, B.C. V8W 3E7.

THREE "LEVI LOGGER'S COLOR BOOK TOURS" about how trees are cut, processed, and used. Alaska Loggers Assoc., 111 Stedman Street, Ketchikan, AK 99901.

CORK: NATURE'S ANSWER is an 8-page booklet about the characteristics of cork (lighter than water, more elastic than plastic) and its use in bridge joints, fishing equipment, shoes, & space shuttles. CORK INSTITUTE OF AMERICA, P.O. Box 1297, Lancaster, PA 17603.

"FOREST SERVICE CAREER PROFILES" (FS-308). USDA Forest Service, P.O. Box 2417, Washington, DC 20013.

AIR TRAVEL BOOKLETS, etc. The Air Transport Association, 1709 New York Avenue NW, Washington, DC 20006.

CESSNA INTERNATIONAL AIR AGE EDUCATION PACKET. Air Education Department, P.O. Box 1521, Wichita, KS 67201.

"HOW AN AIRPLANE FLIES." Public Relations, TWA, Inc., 605 Third Avenue, New York, NY 10158.

"HOW THE HELICOPTER FLIES." United Technologies, Sikorsky Aircraft, Public Relations Dept., North Main St., Stratford, CT 06601.

"THE STORY OF THE WRIGHT BROTHERS." Wright Brothers Memorial, Route 1, Box 675, Manteo, NC 27954.

"THOUGHTS TO PONDER," inspirational messages suitable for framing. Write for information. Chairman, United Technologies, Box 360, Hartford, CT 06141.

"WHAT IS A BOY?" & "WHAT IS A GIRL?" by Alan Beck. New England Life Insurance Co., 501 Boylston Street, Boston, MA 02117.

BIBLE CORRESPONDENCE COURSE "that lets the Bible interpret itself." 12 monthly lessons. No charge, no donations. Worldwide Church of God, Pasadena, CA 91123.

"CHOOSING TOYS." Toy Manufacturers of America, 200 Fifth Avenue, New York, NY 10010.

THE TONKA TOUR BOOK, 8-page booklet with photos about the making of Tonka Toys. FREE. Tonka Toys, Box 100, Mound, MN 55364.

"THE WONDERFUL WORLD OF PLAY," booklet. Hasbro Industries, 1027 Newport Avenue, Pawtucket, RI 02861.

"PICTURE-TAKING, a self-teaching guide," booklet. Eastman Kodak Co., 343 State St., Rochester, NY 14650.

DOLL CASTLE NEWS, magazine, sample copy, $2.00. Doll Castle News, PO Box 247, Washington, NJ 07882.

"BASIC RULES OF CHECKERS"; "Beginners' Corner" Pointers and Positions; "A Description of the American Checker Federation." Send 3 1st class stamps. American Checker Federation, 3475 Belmont Avenue, Baton Rouge, LA 70808.

"CHESS LIFE & REVIEW," sample copy. U.S. Chess Federation, 186 Rt. 9W, New Windsor, NY 12550.

"OFFICIAL RULES" list for all sports. The Athletic Institute, 200 Castlewod Drive, North Palm Beach, FL 33408.

"HOW GIRL SCOUTING BEGAN," sample of Girl Scout Leader Magazine. Girl Scouts of the U.S.A., 830 Third Avenue, New York, NY 10022.

INTRODUCTION TO STAMP COLLECTING KIT. Stamp Division, Postal Service, 475 L'Enfant Plaza West SW, Washington, DC 20260.

"HOW TO COLLECT POSTAGE STAMPS," form a stamp club, find rare old stamps, etc. Littleton Stamp Co., Littleton, NH 03561.

STAMP COLLECTING NEWS, monthly newsletter, FREE. Benjamin Franklin Stamp Club, Box 23584, Washington, DC 20024.

HARMONICA INSTRUCTION -- Books and music for harmonicas. HOHNER CANADA INC., 1969 Leslie St., Don Mills, Ontario M3B 2M3.

"MAGIC SALT CRYSTAL GARDEN." Make a crystal garden with household materials. SASE. Luther Ford and Co., 100 N. Seventh St., Minneapolis, MN 55403.

TEN ANIMAL IRON-ONS, $1 postage. Dog's World, 498 New Rochelle Road, Bronxville, NY 10708.

VENUS FLY TRAP SEEDS, brochure about carnivorous plants. $2.00. Peter Pauls Nurseries, Route 4, Canandaigua, NY 14424.

MAKE TWO WATER PUMPS: "A Balloon and Funnel Pump" and "A Tin Can Pump." Two brochures, $1.00 and a SASE. Boston Children's Museum, 300 Congress Street, Boston, MA 02210.

TREASURE MAP & WEAPONS OF THE PIRATES. Two charts, suitable for framing. $1.00 each. Historical Documents Co., 8 N. Preston, PA 19104.

"SEE HOW THEY RUN" battery experiments, 50¢. Union Carbide Corp., Battery Products Div., Old Ridgebury Road, Danbury, CT 06817.

ROAD ATLAS & TRAVEL GUIDE. Best Western, Inc., P.O. Box 10203, Phoenix, AZ 85064.

THE PRINCIPAL RIVERS and lakes of the world, booklet. U.S. Dept. of Commerce, Rockville, MD 20852.

SHIPPING AND THE SEAS material. The U.S. Dept. of Commerce, Marine Bureau, Educational Services, Washington, DC 20235.

"TRAVEL GAMES," Family Fun Book. $1.00 bill. The Beavers, SR Box 184, LaPorte, MN 56461.

"FACTS ABOUT RUSSIA"; sample copy of Soviet Life magazine. Embassy of the U.S.S.R., 1706 18th Street NW, Washington, DC 20009.

PENPALS IN MORE THAN 30 COUNTRIES: write for information. Student Letter Exchange, 910 4th St., SE, Austin, MN 55912.

"YOUR GUIDE TO INTERNATIONAL YOUTH EXCHANGE" (#501P). Consumer Information Center, P.O. Box 100, Pueblo, CO 81002.

"THE OLYMPIC GAMES," history booklet. U.S. Olympic Committee, 1750 East Boulder St., Colorado Springs, CO 80909.

"TWA GETAWAY GREECE" and Greek vacation brochures. TWA Getaway Greece, Box 25, Grand Central Station, New York, NY 10017.

"ETRUSCAN TOURIST GUIDE" includes history. Italian Government Travel Office, 630 Fifth Avenue, New York, NY 10111.

"AUSTRALIA NOW." "Australia Handbook." Australian Information Service, 636 Fifth Avenue, New York, NY 10020.

"TWENTY CENTURIES OF JEWISH LIFE IN THE HOLY LAND," 68-page booklet. Consulate General of Israel, Suite 1700, 6380 Wilshire Blvd., Los Angeles, CA 90048.

UNITED NATIONS material. U.N. Educational Services Dept., United Nations, New York, NY 10017.

FREE U.N. PAMPHLETS. The United Nations Association in Canada. 63 Sparks St., Suite 808, Ottawa, Ontario K1P 5A6.

ENERGY EDUCATION MATERIALS. Specify Elementary, Junior High, or Senior High. FREE. Educational Programs, American Gas Association, 1515 Wilson Blvd., Arlington, VA 22209.

"ENERGY AND EDUCATION," a free monthly newsletter published by the National Science Teachers Association, 1742 Connecticut Avenue NW, Washington, DC 20009. The NSTA also has a series of instructional packets and fact sheets dealing with energy; write for a free list of publications.

"LIGHT & MAN," 3 booklets. GTE Lighting Products, Sylvania Lighting Center, Danvers, MA 01923.

"SOLAR ENERGY AND YOU," "Learning About Renewable Energy." CAREIRS, P.O. Box 8900, Silver Spring, MD 20907.

SCIENCE ACTIVITIES IN ENERGY SERIES, grades 4-6. Technical Information Center, U.S. Dept. of Energy, POBox 62, Oak Ridge, TN 37830.

"ENERGY ACTIVITIES WITH ENERGY ANT," "Energy Conservation" poster, "Captain America and the Campbell Kids Save Energy" poster. Department of Energy, P.O. Box 62, Oak Ridge, TN 37830.

"ENERGY INFORMATION SERIES," several booklets. American Petroleum Institute, Publications Section, 1220 L Street NW, Washington, DC 20005.

"THE AMAZING STORY OF MEASUREMENT," large colorful chart tracing the history of measuring from prehistory to space age. FREE TO TEACHERS ONLY: use letterhead or rubber stamp! Ford Motor Company, Education Affairs Dept., The American Road, Dearborn, MI 48121.

METRIC CONVERSION, plastic chart-ruler. Consumer Relations, Eli Lily & Co., 307 East McCarty St., Indianapolis, IN 46285.

"CHRISTMAS CAROLS," music and words. John Hancock Mutual Life Insurance, Box 111, Boston, MA 02117.

CATALOG OF CARDS, POSTERS, PHOTOGRAPHS. Library of Congress, Information Office, Box A, Washington, DC 20540.

FILM LOANS; list. Association Films, 866 3rd Avenue, New York, NY 10022.

CONSUMER INFORMATION CATALOG. Free or inexpensive booklets from many federal agencies; many subjects. Consumer Information Center, Pueblo, CO 81009.

CERTIFICATES. Catalog and free samples of 8x10" award certificates, grades 1-8. FOR TEACHERS ONLY (use letterhead or rubber stamp). Achievement Certificates, POBox A, Clarence, NY 14031.

CATALOGS OF ETCHINGS, LITHOGRAPHS, WOODCUTS, more. Associated American Artists, 663 Fifth Avenue, New York, NY 10022.

FREE STUFF FOR KIDS, updated edition. More than 250 free or almost-free items which kids can send for themselves. Stickers, pen bracelet, Christmas stamp pad set, a kazoo, etc. Order #0-68988-6. $4.95 plus $1 postage. MEADOWBROOK PRESS, 18318 Minnetonka Blvd., Deephaven, MN 55391.

MANY MORE "FREE OR ALMOST FREE" ITEMS ARE LISTED IN OTHER SECTIONS -- HISTORY, SCIENCE, ETC. See "Free" in the Index.

RELIGIOUS THOUGHT, WORLD RELIGIONS, THE GREAT THOUGHTS, THINKING

EXPERIENCE

The battery-powered phonograph shuts itself off and I step out into the crunchy morning with the quiet joy of Mozart's thirty-fourth symphony still stirring through my veins. Wispy gray clouds fade away from the dawning sky, and sudden sunlight streaks through the frosty lace of the icy woods around me.

The moment is timeless. I lose myself in the simple magnificence of sparkling crystals, the complex diffusions of exciting light and restful shadows. Saplings and branches and towering trees are bent together under the weight of their jewels, curving together to form countless circles and arches, surrounding me in a cathedral of awe and wonder. Am I inside, looking out? Or outside, looking in?

A chickadee flies above me; a bashful rabbit pauses nearby; a phoebe calls; a hawk circles and soars away. Under the snow and ice over our little foot-bridge, the brook murmurs contentedly. They all have the answer.

Then I have it, too. There is no "inside" and "outside." Those are illusions I create when I separate myself from the reality around me.

MANY PATHS

Whatever we believe or teach our children about God and our relationship to Him, it becomes increasingly important each day that we know and understand what others believe and teach. Whether we believe that ours is the one and only true religion or that there are many different paths to God and truth (or even if we don't believe in God at all), we need to understand at least the basic beliefs and teachings of others in the human family.

Some of the oldest legends and artifacts of human civilization indicate that people have always searched for truth and goodness; that they have always sought to understand the mystery of life, of being.

Religion did not begin two thousand years ago, nor four, nor five. Jesus was not the first to preach the return of good for evil, although others who have taught the same thing have been ignored and disobeyed just as much.

We teach our children that the universe and everything in it are basically good; that often what we call bad is only goodness distorted, or goodness frustrated, or goodness undeveloped. From a God's-eye view, even the most horrible criminals are never beyond redemption. They're just not ripe -- but God has plenty of time. I don't believe that God gambles or experiments or makes mistakes. He won't punish parts of his creation for being slower to develop than others.

A parent may say to a child, "I'm punishing you because I love you," but the Creator of billions of stars and flowers and grains of sand is never so foolish. Kindness, understanding, forgiveness, and patient guidance are facets of love; punishments are not.

What loving parent would sentence his child to eternal fear and suffering, no matter what the transgression? Yet there are still some who suggest that the Being whose love and goodness fill the void between the stars will do so for the crime of mistaken belief. Was Jesus lying, when he told the parable of the prodigal son?

No doubt we are all prodigal -- wasteful and extravagant -- at times. We waste life, we waste time, still arguing -- as did some medieval monks -- about how many angels can dance on the head of a pin. "As if you can kill time," wrote Thoreau, "without injuring eternity."

We teach our children that people everywhere want to know God; that the followers of Buddha do not worship his statue, but that they believe in the Eightfold Path of Right Thought and Right Action as devoutly as Christians believe in the Ten Commandments.

In our home, we don't teach denominational dogma, but we often study about it. Our studies include ancient myths and legends as well as the various holy books which have grown from them. In comparing different religions of the world, our purpose is never to proclaim one better or more true than another, but to find what each has to offer for the betterment of humanity. We're curious about the various beliefs regarding creation and the afterlife, but we're more concerned with the moral and ethical teachings -- as Jesus was. We're far more interested in the many similarities among various religions than in their differences.

All four of our children have attended various church services with their friends, and have made several interesting observations. The preachers all talk about Jesus quite a bit, but seldom say anything about Jesus's own teachings. The nonfundamentalist churches, of course, are not so concerned with damnation and redemption, but even these say little about applying Jesus's teachings to our own everyday lives. Far more is said about joy in eternity than about meaningful relationships here and now. In general, our kids have found the unbelievers are neither more nor less friendly and considerate than devout believers.

CONVERSION

When Susan was in her early teens, she decided to attend Sunday School at the local Baptist Church -- initially just to be with her friends, so we saw no reason not to allow it. We had underestimated the church's techniques of persuasion. Susan was given home-work -- searching for specified Bible verses (almost always dealing with sin and redemption), competing for prizes in Bible-verse memorization contests, and writing short paragraphs about how her "life of lasciviousness and wickedness" could be changed by accepting Jesus as her savior. The church's literature, bought from a mid-Western publishing company, used adolescent psychology as a strong lever, insisting that Susan's awakening body and "confused thoughts" were under the control of Satan, and repeatedly telling her that she was sinful by nature, and unworthy of God's love, which would be given to her only if she accepted God's sacrifice of his son. Recognizing the need of many adolescents to rebel and at the same time to belong to a group, the church distributed stories and articles about "Living With Un-Christian Parents" and "How to Convince Your Parents That They Are Wrong." Susan was encouraged to attend many extracurricular church activities -- gospel concerts, barbecues, youth group meetings, choir practice -- increasingly at the expense of participation in family activities and daily chores. She stayed up late at night, studying the Bible, copying and memorizing passages -- particularly from the Book of Revelations. In the morning, she was tired, cranky, and antagonistic. During our school activities, she doodled on her notebook cover or on scraps of paper -- pictures of a cross, and hearts and banners with the words "Jesus Loves Me," over and over. She lost interest in all school subjects, and flatly refused to participate in any lesson which wasn't in agreement with Baptist teachings, whether it was science, history, literature, or religion.

We told Susan we certainly had no objection to her being a Christian, if that was her choice, but that she should examine the church's teachings, investigate other churches, and learn more about Christianity before accepting the teachings of one particular church. Especially, we said, read the four Gospels; they are supposedly the basis of all Christianity; read them carefully, giving particular attention to the message of Jesus himself. She said there was no need to, because she had already found the truth. She accused us of being against the church only because she had chosen it, and then cried because God was going to throw us into a lake of fire and she would be the only one of our family to go to Heaven. She thought she would lose us. We thought we had lost her.

There are many, of course, who would feel that Susan was the only one of our family who had seen the Light. To us, any light which produces blindness is worse than darkness. After so many years of helping our children gain intellectual freedom, we were frightened by the ease with which others could inject intolerance and bigotry into one of them. We reminded ourselves that we should have known; we should have realized the emotional appeal, especially for a young teenager, of being one of God's Chosen.

Our other children were repulsed by the concept of a God who would throw people into a lake of fire, or simply snuff them out like candles. Susan seemed at times to have trouble believing it, but she tried very hard because it was part of the Package: if you don't accept the entire message, you're in danger of God's anger.

We had read and discussed George Orwell's **1984**, and his concept of Newspeak arose one day when Susan told us of learning that God's chosen will be "raptured up to Heaven." "Be what?" she was asked. "Raptured," she repeated, not knowing what the word meant, but assuming it meant "lifted" or "taken." "Like Star Trek," someone said. "Rapture me up, Scotty." She consented to look the word up in a dictionary, but refused to tell us what she had found, and refused to discuss it any further.

One Sunday, Susan told us the church's preacher had told the congregation that Pete Seeger and Jane Fonda are communists, and he advised anyone who owned Jane Fonda's workout book to throw it away immediately, and to be careful not to listen to any of Pete Seeger's recordings. She was a little puzzled and apprehensive, having enjoyed our Pete Seeger records for years, and having looked through Jane Fonda's book in the public library. The principle of the issue wasn't new to our kids, but we were all a little surprised to see it pop up -- ironically, in 1984 -- in our small rural community in New Brunswick.

In the following week, our speculations about the preacher's concept of communism led into a lively discussion of Senator Joseph McCarthy's

witchhunt of the 50s, the subsequent media blacklist of Pete Seeger, the Weavers, Paul Robeson, and many other entertainers because of their refusal to cooperate with McCarthy's senate committee, and of Jane Fonda's opposition to the Vietnam War.

We discussed the nature and dangers of stereotypes, prejudice, and false or incomplete information; and the humorous possibilities of political contamination from contact with an exercise book or a record of folk songs.

After Susan had been a militant born-again fundamentalist for about two years, her friends began drifting away from the church, and she slowly drifted with them. We hoped that her experience would lead her to investigate other beliefs and other approaches to searching for God, but her interest seemed to be not so much in God as in belonging to the church; and, had it not been for the church's techniques of persuasion, not so much in the church as in being with her friends. We don't know what knowledge about herself she may have gained from the experience; it has never been a subject for discussion. We do know that the church took her away from us for many hours each day, and created in her so much hostility toward her "un-Christian" parents that for over two years she was a member of our family in name only, eating and sleeping in our home, but not participating freely in any of our activities.

We think Susan finally learned, as our other children did -- from the people they knew, from history, from the daily news -- that most people's daily lives are affected very little by the religious beliefs they claim to have. In this week's news magazine, how many reports are there of wars between religious factions -- Arabs and Jews, Catholics and Protestants, Christians and atheists, even Christians against Christians? They also began learning that those who have the most faith, hope, and charity are not always Christians or Jews or Buddhists; that an atheist is not necessarily lacking in love and sympathy and generosity.

CREDO

I sometimes teach about God. Should I say "preach"? My text comes from dozens of holy books; from the many evenings I have lain in my sleeping bag, looking up at the stars; from the smell of new-mown grass; from the births of our children; from Straus's symphony, Also Sprach Zarathustra; from the sparkle of ice crystals on the tree branches; from the drowning sloth who puts her baby on her head to save its life from the flood rising around her shoulders; from the cut on my finger which knits and heals; from my eye, a small mass of fluid and membrane and blood and nerves, which transmits the image of a star or a flower or a sunset or a loved one to my inner self.

What I teach about God is too much for some, not enough for some, all wrong for some.

"Why, who makes much of miracles?" asked Walt Whitman. "To me every hour of the light and dark is a miracle, every cubic inch of space is a miracle."

When we hear or read of miracles, we look for something out of the ordinary, as if everything ordinary were not miracle enough. There is no separation between the natural and the supernatural. God is not a remote being to whom we telegraph our requests, dabbling when he pleases in human lives, granting his favors as arbitrary rewards for obeisance or flattery. God is far more natural and more supernatural than that. God IS. All that is, is God. God is the I Am, the Word, the Way, Tao, the Great Spirit, the Oversoul, the Force, all matter and non-matter, everything seen and unseen, all power and glory forever. Not a star or person or microbe is separate or distinct from God.

The early Greeks personified the earth as Gaia, Mother Earth, and saw all things earthly as being essentially one being, totally interrelated in a global ecology of earth and mind and body and spirit. British scientist James Havelock very seriously proposes the "Gaia Hypothesis" -- that the entire earth functions as a single self-regulating organism. Lyall Watson, in SUPERNATURE, writes, "There is life on earth -- one life, which embraces every animal and plant on the planet. Time has divided it up into several million parts, but each is an integral part of the whole. A rose is a rose, but it is also a robin and a rabbit. We are all of one flesh, drawn from the same crucible."

The God of which I teach is that same all-encompassing ecology -- not only of the earth, but of the entire universe. Each of us is a droplet of water in the vast and unending Ocean of God. There is nothing which is not God. Our belief or unbelief, doctrine or doubt, searching or scoffing are also parts of what is, which is God.

"No man is an island, entire of itself," wrote John Donne. "Every man is a piece of the continent, a part of the main; if a clod be washed away by the sea, Europe is the less, as well as if a promontory were, as well as if a manor of thy friends or of thine own were. Any man's death diminishes me, because I am involved in mankind; and therefore never send to know for whom the bell tolls; it tolls for thee."

Those words, for me, are literally true, not only in a global sense, or only human, but referring to all things that exist, everywhere.

And how do we "pray"? The ancient psalmist told us: Be still--

"Be still, and know that I am God."

Not with words of supplication, or even of praise, but with surrender and quietness, with openness to let peace and love flow through us and become us.

LESSON

When Karen was twelve, she stayed overnight with a friend and went to church with her the next morning.

"The preacher asked how many were praying and their prayers weren't being answered," Karen told us. "A lot of people raised their hands. So the preacher told them their mistake was in saying, 'If it be Thy will.' Instead, he told them, they should praise God, tell him how much they love him, and then he'll give them what they want."

"Do you agree?" we asked her.

"That's just trying to butter God up," Karen said firmly, "and make him feel good, so he'll give us what we want. God is too smart for that."

IN THE LIGHT

Officer Archie O'Henry, on a routine patrol one evening, spotted a potted gentleman crawling on hands and knees under the streetlight.

"Can I help you, sir?" he called through his rolled-down window.

The man looked up and finally managed to focus on Officer O'Henry. "Lost my car keys," he explained.

The officer sighed, shut off his motor, and went to help. "Are you sure you lost them here?" he asked.

"Nope," said the man, "lost 'em over there, under that tree. Or maybe that one over there."

The officer scratched his chin. "I hope you won't think I'm being too critical, sir," he said, "but if you lost them over there, wouldn't it make more sense to look for them over there?"

The man hiccoughed and took a deep breath and said indignantly, "'Course not. There's no light over there."

SERMON

Calvin Coolidge, the Vermonter who became the thirtieth American president, was asked one day what the preacher had talked about in church that morning.

"Hell," Coolidge replied.

"Oh? What did he say about it?"

"He's ag'in it," Coolidge replied.

LAST WORDS

Preacher Jones, the traveling pastor, had decided to retire, and had finally found a buyer for his horse.

"Joe," he said, "I'm disappointed that you've never come around to be saved, but if you've got the money, the horse is yours."

Joe handed over the money and Preacher handed Joe the reins.

"By the way, Joe, there are two things I should tell you about this horse. First, when you want him to go, you'll have to say, 'Praise the Lord.' Nothing else will make him move."

Joe frowned, but nodded his understanding.

"The second thing," Preacher said, "is when you want him to stop, you've got to say, 'Amen.' Nothing else will make him even slow down."

Joe frowned again, then nodded, and swung into the saddle. He jabbed his heels into the horse's sides and said, "Giddap!"

The horse lazily turned its head to look at Joe, then stretched its neck down to nibble at some grass.

"Remember what I told you, Joe," Preacher said.

"Oh, all right," Joe said disgustedly. "Praise the Lord!"

The horse took off like a shot, neck stretched in front of him, tail flying behind. Joe grabbed the pommel and barely managed to stay in the saddle as the horse galloped away.

Just as Joe finally got himself settled comfortably in the saddle and was beginning to enjoy the ride, he noticed that the horse was going about forty miles an hour straight toward a cliff and his speed was increasing. Joe pulled back on the reins as hard as he could, shouting, "Whoa! Stop! Whoa!" but the horse galloped on.

Just yards from the cliff's edge, Joe remembered. "Amen!" he screamed frantically. "Amen!"

The horse stiffened its legs, leaned back on its haunches, and slid to a stop, coming to rest two inches from the edge of the cliff, then stood trembling, anxiously waiting for Joe's command.

Joe looked down -- three miles down -- over the sheer cliff.

He sighed, and wiped the sweat from his forehead with his sleeve, and said "Praise the Lord."

DIVINE COMEDY

God, on a routine patrol one day, stalked me as I walked through the winter woods.

"Can I help you, sir?" he called through a curious chickadee.

I looked up. "I've lost the secret of the universe," I explained.

God sighed in a breeze, circled in a hawk, and came to help in a little flurry of snowflakes. "Are you sure you lost it here?" he asked.

"No," I said. "I think it was in one of those philosophies over there. Or maybe in one of those religions."

God chuckled in the brook. "I hope you won't think I'm being too critical, sir," he said, "but if you lost it in a thought, why are you searching for it in the woods?"

"The light is better here," I answered.

"Trying to butter me up?" God asked.

"No," I answered. "When Adam asked for creatures, you thought he said preachers, so you gave him a lot."

God chuckled in the brook. "Not bad," he said.

"Thank you," I said.

"Not _very_ bad," God amended. "Have you heard the story about Calvin Coolidge?"

PILGRIMAGE

Our children must form their own relationships with the universe. Knowledge of God can't be taught; it must come from within. Trying to describe God with words is like dipping a bucket into the rushing brook beside our house: the water in the bucket, captured and held, is no longer the same as it was; it no longer bubbles and breathes and gurgles. We can hint, and point a general direction, commensurate with our own understanding; but our children must find their own ways by themselves, when they're ready.

We agree with Thoreau: "They who know of no purer source of truth, who have traced up its stream no higher, stand, and wisely stand, by the Bible and the Constitution, and drink at it there with reverence and humility; but they who behold where it comes trickling into this lake or that pool, gird up their loins once more, and continue their pilgrimage toward its fountainhead."

We hope to give our children the strength and desire to continue that pilgrimage.

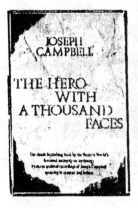

IN THE BEGINNING: Creation Stories from Around the World, compiled and edited by Virginia Hamilton. 25 intriguing stories from cultures around the world about the creation of the world and mankind. Illustrated with beautiful watercolors by Barry Moser. All ages. $18.95. Code HBJ. BROOK FARM BOOKS.

THE OXFORD BOOK OF PRAYER, edited by George Appleton. A selection of prayers combining traditional with modern, with material from the Bible and the Book of Common Prayer to a Ghanaian fisherman's prayer, including prayers from great non-Christian religions. The compilers looked first for spiritual quality; secondly, for literary merit, whether of eloquence or simplicity; and, thirdly, for "a living relevance," asking, "Does it ring true?" The prayers are arranged in subject groupings; complete index. 416 pages. $18.95. Code OX. BROOK FARM BOOKS.

BIBLE COLORING BOOKS --
A COLORING BOOK OF THE OLD TESTAMENT -- Scenes from the Tickhill & other Psalters, reproduced from manuscripts of the 13th and 14th centuries; interesting introduction to medieval art.
A COLORING BOOK OF THE NEW TESTAMENT -- Ready-to-illuminate illustrations from the renowned St. Alban's Psalter and other Romanesque manuscripts.
BIBLE COLORING BOOKS, $2.95 each. Code BB. BROOK FARM BOOKS.

DICTIONARY OF WORLD RELIGIONS-- A concise, authoritative compendium of information on the world's living religions, including Christianity, Judaism, Buddhism, Hinduism, and many others. More than 1600 cross-referenced entries, with many key creeds, prayers, and mantras given in full. 848 pages, 131 black-&-white photographs and illustrations, eight pages of color maps, more. $22.95 plus $2 postage. BROOK FARM BOOKS.

THE HERO WITH A THOUSAND FACES, by Joseph Campbell. This audio-cassette adaptation of Joseph Campbell's bestselling book and popular PBS television show brings to life his insightful, poetic interpretation of mythology. Drawing on myths & legends from around the world, Campbell describes "the universal hero," asserting that myths are not merely enchanting fairy tales filled with demons, rituals, and romance, but are allegories which can help us make sense of the timeless mysteries of humankind's physical and spiritual worlds. Weaving traditional wisdom of the past with the modern struggle for identity and spiritual growth, Campbell demonstrates that folklore and mystic literature are potent sources of universal meaning that can serve as spiritual metaphors for modern man. Two cassettes, 2 hours. $16.95. Code STM. BROOK FARM BOOKS.

THE PROPHET, Kahlil Gibran. This beautiful and simple book of poetic prose tells us that work without love is worse than begging; that if there is a despot we would dethrone, we should see first that he is dethroned in our minds; and that children are the arrows of God, and we are His bows. "What is it to make laws but to trace around our own shadows on the ground? But what law binds him who walks facing the sun?" A book to read, re-read, and browse in often. **$12.95. Code RH. BROOK FARM BOOKS.**

THE BOOK OF JOB. Translated by Stephen Mitchell; read by Peter Coyote. Excellent performance captures the great spiritual and human power of this ancient Hebrew legend, bringing new meaning and understanding of the original. Unabridged; 1 hour 13 minutes. $9.95. Code TSP. BROOK FARM BOOKS.

THE ILLUSTRATED BIBLE, complete text from THE LIVING BIBLE, with over 400 color illustrations; various bindings available. DAVID C. COOK PUBLISHING CO., 850 No. Grove Ave., Elgin, IL 60120.

PICTURE BIBLES, biblical and inspirational books for all ages. ST. PAUL BOOKS & MEDIA, 50 St. Paul's Avenue, Boston, MA 02130.

THE BOOK OF THINK, or How To Solve a Problem Twice Your Size (a Brown Paper School Book), by Marilyn Burns. Did you ever have a traffic jam in your head? Did you ever feel as if on some days you just won't do anything right? Did you ever get yourself into a corner and know that whichever way you tried to get out was going to be the wrong way? If the answer to any of those questions is "Yes," then this book is for you. This book is about what to do when you are puzzled, or perplexed, or stumped, or can't get there from here. It's about using your noggin. It's about being smart even when you feel dumb. This book is about how to think even when you know you're fresh out of ideas. If you are a person who never has a problem, then don't read this book. $9.95. Code LB. BROOK FARM BOOKS.

RETURN OF THE INDIAN SPIRIT, Vinson Brown. A young Indian boy, raised in the city, visits the reservation and is inspired to attain the knowledge of his forefathers. Children and adults. $5.95. Code TSP. BROOK FARM BOOKS.

NEW OXFORD REVIEW, 1069 Kains Ave., Berkeley, CA 94706. Ecumenical, intellectual "return to religion," praised equally by conservatives such as George Will and Newsweek and by liberals such as Utne Reader. Suggests that "the answers" are in the tradition of Moses, Jeremiah, Jesus, Augustine, Dante, Aquinas, Tolstoy, Kierkegaard, Buber, Niebuhr, Dorothy Day, and Mother Teresa. 1 year/$14. 2 years/ $23. Sample, $3.50.

GREAT IDEAS THAT HAVE SHAPED OUR WORLD -- Excellent cassette programs presenting the ideas of Paine, Jefferson, Thoreau, Garrison, Adam Smith, Mill, Burke, Hamilton, Hobbes, Locke, de Tocqueville, and others. See this title under History.

GREAT CHRISTIAN BOOKS, 1319 Newport Gap Pike, Wilmington, DE 19804. Christian books, music, records, cassettes.

PILGRIM'S PROGRESS, by John Bunyan; dramatized, with music & sound effects; six hours on audio cassettes. $33.00 ppd. COMPANY ONE, Box 1, Angwin, CA 94508. (A religious drama ministry.)

EASTERN THOUGHT AND RELIGION -- Books on karma, Universal Brotherhood, reincarnation, etc. THE THEOSOPHY COMPANY, 245 West 33rd Street, Los Angeles, CA 90007.

GREAT CLASSICAL MYTHS.
THE CITY OF GOD, St. Augustine.
THE WISDOM OF CONFUCIUS.
THE WISDOM OF LAOTSE.
THE WORKS OF PLATO.
  See Literature, "Modern Library."

ATLAS OF THE BIBLE LANDS. See History & Geography.

A BRIEF HISTORY OF TIME, by Stephen Hawking -- See my description and review of this book and six-hour cassette package under "Science." I mention it here because science and religion are both searching to understand the nature of the universe, and because Hawking's book might also be a brief history of God, although he only hints that this might be so.

THE VARIETIES OF RELIGIOUS EXPERIENCE, by William James. A comprehensive masterpiece that explores the personal, subjective, and mystical aspects of religion, considering religion not as a series of doctrines and beliefs, but as a direct experience of that force or essence of being which we call "God." Modern Library edition. $17.50. Code RH. BROOK FARM BOOKS.

THE PRINCIPLES OF PYSCHOLOGY, William James. Although written a hundred years ago, this classic study of human psychology is still an excellent introduction to concepts such as stream of consciousness, self-consciousness, instinct, will, perception, memory, and emotion; and psychology related to philosophy, experience, and the arts. Volume I, $9.95. Volume II, $9.95. Code DV. BROOK FARM BOOKS.

ZEN IN THE ART OF ARCHERY, by Eugene Herrigel. This enduring classic in its field demonstrates several of the basic differences between "eastern" and "western" thought; more importantly, it shows how, through archery (or flower arrangement, or fencing, or almost anything) one can become aware of the absolute Oneness of everything. When the archer abandons his feelings of separateness from the target, when he realizes that he and the bow and the arrow and the target are essentially One, then he sees the futility of striving to hit the target -- and the impossibility of missing. $8.95. Code OX. BROOK FARM BOOKS.

The sun, with all those planets revolving around it and dependent on it, can still ripen a bunch of grapes as if it had nothing else in the universe to do.

                              --Galileo

EINSTEIN AND THE BUDDHA -- See this title under Science.

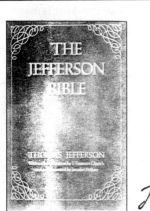

THOMAS JEFFERSON'S LIFE OF JESUS -- Also called "The Jefferson Bible." While president, Jefferson compiled a version of the Four Gospels that eliminated the virgin birth and resurrection, and focused instead on the meaning of Jesus's life and how he lived. Like Thomas Paine and many others of his time, Jefferson was a firm believer in God, but did not accept the doctrines of sin, salvation, and vicarious atonement, and believed (as do many theologians today) that these doctrines were added to the teachings of Christ after he died, and had nothing to do with Christ's actual teachings. Not surprisingly, critics said that Jefferson was only re-writing gospel to suit himself, but he believed he was attempting to restore Jesus's real message. "It is in our lives and not our words that our religion must be read," he wrote. Whether or not one agrees with Jefferson, his LIFE OF JESUS provides an excellent insight into the religious and moral beliefs of one of America's most important early leaders. It may also be useful in the way Jefferson intended it -- as a look at Jesus's actual life and teachings without added doctrinal interpretations. $2.95. Code TG. BROOK FARM BOOKS.

TRY THIS ON YOUR COMPUTER -- IMPORTANT CORRECTION!! In my first edition, I said that in the mid-1800's Bishop James Usher calulated that God finished the creation of everything on October 22, 4004 B.C., at exactly 6:30 AM. I was wrong, on both dates, and I hope my faulty reporting didn't make you late for any appointments. Usher (1581-1656), while Archbishop of Armagh, calculated that God finished the creation on October 22, 4004 B.C., not at 6:30 AM, but at exactly 6:00 PM. However, in 1859, 200 years later, Dr. John Lightfoot, Vice Chancellor of the University of Cambridge, said Usher was wrong anyway. "Heaven and earth and man," he said, "was created by the Trinity on twenty-third of October, 4004 B.C., at nine o'clock in the morning." (Now that that's settled, let's work on our grammar.)

gy=c -- Look for this item under "Science" (check the Index if you can't find it) to learn why this might be God's signature.

I have hardly ever known a mathematician who was capable of reasoning.

Plato

I have gained this by philosophy: that I do without being commanded what others do only from fear of the law.

Aristotle

I would not have believed the gospel had not the authority of the Church moved me.

St. Augustine

Three things are necessary for the salvation of man: to know what he ought to believe; to know what he ought to desire; and to know what he ought to do.

St. Thomas Aquinas

Nature abhors a vacuum.

Baruch Spinoza

THE GIANTS OF PHILOSOPHY -- "Moderation in all things." "I think, therefore I am." "The unexamined life is not worth living." "And it is this that everyone understands to be God." These are the men whose thoughts have formed much of our Western civilization -- Plato, Aristotle, St. Augustine, Immanuel Kant, and nine others. These are the men who have contributed greatly to the ideas we now have about happiness, love, art, God, morality, reason, justice, goodness, and evil.

The format of these presentations is the same as that of the "Great Ideas That Have Shaped Our World" (see History). The cassette tapes of The Giants of Philosophy are dramatized, with multiple voices portraying the author, contemporary observers, and critics, drawing on actual writings and quotations of the time and later history, with an overview narrated by actor Charlton Heston. Each tape is about 90 minutes long, divided into shorter segments, about 20 minutes each, for more convenient study. The social and historical background of each work is presented, as well as the effects, both immediate and long-term, which the work had on other thinkers and on society. There are numerous references to other works and historical events, demonstrating the continuing influence of the author's ideas.

Listening to these tapes is much better than simply reading the works which are discussed. The full background of the works and their influences on contemporary and future society are fully explored, giving a much deeper understanding than could be gained from the works by themselves.

Set 1. PLATO (ca. 430-350 B.C.), Greece. Plato, the first great Western philosopher, thought that existing things are modeled on changeless, eternal forms. To Plato, human beings consist of an immortal soul and a mortal body; the soul has a love for the eternal, the good, the true, and the beautiful; these give live purpose, stability, and meaning.

Set 2. ARISTOTLE (384-322 B.C.), Greece. In revising Plato's ideas, Aristotle thought human beings are one with the rest of nature, yet set apart from it by their ability to reason. Aristotle codified the laws of thought, gave a complete account of nature and of God, and developed an attractive view of the Good Life and the Good Society. He was the first to describe physics, biology, psychology, and the standards of literature systematically.

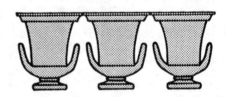

Set 3. ST. AUGUSTINE (354-430 A.D.), Rome. St. Augustine, the first great systematic Christian philosopher, thought of Plato's eternal forms as ideas in the mind of God; he believed Christ provided the light of knowledge to the human mind. His detailed description of the "City of God" portrayed a divine ordering of human affairs.

Set 4. ST. THOMAS AQUINAS (1224-1274), Italy. The Summa Theologica was St. Thomas Aquinas' monumental summation of the facts of Christian faith and knowledge. He offered proofs of the existence of God and set limits to the power of reason; he gave an account of the nature and constitution of the world, and outlined the soul's road to blessedness.

Set 5. BARUCH SPINOZA (1632-1677), The Netherlands. Spinoza took the unorthodox view that God, an eternal and infinite being, is identical with the world, and that we are therefore merely parts of the Deity. Human fulfillment is possible, he believed, only by rejecting our finite, flawed selves and identifying with the eternal within us.

Set 6. DAVID HUME (1711-1776), Scotland. Hume thought the entire world is constituted of the perceptions from our sense-experience. He had profound doubts about our ability to know anything with certainty; he was skeptical of science, and vigorously attacked others' proofs of the existence of God. He thought reason is a slave to our passions, yet was optimistic about human nature.

Beauty in things exists in the mind which contemplates them.

David Hume

Morality is not properly the doctrine of how we may make ourselves happy, but how we may make ourselves worthy of happiness.

Immanuel Kant

What experience and history teach is this -- that people and governments never have learned anything from history, or acted on principles deduced from it.

Georg Wilhelm Friedrich Hegel

Every man takes the limits of his own field of vision for the limits of the world.

Arthur Schopenhauer

Life can only be understood backwards; but it must be lived forwards.

Soren Kierkegaard

Man is a rope stretched between the animal and the Superman -- a rope over an abyss.

Friedrich Nietzsche

...The school is primarily a social institution; education, therefore, is a process of living and not a preparation for future living.

John Dewey

Man is not the sum of what he has but the totality of what he does not yet have, of what he might have.

Jean Paul Sartre

Set 7. IMMANUEL KANT (1724-1804), Germany. Kant believed that reason, the most fundamental human faculty, creates a world in which all events are causally connected; it enables us to act morally, to enjoy beauty, and to appreciate nature's magnificence. He forecast the possibility of a purely rational religion, and believed that the rule of reason might lead to permanent international peace. Kant believed that God's existence cannot be known, but he saw evidence of God in the moral order of the world.

Set 8. GEORG WILHELM FRIEDRICH HEGEL (1770-1831), Germany. Hegel aimed to make philosophy a comprehensive science and to restate the truth of Christianity in more precise language. For him, the state represents the divine on earth; our lives have meaning only as small parts of this larger entity. Hegel saw progress as the work of reason and of the "dialectic" - a historical process moving us through struggle and contradiction to a higher synthesis.

Set 9. ARTHUR SCHOPENHAUER (1788-1860), Germany. Schopenhauer was the most articulate and influential philosophical pessimist in the history of human thought. He believed the space and time of ordinary life are illusions, and that we can flourish only at each other's expense. Life, therefore, is evil to the core, and pain and suffering are unavoidable; the price of escape is the total surrender of ambition, desire, and choice. (Compare this with the revelations which came to Siddhartha Gautama, bringing him to the realizations which made him the Buddha.)

Set 10. SOREN KIERKEGAARD (1813-1855), Denmark. Kierkegaard believed that truth emerges only from our subjective, private lives; but neither the selfish search for pleasure nor a responsible social life can fully satisfy us. A deeply religous thinker, he believed God's existence cannot be proven, but that only a religious leap of faith can make our own finitude bearable and endow life with meaning.

Set 11. FRIEDRICH NIETZSCHE (1844-1900), Germany. Nietzsche announced in 1883 that God is dead, reasoning that the world's injustices and suffering could not exist if God were still alive. He also believed that truth is relative, and proposed to replace the values of traditional morality with the idea that creative human beings can use their energy, strength, and intelligence to give purpose and meaning to their own lives.

Set 12. JOHN DEWEY (1859-1952), The United States. Dewey believed that the scientific method, when applied to human affairs, can enhance personal happiness and community cooperation. Dewey believed that democracy is not so much a political organization as a way of life; it is best promoted by a rational and effective educational system. Dewey's educational theories which grew out of his philosophy have been greatly criticized, but are still very influential.

Set 13. JEAN-PAUL SARTRE (1905-1980), France. Sartre was a leading advocate of existentialism -- the view that we must establish our own existence, and individual dignity, despite a meaningless life and a final death. Sartre asserted the ultimate reality of human freedom and the desperate need for personal responsibility.

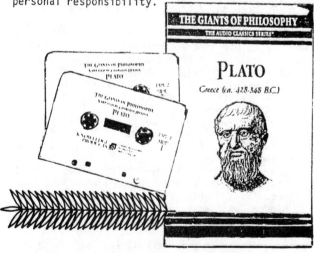

THE GIANTS OF PHILOSOPHY
THE AUDIO CLASSICS SERIES

PLATO
Greece (ca. 428-348 B.C.)

EACH SET (two cassettes, approximately 3 hours), $15.95. Postage: $2.00 for the first set, and $1.00 for each additional set. Specify "Giants of Philosophy," set number and title (e.g., "Set #11, Nietzsche.") Order from BROOK FARM BOOKS.

WALDEN, or Life in the Woods
by Henry David Thoreau

I spent many of my childhood and teenage weekends and summers hiking and camping in the woods of southern Vermont, sometimes with one or two friends, but more often by myself. One day, my sophomore English teacher, Walter Cohen, had written the title of this book on the chalkboard, and the sub-title made me wait eagerly for his explanation -- which never came. At the end of the day, the note was erased. I realized much later he had been sowing a random seed, and I may have been the most fertile ground in that particular class.

About that time, the early 50's, some of the world's best literature was being published in inexpensive paperbacks for the first time. Browsing in a bookstore one afternoon (a favorite pastime), I recognized that title, and bought it -- for 35¢ -- and soon entered into one of the most important revolutions of my life. The first pages told me the book wasn't about camping at all, and not very much about life in the woods. It was about life in society, life in the world, life in the universe, life within oneself. How should I live my life? To whom or to what do I owe allegiance? How should I relate to other people, to society, to government, to my own existence?

"Why should we be in such desperate haste to succeed," Thoreau asked, "and in such desperate enterprises? If a man does not keep pace with his companions, perhaps it is because he hears a different drummer. Let him step to the music which he hears, however measured or far away" -- not meaning, as many would have it today, that one should act capriciously or merely for self-gratification, but that one should listen for, and be guided by, the inner voice of conscience, of principle, of higher laws than those devised by governments. "I think that we should be men first, and subjects afterward. It is not desirable to cultivate a respect for the law, so much as for the right."

I devoured the book; it devoured me. What I felt was not so much agreement as recognition, as if many of Thoreau's thoughts were already in my mind and soul, hidden, waiting only to be called forth by an expression of them far greater than I would ever achieve.

Thoreau refused to pay his poll tax to Massachusetts, because that state supported the Fugitive Slave Act and the Mexican War, both of which he believed were wrong. For a while, he was a schoolmaster, but was fired for taking his students on nature walks, and for refusing to whip them periodically to keep them in line.

Thoreau's essay "Civil Disobedience" has encouraged thousands, perhaps millions, to resist injustice, not through bloodshed and violence, but by personal withdrawal from the injustice. You can't stop the machinery of government, he said, but your deliberate opposition to its tyranny may throw a little sand in the gears. Gandhi, Tolstoy, and Martin Luther King, Jr., credit their reading of "Civil Disobedience" as a turning point in their own education and careers. No one, before or since, has so eloquently and accurately summed up the ideal relation of a person to society, to government, and to oneself.

Thoreau used words carefully and exactly, never settling for an approximation of what he meant, always choosing the word which precisely conveyed his meaning. He was a classical scholar, and likened the tending of his bean field to ancient battles -- "Daily the beans saw me come to their rescue armed with a hoe, and thin the ranks of their enemies, filling up the trenches with weedy dead. Many a lusty crest-waving Hector, that towered a whole foot above his crowding comrades, fell before my weapon and rolled in the dust." He enjoyed puns -- "If you are chosen town clerk, you cannot go to Tierra del Fuego this summer; but you may go to the land of infernal fire nevertheless."

WALDEN and "Civil Disobedience" shouldn't be required reading, because the person who isn't ready for them will get little from them, but every thinking person should have a copy, and browse in it occasionally, ready for the moment when Thoreau's words suddenly open the shutters and let the sunlight in.

I've read WALDEN several times, and re-read bits of it -- a sentence here, a paragraph there, often becoming absorbed and finishing the chapter -- scores of times. I always discover something new in myself.

There are many editions of WALDEN and Thoreau's other works. I recommend the Modern Library edition, WALDEN AND OTHER WRITINGS BY HENRY DAVID THOREAU, which includes his two other books -- A WEEK ON THE CONCORD & MERRIMACK RIVERS and CAPE COD -- and six of his most important essays -- "The Allegash and East Branch," "Walking," "Civil Disobedience," "Slavery in Massachusetts," "A Plea for Captain John Brown," and "Life Without Principle." This is a durable, hardcover book, with clear text, and a reasonable price. $18.50. Code RH. BROOK FARM BOOKS.

A MAN NAMED THOREAU, by Robert Burleigh. An excellent introduction to Henry David Thoreau for ages 8 and up, but also very interesting for older readers, including adults. Quotations from WALDEN have been woven with biographical facts and bits of Thoreau's philosophy to give an intriguing picture of an unusual man & his examination of conventional society. Many difficult concepts have been simplified without loss or distortion of meaning, making this a very good introduction to many questions of ethics and morality, as well as a portrait of Thoreau. Many illustrations by Lloyd Bloom. Hardcover, 48 pages. $12.95. Code MAC. BROOK FARM BOOKS.

HENRY THOREAU: A Life of the Mind, Robert Richardson. The author's narrative unites several selections from Thoreau's journals, presenting a compelling picture of Thoreau's spiritual and intellectual life. Woodcuts by Barry Moser. $10.95 plus $2 postage. BROOK FARM BOOKS.

WALDEN, Henry David Thoreau. Brief selections from WALDEN, illustrated with full-color lino-cuts. In March 1845, Henry David Thoreau borrowed an axe from Bronson Alcott (father of Louisa May Alcott, author of LITTLE WOMEN) and built a small cabin next to Walden Pond in Concord, Massachusetts, in which he lived for two years, two months, and two days. His purpose, he wrote later, was to live simply, and to discover exactly what things are truly essential in life. These selections by Steve Lowe and illustrations by Robert Sabuda portray some of the most peaceful moments of Thoreau's life in the woods, building his cabin, tending his bean field, swimming in the pond at dawn, and playing his flute in the evening. An excellent introduction to Thoreau and many of his ideas, for children and adults, and a very enjoyable companion to full-text editions of WALDEN. $15.95. Code BT. BROOK FARM BOOKS.

RELIGION, SCRIPTURES, AND SPIRITUALITY -- Since the dawn of civilization, religions have expressed the concerns at the core of human existence -- life's meaning and purpose, the significance of birth and death, moral commitments, and the proper conduct of life. Religion transcends <u>making a living</u> to guide us in <u>how we should live</u>. It involves us with what some theologians call "an other" -- an inexpressible, non-rational part of existence that may be an emotional refuge or a source of spiritual nourishment and enlightenment. The history of the world is intertwined with religion, and can never be fully understood without a basic knowledge of the beliefs that have shaped it.

Each of these programs consists of two 90-minute cassette tapes, narrated by actor Ben Kingsley, and featuring dozens of dramatizations and characterizations of great religious leaders, theologians, historians, and readers of the various scriptures.

<u>Set #1</u>. ORTHODOX AND ROMAN CATHOLIC CHRISTIANITY. Both of these churches have their roots in first-century Christianity; their basic doctrines were summarized in the great Councils of the Churches, yet Orthodoxy and Catholicism have diverged through the centuries as each embraced different ideas about worship, ethics, and relations to politics and culture.

<u>Set #2</u>. PROTESTANT CHRISTIANITY. Since the sixteenth century, Christianity has flourished in a third form called Protestantism. In the Protestant Reformation, four distinct forms of religious expression emerged -- Lutheran, Reformed, Anglican, and various radical extensions of those three initial movements. Succeeding developments extended this variety over the centuries, leading to the many sects and denominations of today.

<u>Set #3</u>. JUDAISM. Judaism is both a religion and a way of life. It has several major forms or traditions (Orthodox, Conservative, Reform, and Reconstructionist); it is also the parent religion of both Christianity and Islam. Jewish sacred literature preserves the ancient oral tradition through the Hebrew Bible (Christianity's Old Testament), and other writings (in particular, the Talmud). Judaism exalts the divine gifts of the Torah, God's teaching or instruction.

<u>Set #4</u>. ISLAM. Islam began in the seventh century, and has evolved into various forms -- Sunni, Shi'ah, Sufi mysticism, etc., and is now a rapidly-growing religion. This program also discusses the backgrounds and connections of related groups such as the Druse, Baha'i, the Nation of Islam, etc.

<u>Set #5</u>. HINDUISM. Hinduism began in India about 1800 B.C.; several other religions and philosophies have sprung from it, including Buddhism and the Jain tradition (both 6th century B.C.) and the Sikh tradition (15th century A.D.). Vedanta, Yoga, transcendental meditation, and other spiritual and meditative exercises are also related to Hinduism.

<u>Set #6</u>. BUDDHISM. Buddhism began with Siddhartha Gautama in the 6th century B.C., and has developed two chief forms: Theravada (or Hinayana) is found especially in Asian countries; Zen, a more recent form of Buddhism, is found throughout the world.

<u>Set #7</u>. SHINTO AND JAPANESE NEW RELIGIONS. Traditional Shinto was present in Japan from prehistoric times, and has greatly influenced Japanese culture. This program discusses various forms of Shinto, as well as new Japanese religions formed during the last 150 years.

<u>Set #8</u>. CONFUCIANISM AND TAOISM. Confucius, in the 6th century B.C., stressed family ethics and humanistic virtues and values. Taoism, beginning only a little later, is concerned with universal principles as well as social values.

<u>Set #9</u>. NON-LITERATE RELIGIONS. "Primitive" religious practices and understandings -- those without a surviving sacred literature -- are recognized by many to be in no way inferior to other religious beliefs. This program compares various non-literate religions, along with a discussion of their geographical concentrations and historical development.

<u>Set #10</u>. CLASSICAL MEDITERRANEAN RELIGIONS AND MYTHS. Mesopotamia, Egypt, Asia Minor, Canaan, Greece, and Rome have greatly and continuously influenced all of Western culture and civilization, and the literature and culture of the religions of these areas have also influenced Hebrew and Christian scriptures.

<u>Set #11</u>. AFRICAN AND AFRICAN-AMERICAN RELIGION. The religious ideas & practices of African peoples have much in common with each other, and with related religions in the Caribbean and the Americas.

<u>Set #12</u>. NATIVE RELIGIONS OF THE AMERICAS. This program discusses the religious heritage and cultures of North, Central, & South American Indians.

<u>Set #13</u>. SKEPTICISM AND RELIGIOUS RELATIVISM. Humanism, agnosticism, & atheism have always challenged traditional religious doctrines, yet reason alone -- like religious faith alone -- often raises more questions than answers. Can a religious commitment be reconciled with life in a rational, skeptical world?

EACH SET (approximately 3 hours), $15.95. Order by number and title. POSTAGE: $2.00 for the first set, and $1.00 for each additional set. Order from BROOK FARM BOOKS.

There is in all things an inexhaustible sweetness and purity, a silence that is a fountain of action and joy. It rises up in wordless gentleness and flows out to me from unseen roots of all created being.
Thomas Merton

Our life is what our thoughts make it.
Marcus Aurelius

Physical bravery is an animal instinct; moral bravery is a much higher and truer courage.
Wendell Phillips

Every day one should at least... read one good poem, see one fine painting and -- if at all possible -- speak a few sensible words.
Goethe

Every religion is good that teaches man to be good.
Thomas Paine

...Ministers who spoke of God as if they enjoyed a monopoly of the subject.
Henry David Thoreau

Our humanity were a poor thing but for the divinity that stirs within us.
Francis Bacon

The world is my country, all mankind are my brethren, and to do good is my religion.
Thomas Paine

Do not be too moral. You may cheat yourself out of much life so. Aim above morality. Be not simply good; be good for something.
Henry David Thoreau

We have been judging and punishing ever since Jesus told us not to, and I defy anyone to make out a convincing case for believing the world has been made better than it would have been if there had never been a judge, a prison, or a gallows in all that time.
George Bernard Shaw

The Lord's Prayer contains the sum total of religion and morals.
Duke of Wellington

The devil loves nothing better than the intolerance of reformers.
James Russell Lowell

I hate people who are intolerant.
Laurence J. Peter

All are but parts of one stupendous whole,
Whose body Nature is, and God the soul.
Alexander Pope

Humanity is the Son of God.
Theodore Parker

The test of a preacher is that his congregation goes away saying, not What a lovely sermon, but, I will do something!
St. Francis de Sales

Adam and Eve had many advantages, but the principal one was that they escaped teething.
Mark Twain

The care of every man's soul belongs to himself. I cannot give up my guidance to the magistrate, because he knows no more of the way to heaven than I do.
Thomas Jefferson

When angry, count ten before you speak; if very angry, a hundred.
Thomas Jefferson

When angry, count four; when very angry, swear.
Mark Twain

There was never yet philosopher that could endure the toothache patiently.
William Shakespeare

A CHILD IS BORN: The Drama of Life Before Birth. Photographs by Lennart Nilsson; text by Jirjam Furuhjelm, Axel Ingelman-Sundberg, and Claes Wirsen. This is an awesomely-beautiful photographic record of life developing inside the womb, from conception to birth, and of birth itself. Children and adults of all ages will feel as if they're gazing into a magical world in the pictures, all in full color in this new edition. Imagine: this is what you looked like inside your mother when you were five weeks old. $25.00. Code DD. BROOK FARM BOOKS.

HUSBAND-COACHED CHILDBIRTH, Robert A. Bradley, MD; foreword by Ashley Montagu. In 1966, when our first daughter was born, the husband's participation in childbirth was considered very radical; today, in many areas at least, it has become common. This book is one of the very best in discussing the father's role and the ways in which his presence and participation contribute during both pregnancy and childbirth. Ill effects of drugs are discussed. We recommend this book very highly to all couples expecting a baby. New revised edition, hardcover. $18.95. Code HR. BROOK FARM BOOKS.

THE ILLUSTRATED DICTIONARY OF PREGNANCY & CHILDBIRTH by Carl Jones. Defines and explains over 1500 technical terms used in referring to pregnancy & childbirth, with explanations and recommendations regarding discomfort, circumcision, electronic fetal monitoring, false labor, etc. #0-671-68993-2. $7.95 plus $1 postage. MEADOWBROOK PRESS, 18318 Minnetonka Blvd., Deephaven, MN 55391.

BIRTHING SUPPLY CATALOG -- Everything you'll need (and a lot you won't need) for a safe, happy, knowledgeable birth, and afterward. Thermometers, bed pads, stethoscopes, ear scopes, baby food grinder, speculums, disposable gloves, herbal tea, much more, and scores of books on pregnancy, birth, and breastfeeding. Also several "emergency" items, such as resuscitation equipment and hemoglobinometers, which are probably for professional midwives. If you're getting ready for a birth, read a lot of good books about it, and don't buy a lot of gimmicks without knowing what they're really for, or if you'll really need them. NATURPATH MEDICAL & BIRTHING SUPPLIES, RR 1 Box 99C, Hawthorne, FL 32640.

MOTHERING, P.O. Box 1690, Santa Fe, NM 87504. The leading international magazine devoted to natural childbirth, child-raising, nursing, midwifery, with articles, photographs, book and product reviews, and useful advertisements of books, childbirth resources, education, health, herbs, music, natural beauty care, services, toys, etc. Quarterly. $18 per year.

YOUR PRESCHOOL CHILD, Robyn Gee and Susan Meredith. A one-volume combination of two books. ENTERTAINING AND EDUCATING BABIES AND TODDLERS has hundreds of activity and toy ideas, all easy and inexpensive, with attractive and detailed drawings on every page. Sections cover things to look at and listen to, things to feel and hold, learning to talk, books and stories, energetic and messy play, imitating and pretending, things to fit together and take apart, walks and trips, and more. ENTERTAINING AND EDUCATING YOUNG CHILDREN has hundreds more ideas and activities, covering art, books, music, cutting, building, sand and water play, dressing up and pretending, animals, collecting, parties, vegetable printing, growing hair on an eggshell clown, making books, and more. $11.95. Code EDC. BROOK FARM BOOKS.

IMPRINTS -- A catalog-newsletter with reviews of books about pregnancy, birth, childraising, health, home education. Books, records, tapes, magazines, pamphlets. Free sample. IMPRINTS, Birth & Life Bookstore, P.O. Box 70625, Seattle, WA 98107.

SPECIAL DELIVERY: The Complete Guide to Informed Birth, Rahima Baldwin. For couples who want to take greater responsibility for the birth of their baby, whether at home, in a birth center, or in the hospital. Couples have come to see birth as a natural process, not a "sickness" or abnormal condition, and any birth carried out with this awareness, with the focus on the people rather than on the technology, is a special delivery. 8½x11", 30 photographs, bibliography, index, drawings. $12.95. Code TSP. BROOK FARM BOOKS. (See also Education, YOU ARE YOUR CHILD'S FIRST TEACHER, by Rahima Baldwin.)

THE COMPLEAT MOTHER, The Magazine of Pregnancy, Birth, and Breastfeeding. Quarterly. $10/yr; $18/2 years. THE COMPLEAT MOTHER, RR 2, Orangeville, Ontario, Canada L9W 2Y9.

ABSENTEE PARENTS? Sociologists predict that by the year 2000, 80 percent of new work force members will be women, 80 percent of all two-parent families will have both parents working outside the home, and four out of five children under the age of one will have a mother in the work force.

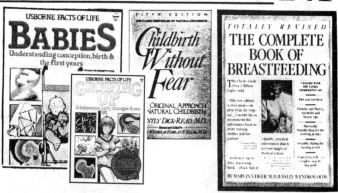

LOVE AND SEX AND GROWING UP, by Eric and Corinne Johnson. More and more "sex education" books for adolescents reflect society's growing attitude that anything is okay if you feel like doing it. This was one of the few books on the subject which I felt like recommending -- very highly -- in my previous edition, because it not only presented the basic facts of life in an objective, understandable way, but also because it emphasized the importance of married and family love. The book is now in a brand new "updated" edition, complete with updated information and opinions. Some of the new information, as such, is okay; homosexuality and AIDS have become inescapable subjects in newspapers and on TV, and our kids need to know about them; perhaps it will even satisfy a legitimate curiosity to know the basic mechanics of homosexuality. But the authors go on to say that ten percent is a conservative estimate of the percentage of homosexuals in society, seeming to imply that because so many people are engaged in it, it must be all right; and, further, that "evidence" seems to show that homosexuality is probably determined genetically, not psychologically or environmentally. The authors also mention that the word "lesbian" comes from the Isle of Lesbos, where the female inhabitants "en-joyed" lesbian relationships, as if such an historic precedent also gives respectability to the practice. Such arguments justifying homosexuality have no place in a supposedly objective introduction to the subject of sex. The book also joins the multitude of other "modern" books in referring to "relationships" rather than marriage, and various social aberrations as "alternative lifestyles" or "personal orientation." Much less than ten percent of this book is concerned with these modern concepts, but even one percent would be enough to cause me to junk it. I don't believe homosexuality is "natural" or an acceptable "orientation." I could probably write pages of my reasons, but you either agree with me or you don't. In either case, I no longer recommend this book, and I won't sell it. Which has left me with the problem of finding suitable substitutes for it -- and believe me, there aren't many being published these days that I'd let our dog read.

BORN TO LOVE, 21 Potsdam Road, Unit 61, Downsview, Ontario, Canada M3N 1N3. A small but comprehensive advertising booklet, with ads and short articles mostly from Canada, but with products available by mail to U.S. customers also.

BABIES: Understanding conception, birth, and the first years and **GROWING UP: Adolescence, body changes & sex** -- These two excellent books explain in clear text and accurate, tasteful illustrations important aspects of the human body and reproduction, and are especially suitable for ages 10 or so and up. BABIES traces the growth and development of a baby from conception to birth, and during the first years of life. GROWING UP describes the emotional and physical changes that occur during puberty, and includes sections on sex, contraception, and common problems of adolescence. Very well-done, very informative, and not at all objectionable to me. $6.95 each or both in one volume for $12.95. Code EDC. BROOK FARM BOOKS.

CHILDBIRTH WITHOUT FEAR: The Original Approach to Natural Childbirth, Grantly Dick-Read, M.D. All four of our children were born at home, and we did a lot of research before making that decision. This book doesn't advocate home-birth, but it was one of the few good books about birth available in 1966, when Cathy was born. Now an international classic in its field, it's still one of the most important and most informative books about undrugged birth. The author explains how childbirth can be a joyful and rewarding experience for both baby and mother when the mother is freed of anxiety and doubts -- without drugs. Jean and I can testify that it's entirely true. 420 pages, illustrated, index. $8.95. Code HR. BROOK FARM BOOKS.

THE COMPLETE BOOK OF BREASTFEEDING, by Marvin S. Eiger, M.D., and Sally Wendkos Olds; completely revised. Advice and information on nearly every aspect of breastfeeding, including new chapters on sexuality, special needs of single and working mothers, the role of the father, drugs, exercise, nutrition, and nursing premature babies. $7.95. Code BT. BROOK FARM BOOKS.

HOW YOU WERE BORN, by Joanna Cole; illustrated by Hella Hammid. Clear text and beautiful photographs answer young children's questions about how an egg cell becomes a baby, how a baby lives in the uterus, and how a child is born. Hardcover. $11.95. Code WM. BROOK FARM BOOKS.

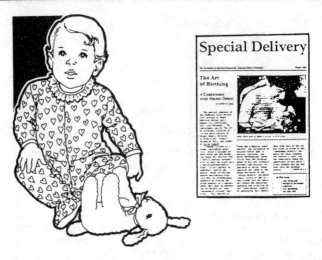

THE NEW NATIVITY, quarterly news-magazine, edited by Marilyn Moran. Although this little magazine is dedicated to home-birth, it will be interesting to parents-to-be who prefer to have their babies in a hospital. Besides home-birth, the emphasis is on a strong and healthy relationship between husband and wife -- before, during, and after pregnancy. For current price and description, write to: THE NEW NATIVITY, P.O. Box 6223, Leawood, KS 66206.

The hand that rocks the cradle is the hand that rules the world.

William Ross Wallace

SPECIAL DELIVERY, P.O. Box 3675, Ann Arbor, MI 48106. Newsletter of Informed Homebirth/Informed Birth and Parenting. Pregnancy, birth, early childhood, alternative education; letters, news, events, book reviews, classified ads. $12/yr. Free sample.

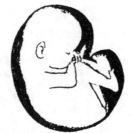

PRO/ANTI-CHOICE. As I've said elsewhere, I sometimes send contributions to World Wildlife Fund, Amnesty International, UNICEF, and similar organizations.

My small contributions of money or effort should indicate that I'm opposed to nuclear war, pollution of the earth, the torture and unlawful imprisonment of peaceful civilians, and the slaughter of whales, elephants, and dolphins.

As mailing lists get traded around, other organizations solicit my support, having inferred, through some sort of logic which I can't follow, that my opposition to wanton slaughter of animals and to irresponsible use of the earth means I also favor the killing of babies.

The few churches which still believe in the sanctity of life -- human life, at least -- oppose abortion, so pro-abortionists claim it's a religious issue only, and therefore protected by the First Amendment.

Does the study of law include a study of logic? The writers of the First Amendment, reacting in part to the theocratic monarchies of Europe, stipulated that the federal government may not establish a religion, so today's students of law and justice infer that "separation of church and state" means the government should have no jurisdiction over the subject of abortion -- because, they say, it's a religious matter.

Most religions also oppose suicide, stealing, and murder. Does that mean governmental legislation on these issues constitutes interference in religious matters? If the killing of unborn babies is a "personal" or "religious" matter, and therefore protected by the First Amendment, how long will it be before the killing of an unwanted five-year-old is also a "personal" or "religious" matter?

Those who say abortion should be made legal because women will get abortions anyway (and shouldn't be "forced" to risk their lives with illegal methods), might as well use the same argument for speeding on the highway, robbing banks, and forcing children into prostitution. The logical extension of their argument is that some people will do those things anyway, so let's make them legal.

In most cases, once conception has taken place, a choice has been made, whether carelessly or deliberately. From that moment on, there are many choices and decisions to be made, but murder should not be one of them. Killing a baby isn't made into something less by hiding it under a bushel of evasive impersonal euphemisms such as "fetus" and "product of conception."

Now you know why I just drop some of my mail into the waste basket. And I'll even risk being put on a right-wing mailing list by suggesting that if you think killing unborn people is wrong, write to THE NATIONAL RIGHT TO LIFE COMMITTEE, 419-7th Street N.W., Suite 500, Washington, DC 20004, to learn more about what's being done about it and what can be done. A year's subscription to the biweekly NRL NEWS costs only $16.00.

WHY WE CLOSED ONE OF OUR BANK ACCOUNTS, ACCOUNTING, BOOKKEEPING, MONEY

WHY WE CLOSED ONE OF OUR BANK ACCOUNTS
and discontinued business as our own ad agency--

BROOK FARM BOOKS
GLASSVILLE, NEW BRUNSWICK EOJ 1LO

Assistant Manager
Bank of Nova Scotia
Florenceville, N.B. EOJ 1KO

Sir:

In reply to your letter stating that my other business account, J-D Advertising Associates, is currently overdrawn 86¢, please find enclosed herewith a check from myself as a client of J-D Advertising Associates to myself as a partner in J-D Advertising Associates, in the amount of $1.00, which should restore said account to a state of solvency.

As I explained to the teller when setting up the account, it is not really a business. It is my left pocket, into which I put money which I have taken from my right pocket. In the course of trying to make a living without robbing banks, I sometimes place advertisements in various publications, some of which allow discounts to advertising agencies. I therefore hired the printing of ad agency order forms, transforming myself into what the media call "a house agency" -- meaning that I function as an ad agency in placing my own ads. These forms entitle me to a discount. So far, I have paid myself one commission of $6.00, the amount of discount allowed on a certain ad. That $6.00 was the deposit with which I opened an account in the name of myself as an ad agency, and paid out of my regular account which I maintain in my other guise as myself. Within a few days, I received a bank statement, noting that $1.50 has been deducted as a service charge, making my balance $4.50.

A few days later, I received some personalized checks which had been printed incorrectly. I returned them promptly to the bank, explaining the error. I assumed I would not be charged for these checks, which should indicate how naive I am when it comes to matters of high finance. As I have written no checks on this account, and have not withdrawn any money from it in any other way, I am now assuming that I have already been charged for the incorrectly printed checks. Since my previous balance was $4.50, and you say the account is now in the red to the tune of 86¢, I compute the cost of the checks to be $5.36. Is that a penalty imposed on me for not accepting the checks? How much more will it cost me to have some checks printed correctly? Let me know quickly, before my account becomes overdrawn again, so that I can mail myself a check to cover the amount.

Incidentally, there is no use trying to get money from me as a partner in J-D Advertising Associates. The only money ever owned, even fleetingly, by me as an ad agency is in the account. The next time the ad agency's account slips down out of the black, you should write to me as myself and not to me as the ad agency. If your accounts say the ad agency is bankrupt, then it is really so. Write to me, and I'll have a word with myself, and loan myself a little money to get over the hump. Which I am now doing, with the enclosed check for $1.00. That is not a commission for anything, so I have to regard it as a loan, which I will have to pay back to myself as soon as I pay myself enough commissions to do so. That may take quite a while, because so far I have put money into the account and have taken none out, but you have been taking money out of it faster than I can put it in.

I wonder if you have any little pamphlets explaining to me the benefits of a business account. So far, the only benefits I have noticed seem to be to the bank. How much more must I invest in the bank before some of the benefits come to me?

I hope some of my questions will be answered soon, unless such attention will result in more service charges, in which case I'll be better off if you leave me wondering.

Sincerely yours,
Donn Reed

MAKING CENTS: Every Kid's Guide to Making Money, by Elizabeth Wilkinson. A Brown Paper School Book. How can kids have fun making money in their spare time? By starting with this book, which gives a kid's-eye view of money, where it started, what it represents, how it's spent, and (best of all) how to earn it. $8.95. Code LB. BROOK FARM BOOKS.

WHATEVER HAPPENED TO PENNY CANDY? by Richard J. Maybury, Global Affairs Editor for Moneyworld. Highly-acclaimed, clear introduction for ages 12 through adult to the causes of inflation, recession, and wage and price controls. Topics include the origin and history of money, the economic behavior of government, investing, business cycles, recessions, depressions, etc., as they relate to several areas of history, social studies, and even science. $4.95 plus $1.50 postage. BLUESTOCKING PRESS, P.O. Box 1014, Placerville, CA 95667.

"COINS AND CURRENCY," 22-page booklet tracing money from its origin as trinkets, then bartered goods and services, to present-day form. FREE. FEDERAL RESERVE BANK OF NEW YORK, Public Information Dept., 33 Liberty St., New York, NY 10045.

YOU CHOOSE, workbook with cartoon characters explaining how a business is organized to produce goods and services; grades 3-5. ARTHUR'S IDEA, coloring-activity book for grades 1-4, teaches how people's needs and wants are met through production of goods and services. 70 cents each. Free catalog of other materials on economics. NATIONAL SCHOOLS COMMITTEE FOR ECONOMIC EDUCATION, P.O.Box 295, Cos Cob, CT 06807.

An allowance? No, we have something better. Dad pays each of us a nickel for each mistake of spelling, punctuation, or grammar which we find in letters from school authorities and speeches of school officials.

BOOKKEEPING AND ACCOUNTING COMPUTER COURSE, using "made easy" software. Computer (unless you already have one) with the course. Catalog. McGRAW-HILL SCHOOL OF BOOKKEEPING AND ACCOUNTING, 3939 Wisconsin Ave. NW, Washington, DC 20016.

INTERNATIONAL CORRESPONDENCE SCHOOLS (ICS), Scranton, PA 18540. Correspondence courses in several business, trade, and professional fields, including Business Management, Mechanical Engineering, Electronics Technology, Accounting,Computer Programming, **HIGH SCHOOL,** Medical or Dental Assistant, Drafting, Travel Agent, Police Sciences, Art, Wildlife and Forestry, TV/VCR Repair, and many more. Write for free information.

NATIONAL HOME STUDY COUNCIL, 1601 18th St. N.W., Washington, DC 20009. "Directory of Accredited Home Study Schools," free brochure listing more than 100 schools offering correspondence courses in three times as many career choices, from Accident Investigation to Zoology. (Many excellent schools haven't applied to the NHSC for accreditation, so their absence from this list doesn't mean they aren't good schools.) Most courses listed are suitable for late high school and adult study.

BOOKKEEPING MADE SIMPLE, Louis W. Fields; revised by Richard R. Gallagher. Complete accounting course from journals and ledgers to merchandising accounts, depreciation, payroll records, partnerships, computer use, new financial regulations, etc. The most comprehensive, basic guide available. $12.00. Code DD. BROOK FARM BOOKS.

HOME BUSINESS ADVISOR, bimonthly with features on alternative work options, telecommuting, and working at home. $24/year. NEXT STEP PUBLICATIONS, 6340 34th Avenue SW, Seattle, WA 98126.

To succeed in the world, it is not enough to be stupid, you must also be well-mannered.
Voltaire

COLLEGE BUSINESS COURSES-- Relatively easy-to-follow formats emphasize real-life business situations. Concise chapter-by-chapter summaries highlight fundamental concepts. The format of these books makes them easy to use as supplements to college courses or as self-teaching texts.
ACCOUNTING, by Peter J. Eisen
BUSINESS LAW, by Hardwicke and Emerson
BUSINESS STATISTICS, by Downing and Clark
ECONOMICS, by Walter J. Wessels
FINANCE, by Groppelli and Nikhbakht
MANAGEMENT, by Montana and Charnov
MARKETING, by Richard L. Sandhusen
Each book (384 to 456 pages), $8.95. Code BE. BROOK FARM BOOKS.

OUR WORKING SCHEDULE

Starting Time	8:00 a.m.
Morning Coffee Break .	9:00-11:30 a.m.
Lunch Hour .	11:30 a.m.-1:30 p.m.
Afternoon Coffee Break .	2:00-4:30 p.m.
Quitting Hour	5:00 p.m.

A NOTICE RECEIVED FROM A PUBLISHER --

IMPORTANT NOTICE
TO: ALL RETAIL ACCOUNTS
RE: QUALIFYING DISCOUNTS
THE PERIOD FOR ESTABLISHING YOUR NEW QUALIFYING DISCOUNT WILL BE FROM 5/1/93 THROUGH 8/31/93. DURING THIS TIME FRAME, YOUR CURRENT QUALIFYING DISCOUNT WILL REMAIN IN EFFECT. ON 9/1/93, IF YOU HAVE NOT RE-QUALIFIED, THE OLD QUALIFYING DISCOUNT WILL BE DELETED FROM THE SYSTEM. THE NEW QUALIFYING DISCOUNT WILL REMAIN IN EFFECT FROM 9/1/93 THROUGH 8/31/94. FOR EACH PRODUCT GROUP, IF A SUBSEQUENT ORDER IS RECEIVED WITHIN THE FISCAL YEAR WHICH CARRIES A HIGHER DISCOUNT THAN THE ORIGINAL QUALIFYING ORDER, IT WILL RECEIVE THE HIGHER DISCOUNT AND BECOME THE NEW QUALIFYING DISCOUNT FOR THAT PRODUCT GROUP. THE HIGHEST DISCOUNT WILL REMAIN IN EFFECT UNTIL AUGUST 31/1994. PLEASE CONTACT YOUR SALES REPRESENTATIVE OR CUSTOMER SERVICE REGARDING ANY QUESTIONS ON THE ABOVE.

MORE EXPENSIVE BY THE DOZEN

Rural New Brunswick is very similar to the Vermont of my boyhood (in the 40's and early 50's), and Canada is pretty much what the United States would have become without the Boston Tea Party. The majority in both countries speak some form of English, and tabloids in both countries entertain us weekly with the latest adventures of British royalty. (It puzzles us sometimes that the longer we live in Canada the more American we feel, but we have a nice home and good neighbors, and we live just a few miles from the United States border, so we exercise our Americanism mostly on frequent visits to our post office box in Maine.)

One of the more significant differences we've found between the two countries is that Americans still believe (or so they claim) in free enterprise, while Canada has "marketing agencies," which establish quotas and set prices and in many other ways regulate the production and sales of milk, eggs, lumber, and countless other consumer goods, all of which may be enterprising but is certainly not free. You don't cut costs by increasing the number of middlemen.

Government agencies often do funny things, but that doesn't mean their actions are humorous, and sometimes the public is severely taxed to find a single smile in a shovelful of government edicts. ("Shovelful," of course, isn't a metric term, and is therefore probably illegal in Canada now, but at present I can't think of a polite metric form of measurement to use for political excretions.)

Take, for example, the Canadian Egg Marketing Agency.

We all know that Saudi Arabia is one of the poorest nations in the world, so no sensible person would have protested a few years ago when the Egg Marketing Agency sold that country millions of Canadian eggs for half the price Canadians had to pay. It was only fair, of course. After all, don't we always get their oil for half price?

When one of the Agency's shipments to Saudi Arabia of four million eggs (or 333,333 dozen, with four left over) got sucked into the Twilight Zone by high-seas hijinks, who could blame the Saudi Arabians for being reluctant to pay the bill? After all, the CEMA was charging them five cents per egg, or 60 cents a dozen. That was $200,000 for the whole kit and cockadoodle, which must be nearly half a week's wages for some of those middle-class oil dealers.

The Marketing Agency lost the eggs, the Saudis refused to pay for them, so the Agency charged the Canadian public by raising the price of eggs sold at home. A neat solution to a problem which might have left the Agency with egg on its collective face.

According to one of its humorous -- I mean, funny -- press releases at the time, the purpose of the Egg Marketing Agency is the "orderly marketing of egg production at a fair price to both producers and consumers." In line with that purpose, the Agency offered farmers a price increase of one to three cents per dozen to help meet rising costs of feed and labor. (This was one of the points in the bill I sent to the Agency, which I'll explain in greater detail later on.)

Next, faced with more eggs than they could lose at sea, and fearing that the price per dozen on a glutted market might drop as low for Canadians as they had set it for the Saudi Arabians, the Agency's managers played with their pocket calculator and found another logical solution. They offered poultry farmers $2.07 per hen to kill off one and a half million laying hens, and to refrain from raising more hens for sixteen weeks.

My own calculator, which I wear under my hat, ran that through twice and came up with the news that the Agency was sticking taxpayers for $3,105,000 for eggs they would never eat, in order to make them pay more than 10 cents for each egg they did eat.

Naturally, I could see great possibilities in this for myself, and I went to discuss it with the Brook Farm Ladies Aid & Missionary Society, which lives in our barn and gives us an average of 20 eggs a day. The society has one rooster, named Hamlet, but he doesn't get out much, so I do most of his missionary work. Just to make it proper, I sent away $3.00 and received a card in the mail announcing that I am now fully ordained and should be addressed as "Reverend," and I have

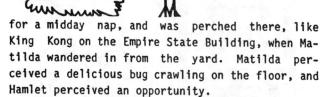

full authority to preside over marriages, baptisms, and funerals. So far, I have exercised that authority over 18 marriages (all bigamous, I'm afraid) and three funerals, all in my henhouse. I have yet to conduct a baptism, although I was surprised one day by a hen sticking her head into my boot, and I accidentally poured a bucket of water over two others.

When I told the ladies about the Marketing Agency's patriotic offer, they laughed so hard that one of them nearly turned inside out. Apparently it's difficult to live with a prolapsed intestine, which accounted for the first $2.07 I thought the Agency should pay me, and I went back to the house right away to prepare a bill, along with a letter to explain, itemize, and justify the total amount of $7.21 for which I finally billed the Agency.

I showed another hen, I wrote, what happens when the axe meets the chopping block, making another $2.07 the Agency owed me.

Matilda, with white flecks on her red feathers and beady black eyes, was a cute little thing, and Hamlet had had his gimlet eyes on her for some time. Whenever he tried to show his affection, however, she would glance shyly at the nest of eggs and say, "Please, dear, not in front of the children." So Hamlet took cold showers (not under my baptismal authority) and waited for us to collect the eggs.

One day, Hamlet fluttered up to the top roost for a midday nap, and was perched there, like King Kong on the Empire State Building, when Matilda wandered in from the yard. Matilda perceived a delicious bug crawling on the floor, and Hamlet perceived an opportunity.

Hamlet has responded to countless magazine ads that promised to enlarge his biceps, triceps, forceps, and brain capacity. The courses have done wonders for him -- all but the last. Nearly two feet tall at the shoulders and built like a ham, Hamlet is a 97-pound idiot.

He leaped off the roost, travelling eight feet out and six feet down, and landed squarely on Matilda's back. She surrendered meekly, and Hamlet bragged for weeks about his brilliant strategy.

What he didn't realize was that Matilda's neck was broken, making it a total of $6.21 the Agency owed me.

With an average of 20 eggs a day, our hens give us about 600 eggs a month. That's 50 dozen, believe it or not, with which we could have helped to glut the market if we didn't use them to glut ourselves. (I hasten to tell you that this was before our kids grew up and flew the coop.) By eating all our eggs -- fried, scrambled, boiled, and in bread, cookies, and doughnuts -- instead of selling them, we were doing our part to help the Agency inflate the market. This was a hardship we would gladly endure if it would help the national economy.

However, we still had to provide feed and labor, and here I called the Agency's attention to its offer of one to three cents per dozen.

My third grade teacher used to insist that we can't multiply apples by oranges, but the government frequently proves that much of our education is worthless, so I cheerfully followed the Agency's example, as follows: The average of "one to three" is "two," and two cents multiplied by 50 dozen equals 100 cents, which I rounded off to an even dollar.

"There you have it," I wrote. "My bill for this month: $6.21 for the demise of three hens, and $1.00 for grain fed to the remaining hens to help them produce eggs which I promise not to sell -- total, $7.21."

"Please remit promptly," I said, "as additional billing will increase my operating expenses, making me an even greater burden on the taxpayers."

You think the U.S. mail is slow sometimes? You should try Canada Post. I sent my bill to Ottawa six years ago, and I'm still waiting for a reply.

ART, ARTS & CRAFTS, ACTIVITIES, GAMES, HOBBIES

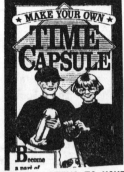

NECESSARY ITEMS TO HAVE ON HAND -- Paper, pencils, crayons, watercolors, poster paints, fingerpaints, scissors, ruler, glue, paste, colored construction paper. Our kids never liked the oversized pencils and crayons supposedly meant for "little fingers." For older kids, ballpoint pens, colored pencils, and felt-tip markers.

MAKE YOUR OWN TIME CAPSULE, by Steven Caney. Preserve the past, send a message to the future! The screw-top time capsule is made of shatterproof silver plastic, is roomy enough for dozens of artifacts -- photographs, tickets, a diary, and many other keepsakes. The instruction & idea book tells how to prepare materials, shows how to mark, map, and commemorate a time capsule. The book also includes a log, map grids, and forms to fill in; a sealing label with a serial number; envelopes, and identification tags. Ages 7 up. $12.95. Code WKM. BROOK FARM BOOKS.

FINGER MAGIC BOOKS -- I don't know which are better, the books or the finger puppets that come with them. The books are made of heavy, laminated cardboard. Each book has a simple, rhyming story which suggests actions for the child to perform as he listens to the story being read, and soon repeats himself. Each book -- BUNNY MAGIC, SPIDER MAGIC, TURTLE MAGIC, and BEAR MAGIC -- has a friendly felt finger puppet to join in the activity. Recommended for ages 9 months to 4 years. We asked our two-year-old granddaughter to review SPIDER MAGIC, because she already knows about the eency, weency spider who climbed up the water spout. She praised it very enthusiastically. She also indicated that she'd like to review it several more times, and would like to take the finger-puppet spider to bed with her. We'll have her written report a few years from now. $5.95 each. If you have a house full of kids and want to have a barrel of fun, order the Story Time Set, one book and ten puppets, for $21.95. Add $3 postage for any order up to $50.00. Order from: SCHNEIDER EDUCATIONAL PRODUCTS, 2880 Green St., San Francisco, CA 94123.

HOW TO DRAW SERIES, ages 8 and up. Valuable tips on style and technique, along with interesting information about the subjects. Eighteen 32-page books:
HOW TO DRAW--
BABY ANIMALS -- CARS & TRUCKS -- BIRDS -- BOATS, TRAINS & PLANES -- THE CIRCUS -- CATS -- DINOSAURS -- DOGS -- FARM ANIMALS -- FLOWERS -- FOREST ANIMALS -- HORSES -- GHOSTS, GOBLINS & WITCHES --INDIAN ARTS & CRAFTS -- SEA CREATURES -- FUNNY PEOPLE -- ZOO ANIMALS -- YOU CAN DRAW FUNNY ANIMALS
$1.95 each. Code TRL. BROOK FARM BOOKS.

A YOUNG GIRL'S NEEDLEWORK TREASURY-- The first part of the Treasury is an 18" old-fashioned rag doll to be completed by an adult (with the child or as a surprise), appropriate clothing, & the doll's four-poster bed. The second part of the Treasury is a year's subscription to monthly needlework projects, for the doll and for the doll's owner, including simple items of clothing, a quilt, Christmas gifts, and many other items; and introducing the child to skills in patchwork, counted embroidery, stitchery, crocheting, bead embroidery, needlepoint, heirloom sewing, crazy quilting, applique, knitting, and blackwork. Projects range from very easy to more challenging. Costs: $39 for the doll (and accessories) and bed, and $16.50 monthly for the projects, full instructions, and all necessary materials. For more information or to order: Jeannette Fields & Co., Bean Hill, Northfield, NH 03276. (Order with a credit card, toll-free, 1-800-735-4661, 3:30 to 10:00 PM.)

STEVEN CANEY'S TOYBOOK, Steven Caney. My dad used to make racing spools for me, and a little while ago I tried to remember how he did it. They're simple gadgets -- a spool, a rubber band, a thumbtack, and a wooden match -- but the secret kept eluding me. TOYBOOK to the rescue. Racing spools, clothespin wrestlers, a water lens, pocket parachute, tube telephone, bull roarer, and much more. 50 very simple, inexpensive (or free, from household throwaways) Games, Pretending Toys, Building Toys, Action Toys, Discovery Toys. Ages 2 to 12, and older kids will enjoy making these things for younger ones, or even for themselves on a rainy day. 176 large pages; many photos and line drawings. $10.95. **Code WKM. BROOK FARM BOOKS.**

STEVEN CANEY'S PLAY BOOK, Steven Caney. Another great book for kids of nearly any age, especially 3 to 12. How to turn cardboard, rocks, noodles, pencils, bottles, nails, and more into toy boomerangs, rings, salt gardens, sun clocks, bottle sandwiches, nail chimes, even a hammock made of 96 plastic six-pack carriers strung on clothesline. (Yucko. That's 576 cans of whatever. Better ask the neighbors if they'll help you guzzle.) 240 large pages, many photos and line drawings. $10.95. **Code WKM. BROOK FARM BOOKS.** (See also History, STEVEN CANEY'S KIDS' AMERICA; & Science, STEVEN CANEY'S INVENTION BOOK.)

PUNCH-OUT STENCILS-- No scissors or craft knife required; just punch out and trace. Several titles: FARM ANIMALS -- REPTILES AND AMPHIBIANS -- WILD ANIMALS -- ZOO ANIMALS -- ABC -- ANIMAL FRIENDS -- CARS AND TRUCKS -- CHRISTMAS -- CIRCUS -- CLOWN MASKS (to trace on to paper bags) -- SHIPS AND BOATS -- BIRDS -- FLOWERS -- SEA LIFE -- DINOSAUR. EACH BOOK, $3.95. Code DV. BROOK FARM BOOKS.

When one has much to put into them, a day has a hundred pockets.

Friedrich Nietzsche

CUT AND MAKE MASKS -- All on sturdy 9¼x12¼" card stock, in full color, ready to cut out and wear.
CUT AND MAKE CIRCUS CLOWN MASKS. Six masks based on the comic make-up created by famous circus clowns. $2.95.
CUT AND MAKE NORTH AMERICAN INDIAN MASKS. Eight full-color masks based on authentic designs: Hopi corn man, Kwakiutl human-bear mask, Aztec fire god mask, five others. $4.95.
CUT AND MAKE ANIMAL MASKS. 15 very lifelike animal masks -- dog, cat, rabbit, raccoon, koala, panda, lion, tiger, more. $4.95.
CUT AND MAKE CAT MASKS. Ten easy-to-make Victorian cat masks -- Persian Princess Cat, Marie Antoinette Cat, Gypsy Cat, Billy the Cat, Indian Chief Cat, more. $4.95.
CUT AND MAKE MONSTER MASKS. Ten wonderfully gruesome masks include a blood-sucking vampire, a sadistic cat woman, Quasimodo, seven more. $4.95.
CUT AND MAKE "WIZARD OF OZ" MASKS. Eight masks to wear or put on your wall, including Dorothy, Toto, Scarecrow, Cowardly Lion, Tin Man, and others. $4.95.
All "Cut and Make Masks," prices as indicated above. Code DV. BROOK FARM BOOKS.

THE RAINY DAY SURVIVAL GUIDE: Entertaining Activities for Two- and Three-Year-Olds. 78-page activity book with dozens of ideas, arts, crafts, homemade toys & games; useful list of publications and other resources. $7.95 + $1 postage. PARENTING INSIGHTS, P.O. Box 120, Ridgewood, NY 11386.

EASY-TO-MAKE NOAH'S ARK IN FULL COLOR -- Cut and assemble an 11" model of Noah's Ark, along with Noah, his family, & several animals, all two-by-two: polar bears, camels, ostriches, crocodiles, elephants, zebras. The pieces are printed in full color on both sides of heavy stock. Full instructions. $2.95. Code DV. BROOK FARM BOOKS.

BARE BOOKS -- Blank books, for kids or adults. Real books with sewn binding, hard covers, and blank, unlined pages. Some covers are blank, for your own design or title; others have line drawings to color or draw on. Good for recipes, poems, journals, pictures, essays, stories, anything. Sample book and descriptive brochure, $1.50 to: TREETOP PUBLISHING, 220 Virginia Street, Racine, WI 53405.

EASY CRAFTS AND PROJECTS. Sixteen 48-page colorful books with fun-to-do crafts and activities for all ages, including nature and holiday crafts, cooking, and mask-making.

DETECTIVE TRICKS YOU CAN DO -- DOLLHOUSE FURNITURE YOU CAN MAKE -- FUN-TO-MAKE NATURE CRAFTS --FUN WITH PAPER -- GREAT GIFTS TO MAKE -- HAPPY DAY! THINGS TO MAKE AND DO -- MAGIC TRICKS YOU CAN DO -- MORE MAGIC TRICKS YOU CAN DO -- SCIENCE SECRETS -- MORE SCIENCE SECRETS -- PLENTY OF PUPPETS TO MAKE -- QUICK & EASY COOKBOOK -- RAINY DAY SURPRISES YOU CAN MAKE -- SPRINGTIME SURPRISES TO MAKE AND DO -- STOP & LOOK! ILLUSIONS -- THINGS THAT GO! TOY BOATS, CARS, PLANES

Each title, $3.50. Specify "Easy Crafts" and title. Code TRL. BROOK FARM BOOKS.

CREATIVITY FOR KIDS, 1600 East 23rd St., Cleveland, OH 44114. Several "Let's Pretend" kits -- Office, Restaurant, Store, Theater, School, Travel--with appropriate forms and paper "hardware" such as menus, credit cards, order pads, signs, tickets, badges, play money, etc. A DRAMA KIT in a cardboard trunk. CARTON CONSTRUCTION, with connectors, wheels, license plates, and stickers to turn empty boxes into cars, computers, theatres, appliances, more. Doll making, rubber stamp making, quilt making, much more. Small catalog of great stuff, with reasonable prices. Almost makes us wish our kids were younger again.

658 THINGS FOR KIDS TO DO! Creative crafts from inexpensive, readily-available materials. $12.95 postpaid. HIGHLIGHTS FOR CHILDREN, P.O. Box 269, Columbus, OH 43272.

RAINY DAY PROJECTS FOR CHILDREN, Gerri Jenny and Sherrie Gould. Why wait for a rainy day? Thirty-four projects for parents and children ages about 4 to 8, making puppets, building a city, making gifts, and many other crafts. Full-size patterns, fully illustrated. Each project takes from 45 minutes to two hours. "Fun City," with buildings, houses, street signs, etc., will take considerably longer, and may be a continuing project for several days. $10.95 plus $2 shipping. BROOK FARM BOOKS.

TOYS AND GAMES FOR CHILDREN TO MAKE, Gerri Jenny and Sherrie Gould. Thirty-two projects, ranging from simple Stick Puppets to making a set of adjustable stilts, an imaginative "Castle Scene" (complete with clothespin alligators), and many other toys, games, and activities. Full-color photographs and illustrations, easy directions. $10.95 plus $2 postage. BROOK FARM BOOKS.

THE KIDS' ENCYCLOPEDIA OF THINGS TO MAKE AND DO, Richard and Ronda Rasmussen. <u>1,866</u> arts, crafts, and activities for young children and their parents, using bottle caps, plastic bottles, buttons, cardboard boxes, egg cartons, juice cans, old socks, paper bags, spools, string, yarn, and similar items. Short, clear directions; many illustrations. A fantastic collection. $17.95 plus $2.50 postage. BROOK FARM BOOKS.

PLAYDOUGH, 32 pages of interesting playdough ideas and activities for parents and their children from 3 to 6 years old. All projects will encourage imagination, creativity, manual dexterity, and discussion. Profusely illustrated. $4.95. Code EDC. BROOK FARM BOOKS.

PAPERPLAY, 32 pages of interesting ideas and activities in paper craft, for parents and their children from 3 to 6 years old. All projects will encourage imagination, creativity, manual dexterity, and lots of discussion. $4.95. Code EDC. BROOK FARM BOOKS.

GRYPHON HOUSE, P.O. Box 275, Mt. Rainier, MD 20712. Many excellent books such as TEACHABLES FROM TRASH-ABLES (making toys that teach), MUDPIES AND MAGNETS, HUG A TREE, and many more, for pre-school and elementary children, using exciting activities & crafts to introduce concepts of peacemaking, conservation, alternative power (with experiments in solar, wind, and water power). Games, crafts, holiday celebrations, etc. Free catalog.

CRAYON PROJECTS IDEA BOOK--"Colorfun Project Ideas," FREE from BINNEY & SMITH, Crayola Products Division, P.O. Box 431, Easton, PA 18042.

THE USBORNE STORY OF PAINTING -- Children age 10 and up are introduced to the world of great paintings, the development of styles throughout the years, changing tastes and improved materials, and the ways of life of the "old masters." $5.95. Code EDC. BROOK FARM BOOKS.

ART HISTORY STUDIES -- 7,400 prints of paintings and other art objects throughout history, edited by art authorities and continually updated. The collection is a survey of virtually all areas of art history. The prints are 5½x8 inches. Black and white prints are 5¢ each; color prints are 10¢ each. Choose those you want, any quantity, from the titles and subjects listed. Complete catalog, 246 pages, listing all titles by period, school, and artist, $2.00. THE UNIVERSITY PRINTS, Box 485, Winchester, MA 01890.

ART REPRODUCTIONS of well-known prints: Mona Lisa, Blue Boy, etc. Most are only $2 to $6; some a little higher. Ten prints or more at one time, preferably ordered on a good letterhead, may qualify for discounts averaging 50%. Catalog, $2 (refunded with first order). DECOR PRINTS, Box 502, Noel, MO 64854.

ARTDECK, The Game of Modern Masters, Impressionism to Surrealism. Learn about art while enjoying an afternoon or evening card game. ARTDECK contains a miniature collection of modern art by 13 of the world's greatest artists, from Monet to Miro. There are 52 cards depicting 4 major works of art of each artist represented, 13 artist cards which feature information about the artists and their work, 2 jokers, 1 die, 4 card holders, and game instructions. The 52 paintings depicted are from 16 of the world's great museums, including The Louvre, London's National Gallery, The Metropolitan Museum of Art, Boston's Museum of Fine Arts, and The National Gallery of Art, Washington, D.C. Play the game as directed, make up your own game, or just enjoy the artwork. Ages 12 to adult; 2 to 4 players. $25.00 plus $3.00 shipping. BROOK FARM BOOKS.

FINE ART POSTERS AND PRINTS -- ART POSTER CO., 29555 Northwestern Hwy., Ste. 234, Southfield, MI 48034.

ART REPRODUCTIONS-- 50-page catalog (interesting and informative, even if you don't buy anything from it), $1.00. THE MUSEUM OF FINE ARTS, P.O. Box 1044, Boston, MA 02120.

INSTRUCTOR'S PRE-SCHOOL BOOK CLUB, P.O. Box 10339, Stamford, CT 06904. Seven-book set -- FUN WITH FAIRY TALES, FUN WITH NURSERY RHYMES, FUN WITH THE ALPHABET, FUN WITH BOOKS, COLORS AND SHAPES, MOTHER GOOSE NURSERY RHYMES, and COUNTING SETS -- all for less than $4 with membership in the Club, which offers a wide variety of books filled with activities, games, lessons, bulletin board materials and ideas, activity sheets; picture books, records, cassettes, toys, puppets, puzzles, board games, more. Inquire about membership.

ART TODAY AND EVERY DAY-- More than 200 ready-to-use art activities especially suitable for use from September through June: vegetable and fruit printing, crayon batik, tissue leaf rubbings, weaving, space pictures, owl puppet, dancing witch, explorer's ship, jack-o'lantern mobile, chalk stencil ghosts, cat mask, puzzles, Indian headdress, rolled fruit, 3-D turkey, cornucopia, walnut people, paper fruit wreath, macaroni tree ornaments, starch poinsettia, Rudolph mask, sponge painted snowman, name designs, watercolor sparkle tree, string painting, penguin puppet, crayon mosaic, animals in cages, leprechaun, patriotic hat, newspaper cities, Valentine basket, shadow box Valentines, marbled chalk, bunny mask, newspaper carp kite, clown, insect puppets, happy sun faces, papier-mache egg, and more and more and more. $18.95 to PARKER PUBLISHING COMPANY, Book Distribution Center, Route 59 at Brookhill Drive, West Nyack, NY 10995-9901.

DRAWING WITH CHILDREN, A Creative Teaching & Learning Method That Works for Adults, Too; Mona Brookes. Hundreds of very helpful tips on techniques and art materials, used with great success even with very young children. $13.95. Code PG. BROOK FARM BOOKS.

ALPHA-BETICS, math & grammar games for two players. SASE to MINA ARNOLD YOUNG, 4412 Park Avenue, Fort Smith, AR 72903.

DISCOVERY CARDS: 180 cards, 6x9", each with an interesting activity in reading, writing, math, social studies, science or art (30 in each category.) Grades 3-6. Easy directions, list of required materials (easily acquired), illustrations, and suggested follow-up activities. $14.95 from THE CENTER FOR APPLIED RESEARCH IN EDUCATION, INC., P.O. Box 130, West Nyack, NY 10995.

DISCOVER! You supply an ordinary object, hand your student the corresponding set of cards, and watch the unfolding of observation, evaluation, & thinking. Ages 8 up. 20 cards per set. Order by Name of Set: Discover (a): Pencil, Comb, Spoon, Popcorn, Crackers, Scissors, Paper Clip, Handkerchief, Tape Dispenser, Egg Carton, Paper Bag, Table Knife. Each set, $1.50. Orders under $5, add $1 postage; orders over $5, add $1.50. All 12 sets, $18 postpaid. TIN MAN PRESS, P.O. Box 219, Stanwood, WA 98292.

TOUCHSTONE ART MAGIC, Gary Layman. Children easily develop drawing and painting skills using construction paper, crayons, markers, and other common art materials. More than 150 projects for all grade levels, with suggestions for integrating the projects with history, social studies, science, math, & language arts. Write for information. TOUCHSTONE ART MAGIC, 1106 Paradise Lane, Ashland, OR 97520.

CHALKBOARDS -- Washable hardboard "slates," 11x13", lined for either vertical or horizontal use. Chalk wipes off easily with cloth. $2.95 each plus $1.50 postage. 12 or more, only $1.89 each plus 10% postage. WORLD RESEARCH COMPANY, 307 S. Beckham, Tyler, TX 75702.

THE NEW TEACHER'S ALMANACK, A Complete Guide to Every Day of the School Year. Ready-to-use activities and ideas, including a daily calendar of famous peoples' birthdates, holidays, special weeks, and historical events; sayings and quotations by famous people born during each month; historical facts and teaching suggestions; biographical material; bulletin board ideas with holiday, seasonal, and content themes; special projects; recipes, games, 150 sources of free or inexpensive material; more. If you don't want to keep it, return it within 10 days for a full refund. $17.50 + $1.50 postage. THE CENTER FOR APPLIED RESEARCH IN EDUCATION, INC., P.O. Box 430, West Nyack, NY 10995.

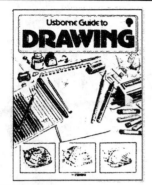

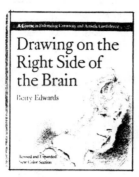

USBORNE ART GUIDES -- Written and fully illustrated to introduce the complete beginner to the basic knowledge and skills of each subject, from choosing and using equipment to increased understanding and enjoyment. Lots of interesting background information, many helpful hints and tips. Age 10 and up.
  USBORNE GUIDE TO PAINTING
  USBORNE GUIDE TO DRAWING
Each book, $5.95. Code EDC. BROOK FARM BOOKS.

EDUCATIONAL CARD GAMES -- AC/DC, a game of electric circuitry; GOOD HEAVENS!, a game of astronomical fun & trivia; KRILL, A Whale of a Game; O! EUCLID, fun with geometry; OH WILDERNESS!, PREDATOR, and THE POLLINATION GAME. $7.95 each. Write for information and catalog: AMPERSAND PRESS, 691 26th St., Oakland, CA 94612.

BOARD & TABLE GAMES FROM MANY CIVILIZATIONS by R.C. Bell. Encyclopedic work on 182 different games -- Majong, Hazard, Wei-ch'i (Go), Backgammon, Pachisi, many others. Over 300 illustrations. 448 pages. $6.50. Code DV. BROOK FARM BOOKS.

DRAWING ON THE RIGHT SIDE OF THE BRAIN, A Course in Enhancing Creativity and Artistic Confidence, revised edition, by Betty Edwards. I seldom think about which side of my brain I'm using, but a few years ago when Karen was feeling frustrated by the elusiveness of a tricky subject she was trying to draw, we got out this book and tried its techniques. Hooray, Karen captured the subject she was after with little trouble, and went on to use the book's ideas to improve her artwork immensely. We both give it our wholehearted endorsement. $13.95. Code PG. BROOK FARM BOOKS.

ClassWorks!! Every other month, 80 pages with a reproducible activity on one side and answers, plans, and extension activities on the other; games, background information, and 22x34" poster; subjects include dinosaurs, robots, space, nutrition, presidents, weather, fractions, story starters, more. Grades 3-5. $11.95 plus $2 postage for each kit. Cancel anytime; return unwanted kits; no minimum to buy. Write for information and introductory offer (many things free): CLASSWORKS!!, Scholastic Teacher's Resource Club, P.O. Box 11413, Des Moines, IA 50380.

THE MAILBOX, bimonthly teachers' magazine with art activities, bulletin board ideas, reproducible worksheets, teaching units, seasonal and holiday activities; pull-out posters, learning centers, and gameboards; teaching tips from readers. Three levels: Preschool and kindergarten; Primary (grades 1-3); & Intermediate (4-6), each $16.95/ year. THE EDUCATION CENTER, INC., 1410 Mill St., Greensboro, NC 27408.

PALMLOOM-- Interesting handicraft for all ages. Make scatter rugs, table pads, hat ornaments, applique coasters, rosettes, belts, chair & table coverings, and much more. The Palmloom Kit will fit into a pocket or purse, ready to use any time. It's fast & easy: just wind strips of any type or weight of remnant materials -- yarn, cord, cloth; wool, cotton, nylon -- on the Palmloom; then bind it through the slots, and you have one finished unit. Join several units to make the finished product you want. Full directions included. $5.50 each or 2 for $10.00, postpaid. BROOK FARM BOOKS.

LEICHTUNG WORKSHOPS, 4944 Commerce Parkway, Cleveland, OH 44128. Clamps, saws, drills, sanders, routers, clock parts, wooden car and truck kits, woodworking plans, dollhouse kits & furniture, plans for rocking horses, a rocking cow, etc. For amateur or professional. Catalog.

WOODEN BUILDING BLOCKS, hard maple. MARVELOUS TOY WORKS, 2111 Eastern Ave., Baltimore, MD 21231.

EARLY LEARNING BOOK CLUB -- Reproducible patterns in titles such as Art for Winter, Art for Spring & Summer, Animal Faces, Paper Animals, many more. Monthly catalog, from which you select. Projects to color, cut, paste and assemble, play with, give as gifts. The Club's "introductory offer" varies from time to time, but you receive about $35 worth of books for less than $5 when you join and agree to buy only three more books at discounted prices within 12 months. Information from: EARLY LEARNING BOOK CLUB, Riverside, NJ 08075.

MACMILLAN EARLY SKILLS PROGRAM -- For $11.95 plus postage (about $2.00), you receive a set including at least 100 ideas and activities, printed on 8½x11" cardboard, and a full-color teaching aid (game, poster, bulletin board project, etc.). With your first order, you receive a large plastic file box to hold future sets. Ideas and activities include arts and crafts, storytelling, listening skills, nature and science, and small motor skills. The activities are planned for early pre-school through second grade. Sets come to you every other month; and any sets you don't want may be returned without charge. No minimum number of sets to buy; you may cancel your subscription anytime. Write for current details: MACMILLAN EARLY SKILLS PROGRAM, P.O. Box 938, Hicksville, NY 11802.

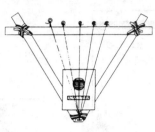

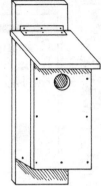

CLIP ART CAROUSEL, four books filled with a great variety of eye-catching illustrations (many of which you'll see throughout this book), including animals, plants, transportation, music, careers, awards, national costumes, ancient Greece and Egypt, and much, much more. Subjects include All-Purpose Art (#139), Holidays and Celebrations (#140), Science and Math (#141), and People and Places (#142). The hundreds of illustrations will add zest and interest to your family newsletters, awards and certificates, students' stories, homemade bookmarks and note paper, activity sheets, holiday greeting cards, party invitations, worksheets, and scores of uses I haven't thought of yet. Illustrate your own story books. Impress the Department of Education with how "professional" your activity sheets are. Just clip the illustrations you want, glue them to your master copy along with your own typed or handwritten material, and take to your local photocopy service for as many copies as you want. Useful for all grades & adults. Each book is $4.95. Minimum postage fee is $2, for one or all four. Order from: THE LEARNING WORKS, P.O. Box 6187, Santa Barbara, CA 93160. (See also Science, "Reproducible Science Series," and Teaching Aids, "The Learning Works.")

SPIZZIRRI PUBLISHING, INC., P.O. Box 9397, Rapid City, SD 57709. Excellent coloring books about dinosaurs, sea life, birds, mammals, Indians, dogs, cats, endangered species, rockets, ships, dolls, and many other subjects; several with complementary cassettes (not read-alongs, but with a similar theme, with music, sound effects, and voice). A wall chart "life line," covering 600 million years of life on earth, with 207 different life forms to color. Many other products, also -- animal masks, posters, etc. Very low prices. Catalog.

DAY BY DAY, A Learning Ideabook, with 300 seasonal & calendar-related activities & projects, featuring a calendar with daily highlights, activities in all curriculum areas, bulletin board and craft ideas, resources for kids and teachers, reproducible worksheets. Grades K-6; 240 pages. $13.95. PITMAN LEARNING, INC., 6 Davis Drive, Belmont, CA 94002.

TOTLINE PRESS, P.O. Box 2255, Everett, WA 98203. Free catalog of many art books and materials for children, emphasizing process rather than product.

CURIOSITY KITS -- Very inexpensive craft kits for young children, with all materials needed (including tools, such as scissors, screwdriver, or glue), full instructions, and historical and/or scientific background information. Each project takes approximately two hours to complete. Kits include an Early American folk art rabbit, a lyre, insect house, bluebird house, African mask, Amish heart basket, and others. Especially for children 6 to 10, but younger and older kids will enjoy them, too. For more information and prices, send a #10 SASE to: CURIOSITY KITS, P.O. Box 811, Cockeysville, MD 21030.

EVERY DAY IS SPECIAL, 1602 Naco Place, Hacienda Heights, CA 91745. A monthly calendar, with an entry for each date that tells about an historical event that happened on that day, or a famous birthday or holiday. Art activities, projects, puzzles, games, contests. Many activities involve outdoor and nature resources. Clear, interesting illustrations. Sample copy, $1. Annual subscription (12 issues), $12.00.

SCIENCE & MATH ENRICHMENT ACTIVITIES FOR THE PRIMARY GRADES, Elizabeth C. Stull and Carol L. Price. Hundreds of activities on 183 reproducible pages & 178 ready-to-use pages, using writing, graphing, creative thinking, and math manipulatives in learning about birds, dinosaurs, fruits, vegetables, insects, careers in math & science, monsters, foods, rodents, space travel, sea life, seeds, plants and flowers, tools, transportation, wind, computers, and robots. ON SCHOOL LETTERHEAD OR ORDER FORM, IF POSSIBLE, ask for "Free Trial Exam Copy," stating that you agree to pay $19.95 plus postage and handling if you keep the book; or return it within 15 days and owe nothing. CENTER FOR APPLIED RESEARCH IN EDUCATION, Book Distribution Center, Rte. 59 & Brookhill Drive, West Nyack, NY 10995.

DEVELOPMENTAL ARTS, P.O. Box 389, Arlington, MA 02174. Enrichment activities for young children. Free catalog.

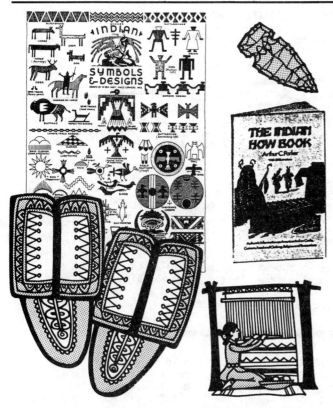

THE COMPLETE HOW-TO BOOK OF INDIANCRAFT, by W. Ben Hunt. 68 projects for authentic Indian crafts, clothing, musical instruments, totem poles, snowshoes, sleds, wigwams, bows and arrows, more. Clear text and detailed drawings and diagrams. $9.95. Code MAC. BROOK FARM BOOKS.

THE INDIAN HOW BOOK, Arthur C. Parker (Gawaso Wanneh). How Indians made canoes, tepees, traps, arrowheads, pottery; Indian dances, songs, rituals; hunting, cooking, much more. One of the classics in the field, by a man who spent much of his life with the Indians before their way of life was completely changed by "civilization." 51 illustrations. 335 pages. $5.95. Code DV. BROOK FARM BOOKS.

INDIAN CRAFTS --
PLUME TRADING SALES CO., P.O. Box 585, Monroe, NY 10950. 35-page catalog, $1. Inexpensive crafts and supplies; lots of kits.
AKWESASNE NOTES & PRODUCTS CATALOG, Mohawk Nation, via Rooseveltown, NY 13683. $1 for comprehensive catalog. Finished craft items for sale; also a good selection of posters and books for children and adults.
GREY OWL, 113-15 Springfield Blvd., Queens Village, NY 11429. $1 for 186-page catalog. Lots of kits and books; very large selection; low prices.
CRAZY COW TRADING POST, Box 314, Denison, TX 75020. Great catalog, $2. Patterns for historic clothing and usable historic and western tools, as well as Indian crafts.
LAKOTA DEVELOPMENT COUNCIL, 1100 North Jasper St., Chamberlain, SD 57326. Sioux arts and crafts. Quilting, jewelry, beadwork, dolls, silver. Catalog, $1.
AMERICAN INDIAN ART, Box 5896, Sherman Oaks, CA 91413. Masks, graphics, sculpture, kachinas, rugs. Catalog.
BASKETS & POTTERY, Box 73, St. John, IN 46373. Contemporary crafts and artifact reproductions; jewelry. Photos and catalog, $3.50.

THE USBORNE GUIDE TO PLAYING CHESS. Profusely illustrated introduction to chess, with clear step-by-step instruction in basic and more advanced techniques. Age 10 and up. $5.95. Code EDC. BROOK FARM BOOKS.

BEGINNER'S BOOK OF CHESS and Beginner's Chess Set, by Harvey Kidder. The origins of chess, patterned after medieval battlefields, help explain the movements of its pieces. Pawns, the common infantry, advance step by step. The Knight's leaping L-shaped move is the warrior on his charging horse. Powerful Bishops line up beside the Queens and Kings, as in the Middle Ages' alliance of Church and State. Readers are led through the fundamentals of beginning, middle, and end game, and shown winning strategies for offense and defense -- how to castle, how to protect pieces, how to control the center of the board, how to identify the opponent's key square and bear down with an attack until check mate. The book is accompanied by a full 32-piece chess set, with a **folding chess board.** $14.95. **Code WKM.** BROOK FARM BOOKS.

KID PRINTS. A "complete" home program for teaching the fine arts. Easy activities, famous art and artists, lesson plans. Not complete, but very good, and fun. SASE for information and price. KidsArt, 912 Schilling Way, Mt. Shasta, CA 96067.

KidsArt NEWS. Quarterly ideas, reviews, art prints, activity sheets, art calendar, much more. Send #10 SASE for free sample. KidsArt NEWS, 912 Schilling Way, Mt. Shasta, CA 96067.

"SEE THE PAINTINGS!" Art appreciation program, encourages children to observe and compare colorful art prints and other materials; also integrate with language arts, social studies, math, and science. The intended use is too contrived, but may work for some people. Free brochure. MODERN LEARNING PRESS, Rosemont, NJ 08556.

FINE ARTS ON VIDEO-- Art & artists, concerts, opera, literature, ballet, and many other special interest video tapes; many produced in cooperation with the National Gallery and the Metropolitan Museum of Art. Colorful catalog. HOME VISION, 5547 N. Ravenswood Ave., Chicago, IL 60640.

ORIENTEERING-- Outdoor fun with a map and a compass, learning geography and science, and building health & self-confidence. Free information kit. ORIENTEERING SERVICES, P.O. Box 1604, Binghamton, NY 13902.

ARTS IN RESIDENCE, 235 Pasadena, Tustin, CA 92680. Monthly newsletter to help parents give their children basic knowledge of the arts. $15/year (12 issues). Sample, $2.00.

There are more valid facts and details in works of art than there are in history books.

Charlie Chaplin

NON-COMPETITIVE GAMES -- Lots and lots of games in which no one loses and everyone wins.
ANIMAL TOWN GAME COMPANY, Box 2002, Santa Barbara, CA 93120.
FAMILY PASTIMES, RR #4, Perth, Ontario, Canada K7H 3C6.

ARTS & CRAFTS PACK for just 99¢ when you join the TEACHER BOOK CLUB. Monthly selections include container crafts, animals, holiday art, seasonal themes, relating to math, reading, & science. Information from TEACHER BOOK CLUB, Riverside, NJ 08075.

BITS & PIECES, 1 Puzzle Place, Stevens Point, WI 54481. Beautiful, unusual jigsaw puzzles, games, books, model kits (e.g., a replica of the Notre Dame Cathedral), crossword puzzles, Dragonfly Optiscope (see 24 undistorted images of everything you look at), blank jigsaws to draw your own picture on. World's Most Difficult Jigsaw Puzzle: the same artwork on both sides, but rotated 90 degrees, with all pieces cut so it's impossible to distinguish one side from the other. Just the thing for a long winter's evening (or month, or all winter). Over 200 fascinating items. Catalog.

SUPPLIERS OF ARTS & CRAFTS MATERIALS

AMERICAN FOLK ART, Box 2560, Youngstown, OH 44507. Reproductions on paper and canvas, framed or unframed. Brochure $2.00.

AMERICAN HANDICRAFTS, Box 791, Fort Worth, TX 76101. Supplies, kits, books, tools, more. Needlepoint, cross-stitch, quilting, embroidery, latch hook, basketry, craft sticks, crochet, knitting, string art, wooden frames, ribbons, doll making, stained glass, baking crystals, candle making, woodburning, clock parts, decoupage, plaques, paints, calligraphy, molding, sculpting, macrame, music box movements, more. Free catalog.

AMERICA'S HOBBY CENTER, 146 West 22nd St., New York, NY 10011. Discounts to 40%. Catalog $1.50.

ARTEXT PRINTS, INC., Box 403, Greenwich, CT 06830. Catalog of small reproductions of famous paintings and sculptures.

THE BASKET WORKS, 4900 Wetheredsville Road, Baltimore, MD 21207. Basketry books, kits, supplies.

CANVASBACK ART COMPANY, INC., 30 Perseverance Way, Hyannis, MA 02601. Framed canvas reproductions. Brochure, $1.00.

COHASSET COLONIALS, 124AX Ship St., Cohasset, MA 02025. Framed reproductions. Catalog $1.00.

CRAFTSMAN, 1735 West Cortland Blvd., Addison, IL 60101. General crafts; also kits for making your own musical instruments.

CURRICULUM RESOURCES, INC., Box 828, Fairfield, CT 06430. Basketry, yarn crafts, weaving, etc.

DICK BLICK, P.O. Box 1267, Galesburg, IL 61401. Creative materials, including paints, brushes, paper, ceramics, jewelry, stitchery, silk screen, etc. Some prices are somewhat high, but the selections and quality are very good.

DIDAX, INC., 6 Doulton Place, Peabody, MA 01960. Excellent materials for art and other subjects (arithmetic, reading, etc.).

HEDGEROW HOUSE, 230 Fifth Avenue, New York, NY 10001. Unframed reproductions, paper. Free brochure.

HERRSCHNERS, INC., Hoover Road, Stevens Point, WI 54481. Large catalog of craft materials, yarn, knitting, crocheting, kits; mostly needlecrafts.

J & A HANDY-CRAFTS, INC., 210 Front St., Hempstead, NY 11550. Large selection of materials for most handicrafts.

LEATHERCRAFTERS SUPPLY CO., 25 Great Jones Street, New York, NY 10012. Discounts up to 40% on leathercraft supplies, tools, equipment, books. Minimum order $25. Catalog and price list, $2.00.

LEWISCRAFT, 40 Commander Blvd., Scarborough, Ontario, Canada M1S 3S2. Mail-order catalog with over 12,000 items. (Canada only, unfortunately!)

MARCIA LYMAN, Brainard Hill Road, Higganum, CT 06441. Hand-painted copies, framed. Catalog, $1.00.

NEW YORK GRAPHIC SOCIETY, 95 East Putnam Avenue, Greenwich, CT 06830. Catalog of art supplies.

OLD GRANGE GRAPHICS, P.O. Box 297, Hopewell, NJ 08525. Canvas reproductions, frames available. Catalog $2.00.

PEARL PAINT, 308 Canal St., New York, NY 10013. Very large catalog ($1.00) of nearly everything you might need for painting. One of the best <u>discount</u> sources of art and craft supplies, with discounts from 10% to 50%. Minimum order, $50. Excellent if you're seriously buying art supplies.

R. B. WALTER, P.O. Box 920626, Norcross, GA 30092.

SAX ARTS & CRAFTS, P.O. Box 51710, New Berlin, WI 53151.

SCULPTURE HOUSE, 38 E. 30th St., New York, NY 10016. Clay and sculpture supplies.

TRIARCO ARTS & CRAFTS, 14650 28th Ave. N., Plymouth, MN 55441.

UTRECHT LINEN CO., 33 Thirty-fifth St., Brooklyn, NY 11232. Professional supplies and equipment for art, sculpture, printmaking. Oils, acrylics, solvents, canvas, brushes, etc., etc. Minimum order, $40. Free catalog.

"efficient instruction elsewhere," by Donn Reed. As you must realize by now, Jean and I take education very seriously, but laughter is high on the curriculum in our school. I've always wondered at the lack of humor in most home-school books and other publications. The only other home-school writers who seem to have much sense of humor are Earl Stevens, who writes a column for Home Education Magazine, and Mario Pagnoni, whose book, THE COMPLETE HOME EDUCATOR, is out of print. Mary Pride is witty sometimes, but not funny. A lot of others are "funny," but not humorous. Home-schooling is usually treated as if it's too sacred to speak of lightly. Despite the slings and arrows of my outrageous family, I published this book of cartoons about confrontations with suspicious school authorities, disapproving relatives, curious neighbors, and the continuing challenge of providing "efficient instruction elsewhere." Several publications asked to borrow a few of the cartoons, including Home Education Magazine, the first edition of Don Hubbs' HOME EDUCATION RESOURCE GUIDE, and several newsletters. On the other hand, John Holt wasn't impressed. Most of the cartoons are now in this book, which saves me the bother of printing and binding a separate book, and saves you the bother of writing out another check (in case you'd be tempted to).

HOLT ASSOCIATES, INC.

Dear Donn,
    First of all, I want to say what a pleasure it was to meet your very nice daughter Karen, when she came into the office... What a nice young person!
    On this matter of EFFICIENT INSTRUCTION ELSEWHERE, I have been stalling around for a while, but guess I can't stall around any longer. I just don't think it's funny... Your book is full of sayings which are certainly true enough, but, for whatever reason, they just don't strike me as particularly funny. I don't even get a smile out of them, much less a guffaw. The other thing that might redeem the book would be if the cartoons were unusually well-drawn, but I am not telling you anything you don't already know if I say they are barely beyond the stick-figure stage.
    I think it is a worthy effort, and if other people are buying it, more power to them and you. But I don't add something to our list until on a scale of 1 to 100 I am about 95% enthusiastic, and my enthusiasm for your book of cartoons falls quite a bit short of that. Hope this won't offend you, or lessen in any way my admiration for the many kinds of good work you are doing.
    Good luck to you and all the family.
                                        Best,
                                        John Holt

Without music life would be a mistake.
Friedrich Nietzsche

FIRST MUSIC BOOKS -- Colorfully illustrated books for beginners, age 8 and up.

EASY RECORDER TUNES

EASY PIANO TUNES -- Many traditional and original tunes in both books for beginning players.

THE FIRST BOOK OF THE RECORDER

THE FIRST BOOK OF THE PIANO -- Friendly cartoon characters in both books introduce simple music theory, beginning techniques, interesting facts about the instruments, and a few tunes to practice.

Each book, $7.95. Code EDC. BROOK FARM BOOKS.

BIG EARS AND HIS TRIP TO ORCHESTRA HALL. 24-page coloring book, in which a rabbit plays various instruments, including strings, brass, percussion, and woodwinds. Instrumental "families" and their places in the orchestra are also shown. $1.40 postpaid. EDGEHILL ASSOCIATES, 3200 Edgehill Road, Ft. Worth, TX 76116.

THE USBORNE CHILDREN'S SONGBOOK, with music for piano, recorder, and guitar. 64 pages. Ages 3 up. $6.95. Code EDC. BROOK FARM BOOKS.

EARTH MOTHER LULLABIES FROM AROUND THE WORLD -- Lullabies from many ethnic groups and traditions, including Japanese, Russian, Swedish, Icelandic, Slovakian, Yiddish, Iroquois, Afro-American, Spanish, & others, including what is believed to be the oldest musically-notated song ever translated. Vocal by Pamala Ballingham, with flute, guitars, harp, keyboard, and Tibetan bell. Two cassettes. Infant to adult. $19.95. Code JN. BROOK FARM BOOKS.

UNDERSTANDING MUSIC (An Usborne Introduction). This complete introduction to music covers every style from classical to punk (yuck). It highlights the main features of each kind of music, and the life and times of those who wrote and first performed it, and explains the theory and science of music. A full description of instruments and instrumental groupings is given, and suggestions for music to listen to. Age 9 and up. $6.95. Code EDC. BROOK FARM BOOKS.

THE USBORNE STORY OF MUSIC -- Children age 10 and up are introduced to the world of classical music, the development of styles throughout the years, changing tastes and instruments, and the ways of life of the great composers. Lavishly illustrated. $5.95. Code EDC. BROOK FARM BOOKS.

A GENTLE WIND, Box 3103, Albany, NY 12203. Very good children's recordings. Free catalog.

STORIES AND SONGS FOR LITTLE CHILDREN, told and sung by Pete Seeger. Audio cassette with many of his best songs for kids (and playful adults), including Abiyoyo, Froggie Went A-Courting, more. $9.98 plus $1.50 postage. HIGH WINDY AUDIO, P.O. Box 553, Fairview, NC 28730.

RECORDINGS FOR CHILDREN. ALACAZAM! PRODUCTIONS, P.O. Box 429, Waterbury, VT 05676.

EARLY CHILDHOOD MUSIC, bimonthly newsletter with games, songs, crafts, and other musical activities for young children; articles on music, reviews of books and tapes, directions for making a simple musical instrument, much more. One copy, $3.95. One year (six issues), $19.50. MISS JACKIE MUSIC CO., 10001 El Monte, Overland Park, KS 66207.

MUSIC!-- A "Young Discovery Library" book. Discusses the origins and forms of music since ancient times, including all kinds of instruments around the world. A compact, comprehensive introduction to Western music, including information about foreign orchestras and U.S. jazz bands. 40 pages, hardcover, with brief but very informative text and brilliant, detailed pictures. The author and illustrator worked in collaboration with a musicologist to ensure accuracy in both the text and illustrations. Especially suitable for ages 5 to 10, but very interesting for older kids and adults, too. $4.95. Code YD. BROOK FARM BOOKS. (For other books in the Young Discovery Library series, see History and Science.)

KEY TO THE KEYS, by Gale Pederson. This basic home-study course provides an easy, enjoyable way to learn to play the piano, for children and adults.
 VOLUME I: the basics of fingering and chords, and the playing of simple melodies. One cassette and illustrated booklet. $15.95.
 VOLUME II: Increasingly-advanced piano-playing skills. Two cassettes and illustrated booklet. $21.95.
 BOTH VOLUMES, I and II, $35.00.
 KEY TO THE KEYS, prices as indicated. Code JN. BROOK FARM BOOKS.

LEARNING TO READ MUSIC -- An 80-minute cassette program, with a booklet containing 90 diagrams, that teaches the basics of reading notes, musical staff, time signatures, sharps & flats, repeats, naturals, rests, clefs, etc. Excellent beginner course or refresher course for children and adults. $15.95. Code JN. BROOK FARM BOOKS.

THE AMERICAN ORFF-SCHULWERK ASSOCIATION. Movement, speech, song, and instrument playing are integrated to teach the elements of music; improvisation is encouraged to develop creative thinking. CINDI WOBIG, AOSA Executive Secretary, P.O.Box 391089, Cleveland, OH 44139.

MUSICAL BINGO--A game of bingo that replaces numbers with elements of music; provides practice in basic skills of note reading, rhythm, terms, and signs; easy to play, 5 years to adult; designed specifically for keyboard students, but helpful for all music students. Available in two levels: Basic Preparatory and Sharps Added. Each game package contains 10 Musical Bingo cards, tally card, 75 bingo markers, 44 number chips, and instructions. Each game (one level), $6.00 plus $1.50 postage. JAYMAR PUBLICATIONS LTD., P.O. Box 6160, Depot C, Victoria, B.C., Canada V8P 5L5.

OLD MAN NOAH -- Music tape and guide, composed and written by Johnie Eager; sung by various artists. Musical games and activities to introduce and reinforce musical concepts; some with built-in morals, but not tiresome or preachy. "Day Star," folk song about the earth's rotation and the sun's effect on living things; "Ode to Joy," introduction to one of Beethoven's classics, teaching basic musical structure; eight others. 50-page guide, discussion, glossary, and bibliography. $15.00 plus $1.50 postage to EAGER PRODUCTIONS, P.O. Box 306, Mound City, KS 66056; or send SASE for more information.

CHILDREN'S SONGS OF MEXICO -- Niños Cantores de la Ciudad de México (Children's Choir of Mexico City) sings 12 traditional favorites in Spanish. The selections give an introduction to the language and folk heritage of Mexico. One cassette and a booklet of bilingual lyrics. $14.95. Code JP. BROOK FARM BOOKS.

MUSIC MINUS ONE, 423 West 55th St., New York, NY 10019. Long-play recordings of an orchestra or professional group with one part missing -- piano, violin, bass, clarinet, French horn, percussion, voice, etc. --your choice. Learn the piece, then play along as part of a full orchestra! About $10 each. Write for a free brochure and title listing.

MUSIC FOR LITTLE PEOPLE, Star Route, Redway, CA 95560. Musical instruments & materials for children. Catalog.

MUSIC MAESTRO, The Game of Musical Instruments, Past and Present. Learn the sounds, shapes, and functions of 48 instruments played in classical, bluegrass, rock, and jazz ensembles. Two high-quality cassette tapes, featuring the Oberlin College Conservatory of Music, present instrument sounds. Contents include puzzle game board, 48 instrument cards, ensemble and conductor cards, two cassette tapes, & instructions for five games of graduated difficulty. Preschool through adult; 2 to 6 players. $25.00 plus $3 shipping. BROOK FARM BOOKS.

THE GAME OF GREAT COMPOSERS. A colorful introduction to compositional style, medieval to modern. Players travel with 32 great composers, collecting travel and works cards by period. Active player interaction assures a lively play and stimulating information exchange. A cassette tape of keyboard selections, performed by faculty members of the University of Michigan School of Music, illustrates the compositional styles. Contents: composer cards, gameboard, period cards, travel cards, works cards, cassette tape, playing tokens, dice, Great Composers Booklet with a summary of information presented in the game, and instructions. Age 10 to adult. 2 to 4 players. $25.00 plus $3 shipping. BROOK FARM BOOKS.

HARPS OF LORIEN, 610 North Star Route, Questa, NM 87556. Very high-quality musical instruments, many of them difficult to find elsewhere, including harps, lyres, drums, guitars, recorders, flutes, and many more. Cassette recordings for children and adults. Send a #10 SASE for more information.

THE LAURA INGALLS WILDER SONGBOOK: Favorite Songs from the "Little House" Books, compiled and edited by Eugenia Carson; arranged for piano and guitar by Herbert Haufrect; pictures by Garth Williams. Words, music, and historical notes for 62 songs that play an important part in the Little House books (see History), including folksongs, gospel tunes, ballads, minstrel-show tunes, and hymns. $14.95. Code HR. BROOK FARM BOOKS.

MUSIC COLORING BOOKS--
WOLFGANG AMADEUS MOZART COLORING BOOK -- Portraits of Mozart and his family, suitable for framing after coloring; with interesting, informative text. $2.50.
A COLORING BOOK OF EARLY COMPOSERS--Schutz, Lully, Purcell, Scarlatti, Corelli, Couperin, many more. $3.50.
A COLORING BOOK OF GREAT COMPOSERS, Book I -- Rameau, Weber, Beethoven, Mendelssohn, Mozart, Scarlatti, Schubert, Gluck, and others. $3.50.
A COLORING BOOK OF GREAT COMPOSERS, Book II -- Schumann, Liszt, Wagner, Verdi, Smetana, Brahms, Bizet, Dvorak, Rossini, and other 19th-century composers. $3.50.
A COLORING BOOK OF GREAT COMPOSERS, Book III -- Debussy, Bartok, Richard Straus, Prokofiev, Delius, Milhaud, Poulenc, Sibelius, Vaughan Williams, Rachmaninoff, Elgar, Ravel, and more. $3.50.
A MUSICAL ALPHABET -- Very interesting portraits and caricatures of several well-known composers, arranged alphabetically, for coloring or plain enjoyment as they are. $3.50.
LUDWIG VAN BEETHOVEN COLORING BOOK -- Beethoven's life story in pictures. $3.50.
WOMAN COMPOSERS COLORING BOOK -- From the Middle Ages to the present, some famous, some less known. $3.50.
A COLORING BOOK OF PETER & THE WOLF BALLET-- Drawn from Nicholas Benois' famous ballet of 1947 at La Scala. Great pictures of Prokofiev's story, along with amusing, informative text about musical instruments. $3.50.
NUTCRACKER BALLET COLORING BOOK-- The story of the ballet and of its different productions, with illustrations by Alexandre Benois. $3.50.
A COLORING BOOK OF GREAT DANCERS -- A history of dance and dancers, with a portrait of each great dancer's greatest role. $3.50.
A COLORING BOOK OF THE SLEEPING BEAUTY BALLET -- The famous, elegant costumes by Leon Bakst for Diaghilev's production of this ballet a grand spectacle. $3.50.
ALL "MUSIC COLORING BOOKS," prices as indicated. Code BB. BROOK FARM BOOKS.

THE AMERICAN SONGBAG, edited by Carl Sandburg. A collection of 280 songs, ballads, and ditties which people have sung in the making of America. Piano accompaniments. 495 pages. $12.95. Code HBJ. BROOK FARM BOOKS.

FOLK SONGS OF NORTH AMERICA, by Alan Lomax. The origins, lyrics, & music of more than 300 of America's favorite songs; true history set to music. Melodies and guitar chords transcribed by Peggy Seeger; with 100 piano arrangements by Matyas Seiber & Don Banks. "The intention of this volume," writes Lomax, "is to put a choice selection of our folk songs into their historical and social setting so that they tell the story of the people who made them and sang them-- to compose a folk history, or a history of the folk of America." Frequent anecdotes and historical notes, often as interesting as the songs, cover the social, religious, and political growth and changes of the people. Songs cover: THE NORTH: Old Colony Times, Yankee Soldiers and Sailors, Shouters and Shakers, Pioneers, Timber Tigers, Workers and Farmers, & the Maritime Provinces; THE SOUTHERN MOUNTAINS & BACKWOODS: Across the Blue Ridge, the Old Ballads, Lonesome Love Songs, White Spirituals, Rowdy Ways, Murder Ballads, Hard Times and the Hillbilly; THE WEST: Beyond the Mississippi, Plainsmen & 49'ers, Soldiers and Renegades, Cowboys, Prairie Farmers, Railroaders and Hoboes, The Last West; THE NEGRO SOUTH: Spirituals, Reels, Work Songs, Ballads and Blues. Five appendices, including a guitar and banjo guide, and bibliographies of books and records. Profusely illustrated. Giant paperback, 623 pages. $19.95. Code DD. BROOK FARM BOOKS.

LARK IN THE MORNING, P.O. Box 1176, Mendocino, CA 95460. Catalog and newsletter featuring musical instruments (zithers, flutes, harps, bagpipes, mandolins, dulcimers, etc.); records, tapes, books, videos, more.

THE INTERNATIONAL PREVIEW SOCIETY, P.O. Box 91405, Indianapolis, IN 46291. Recorded music "club": symphonic, classical jazz, big band, easy listening. Reasonable prices if you watch for frequent promotional sales and discounts. Each purchase earns a half-price bonus coupon to use on future purchases, so you really get three for the price of two. Write for information.

> Wagner's music is better than it sounds.
> Bill Nye

THE INSTRUMENT WORKSHOP, 8023 Forest Drive NE, Seattle, WA 98115. Kits, tools, and plans for making reproductions of early keyboard instruments. Catalog, $1.00.

DISCOUNT MUSIC CLUB, Box 2000, New Rochelle, NY 10801. Discounts up to 73% on tapes and records; all labels; no purchase obligations. Free details.

HEARTSONG REVIEW, P.O. Box 1084, Cottage Grove, OR 97424. Music for healing, massage, yoga, meditation, dance, aerobics, group singing, driving, working; reviews of music, including electronic, acoustic, folk, rock, children's, peace. Sample, $4. 1 yr (2 issues), $6. 2 years (4 issues), $10.00.

SHEET MUSIC MAGAZINE, 352 Evelyn St., Paramus, NJ 07652. 1 year (9 issues), $13.97; 2 years (18 issues), $25.00. Each year includes more than 100 songs -- pop, standards, jazz, show tunes, folk, country, tin pan alley, movie songs, classics, ragtime, blues, more; keyboard clinic, guitar workshop, sight-reading, playing by ear, theory & harmony, rhythm workshops, more. Choose piano/guitar or organ edition; choose Easy or Standard.

"HOW TO ENJOY A SYMPHONY," booklet naming classical composers whose music has been used in movies, commercials, and rock tunes; miscellaneous facts about symphonies, activity ideas, etc. FREE. HERSHEY CHOCOLATE USA, Dept. "Symphony," P.O. Box 800, Hershey, PA 17033.

KEYBOARD CAPERS. Suzuki method at home, all grades and ages, from beginner to advanced; with 100 activities, games, and cutouts. Write for information and price. THE ELIJAH COMPANY, P.O. Box 12483, Knoxville, TN 37912.

SUZUKI MUSICAL INSTRUMENTS, P.O. Box 261030, San Diego, CA 92126. High-quality musical and rhythm instruments, primarily for elementary schools. Recorders ($2.50 & up), xylophones (soprano, alto, bass), metallophones, glockenspiels, melodians, percussion instruments, tone bells, digital pianos, omnichords, a piano that can sound like 20 different instruments including a human voice, musical instruction books, song books, more. Not necessarily for the Suzuki Method of learning. Catalog.

CHILDREN'S MUSIC CENTER, 5373 West Pico Blvd., Los Angeles, CA 90019. Good source of records and books on multi-ethnic and multi-cultural education (Spanish, Black, American, Asian, Pacific).

LIVES & MUSIC of great composers. Four-year cassette tape course for children. Free brochure. MUSIC & MOMENTS WITH THE MASTERS, The Cornerstone Curriculum Project, 2006 Flat Creek Road, Richardson, TX 75080.

CHILDREN'S BOOK AND MUSIC CENTER, P.O. Box 1130, Santa Monica, CA 90406. Music & rhythm instruments, thousands of music titles on tape including classical dance and ballet, much more. Catalog.

> Of all noises I think music is the least disagreeable.
> Samuel Johnson

THE BEST WAY TO LEARN A LANGUAGE is to grow up with it. The next best way, we're often told, is to live in the country in which the desired language is spoken. I think the next best way is to live in the country AND use some good books, tapes, or other study guides. I became fairly fluent in Spanish while living in Mexico, but if I hadn't studied grammar and vocabulary at the same time, my Spanish would have been limited to that of the uneducated, poor people with whom I spent most of my time. The same is usually true even in learning one's native language: if one's family and everyday associates speak ungrammatically, one's own speech will be the same unless an effort is made to improve it through study and practice. If you want to learn a language but don't expect to be living where it's spoken, or you want to learn some of it before you go, there are many different ways of learning -- tapes, phrase books, classroom studies, and so on. We've investigated and tried several, and we believe the selections we've made are among the best language-learning aids available.

BEGINNER'S FOREIGN LANGUAGE DICTIONARIES --
  BEGINNER'S GERMAN DICTIONARY
  BEGINNER'S SPANISH DICTIONARY
  BEGINNER'S FRENCH DICTIONARY
Each book, 128 pages; fully illustrated; for ages 11 and up. **$9.95 each.** Code EDC. BROOK FARM BOOKS.

"SPRINGBOARD" LANGUAGE COURSES FOR CHILDREN introduce young children to foreign languages in an active, play-oriented way. Ideal for ages 4-8. Adult guidance is usually needed, but familiarity with the foreign language is not necessary; everything is on the cassettes. It's like playing "Simon Says" in another language. Activities include songs, coloring, playing games, & cutting out shapes. Two cassettes and a 40-page book. Order #F700 French, #G700 German, or #S700 Spanish. $19.95 each plus $2 shipping. BROOK FARM BOOKS.

STORYBRIDGES FOR CHILDREN-- Children learn French or Spanish by joining Sadie & Sydney, the storyteller's young helpers, in repeating key foreign language words and phrases spoken in the context of familiar stories-- Goldilocks and the Three Bears, Little Red Riding Hood, The Turtle's Music, The Nightingale, The Shoemaker & the Elves, and Peter and the Wolf. Each program consists of three cassettes in an attractive album. Order "Storybridges"; specify French or Spanish. $19.95. Code JN. BROOK FARM BOOKS.

"BIEN TRABAJO," "BUENO," and other Spanish & French stickers to tell your students how well they're doing (or not well, but I'd toss out the "You can improve" stickers). Each package has 64 stickers (32 designs). Specify language; $1 per package, plus $2 postage for any size order. WOODY'S COUNTRY STORE, P.O. Box 248, Clear Lake, MN 55319. Free catalog.

CORRESPONDENCE COURSES IN FRENCH-- Elementary school courses, all subjects, completely in French, for Francophones or advanced students of French. A few years ago, the cost was about 825F, or approximately $110 US. Write for information to: Ministere de L'Education Nationale, Centre National D'Enseignement par Correspondence, 109 rue Vauquelin, 31100 Toulouse, France.

LIVING SPANISH & LIVING FRENCH for Children-- Learning Spanish or French is fun and easy with this method, which is especially suitable for children of all ages who can read. 40 lessons centered around everyday activities such as going on a picnic, having a birthday party, and visiting a circus. Each program includes an illustrated read-along book, two 1-hour cassettes, & an illustrated picture dictionary. Lessons include songs, poems, and well-known children's stories. Order "Living Spanish" or "Living French." $18.95 each plus $2 shipping. BROOK FARM BOOKS.

TOPSY TURVY/PATAS ARRIBAS. A unique 8-page Spanish-English newspaper for children; also interesting to anyone learning Spanish. $6 for 12 issues. BK PUBLICATIONS, 7060 Calle del Sol, Tucson, AZ 85710.

"BUENO," free sample bilingual (English-Spanish) newsletter with bilingual notes, recipes, offerings of many other products. Send #10 SASE with your request to: In One EAR Publications, 29481 Manzanita Drive, Campo, CA 91906-1128.

FRENCH FOR TOTS -- For ages 2½ and up. I don't think this course is quite as good as the "Springboard" series (above), but it's being sold widely in many stores and kids are learning French with it. The course has two cassettes with original songs and music, activity book, and parent's guide. Write for more information or send $19.95 plus $2 shipping to OPTIMALEARNING LANGUAGE LAND, 88-D Belvedere Street, San Rafael, CA 94901.

CHINESE & JAPANESE SOFTWARE, video tapes, language programs, dictionaries, movies. Catalog. CHENG & TSUI COMPANY, 25 West St., Boston, MA 02111.

LANGUAGE/30 -- Based on the U.S. military "speed-up" methods designed for military and embassy personnel, each LANGUAGE/30 course includes two 45-minute cassettes with all phrases spoken in both English and the target language by native speakers, with a convenient phrasebook. Edited by the world-famous linguist Charles Berlitz, LANGUAGE/30 offers one of the most effective "quick" courses available, with which you could master a basic conversational level within 30 days or less. Stressing conversational and useful words and phrases, the course offers one-and-a-half hours of guided, repeated practice in greetings, introductions, requests, general conversations; native speakers with perfect pronunciation; two short sections by Charles Berlitz, one introducing the course with helpful tips on its use, and another on the social customs & etiquette of the country. LANGUAGE/30 is available in the following languages:

AFRIKAANS -- ARABIC -- CZECH -- DANISH -- DUTCH -- FINNISH -- FRENCH -- GERMAN -- GREEK -- HEBREW -- HINDI -- IRISH -- INDONESIAN -- ITALIAN -- JAPANESE -- KOREAN -- MANDARIN CHINESE -- NORWEGIAN -- NORTHERN SOTHO -- PERSIAN -- POLISH -- PORTUGUESE -- RUSSIAN -- SPANISH -- SERBO-CROATIAN -- SOUTHERN SOTHO -- SWAHILI -- SWEDISH -- TAGALOG (FILIPINO) -- THAI -- TSWANA -- TURKISH -- VIETNAMESE -- XHOSA -- YIDDISH -- ZULU.

Each LANGUAGE/30 COURSE (book with two cassettes), $17.95 plus $2 postage. BROOK FARM BOOKS.

MADRIGAL'S MAGIC KEY TO SPANISH, by Maria Madrigal. This is THE book with which to study Spanish, along with a good cassette course (such as LANGUAGE/30) to help you learn the proper accent and pronunciation. "At this moment you know several thousand Spanish words even if you have never seen or heard a Spanish word," says the author in her preface. Many of those words are identical in spelling and meaning to the English, such as popular, capital, animal, hotel, radio, conductor, probable, cable, actor, ideal, flexible, and central. Many others are different only by one or two letters, such as Atlantico, Pacifico, dramatico, atractivo, restaurante, importante, presidente, permanente, medicina, constructivo, optimista, dentista, artista, and invitacion. Spanish is a very phonetic language, with very few exceptions to spelling and grammatical rules. This book will teach you how to recognize words which are identical in both languages, how to make Spanish words from the English words you already know, and how to form easy sentences right away. Before our kids were born, Jean and I took this book with us to Mexico, and received many compliments on our quick grasp of Spanish. When our daughter Cathy was 21, she spent several months traveling in Mexico, alone and with a friend, after studying this book and the LANGUAGE/30 Spanish course, and she agrees that they are an excellent combination. NEW REVISED EDITION, 496 pages, paperback. $12.00. Code DD. BROOK FARM BOOKS.

TRANSLATOR-8000. Your pronunciation may bring smiles and your conversation may be punctuated with frequent pauses, but you will "Speak A Foreign Language In Seconds," as the manufacturers of this handy little gadget promise. TRANSLATOR-8000 is a pocket-sized, electronic translating machine, measuring less than 3x5 inches. It provides a nearly-instant, 4-step translation of an English word into a foreign language, or a foreign word into English. Turn it on, selecting English-to-foreign or foreign-to-English, and press the ABC1 button until the first letter of the word you want appears on the screen. Then press the ABC2 button until the second letter of the word you want appears. Now press the "Search" button; all words beginning with those two letters will scroll rapidly across the screen; when your word appears, stop. Push the "=" button for an immediate translation. Available in French, German, and Spanish, with an 8000-word vocabulary (4000 English, 4000 foreign) of the most commonly-used words in travel and business. Use it for study before traveling (like electronic flash cards), and take it with you to help decipher menus and ask (and understand) directions. It's also a full-function calculator, which will help with currency conversions.

TRANSLATOR-8000. Specify French, German, or Spanish. $79.95 plus $4 postage. BROOK FARM BOOKS.

AROUND THE WORLD WITH 80 WORDS, by Charles Berlitz. Study this book before you go or carry it with you to help you feel at home wherever your plane lands. The basic words and colloquial phrases in 25 different languages that will help you find your way, ask and receive directions, and be a traveler instead of just a tourist. $15.95. Code BT. BROOK FARM BOOKS.

GREEK and LATIN -- All levels, beginner to very advanced. Textbooks, literature, easy readers, filmstrips, cassettes, buttons ("Litterae non dant panem" -- "Literature does not earn bread"). Classical Greek and Latin literature, in the original and in translation. Catalog: BOLCHAZY-CARDUCCI PUBLISHERS, 44 Lake Street, Oak Park, IL 60302.

LATIN--Beginning and advanced courses, readings from Latin writers, workbooks, etc. Request "School Catalog, grades 4-12." LONGMAN INC., 95 Church St., White Plains, NY 10601.

"LATIN LIVES ON" -- 333 common words, identical in Latin and English, arranged alphabetically on one sheet of paper (suitable for photocopying). You can say, "These ordinary words I use every day were used by Nero, Caesar, and Cicero!" Accompanied by "Latin Lives On," an article by Bruce D. Price, originally published in Princeton Alumni Weekly, which discusses the educational implications & uses of the list. $5.00 postpaid. WORD-WIDE EDUCATIONAL SERVICES, Box 21212, Midtown Station, New York, NY 10129.

TELA CHARLOTTAE, Fabula quae scripta est ab E. B. White. In sermonem latinum conversa ab Bernice L. Fox. CHARLOTTE'S WEB in Latin! Complete vocabulary list in back. For students with a background of two years of high school Latin. $10 plus $1 postage. BERNICE L. FOX, 1025 Cramer Ct., Monmouth, IL 61462.

ADVANCED LANGUAGE COURSES -- We have more extensive courses, including basic, intermediate, and advanced lessons, in nearly 50 languages. Please send two first-class stamps for information. Be sure to specify the language in which you're interested. BROOK FARM BOOKS.

COMPUTERS

TO: Our Customers
FROM: Shipping Dept.
RE: Packing Slips

Please accept our apology for using a duplicate of your purchase order for a packing slip. We are presently updating our computer system which necessitates temporary manual order processing.

"Computers are man's most beautiful creation," says U. S. Navy Captain Grace M. Hopper, who sets the standards of computer language for the Pentagon. "All children older than four should have their own computers. We may even get a generation that can spell."

That's like saying anyone who owns a gun will know how to make bullets.

Captain Hopper must mean that all previous generations, those unlucky enough to have grown up computerless, can't spell. She may be right. A little while ago, I was looking through the diary my grandmother kept during her first year as a school teacher. That was more than ninety years ago, and my grandmother was sixteen. Not once in the diary did she spell "computer" correctly. In fact, she avoided the word completely.

Although excessive love of gadgets and gimmicks is the root of much evil in the world, it's good to be familiar with the basic usages of some of those gadgets. Books are tools of communication and learning; cars and planes take us to interesting places; telephones help us to reach out and touch someone. We try to help our children become book-literate, telephone-literate, and even airplane-literate.

(See what happens when a word is suddenly uprooted and transplanted into foreign soil? "Literacy" used to be related only to the ability to read and write. Then computer folk tacked it on to the word "computer," with the guilt-trip implication that if you're not able to operate one of the new-fangled gadgets, it's tantamount to the other kind of illiteracy. In other words, "literacy" came to mean "competency," which gave it an added dimension, but also robbed its original meaning of much of its potency. E. D. Hirsch, Jr., compounded the felony by tacking the word to "cultural," with the implied parallel suggestion that a lack of cultural knowledge and awareness is as serious as the inability to read and write. Okay, then, why can't I say "telephone-literate" and "airplane-literate"?)

We have little interest in computer-literacy. Computers are undoubtedly very useful tools, but I am unconvinced that they're essential to a happy life or a creative career. An apple a day may keep the doctor away, but an Apple a day may increase society's need for psychiatrists.

On the larger scale, computerized society becomes increasingly impersonal, and the value of life becomes reduced each day by a few more decimal points. On a smaller scale, people who use computers a great deal tend to think in computer-like patterns, in which life becomes a series of problems to be dealt with in a systematic, orderly manner, with a logical solution to each problem at the end of each operation. Life is seldom that orderly and logical. Solutions are often reached by feelings, hunches, and intuitive empathy as often as by orderly examination.

To give the devil his due (to use one of those strange phrases that seem to make sense until you examine them), Mario Pagnoni almost convinces me, in THE COMPLETE HOME EDUCATOR, that computers are not the bad guys I think they are. His explanation of the uses and values of a computer, especially as a learning tool, is the clearest and most convincing I've found. I'm just as suspicious of computers, and as concerned about their detrimental influences on human ways of thinking, but Mario's book has shown me that computers can be controlled and can have a proper place in the home or homeschool. Maybe.

The greatest advances in art, music, literature, philosophy, and science have been made by men and women who were open to inspiration, hunches, and wild guesses. Computers often do away with the need of creative thinking: just feed the problem into the keyboard, and wait for the computer to find the solution. This approach may produce rapid and astonishing advances in the already-existing arts and sciences, but it is incapable of producing truly new arts and sciences. The computer's "reasoning" can be based only on information and procedures which are fed or built into it; a human being -- genius, mystic, or you or I -- unfettered by controls and programs, with circuits and synapses of flesh and spirit infinitely greater than anything of silicone and magnetic impulses will ever be, can leap lightyears while the computer is still singing "Daisy, Daisy."

The possibilities of extrapolation open to a computer may be nearly infinite; but that extrapolation must still be based upon existing data. Any situation or problem of life processed from a computer's view is reduced to a paint-by-number picture. No matter how the combinations or choices of colors are varied, the end result is still no more, and usually less, than the original.

We don't want paint-by-number lives, for our-selves or for our children. We're willing to accept the benefits and beneficial possibilities of computers, but we're not convinced that they will make any significant contributions to the world in any terms of real human progress. The art of living, if reduced to lines and numbers, would no longer be art and hardly living.

COMPUTER BOOKS FOR BEGINNERS -- Very basic introductions and programs that will run on most home computers, especially for age 11 and up, but good for the absolute beginner of any age because they clearly explain all necessary steps and concepts, progressing steadily toward increased competence and understanding. 48 pages each, except COMPUTERS, which has 32.

    CREEPY COMPUTER GAMES $2.95
    WRITE YOUR OWN ADVENTURE PROGRAMS $3.95
    GUIDE TO BETTER BASIC $3.95
    COMPUTER BATTLE GAMES $3.95
    COMPUTER-CONTROLLED ROBOTS, hardcover, $10.95
    COMPUTER FUN $3.95
    COMPUTERS: A Simple Introduction   3.95
    COMPUTER GAMES $3.95
    COMPUTER SPACE GAMES $3.95
    PRACTICAL THINGS TO DO WITH MICROCOMPUTER $3.95
    PRACTICE YOUR BASIC $3.95
Specify "Beginner Computer Books" and title. Code EDC. BROOK FARM BOOKS.

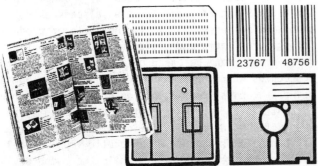

COMPUTER EQUIPMENT AND TOOLS -- Workstation kits, LAN equipment, diagnostic software, cabling accessories, test equipment, much more. Free catalog. JENSEN TOOLS INC., 7815 South 46th Street, Phoenix, AZ 85044.

COMPUTER WIMP NO MORE, by John Bear, Ph.D., & David M. Pozerycki. This is Bear's revised, updated version of his very popular COMPUTER WIMP, in which he summed up his search in 1974 for "the perfect personal computer" as "frustrating" and "fatiguing." This definitive resource guide will help potential buyers choose the right PC by analyzing their computer needs and capabilities. It's filled with simple practicalities (such as the differences between IBM & Macintosh systems), information on software, hardware, viruses, computer crimes, health issues, a 30-page buyer's guide (with PC prices, makes, and models), and even a section called "Computer Consumer Karate" to help if things go wrong. 320 pages. $14.95. Code TSP. BROOK FARM BOOKS.

ACCESS ERIC, free service of Educational Resources Information Center, which is part of the U.S. Department of Education. Call 1-800-LET-ERIC to learn what resources are available; also to request two free booklets, "A Pocket Guide to ERIC" and "All About ERIC."

THE COMPLETE HANDBOOK OF PERSONAL COMPUTER COMMUNICATIONS, Alfred Glossbrenner. Revised, updated 3rd edition. The latest information on online utilities -- CompuServe, The Source, Delphi, GEnie, BIX, People/Link, Quantaum/Link, Prodigy, EasyLink, Minitel, and the latest on online information services, including updated sections on DIALOG, Dow Jones, BRS, Orbit, NewsNet, VU/TEXT, Data Times, Lexis/Nexis, & other essential systems. Hands-on coverage of electronic mail (via MCI and others), computerized conferencing, how to plug into the worldwide Telex network, and the latest on how to send and receive facsimile (FAX) messages with any computer. Other new information includes: how to go online from a remote location using radio links circling the globe, insightful advice on micro-to-mainframe connections, a primer on LANs (Local Area Networks), and updates on online shopping, banking, and stock trading; working at home through "telecommuting"; and how to tap into the nation's 14,000 bulletin board systems (BBSs) or set up one of your own. Considered by many authorities to be essential reading for all computer owners who use telephone modems to go online with the world. Hardcover, 400 pages, glossary, index. $24.95. Code STM. BROOK FARM BOOKS.

TECHNOSTRESS: The Human Cost of the Computer Revolution, by Craig Brod. An in-depth look at the ways in which the new technology may adversely affect our lives at work, school, home, and play. The author says that as life becomes increasingly centered around the computer, people are likely to experience eye strain, boredom, and headaches; alienation from spouse and family; frustration with perpetually changing work routines; fear of being left behind by the technological revolution; and impatience with human imperfection. The author also discusses strategies for incorporating computers into a happy, balanced, human-oriented life. Older teens and adults. $16.95. Code AW. BROOK FARM BOOKS.

THE ELECTRIC CONNECTION: Its Effects on Mind & Body, by Michael Shallis. The author, an astro-physicist lecturing on External Affairs at Oxford University, explores the nature of a form of energy that is a feature of the life force itself. Electricity can be found in every animate and inanimate thing on earth. The electric fields surrounding rocks, trees, and ourselves are measurable and can be monitored. There are clear correspondences between the character of such fields and our moods and our state of health. Natural electricity is a beneficient force, controlled as it is by magnetism. But the electricity that now pulses through the cables in our homes, offices, and factories, beneath our feet and above our heads, has been unleashed from magnetic bonds; even the electrical industries acknowledge that prolonged exposure to it is harmful. In our everyday lives it can make us ill; we can develop severe allergies to it. In its purest, strongest form -- in the computer world -- it can influence our minds, alter our characters, and markedly affect our health. Physicians now recognize a painful and dangerous physical syndrome that attends intense and protracted work with a computer. As computer applications proliferate, and greater numbers of people use computers at work and in their homes, "computer syndrome" may become endemic. Even worse, a change in consciousness and character that has already been observed may affect a much larger segment of humanity. Hardcover, 287 pages. $18.95 plus $2 postage. BROOK FARM BOOKS.

THIS PERFECT DAY, by Ira Levin. A dramatic, thought-provoking reading about a time in the future when all people of the earth are members of a world-wide "family" that is ruled by a computer... 2 CASSETTES. $14.95. Code BT. BROOK FARM BOOKS.

HUG-BBS -- The Home-Education Computer User's Group Electronic Bulletin Board. (Say it 10 times, fast.) HUG-BBS "is dedicated to home-schooled children and those with a serious interest in the education of children in the home environment...[and] is intended to be used for the free exchange of information relevant to home education." For information, send a first class stamp to: JIM MAYOR, 26824 Howard Chapel Drive, Damascus, MD 20872.

EXCEL-ED, P.O. Box 380154, San Antonio, TX 78280. Educational data bank providing extensive library of computer programs at low cost. One-time registration fee (about $50) pays for four programs, specialized access programs, catalogs, & continual information updates. Thereafter, each program costs only $2.50 plus telephone transmission time (4 to 6 minutes) to download the program to your own computer (transmission costs are about $5 or $6 per hour during non-peak times, 6PM to 7AM. Write for current information and registration form.

CLASSROOM COMPUTER LEARNING, 2451 East River Road, Dayton, OH 45439. 8 issues (school year); introductory price $13.95. Curriculum planning, system development, teaching and computing. May be of use to homeschoolers. Request a sample.

SOFTWARE FOR KIDS. Maneuver and land airplanes with Air Trax. Math problems. IBM or compatible. DATA-WARE, 5737 64th St., Lubock, TX 79424.

SOFTWORLDS FOR CHILDREN -- Bimonthly "report on Macintosh software for fun & learning." Each issue has reviews of several different programs, recommended programs, and editorial comments. Having tried to follow an article or two in various computer publications, I'm very impressed by the clarity of writing in these reviews, and the absence of surplus jargon. The publisher's editorial position -- which I'd characterize as "subjective objectivity" -- is similar to ours: i.e., do we like it or not? And why, or why not? The bigger, more-commercial publications depend on advertising revenue, which makes real objectivity a luxury for them, with the result that their "reviews" can seldom be trusted. Not depending on advertisers, SoftWorlds is under no such economic pressure. Regular subscription is $32 per year, but SoftWorld's publisher, Gary E. Bloom, offers a special discounted price of $25 to home-schoolers who mention that they learned of his program in THE HOME SCHOOL SOURCE BOOK. Send payment with your order to: Soft-Worlds, P.O. Box 219, Edmonds, WA 98020.

CHILDREN'S SOFTWARE REVUE, bimonthly newsletter with reviews and ratings for twelve software programs, each one "kid-tested" and evaluated according to its educational value, ease of use, etc. Also news and tips for choosing software. For parents and teachers of children age 3 to 10. Sample issue, free. Annual subscription, $24.00. CHILDREN'S SOFTWARE REVUE, 520 N. Adams St., Ypsilanti, MI 48197.

PUBLISHERS OF EDUCATIONAL SOFTWARE --

ACADEMIC HALLMARKS, P.O. Box 998, Durango, CO 81302

ACTIVE LEARNING SYSTEMS, 5365 Avenida Encines, Carlsbad, CA 92008

ADDISON-WESLEY PUBLISHING CO., Software Sales, Reading, MA 01867

ADVANCED IDEAS, 2902 San Pablo Avenue, Berkeley, CA 94702

APPLE: For the name of the dealer nearest you, call 1-800-538-9696. In California, 1-800-662-9238

ARTSCI, INC., 10432 Burbank Blvd., North Hollywood, CA 91325

BOBBS-MERRILL EDUCATIONAL PUBLISHING, P.O. Box 7080, Indianapolis, IN 46206

BRITANNICA SOFTWARE, 345 Fourth St., San Francisco, CA 94107

BRODERBUND SOFTWARE, 17 Paul Drive, San Rafael, CA 94903

C & C SOFTWARE, 5713 Kentford Circle, Wichita, KS 67220

CHASELLE, INC., 9645 Gerwig Lane, Columbia, MD 21046

CLARIS, 440 Clyde Ave., Mountain View, CA 94043

CLASSROOM COMPUTER LEARNING, 5615 W. Cermak Road, Cicero, IL 60650

COMPress, P.O. Box 102, Wentworth, NH 03282

COMPU-TATIONS, P.O. Box 502, Troy, MI 48099

COMPUTER SOFTWARE STORE, 2549 Cleveland Ave., Granite City, IL 62040

CUE SoftSwap, P.O. Box 271704, Concord, CA 94524

CUISENAIRE COMPANY OF AMERICA, INC., 12 Church St., New Rochelle, NY 10805

D. C. HEATH SOFTWARE, 2700 N. Richardt St., Indianapolis, IN 46219

DAVIDSON & ASSOCIATES, 3135 Kashiwa St., Torrance, CA 90505

DAYBREAK SOFTWARE, 1951 Grand Ave., Baldwin, NY 11510

DEVELOPMENTAL LEARNING MATERIALS, P.O. Box 4000, Allen, TX 75002

DIDATECH SOFTWARE LTD., 3812 William St., Burnaby, B.C., Canada V5C 3H9

EDUCATIONAL ACTIVITIES, P.O. Box 392, Freeport, NY 11520

EDUCATIONAL MATERIALS & EQUIPMENT CO., P.O. Box 17, Pelham, NY 10802

EDUCATIONAL RESOURCES, 2360 Hassel Road, Hoffman Estates, IL 60195

EDU SOFT, 4639 Spruce St., Philadelphia, PA 19139

FOCUS MEDIA, P.O. Box 865, Garden City, NY 11530

GROLIER ELECTRONIC PUBLISHING INC., Sherman Turnpike, Danbury, CT 06816

HARTLEY COURSEWARE, 133 Bridge St., Dimondale, MI 48821

HOUGHTON MIFFLIN, Educational Software Division, P.O. Box 683, Hanover, NH 03755

HRM SOFTWARE, 175 Tompkins Avenue, Pleasantville, NY 10570

IBM EDUCATIONAL SOFTWARE, 1 Culver Road, Dayton, NJ 08810

LAWRENCE HALL OF SCIENCE, University of California, Berkeley, CA 94720

LEARNING TECHNOLOGIES, INC., 4255 LBJ Freeway, Suite 131, Dallas, TX 75244

LOGO COMPUTER SYSTEMS, 121 Mount Vermon, Boston, MA 02108

MERLAN SCIENTIFIC, LTD., 247 Armstrong Ave., Georgetown, Ontario, Canada L7G 4X6

MINDSCAPES, 3444 Dundee Road, Northbrook, IL 60022

MONTESSORI WORLD EDUCATIONAL INSTITUTE, P.O. Box 3808, San Luis Obispo, CA 93403

MECC, 3490 Lexington Ave. N, St. Paul, MN 55126

MIDWEST SOFTWARE, Box 214, Farmington, MI 48332

MILLIKEN PUBLISHING COMPANY, P.O. Box 21579, St. Louis, MO 63132

MINDSCAPE, 3444 Dundee Rd., Northbrook, IL 60062

QUEUE, 562 Boston Ave., Bridgeport, CT 06610

RESTON PUBLISHING CO., 11480 Sunset Hills Rd., Reston, VA 22090

SOUTH-WESTERN PUBLISHING, 5101 Madison Road, Cincinnati, OH 45227

SCHOLASTIC, P.O. Box 7501, Jefferson City, MO 65102

SOUTH WESTERN PUBLISHING CO., 5101 Madison Road, Cincinnati, OH 45227

SPRINGBOARD SOFTWARE, 7808 Creekridge Circle, Minneapolis, MN 55435

SUNBURST COMMUNICATIONS, 39 Washington Ave., Pleasantville, NY 10570

SPINNAKER SOFTWARE, 1 Kendal Square, Cambridge, MA 02139

TERRAPIN, 400 Riverside St., Portland, ME 04103

TEXAS INSTRUMENTS, INC., P.O. Box 10508, Lubbock, TX 79408

THE LEARNING COMPANY, 6493 Kaiser Drive, Fremont, CA 94555

THE TEACHING COMPUTER, 67 Barbara Dr., Centereach, NY 11720

TOM SNYDER PRODUCTIONS, 90 Sherman St., Cambridge, MA 02140

WEEKLY READER SOFTWARE, 10 Station Place, Norfolk, CT 06058

XEROX EDUCATIONAL PUBLICATIONS, 245 Longhill Rd., Middletown, CT 06457

SUNBURST COMMUNICATIONS, 39 Washington Ave., Pleasantville, NY 10570. Educational computer courseware & other instructional materials, preschool to adult.

HOWARD W. SAMS & CO., INC., P.O. Box 7092, Indianapolis, IN 46206. Leading publisher of technical books, from consumer electronics to microcomputers to the design and application of 16-bit microprocessors. Available in bookstores, computer stores, from electronic distributors, or by direct mail. Catalog. (In Canada, write to LENBROOK INDUSTRIES, 1145 Bellamy Road, Scarborough, Ontario M1H 1H5.)

CHINESE & JAPANESE SOFTWARE, video tapes, language programs, dictionaries, movies. Catalog.   CHENG & TSUI COMPANY, 25 West St., Boston, MA 02111.

MICROCOMPUTER REFERENCE MANUALS & HANDBOOKS. Catalog. INTEL LITERATURE SALES, Box 58130, Santa Clara, CA 95052.

SCHOOL OF COMPUTER TRAINING, Scranton, PA 18515. Fairly comprehensive correspondence course in computer programming; includes a keyboard (to connect to your own TV), cassette recorder and tapes, charts, worksheets, user manual, more. About $600. Monthly payment option (about $30) available. Write for current information.

COMPUTER SERVICING COURSE. Build a complete computer system, step by step; learn to program, interpret, & service in a home-study program. Free catalog of this & other careers (robotics, data communications, radio, TV, video, more). NRI SCHOOLS, McGraw-Hill Continuing Education Center, 3939 Wisconsin Ave., Washington, DC 20016.

I disagree with the fairly common belief that many kids of today can't read because they watch too much television. I think they watch too much television because they can't read, which is not the same thing.

The great public furor over "why Johnny can't read" began before TV became a common household appliance. Public school teachers, not realizing the teaching methods they had learned were different from those of the previous generation, and feeling perplexed and frustrated by their students' reading failures, thought they had finally discovered the reason for those failures.

Like many other things, television can be a useful tool of learning (as well as a source of good entertainment), or it can be an escape from life. There are times when I resent its intrusion into our lives, even with good programs, and I can understand and sympathize with those who choose not to have a television. On the other hand, I'm just as impatient with those who preach against it as I am with those who watch it for ten or twelve hours a day. If your kids' minds are being turned into soggy oatmeal by too much television, there's no need to throw away the television, as many critics suggest; just cut down on the viewing time. If you can't control your kids' television use, how will you control anything else in their lives?

The number of hours we spend, as a family, in watching television varies from year to year, depending somewhat on our other activities and somewhat on the programs available. Our choices are limited to the programs available in our area, through one Canadian network, one American network, and the American Public Broadcasting System. We check the TV guide in the local newspaper for National Geographic specials, wildlife and science shows, vintage movies, and occasional music or movie specials. Our average, over the years, has been about ten or twelve hours a week.

In 1985, the year I wrote the first draft of this chapter, Jean and I chose about a fourth of the programs (although the kids might have chosen the same ones, if we hadn't) -- M*A*S*H and Hill Street Blues; three and a half hours each week. The kids' own choices, sometimes with our encouragement and sometimes not, were Magnum (alternating weekly with Remington Steele, because of a difference of opinion about which was better, two of us favoring one, and four of us favoring the other), The A-Team (stupid, but sort of funny), Knight Rider (yuk), Walt Disney, Fall Guy (usually stupid, sometimes amusing), Simon & Simon (not on our channels anymore, and we miss it), Dallas

(triple yuk; the only soap opera we allowed), and Highway to Heaven (surprisingly good sometimes) -- eight hours. That brought our total regular viewing to eleven and a half hours a week, although we didn't always watch all the shows together. A "special," such as The Ten Commandments, would add to our time.

Some of the kids wanted to watch Love Boat, Fantasy Island, Three's Company, and other similar shows, but we discussed them all democratically and then Jean and I democratically ruled them out.

Some people say that kids will eventually tire of too much television, and shut it off without adult direction. We experimented with that approach a few times, but neither Jean nor I had the stamina to follow through. Many of our kids' friends were hooked on soap operas, and talked of the characters of Dynasty, Knott's Landing, and Falcon Crest as if they were real acquaintances. If there was a saturation point for them, they hadn't reached it.

Our kids have always spent at least three or four hours reading for every hour spent watching television. They read before TV, after TV, and even during commercials. They also knit, crochet, and draw both during the programs and the commercials.

One evening, after an episode in Hill Street Blues in which a character mentioned casually that a certain situation was "like something out of Kafka," Cathy said she had recently read one of Kafka's stories which didn't seem to fit the allusion. Our discussion of the subject added new dimensions to her studies as well as to the television program.

Sometimes we have discussed the shows, especially if we thought the kids might need help in putting them into useful or healthy perspectives. Some of the situations and people in many of the big-city settings would have been confusing or even incomprehensible to kids whose only contact with cities had been brief visits to relatives in New York, Chicago, and Boston.

Sesame Street was a favorite when the kids were younger. We assumed, like millions of other parents, that it was Good For Them, but after a while we no longer thought so, and we were glad when the kids finally tired of it. John Holt has criticized the show's flashy bombardment of letters and numbers, and we agree with him, but we became more concerned with the relationships of the characters. Most of them are selfish, sarcastic, and inconsiderate. They criticize each other constantly, usually in a bossy or nagging way, or whine about their own misfortunes. Our kids always needed at least an hour of active physical play to counteract each hour of Sesame Street.

The only children's show which never disappointed us was Mister Rogers' Neighborhood. Mister Rogers' cheerfulness is never artificial, and he really believes that you -- you, to whom he is speaking -- are a very special person, just as you are. We were sorry when the kids eventually outgrew it, and wished there might be a similar show for older kids.

Even on the programs we enjoy and think are "worthwhile," we are often jolted by the subjects of drugs, violence (both physical and psychological), sexual promiscuity, homosexuality, prostitution, and rape; but we never reject shows just because of them (although we used more "parental discretion" when the kids were younger). Such subjects, unfortunately, are part of everyday conversation throughout society, and our kids need to know how to deal with them. Playing ostrich won't help. So we judge each show by its treatment of such subjects: is it realistic and accurate? What is the attitude of the show's main protagonist? We accepted the early Dallas shows because the "good" characters tried to lead moral lives. We reject Three's Company because promiscuity and homosexuality are treated lightly, with double-meaning jokes and naughty winks. Our children's friends who attend public school and watch television for forty hours a week won't keep their "knowledge" secret, so we have the choice

of helping our kids understand the subjects or moving to a remote island.

We never tried to develop a formal philosophy about television, but we soon reached several informal rules:

Television, like most other tools, is neither good nor bad in itself. For us, the weekly average of ten to twelve hours has never seemed harmful, and at least half that time has been either directly or indirectly informative and educational, as well as entertaining. We always try not to be arbitrary in our decisions about which shows will be allowed. We're always willing to try a new show if the kids want it, and then we discuss it, although Jean and I retain final veto authority. In limiting viewing time or choosing programs, we always discuss it with the kids; they may disagree with us, but they understand our viewpoint, and usually accept our decision graciously. We don't grant viewing as a reward, or withhold it as a punishment. We don't use television as a babysitter.

There are many good shows on television -- art, nature, science, history, sociology, music, theatre -- and throwing away the TV in spite of them would be like throwing away all our books because there are so many bad books being published.

We live in a small rural community, fairly isolated, both geographically and culturally, which makes television especially valuable for us; but in any situation, the judicious use of television can be very broadening, showing us other coun-

tries and ways of life, the deep sea adventures of Jacques Cousteau, and the exploration of outer space.

Television is certainly not a substitute for books; but neither are books a substitute for television.

One evening, through the combined miracles of intrauterine filming and television, we watched the hazardous journey of a sperm, its union with an ovum, the magical growth of the resulting single cell into a human being, transparent, without eyes or ears, rapidly developing features and losing its atavistic tail, floating weightlessly inside every mother that has ever lived.

We've watched births and deaths, and thousands of lives, both animal and human. We've attended concerts, not sitting somewhere back in the balcony, but wandering freely through the orchestra, savoring each instrument's voice, then standing with the conductor to hear the blended sounds. Sometimes we spend a few minutes with Grand Prix racing or a prize fight or Billy Graham -- not because they have particular meaning in our own lives, but because seeing them increases our knowledge and understanding of those who consider them to be of great importance. We've seen presidents, dictators, winos, junkies, and saints.

Through that little black window, we travel in time and space, and our little home in the woods is everywhere in the world and the universe.

HISTORY & LITERATURE ON VIDEO -- Also science, art, travel guides, ballet, and opera. These are among the best sources of video tapes, including several movies of classic literature, history, and historical fiction (along with standard, popular movies & a lot of junk).

PACIFIC ARTS, 11858 La Grange Ave., Los Angeles, CA 90025. Videos from PBS, with prices beginning at $19.95.

CRITICS' CHOICE VIDEO, P.O. Box 749, Itasca, IL 60143. Thousands of video titles; most prices as low as $19.95.

COLUMBIA HOUSE VIDEO CLUB, 1400 North Fruitridge Avenue, Terre Haute, IN 47812. Large quarterly catalogs and smaller monthly catalogs offering thousands of titles, often with special offers such as "Buy 1 at $19.95 and take 2 at $9.99 each."

THE VIDEO CATALOG, P.O. Box 64267, St. Paul, MN 55164. "The Count of Monte Cristo," "Antony & Cleopatra," "The Man in the Iron Mask," "A Tale of Two Cities," "The Scarlet Pimpernel," and many other fine movies of historical fiction for only $19.95. Travel, documentaries, performing arts, and travel. "A Brief History of Time," based on the book by Stephen Hawking (see Science), only $19.95.

TIME WARNER VIEWER'S EDGE, P.O. Box 3925, Milford, CT 06460. Most movies only $9.95, including a monthly special such as (this month) "Ben Hur." A few movies cost more, and some are as low as $7.49.

BARNES & NOBLE, 126 Fifth Avenue, New York, NY 10011 has scores of classic films, including the original "Tale of Two Cities," which is far better than the modern re-make.

LITERATURE ON VIDEO--See History, HISTORY ON VIDEO.

THE AVERAGE AMERICAN CHILD watches 18,000 television murders before graduating from high school.

SUPPLIERS OF INSTRUCTIONAL VIDEO PROGRAMS --

AGENCY FOR INSTRUCTIONAL TECHNOLOGY, 1111 W. 17th St., Bloomington, IN 47402.

BARR FILMS, P.O. Box 7878, Irwindale, CA 91706.

BEACON FILMS, INC., 930 Pitner, Evanston, IL 60202.

DIRECT CINEMA, LTD., P.O. Box 69799, Los Angeles, CA 90069.

INTERMEDIA, 1600 Dexter Ave. N, Seattle, WA 98109.

LUCERNE MEDIA, 37 Ground Pine Road, Morris Plains, NJ 07950.

MTI FILMS AND VIDEO, 108 Wilmot Road, Deerfield, IL 60015.

PYRAMID FILM AND VIDEO, P.O. Box 1048, Santa Monica, CA 90406.

SOCIAL ISSUES RESOURCES SERIES, INC., P.O. Box 2348, Boca Raton, FL 33427.

WORLD BOOK, INC., Customer Service, Stn. 58, Merchandise Mart Plaza, Chicago, IL 60654.

If you read a lot of books, you're considered well-read. But if you watch a lot of TV, you're not considered well-viewed.

Lily Tomlin

PROGRAM GUIDES -- 30 educational-TV program guides each year, giving advance notice of coming shows, synopses, individual projects, discussion questions, recommended resources. $15/year. Prime Time School Television, 120 So. LaSalle, Chicago, IL 60603.

3-2-1 CONTACT -- Teacher's guide, designed to help educators use the TV program "3-2-1 Contact" as a supplement to a science curriculum. Previews, related activities, background information; instructions for demonstrations, long-term science projects, etc. CTV WORKSHOP, 1 Lincoln Plaza, New York, NY 10023.

DISCOUNT VIDEOS -- Over 1000 how-to, travel, and other educational videos; also VCRs, TVs, blank tapes, etc. No membership fee, no minimum purchase, no obligation. TEACHERS VIDEO CLUB, 3230 Nebraska Ave., Santa Monica, CA 90404. Catalog, $1.00.

THE VIDEO SCHOOLHOUSE, P.O. Box 5101, Carmel, CA 93921. Rent or buy over 5,000 "how-to" videotapes on gardening, cooking, arts and crafts, hobbies, hunting, fishing, self-improvement, sports, academic subjects, mechanics, home improvement, business, and much more. Catalog, $3.00.

PESKY PRONOUNS, GENDER BLENDING, & THE NON-SEXIST NAMES OF GOD

In 1850, the British Parliament -- perhaps afloat on a sea of verbiage, as is often the fate of such bodies -- enacted "An act for shortening the language used in acts of Parliament," decreeing that "in all acts, words importing the masculine gender shall be deemed and taken to include females."

This is an example of "theoretical English," which tacitly stipulates that which is not explicitly stated, as in "Each student should open his book."

A few years earlier, when the Boston Patriots symbolically dumped King George overboard and coffee suddenly became the national drink, those colonists who still preferred tea either escaped to Canada or were hanged. (To this day, the only Americans who drink tea are secret Loyalists. Britons and even Canadians have periodic teatimes, but real Americans never observe anything but a coffee break, even if it's only to nibble a Kit-Kat or sip a diet cola.) It's the nature of Americans, however, to be forgiving (with the exception of certain high executives, who are merely forgetful), and by 1850 sufficient detente had been regained to allow a few English words and speech conventions into the American language. One of the most significant conventions acquired -- the generic pronoun, as it's called these days -- although steeped in common English usage and further strengthened by Parliamentary edict, was prohibited by the belated First Amendment from a similar Congressional edict.

That Parliamentary edict is still upheld today by major dictionaries (although their editors are beginning to look warily over their shoulders). One dictionary says: "he, pronoun. 1. the male person or animal mentioned. 2. a person of unspecified sex, [as in] He who hesitates is lost." Another dictionary agrees: "2. used in a generic sense or when the sex of the person is unspecified [as in] 'He that hath ears to hear, let him hear.'"

Feminists don't want women to be included in words that sometimes refer exclusively to males. They say it's discriminatory, because they're not receiving specific recognition; demeaning, because it still relegates them to a subordinate position; and confusing, because when someone says, "Look at that man," the reference is obviously to an adult human male, but when someone says, "Man will go to the stars someday," they don't know if women will be invited. (People, men or women, who are so easily confused must have a hard time with homonyms. If they hear of someone telling a bare-faced lie, they'll expect to see an animal costume.)

I heartily approve of equal opportunity, equal liability, equal rights, equal everything, including equal pay for equal work, and if Jean seriously wants to shovel out the barn while I sweep the kitchen floor, I won't argue very hard. I realize there's still a long way to go before this fair and logical equality is fully achieved, but let's not get wound up in such a strictly literal interpretation of words and phrases that we lose sight of the real problems.

Many words and phrases in English certainly are "sexist"; that is, discriminatory against either men or women. Feminists claim that women are the targets more often than men, which may be true. They also claim that it's part of an age-old male conspiracy to demean and subjugate women, which is sexist hogwash. It's simply the way the language evolved. They claim that the changes they want in the language -- right now -- are just further steps in its evolution. More hogwash. It isn't evolution; it's erosion.

Attitudes, especially of multitudes, change slowly, and the changed attitudes will be reflected in a slowly-changing language. But the feminists want to reverse the process; they want to change the attitudes by changing the language.

George Orwell's **1984** vividly illustrates how the feminists' strategy could easily succeed. The best way to control people's thoughts, he points out, is to control their vocabulary. If all the ways of expressing a certain concept are removed from people's knowledge, then it will be impossible for them to entertain the concept, except perhaps in vague circumlocution. Even that possibility can be eliminated by letting the words remain, but with all meaning removed, as in the slogan, "War is peace." Once people have been fully taught that war is peace and peace is war, how can they express a thought about a state of non-war?

(On the other hand, erasing words to express emotions -- love, hate, fear -- will not erase the emotions.)

Marie Shear, in an article about "Solving the Great Pronoun Problem," ho ho, complains that she heard a radio announcer refer to a wire-chewing squirrel as "he." "Had a reporter been to the morgue," she asks, "to check the corpse's sex?" Pausing only to start another paragraph, she answers her own question: "Of course not. Like lots of other organizations and individuals, the radio station had simply assumed that anything worth mentioning is male, until proved otherwise. That assumption creates The Great Pronoun Problem."

Turning a squirrel into The Great Pronoun Problem is giving him quite a big responsibility, and seems close to making a mountain out of a mole-hill. It even skirts pretty close to exactly the same sort of assumption Ms. Shear objects to. Did she check to see if the writer of the announcement was male or female, or did she simply assume that only a male would be guilty of such a sexist offense? Would her antennae have twitched any less if the reporter had referred to the squirrel as "she," or would Ms. Shear then have complained about the assumption that any mischief-making worth mentioning is female, until proved otherwise?

Male and female, man and woman, and boy and girl, say the feminists, refer to biological sex -- the function of reproduction and (if the weather doesn't change) its attendant duties, such as breastfeeding. Period. The words should not be used in conjunction with any person or activity in which this specific function is not relevant. "Woman police officer" or "male nurse" are offensive because being a police officer or a nurse has nothing to do with being male or female. That's true, of course, and rightly so. But try to explain to the feminists that it has not always been so, and that those expressions were not used to reinforce stereotypes but to dispel them, and you'll get your lip buttoned. The next time you hear the word "nurse," feminists want you to picture a generic human being, neither male nor female, because that human being's reproductive functions have nothing to do with his/her/its ability to be a nurse.

This sort of discussion can easily engender -- whoops -- confusion, but I'm trying to make it as clear as I can.

When I was little, my grandmother told me that a dragonfly would sew up my lips if I told a fib. I don't think I fibbed any more than most little boys, possibly a little less, but whenever I saw a dragonfly I'd cover my mouth and go the other way, not knowing how fair the dragonfly's judgement might be. I tried to avoid fibbing, but I also avoided dragonflies, in case I'd slipped up without knowing it. When I say now that I try in the same way to avoid active confrontation with feminists, I don't mean to imply that feminists are like dragonflies. The problem is, the minute you let slip what you think is an innocent phrase such as "hired man" or "woman's work is never done," some Feminist Thought Police Person is ready to threaten you with something worse than dragonflies. You should say "hired person" or "worker," unless that person's biological sex is specifically involved in the work being done, in which case you're in a whole different kettle of fish about which feminists are also very sensitive. I have always thought the old saying, "A man works from sun to sun, but woman's work is never done," was either a woman's complaint or a man's tribute, or a little of both, or just a statement of unfortunate fact, but the feminists claim it shouldn't be said even if it's true, because it shouldn't be true. Sort of like hearing a noise at night; if you ignore it, maybe it will go away.

I don't know if all states have a position known as Revisor of Statutes, but there is one in Minnesota, and in 1984 that Revisor was ordered by the state legislature to remove "gender-specific language" from the state statutes. Without changing the meaning of the law, of course.

It was an excellent example of Your Tax Dollars At Work. The whole process took two years, and the Revisor and his staff must have been as happy as pigs in a mud puddle. They removed 20,000 "nonsubstantive gender-specific" pronouns. "His" was changed more than 10,000 times. "He" was eliminated 6,000 times. 100 gender-specific nouns and adjectives (such as "chairman," "foreman," and "fisherman") were eliminated about 1,400 times. The Revisor reported to the legislature that a few gender-specific words, such as "manhole," were allowed to remain "because every proposed substitute has drawn so much bad press." (Well, yes, I can imagine a few editorial comments which might have been made, hee hee.) The Revisor's report ends with the humble opinion that "We are confident that the revised statutes are no worse than the originals. In many cases they are improved."

One down; forty-nine to go.

But feminists aren't happy attacking only generic pronouns and gender-specific work descriptions. They want to eliminate from the language all gender-specific references. Trying to keep abreast of feminist thought ("Forewarned, forearmed," Don Quixote advised), I've invested a few dollars in a couple Non-sexist Dictionaries. I can entertain Jean for hours, without reading a single word aloud. She is not a feminist, and wouldn't dream of asking me why I read the book and laugh and then read the book and cry and then read the book and bang my head on the wall and then read the book and throw it across the room.

--Let's rewrite Shakespeare: "The evil people do" instead of "the evil men do."

--Avoid "hysteria," which not only comes from the Greek word meaning "womb" (a female organ), but is almost always used (say the feminists) in referring to women.

--"Jack of all trades" uses a man's name. Sexist. Don't use.

--"Hit the jackpot." Another man's name. Substitute "strike it rich."

--"Hobson's choice." Ignore the historical basis for this phrase; it uses a man's name, so substitute a non-sexist phrase such as "No choice at all."

--"Jekyll and Hyde personality." Two masculine names! Substitute "split personality."

--"The patience of Job." You guessed it, Job was a man. Say instead, "long-suffering," "very patient," or "uncomplaining."

--What about sexism in the barnyard? Feminists object to "Mad as a wet hen" (although many of them are), and want to substitute "Mad as a hornet." I've known several wet hens over the years, and have had a passing acquaintance once or twice with several mad hornets. Given a choice, I'll take the wet hens.

--"Man overboard!" is obviously sexist, unless you're sure it's a man; and, even then, it wasn't his maleness which made him go over, so substitute "Person overboard!" and hope he or she or it doesn't drown while you get it right.

--Don't call a dog "man's best friend" because the only similar phrase referring to women is in the popular song of a few years back, "Diamonds are a girl's best friend," which makes women seem greedy and materialistic, which isn't fair, so don't call a dog man's best friend. (Honest. I'm not making this up.)

--"Motherly," "fatherly," "sisterly," and "brotherly" are gender-specific, which makes them sexist, and should be replaced by more precise adjectives, such as "loving," "kind," "supportive," etc., which can be applied to anyone regardless of gender.

Those are probably enough examples to help you understand why Jean is so entertained by my reactions.

Wait. Let's not forget our Father in Heaven. Why not Mother in Heaven, the feminists indignantly want to know? In fact, since gender is an attitude learned from one's culture, God probably doesn't have gender, and is neither masculine nor feminine. God can't be male or female, either, because those words refer to biological function, and let's not get absurd. Therefore, the proper reflexive pronoun for God is "it." But calling God "It," even with a capital I, somehow doesn't sound right, so let's not give God a reflexive pronoun. Instead, let's search our little heads for other gender-fair, non-sexist, divine nouns and pronouns for God, such as Author, Being, Good Parent, Guide, God of Abraham and Sarah (we need Sarah, for non-sexist balance), Heavenly Parent, and so on. The Coordinating Center for Women in Church & Society (1400 N. 7th Street, St. Louis, MO 63106) has a report called "Inclusive Language Guidelines for Use and Study in the United Church of Christ," which explains the whole problem and lists 196 gender-free, non-sexist names, titles, and phrases referring to God. You can order a copy for a mere $2.00, postpaid.

"He or she who hesitates is lost" and "He or she that hath ears to hear, let him or her hear" are grammatically correct, and are acceptable to feminists, but they're awkward verbosities, as well as mangled corruptions of the originals.

"He or she," "him and her," "his or hers," and similar constructions always have at least three words for gender-clarity where previously there was no doubt or confusion; hence, no need for clarification. The advantage, as with Russia's missiles in Cuba, is merely political, not strategic.

At first, some writers attempted compromise by putting "her" in parenthesis after "his," but feminists objected right away that this still included women only as an afterthought. Next came the slash, or diagonal, mark separating (or joining?) the two words, thus creating compound bisexual pronouns such as "his/her," "he/she," and so on. Sometimes the slash is called a stroke; sometimes it almost causes one. I'll return in a moment to the slash/stroke/diagonal.

Some hurried writers have harried us with another gelded pronoun, created by juxtaposing "he/she" and omitting the duplicated letters, thus arriving at "s/he," which can be pronounced aloud only as a sibilant hiccough; and can be read silently only with a slight mental back-flip, as one tries to define it: A split personality? A bearded lady? A gender blender?

Many writers alternate the masculine and feminine pronouns from paragraph to paragraph, or even sentence to sentence, so they always have a fifty percent chance of being right, and the reader always has a fifty percent chance of being satisfied. Also a fifty percent tendency to skip every other paragraph. A book on parenting, for instance, is very disconcerting when the sex of your child keeps changing from male to female and back again.

I sometimes receive letters addressed to "Dear Sir or Madam," which is understandable and appropriate, since the writer doesn't know which I am; but many letters, third-class in particular, address me as "Sir/Madam," as if I might be half-and-half. That may be appropriate these days for some people, but it is definitely not for me.

In reading sentences such as "Each student must bring his/her book," some readers skip over the punctuation, reading it as "his her book," but with a slight pause between the pronouns to indicate an awareness that something isn't quite right; some supply the supplanted conjunction, as if the diagonal line were a grammalogue representing "or" -- "his or her book"; and some others name the oblique punctuation as if it were a synonym for "or," thus: "Each student should bring his slash her book."

Apparently, not many people know that the tipsy line's real name is "virgule," which is just as well. Things are bad enough already. We don't need people saying, "bring his virgule her book." It sounds like a tropical fish. Why not stick to "or"?

Better yet, let's go back to one of the most intelligent enactments of the British Parliament. If men are gracious enough to allow the temporary emasculation of masculine pronouns, women should be gracious enough to accept their chivalry with dignity and even a slight smile of appreciation.

Please, before we all become he/shes and sir/-madams.

Some readers write to me, "Dear Person," which solves the problem neatly, and has little chance of being wrong.

Phantom conjunctions, bisexual pronouns, and conjunctive virgules are not the only language slashers lurking behind the bushes. Enter the plural singulars, rapidly increasing in popular usage. "Everyone should bring their book," "Each person should get their share," and "Everyone should watch their language." New math or not, "one" is singular and "their" refers to more than one -- "of or belonging to them," which is also

more than one -- and never the twain should meet. Feminists say it's better to be wrong in quantity than confused in gender, but we could be correct in both if feminists didn't insist on redefining words to suit themselves.

The speech of radio and television announcers abounds with singular forms which suddenly become plural in the middle of the verbal stream. English teachers, without blushing, use this abrupt shift of number not only in their speaking, but also in their writing. They know it's grammatically incorrect but, because it's in common usage, they say it's "permissible."

It shouldn't be. There are many speech and writing habits which are "in common usage," but shouldn't be. Sloppy English from a teacher makes us think he/she doesn't know their business.

In our home-school teaching, and in my books, I follow the edict of the British Parliament, although I'm not a Loyalist, and I don't drink tea.

If anyone wants to write me about this, he/she is welcome to send their letter.

GENDER BLENDING: Confronting the Limits of Duality, Holly Devor. I haven't read this book, and don't intend to. The publisher's description of it is enough to make me wander about muttering and bumping into things. A recent "Help Wanted" ad in our local newspaper said, with italic emphasis, that applicants "must be either male or female." At the time, I didn't think that would be too difficult, although I realize some people seem to be a little confused on the matter. Then along came this book, whose author, says the publisher, "...interprets gender as a social distinction related to, but different from, biological sex... Gender is... learned by displaying the culturally defined insignia of the gender category with which one identifies ..." The book is also about "fifteen women who have...rejected traditional femininity, but not their femaleness... [are] sometimes mistaken for men... minimize their female vulnerability in a patriarchal world by minimizing their femininity... [T]heir gender identity does not fit either of the two roles socially and culturally defined as feminine and masculine." Hmmm. Let me see if I've got this, now. If you're dissatisfied with your gender but can't get a refund, you should homogenize yourself? Bob Hope once said the Old West was where men were men and women were women "-- and I like it that way!" Me, too. You can buy this study of neutered neutrality from INDIANA UNIVERSITY PRESS, 10th & Morton, Bloomington, IN 47405. $35.00.

HIGH SCHOOL, COLLEGE, AND BEYOND

HOME STUDIES, CORRESPONDENCE COURSES, WORK, TRAVEL

Unique Graduation Ceremony
[THE OBSERVER, Hartland, New Brunswick, Wednesday, June 20, 1984]

Brook Farm School celebrated its first high school graduate, Catherine Barbara Reed, 17, at a unique graduation ceremony held at the Women's Institute Hall in Knowlesville, Saturday, June 16. A family enterprise, Brook Farm School is operated by Donn and Jean Reed.

Donn Reed opened the Commencement and Awards Ceremony, and welcomed the 35 guests present. He then presented certificates to Catherine and Karen for maintaining exceptional standards of study, workmanship, perseverance, and independent endeavor, and to Susan and Derek for outstanding work and progress in specific areas of investigation, study, and accomplishment. Notes of appreciation were given by the four children to their parents.

Rev. Maynard Rector offered the Baccalaureate, after which Mr. Reed presented Catherine with her diploma. In his address, Mr. Reed said, in part, "Basic academic skills...are all parts of the education in our school. Several other subjects are just as much a part of our education -- the study of other countries and their people, other ways of thinking, other beliefs about humanity and God and the universe. Activities such as daily chores, ball games, participation in 4-H and youth groups, jobs away from home, are invaluable parts of education."

Presenting the Class History, Mr. Reed said, "Through the modern miracles of airplanes, buses, satellite television, and first class mail in less than three weeks, Brook Farm School has drawn freely upon resources and instructors from around the world."

In the Valedictory Address, Catherine said, "I think my education has given me imagination, a sense of truth, and a feeling of responsibility -- which I hope to share with people wherever I go."

Following the reading of the Class History, the Last Will and Testament, and the Class Prophecy, the ceremony ended, and guests sat down to a pot luck supper. A copy of Catherine's year book was presented to each guest.

Catherine is leaving shortly to work as a camp counselor at a private girls' camp in the States, after which she plans to continue her education.

HIGH SCHOOL AT HOME

We have found that basic academic skills and very general knowledge of the world -- reading, writing, arithmetic, history, geography, government, science, and beginning literature -- fit well into the ages from six or seven to thirteen or fourteen, roughly equivalent to the ages spent in the first eight grades of public school. Our approach to many of the subjects, as you have seen, is often very different; sometimes oblique, as with Derek's study of sharks. We often introduce new subjects, or new facets, and we lead, guide, instruct, and question -- but we let the kids' own interests determine the scope and direction of our leadership. Sooner or later, their interests usually lead them not only to all the fields and subjects prescribed by law or convention, but to many others as well, and often beyond the levels expected in public schools.

Since the kids were never taught to read, they read constantly -- fiction, history, science, travel, animals, humor, poetry. Their choices of reading material were often of "high school" level by the time they were nine or ten. Their academic skills have been very good in some subjects, and very low in others, since we haven't tried to fit them into a norm based on age.

There are no other home-schoolers in our area, so in relating to their acquaintances our kids tend to think in terms of grade levels, with a definite division between elementary school and high school, based on their ages more than on their actual studies and achievements.

The children's own desire and capacity for a deeper and broader educational base -- which we may call "high school" -- are roughly concurrent with adolescence.

From the time they could move about freely, the kids have played at many roles -- father, mother, dog, lion, cowboy, nurse, clown, super hero -- testing each one, experimenting with their own possible roles in society. Throughout, they have felt secure in their knowledge of belonging to the family. Actually leaving the family someday has never been a serious reality.

At puberty, as the body begins rapid changes and emotions become stronger, the mind also grows suddenly and rapidly. The children begin to realize that they really will leave home someday, and the world is still a huge intimidating mass of uncertainties. They look forward to being on their own as adults, but at the same time are apprehensive about it. They want more time, more preparation, and more practice.

Once again, they try on different roles, this time outside the home -- testing themselves in community functions, clubs, traveling alone, fitting into groups larger than the family and separate from it. Some of them experiment with popular teen fashions -- dress, makeup, slang, music, and opinions.

They see many of their friends moving steadily, or so it seems, toward definite goals, but they don't envy them, whether the goals are college, careers, the military, or working in the local frozen food plant. They know that most of their friends have been programmed by parents, teachers, aptitude tests, guidance counselors, or even economic necessity to make early decisions, often based on narrow or incomplete data, and will probably be frustrated and unhappy adults.

We try to show our children the broadest fields of possibilities, always emphasizing that there's no need to make a choice; that following one's own interests and instincts, not as a goal but as an exciting journey, will lead naturally to a happy, creative life. If a child of ten or fifteen has a particular talent or interest, and is determined to follow it, that's good -- provided that determination doesn't become a dutiful consistency without a continuing interest. How many adults would like to change careers or lifestyles when they're thirty or forty or fifty, but don't dare to, or don't feel capable of doing so? Any early choices made should allow for the possibility of a more desirable alternative suddenly popping up at any time, and the freedom of thought and circumstance to accept that alternative.

Some public schools encourage children as young as eleven or twelve to choose their academic and vocational futures. Twice that age is a much better time for such choices, if they must be made. We encourage our kids not to make choices and decisions, but to watch and explore their own feelings and desires; to watch their general inclinations, and follow them, but without committing themselves beyond their present interests.

With high school, as with earlier learning, the children's own interests and preferences are the best indications of the direction their studies should take. Working with them, we can help them discover and develop subjects of study which will give them broad and solid foundations for nearly any career or lifestyle they may pursue, as well as the knowledge, skills, and self-confidence to develop other foundations if their interests change.

Many of the conventional high school subjects are part of a good beginning. Cathy enrolled in American School of Chicago, possibly the best-known of the many correspondence high schools. At that time, the entire four-year course cost about five hundred dollars, which we were allowed to pay in small monthly installments. Each of this school's courses consists of a basic textbook and an examination booklet, sometimes including a brief study guide. Cathy read a chapter, wrote out a test, and mailed it in; the test was graded by the school and returned, usually with brief comments. Cathy had three or four courses at one time; when one was completed, she began another. The textbooks are average; i.e., not outstanding, but adequate. Her algebra text was based on "new math," which none of us liked, and her general science book seemed to be poorly written and confusing.

After we had seen half a dozen of Cathy's courses, we realized we could provide a much better education ourselves, choosing our own textbooks, and, not so incidentally, save at least two hundred dollars. We sent for and studied the catalogs of several correspondence high schools, and found that most of those which, like American School, are advertised in magazines offer little more than fifteen or sixteen textbooks, a series of short tests (most of which can be completed quite easily by reading the questions and then searching the text for the answers), a few brief study guides, and a diploma. A conscientious student can learn a great deal from them; a lazy student can receive high marks and a diploma almost as easily. Most of the schools offer some individual attention if the student has problems or specific questions.

Extension courses offered by universities and state departments of education usually have a much wider range of subjects, sometimes with laboratory materials (when appropriate), and more personalized tutoring, by mail or telephone. A supervisor approved by a local school official is often required for courses taken for credit. Noncredit courses require no supervision, and usually cost much less.

None of the high school programs we examined seemed to meet our needs. We felt, and feel, that the education itself is far more important than the diploma, and all the correspondence courses lack many of the subjects we feel are most desirable or necessary. As thousands of functional illiterates receive fully accredited diplomas from public schools, more and more colleges and employers realize that the decorated parchment may mean nothing at all except that the student has met minimal attendance requirements.

At least half of the correspondence high schools whose catalogs we received were not accredited, which often meant only that they had not yet been "certified" by an independent examining board, although their curricula may be identical or at least very similar to those of the schools which are accredited. Their diplomas would readily be accepted by most colleges and employers. The diplomas from these non-accredited schools are genuine, and represent at least as much study and learning as most students will have in a public school.

We decided that our own curriculum was superior in many ways to that of almost any public or correspondence school, and that a diploma from Brook Farm School would have at least as much moral validity as theirs. We wrote a rough draft, had the local print shop set it in type and print it on a standard diploma form. It cost about twenty dollars, and to us is much more valuable than others which might have cost us several hundred dollars, but would have represented much less work and learning.

Cathy continued her American School studies, but augmented them substantially with our own materials, and we had learned an important lesson. We sat down with Karen and worked out her first year's high school course, and then sent away for books and other materials. The skeleton of her academic work for two years was HIGH SCHOOL SUBJECTS SELF TAUGHT, edited by Lewis Copeland, a comprehensive distillation of 28 subjects (now out of print, unfortunately). A few subjects needed supplementation, for which we used several of the "Made Simple" series, and various other books especially pertinent to Karen's interests. Karen finished all 28 courses in HIGH SCHOOL SUBJECTS SELF TAUGHT in two years, and went on to expand her studies in literature, psychology, art, and miscellaneous reading. With a few books from the public library, Karen had a very complete high school education for less than three hundred dollars. (Not including all the books and other materials we already had on hand.)

One's education is neither more nor less than all of what one learns, whether or not the learning is planned and intentional, and regardless of the setting in which it occurs. Much of our education is introspective; that is, we frequently examine what we're doing as we do it, continually looking for ways to improve our learning, abandoning methods or materials that aren't working well, and searching for others that are better. We have read and discussed John Holt's HOW CHILDREN LEARN, applying it to ourselves, testing it against our own experience. Despite the title, many of John's observations can be applied to how <u>anyone</u> learns, at any age.

We read literature together -- poems, stories, novels -- and discuss it, talking about the ideas and characters, the authors and the times in which they lived; how they were influenced by the people and events around them; and how they in turn influenced their times and the world. We talk about the meaning of life, both in the totally abstract and in the intensely personal. We read and discuss magazines -- news, science, nature, psychology. We discuss the news on television, and relate it to ourselves and to history.

We play cassette tapes of old radio programs, poetry, dramatized history, and recorded novels. We study languages (French and Spanish at present, as well as English). Jean and the kids all play musical instruments -- guitars, recorder, and flute -- and sing together. (Sometimes they talk me into joining them, although I usually prefer to listen.)

Other activities, many of which are discussed elsewhere in this book, are just as much a part of our education: youth groups, 4-H, ball games, skiing, skating, sliding, carrying firewood, churning butter, building our barn, building our house, gardening, cooking, washing dishes, caring for our farm animals, gathering maple sap, and on and on. The kids have jobs at times -- in a grocery store, picking potatoes, picking rocks, babysitting -- and they learn how to save money and how to spend it; how to study catalogs and decide what to buy, and to evalute their purchases afterwards.

We always sought ways to expand the children's knowledge and experience far beyond that of our rural home. Cathy and Karen participated in national 4-H exchange programs, Cathy traveling to Alberta and Karen to Manitoba. Cathy worked once a week as a volunteer helper in a public library, and the following summer was hired as a full-time assistant. The next year she was a counselor in a girls' camp in Vermont. Karen visited relatives in Vermont and New York, went to Virginia and New Hampshire for two-week visits with families we had "met" by correspondence, and worked for a few hours in John Holt's office in Boston. Susan won a trip into the past at New Brunswick's Kings Landing Historical Settlement [see Writing], and went on a month-long Outward Bound trip in the mountains and rivers of Maine; and, two years later, another month with Outward Bound in Arizona.

Derek cleaned horse stalls to pay for riding lessons and the opportunity to be near horses, saved his money until he could buy his own horse, and within a year was winning ribbons and trophies in both Western and English competitions, was training horses and riders, and a year later went to a riding camp in Virginia as a Counselor in Training.

As the kids leave home, one by one, at first for very short periods, then for increasingly longer periods of time, they continue to find that the entire world is their school, and that no matter where they are, life is learning. It's exciting and challenging, and sometimes very different from what they or we have expected.

Cathy had planned tentatively to work in Third World countries, and is now a full-time librarian in a large town library, although she still considers her earlier plans to be definite possibilities for the future.

Karen insisted on leaving home and going to New York City before we felt she was ready to cope with full independence, especially in a large city, but we couldn't hold her back. Her few months in New York were as disastrous as we had feared they would be, but after a few months at home she was ready for the world again. She entered a college in Florida, where she received very high marks and was on the dean's list. Then she got married, had a baby, and got divorced, which is never in anyone's plans. Karen is now working in a newspaper office in southern Vermont, spending a lot of time with her daughter, and coping very well with the challenges she faces in life on her own.

When Susan was sixteen, she wanted to enroll in the local high school, which we rejected. We compromised on a small private school in New Hampshire, which she attended for two years. Jean and I are still not sure if it was a mistake or not. The school's "alternative education" included very few of the subjects we felt a supposedly-Quaker school would teach, and its approach to standard subjects such as history and literature made them seem, to us, almost totally unrelated to the subjects as we know them. The school's social atmosphere seemed to us to be an unending adolescent soap opera. Nonetheless, Susan made many friends there, and feels very loyal toward the school. She spent the next year working, saving money, and traveling around the country with friends in a $1000 car, which almost made it back home. As I write this, she has been accepted by Prescott College in Arizona, is working through the summer as a waitress and chambermaid to help pay her expenses, and plans to pursue a career in working with people in outdoor situations, such as camping and Outward Bound.

Working part-time in a grocery store, Derek saved money for a car, besides buying all his own clothing and other incidental needs. In his last year at home, he drifted away from academic studies, although he still reads a great deal. He now has a job which fulfills a long-time ambition -- training horses and riders, helping to tame and train two wild mustangs in a program initiated by the Department of the Interior, receiving advanced riding lessons, and receiving instruction and practice in stable management.

After twenty-four years of raising children and teaching them at home, Jean and I stand back (as we have frequently done through the years), and ask ourselves if we have achieved what we had hoped to achieve. Have we prepared our children adequately for life on their own? Has the education they have received with us really been a better preparation for them than public education would have been? We made many mistakes, although we watched for them, and tried to correct them as soon as we were aware of them. Sometimes we set our goals too high, for our children and for ourselves; other times, our goals may not have been high enough. We listened to our children constantly, and watched them, trying to anticipate and meet all their needs, academic, intellectual, social, physical, and spiritual, both immediate and eventual. Most of the time, I think, we succeeded, although we always wished we could do better. We aimed for perfection, for ourselves and for our children, knowing it would never be reached, but also knowing that the higher our aim, the higher our achievements would be.

Despite setbacks, problems, and occasional disappointments, we have enjoyed these twenty-four years, and have no regrets at all about having chosen to teach our children at home. Not to have done so would have left us with much less meaning and happiness in our lives, then and now. We and our children continue to be very close, regarding each other as good friends as well as loving parents, daughters, son, sisters, and brother. That alone is great success and wealth. With the wisdom of hindsight, we know there are many changes we'd make if we could, but we're not sure exactly what they would be.

"By their fruits ye shall know them," says the Bible, which I guess means the final judgement rests not with us, but with our children, and with the people who will know them through their lives. The real measure of our children's education at home will be the degree to which they achieve success and happiness in their own lives, and in the influence they have on the world around them. Jean and I are confident that they will continue to make us proud of them, and we'll feel honored to be judged according to the people our children are and are still becoming.

I think that's the best any parents can hope for.

HIGH SCHOOL CORRESPONDENCE COURSES --
AMERICAN SCHOOL, 850 East 58th Street, Chicago, IL 60637.
CLONLARA HOME BASED EDUCATION PROGRAM, 1289 Jewett Street, Ann Arbor, MI 48104.
HOME CENTERED LEARNING, P.O. Box 92, Escondido, CA 92025.
NEWPORT/PACIFIC HIGH SCHOOL, 925 Oak Street, Scranton, PA 18515.
SETON HOME STUDY SCHOOL, One Kidd Lane, Front Royal, VA 22630.
THE SYCAMORE TREE, 2179 Meyer Place, Costa Mesa, CA 92627.
UNIVERSITY OF NEBRASKA AT LINCOLN, 33rd and Holdredge Streets, Lincoln, NE 68583.

PHOENIX SPECIAL PROGRAMS, 3231 W. Clarendon, Phoenix, AZ 85017. Nationally accredited nontraditional courses, high school level. Free brochure.

ACCELERATED LEARNING PROGRAMS -- Several video and audio cassette programs which promote enhanced skills and achievements in reading, memory, note-taking, test preparation, math and algebra, communications, confidence, and motivation. The materials have been used & tested by thousands of high school students, whose scores jumped very dramatically. For more information & a catalog, write LEARNING FORUM, 225 Stevens Ave., Ste. 103, Solana Beach, CA 92075.

THE EXPEDITION INSTITUTE, Sharon, CT 06069. Environmental and ecological expeditions; liberal arts studies; school credit; junior and up.

Training is everything. The peach was once a bitter almond; cauliflower is nothing but cabbage with a college education.

Mark Twain

THE EDUCATIONAL REGISTER. Descriptive listings of hundreds of private schools, boarding schools, summer study programs (academic, remedial, music, computer, etc.), and summer camps and trips, listed by geographic area (e.g., Northern New England, Mid-Atlantic, Canada, Abroad). Descriptions include curriculum, programs, extra-curricular activities; number, age, and gender of students; and cost. Many listings seem to be for upper-middle incomes, but scholarships are often available. When Derek was 15, we looked for a summer riding camp we could afford -- meaning one with almost no fee. Nonexistent, of course. The description in THE EDUCATIONAL REGISTER of Hazelwild Farm Camp, in Fredericksburg, Virginia, seemed just right, except the $400 per week fee. Derek wrote to the camp's director, telling of his experiences in riding, training horses, winning trophies, and teaching other riders. He was accepted as a Counselor In Training, and spent eight weeks riding, coaching, training, and making friends; and paid $200 (which he had earned the previous winter) for the entire summer. THE EDUCATIONAL REGISTER is FREE to parents and educators. Request a copy from: VINCENT/CURTIS, 224 Clarendon Street, Boston, MA 02116.

INSTITUTE OF LIFETIME LEARNING, American Association of Retired Persons, 1909 K Street NW, Washington, DC 20049 offers several FREE booklets on many subjects, including art, anthropology, history, literature, philosophy & physics, with suggestions for further study and self-tests. Free information and full list of subjects.

Learning is the very essence of humility, learning from everything and from everybody. There is no hierarchy in learning. Authority denies learning and a follower will never learn.

Jiddu Krishnamurti

COLLEGE

The October 1983 issue of Home Centered Learning (no longer published, unfortunately) reproduced the following editorial from the Marin County (CA) Independent Journal:

"Home-educated youths do well

"When Grant Colfax, 18, of Boonville was accepted for the fall term at Harvard University, we thought of Brian Pacula, going on 5, since both youngsters share the same alternative 'schooling' -- being tutored at home by parents. We assume the parents of the two boys are not anti-education, since both fathers are scholars. Grant's dad holds a doctorate (and is a former college professor) and Norman Pacula is an instructor at College of Marin. Apparently, the parents decided that they could do a better job of teaching their children -- and did just that. A few weeks before carrying the news about Colfax, who raised goats while learning at home, the Independent Journal ran an interesting -- if controversial -- story about Brian's advanced home classes with his mother, Pam Pacula. **IJ** letter writers, although commending the Pacula pioneer spirit, usually ended with the question: 'Since Brian will grow up without the advantages of going to school, how on earth can he ever hope to be admitted to Stanford or Cal?' We still can't answer the question, of course, but we assume that Harvard is always a possibility."

Grant Colfax has since graduated. Two of his brothers have been accepted by Harvard, and scores of other homeschoolers have been accepted by many different colleges and universities. Whether or not Stanford or the University of California will now accept homeschoolers, there are certainly many other possibilities.

COLLEGE AT HOME--The cheapest and possibly simplest way to get a good college education at home is to send for the catalogs of several colleges and universities, look over the subjects offered, then spend your days in a local library, reading all you can find on the subjects which interest you. If you live in or near a city or large town, or even many small towns, there are undoubtedly seminars, art shows, museums, and adult education courses. Unless you need the full equivalent of a conventional college curriculum, you may as well eliminate the subjects which don't interest you or seem of value to you. If various required courses are of no use to you, why waste time on them? If one wants or needs a degree, but doesn't have the time or money to spend on full-time residence in a conventional college, there are several ways to combine home-study, using one's own curriculum and materials, with correspondence courses and, perhaps, some time on a college campus.

COLLEGE WITHOUT COLLEGE -- Fully-accredited college degrees may be granted for non-college work, general life experience (travel, military service), or proficiency in specific areas of knowledge (such as writing, math, or a foreign language). One of the best of several institutions offering such degrees is THE UNIVERSITY OF THE STATE OF NEW YORK, Albany, NY 12230. Write for free information about the College Proficiency Examinations and the Regents External Degrees Program. This isn't a program for which a recent high school graduate would qualify, but is a practical possibility for anyone to consider for the future, if one foresees a need for a degree but prefers to spend a few years in work or travel.

A DEGREE FROM AN EXPENSIVE COLLEGE WITHOUT PAYING THE FULL PRICE -- Most colleges and universities will accept up to three years' worth of credits from other colleges and universities, including accredited correspondence courses. If you have enough money for one year at an expensive school, make it your last. Build credits in cheaper schools or by correspondence, or both, and then transfer to the more expensive school for your degree.

COLLEGE CREDIT "BANKING" -- The Regents Credit Bank of The University of the State of New York, Albany, NY 12230, for a very reasonable fee, will keep records of all college credits you earn through any accredited institution, including correspondence courses, and will send a complete transcript to any institution or agency at your request. In this way, credits earned through several different institutions or life situations can be combined into a single transcript. Information about this program

COLLEGE BY CORRESPONDENCE-- For those who prefer to continue their studies at home, there are hundreds of institutions which offer college-level credits, and even grant fully-accredited degrees, mostly or entirely by correspondence. The cost is far below that of an on-campus education. Usually, the correspondence program can be completed in a shorter time than an on-campus program would take, but may also be stretched over a longer period if limited time or money require it. The credits and degrees thus earned are completely legal and are recognized throughout the world as being just as good as if they were obtained on campus. One can earn a Bachelor of Arts, a Bachelor of Science, a Master's in several fields, even a law degree and several doctorates -- all without ever attending a school except through a post office. It is often possible to earn a full degree without taking any courses, by having one's work, hobbies, previous training and study, military service, and travel experiences evaluated.

Some of the best college-by-correspondence programs are offered by:

THE UNIVERSITY OF THE STATE OF NEW YORK, Albany, NY 12230.

HOME STUDY INTERNATIONAL, 6940 Carroll Avenue, Takoma Park, MD 20912. Doesn't grant degrees, but courses are fully accredited. Make arrangements with a local college or university to earn its degree using some or all courses from HSI.

UNIVERSITY OF NEBRASKA AT LINCOLN, College Counselor, Division of Continuing Studies, 511 Nebraska Hall, Lincoln, NE 68588. The College Independent Study program offers the opportunity for students who are still high school juniors or seniors to earn college credit while still in high school; who are attending on-campus college classes to make up academic deficiencies; who are off-campus (at home or elsewhere) to expand their academic background without attending classes. Over 100 courses are offered. Non-credit college-level courses are also offered in specific professional and personal interest areas. Counseling for students is available.

IN CANADA: ATHABASCA UNIVERSITY, 150 15-123 Ave., Edmonton, Alberta T5V 1J7. Very comprehensive and inexpensive. Full degree programs entirely by mail. For residents of Canada only (unfortunately). A 4-year graduate program (BA or BS) costs less than $1000 per year. Write for current catalog.

<u>ALSO IN CANADA</u>: UNIVERSITY OF GUELPH, Independent Study, Guelph, Ontario N1G 2W1. Several very good courses.

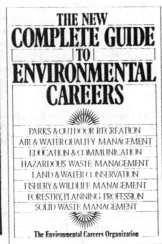

COLLEGE DEGREES BY MAIL (Revised), by John Bear, Ph.D. A completely revised and updated edition of the original guide to the 100 best non-traditional institutions which grant degrees at undergraduate or graduate levels without requiring attendance on campus. 216 pages. $12.95. Code TSP. BROOK FARM BOOKS.

THE COMPLETE GUIDE TO ENVIRONMENTAL CAREERS, by The Environmental Careers Organization. Very comprehensive overview of the entire range of environmental career fields -- parks and outdoor recreation, air and water quality management, education and communication, land and water conservation, fisheries and wildlife management, forestry, and much more. This is probably the most complete and reliable source of information today for students, recent college graduates, volunteers, career counselors, and anyone interested in working to protect the environment. 364 pages, photos, index. $15.95. Code PI. BROOK FARM BOOKS.

COLLEGE ADMISSIONS: A Guide for Homeschoolers, by Judy Gelner. Written and compiled especially for college-bound homeschoolers. Detailed information about applying to colleges without "official" transcripts and diplomas; how to go about it; necessary preliminary tests, & where to take them; financial aid; college admission guides; much more. Why bang your head against brick walls when Judy and her family have already banged their heads for you? $7.95 plus $1.20 postage. POPPYSEED PRESS, P.O. Box 85, Sedalia, CO 80135.

PETERSEN'S GUIDES, P.O. Box 2123, Princeton, NJ 08543. Free catalog of annually-updated guides to secondary schools, colleges, universities, camps, private schools, and career education courses, such as GUIDE TO TWO YEAR COLLEGES, SAT SUCCESS, SUMMER OPPORTUNITIES FOR KIDS AND TEENAGERS, INDEPENDENT STUDY CATALOG, and many more.

BARRON'S STUDENT'S CONCISE ENCYCLOPEDIA -- Subtitled "A Complete Reference Guide for Home & School," this is a single-volume encyclopedia of "essential information" for high school and college students. A review of all major subjects is presented in the form of A-to-Z entries within these general academic sections:

THE LIBERAL ARTS: Music, Art, Language and Literature, Philosophy, and Religion.

SOCIAL STUDIES: American & World History, Government, Geography, Economics, and Business.

MATHEMATICS AND COMPUTER SCIENCE.

SCIENCE: Astronomy, Biology, Chemistry, Earth Sciences, Technology, Physics, Psychology.

In general, the information presented is reliable and comprehensive. An important disadvantage is that most information (except in Mathematics and a few other subjects) is arranged <u>alphabetically</u>, as in an encyclopedia, rather than chronologically or around a central theme, which makes study somewhat difficult -- in history, for instance, in which the chronological sequence of cause and effect is of major importance. However, these sections still serve very well as mini-reviews, refresher courses, and -- the best use of this book -- basic reference points and starting guides for more intensive study using other materials (library books, encyclopedia, etc.).

The Mathematics section is very complete, from simple arithmetic to calculus and trigonometry, but is also very brief. For more detailed study, which you'll probably want, we recommend SURVIVAL MATHEMATICS or ARITHMETIC MADE SIMPLE for high school math.

The U.S. History is fairly complete, but brief; World History is very skimpy.

Another section, "Study and Learning Workshops," provides advice and guidelines to help students make efficient use of study time, and to achieve their highest possible marks when taking tests. Detailed instructions are given for writing term papers and for making full use of library research facilities.

A section on "life outside the classroom" contains information -- some of it very useful -- about basic health and nutrition, exercise programs, first aid, and practical tips for managing personal finances. The book also contains many excellent maps, including historical maps, and many charts & tables, including weights and measures, metric conversions, holidays, and time zones.

Hardcover, approximately 1,200 pages. $29.95. Code BE. BROOK FARM BOOKS.

NANNIE NETWORK, INC., P.O. Box 2423, Darien, CT 06820. Teenage and young adult women work on Long Island Sound in southern Connecticut, five or five-and-a-half days a week, about ten hours per day, caring for children and doing light housekeeping (preparation of children's meals, laundry, & "generally helping to maintain the household"; no heavy housework.) A one-year commitment is usually required, but shorter terms are sometimes available. Live as a member of the family, receive a minimum weekly salary of $150, paid vacation (usually 1 or 2 weeks), room and board, free time during evenings and weekends, and sometimes use of a car. About an hour from New York City; short train or bus ride to Boston & Washington, D.C. The NANNIE NETWORK matches applicants with host families; no placement fees are charged. Write (or phone 1-800-US-NANNY) for more information, application and reference forms.

By working faithfully eight hours a day you may eventually get to be boss and work twelve hours a day.

Robert Frost

Banking establishments are more dangerous than standing armies.

Thomas Jefferson

AUTO REPAIR FOR DUMMIES, Deanna Sclar; 2nd revised edition. Auto repair is conventionally in the male domain, and I'm a total ignoramus once the hood is up, and here's a book by a woman that makes it almost clear to me. Boy, am I embarrassed. This book is the answer for those of us (male or female) not born with wrenches in our hands. Concise, direct, simple explanations help the reader understand the major systems of an automobile and take the fear out of dealing with maintenance and repair. If you don't like greasy hands, at least you'll be able to talk to a mechanic as if you know what you're talking about; but probably, with this book, you won't need a mechanic. Over 300 illustrations. 480 pages, comb bound (so it will lie flat while you refer to it as you work, so you won't get grease all over it). $17.95. Code TSP. BROOK FARM BOOKS.

HOMESTEADING BOOKS -- Just about everything you need to know about gardening, cooking, preserving, building and maintaining a home, raising and caring for animals, home crafts, and alternate energy. Scores of books by some of the most respected authors in the field. Catalog. GARDEN WAY PUBLISHING, Schoolhouse Road, Pownal, VT 05261.

HOMESTEADING -- Formal apprenticeship programs in homesteading skills. #10 SASE for information. LEARNING & HOMESTEADING CENTERS, 33 East Minor St., Emmaus, PA 18049.

IS A CAREER DESIRABLE? Common opinion these days -- or "conventional wisdom," as it's sometimes called, although it's seldom very wise -- is that it's important to decide upon a career as early in life as possible, and to work diligently to achieve that career and to advance in it. In the United States and Canada, the question, "What do you do?" usually means "What do you do <u>for a living</u>?" In most other parts of the world, although the earning of money is considered a necessary part of one's life, "What do you do?" refers to one's hobbies, avocations, or personal interests -- "What do you do for enjoyment?" Not everyone is fortunate enough to have his strongest interests coincide with means of earning money; many people resign themselves to working for money at jobs they don't care for, but are able to fill their other hours with more interesting activities, and don't feel their lives are wasted. Many people are content to have a variety of jobs during their lifetimes, although much of society sees this as being unsettled and indecisive, if not downright shiftless. "Jack of all trades, master of none" used to be the common pejorative applied to someone who didn't stay settled in one line of work.

I have never had a desire for any one career. Since I left high school, I've worked at many things -- road construction, newspaper editor, psychiatric aide, migrant farm worker, freelance columnist, sawmill edgerman, etc. Usually, I stayed with the jobs for as long as I enjoyed them; when my enjoyment began to wane, I moved on to something else. Many times I have had the opportunity of staying with a job and advancing in it -- "making a career" of it -- but I knew I'd soon become bored and wish I were doing something else. "A foolish consistency," said Emerson, "is the hobgoblin of little minds." Not <u>consistency</u>, but "a <u>foolish</u> consistency," being consistent just for the sake of being consistent.

Even now, although most of my monetary income is derived from my books and our mail-order book service, not all of our <u>living</u> comes from them. We have a cow and chickens and pigs and a garden, and a great deal of our living comes from a sort of part-time farming, although it doesn't bring us any money. The monetary value of the food we produce through our own efforts could be expressed as the amount of money we would have to spend to buy it, but that doesn't say anything about our enjoyment and satisfaction in raising it. We'd rather put the time and labor into milking the cow and collecting eggs than half the time into earning money with which to buy milk and eggs produced by someone else.

There is nothing dishonorable in having a variety of work, either concurrently or consecutively; a peripatetic career can be as remunerative and often more satisfying than the single-minded pursuit of only one kind of work.

Choosing a career should be done only if one wants a career.

Books seem to me to be pestilent things, and infect all that trade in them... with something very perverse and brutal. Printers, binders, sellers, and others that make a trade and gain out of them have universally so odd a turn and corruption of mind, that they have a way of dealing peculiar to themselves, not conformed to the good of society and that general fairness that cements mankind.

John Locke (letter to
Anthony Collins, 1704)

DIRECTORY OF AMERICAN YOUTH ORGANIZATIONS, by Judith B. Erickson, Ph.D., Indiana Youth Institute. Updated and expanded, this directory is the most comprehensive guide available to adult-sponsored, nonprofit youth organizations in the United States. From the Academy of Model Aeronautics to the Zenith Clubs, this directory lists and describes hundreds of possibilities for fun, friendship, and social action: hobby, special interest, sports, & religious groups; patriotic, political, and social organizations; conservation and ethnic heritage groups; character-building and service groups; and many more. Includes information about extensive resources for administrators and leaders, and a list of related readings. 192 pages, paperback. $18.95. Code FS. BROOK FARM BOOKS.

"WHEN I GROW UP," a videotape with 22 one-minute vignettes featuring people talking about their careers and what they had to learn in preparation; poster; teacher's guide. $9.75 plus $2.25 postage. CUSTOMER RELATIONS, McDonald's Corporation, One McDonald Plaza, Oak Brook, IL 60521.

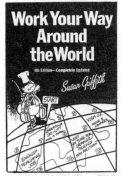 

WORK YOUR WAY AROUND THE WORLD, edited by Susan Griffith. Information and tips on types of temporary jobs that can be found in Britain, Europe, New Zealand, Canada, Australia, Latin America, Africa, Israel, Turkey, Asia, and the United States. Jobs covered include picking oranges, teaching English, fishing for prawn, babysitting, building, and many more, with first-hand accounts of what the experience is like; how to travel free by working a passage by land, sea, and air; how to travel cheaply, taking advantage of little-known travel bargains; and how to survive when your money runs out. Regularly updated. 432 pages. $12.95 plus $2 postage. WRITER'S DIGEST BOOKS, 1507 Dana Avenue, Cincinnati, OH 45207

THE AU PAIR & NANNY'S GUIDE TO WORKING ABROAD, Susan Griffith & Sharon Legg. See the world, and get paid for it! This is a complete international handbook for au pairs and nannies, with information on training and experience of applicants; arranging placement; preparing for interviews; working conditions; how to cope with culture shock; and more. Full listing of nanny and au pair opportunities in Britain, Ireland, France, Spain, Greece, Italy, Switzerland, and Canada. Details of regulations & necessary documentation (visas, taxes, etc.); geographical distribution of hiring families; recreational time and working contracts; alphabetical list of agencies which specialize in each country. $12.95 plus $2 postage. WRITER'S DIGEST BOOKS, 1507 Dana Avenue, Cincinnati, OH 45207

CAREERS IN CAMPING, pamphlet describing several professional camp jobs (administrator, trip leader, program director, etc.), with advice on the necessary training and how to get it, where to find the jobs, etc. Free. AMERICAN CAMPING ASSOCIATION, Bradford Woods, 5000 State Road 67 North, Martinsville, IN 46151.

THE TEENAGER'S GUIDE TO STUDY, TRAVEL, AND ADVENTURE ABROAD, from the Council on International Educational Exchange (CIEE). New edition, fully revised. The most up-to-date and exciting guide to world travel opportunities for students in junior and senior high school. The book describes more than 200 programs, from hiking in the USSR to studying the Spanish language in Madrid. Listings include information on sponsors, supervision, orientation, housing, finding the best program, preparing for the trip, academic credit, and interviews with past participants. 304 pages. $11.95. Code STM. BROOK FARM BOOKS.

THE TEENAGE ENTREPRENEUR'S GUIDE, by Sarah L. Riehm. This book is written primarily for teens, but has many ideas which would be very useful to adults who want to be self-employed, either part- or full-time. Fifty job ideas, with full descriptions and step-by-step guides, including materials needed, marketing methods, expected income, and time required. All suggested ventures can be run from one's home, with little or no investment. Special section on setting up a business, bookkeeping, and taxes. $10.95 plus $2.00 shipping. SURREY BOOKS, 230 East Ohio, Suite 120, Chicago, IL 60611.

TRAVEL AND GET PAID FOR IT -- Eight-week training course for many aspects of hospitality and travel industries -- hotels, motels, airlines, steamships, etc. Classes taught by training staffs from Hilton, Sheraton, TWA, Princess Cruises, etc. The school claims 92% job placement after graduation. I wouldn't recommend this work for a lifetime career for creative people, but there are often temporary work positions in these fields which might enable young people to receive substantial discounts or even be paid for traveling. Information: ECHOLS INTERNATIONAL & TRAVEL SCHOOLS, 303 East Ohio St., Chicago, IL 60611.

"HOW TO STUDY" PROGRAM, by Ron Fry. Unlike most books with similar subjects and titles, which I wouldn't give shelf (or review) space, this series is really useful for all high school students, and especially for home-school students who plan to go to college. The author's style is informal, encouraging, and often funny, and his advice and suggestions are practical and easy to employ.

  HOW TO STUDY, 192 pages. $8.95.
  IMPROVE YOUR READING, 96 pages. $5.95.
  WRITE PAPERS, 96 pages. $5.95.
  TAKE NOTES, 96 pages. $5.95.
  MANAGE YOUR TIME, 96 pages. $5.95.
  IMPROVE YOUR MEMORY, 96 pages. $5.95.
  "ACE" ANY TEST, 96 pages. $5.95.
All titles, Code CAR. BROOK FARM BOOKS.

DIRECTORY OF OVERSEAS SUMMER JOBS-- An excellent way to travel to other countries, get to know the people and cultures of many countries, and sometimes even get paid for it. This directory (updated annually) lists more than 50,000 jobs around the world, most of them lasting from a few weeks to a few months. Each listing is prepared by the employer, and provides you with complete data about the length of employment, the number of openings available, the rate of pay, how & when to apply, explanation of duties, qualifications sought, suggestions for an effective application, and the address to whom you should send your application. The directory also includes information on visa and work permit regulations and procedures. Most of the book lists full-time summer work, but many shorter jobs are also listed. The book also lists agencies and organizations which can arrange jobs with other employers. Opportunities for paid summer employment are few in Eastern Europe and underdeveloped countries, so the listings for these areas are mostly for voluntary work organizations which are willing to accept unskilled labor for short periods. There are also listings of organizations or agencies which can give advice and suggestions about travel arrangements. In most cases, the cost of transportation (or more) will be earned back on the job. $9.95 plus $2 postage. WRITER'S DIGEST BOOKS, 1507 Dana Avenue, Cincinnati, OH 45207

ADVENTURE CAREERS, Alex Hiam and Susan Angle. "Your Guide to Exciting Jobs, Uncommon Occupations, and Extraordinary Experiences." How to get a grant to teach public health in Nepal, apply to the Peace Corps, work on a <u>kibbutz</u>, support yourself during a year of travel through Europe or Africa, and much more. Lots of practical how-to information, lists of contacts and phone numbers, and first-hand accounts of experiences of a number of teen and young adult adventurers who didn't want just a "secure" and comfortable career niche. Teens and adults. $9.95. Code CAR. BROOK FARM BOOKS.

AMERICA'S LOWEST-COST COLLEGES, Nicholos A. Roes. The most up-to-date information on more than 1,000 fully-accredited colleges and universities with low or no tuition -- where they are, what they offer, requirements, etc. $9.95. Code CAR. BROOK FARM BOOKS.

Dear Mr. Reed,
  As you can see I am returning your Home School Source Book. I have read about half of it which is why it may look a little used. I found your cartoons and comments confusing and offensive. I would not like my young children to find your book and be exposed to your philosophy. I am however interested in purchasing two books listed, Understanding Music and The Story of Music. Please transfer my refund for this book to the two music books. Thank you.

I MET HER ON THE BUS

She was going two hundred miles, back to college from a weekend visit with her grandmother. I was going ten miles, home from the store. Her guitar case was on the luggage rack and she had long blond hair and I sat beside her. Three months later, on Groundhog Day, 1963, we were married.

When we built our first home, we worked together, hauling and lifting logs, fitting, chinking, and nailing on the roofing. We've built other homes since then, and we've worked together to make them strong and warm.

With an affluent, suburban childhood, she had no home-making skills. She taught herself to sew and mend, to make shirts and darn socks; to cook on a woodstove; to bake pies, cookies, cakes, and bread; to churn butter and make cottage cheese.

When we decided to start a family, we wanted to share the experience of childbirth, but every doctor we consulted refused my presence in the delivery room -- "We can't have fainting husbands all over the floor."

We went to the bookstore and the library, and we studied obstetrics, gynecology, and yoga breathing. We delivered our first child, Cathy, in a small log cabin, miles from the nearest neighbor. In following years, we delivered Karen, Susan, and Derek, all at home, all four without complication or pain.

She nursed each of the children at least a year, and we carried them everywhere, and they always knew they were loved and wanted.

We've worked together in the garden, the hay-field, the barn. She can milk a cow, nurse a sick calf, pitch hay, shovel manure, catch runaway pigs and be midwife for a pig.

Her pie crusts are light and flaky; a slice of her bread makes a meal complete; and her doughnuts are my special reward.

She has stood spell-bound by the Northern Lights, entranced by the call of wild geese flying north, and breathlessly excited by the musical howl of northwestern timber wolves.

Her fingers fly on her guitar and her singing is magic, whether playing classical or folk, Bach or Dylan, loving or growling.

She's five-foot-five, still slim and shapely, and becoming more beautiful every day. Her golden hair is silvery now, but still falls free and long, like spring rain and the morning mist. Her eyes sparkle, she smiles, she laughs, she works and plays, she hugs our children, and she's the best there is. She's a natural woman, whose love flows like a river, warm as summer, strong as a mountain.

With her, my fields are always green, my skies are blue; she nourishes me, feeds my soul. We are two shafts of grain, blown by the wind, north or south or east or west, leaning together, in sunrise and sunset, under clouds and rain and storms, under clear skies and stars, sunlight, moonlight, dark-ness, whispering together in the breezes, our roots intertwined in the earth, our stalks together in the air, our heads together in the sky.

Sometimes I think I will burst with the awesome mountain of love I have for her; and when I feel her love, I am grateful: thank you, Jean.

And humble: bless me, wife.

And glad: let's dance! dance! dance!

And proud: look, world, look at this woman of mine, there's no better woman anywhere; she's the one I'll take to the stars with me--

Oh yes oh yes oh yes.

POSTAGE

Listings which don't include postage or specify "postpaid" have a letter code just before the words "Brook Farm Books." Believe it or not, the letter codes are set up to save you money.

For the **first item** in each letter group, add $2.50 for postage. For **each additional item** with the same letter code, add 25¢. The more you order within any one letter group, the less the postage is per item. (These fees are about half the packaging and shipping costs we actually pay.)

IMPORTANT! If your order totals $100.00 or more before adding postage fees, deduct five percent from the total AFTER adding the postage fees.

HOW TO ORDER

Use this sample as a guide in ordering from Brook Farm Books. All information is essential for accurate filling of your order. Please PRINT or TYPE your order, unless you have exceptionally clear handwriting!

Brook Farm Books   (Date)
P.O. Box 246
Bridgewater, ME 04735

Please send me the following items:

Qty.	Title	Price	Code	Postage
1	Red badge of courage (Modern Library)	13.50	RH	2.50
1	Great Classical myths (Modern Library)	15.00	RH	.25
2	Palmlooms	10.00	--	ppd.
1	Atlantis world globe	38.95	--	4.00
1	Illustrated U.S. history	36.00	--	3.00
1	French Language/30	17.95	--	2.50
1	What Your 1st grader needs	10.95	DD	2.50
1	What Your 2nd grader needs	10.95	DD	.25
	Sub-totals	153.30		15.00
		+ 15.00		
	Total	168.30		
	Minus 5%	- 8.42		
	Total enclosed	159.88		

Thank you!   Mrs. Marion Homeschooler
                              123 Maple Lane
                              Mytown, State Zip

PAYMENT

Most of our suppliers and most of our customers are in the United States, so all prices of items we sell are listed in U.S. dollars. U.S. orders should be sent to:

BROOK FARM BOOKS
P.O. Box 246
Bridgewater, ME 04735.

Canadian orders may be paid in U.S. dollars by postal money order or in Canadian funds by check or money order. If you pay in Canadian funds, please add **30%**. WE DO NOT CHARGE GST. Send Canadian orders to: BROOK FARM BOOKS
Glassville, N.B. E0J 1L0

SHIPPING

Items in stock are usually shipped within three days of our receipt of your order. Allow two to four weeks for 4th Class mail; sometimes longer, depending on the season and how the postal workers feel. ("Christmas rush" doesn't mean things move faster.)

PRICES

Our suppliers all note that their "Prices are subject to change without notice," which means we have to tell you the same thing. Most prices are relatively stable, but of course they do increase sooner or later. If the price increase on an item you order is small (5% or so), we usually won't charge you for it, or we'll just mention it in a note to you and let you decide if you feel like paying it. If it's more, we'll ship your order and bill you for the difference. If the increase is very great (30% or more), we'll usually check with you before shipping.

THREE KINDS OF "OUT OF STOCK"

The first two aren't bad.

First kind: We have a very small business and can't keep all items in stock all the time. When an item is out of stock with us, we just order it from a publisher or supplier and usually have it within a week or two. If an item is out of stock but already on order and we expect to ship within 30 days, we probably won't notify you about the delay. If we expect shipment to be later than 30 days, we'll send you a note saying so. Expected shipping dates are only approximate, because we're dependent on the whims of the publishers. Most publishers and other suppliers are very prompt and thoughtful, but a few are consistent in sending late and/or incomplete shipments, often with no explanation.

Second kind: Our regular supplier is out of stock, and follows the same procedure, ordering from the publisher and sending the item on to us, still within a week or two.

Third kind: the publisher is out of stock, which really means the current printing is sold out and the book is being reprinted, and anyone who knows when the book will again be available has been sworn to secrecy. This doesn't happen often, but when it does, it could be a long wait. Usually we'll refund your money and suggest you try something else.

OUT OF PRINT

Publishers' minds often seem on a par with those of public educators. They undoubtedly have very good reasons for discontinuing publication of some very good books -- such as most of the Made Simple series, HIGH SCHOOL SUBJECTS SELF TAUGHT, Ivan Illich's DESCHOOLING SOCIETY, and many others. I wish the publishers could share some of the embarrassment I feel when I have to tell you that a book you've ordered (on my recommendation) is now out of print. Luckily for all of us, it doesn't happen often. When it does, I'll try to suggest a substitution to you, but I won't substitute without your permission unless the substitution is really comparable, in both content and price. If you don't like the substitution, just return it for a full refund, including postage.

If we write you that many (perhaps even all) of the items you've ordered are out of stock, please bear with us. All the items will already be on order and will be sent to you as soon as possible. We have a very small company -- just Jean and me, with a little help (very little) from Gus -- and we just can't keep all the items we sell in stock all the time. We try to keep the most popular items in stock, but even those sometimes sell out unexpectedly, and we scramble to rebuild our stock. Rather than hold up your entire order to ship all at once (if you've ordered several items), we'll probably ship items to you as we receive them, so you may receive your order in installments. We're a lot friendlier than computers even if we aren't as efficient.

I've tried to make this index fairly comprehensive, but it isn't exaustive. Many items, such as indiviual organizations, suppliers, etc., are not listed; look for them under related entries. Many individual titles and their authors are not listed; look for them in appropriate sections -- e.g., literature, history, etc., Most titles of books in series, such as Tintin and the Little House Books, are not listed individually. Titles and subjects not in the index can sometimes be found by scanning the page-top headings. Be adventurous; browse and explore.

I have omitted the initial articles (*a, an, the*) from the beginnings of titles; thus, A TALE OF TWO CITIES is listed simply as TALE OF TWO CITIES. Book titles are printed in CAPITAL LETTERS. Magazines and other periodicals are printed in *italic*.

Categories frequently overlap: early science and early history books are also excellent early readers. History and literature are hopelessly intertwined, because of my own idiosyncracies; you may have to search both catagories to find the items you want.

An important news item:

Police called in
to quell librarians

An important news item:

President Bush briefed on drought; says rain is needed to end it

An important news item:
Unemployment not working, critics say

An important news item:

Farm forecasters predicting a good year, or possibly a bad year

An important news item:

Town council votes to buy shredder to aid in record keeping